INTERNATIONAL
BUSINESS

INTERNATIONAL BUSINESS
THEORY AND PRACTICE

—— 2ND EDITION ——

RIAD A. AJAMI
University of North Carolina at Greensboro

KAREL COOL
INSEAD, Fontainebleau, France

G. JASON GODDARD
Wachovia Corporation

DARA KHAMBATA
American University

M.E.Sharpe
Armonk, New York
London, England

1004907785

Library of Congress Cataloging-in-Publication Data

Ajami, Riad A.

International business : theory and practice / by Riad A. Ajami, . . . [et al.].—2nd ed.
   p. cm.
Includes bibliographical references and index.
ISBN 13: 978-0-7656-1780-4 (cloth : alk. paper)
ISBN 10: 0-7656-1780-3 (cloth : alk. paper)
   1. International trade. I. Title.

HF1379.A6835 2006
658'.049—dc22
                                           2005037167

Dedicated to:

ALI R. CHARLES AJAMI

ANNE-MARIE KOOL

LEILA GODDARD

FARIDA KHAMBATA

Brief Contents

Detailed Contents

PART V. SOCIAL AND ETHICAL ISSUES AND THE FUTURE OF INTERNATIONAL BUSINESS

17. Ethical Concerns: Multinationals and the Earth's Environment

Preface

International business and multinational corporate activities have grown significantly during the past two decades. The rapid and continuous growth of cross-border economic linkages have contributed to the importance of the study of international business. Furthermore, the mandates by the international Assembly of the Collegiate Schools of Business (ACSB) regarding the globalization of the business curricula added to the relevance and importance of international business teaching. The objective of this text is to present an overview of international business teaching as a balance between international business environments and the functional area knowledge of international finance, international accounting, and international management.

The textbook is divided into five parts. Part 1 deals with the scope of international business and the multinational corporation. Part 2 presents the institutional framework of economic theories and global strategies. It includes discussion of both classical theories of economic development by such noted scholars as Adam Smith and David Ricardo, as well as modern theories by economists such as Albert Hirschman, John Kenneth Galbraith, and Amartya Sen. This section of the book also includes the functioning of the international monetary system and the foreign exchange markets, as well as a discussion of supranational organizations such as the World Trade Organization, the International Monetary Fund, and the World Bank. Part 3 evaluates the environmental constraints in international business, as they are applied to international business operations. In particular, it focuses on analyzing national economies, market demand forecasting, international law, intellectual property rights, sociocultural factors in international business, as well as the researching of risk in foreign investment. Part 4 deals with the functional operations aspect of multinational corporate activities with particular focus on international finance, accounting, taxation, marketing, international staffing and labor issues, as well as the management of technology and operations. Part 5 covers social and ethical issues as well as the future of international business. The first chapter in Part 5 discusses emerging environmental concerns, the responses to those concerns by multinational firms, and the social responsibility of business in the modern world. The last chapter provides a thought-provoking discussion concerning future trends affecting international business and the impacts of those trends on the multinational firm. The book concludes with a section of case studies that provide a distinctly European focus. The case studies present real-world examples of business problems facing multinational firms and include cases on Michelin, AXA, Bang & Olufsen, Arcelor, ABX, as well as a technological case on Smart Cards in the Netherlands.

The distinctive features of this book are the chapters focusing on economic development, and analyzing national economies, as well as the chapter on the environment and ethics. The book also contains an analysis of issues of importance in today's global economy, such as outsourcing, and the continued importance of world energy markets. Moreover, the richness of the case studies and the cross-regional geographic focus presents a bridge between globalization, corporate strategies, and environmental and social concerns.

Many colleagues have given the authors invaluable assistance in the preparation of this book. Our deep appreciation goes to the many who are too numerous to mention individually by name from the Bryan School of Business and Economics at the University of North Carolina at Greensboro, INSEAD, and the American University in Washington, DC. Our deep appreciation also goes to the following colleagues: Kamel Abdallah of the American University, Beirut; Gail Arch, Curry College; James T. Goode, Osaka International University, Japan; Hanne Norreklit, Aarhus School of Business, Denmark; C. Bulent Aybar, Southern New Hampshire University; Frederic Herlin, Center for Creative Leadership, Brussels, Austria, and

Greensboro; Mary Lynn Briddell, Executive in Residence at the Center for Global Business Education and Research, University of North Carolina at Greensboro. The authors are grateful for the case study submitted by Frederic Herlin, as well as for the case study jointly submitted by Frédéric Le Roy, M'hamed Merdji, Saïd Yami, and Franck Seguy. The authors are further grateful for the guidance of Allen Mandelbaum, W.R. Kenan Endowed Professor of English and Humanities, Wake Forest University and Professore per chiara fama di Storia della Critica Letteraria Università di Torino, Italy.

The authors are also indebted to the University of North Carolina at Greensboro's Bryan School of Business and the support staff of the Center for Global Business Education and Research, in particular Rodney Ouzts and the research assistant team, including Maria Chavez, Sylvan Allen, and Josh Exoo.

Finally, the authors are grateful for the careful editing provided by Edward G. Clarke, who patiently read each chapter during the draft phase, and offered sound advice on improving both the content and the format of the chapters that follow.

PART I

SCOPE OF INTERNATIONAL BUSINESS AND THE MULTINATIONAL CORPORATION

CHAPTER 1

An Introduction to International Business and Multinational Corporations

> "The first thing to understand is that you do not understand."
> *Søren Kierkegaard*

CHAPTER OBJECTIVES

This chapter will:

- Present the historical context of international business and establish the role of multinational corporations in the current business environment.
- Describe the various operating advantages and disadvantages facing the multinational corporation.

The quote by the Danish philosopher Kierkegaard was intended for a philosophical interpretation, but it could just as easily apply to international business. There are countless examples of businesses that failed in their international expansion efforts because they did not heed the basic tenet ingrained in these words. It is critical for both students and business professionals to understand that the successful entry into foreign markets comes only with the realization that circumstances in foreign markets are not necessarily the same as those in the domestic market. This first chapter will provide examples of some companies that have been successful by learning how to profitably compete in today's global marketplace. But first, the subject of international business must be discussed in its historical context.

CURRENT SCOPE AND HISTORICAL ANTECEDENTS

In the world of business in the twenty-first century, vast business interrelationships span the globe. Far more than ever before, products, capital, and personnel are becoming intertwined, as business entities increasingly consider their market areas as being global rather than simply domestic or even foreign. More and more companies, some of which have annual sales levels larger than the *gross national products (GNP)* of some countries, consider every corner of the globe a feasible source of raw materials and labor or a new market possibility.

As business has expanded across national borders, banks and financial institutions have followed it to meet its need for capital for investment and operations around the world. Financial markets have also become intricately linked, and movements and changes in the U.S. stock market have a direct impact on equity markets in other parts of the world.

Today, only a naive businessperson would believe that an enterprise can grow and prosper entirely within the confines of its domestic market borders. Domestic business must at least be aware of international sources of competition, because they are an ever-present and growing threat as international business relationships become increasingly intricate and complex. The source of these changes in the dynamics of world markets and economies is the international business activity being pursued around the globe.

WHAT IS INTERNATIONAL BUSINESS?

In its purest definition, international business is described as any business activity that crosses national boundaries. The entities involved in business can be private, governmental, or a mixture of the two. International business can be broken down into four types: foreign trade, trade in services, portfolio investments, and direct investments.

In foreign trade, visible physical goods or commodities move between countries as exports or imports. Exports consist of merchandise that leaves a country. Imports are those items brought across national borders into a country. Exporting and importing comprise the most fundamental, and usually the largest, international business activity in most countries.

In addition to tangible goods, countries also trade in services, such as insurance, banking, hotels, consulting, and travel and transportation. The international firm is paid for services it renders in another country. The earnings can be in the form of fees or royalties. Fees are generated through the satisfaction of specific performance requirements and can be earned through long- or short-term contractual agreements, such as management or consulting contracts. Royalties accrue from the use of one company's process, name, trademark, or *patent* by someone else.

One example of a fee situation is the *turnkey operation*, in which a foreign government or enterprise hires the expertise appropriate to starting a new concern, plant, or operation. The turnkey managers come into a foreign environment and get an operation up and running by designing the plant, setting up equipment, and training personnel to run the business. The foreign firm can then merely take over the reins of management and continue operating the facility. Alternatively, a firm can earn royalties from abroad by licensing the use of its technology, processes, or information to another firm or by selling its franchise in overseas markets.

Portfolio investments are financial investments made in foreign countries. The investor purchases debt or equity in the expectation of nothing more than a financial return on the investment. Resources such as equipment, time, or personnel are not contributed to the overseas venture. *Direct investments* are differentiated by much greater levels of control over the project or enterprise by the investor. The level of control can vary from full control, when a firm owns a foreign subsidiary entirely, to partial control, as in arrangements such as joint ventures with other domestic or foreign firms or a foreign government. The methods of conducting interna-

Figure 1.1 **World FDI Inflows, 1988–2003**

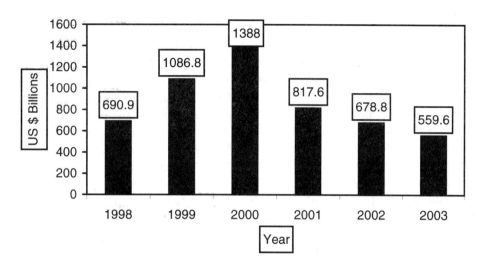

Source: United Nations Conference on Trade and Development (UNCTAD), *World Investment Report 2004* (New York: United Nations, 2004).

tional business are discussed more thoroughly in subsequent chapters. As illustrated in Figure 1.1, the level of foreign direct investment (FDI) peaked in 2000 at $1.388 trillion, although the worldwide economic slowdown since 2000 has somewhat slowed FDI growth.[1] Additionally, the European Union has become a leading destination for FDI over the past few years, while FDI into the United States fell by 12 percent in 2003.[2] The downward trend for FDI into the United States was reversed in 2004, with FDI increasing by 2.50 percent

BRIEF HISTORY OF INTERNATIONAL BUSINESS

International business is not new, having been practiced around the world for thousands of years, although its forms, methods, and importance are constantly evolving. In ancient times, the Phoenicians, Mesopotamians, and Greeks traded along routes established in the Mediterranean. Com-

merce continued to grow throughout history as sophisticated business techniques emerged, facilitating the flow of goods, resources, and funds between countries. Some of these business methods included the establishment of credit for exchange, banking, and pooling of resources in joint-stock ventures. This growth was further stimulated by colonization activities, which provided the maritime nations with rich resources of raw materials as well as enormous potential markets in the new worlds.

The Industrial Revolution further encouraged the growth of international business by providing methods of production for mass markets and more efficient methods of utilizing raw materials. As industrialization increased, greater and greater demand was created for supplies, raw materials, labor, and transportation. The flow and mobility of capital also increased as expanded production provided surplus income, which was, in turn, reinvested in further production domestically or in the colonies.

The technological developments and inventions resulting from the Industrial Revolution accelerated and smoothed the flow of goods, services, and capital between countries.

By the 1880s the Industrial Revolution was in full swing in Europe and the United States, and production grew to unprecedented levels, abetted by scientific inventions, the development of new sources of energy, efficiencies achieved in production, and improvements in transportation, such as domestic and international railroad systems. Growth continued in an upward spiral as mass production met and surpassed domestic demand, pushing manufacturers to seek enlarged, foreign markets for their products. It led ultimately to the emergence of the multinational corporation (MNC) as a new organizational entity in the international business world.

THE MULTINATIONAL CORPORATION

During its early stages, international business was conducted in the form of enterprises that were owned singly or in partnerships. As the size of organizations grew with industrialization and companies' needs for capital increased, corporations began to displace privately held firms. These corporations had the distinct advantage of being entities with a separate legal identity, consequently limiting the liability of the principals or owners. At the same time, by issuing shares of stock, the corporation could tap an enormous pool of excess funds held by potential individual investors.

With the emergence of the multinational enterprise in the late 1800s and early part of the twentieth century, the corporation underwent yet another modification.[3] Some early multinational enterprises sought resources and supplies abroad, such as oil in Mexico (Standard Oil), precious minerals in South Africa (Amalgamated Copper, International Nickel, Kennecott), fruit in the Caribbean (United Fruit), and rubber in Sumatra (U.S. Rubber). Other firms entered the international business arena in a search for markets to absorb their excess domestic production or to obtain economies of scale in production. Some of these early market seekers from the United States were Singer, National Cash Register Company, International Harvester (now Navistar International), and Remington, which sought to use their advantages of superior metal production skills against European producers.

These early entrants were quickly followed by companies with other areas of expertise, such as Cable Telephone (now Chequamegon Communications), Eastman Kodak, and Westinghouse. All these early U.S. multinational firms marketed their products primarily in the neighboring countries of Canada and Mexico and in European markets.

DEFINITION OF A MULTINATIONAL CORPORATION

There is no formal definition of a multinational corporation, although various definitions have been proposed using different criteria. Some believe that a multinational firm is one that is structured so that business is conducted or ownership is held across a number of countries, or one that is organized into global product divisions. Others look to specific ratios of foreign business activities or assets to total firm activities or assets. Under these criteria, a multinational firm is one in which a certain percentage of the earnings, assets, sales, or personnel of a firm come from or are deployed in foreign locations. A third definition is based on the perspective of the corporation, that is, its behavior and its thinking. This definition holds that if the management of a corporation has the perception and the attitude that the parameters of its sphere of operations and markets are multinational, then the firm is indeed a multinational corporation.

In his study of the topic, Howard Perlmutter looks at this attitude held by the decision makers of an organization and differentiates among ethnocentric, polycentric, and geocentric organizational types.[4]

Ethnocentric organizations are those that are focused in a home or domestic environment and therefore exclude MNCs. *Polycentric* organizations have investments, operations, or markets in several countries but do not integrate the management of these international functions. *Geocentric* organizations are integrated and have a world perspective regarding the breadth and reach of possible organizational operations. Some students of international business (and sticklers for linguistic accuracy) dispute the use of the terms "global" or "world" corporation in reference to MNCs. They argue that a truly global corporation or enterprise looks to every market in the world as a potential market and allocates resources without regard for the location of its home country. Under this definition, for example, an international corporation with subsidiaries and markets in Europe and South America would not be considered a global enterprise. As the *globalization* of international *markets* has continued, more firms have realized that the key to their future success depends on increasing their business activities in other parts of the world (including China, India, and Southeast Asian nations).

The existence of different definitions for multinational corporations is not surprising. There are many different types of multinational corporations, and most definitions characterize only a particular type. Because there are so many possible ways in which a corporation can be organized and can transact business across national borders, it is indeed very difficult for any one definition to adequately describe all forms of multinational corporations.

Another problem in standardizing the definition of a multinational corporation is the gradual evolution of purely domestic companies to multinational status. In this process, the point cannot be clearly demarcated when a company becomes a multinational. Such demarcations, if at all possible, also cannot explain or describe adequately the wide differences that corporations may have in the extent to which they have gone international.

The United Nations does not use the terms "multinational corporations" or "multinational enterprises." Instead, it calls these organizations "transnational corporations," but this term is not used widely. This text will use the term "multinational corporation" to identify a firm that conducts international business from a multitude of locations in different countries.

MULTINATIONAL CORPORATIONS COME OF AGE

The multinational corporation began to flourish in the decade following World War II, primarily in the United States. It was spurred by reconstruction efforts in Europe and an inflow of U.S. dollars geared to take advantage of new opportunities, as countries of the ravaged continent attempted to rebuild their economies. U.S. corporations, having prospered through wartime demand, channeled investments into other countries, notably in Europe and Canada. During the period from 1950 to 1970, the book value of U.S. direct foreign investments skyrocketed from $11.8 billion to $78.1 billion.[5]

As the European economy strengthened during this period, the motives of U.S. companies doing business there switched from an aggressive market- and profit-seeking stance to a defensive position of protecting European market share and shielding domestic and U.S. markets from encroachments by increasingly strong European competitors. In the 1960s, U.S. firms also began to take advantage of the availability of new capital and debt markets: the *Eurodollar* and *Eurobond* markets emerging in that part of the world. During this period, the orientation of U.S. MNCs also began to change, from seeking raw materials and being involved in the extractive industries to focusing more on overseas manufacturing industries.

By the 1970s the United States had lost its nearly complete dominance of multinational industry, partially because of the reemergence of strong European

Table 1.1

Top Twenty Multinational Corporations, 2005
(US $ billions)

Company	Revenue
1. ExxonMobil	$328
2. Wal-Mart Stores	312
3. Royal Dutch/Shell Group	306
4. BP	249
5. General Motors	192
6. Chevron	185
7. Ford Motor	178
8. DaimlerChrysler	177
9. Toyota Motor	173
10. ConocoPhillips	162
11. General Electric	150
12. Total	145
13. ING Group	137
14. Allianz Worldwide	124
15. Citigroup	120
16. AXA Group	115
17. Volkswagen Group	113
18. American International Group	107
19. Nippon Telegraph and Telephone	101
20. Carrefour	99

Source: "Forbes Global 200," *Forbes,* April 17, 2006.

concerns, but also due to Japan and the other emerging giants of the East. As presented in Table 1.1, as of 2005, only 9 of the top 20 multinational companies were from the United States. The rest of the top 20 companies were from Europe and Japan.[6]

Until 2005, Wal-Mart was the world's largest company from a revenue perspective. This mass retailer has stores in the United States, Argentina, Brazil, Canada, Germany, Korea, Mexico, Puerto Rico, and the United Kingdom. The fact that Wal-Mart is one of the largest companies in the world without yet completely penetrating the European market shows just how successful this company has been in North America. ExxonMobil surpassed Wal-Mart in total revenues in 2005. This was largely

attributed to the increase in oil and gas prices during the year. As an interesting side note, of the top 20 companies in the world, 11 of them are in either the oil or the automobile industry. BP, ExxonMobil, Royal Dutch/Shell Group, Total, ChevronTexaco, and ConocoPhillips are all in the oil industry, while General Motors, Ford Motor, DaimlerChrysler, Toyota Motor, and Volkswagen are in the automobile industry. Financial services and insurance companies are also well represented in the top 20, with Citigroup, Allianz, ING Group, AXA, and American International Group appearing there.

A Look at Present-Day Multinationals

To understand the complexities of the operations pursued by multinational firms, it is helpful to look at the structure and operations of actual multinational business organizations. In this way, the student of international business can envision the enormity and complexity of operations for a global bank, a multinational manufacturing company, and an international conglomerate: Citigroup, Sony, and Nestlé.

Citigroup (United States)

Citigroup is a prime example of a truly global corporation. Indeed, the company calls itself a global financial services company and attempts to provide a full range of banking services in all parts of the world. In 2003, Citigroup derived 64 percent of its revenues from North America, and global business accounted for 32 percent of its revenue (with 10 percent coming from Asia). This revenue was diversified in the following manner: consumer banking (55 percent), corporate and investment banking (31 percent), global investment management (10 percent), and private client services via Smith Barney (4 percent). Citigroup was the largest bank in the world in terms of market capitalization in 2004, with a market value of nearly $8 billion.[7] The bank achieved revenue levels of $94.71 billion in 2003, as well as net profits of $17.85 billion. By year-end of 2003, Citigroup held total assets of $1.264 trillion, employed 275,000 people, and managed 200 million customer accounts in more than 100 countries on six continents.[8]

The Citigroup's Global Consumer Group acquired the Sears and Home Depot credit card portfolios in 2003, making it the leading private label provider in the United States. Citigroup also became the first international bank in Russia to offer credit cards to consumers. In 2004, Citigroup acquired Washington Mutual's consumer finance business, which helped to increase the bank's position as the leading community-based lender in the United States. In 2003, Citigold Wealth Management programs were launched in the Czech Republic, Egypt, France, Hungary, Poland, Russia, Turkey, and the United Arab Emirates. Citigroup also launched the Banamex Tricolor card, which makes it easier and more affordable for people in Mexico to receive funds from their friends and relatives in the United States.

Citigroup's Global Corporate and Investment Banking Group advised on four of the world's eight largest merger and acquisition transactions in 2003. The group also settled more than one million transactions in international trade related to the movement of goods. All of this shows that Citigroup is an organization with a global approach that has been very successful by finding ways to cater to various markets throughout the world.

In recent years, the company's advertising campaign centered on the slogan "Live richly," and this was communicated in English, Chinese, Spanish, and many other languages throughout the world.

Sony Corporation (Japan)

Sony Corporation, based in Tokyo, Japan, is a major world manufacturer of televisions, DVD players, gaming systems, and semiconductors. While Sony's reach is not as wide as Citicorp's in terms of international scope, product line, or diversity, the company's success since its incorporation in 1946 is still remarkable. Since the 1940s, Sony has constantly continued its growth and development in the electronics and telecommunications fields, producing in Japan in 1950 the first tape recorder and magnetic tape. This accomplishment was followed by the production of transistors in 1954, the technology of which was applied to radios, televisions, and tape recorders. This period was followed by a growth period in the 1960s, culminating with the production of the Trinitron color television tube in 1968. Advances followed in video equipment that led to the introduction of the Betamax in 1975 and the subsequent introduction of the Walkman personal cassette tape player and radio.

Sony's enormous growth was evidenced in a quintupling of sales in the decade from 1972 to 1981. By 2003, Sony's revenues had reached $47 billion (an increase from $5 billion in 1985), and total assets had reached $87.41 billion. Today, 62 percent of Sony's revenues come from its electronics segment. This segment includes digital cameras, DVD players, and various television and home audio systems. Ten percent of Sony's revenues come from the video-game segment. This primarily includes the Sony PlayStation 2 (PS2) video-game consoles and software. In 2003, Sony surpassed 70 million units sold for the PS2 product. Sony also achieves revenue from the music segment (7 percent of total revenues), the picture segment (10 percent of total revenues), and the financial services segment (7 percent of total revenues).[9]

Sony's financial success lies in its enormous research and development (R & D) strengths, its international revenue diversity, and its ability to find successful partnerships and methods of increasing the breadth of its sales to a given consumer. Sony's R & D strategy is based on creating an environment of freedom and open-mindedness in which its researchers and developers can use their imaginations freely, while also efficiently focusing management resources in strategic fields. Over the next few years, Sony is focusing its R & D efforts on semiconductors, displays, and home servers. The company will concentrate on the CCD semiconductor, a product that Sony currently holds the number one world market share in producing, and on semiconductor lasers.

While it is not as globally diverse as Citigroup, 30 percent of Sony's revenues come from Japan, while 28 percent of its revenues come from the United States. European sales account for 24 percent of total revenues, with the remainder coming from sales elsewhere in the world. In terms of production facilities, Sony has the majority of them in Asia but does have a presence in both Europe and North America as well.

To continue to succeed in today's global marketplace, Sony has set as a goal the successful implementation of "Transformation 60," a program scheduled for completion in 2006 (Sony's sixtieth anniversary). The objective was to position Sony as a global company, but to ensure that this diversity provided the company with the ability to withstand dramatic shifts in the world economy. The company instituted fixed cost cuts via downsizing of non-value-added areas of its company, and also promoted the idea of "convergence" and centralization of management resources within the Sony group. Such convergence initiatives again relied on the company's core strength in R & D. The plan was to use the role of the television as the centerpiece of the living room to sell other products that could link with the television. Other future plans include using the benefits of a successful joint venture with Sony Ericsson Mobile Communications AB to converge mobile electronic devices and audio-video functions (similar to what has already been done with cell phones).

Nestlé SA (Switzerland)

Nestlé is the world's leading food processor and, like Citigroup, is a truly global corporation. Based in Vevey, Switzerland, the company operates 511 factories in 86 countries around the world.

Nestlé originated in Switzerland with the founding by chemist Henri Nestlé of a condensed-milk factory in the mid-1800s and a factory to manufacture a milk-based baby food product. In the early 1900s, these two factories merged and rapidly expanded their operations and manufacturing facilities to all of Europe, the United States, and Latin America.

In the 1930s, the firm's fortunes were abetted by its move into the instant-drink market with one of its major products, Nescafé instant coffee, which was introduced in 1938. Since then, the company has continued to grow because of its strategies of diversification, market expansion, and product development. At present, Nestlé's product line includes instant drinks, dairy products, culinary products such as bouillon, soups, spices, and dehydrated sauces, chocolate and candy, frozen foods and ice cream, infant and dietetic products, and liquid drinks. In addition, the company manufactures pharmaceutical products, such as instruments and medicines, owns and runs restaurants and hotels in the United States and Europe, and has a minority share in L'Oréal, a producer of cosmetics, perfumes, and beauty products.[10]

In 2003, Nestlé achieved annual revenues of $65.46 billion. Thirty-three percent of these revenues were in Europe, 31 percent were in the Americas, and 16 percent were in Asia and Africa. Beverages accounted for 27 percent of the revenue worldwide, followed by milk products and nutrition (26 percent), prepared dishes (18 percent), chocolate and biscuits (12 percent), pet care (11 percent), and pharmaceuticals (6 percent). Six worldwide brands, Nestlé, Nescafé, Nestea, Maggi, Buitoni, and Purina, account for approximately 70 percent of the company's sales.

Of Nestlé's 511 factories, 170 of them are located in North and South America. These plants produce such familiar products as Ovaltine, Nescafé, Stouffer's frozen foods, Poland Spring bottled water, Libby's vegetables and other canned foods, Beech-Nut baby food, and Taster's Choice coffee. In addition, the company produces dairy products, such as cheeses, chocolates, candies, cookies, and their own cans for fruit and vegetable packing. Nestlé also produces Friskies and Alpo pet foods.

Nestlé's desire to produce healthy, nutritious products is shown in its current advertising slogan, "Good food, good life." The company is seeking to transform itself from the world's leading food company to the world's leading food, beverage, nutrition, health, and wellness company. Many of its R & D efforts are currently focusing on producing more healthy and nutritious products. The company has tried to strengthen its credibility in the medical community by producing quality products in its pharmaceutical product line.

An example of the company's emphasis on health is its continued focus on the bottled water market. In July 2004, Nestlé announced a bottled water joint venture with Coca-Cola in Indonesia. Indonesia is the second largest bottled water market in Asia (after China), and the seventh largest bottled water market in the world. This joint venture will increase Nestlé's global bottled water presence. The company is present in 130 countries across the world and has a portfolio of 77 brands. This has led Nestlé to the number one position in the world bottled water market.[11]

OPERATING ADVANTAGES AND DISADVANTAGES OF MULTINATIONALS

MNCs have certain unique advantages and disadvantages in their operations that make them quite different from purely domestically oriented companies. The international success of the MNCs is primarily because of their ability to overcome the disadvantages and capitalize on the advantages. The advantages, as well as the disadvantages, depend to a large extent on the nature of individual corporations themselves and on each of their types of businesses. Studies of MNCs, however, show that a pattern of common characteristics exists across the broad spectrum of different corporations operating around the globe.

Advantages Gained by MNCs

Superior Technical Know-how

Perhaps the most important advantage that MNCs enjoy is patented technical know-how, which enables them to compete internationally. Most large MNCs have access to higher or advanced levels of technology, which was either developed or acquired by the corporation. Such technology is patented and held quite closely. It can be in the areas of production, management, services, or processes. Widespread application of such technology gives the MNC a strong competitive advantage in the international market, because it results in the production of efficient, hi-tech, low-priced products and services that command a large international market following. The Banamex Tricolor card technology developed by Citigroup is an example of how an MNC can obtain a competitive advantage by developing, patenting, and then exploiting an advanced technology.[12] Further examples include IBM and Microsoft in computers, Boeing in aviation, and DuPont in chemicals.

Large Size and Economies of Scale

Most MNCs tend to be large. Some of them, such as Wal-Mart and ExxonMobil, have sales that are larger than the gross national products of many countries. The large size confers the advantage of significant economies of scale to MNCs. The high volume of production lowers per-unit fixed costs for the company's products, which are reflected in lower final costs. Competitors who produce smaller volumes of goods must price them higher to recover higher fixed costs. This situation is especially true in such capital-intensive industries as steel, petro-chemicals, and automobiles, in which fixed costs form a substantial proportion of total costs. Thus, an MNC such as Nippon Steel of Japan can sell its products at prices much lower than those of companies with smaller plants.

Lower Input Costs Due to Large Size

The large production levels of multinationals necessitate the purchase of inputs in commensurately large volumes. Bulk purchases of inputs enable MNCs to bargain for lower input costs, and they are able to obtain substantial volume discounts. The lowered input costs imply less expensive and, therefore, more competitive finished products. Nestlé, which buys huge quantities of coffee on the market, can command much lower prices than smaller buyers can. Wal-Mart is able to sell its products at low prices relative to its competition due to both its bulk purchasing and its effective inventory control. By understanding which products are selling effectively, Wal-Mart combines low-cost purchasing with the effective movement of inventory to achieve competitive advantage in the retail consumer products market.

Ability to Access Raw Materials Overseas

Many MNCs lower input and production costs by accessing raw materials in foreign countries. In many of these cases, MNCs supply the technology to extract or refine the raw materials, or both. In addition to lowering costs, such access can give MNCs monopolistic control over the raw materials because they often supply technology only in exchange for such monopolistic control. This control gives them

the opportunity to manipulate the supply of the raw materials, or even to deny access, to the competitors for this raw material.

Ability to Shift Production Overseas

The ability to shift production overseas is another advantage enjoyed by MNCs. To increase their international competitiveness, MNCs relocate their production facilities overseas, thereby taking advantage of lower costs for labor, raw materials, and other inputs, and, often, utilizing incentives offered by host countries. MNCs exploit the reduced costs achieved at these locations by exporting lower-cost goods to foreign markets. Several major MNCs have set up factories in such low-cost locations as China, India, and Mexico, to name only a few. This advantage is unique to MNCs, and it gives them a distinct edge over purely domestic corporations.[13]

Scale Economies in Shipment, Distribution, and Promotion

Scale economies allow MNCs to achieve lower costs in shipment expenses. The large volumes of freight they ship permit them to negotiate lower rates with the shippers. Some of the very large corporations, especially the oil giants, have operations that are large enough to justify the purchase of their own ships, which is an even more effective way to reduce costs.

Distribution and promotion costs are also lower for MNCs because of their high volumes of production. The *distributors* in different countries charge lower commissions to move the products because they are able to make substantial profits on their high volumes. A similar lowering of costs accrues with promotional expenses. MNCs have large advertising budgets and are valuable clients for advertising agencies and the media. Consequently, they are able to obtain cheaper rates. More important, MNCs are often able to standardize a promotional message and use it in different countries (for example, the Marlboro cigarette advertisements or several Coca-Cola promotions that have been released in different countries using standardized messages).

Brand Image and Goodwill Advantages

Many of the MNCs possess product lines that have established a good reputation for quality, performance, value, and service. This reputation spreads abroad through exports and promotion, which adds to an MNC's arsenal of potent weapons in the form of brand image or goodwill, which it is able to use to differentiate its own products from others in its genre. MNCs are able to leverage this goodwill or brand image by standardizing their product lines in different countries and achieving economies of scale. For example, Sony PlayStations do not have any special modifications for different countries (except for voltage) and the home-based plant churns out standardized products for the world market. Similarly, Levi Strauss is able to market its standard denim jeans around the globe even though clothing fashions vary widely within different cultures. Moreover, goodwill and brand names allow the company to charge premium prices for its products (e.g., Sony), because the customers are convinced that the products are good values even at premium prices.

Access to Low-Cost Financing

As a result of their size, MNCs require large amounts of financing, and generally they are excellent credit risks. Therefore, they are the favored customers of financial institutions, which lend to them at their best rates. The lower cost of financing for the MNCs adds to their competitive strength. MNCs also have the advantage of access to different financial markets, which allows them to borrow from the source offering the best deal; the funds are then transferred internally to required

locations. This access enables MNCs to avoid some countries' credit rationing and to obtain financing at costs lower than those available to their domestic-oriented competitors.

Financial Flexibility

MNCs also have an advantage in being able to manipulate their profits and shift them to lower-tax locations. This greater financial leverage can be used to artificially lower prices to enter new markets or to increase market shares in existing ones. The manipulation of profits to save taxes is generally accomplished through transfer pricing, in which the overseas subsidiaries are charged artificially higher prices for products supplied to them by the parent company. MNCs also utilize several financial mechanisms with the objectives of shifting profits and manipulating taxes.

Information Advantages

Multinationals have a global market view and are able to collect, process, analyze, and exploit their in-depth knowledge of worldwide markets. They use this knowledge to create new openings for their existing products or to create new products for potential market niches. Their special knowledge is used to diversify and expand the market coverage of their products and to design strategies to counter the marketing efforts of their competitors. Moreover, excess production can be sold off, as the company can quickly find new markets through its global search-and-marketing mechanism.

The information-gathering abilities of MNCs are an advantage not only in marketing but also in all other aspects of their operations. An MNC is able to gather commercial intelligence, forecast government controls, and assess political and other risks through its information network. The network also provides valuable information about changing market and economic conditions, demographics, social and cultural changes, and many other variables that affect the business of MNCs in different countries. Access to this information provides MNCs with the opportunity to position themselves appropriately to respond to contingencies and exploit opportunities.

Managerial Experience and Expertise

Because MNCs function simultaneously in a large number of very different countries, they are able to assimilate a wealth of valuable managerial experience. This experience provides insights into dealing with different business situations and problems around the globe. MNCs also acquire expertise in different ways of approaching business problems and can effectively apply this knowledge to multiple locations. For example, a multinational located in Japan can acquire in-depth knowledge of Japanese management methods and apply them successfully elsewhere. MNCs also develop expertise in multi-country operations management as their executives gather experience working in different countries on their way to senior management positions.

Diversification of Risks.

The simultaneous presence of MNCs in different countries allows them to more effectively bear the risk of cyclic economic declines. Generally these cycles are not the same among different countries. Thus, losses in one country can be offset by gains in other countries. Simultaneous operations also provide considerable flexibility to MNC operations, which enables them to diversify the political, economic, and other risks that they face in different countries. Thus, if an MNC is not able to keep up production levels in one country, it can still retain its market share by serving the market with products from a factory located in a different country. In another instance, if raw material supplies are stopped from one source, the global presence of the MNC assures supplies from alternative sources. In the

oil market, for example, if a Russian pipeline is shut down unexpectedly, nations such as Saudi Arabia have the necessary spare capacity to temporarily increase the supply of oil on the world markets in an effort to stabilize prices over the short term.

Disadvantages Faced by MNCs

Business Risks

MNCs have to bear several serious risks that are not borne by companies whose operations are purely domestic in nature. Since MNCs conduct business outside the borders of their own countries, they deal with the currencies of other countries, which renders them vulnerable to fluctuations in exchange rates. Violent movements in exchange rates can wipe out the entire profit of a particular business activity. Over the long run, MNCs often have to live with this risk because it is extremely difficult to eliminate it. Over the short run, however, there are market mechanisms such as *currency swaps* and forward contracts that allow an MNC to minimize the movement of exchange rates for a particular business transaction. Companies that engage in these forms of financial contracts understand that they are not in the currency-risk business and that it makes sense to minimize this risk when at all possible.

Host-Country Regulations

Operating in different countries subjects MNCs to a myriad of host-country regulations that vary from country to country and, in most cases, are quite different from those of the home country. The MNC has the difficult task of familiarizing itself with these regulations and modifying its operations to ensure that it does not overstep them. Regulations are often changed, and such changes can have adverse implications for MNCs. For example, a country may ban the import of a certain raw material or restrict the availability of bank credit. Such constraints can have serious effects on an MNC's production levels. In many developing countries, national controls are quite pervasive and almost every facet of private business activity is subject to government approval. The MNCs of developed countries are not used to such controls, and their methods of doing business are not geared to work in this type of environment.

Different Legal Systems

MNCs must operate under the different legal systems of different countries. In some countries the legislative and judicial processes are extremely cumbersome and contain many nuances that are not easily understood by non-natives. Some legislation can also prohibit the type of business activity the MNC would regard as normal in its home country.

Political Risks

Host countries are sovereign entities and their actions normally do not admit any appeals. There is little that an MNC can do if a host country is determined to take actions that are inimical to its interests. This *political risk*, as it is known, increases in countries whose governments are unstable and tends to change frequently.

Operational Difficulties

Multinationals work in a wide variety of business environments, which creates substantial operational difficulties. Unwritten business practices and market conventions often prevail in host countries. MNCs that lack familiarity with such conventions find it difficult to conduct business in accordance with them. Often the normal methods of operation of an MNC can be quite contrary to a country's business practices. A typical example is informal credit. In many countries retailers agree to stock goods of a manufacturing company only if they are offered a market-determined period of credit that is not covered by a written document. The accounting and sales policies of an MNC may not permit such arrangements. On the other hand, doing business in that country may not be at all possible without such arrangements. The multinational must therefore adjust its business practices or lose business entirely.

Cultural Differences

Cultural differences often lead to major problems for MNCs. Many find that their expatriate executives are not able to turn in optimal performances because they are not able to adjust to the local culture, both personally as well as professionally. On the other hand, local managers of MNCs often have difficulties in dealing with the home office of an MNC because of culturally based communication problems. Inability to understand and respond appropriately to local cultures has often led MNC products to fail. Misunderstanding of local cultures, work ethics, and social norms often leads to problems between MNCs and their local customers, their business associates, government officials, and even their own employees.

Many of the problems and challenges of conducting international business center around overcoming disadvantages and capitalizing on advantages that arise when corporations go international. These problems and challenges are discussed in detail in subsequent chapters.

RECENT TRENDS IN WORLD TRADE

EXPANDING VOLUME

The sheer volume of trade among nations has grown enormously since World War II. In 1948 the volume of world trade was only $51 billion. It rose to $331.72

Figure 1.2   **Growth in World Trade Volume**

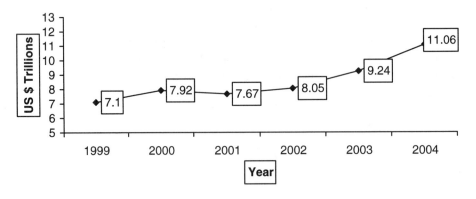

Source: World Trade Organization (WTO), "Statistics Database," 2006, http://www.wto.org, accessed April 10, 2006.

billion in 1970 and to $11.06 trillion in 2004 (see Figure 1.2). The international trade arena continues to be dominated by the industrialized countries, which account for as much as 73.5 percent of world trade.[14] Major changes have occurred in trading patterns within the industrialized countries, however. For example, China increased exports by an average of 19 percent from 1990 to 1995 and saw an increase of 35 percent in 2003. China now accounts for 6 percent of the world's exports, a statistic that is sure to increase over time. On the other hand, the U.S. share of world exports declined from 13.7 percent in 1970 to 10 percent in 2003. These trends have very important implications for international business. It is clear that the world trading environment is now truly international, in the sense that it is no longer dominated by any one country. There has, in fact, been a reversal of roles for some countries, most significantly the United States, which incurred huge trade deficits in the 1980s and has moved from being the world's largest creditor to being the world's largest debtor. There are many reasons for this dramatic change. During the 1990s, the U.S. budget did return to a surplus position, only to fall back into deficits in the past few years. The trade deficits that began in the 1980s still persist, though.

The United States faces intense competition in its home market as well as in foreign markets from several countries, especially China, India, Germany, and Japan. Apart from these challenges, new competition has surfaced in the form of the newly industrializing economies of the Pacific Rim, popularly known as the *four tigers*. These countries, Hong Kong, South Korea, Taiwan, and Singapore have been rapidly increasing their share of world trade. In 2003, these nations increased their exports by 11 percent and now account for 6.2 percent of world trade volume. As Figure 1.3 illustrates, the developing countries of Asia and the transition economies of central and eastern Europe have begun to experience large gains in trade volume over the past few years.

INCREASED COMPETITION

Competition on the international trade front is likely to intensify. The emergence of the European Union in 1992, the further strengthening of Asian exporting capabilities, and the continuing increase in Chinese exports are likely to put further pressures on the United States. To respond to these pressures, the United States will have to take a more active and positive approach to international business. The

Figure 1.3 **Real Merchandise Trade Growth by Region, 2004** (annual percentage change)

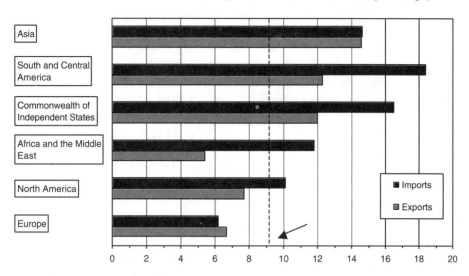

Source: WTO. http://www.wto.org/english/news_e/pres05_e/pr401_e.htm.

Note: The numbers represent annual change percentages.

realization that we live in an integrated world must become more deeply rooted. Increased attention to international business is therefore not only likely but also necessary.

INCREASING COMPLEXITY

The nature of international business also continues to grow more complex. As more and more nations industrialize, they offer both opportunities as well as threats in the field of international business. Many developing countries, such as Mexico, China, and India, have large corporations that are now competing for export markets as well as FDI opportunities in other countries. Most of the ex–socialistic bloc countries are selectively opening their economies for trade with the rest of the world. There is also increasing emphasis on boosting the trade participation of the heavily indebted countries of Latin America and sub-Saharan Africa, as that is seen to be an important solution to their current debt crises. Many developing

countries, disappointed by the performance of commodities trade, which had been their mainstay, are shifting their emphasis to the production and export of manufactured goods. This shift opens new opportunities for relocating production facilities, thereby establishing international manufacturing and trading arrangements. As these economies mature, they are better able to offer infrastructural facilities that provide electricity, transportation, communications, and labor and that can support large-scale manufacturing facilities. Low labor costs and government incentives are attracting overseas investments on a large scale to such countries. While FDI grew during the 1980s and 1990s in support of such activities, global inflows of FDI declined in 2003 for the third consecutive year. This was again due to a fall in FDI flows to developed countries. Worldwide, 111 countries saw a rise in flows, and 82 a decline. In the United States, FDI fell by 53 percent, to $30 billion, the lowest level in the past 12 years. In 2004, FDI flows improved slightly worldwide.

FDI into the United States rose by 69 percent in 2004 due to an increase in cross-border mergers and acquisitions, improved economic growth, and improved corporate profitability. One trend that did not reverse was the movement to services. In 1990, FDI services inflows accounted for 49 percent of the total FDI; in 2002, services accounted for 60 percent of inward FDI flows.[15]

TRADE IN SERVICES

The revolution in communications ushered in by the use of satellite-based computer networks has enabled almost instantaneous transmission of information from any part of the world. This development has resulted in an enormous expansion of the services industry—banking, travel and tourism, and consulting—all of which have expanded rapidly across the world, integrating trade in services more than ever into a global business framework.

THE FIELD OF INTERNATIONAL BUSINESS STUDIES

The large volumes of trade, the existence of huge multinational business entities, and the rapidly changing international business environment merely emphasize the fundamental interrelationships of business firms, governments, economies, and markets in the world today. Thus, the study of international business and the knowledge of the forces operating in the world have direct implications for everyone in the modern world: from consumers who are presented with an increasing array of foreign product choices, to political leaders who find more and more that political concerns are directly tied to economic and international trade concerns, and, naturally, to business managers, who face increasing competition from not only domestic but also foreign producers of goods and services, who, despite many disadvantages, have many factors working in their favor.

The study of international business also provides the modern business manager with a greater awareness of wider business opportunities than those available within local borders, which, in strategic management terms, means that the parameters of the manager's external environment, as well as the possible configuration of that external environment, have expanded for the modern and progressive firm.

The study of international business, however, does not merely expand the parameters of the external environment of the modern business firm. It stimulates a more basic, attitudinal change in doing business in this larger environment. The business manager is exposed to the problems that inward-looking attitudes—ethnocentrism and parochialism—can and do create for international business. The business manager is encouraged to become aware of these constraints and to overcome them by seeking practical solutions in the real world. Promotion of the awareness that people and cultures do differ around the globe and that these differences are sometimes crucial to the conduct of international business is very important. It is the starting point for developing attitudinal changes that move business managers to flexibility and adaptability in dealing with the varied situations that arise in the conduct of international business.

These developments over the past 50 years, a time of unparalleled growth and activity, provide a fascinating area of study for the student of international business. The trend is likely to continue upward, with increases in the flow of goods, capital, investments, and labor across national borders, and the growth of truly global industries and corporations.

DISCUSSION QUESTIONS

1. Why has international business become so important in today's environment?
2. What are some of the reasons that corporations choose to develop international operations?

3. What differentiates the modern multinational corporation from the import-export firm?

4. What factors make international business more complex than domestic business?

5. Obtain the annual report of a large multinational corporation and identify the scope of its international operations and the countries in which it currently operates.

6. What are some of the conflicts that may occur between a multinational corporation and the local government hosting the multinational?

7. How can increases in world trade affect the small businessperson in your hometown?

8. How can studying international business increase your understanding of the world around you?

NOTES

1. United Nations Conference on Trade and Development (UNCTAD), *World Investment Report 2004*.
2. "Foreign Direct Investment," *Economist*, September 23, 2004.
3. Wilkins, *Emergence of the Multinational Enterprise*.
4. Perlmutter, "Tortuous Evolution of the MNC."
5. U.S. Department of Commerce Bureau of International Commerce, *Trends in Direct Investment Abroad by U.S. Multinational Corporations*, 1975.
6. "Forbes Global 200," *Forbes*, April 17, 2006.
7. *Economist*, May 13, 2004.
8. Citigroup, *Citigroup 2003 Annual Report*.
9. Sony, *Annual Report 2003*.
10. Nestlé, "General Information."
11. Nestlé, "Indonesia: Bottled Water Joint Venture Between Nestlé and Coca-Cola," press release, July 20, 2004.
12. Some texts use the term "proprietary technology" for technology that has been patented by a firm.
13. World Trade Organization (WTO), "Statistics Database," 2004 (includes total exports and reexports), http://www.wto.org.
14. WTO, *World Trade Report 2004*, 20, Appendix Table 1A.1. http://www.wto.org. Accessed on April 5, 2006.
15. UNCTAD, *World Investment Report 2005*.

BIBLIOGRAPHY

Citigroup. *Citigroup 2003 Annual Report*. 2004.
"Foreign Direct Investment." *Economist*, September 23, 2004.
Nestlé. "General Information." *Management Report 2003*. 2003.
———. "Indonesia: Bottled Water Joint Venture Between Nestlé and Coca-Cola." Press release, July 20, 2004.
Perlmutter, Howard. "The Tortuous Evolution of the MNC." *Columbia Journal of World Business*, January–February 1969, 9–18.
Sony. *Annual Report 2003*. 2003.
Stopford, John M. *The World Directory of Multinational Enterprises, 1982–83*. Detroit: Gale Research Company, 1984.
United Nations Conference on Trade and Development (UNCTAD). *World Investment Report 2004*. New York: United Nations, 2004.
U.S. Department of Commerce. *Survey of Current Business*. Washington, DC: Government Printing Office (published quarterly).
U.S. Department of Commerce Bureau of International Commerce. *Trends in Direct Investment Abroad by U.S. Multinational Corporations*. Washington, DC: Government Printing Office (published quarterly).
Whiteside, David E., Otis Port, and Larry Armstrong. "Sony Isn't Mourning the 'Death' of Beta-max." *Business Week*, January 25, 1988, 37.
Wilkins, Mira. *The Emergence of the Multinational Enterprise: American Business Abroad from the Colonial Era to 1914*. Cambridge, MA: Harvard University Press, 1970.
World Bank. *The World Development Report, 1990*. Washington, DC: Oxford University Press, 1990.
World Trade Organization. *World Trade Report 2004*. Geneva: WTO, 2004, 20, Appendix Table 1A.1.

CASE STUDY 1.1
TRANSWORLD MINERALS, INC.

John Wright fully reclined his first-class seat and pulled a sleeping mask over his eyes; he wanted to relax, he told the stewardess, and would not have dinner for the next two or three hours. Wright was anything but relaxed, however. A senior vice president in charge of international investment planning with Transworld Minerals, Inc., a large multinational corporation based in Dallas, Texas, he was returning from a business trip to Salaysia, a small, mineral-rich country in Asia. His company was considering a major investment there in a new coal-mining project, using Transworld's recently developed advanced technology that highly automated all operations. Wright had just finished a preliminary evaluation of the prospects.

On the face of it, it looked like a great investment that would generate substantial revenues in the long run. Salaysia had enormous deposits of coal in the northeastern parts of the country, located principally in the Nebong Province. Most of these deposits had been recently discovered as the result of sustained geological exploration undertaken by Salaysia with the help of a large exploration firm from Australia. Most of the deposits were of high-quality anthracite coal, which was in considerable demand in steel manufacturing plants in China, Japan, and other, newly industrializing economies of Southeast Asia.

The government seemed encouraging, primarily because it did not have the technology to exploit these reserves and was badly in need of additional export revenues to meet the deficits in its balance of payments, which meant, however, that much of the project would have to be financed by Transworld.

Transworld had substantial financial resources. Its net working capital had been expanding steadily over the past five years, and it had been on schedule in repayment of all its loans from leading international banks in four countries: the United States, the United Kingdom, Japan, and China (via Hong Kong). It had an excellent credit standing, and two years ago, it had floated a successful bond issue in the UK market that raised £150 million to finance a major project in Zambia. It had good working relationships with banks in Singapore and Hong Kong, two leading financial centers in the region. Wright also had had discussions with the local branches of three multinational banks in Salaysia, and they appeared to be interested, at least on a preliminary consideration basis.

Transworld was the world leader in advanced coal-mining technology: Its latest processes resulted in high-speed extraction, that is, the stacking and loading of coal from depths that were not accessible to most of the existing mining techniques. Because the technology was highly automated, there were substantial economies resulting from saved labor costs. Most of the operations would be optimized by Transworld by using its sophisticated, computer-based optimization models, which would generate the best possible sequencing, timing, and coordination of different operations; these methods would be at least 20 percent more efficient than the technology currently in use in Salaysia.

The company had substantial marketing strength. It ran coal-mining operations in several countries in Asia and Africa and had other

continued

Case 1.1 (*continued*)

mineral extraction operations in Latin America. Most of the products were sold to industrial consumers in Japan, Italy, and France. Transworld had strong business relationships with major shipping lines and considerable strength at the bargaining table while negotiating pricing for shipping its products.

The world market for coal was expected to remain strong, and Transworld could reasonably expect to make at least an average level of profit on the exports of Salaysian coal.

There were a few problems. Salaysia's local coal-mining company was exerting substantial pressure on the home government to allow it to run the new project. It argued that it could access a similar level of technology by entering into a joint venture with Intermetals, an Australian mining company from which it could obtain the technical know-how, while the local implementation of the entire project would be in its hands. This venture would mean that Salaysia would be buying only the technical know-how from Australia, and the entire mining, extraction, processing, shipping, and marketing operations would be carried out by the Salaysian Coal Mining Company. The company had access to relatively dated machinery and extraction processes, but it had considerable

financial strength and good relations with the labor force. Although it was relatively unknown abroad, the company was a major force in Salaysia's domestic mining industry. The management of the Salaysian Coal Mining Company also had good relations with the current minister of industries and was attempting to convince him that placing the entire project into the hands of multinational Transworld would be detrimental to the national interest and that it could lead to foreign domination of the domestic coal-mining industry.

The Industries Ministry was weighing the two alternatives and had called for additional details before the proposals could be submitted to the Industrial Approvals Board of the Salaysian government for a final decision.

DISCUSSION QUESTIONS

1. What additional incentives should Wright suggest to improve the attractiveness of Transworld's proposal to the Industries Ministry?
2. What strategy should Transworld adopt to offset the political advantage enjoyed by the Salaysian Coal Mining Company?

CHAPTER 2

The Nature of International Business

"The individual serves the industrial system not by supplying it with savings and the resulting capital; he serves it by consuming its products."

John Kenneth Galbraith

CHAPTER OBJECTIVES

This chapter will:

- Explain the difference between the domestic and international contexts of business.
- Introduce the various entry methods a corporation may use to establish international business.
- Relate the changes in world trade patterns in terms of countries, products, and direct investment.
- Discuss the role of central governments in establishing trade policy and providing environments that support or restrict international trade.

DOMESTIC VERSUS INTERNATIONAL BUSINESS

The student of business is certainly familiar with the nature of doing business in a domestic market economy. A firm needs to identify its potential market, locate adequate and available sources of supplies of raw materials and labor, raise initial amounts of capital, hire personnel, develop a marketing plan, establish channels of distribution, and identify retail outlets. As an overlay upon this comprehensive system, the firm must also establish management controls and feedback systems, as well as accounting, finance, and personnel functions.

Not only must novice international businesspeople contend with establishing an international component to add to domestic operations, but they must also contend with the fact that international business activities are conducted in environments and arenas that differ from their own in all aspects: economies, cultures, government, and political systems. The differences range along a continuum. For example, economies can range from being market oriented to being *centrally planned*, and political systems from democracies to autocracies. As an example, the African nation of Zimbabwe, under the rule of Robert Mugabe, would be considered a centrally planned, autocratic government. Countries are widely divergent in cultural parameters such as ethnic varieties, religious beliefs, social habits, and customs. The difficulties these differences generate are exacerbated by problems of distance, which complicate the firm's ability to communicate clearly, transmit data and documents, and even find compatible business hours, because of office locations in different time zones. A U.S. firm with a subsidiary operation in the Far East faces a 15-hour time difference: The company's U.S. standard hours of 9 A.M. to 5 P.M. would be the equivalent of midnight to 8 A.M. in its Far East office.

Business activities require vast investments of time, energy, and personnel on the domestic level. Adding an international component merely intensifies the number of steps necessary and the length and breadth of the firm's reach of effort and activity. Imagine establishing international components for all business functions as separate and discrete units. The prospective commitment is staggering and is generally avoided by many domestic businesses.

It is more likely that domestic firms enter foreign markets in a progressive way, beginning with exporting, which involves the least amount of resources and risk, before moving to a full-scale commitment in the form of establishing wholly owned overseas subsidiaries. A concern must take many factors into consideration before deciding whether or not to move overseas. It must evaluate its own resources—personnel, assets, experience in overseas markets—and the suitability of its products or organization for transplantation overseas. It is also crucial that a firm decide on the minimum and optimum levels of return it wishes to receive, as well as the amount of risk it is willing to bear. A firm must also evaluate the level of control necessary to manage an overseas operation. These factors must be reviewed in light of the competition expected in

markets abroad and the potential business opportunities that are to be created by the international operation.

All these factors must be weighted in terms of the overall short-term and long-term strategic goals and objectives of the firm. For example, a firm may have a long-term goal to build a production facility abroad to serve a foreign market within ten years. Consequently, it would be unwise for the firm to enter into a short-term licensing agreement in that overseas market that would monopolize the use of its rights for a long period of time.

METHODS OF GOING INTERNATIONAL

EXPORTING

Exporting requires the least amount of involvement by a firm in terms of resources needed and allocated to serving an overseas market. Basically, the company uses existing domestic capacity for production, distribution, and administration and designates a certain portion of its home production to a market abroad. It makes the goods locally and sends them by air, ship, rail, truck, or even pipeline across its nation's borders into another country's market.

Entrance into an export market frequently begins casually, with the placement of an order by a customer overseas. At other times, an enterprise sees a market opportunity and actively decides to take its products or services abroad. A firm can be either a direct or an indirect exporter. As a direct exporter, it sees to all phases of the sale and transmittal of the merchandise. In indirect exporting, the exporter hires the expertise of someone else to facilitate the exchange. This intermediary is, of course, happy to oblige for a fee. There are several types of intermediaries: manufacturers' export agents, who sell the company's product overseas; manufacturers' representatives, who sell the products of a number of exporting firms in overseas markets; export commission agents, who act as buyers for overseas markets; export commission agents, who act as buyers for overseas customers; and export merchants, who buy and sell on their own for a variety of markets.

Sales contacts within the foreign market are made through personal meetings, letters, cables, telephone calls, or international trade fairs. Some of these trade expositions take unusual forms; for example, in an attempt to promote the sale of U.S. products in Japanese markets, the Japanese government established a traveling trade show on a train. In the initial stages, the objective of the exporter is to develop an awareness of outstanding features of the firm's products, such as competitiveness against local products, innovation, durability, or reasonable prices.

The mechanics of exporting require obtaining appropriate permission from domestic governments (for example, for food products, and for some technology and products considered crucial for national security); securing reliable transportation and transit insurance; and fulfilling requirements imposed by the importing nation, such as payment of appropriate duties, declarations, and inspections. Prior to the completion of the transaction, payment terms must be negotiated. The parties must establish the terms of the sale and whether the buyer will be extended credit, must open a letter of credit, will pay in advance, or will pay cash on delivery. In addition, the participants in the sale must determine which currency will be used in the exchange. The currency used is especially crucial in light of fluctuations in exchange rates between countries. Sometimes the facilitation of an international transaction is difficult if the two currencies involved (of the buyer and the seller) are not actively traded on the world markets. One method of completing the transaction is to use the U.S. dollar as an intermediary currency (the buyer converts his or her home currency into dollars and pays the seller in dollars; then the seller converts the dollars received into his or her

domestic currency). In this way the U.S. dollar has become a very important currency in international business today.

Advantages of Exporting

The prime advantage of exporting is that it involves very little risk and low allocation of resources for the exporter, who is able to use domestic production toward foreign markets and thus increase sales and reduce inventories. The exporter is not involved in the problems inherent in the foreign operating environment; the most that could be lost is the value of the exported products or an opportunity if the venture fails to establish the identity or characteristics of the product in the foreign market.

Exporting also provides an easy way to identify market potential and establish recognition of a name brand. If the enterprise proves unprofitable, the company can simply stop the practice with no diminution of operations in other spheres and no long-term losses of capital investments.

Disadvantages of Exporting

Exporting can be more expensive than other methods of overseas involvement on a per-unit basis because of not understanding the differences of the local market relative to the home market of the firm, and the costs of fees, commissions, export duties, taxes, and transportation. In addition, exporting could lead to less-than-optimal market penetration because of inappropriate packaging or promotion. Exported goods could also be lacking features appropriate to specific overseas markets. Relying on exporting alone, a firm may have trouble maintaining market share and contacts over long distances. Additional market share could be lost if local competition copies the products or services offered by the exporter. The exporting firm also could face restrictions against its products from the host country.

While some of these problems can be addressed by establishing direct exporting capability through the establishment of a sales company within the foreign market to handle the technical aspects of export trading and keep abreast of market developments, demand, and competition, many firms choose instead to expand their operations in foreign spheres to include other forms of investments.

LICENSING

Through *licensing*, a firm (licensor) grants a foreign entity (licensee) some type of intangible rights, which could be the rights to a process, a patent, a program, a trademark, a copyright, or expertise. In essence, the licensee is buying the assets of another firm in the form of know-how or R & D. The licensor can grant these rights exclusively to one licensee or nonexclusively to several licensees.

Advantages of Licensing

Licensing provides advantages to both parties. The licensor receives profits in addition to those generated from operations in domestic markets. These profits may be additional revenues from a single process or method used at home that the manufacturer is unable to utilize abroad. The method or process could have the beneficial effect of extending the life cycle of the firm's product beyond that which it would experience in local markets.

Additional revenues could also represent a return on a product or process that is ancillary to the strategic core of the firm in its domestic market; that is, the firm could have developed a method of production that is marketable as a separate product under a licensing agreement. In addition, by licensing, the firm often realizes increased sales by providing replacement parts abroad. Also, it protects itself against piracy by having an agent (the licensed user) who watches for copyright or patent infringement.

The licensee benefits from acquiring the rights to a process and acquires state-of-the-art technology while avoiding the R & D costs.

Disadvantages of Licensing

The prime disadvantage of licensing to the licensor is that it limits future profit opportunities associated with the property by tying up its rights for an extended period of time. Additionally, by licensing these rights to another, the firm loses control over the quality of its products and processes, the use or misuse of the assets, and even the protection of its corporate reputation.

To protect against such problems, the licensing agreement should clearly delineate the appropriate uses of the process, method, or name, as well as the allowable market and reexport parameters for the licensee. The contract should also stipulate contingencies and recourse, should the licensor or licensee fail to comply with its terms.

FRANCHISING

Franchising is similar to licensing, except that in addition to granting the franchisee permission to use a name, process, method, or trademark, the firm assists the franchisee with the operations of the franchise or supplies raw materials, or both. The franchisor generally also has a larger degree of control over the quality of the product than it does under licensing agreements. Payment under franchising agreements is similar to the payment scheme in licensing agreements in that the franchisee pays an initial fee and a proportion of its sales or revenues to the franchising firm.

The prime examples of U.S. franchising companies are service industries and restaurants, particularly fast-food concerns, soft-drink bottlers, and home and auto maintenance companies (for example, McDonald's, KFC, Holiday Inn, Hilton, and Disney in Japan).[1] Keep in mind that only companies with models that have been successful in the domestic market should consider franchising internationally. If the franchisor has not had success in the domestic market, it would not be wise to consider an international franchising program.

Advantages and Disadvantages of Franchising

The advantages accruing to the franchisor are increased revenues and expansion of its brand-name identification and market reach. The greatest disadvantage, as with licensing, is coping with the problems of assuring quality control and operating standards. Franchise contracts should be written carefully and provide recourse for the franchising firm, should the franchisee not comply with the terms of the agreement. Other difficulties with franchises come with their need to make slight adjustments or adaptations in the standardized product or service. For example, some ingredients in restaurant franchises may need to be adapted to suit the tastes of the local clientele, which may differ from those of the original customers.

MANAGEMENT CONTRACTS

Management contracts are contracts under which a firm basically rents its expertise or know-how to a government or company in the form of personnel who enter the foreign environment and run the concern. This method of involvement in foreign markets is often used with a new facility, after *expropriation* of a concern by a national government, or when an operation is in trouble.

Management contracts are frequently used in concert with turnkey operations. Under these agreements, firms provide the service of overseeing all details in the startup of facilities, including design, construction, and operation. These projects are usually large in scale, for example, production plants or utility constructions. The problem faced in turnkey operations is often the time length of the contract,

which yields long payout schedules and carries greater risk in currency markets. Other problems can arise in the form of an increase in potential competition as overseas capacity is increased by the new facilities. Turnkey operations also face all the problems of operating in remote locations.

CONTRACT MANUFACTURING

Contract manufacturing is another method firms use to enter the foreign arena. In this case, an MNC contracts with a local firm to provide manufacturing services. This arrangement is akin to *vertical integration*, except that instead of establishing its own production locations, the MNC subcontracts the production, which it can do in one of two ways. In one scenario, the MNC enters into a full production contract with a local plant producing goods to be sold under the name of the original manufacturer. In a second scenario, the MNC enters into contracts with another firm to provide partial manufacturing services, such as assembly work or parts production.

Contract manufacturing has the advantage of expanding the supply or production expertise of the contracting firm at minimum cost. Essentially, the MNC can diversify vertically without a full-scale commitment of resources and personnel. By the same token, the firm also forgoes some degree of control over the production supply timetable when it contracts with a local firm to provide specific services. These problems are, however, no more substantial than those that accompany standard raw material supplier contracts.

DIRECT INVESTMENT

When a company invests directly within foreign shores, it is making a very real commitment of its capital, personnel, and assets beyond domestic borders. While this commitment of resources increases the profit potential of an MNC dramatically by providing greater control over costs and operations of the foreign firm, it is also accompanied by an increase in the risks involved in operating in a foreign country and environment.

As with other forms of international activity, direct investment runs a continuum from *joint ventures*, in which risk is shared (as are returns), to *wholly owned subsidiaries*, in which MNCs have the opportunity to reap the rewards but must also shoulder the lion's share of the risk. Multinationals decide to make direct investments for two main reasons. The first is to gain access to enlarged markets. The second is to take advantage of cost differentials in overseas markets that arise from closer production resources, available economies of scale, and prospects for developing operating efficiencies. Both reasons lead to the enjoyment of enhanced profitability. Alternatively, a firm enters a foreign market for defensive reasons, to counter strategic moves by its competitors or to follow a market leader into new markets.

STRATEGIC ALLIANCES

Strategic alliances (or joint ventures) are business arrangements in which two or more firms or entities join together to establish some sort of operation (recall our discussion in Chapter 1 concerning Sony's cellular phone joint venture with Ericsson). Strategic alliances may be formed by two MNCs, an MNC and a government, or an MNC and local businesspersons. If there are more than two participants in the deal, the relationship can also be called a consortium operation.

Each party to these ventures contributes capital, equity, or assets. Ownership of the joint venture need not be a 50-50 arrangement and, indeed, percentage of ownership ranges according to the proportionate amounts contributed by each party to the enterprise. Some countries stipulate the relative amount of ownership allowable to foreign firms in joint ventures. Vietnam is an example of a country that has historically had foreign ownership limits with regard to joint ventures. The recently signed United States–Vietnam Bilateral Trade Agreement allows the 50 percent U.S. ownership of joint ventures in Vietnam to continue for three years. After five years, this requirement is lessened in the majority of industries, and U.S. companies will be able to own 51 percent of a joint venture in Vietnam. In some industries, such as hotels, restaurants, and travel agencies, the United States will have no equity-limit restrictions after five years.[2]

Advantages of Strategic Alliances

Strategic alliances provide many advantages for both local and international participants. By entering a local market with a local partner, an MNC finds an opportunity to increase its growth and access to new markets while avoiding excessive tariffs and taxes associated with importing products. At the same time, joining forces with local businesses often neutralizes local existing and potential competition and protects the firm against the risk of expropriation, because local nationals have a stake in the success of the operations of the firm. It is also frequently easier to raise capital in local markets when host-country nationals are involved in the operation. In some cases, host governments provide tax benefits as incentives to increase the participation of foreign firms in joint enterprises with local businesspersons.

Disadvantages of Strategic Alliances

The involvement of local ownership can also lead to major disadvantages for overseas partners in strategic alliances. Some of the problems that can be experienced by MNC partners are limits on profit repatriation to the parent office; successful operations becoming an inviting target for *nationalization* or expropriation by the host government; and problems of control and decision making. For example, different partners might have different objectives for the joint ventures. An MNC might have a goal of achieving profitability on a shorter timetable than its local partner, who might be more concerned about long-term profitability and maintaining local employment levels. It is necessary, therefore, that firms establish guidelines regarding the objectives, control, and decision-making structures of joint ventures before entering into agreements.

Joint ventures tend to be relatively lower-risk operations because the risks are shared by individual partners. Nevertheless, not having full control of the operation remains a predominant problem for the overseas participants in these ventures. A firm can achieve full control over operations, decision making, and profits only when it establishes its own wholly owned subsidiary on foreign soil.

WHOLLY OWNED SUBSIDIARIES

By establishing its own foreign arm, a firm retains total control over marketing, pricing, and production decisions and maintains greater security over its technological assets. In return, it is entitled to 100 percent of the profits generated by the enterprise. Although it faces no problems with minority shareholders, the firm bears the entire risk involved in operating the facility. These risks are the same as those customarily encountered in domestic operations, but with an additional layer of special risks associated with international operations, such as expropriation, limits on profits being repatriated, and local operating laws and regulations, including the requirement to employ local labor and management personnel. In these cases, the MNCs do not have the benefit of local shareholders to run interference for them with local governments.

In establishing a subsidiary, a firm must choose either of two routes: acquire an ongoing operation or start from scratch and build its own plant. Buying a firm (also known as the *brownfield strategy*) has the advantage of avoiding startup costs of capital and a time lag. It is a faster process that is often easier to capitalize at local levels and generally cheaper than building. Buying also has the advantages of not adding to a country's existing capacity levels and of improving goodwill with host-country nationals.

A company may decide to build a new plant (also known as the *greenfield strategy*) if no suitable facilities exist for acquisition or if it has special requirements for design or equipment. Although building a plant may avoid acquiring the problems of an existing physical plant, the firm may face difficulties in obtaining adequate financing from local capital markets and may generate ill will among local citizenry.[3]

GLOBALIZED OPERATIONS

Some theorists believe that consumers around the world are becoming increasingly alike in their goals and requirements for products and product attributes.[4] As a result, the world is moving toward becoming a global market in which products would be standardized across all cultures, which would enable corporations to manufacture and sell low-cost reliable products around the world. Such firms would be characterized by globalized operations, as distinct from multinational operations. A firm that has globalized operations would be able to take advantage of business opportunities occurring anywhere in the world and would not be constrained to specific sectors. Indeed, some firms have been able to achieve substantial globalization of operations as their products cross national borders, without being adapted to individual country preferences. Prime examples include Levi Strauss, PepsiCo, Coca-Cola, and several other companies ranging from consumer goods to fast food.

PORTFOLIO INVESTMENTS

Portfolio investments do not require the physical presence of a firm's personnel or products on foreign shores. These investments can be made in the form

Figure 2.1 **Global Diversification**

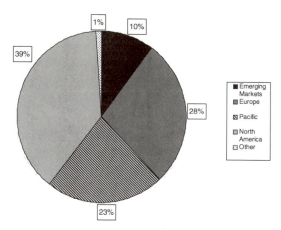

Source: Regional Allocations of Global Equity Fund as of March 31, 2006. Vanguard Group Company website.

of marketable securities in foreign markets, such as notes, bonds, commercial paper, certificates of deposit, and noncontrolling shares of stock. They can also be investments in foreign bank accounts or as foreign loans. Investors make decisions to acquire securities or invest money abroad for several reasons: primarily to diversify their portfolios among markets and locations, to achieve higher rates of return, to avoid political risks by taking their investments out of the country, or to speculate in foreign exchange markets.

Portfolio investments can be made either by individuals or through special investment funds. These investment funds pool local resources for investment in overseas stock and financial markets. Many mutual fund companies, such as Fidelity and Vanguard, have funds with an international focus. These funds invest in companies in a specific region of the world for investors in the United States. This allows both individuals as well as institutional investors to diversify their investments geographically. The Vanguard Global Equity Fund, for example, invests in a total of 553 companies worldwide and has current assets of $3.5 billion. Figure 2.1 shows how this fund is geographically disbursed in terms of its portfolio of investments.[5]

Over the last few years, some emerging economies have reformed the rules and regulations to encourage foreign investment.[6] Most developed countries allow free access to their stock markets to overseas investors. Other developing economies allow less access to their stock markets. Overall, the countries of the developing world range from being less restrictive than they have been in the past, to providing an open market system for foreign investors.

There are several factors that determine the degree to which a particular country will be able to attract portfolio investments. Political stability and economic growth are the most basic factors. The size, liquidity, and stability of stock markets, the level of government taxes, and the nature of government regulation are also important determinants. The degree of restrictions on repatriation of income and capital invested are other major variables that affect the attractiveness of a country to overseas portfolio investors. Most international portfolio investment is concentrated in the industrialized countries, and the United States, Japan, France, the

Figure 2.2   **Growth in World Trade**

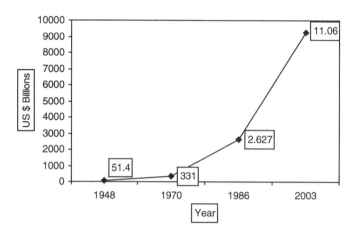

Source: World Trade Organization (WTO), "Statistical Database," 2004, http://www.wto.org.

United Kingdom, Switzerland, the Netherlands, and Canada receive substantial amounts of portfolio investments in their markets. Some emerging stock markets, such as those in China, India, Malaysia, Indonesia, and Taiwan, have been able to attract significant amounts of foreign portfolio investment. In 2003, the United States received portfolio investments of $544.5 billion. The European Union received $342.7 billion, and the United Kingdom alone received $149.3 billion. In contrast, the emerging markets and developing countries of the world received portfolio investments of $62 billion, which was the highest such total since 1996.[7]

One of the reasons that the majority of portfolio investments are received in the developed world is due to the soundness of the financial system. During the first quarter of 2004, the United States' banking sector had only 1.1 percent of its total loans classified as nonperforming (past due or in collection or liquidation status). Comparatively, Argentina and Ukraine had 28 percent of their total bank loans in nonperforming status. Portfolio investment fell in these countries accordingly.[8]

RECENT TRADE PATTERNS AND CHANGES IN GLOBAL TRADE

As the world has become more industrialized and as markets have become global entities, trade has increased proportionately and grown tremendously in both volume and dollar terms. Concomitantly, patterns in trade have also changed, as new nations enter the world-trading arena. In 1948 world trade totaled $51.4 billion. This figure rose to $331 billion in 1970, increased to $2.627 trillion in 1986, and reached $11.06 trillion in 2004.[9] This increase in world trade volume can be best illustrated by Figure 2.2.

Most of the world's trade is carried out among the industrialized countries. This group of countries, comprising western Europe, North America, and Japan, currently accounts for 65.2 percent of exports sent to other countries and receives 68 percent of all imports.[10] In comparison, developing countries account for only 28.2 percent of exports and take in 25.6 percent of imports. These figures include the volumes attributed to members of the Organization of the Petroleum Exporting Countries (OPEC),[11]

Table 2.1

OPEC's Share of the World Market, 2003
(in percent)

	Crude Oil	Natural Gas
Reserves	78	49
Production	40	16

Source: Organization of the Petroleum Exporting Countries (OPEC), *OPEC Annual Statistical Bulletin, 2004* (Vienna: OPEC, 2005).

Table 2.2

World's Leading Exporters

Country	% of Total World Exports (goods and services)
1 European Union	17.16
2 United States	13.59
3 Germany	9.11
4 United Kingdom	6.63
5 Japan	6.11
6 France	5.23
7 China	4.13
8 Italy	3.95
9 Canada	3.55
10 Netherlands	3.35

Source: The Economist Pocket World in Figures, 2005 Edition (London: Economist, 2005), 34.

which account for 5.1 percent of world exports and 2.8 percent of imports. Table 2.1 itemizes OPEC's importance in the global economy.

OPEC's participation in world trade declined in the second half of the 1980s because prices and demand for oil had fallen since the early 1970s. Given the recent upswing in the demand for oil (due to the expansion of the Chinese economy and the continued demand of the United States) and the price per barrel of oil, OPEC retains a major proportion of the share of developing countries' exports in world trade. Without the contribution of OPEC, the share of the remaining developing countries' exports in world trade is only 24.7 percent.[12]

This pattern of trade is changing, however, as the fortunes of nations change in different trading regions. While high-income, developed countries continue to hold the lion's share of world trade, greater portions of activity are being taken over by new entrants into the world market. The most notable, historically, is Japan, which completely reversed its fortunes, prospects, and future since its reconstruction and growth after World War II. In 1950 Japan had merchandise exports of $820 million and imports of $974 million; by 1970 these levels had risen to exports of $19.318 billion and imports of $8.881 billion. By 2003 Japan was exporting $542 billion worth of products and services in world markets and importing products and services valued at $493 billion.[13]

Japan is being joined by other countries that are nipping at the heels of the wealthy, industrialized nations and rapidly increasing their levels of industrialization, production, and exports. Some of Japan's increased exports were imported by the rapidly developing Chinese economy. The value of Chinese exports of goods and services in 2003 was $483 billion, while its imports had a value of $467 billion. Given China's strong projected gross domestic product (GDP) growth over the next decade, this trend is sure to continue. Other challengers to Japan include the so-called four tigers, or *newly industrialized countries (NICs)*: South Korea, Taiwan, Singapore, and Hong Kong. Trade activity by these nations is slowly moving the focus of international trade patterns away from traditional routes of north-north activity, between developed countries, to those of increased trade between north and south, that is, between developed and developing nations. Similarly, the growth in trade by less-developed countries is increasing, as economic development and increases in standards of living provide citizens of those nations with higher incomes and surplus resources to spend on goods other than basic necessities.

These trends in the trade patterns of the twentieth century indicate a reduction of U.S. and European dominance in the world trade arena. On the other hand, the Asian and Middle Eastern countries are increasing their participation in world trade because of their rapid industrialization and the importance of petroleum and petroleum products. U.S. trade with these countries has also been increasing significantly, marking a departure from its traditional trading pattern that relied to a very large extent on trade with European trading partners. Furthermore, changes in the international political climate, especially the thawing of relations with countries with centrally planned economies as they move toward market economies, has led to marked increases in U.S. trade with Russia and the former Soviet bloc countries and the People's Republic of China. Rapid and far-reaching technological developments have also affected trade patterns, because raw material monopolies have been shattered by hi-tech substitutes, such as synthetic products. Countries that were major exporters of such raw materials have had to look for other products to export, and export market shares have shifted dramatically in these commodities, for example, rubber and metals.

PRODUCT GROUPS

In world trade, the major product categories of goods are manufactured goods, machinery, and fuels, which account for 80 percent of all world commodity trade. The remaining 20 percent of commodity types are crude commodities, agricultural products, and chemicals. Until 1972, manufactured goods continued to increase in relative importance in world trade. After that, they began to decline in importance because of the increase in oil prices and the worldwide recession that followed. The developed countries account for the largest proportion of goods traded in world markets. The European Union emerged as the world's leading exporter, but the United States was the largest single-country exporter. The United States is the world's leading exporter of services as well.

Less-developed countries have increased their relative shares of world trade. Non–Middle Eastern Asian countries slightly increased their exports during the period 1980 to 2003 (to roughly 9 percent of world commodity exports), as compared to an overall decline in total Middle East exports over the same period. The regions of Africa and Central and South America stayed relatively constant over the past two decades, with each accounting for less than 3 percent of the world's commodity exports. China's portion of world commodity exports rose by 35 percent from 2002 to 2003, and China's exports now account for 6 percent of world commodity exports, while its imports rose in the same period by 40 percent and now account for 5.5 percent of world totals.

PATTERNS OF DIRECT INVESTMENT

As trading patterns in merchandise continue to change, so do the patterns of countries investing in resources abroad. Many believe that direct investment activity is a natural adjunct to trading activities in different locations; that is, investment funds follow trade activity. Direct investment can be measured according to the source country of funds or ownership. Generally, foreign direct investment of capital is differentiated from portfolio investments according to levels of managerial involvement and control by owners. Some countries distinguish effective control according to a level of percentage ownership. The United States, for example, in the past has used a level of 10 percent as a criterion.

World FDI levels were $648.1.6 billion by the end of 2004. This figure is misleading, however, because it reflects the book value of the investments, which is the value at which they were acquired, and is a historical figure that does not account for appreciation in value over time or for

Figure 2.3   **FDI into the United States**

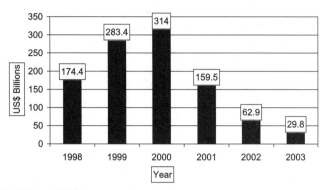

Source: UNCTAD, *World Trade Report*, 2004.

inflation. According to recent studies, the bulk of world direct investment is within the industrialized countries of the world. The United States, France, and the United Kingdom together account for about 43 percent of the world total FDI.[14] Fewer than 20 countries hold more than 95 percent of direct overseas investments. Foreign direct investments are generally made according to two patterns: geographically between countries that are in close proximity to each other, and along traditional lines, such as those based on the strength of historical or political alliances or those made by countries in their former colonies. While FDI into the United States has been trending downward over the past few years, as was discussed in Chapter 1, this tendency was due primarily to a worldwide recession and historically low interest-rate levels in the United States (see Figure 2.3). Also, with the arrival of China and India on the world stage, there are now many other destinations for FDI. While the portion of the U.S. share is decreasing, the amount of FDI worldwide is increasing.

Investments, in general, are made by very large firms and have seen their highest growth in the areas of manufacturing, petroleum, and industries that require high levels of capital assets. The investments are made primarily in industrial countries with the lowest level of risk and the largest possible markets.

GOVERNMENT INVOLVEMENT IN TRADE RESTRICTIONS AND INCENTIVES

All governments attempt to restrict or support international trade or transfers of resources. This intervention can take the form of controlling the flow of trade and transfer of goods, controlling the transfer of capital flows, or controlling the movement of personnel and technology. Rationales for intervention vary but fall into several patterns, all of which are based on the notion that the governmental actions will promote the best interests of the nation.

Governments may be motivated by economic goals, such as increasing revenues or the supply of hard currency in the country. They also may have economic or monetary considerations in equalizing balances of trade or keeping inflation to a minimum. They may cite national objectives, such as maintaining self-sufficiency, economic independence, and national security. There may be specific concerns in the country regarding the welfare of the populace, such as health and safety considerations or full employment goals. Political objectives also play a major role in governmental establishment of trade policy.

PROTECTIONISM

Protectionism refers to government intervention in trade markets to protect specific industries in its economy. Impetus for protecting industries comes from special-interest groups within different sectors of the economy who plead their case for protecting domestic capacity and production facilities. Many believe that calls for protectionism should be interpreted as a need for the country to make structural changes in its industrial base, in order to increase its competitiveness in foreign markets, rather than have government intervention support inefficient industries.

One rationale promulgated for protecting industry is to ensure full employment. This argument holds that the substitution of imports for domestic products causes jobs to be lost at home and that protecting industries is necessary for a strong domestic employment base.

A second rationale is that of protecting infant industries, which is especially pertinent in less-developed and developing countries. The *infant-industry argument* holds that newly established industries cannot compete effectively at first against established giants from industrialized nations. Consequently, the industry is protected (theoretically) until such time as it can grow to achieve economies of scale and operational efficiencies matching those of its major competitors. Under this scenario, difficulties occur when the time comes to withdraw such protection, which by then has become institutionalized and is vociferously defended by industry participants. This argument was first made by Alexander Hamilton, the first U.S. secretary of the treasury, in 1792. Hamilton wanted to protect the fledgling industries of the new nation from European competition (he also advocated the idea of not recognizing foreign patents and copyrights for similar competitive reasons).

A third rationale for protecting specific industries is that the industrialization objectives of a country justify a promotion of specific sectors of the economy in order to diversify the economic structure. Thus, protection and incentives are given to those industries that are expected to grow quickly, bring in investment dollars, and yield higher marginal returns. For this reason, many developing countries attempt to promote the growth of industries that provide high-value-added materials and emphasize the use of locally available agricultural or primary raw materials.

The ultimate rationale for protectionism is more accurately based in emotionalism than in sound economic arguments, and its cost is high. Protectionism leads to higher prices for consumers for imported products and components. It may lead to retaliation by importing countries, which may reduce the home country's exports abroad and employment in local markets. Protectionism also may increase opportunity costs by allocating the resources of a country inappropriately and at the expense of other sectors of the industrial base.

The methods of governmental intervention in markets take several different forms. The primary and most direct method is through the application of tariffs to exports or imports. A less direct method is the application of nontariff barriers.

TARIFFS

Tariffs or *duties* are a basic method of governmental intervention in trade and may be used either to protect industries by raising the price of imports, to bring import prices even with domestic prices, or to generate revenues. Tariffs may be placed on goods leaving the country, as export duties, or on goods entering the country, as import duties. They are the most typical controls on imports. Tariffs are assessed in three different ways:

1. *Ad valorem duties* are assessed on the value of the goods and are levied as a percentage of that value.

2. *Specific duties* are assessed according to a physical unit of measurement, such as on a per-ton, per-bushel, or per-meter rate, and are stipulated at a specific monetary value.

3. *Compound tariffs* are a combination of ad valorem and specific duties.

Determining Tariffs

Tariffs have an advantage as a tool for government intervention in international markets because they can be varied and applied on a selective basis according to commodity or country of origin. Some countries can be assessed higher duties on their imports than others. These duties are prescribed according to tariff schedules. Single-column schedules are those in which the duties on products and commodities are the same for everyone. Multicolumn schedules list tariffs rates for different products and different countries according to trade agreements between the importing and exporting countries.

Some countries that are treated separately are those that have *most-favored-nation (MFN)* status accorded to them. These countries have entered into agreements under which all the signatories are accorded the same preferential tariff status. Countries enter into these agreements to facilitate entry of their own exports and for political and other economic reasons. There are many groups of trading partners in the world, the largest and most important of which began as the General Agreement on Tariffs and Trade (GATT), which was established soon after World War II with an original membership of 19 countries. GATT was replaced by the World Trade Organization (WTO) in 1995, which was expanded to include discussions on services (in addition to merchandise exports); it now includes 149 member nations.

WORLD TRADE ORGANIZATION

The purpose of the WTO is to establish an umbrella under which its signatory members can meet to establish reciprocal reductions in tariffs and the liberalization of trade in a mutual and nondiscriminatory manner. A major objective of the body is to extend tariff accords and MFN status to all members. Under the WTO, methods and rules of trade liberalization are established with provisions for monitoring trade activity, enforcement, and the settling of disputes. WTO rules allow for certain exceptions to reduce trade barriers, such as allowing countries to continue to provide support for domestic agriculture and for developing countries to protect infant industries.

Reductions in trade barriers are achieved through the meeting of the signatories in negotiating sessions, or trade rounds. These meetings are held periodically to discuss the further lowering of barriers to trade. In recent rounds, WTO members have attempted to deal with nontariff problems and other current issues, such as trade in agriculture and services, technology transfer, and nonmonetary barriers put up by countries to discourage free trade. *Doha Agenda*, which began in 2001, is a trade round, focusing on integrating the developing countries into the world economy, and on opening market access between these countries and the developed world. (For a more detailed discussion of the WTO, see Chapter 6.)

REGIONAL TRADE GROUPS AND CARTELS

Trade groups organized along regional or political lines are less pervasive and influential. Two major regional trading groups are the *European Union (EU)*, which is composed of 25 European countries, and the *North American Free Trade Agreement (NAFTA)*, which includes the United States, Canada, and Mexico.

Traditionally, trade groups have also been organized according to specific commodity types and agreements that allow for monitoring or controlling the supply of those commodities, or both. Ten such basic commodities have been identified by the United Nations: coffee, cocoa, tea, sugar, cotton, rubber, jute, sisal, copper, and tin. Some of these commodities are traded on open and free markets, and their prices fluctuate to a great degree. Sales of some of the other commodities on this list, such as sugar, rubber, tin, cocoa, and coffee, have historically come under the aegis of international commodity agreements that promote use of import and export quotas and a system of buffer stocks. In today's marketplace, prices are subject to market pressure, so these types of groups are less meaningful than they have been in the past. Other trade groups are organized among producers, consumers, or both.

Generally, under these agreements prices are allowed to move up and down within a certain range, but if the price moves above or below that range, an outside collective agency is authorized to buy or sell the commodity to support its price. Similarly, a commodity agreement may provide for quotas on exports from individual supply countries to limit supplies of the commodities on world markets, thus shoring up prices.

CARTELS

Another form of a commodity agreement group is the *cartel*, in which a group of commodity-producing countries join forces to bargain as a single entity in world markets. A cartel can be formed only when there is a relatively small group of producers who hold an oligopoly position; that is, they control the bulk of the commodity supply. The most notable cartel in recent years has been the *Organization of the Petroleum Exporting Countries (OPEC)*, which is composed primarily of Middle Eastern countries, such as Saudi Arabia, Qatar, Iraq, Libya, Algeria, Kuwait, the United Arab Emirates, and Iran, as well as other oil-producing countries in the world, such as Venezuela, Indonesia, and Nigeria.

In the early 1970s, OPEC was able to raise the price of crude oil fourfold, from $3.64 per barrel to

$11.65 per barrel, within a single year. It was able to do so because it had a great deal of leverage in the world marketplace; its members controlled more than half of the world production of oil in 1973. World demand for oil was very high, and the top oil-consuming countries were not able to meet the demand with domestic supplies.[15] There were few suitable energy substitutes being utilized around the world. The cartel was also successful because its members adhered to their production and pricing agreements.

Frequently, cartels fail because members violate their agreements by dropping prices or raising production and forcing the other members back into a competitive position. Although this did not occur with OPEC, the cartel's hold on world markets began to slip in the mid-1970s as a worldwide recession, conservation, and the use of energy substitutes reduced the demand for oil. In addition, non-OPEC producers increased their production to take advantage of price escalations in world markets. Political turmoil, the emergence of the Chinese economy, and an insatiable demand for oil by the United States has recently led to an increase in the price of oil to more than $50 per barrel. In 2003, world oil demand was 78.7 millions barrels per day, and world oil supply was 79.3 million barrels per day. North America (led by the United States) accounted for 31 percent of the total demand, but only 18 percent of world oil supply.[16]

NONTARIFF BARRIERS TO MERCHANDISE TRADE

Nontariff barriers have become a controversial topic in trade activity over the past decade. They are a matter of concern because they are not traditional methods of discouraging imports through the application of duties. Instead, they work to slow the flow of goods into a country by increasing the physical and administrative difficulties involved in importing.

Nontariff barriers can take a number of forms that provide effective restraints on trade:

- Government discrimination against foreign suppliers in bidding procedures
- Highly involved and rigorous *customs* and country-entry procedures
- Excessively severe inspection and standards requirements
- Detailed safety specifications and domestic testing requirements
- Required percentages of domestic material content

Some nations regulate the importation of certain products that they deem harmful to their citizens. Canada, for example, has strict entry requirements for individuals and companies that are bringing tobacco products into the country. Other countries attempt to control the amount of a certain product being imported to a country by returning entire shipments of goods just because one sample failed to meet the accepted standards. In the aftermath of the Canadian mad cow disease scare in May 2003, Japanese officials discussed the possibility of requiring that all imported Canadian beef products be inspected, rather than requiring the sampling of just a certain number, which was the typical procedure. Instead of incurring the cost of such inspections, the government of Japan decided to ban future shipments of Canadian beef until the problems surrounding this issue in Canada could be resolved.

Some countries have restrictions on services, such as those that prohibit transportation carriers from serving specific destinations, or those that allow only advertising featuring models of that country's nationality.

QUOTAS

The most widely used method of restricting quantity, volume, or value-based imports is the imposition of *quotas on* imports into a country. These quotas may be unilateral according to commodity and stipulate that only a certain aggregate amount of the import from any source may enter a country. Alternatively, they can be selective on a country or regional basis. A type of quota is an *embargo*, which prohibits all trade between countries. Another type, encountered only in recent trade history, is the voluntary entry restriction, in which foreign countries agree to restrict their exports to a country, but are actually forced into compliance through the use of direct or subtle political pressure by major trading partners.

While the imposition of quotas may impede the flow of imports into a country, it does little to help that country find a level of readjustment; that is, it does nothing in the way of leading to lowered domestic prices. It often leads to higher import prices.

NONTARIFF PRICE BARRIERS

Nontariff and competitive barriers can also be implemented as adjustments in prices. For example, some countries use *subsidies* to enhance the competitiveness of their exports in international markets. In a recent WTO dispute, the United States insisted that Canada had subsidized its softwood lumber industry, a charge that Canada denied. The subsidized industry would have then been able to sell its product in the United States at a much-reduced cost, thereby gaining a competitive advantage. The WTO decided in favor of Canada in July 2004, although the result was disputed by the United States. Some subsidized services, such as export promotion, are permissible according to trade conventions. Others, such as special *tax incentives* or government provisions of fundamental research, are being contested by trading nations as violations of free trade.

The imposition of quotas also causes serious administrative problems for the authorities of both the importing and exporting countries. Once quotas are imposed, the amount of goods to be sent from the exporting country is not determined by market demand but by an arbitrary ceiling. The quantity of goods allowed to be exported under the quota ceilings is often much lower than the normal export levels, which implies that all exporters of the affected country cannot export at their previous levels. The new levels have to be determined by the authorities, which for large and widespread export industries is an expensive and cumbersome process. Problems arise for the importing country because the imported quantities under the quota rules are not adequate to meet market demand, and the government has to take over the role of the market in allocating the available goods imported under quota rules. Apart from the expense and delays of the administrative process that is required to accomplish nonmarket distribution of imported goods, there is also the danger of creating inequities, because it is often difficult to verify genuine needs and claims by the citizens who are demanding access to imported products that are being rationed by the government.

Some countries raise the effective costs of exporting by assessing special fees for importing, requiring customs deposits, or establishing minimum sales prices in foreign markets, thereby making it less profitable for exporters to send goods to their markets. Similarly, the manipulation of exchange rates can affect the position of a country's goods in overseas markets, because undervaluing a country's currency exchange rate will make that country's goods more competitive abroad.

Another type of nontariff price barrier is erected by valuing imports at customs under the ad valorem method of assessing tariffs. Countries can vary their valuation criteria and value goods at their own country's retail prices rather than at the wholesale or invoice prices being paid by the importer.

In determining the appropriate pricing levels for tariffs in the event of disputes, one would first use the invoice price, then the price of identical goods, then the price of similar goods. A particular problem arises when goods are entering a market-based economy from a centrally planned or nonmarket economy where there is no established pricing structure or valuation procedure. A recent example of this problem has involved the Chinese furniture industry. Many U.S. manufacturers have accused China of *dumping*[17] its furniture in the U.S. market in an effort to unfairly gain market share. A similar case occurred when nonmarket economies tried to bring chemical fertilizers into the United States at below-market prices, which was achieved by undervaluing the costs of crucial inputs such as natural gas.

GOVERNMENT RESTRICTION OF EXPORTS

In addition to controlling or taxing national imports, governments often have laws and regulations that limit certain types of exports generally or to specific countries. Governments apply these limits to maintain domestic supply and price levels of goods, to keep world prices high, or to meet national defense, political, or environmental goals. In the United States, under the Export Administration Act of 1969 and its amendments of 1979, U.S. export licenses could be limited because of foreign policy objectives, for the protection of the economy from a drain of limited or scarce resources, or for military use by the recipient nations. Licenses are required for the export of items on the U.S. controlled-commodity list and for the export of any product to communist countries. The administration of these licenses is overseen by the U.S. Department of Commerce in tandem with the Departments of State and Defense.

SUMMARY

International business requires the same basic functional and operational activities as domestic business. As international business crosses borders, however, it encounters different economies, cultures, legal systems, governments, and languages, which must be integrated into business policies and practices. Entry into international business varies along a continuum, beginning with the simplest form, exporting, through other entry methods, which include licensing, franchising, contract manufacturing, direct investment, joint ventures, wholly owned subsidiaries, globalized operations, and portfolio investments.

Recent changes in global trade patterns reveal a reduction in the dominance of the United States and Europe, while Asian (especially Japan and the four tigers) and Middle Eastern countries are increasing their levels of output. Direct investment, 43 percent of which is held by the United States, France, and the United Kingdom, is generally located in the industrialized countries, where risks are lowest and potential returns are high.

The governments of host countries play an important role in either restricting or supporting international trade. Often, international trade policies are determined to achieve economic or monetary goals; maintain national security; improve health, safety, and employment levels; or support specific political objectives. Protectionism, tariffs, nontariff barriers, and government restrictions on exports are direct and indirect methods of restricting international trade.

DISCUSSION QUESTIONS

1. Which factors should a firm consider before it decides to conduct business internationally?
2. Which method of going international would you use if you were

   - An automobile manufacturer?
   - A software developer?
   - An oil exploration-production company?
   - An electrical power plant builder ?
   - A farmer with a large surplus of wheat?
   - A restaurant operator with a new barbecued ribs recipe?

   What were your reasons?

3. When might a corporation "go international" using a joint-venture approach rather than a wholly owned subsidiary approach? Give an example.
4. What type of business transaction generally uses a turnkey operation approach?
5. Identify the top five leading exporting countries.
6. Who are the four tigers?
7. Which country is the leading provider of services in the world?
8. Give a recent example in which China has invested directly in the United States.
9. How might multinational direct investment help or hurt the country receiving the investment?
10. Discuss the methods governments use to protect their domestic business environments.

NOTES

1. D.A. Bell, *Business America*, 1986.
2. U.S.-Vietnam Trade Council, "Vietnam Trade Agreement: Summary of Key Provisions," http://www.usvtc.org.
3. Kitching, "Winning and Losing with European Acquisition."
4. Levitt, "Globalization of Markets."
5. Vanguard Group. Fund-specific information as of March 31, 2006.
   http://flagship4.vanguard.com/VGApp/hnw/FundsSnapshot?FundId=0129&FundIntExt=INT.
6. International Finance Corporation, *Emerging Stock Markets Fact Book*.
7. International Monetary Fund, *Global Financial Stability Report*, September 2004.
8. Ibid.
9. World Trade Organization (WTO), "Statistical Database," 2004 (includes total exports and reexports), http://www.wto.org.
10. WTO, *World Trade Report 2004*, 20, Appendix Table 1A.1.
11. OPEC members include Algeria, Indonesia, Iran, Iraq, Kuwait, Libya, Nigeria, Qatar, Saudi Arabia, United Arab Emirates, and Venezuela.
12. OPEC, *OPEC Annual Statistical Bulletin, 2003* (Vienna: OPEC, 2004).

13. World Trade Organization, *World Trade Report 2004.*

14. UNCTAD, "Country Fact Sheets," 2004.

15. John Daniels and Lee Radebaugh, "The Middle East Squeeze on Oil Grants," *Business Week*, July 29, 1972, 56.

16. OPEC, *OPEC Annual Report 2003* (Vienna: OPEC, 2004).

17. In international trade, dumping is defined as one country selling a product in another country at a price that is less than the cost of production of that same product in the destination country.

BIBLIOGRAPHY

Belassa, Bela, ed. *Changing Patterns in Foreign Trade and Payments.* 3rd ed. New York: Norton, 1978.

Czinkota, Michael R. "International Trade and Business in the Late 1980s: An Integrated U.S. Perspective." *Journal of International Business Studies*, Spring 1986, 127–34.

International Finance Corporation. *Emerging Stock Markets Fact Book.* Washington, DC: International Finance Corporation, 2004.

International Monetary Fund (IMF). *Global Financial Stability Report.* Washington, DC: IMF, 2004.

Kitching, John. "Winning and Losing with European Acquisition." *Harvard Business Review*, March–April 1974, 81.

Levitt, Theodore. "Globalization of Markets." *Harvard Business Review*, May–June 1983, 92–102.

Mirus, Rolf, and B. Yeung. "Economic Incentives for Countertrade." *Journal of International Business Studies*, Fall 1986, 27–39.

Schoening, Niles C. "A Slow Leak: Effects of the U.S. Shifts in International Investment." *Survey of Business*, Spring 1988, 21–26.

Suzuki, Katshiko. "Choice Between International Capital and Labor Mobility of Diversified Economies." *Journal of International Economics*, November 1989, 347–61.

United Nations. *Statistical Yearbook.* New York: United Nations, 2004.

United Nations Conference on Trade and Development (UNCTAD). "Country Fact Sheets," 2004.

UNCTAD. *World Trade Report 2004.* World Trade Organization, Appendix Table 1A.1. http://www.unctad.org/Templates/Page.asp?intItemID=2441&lang=1.

U.S. Department of Commerce. *Survey of Current Business.* Washington DC: Government Printing Office, October 9, 2004.

U.S. Vietnam Trade Council. "Vietnam Trade Agreement: Summary of Key Provisions." http://www.usvtc.org.

Vanguard Group. Fund-specific information as of October 9, 2004 http://flagship4.vanguard.com/VGApp/hnw/FundsSnapshot?FundId=0129&FundIntExt=INT.

World Bank. *World Development Report, 2004.* New York: Oxford University Press, 2004.

World Trade Organization. "Statistical Database." 2004 (includes total exports and reexports in 2003). http://www.wto.org.

CASE STUDY 2.1

ELECTRONICS INTERNATIONAL, LTD.

Electronics International, Ltd., is a large consumer electronics manufacturer based in Southampton, England. Its product line consists of CD players, DVD players, home entertainment systems, and so on. Annual sales in 2004 were $186 million, 44 percent of which came from overseas sales. Most of the company's exports went to developing countries in Asia and Africa, with a small percentage of its products going to Turkey and Greece. Its most important export market is Zempa, a relatively prosperous developing country in the western part of Africa. Exports to Zempa total nearly 26 percent of all export revenues and have been showing an upward trend for the past six years.

Total sales to Zempa in 2005 were $120 million, up from $40 million in 1998 and $110 million in 2004. The company controlled approximately 20 percent of the audio products market in Zempa, with the rest being taken up by other competitors, all of whom were overseas corporations. Zempa has no audio products manufacturing industry, and all domestic requirements were met through imports. Electronics International was the third largest player in the Zempa market, with the top two slots being occupied by a German company and a Japanese company. Electronics International's products were well established and enjoyed considerable customer loyalty.

Recently, some problems have emerged. The government of Zempa has become increasingly concerned about the relatively backward state of its manufacturing industry and wants to rapidly industrialize the economy by attracting overseas investment in key sectors. One of the important priorities for the Zempa government in this connection is the consumer electronics industry. As a part of its policy to develop the local economy by stimulating domestic manufacturing activity, the Zempa government inquired with each of the major exporters of consumer electronics products about setting up domestic production facilities in Zempa. The managing director of Electronics International received a letter from the Zempa government, inviting the company to set up a manufacturing facility in Zempa, and promising considerable official assistance should the company decide to do so.

Electronics International was asked to evaluate this offer and to reply within three months. The Zempa government said that the other leading suppliers were also considering setting up local manufacturing establishments in Zempa.

The idea of setting up a manufacturing operation in Zempa did not appeal initially to the managing director of Electronics International. The company was doing well as an exporter and sales had been increasing each year. There had been no difficulties in shipping its products, and most of the goods were transported by sea and costs were acceptable. True, there were some problems with the local customs authorities, but they were not insurmountable. The distributors were good, reliable people who were pushing sales hard and were meeting their contractual obligations to the company

continued

Case 2.1 (*continued*)

without any major problems. The government's regulations regarding remittance of payments for imports and exports were tedious and at times a little frustrating, but with the help of the company's local agents, most of the issues regarding repatriation of exchange proceeds were resolved in reasonable time. Therefore, why should the company think of setting up manufacturing operations in Zempa? The infrastructure for industry in Zempa was relatively undeveloped. The electricity supply was especially unreliable. There was little trained manpower, and the production of electronic products requires workers who are adept at carrying out delicate assembly tasks. The managing director was about to dictate a letter thanking the government for the invitation to set up a factory and conveying the company's decision to stay on only as an exporter, when he decided to consult Bill McLowan, the strategic planning director at Electronics International. A couple of days later, McLowan presented a seven-page executive memo that differed from the thoughts of the managing director. Five main points were raised in the memo:

1. Zempa is a valuable market for Electronics International, and as the economy of the country develops, the market size is likely to continue to grow rapidly. What is therefore needed is not only an increase in sales volume but also an increase in market share. The memo pointed out that although the sales of Electronics International's products had risen steadily over the past six years, its market share had stagnated while those of its main competitors had increased.

2. The Zempa government not only had invited Electronics International to set up manufacturing facilities, but also had solicited investments from its two major competitors. If both competitors accepted the invitation and set up local manufacturing operations, they could outprice Electronics International from the Zempa market because costs of local production were bound to be lower, given the lower wage rates and other input costs.

3. Zempa was under increasing domestic and external economic pressure. There was considerable inflation, primarily because of a substantial federal budget deficit (the government had not been able to raise required levels of revenues). Although the external balance position had been comfortable in the past five years because of firm commodity prices (commodities were the main exports of Zempa, generating 95 percent of export revenues), indicators of a weakening were already apparent. In the event of a balance of payments crisis, the government was likely to limit imports, and one of the first items to be put on the banned list would be consumer electronics, because they would be deemed nonessential in the face of competing demands from such imports as defense equipment.

4. Although there were some impediments to the establishment of manu-

continued

Case 2.1 (*continued*)

facturing operations, at this stage the government had assured the company of all assistance. If the company went in now and the other competitors did not, it would gain considerable leverage with the home government, which could be used to attack the dominance of the competition.

5. There were certain risks—the local currency might depreciate, and the lack of training of local workers and the state of local infrastructural facilities might impair the efficiency of the plant. Other constraints might be imposed later on the manufacturing operation. Given the emerging scenario, however, these risks were worth taking, and the company should at least in principle accept the invitation from the government of Zempa and prepare for further negotiations.

McLowan's memo seemed to open a new line of thought, but it did not convince the managing director. He asked his secretary to organize a meeting of the international investment committee to discuss the issues of exporting and direct investment in Zempa.

DISCUSSION QUESTIONS

1. What strategy should Electronics International adopt in this situation? Should the company continue exporting or make a direct investment?
2. Are there any other alternatives open for Electronics International?

PART II

INSTITUTIONAL FRAMEWORK AND ECONOMIC THEORIES

CHAPTER 3

Theories of Trade and Economic Development

CHAPTER OBJECTIVES

This chapter will:

- Present the major trade and economic theories that attempt to explain international trade.
- Describe the continuum of political economic development within the global community of nations and identify the first, second, and third worlds.
- Discuss current economic development theory.
- Define the problems facing less-developed countries.
- Briefly discuss the recent dynamic changes occurring in the global economy.

INTRODUCTION TO INTERNATIONAL TRADE THEORIES

Theories of international trade attempt to provide explanations for trade motives, underlying trade patterns, and the ultimate benefits that come from trade. An understanding of these basic factors enables individuals, private interests, and governments to better determine how to act for their own benefit within the trading systems. The major questions to be answered through such an examination of trade are the following:

- Why does trade occur? Is it because of price differentials, supply differentials, or differences in individual tastes?

- What is traded, and what are the prices or terms agreed on in these trading actions?
- Do trade flows relate to a country's specific economic and social characteristics?
- What are the gains from trade, and who realizes these gains?
- What are the effects of restrictions put on trading activity?

The theories discussed in this chapter answer some of these questions. Although no theory by itself offers all the answers, the different theories do contribute significantly to our understanding.

Theories of trade have evolved over time, beginning with the emergence of strong nation-states and the organization of systematic exchanges of goods among these nations. The theories are associated with discrete time periods, and the earliest of these periods was that of mercantilism.

MERCANTILISM

Mercantilism became popular in the late seventeenth and early eighteenth centuries in western Europe and was based on the notion that governments (not individuals, who were deemed untrustworthy) should become involved in the transfer of goods between nations in order to increase the wealth of each national entity. Wealth was defined, however, as an accumulation of precious metals, especially gold.

Consequently, the aims of the governments were to facilitate and support all exports while limiting imports; these goals were accomplished through the conduct of trade by government monopolies and intervention in the market through the subsidization of domestic exporting industries and the allocation of trading rights. Additionally, nations imposed duties or quotas on imports to limit their volume. During this period, colonies were acquired to provide sources of raw materials or precious metals. Trade opportunities with the colonies were exploited, and local manufacturing was repressed in those offshore locations. The colonies were often required to buy their goods from the colonizing countries.

The concept of mercantilism incorporates three fallacies. The first is the incorrect belief that gold or precious metals have intrinsic value, when actually they cannot be used for either production or consumption. Thus, nations subscribing to the mercantilism notion exchanged the products of their manufacturing or agricultural capacity for this nonproductive wealth. The second fallacy is that the theory of mercantilism ignores the concept of production efficiency through specialization. Instead of emphasizing cost-effective production

of goods, mercantilism emphasizes sheer volumes of exports and imports and equates the amassing of wealth with the acquisition of power. The third fallacy of mercantilism concerns the overall goal of the system. If the goal was to maximize wealth from the sale of exports, and if every participating nation had the same aim, the system itself did not promote trade, since all nations cannot maximize exports (and thus gold accumulation) simultaneously.[1]

Neomercantilism corrected the first fallacy by looking at the overall favorable or unfavorable balance of trade in all commodities; that is, nations attempted to have a positive balance of trade in all goods produced so that all exports exceeded imports. The term "balance of trade" continues in popular use today as nations attempt to correct their trade deficit positions by increasing exports or reducing imports so that the outflow of goods balances the inflow.

The second fallacy, a disregard for the concept of efficient production, was addressed in subsequent theories, notably the classical theory of trade, which rests on the doctrine of comparative advantage. Subsequent theories also attempted to address the third fallacy.

CLASSICAL THEORY

What is now called the classical theory of trade superseded the theory of mercantilism at the beginning of the nineteenth century and coincided with three economic and political revolutions: the Industrial Revolution, the American Revolution, and the French Revolution. This theory was based in the economic theory of free trade and enterprise that was evolving at the time. In 1776, in *The Wealth of Nations*, Adam Smith rejected as foolish the concept of gold being synonymous with wealth.[2] Instead, Smith insisted that nations benefited the most when they acquired through trade those goods they could not produce efficiently and produced only those goods that they could manufacture with maximum efficiency. The crux of the argument was that costs of production should dictate what should be produced by each nation or trading partner.

Under this concept of *absolute advantage*, a nation would produce only those goods that made the best use of its available natural and acquired resources and its climatic advantages. Some examples of acquired resources are available pools of appropriately trained and skilled labor, capital resources, technological advances, or even a tradition of entrepreneurship.

The use of such absolute advantage is the simplest explanation of trading behavior. For example, take two trading nations, Greece and Sweden, which both have the capacity to produce olives and martini glasses. In Greece 500 crates of green olives require 100 units of resources (i.e., workers) to produce, from cultivation and harvesting to processing and packaging. Because of the lack of manufacturing facilities and machinery in that country, however, 100 crates of martini glasses (an equivalent value to 500 crates of olives) take 500 resource units to produce because each glass must be handblown. This contrasts with the situation in Sweden, where the production of 100 crates of martini glasses can easily be mechanized and uses only 300 resource units. Because of Sweden's northern climate, however, olives can be grown only in greenhouses under human-made environmental conditions, a very expensive process that requires 600 units to produce 500 crates. Comparison of these figures leads to a clear conclusion as to how trade should be conducted to provide the citizens of Greece and Sweden with the perfect cocktail. Olives should be grown in Greece and traded for glasses produced in Swedish glass factories, because of the number of resource units required for each country to produce olives and glasses:

Country	Olives (500 crates)	Martini Glasses (100 crates)
Greece	100 units	500 units
Sweden	600 units	300 units

If Sweden concentrates on the production of martini glasses and Greece on the production of olives, production costs are minimized for both products at 100 resource units per 500 crates of olives and 300 resource units per 100 crates of martini glasses, for a total of 400 resource units.

The conclusion reached, of course, was that each country should produce the good that it could manufacture at minimum cost. What if, however, a country could produce both or several goods or commodities at costs lower than the other country's? Do both nations still have impetus to trade?

COMPARATIVE ADVANTAGE

This question was considered by David Ricardo, who developed the important concept of *comparative advantage* in considering a nation's relative production efficiencies as they apply to international trade.[3] In Ricardo's view, the exporting country should look at the relative efficiencies of production for both commodities and make only those goods it could produce most efficiently.

Suppose, for example, in our illustration that Greece developed an efficient manufacturing capacity so that martini glasses could be produced by machine rather than being handblown. In fact, since the development of the productive capacity and capital plants were newer than those in Sweden, Greece could produce 100 crates of martini glasses using only 200 resource units as opposed to the 300 units required by Sweden. Thus, Greece's comparative costs would fall below those of Sweden for both products and its comparative advantage vis-à-vis those products would be higher. Therefore, the resource units required to produce olives and glasses would now be:

Country	Olives (500 crates)	Martini Glasses (100 crates)
Greece	100 units	200 units
Sweden	600 units	300 units

Logically, Greece should be the producer of both olives and martini glasses, and Sweden's capital and labor used in making these happy-hour supplies should be directed to Greece, so that maximum production efficiencies are achieved. Neither capital nor labor is entirely mobile, however, so each country should specialize: Greece in olives at 100 resource units per 500 crates, and Sweden in glass production at 300 resource units per 100 crates. Greece is still better off at maximizing its efficiencies in olive production. By doing so, it produces twice as many goods for export with the same amount of resources than if it allocated production to glassmaking, even at the new, more efficient production level.

While Sweden's production costs for glasses are still higher than those of Greece at 300 units per 500 crates, the resources of Sweden are better allocated to this production than to expensive olive growing. In this way, Sweden minimizes its inefficiencies and Greece maximizes its efficiencies. The point is that a country should produce not all the goods it can more cheaply, but only those it can make cheapest. Such trading activity leads to maximum resource efficiency.

The concepts of absolute advantage and comparative advantage were used in a subsequent theory development by John Stuart Mill, who looked at the question of determining the value of export goods and developed the concept of *terms of trade*.[4] Under this concept, export value is determined according to how much of a domestic commodity each country must exchange to obtain an equivalent amount of an imported commodity. Thus, the value of the product to be obtained in the exchange was stated in terms of the amount of products produced domestically that would be given up in exchange. For example, Sweden's terms with Greece would be exporting 100 crates of glasses in return for an equivalent of 500 crates of olives.

WEAKNESSES OF EARLY THEORIES

While the work of Smith, Ricardo, and Mill went far in describing the flow of trade between nations, classical theory was not without its flaws. In our example of Greece and Sweden, the theory incorrectly assumed:

- The existence of perfect knowledge regarding international markets and opportunities
- Full mobility of labor and production factors throughout each country
- Full labor employment within each country

The theory also assumed that each country had as its objective full production efficiency. It neglected such other motives as traditional employment and production history, self-sufficiency, and political objectives.

In addition, the theory is overly simplistic in that it deals with only two commodities and two countries. In reality, given the full range of production by many countries and the interplay of many motives and factors, the trade situation is actually an ongoing dynamic process in which there is interaction of forces and products.

The largest area of weakness in classical theory is that while we considered all resource units used in production, the only costs considered by classical economists were those associated with labor. The theorists did not account for other resources used in the production of commodities or manufactured goods for export, such as transportation costs, the use of land, and capital. This failing was addressed by subsequent trade theorists, who, in modern theory, include all factors of production in looking at theories of comparative advantage.

MORE RECENT THEORIES

FACTOR ENDOWMENT THEORY

The Eli Heckscher and Bertil Ohlin theory of factor endowment addressed the question of the basis of cost differentials in the production of trading nations. Heckscher and Ohlin posited that each country allocates its production according to the relative proportions of all its *production factor endowments:* land, labor, and capital on a basic level, and, on a more complex level, such factors as management and technological skills, specialized production facilities, and established distribution networks.

Thus, the range of products made or grown for export would depend on the relative availability of different factors in each country. For example, agricultural production or cattle grazing would be emphasized in such countries as Canada and Australia, which are generously endowed with land. Conversely, in small-land-mass countries with high populations, export products would center on labor-intensive articles. Similarly, rich nations might center their export base on capital-intensive production.

In this way, countries would be expected to produce goods that require large amounts of the factors they hold in relative abundance. Because of the availability and low costs of these factors, each country should also be able to sell its products on foreign markets at less than international price levels. Although this theory holds in general, it does not explain export production that arises from taste differences rather than factor differentials. Some of these situations can be seen in sales of luxury imported goods, such as Italian leather products, deluxe automobiles, and French wine, which are valued for their quality, prestige, or panache. Like classical theory, the Heckscher-Ohlin theory does not account for transportation costs in its computation, nor does it account for differences among nations in the availability of technology.

Economist Paul Samuelson extended the factor endowment theory to look at the effect of trade on national welfare and the prices of production factors. Samuelson posited that the effect of free trade among nations would be to increase overall welfare by equalizing the prices not only of the goods exchanged in trade but also of all involved factors. Thus, according to his theory, the returns generated by use of the factors would be the same in all countries.[5]

THE LEONTIEF PARADOX

An exception to the Heckscher-Ohlin theory was examined by W.W. Leontief in the 1950s. Leontief found that U.S. exports were less capital-intensive than imports, although the presumption according to the Heckscher-Ohlin theory would have been that the United States had capital-intensive rather than labor-intensive export goods, because capital endowments at that time were proportionately higher than labor in the United States. The reason, as outlined by Leontief, was that these factor endowments are not homogeneous, and they differ along parameters other than relative abundance.[6] Labor pools, for example, can range from being unskilled to being highly skilled. Similarly, production methods can be more technically sophisticated or advanced in different locations within a nation. Thus, it made sense at the time that U.S. exported products were made through the efforts of highly skilled labor and imported products were produced through the efforts of less-skilled workers in other countries.

Thus, Leontief attempted to answer his own paradox by stating that since U.S. workers were more efficient, U.S. imports appeared to be more capital-intensive than U.S. exports. It could also have been due to not expanding the research into other factors of production (to include land, human capital, and technology) or due to protection of labor-intensive industries.

CRITICISMS

Although these more recent theories seem to go far in explaining why nations trade, they have nonetheless come under criticism as being only partial explanations for the exchange of goods and services between nations. Some of these criticisms are as follows:

- The theories assume that nations trade, when in reality trade between nations is initiated and conducted by individuals or individual firms within those nations.
- Traditional theory also assumes perfect competition and perfect information among trading partners.
- The theories are limited in looking at the transfer either of goods or of direct investments. No theories explain the comprehensive dynamic flow of trade in goods, services, and financial flows.
- The theories do not recognize the importance of technology and expertise in the areas of marketing and management.

Consequently, some scholars have looked separately at the reasons that firms enter into trade or foreign investment. One of these theories is the international product life cycle, which looks at the path a product takes as it departs domestic shores and enters foreign markets.

MODERN THEORIES

INTERNATIONAL PRODUCT LIFE CYCLE THEORY

The international product life cycle theory puts forth a different explanation for the fundamental motivations for trade between and among nations.[7] It relies primarily on the traditional marketing theory regarding the development, progress, and life span of products in markets. This theory looks at the potential export possibilities of a product in four discrete stages in its life cycle. In the first stage, innovation, a new product is manufactured in the domestic arena of the innovating country and sold primarily in that domestic market. Any overseas sales are generally achieved through exports to other markets, often those of industrial countries. In this stage, the company generally has little competition in its markets abroad.

In the second stage, the growth of the product, sales tend to increase. Unfortunately, so does competition as other firms enter the arena and the product becomes increasingly standardized. At this point, the firm begins some production abroad to maximize the service of foreign markets and to meet the activity of the competition.

As the product enters the third stage, maturity, exports from the home country decrease because of increased production in overseas locations. Foreign manufacturing facilities are put in place to counter increasing competition and to maximize profits from higher sales levels in foreign markets. At this point, price becomes a crucial determinant of competitiveness. Consequently, minimizing costs becomes an important objective of the manufacturing firm. Production also frequently shifts from being within foreign industrial markets to less costly less-developed countries (LDCs) to take advantage of cheaper production factors, especially low labor costs. At this point the innovator country may even decide to discontinue all domestic production, produce only in third world countries, and reexport the product back to the home country and to other markets.

In the final stage of the product life cycle, the product enters a period of decline. This decline is often because new competitors have achieved levels of production high enough to effect scale economies that are equivalent to those of the original manufacturing country.

The international product life cycle theory has been found to hold primarily for such products as consumer durables, synthetic fabrics, and electronic equipment, that is, those products that have long lives in terms of the time span from innovation to eventual high consumer demand. The theory does not hold for products with a rapid time span of innovation, development, and obsolescence.

The international product life cycle theory holds less often these days because of the growth of multinational global enterprises that often introduce products simultaneously in several markets of the world. Similarly, multinational firms no longer necessarily first introduce a product at home. Instead, they might launch an innovation from a foreign source in the domestic markets to test production methods and the market itself, without incurring the high initial production costs of the domestic environment.

OTHER MODERN INVESTMENT THEORIES

Other theorists explain firms' overseas investing as a response to the availability of opportunities not shared by their competitors; that is, these firms take advantage of imperfections in markets and enter foreign spheres of production only when their competitive advantages outweigh the costs of going overseas. These advantages may be production, brand awareness, product identification, economies of scale, or access to favorable capital markets. These firms may make horizontal investments, producing the same goods abroad as they do at home, or they may make vertical investments, in order to take advantage of sources of supplies or inputs.

Going a step further, some theorists believe that firms within an oligopoly enter foreign markets merely as a competitive response to the actions of an industry leader and to equalize relative advantages. *Oligopolies* are those market situations in which there are few sellers of a product that is usually mass merchandised. Two examples are the automobile and steel industries. In these situations no firm can profit by cutting prices because competitors quickly respond in kind. Consequently, prices for oligopolistic products are practically identical and are set through industry agreement (either openly or tacitly).

Thus, firms within an oligopoly must be keenly aware of the actions, market reach, and activities of their competitors. Unless their response to competitors' actions is to follow the leader, they will yield precious competitive advantages to rival firms. Therefore, it follows that when a market leader in an oligopoly establishes a foreign production facility abroad, its competitors rush to follow suit.

So the impetus for a firm to go abroad may come from a wish to expand for internal reasons: to use existing competitive advantages in additional spheres of operations, to take advantage of technology, or to use raw materials available in other locations. Alternately, the motive might arise from external forces, such as competitive actions, customer requests, or government incentives. The final determinant however, is based in a cost-benefit analysis. The firm will move abroad if it can use its own particular advantages to provide benefits that outweigh the costs of exporting or production abroad and provide a profit.

Michael Porter of Harvard authored *The National Competitive Advantage Theory*. It discusses many of the elements already addressed in this chapter. Porter believes that successful international trade comes from the interaction of four country- and firm-specific elements:

- Factor conditions
- Demand conditions
- Related and supporting industries
- Firm strategy, structure, and rivalry

Factor conditions include land, labor, and capital. Porter also includes education of the workforce and the quality of a country's infrastructure as important factor conditions. Demand conditions relate to the need for strong domestic consumption to spur the innovation of products and services. As mentioned previously, successful international expansion requires having a successful product in the domestic market (that has been sufficiently challenged at home). A successful domestic industry will stimulate local supplier activity. Having numerous local suppliers will tend to lower prices, raise quality, and increase the usage of technology. Thus, the rivalry of domestic industries will help improve the quality of the product or service, which will improve the company's performance. Successful companies will then attempt to expand their products or services internationally. Porter's last dimension is company strategy. As mentioned in Chapter 1, a firm can choose to have an ethnocentric, geocentric, or polycentric strategy. Additionally, there should be some consistency in strategy at home and abroad; this feature is discussed in subsequent chapters.

THEORIES OF ECONOMIC DEVELOPMENT

Beyond merely examining what types of economic systems exist in the world, those involved in international business must place notions about methods of allocating resources within a country in a theoretical framework. How do basically agrarian national economies become producers of sophisticated manufactured goods? How does economic development come about?

Classical economic theory, put forth by economists Thomas Malthus, David Ricardo, John Stuart Mill, and Adam Smith in the late 1700s and early 1800s, held little hope for a nation to sustain its economic growth. This dismal forecast was because of the substantial weakness in the theory (as evidenced by subsequent historical events), which assumed that no developments would be achieved in technology or production methods. Instead, these economists, Malthus foremost among them, predicted that the finite availability of land would limit any nation's development and that the natural equilibrium in labor wages would hover at subsistence levels because of the interaction of labor

supply, agricultural production, and wage systems. For example, these theorists believed that if labor supplies were low, wages would rise and would motivate workers to increase their number. Increases in the size of the population and labor pool would then put stress on finite supplies of food, increase the costs of nourishment, and ultimately lead to decreases in wages because of increased competition for such employment.

In a nutshell, classical theory holds that expanding the labor pool leads to declines in the accumulation of capital per worker, lower worker *productivity*, and lower income per person, eventually causing stagnation or economic decline. Naturally, this theory was proven incorrect by numerous scientific and technological discoveries, which provided for greater efficiencies in production and greater returns on inputs of land, capital, and labor. It was also knocked awry by the growing acceptance of birth control as a means of limiting population size.

ROSTOW'S STAGES OF ECONOMIC GROWTH

A more recent and applicable theory of economic development was provided in the 1960s by Walter W. Rostow, who attempted to outline the various stages of a nation's economic growth and based his theory on the notion that shifts in economic development coincided with abrupt changes within the nations themselves.[8] He identified five different economic stages for a country: traditional society, preconditions for takeoff, takeoff, the drive to maturity, and the age of mass consumption.

Stage 1: Traditional Society

Rostow saw traditional society as a static economy, which he likened to the pre-1700s attitudes toward change and technology experienced by the world's current economically developed countries. He believed that the turning point for these countries came with the work of Sir Isaac Newton, when people began to believe that the world was subject to a set of physical laws but was malleable within these laws. In other words, people could effect change within the system of descriptive laws as developed by Newton.

Stage 2: Preconditions for Takeoff

Rostow identified the preconditions for economic takeoff as growth or radical changes in three specific, nonindustrial sectors that provided the basis for economic development:

1. *Increased investment in transportation*, which enlarged prospective markets and increased product specialization capacity
2. *Agricultural developments*, which provided for the feeding and nourishing of larger, primarily urban, populations
3. An *expansion of imports* into the country

These preconditioning changes were to be experienced in concert with an increasing national emphasis on education and entrepreneurship.

Stage 3: Takeoff

The takeoff stage of growth occurs, according to Rostow, over a period of 20 to 30 years and is marked by major transformations that stimulate the economy. These transformations could include widespread technological developments, the effective functioning of an efficient distribution system, and even political revolutions. During this period, barriers to growth are eliminated within the country and, indeed, the concept of economic growth as a national objective becomes the norm. To achieve the takeoff, however, Rostow believes that three conditions must be met:

1. Net investment as a percentage of net national product must increase sharply.

2. At least one substantial manufacturing sector must grow rapidly. This rapid growth and larger output trickles down as growth in ancillary and supplier industries.
3. A supportive framework for growth must emerge on political, social, and institutional fronts. For example, banks, capital markets, and tax systems should develop, and entrepreneurship should be considered a norm.

Stage 4: The Drive to Maturity

Within Rostow's scheme, the drive to maturity is the stage during which growth becomes self-sustaining and widely expected within the country. During this period, Rostow believes that the labor pool becomes more skilled and more urban and that technology reaches heights of advancement.

Stage 5: The Age of Mass Consumption

The last stage of development, as Rostow sees it, is an age of mass consumption, when there is a shift to consumer durables in all sectors and when the populace achieves a high standard of living, as evidenced through the ownership of such sophisticated goods as automobiles, televisions, and appliances.

Since its introduction in the 1960s, Rostow's framework has been criticized as being overly ambitious in attempting to describe the economic paths of many nations. Also, history has not proved the framework to be true. For example, many LDCs exhibit dualism; that is, state-of-the-art technology is used in certain industries and primitive production methods are retained in others. Similarly, empirical data has shown that there is no 20- to 30-year growth period. Such countries as the United Kingdom, Germany, Sweden, and Japan are more characterized by slow, steady growth patterns than by abrupt takeoff periods.

THE BIG PUSH: BALANCED VERSUS UNBALANCED GROWTH

While Rostow was attempting to place economic development within a sequential framework, the debate during the 1950s and 1960s centered on whether development efforts should center on specific economic sectors within countries or should be made in all major sectors of the economy: manufacturing, agriculture, and service.

Economist Ragnar Nurske advocated that development efforts should consist of a synchronized use of capital to develop wide ranges of industries in nations. He believed that only a concerted overall effort would propel developing nations beyond the vicious circle of poverty, in which the limited supply of capital is caused by low savings rates.

The advocates of channeling capital to all sectors in a balanced approach also support the big-push thesis and believe that these investments cannot be made gradually. They must be made all at once for the positive impetus to be sufficient to overcome significant barriers to development, such as the lack of an adequate infrastructure.

The theory of balanced development has been criticized because it ignores the economic notion of overall benefits accruing from specialization in development and production. It has also been criticized for being unrealistic; that is, if a country had enough resources to invest in all sectors of the economy at once, it would, in fact, not be underdeveloped. The theory also assumes that all nations would be starting from the same zero point, when in reality, their economies may have some historical strengths or investment capacity. The theory has been discredited, to a very significant extent, by the actual progress of LDCs in the 1960s and 1970s. These countries experienced a great deal of growth without any attempts to synchronize simultaneous investments in all sectors, as recommended by proponents of balanced-growth theory, but most remain comparatively underdeveloped.

HIRSCHMAN'S STRATEGY OF UNBALANCE

Some theorists have advocated a strategy of selective investment as the engine of growth in developing countries. Albert O. Hirschman promulgated the idea of making unbalanced investments in economic sectors to complement the imbalances that already exist within the economy of a nation. Hirschman argued that the LDCs do not have access to adequate resources to mount a balanced, big-push investment strategy. Investments should be made instead in strategically selected economic areas, in order to provide growth in other sectors through backward and forward linkages. Backward linkages spur new investments in input industries, while forward linkages do so in those sectors that buy the output of the selected industry. Thus, in Hirschman's scheme, careful analysis must be made of the situation in each country as to what investment constitutes the best means to reach an ultimate balance among all investment sectors.

GALBRAITH'S EQUILIBRIUM OF POVERTY

Many of the theories discussed thus far have illuminated how a developing country can improve its overall standing in the world economy via increasing income levels and exports. While these are commendable aims by themselves, the theories discussed so far have not detailed how a country can create a climate for such growth. Examples of newly industrialized countries such as Singapore and South Korea have been cited as a useful framework for countries throughout the world. While these economies have been very successful, they have also had the levels of political stability and entrepreneurship incentives necessary to create economic expansion. John Kenneth Galbraith was one of the first economists to discuss the mind-set of individuals in developing countries, in a term he coined as the "equilibrium of poverty."[9] Rather than theorizing on how to improve a developing country's economy as if assuming there was a historical precedence in the country for success, or assuming that all that was needed was new technologies in a poor country, Galbraith considered what would happen if neither of these options was available. If there is not an escape from poverty, and there has not been such an escape for generations, many people will simply not be motivated to change their situation. Thus contentment settles in. Galbraith stated that to break the contentment there needed to be education as well as traumas (famines, droughts, etc.) that caused the desire for change. Globalization itself often contributes to showing people in developing countries a better way of life (via radio and television ads). Galbraith then offered the following framework necessary to successfully industrialize a poor economy:

- *Adequate security* against expropriation of property, physical threats, or very high taxation
- *Reliable infrastructure system* of roads, ports, electrical power supplies, and communications
- *Adequate supply of capital* from private investment and public borrowers and an intelligent system for passing on loans
- *State-supported industries* initially, as they have more means in developing countries than do individual firms
- *Training and specialized education* in order to obtain a workforce capable of doing the required tasks of employment

AMARTYA SEN'S DEVELOPMENT AS FREEDOM

Amartya Sen, recipient of the 1998 Nobel Prize in Economics, further improved the framework for

development that Galbraith and others had started. Amartya Sen asked the question, Is the measure of GDP growth the best way to compare the living standards of the world's people? Sen considers the measurement of GDP to be an aggregate measure of the wealth produced within a country, but it does not necessarily account for quality-of-life issues. Sen gained Nobel distinction for his work in welfare economics. He has also questioned the viability of the concept of the "poverty line" and has offered a similar line of reasoning for why this measure, as well as GDP, is unsuitable for developing countries.[10] The concepts of the poverty line and GDP do not consider the amount of political participation and dissent allowed within a given country. These factors are essential characteristics of freedom and thus of a society's ability to improve its quality of life. Sen would rather frame the argument in terms of an individual's "capabilities," which are influenced by such things as being adequately nourished, being in good health, and avoiding escapable morbidity and premature mortality, as well as other quality-of-life issues such as being happy, having self-respect, and taking part in the community as a whole.

With these thoughts in mind, Sen has offered a framework for development as follows:

- Political freedoms
- Economic facilities
- Social opportunities
- Transparency guarantees
- Protective security

Sen views political freedoms as the opportunities for individuals to determine who should govern and on what principles. Political freedoms also encompass individuals' ability to scrutinize and criticize authorities, have freedom of political expression, and enjoy an uncensored press. Economic facilities consist of opportunities to utilize economic resources for the purpose of consumption, production, or exchange, including the access to credit for large and small companies. Social opportunities consist of arrangements that society makes for education and health care, which allow for an improved ability to live better lives. Factors such as illiteracy, high fertility rates, and morbidity are diminished via these freedoms. Sen's framework for development also contains transparency guarantees, which involve the need for openness and the freedom to deal with one another under guarantees of trust. Transparency guarantees help to prevent corruption, financial irresponsibility, and underhanded dealings. While Sen's framework applies mainly to developing countries, developed nations could also improve in this area given the recent corporate scandals that have been in the news in the United States, Canada, and Europe. The final area of Sen's development framework is that of protective security, a social safety net for preventing the affected population from being reduced to abject poverty and misery. Elements of protective security include unemployment benefits, statutory income supplements to the indigent, and emergency public employment to generate income for the destitute (this is similar to the New Deal program for public employment implemented during the Great Depression).

The key to Sen's philosophy is that these freedoms are required prior to development. While it would appear that having a fully functioning health-care system in a developing country is unrealistic, many health-related services are labor-intensive, so fewer resources would be required to provide these basic services in low-wage countries. Sen argues that guaranteed health care and education can achieve remarkable improvements in life span and quality of life. Literacy and numeracy help the participation of the masses in the process of economic expansion. This participation, in turn, improves the productive capabilities of the nation as a whole.

THE GLOBAL CONTINUUM: WHERE NATIONS FALL TODAY

All trading nations of the world fall within the descriptive continuum of political structures, forms of economic organization, and levels of development. The existence of these three descriptive parameters provides for enormous variation in categorizing the world's trading nations.

THE POLITICAL CONTINUUM

Political systems constitute the methods in which societies organize in order to function smoothly, and such orientation provides one such classification continuum. Certainly the student of international business is cognizant of the two extremes of political organization in the global political arena of the 2000s. At one extreme, there exist societies in which all members have significant power in the decision-making process surrounding the activities, policies, and objectives of their government. These systems are often pluralistic (incorporating a number of different views), use the concept of majority rule in deciding major issues, and often employ a system of representative democracy, where officials are elected to represent their regional constituencies. These nations generally afford all of their citizens some degree of liberty and equality.

At the other end of the political spectrum is the totalitarian state, which is identified by a singular lack of decision-making power among the country's individual citizens. In such a political system, decisions regarding policies, objectives, and the direction of the nation are controlled by a select few individuals who generally operate under the auspices of the government. In these states, the activities and liberties of citizens are often restricted.

All nations in the world fall somewhere along this continuum and take various forms within its parameters, from being highly democratized to being nearly entirely totalitarian. Most individuals would recognize that in the past, the two world powers, the United States and the former Soviet Union, represented the two extremes in the modern political world. Some modern-day examples of central-planning-oriented economies are Cuba and North Korea. Some nations, Afghanistan, for example, are in the process of attempting to move toward democracy after many years of tyranny. Other countries, such as the People's Republic of China, are finding new ways of blending a central-planning structure with market-based reforms.

THE ECONOMIC CONTINUUM

The political orientation of a country can also be placed within the scope of its economic structure, which, similarly, runs along a continuum. Economic orientations vary according to two separate dimensions: the degree of private versus public (state) ownership of property; and the level of governmental (versus individual) control over the nation's resources.

At one extreme is capitalism, which relies on the forces of the marketplace in the allocation of resources. In this free-enterprise system, the market, in the form of consumer sovereignty, defines the relationships among prices for goods and services, quantities produced domestically, and overall supply and demand. For example, if supplies of a product are low and public demand is high, the product's price will rise as consumers compete to acquire this scarce resource. Similarly, if there is little or no demand for products, manufacturers will have no motivation to produce them.

In free-market economies, the creation of profit is generally considered to be the operational motive of business, and profitability tends to be the test of success. Capitalist economies also promote the ownership of private property by individuals and theoretically attempt to limit public (state) ownership of property.

In modern free-market countries, however, governments still intervene at some level and own some property. They set legal and regulatory requirements to provide for the general safety and welfare of the populace and levy taxes in order to provide services, such as national defense or a network of highways. They own resource reserves, land, national parks, and large amounts of capital assets. Indeed, governments often provide the largest single market for manufacturers in many capitalist countries.

The appropriate level of government involvement in the play of market forces continues to be the subject of much debate among economists, politicians, and political parties in many countries. This debate is perhaps best exemplified by the policies put in place by President Ronald Reagan and Prime Minister Margaret Thatcher of the United Kingdom during the 1980s, when significant efforts were made to reduce the role of the central government and promote deregulation of many industries.

At the other end of the economic spectrum are the centrally planned, or nonmarket, economies. Within this economic form, the government decides what is to be produced, when and where it will be made, and to whom it will be sold. The state controls the sources and means of production, the raw materials, and the distribution systems. In addition, the state frequently owns many of the basic and integral industries of the country, which are run in the form of state monopolies and include large-scale power-generating facilities, manufacturing industries, and entire transportation systems. In addition to these production and manufacturing monopolies, all trade with the outside world is financed and conducted by a state trading monopoly.

This centrally planned type of economic structure is based on the belief that a single central agency can coordinate economic activity to provide harmony in the interrelationship of all sectors of the economy. Before 1989, the world's centrally planned, or nonmarket, economies were most strongly represented by the members of the former COMECON, or former communist nations of the world, which included the Soviet Union, Poland, Romania, the former Czechoslovakia, the People's Republic of China, Cuba, and Vietnam, among others. COMECON was disbanded in 1991, and the majority of the former members have become more oriented toward a free-market system (with the notable exception of Cuba).

The nonmarket form of economic organization is not without its problems. The most significant of these are the difficulties arising from attempts to coordinate all factors of production. Frequently, governments attempt to reach their objective of harmonious economic activity by developing complex and extensive goals in the form of long-term (five-year or longer) plans for the nation. They attempt to affect production and outcome by setting manufacturing quotas, but these quotas can lead to high costs. For example, production may be geared toward reaching quota levels, not toward achieving efficiencies, which can result in high production costs.

In addition, nonmarket economies also experience problems farther down the line, especially with the procurement of raw materials for production. They often encounter either insufficient supplies of raw materials or mismatches of the timing of supply deliveries and the need for the supplies. Another problem is insufficient long-term planning, especially at the level of the local production facility. Manufacturing operators have incentives to reach only their production goals for the season or the year; future, long-term production capacity or technological developments are less relevant. Nonmarket economies also face the problem of determining appropriate prices for goods and services produced within their borders. These valuation problems stem from the absence of external criteria of worth, as supplied through consumer demand for products or through prices paid for input resources and raw materials. Thus, in these economies prices are set primarily according to the amount of labor involved in their production and are often as much

a product of politics and ideology as of actual production costs.

Between these two extremes are mixed economic systems, which combine features of both market and nonmarket systems. These nations combine public and private ownership in varying amounts. Their intention is to provide economic security for the country as a whole, by having some amount of public resource ownership or government involvement in decision making, or both. In these systems, public involvement often takes the form of state ownership of utilities or energy sources. The welfare state and heavy involvement of government in the economic planning of the nation are also basic features of mixed economies. An example of this kind of system exists in modern-day Canada, where the government (public sector) administers a national health-care system for all its citizens, while the benefits of a free-market system (private sector) are seen in many other industries that are represented on the Toronto Stock Exchange or in the private sector in general.

To a lesser extent, Japan is also a mixed economy. While there is less government ownership of resources, the state, through its Ministry of International Trade and Industry and Ministry of Finance, is intimately involved in business decisions regarding investments, disinvestments, production, and markets. The government is also intricately involved in conducting basic R & D and deciding long-term and short-term future direction. The government does this by organizing major companies into research consortia, which join together to conduct applied research on new technology. When that research bears fruit, in the form of marketable applications, the consortium disbands and each company takes the technology back to its own labs to use in product development.

INTEGRATING THE CONTINUA

The two ranges of political and economic organization of nations can be put together in a general framework. Overall, democratic societies tend to be oriented toward a free-market, capitalist perspective. Supply and demand in production are determined to a degree by consumers in the marketplace; sources of supply and the means of production are owned by private interests or individuals. In contrast, totalitarian societies are characterized by government allocation of resources and state ownership of the means of production. As you will recall from Chapter 1, Zimbabwe is an example of a totalitarian economy. The results of this sort of governmental structure have not been good, as is exhibited by Zimbabwe's drop in GDP for each of the last four years.[11]

It appears, however, that as nations of the world become more and more interdependent, the boundaries begin to blur between political and economic descriptions. More and more governments are moving toward a mixture of both public and private ownership of property and allocation of resources. This convergence can perhaps be accounted for by the increasingly apparent knowledge that none of the existing systems provides equitably for all segments of society.

The place each country holds in both the economic and political continua is an important consideration for foreign firms when they are considering with whom to do business. The decision maker must take into account, for example, whether the political structures of the home and host countries are complementary, whether the tendency is toward private or public ownership of resource allocation and production, and to what degree the state controls the daily operations of business firms.

Patterns of World Development

Background: The Role of Gross National Income

Traditionally, countries of the world have been divided into three separate categories, known as the first, second, and third worlds. Their assigned categorizations are based on specific economic criteria, such as the *gross national income (GNI) per capita*.[12] *GNI per capita* is a benchmark used in determining levels of development, because it represents a measure of production relative to population that can be compared across nations. GNI is determined by totaling the dollar value of the goods and services a country produced in one year, for example, and dividing that number by the country's population, thereby providing a measure of the country's economic activity level as a per-person value. In addition to GNI per capita, development-level determinations include assessments of annual export levels, relative growth over time, energy consumption per capita, and the relative percentage of agriculture in total production and employment.

In addition, development levels are ascertained according to social criteria, such as life expectancies, infant mortality levels, the availability of health and educational facilities, literacy rates, demographic and population trends, and standards of housing and nutrition. This is where Amartya Sen's human-capabilities focus comes into play, as previously discussed.

The Developed Countries

The industrialized, or developed, countries are commonly referred to as the *first world* (or the high-income countries). These nations generally have economies that are based in industrial manufacturing and are the wealthiest in the world in terms of incomes and standards of living. The industrialized countries are largely in the Northern Hemisphere. They are the United States and Canada in North America and the nations of western Europe. Beyond these two geographic areas, only New Zealand, Australia, Japan, and perhaps the Republic of South Africa represent the east, or the Southern Hemisphere, in this group.

Table 3.1

GNI per Capita, 2003

Income Level	US$
High income	29,450
Middle income	6,000
Low income	2,190
World average	8,180

Source: World Bank, "GNI per Capita—Purchasing Power Parity," *World Development Indicators*, September 2004. http://web.worldbank.org

In the developed countries, the average GNI per capita is $29,450.[13] This compares to other areas of the world as shown in Table 3.1.

In addition to high production capacity per person, each of these countries has levels of adult literacy reported in the ninetieth percentile, large values of exported products, low infant-mortality figures, and low citizen-per-physician ratios.

EMERGING ECONOMIES

The so-called, emerging economies, or second world, consist of countries such as China, Turkey, much of the Middle East, Indonesia, South America, and central European nations. Based on the countries just mentioned, there is a wide variety of cultural and economic factors at play within this segment. Some countries, such as China, have moved up the world economic standings rather quickly, while others, such as many South American nations, have seen stagnant economic growth levels over the past 20 years due in large part to economic overregulation by the government.[14] As you can see from Table 3.1, there is also a large gap in terms of GNI per capita between the high-income and middle-income nations. Literacy rates for these nations are reported to be about 90 percent.

THE THIRD WORLD

The *third world* is generally considered to include developing, less-developed, and underdeveloped countries. More recently, this enormous majority of countries has been recategorized, according to income, as low-income countries. These categorizations, determined by the World Bank, designate countries with per capita GNI of less than $765 as low income and countries with per capita GNI greater than $765 but less than $3,045 as lower-middle income.[15]

The poorest nations of the world are generally found on the continents of Asia and Africa and in parts of Central America. Their poverty is evidenced by inadequate diets, primitive housing, limited schooling, and minimal medical facilities. The common features of most LDCs are low per capita GNI and the division into two very disparate classes: a very rich upper class and a very poor lower class. There is hardly any middle class between them. The richer elements have more access to, and are affected by, the Westernization of ideas and values, whereas the lower classes, with less education and awareness of externalities, tend to cling to traditional values, which leads to inherent conflicts between the two. As Figures 3.1 and 3.2 indicate, there is a wide disparity between where the world's people live and where the majority of the world's income is produced.

LDCs have widely varying political systems, which run the gamut from communist countries, such as North Korea, to democracies, such as India and Costa Rica, and autocratic regimes, such as Zimbabwe. They also have a number of problems in common, which essentially center on the difficulties of achieving greater industrialization in light of increasing levels of population growth and limited resources.

A major problem in LDCs is that their populations are growing rapidly, as compared to the rate of growth per year in the industrialized countries. This

Figure 3.1 **World GDP, 2003**

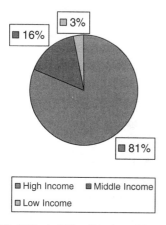

Source: World Bank, "Classification of Economies," 2004, http://www.worldbank.org/data/countryclass.

Figure 3.2 **World Population, 2003**

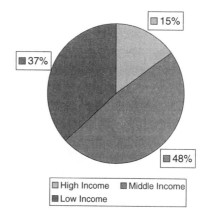

Source: World Bank, "Classification of Economies," 2004, http://www.worldbank.org/data/countryclass.

growth forces LDCs to continue allocating scarce resources for providing the basic necessities of food, clothing, and shelter for their populace. As a result, few resources remain within these countries for increasing development, income levels, education, and training. Consequently, these nations are frequently faced with unemployment, underemployment, and a relatively unproductive labor force.

Similarly, most LDC economies are dependent on agriculture, which often suffers from low productivity but employs the major portion of the workforce. This dependency is often coupled with limited or scarce natural resources, as well as severely limited capital bases to fund ongoing development efforts. Thus, exports are often limited, basic, low-valued-added products that are vulnerable to the violent fluctuations of world commodity prices. This problem is exacerbated by the agricultural protectionism that persists in much of the developed world.

Thus, the situation in LDCs is a continuous vicious cycle. As populations increase, economic activity continues to focus on limited and low-profit agricultural and natural resource production. Because of low savings rates, insufficient capital is available. More improvements in the labor pool

and diversification of the export base are extremely difficult. Added to these problems, LDCs frequently have underdeveloped banking systems, high levels of bureaucratic graft, political instability, serious international debt problems, severe hard-currency needs, and high levels of inflation.

THE SUBTERRANEAN ECONOMIES

While the United Nations and the World Bank consistently use the identification of gross national income per person to evaluate the relative wealth of a nation vis-à-vis its neighbors and trading partners, this figure may not be fully representative of the actual production of a nation, because in many countries, even the United States, there exists an underground economy in which transactions do not enter official records and are not, therefore, shown in the overall figures of the nation's GNI. Unofficial sales and purchases of goods and services are commonly known as black-market transactions, and they make the official GNI figure somewhat lower than it actually is.

Alternately, goods can be traded in *barter* systems, in which no money changes hands but

Figure 3.3 **How Much Dead Capital?**

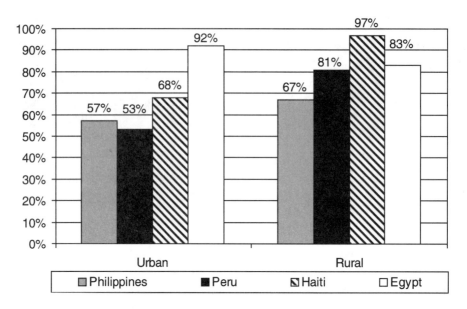

Source: Hernando DeSoto, *The Mystery of Capital*, 2003.

an economic exchange has been made, or transfers are made between currencies in exchange rates that differ from officially cited rates. These systems also lead to a distortion of aggregate economic data and tax evasion by the participants. They are ubiquitous in third world nations and are called shadow, second, or submerged economies, or black work, as the underground economy is called in France.

In a recent book by Peruvian economist Hernando DeSoto, one of the causes for the lack of economic growth in the third world is the amount of "dead capital" in the system.[16] Dead capital refers to the lack of a legal system of private land-ownership in much of the third world. DeSoto has found that there is a large underground economy in many lower-income countries, but that these poor citizens cannot transfer real property as an asset, or use it as collateral for bank financing.

Thus, many small companies are unable to obtain the necessary working capital required to finance business development efforts. This system of legal apartheid must be ended before many third world nations are able to successfully improve their economies. Figure 3.3 illustrates the percentage of dead capital in some select low-income countries. The percentages represent the amount of real estate that is not individually owned and is thus unable to be borrowed against for the growth of any prospective small-business owners in the third world.

How Much Dead Capital?

In his book, DeSoto states that the only solution to this problem is to do what was done in the United States in the nineteenth century: simplify the methods for obtaining legally owned land, and legalize the claims of those in possession of land now.

Parallel Tracks: The Continued Diversity of the World Economy

Since the 1960s, the world has seen dramatic changes in the patterns of world trade and, indeed, in the relative importance of groups of trading nations and historical trade leaders. The past 20 years or more have seen a shift in trading patterns away from the industrialized countries and toward greater involvement of the LDCs and the rising stars in the world, the four tigers of Asia: South Korea, Hong Kong, Taiwan, and Singapore. Even more recently, the world economy has seen the rise of India and China as well. In every category, except perhaps agriculture, where the benefits of the latest in technological development and the use of high-yield fertilizer products are being realized, the developed countries of the world have lost market share primarily to LDCs and to the newly industrialized countries. The Chinese market share is especially remarkable in this scheme, as it shows increases in technology-intensive manufacturing and the transportation trade, while labor-intensive clothing and textile products and land-intensive agricultural production have also increased.

The Chinese economy has grown annually at 8 percent, while the Indian economy has been growing at an average of more than 6 percent over the last decade. This is very high as compared with countries such as the United States, which has seen growth over the same period at less than 4 percent.

The trend of increasing competition to the pre-eminence of the United States is likely to continue in the foreseeable future. With the increasing globalization of the world economy, there will continue to be an increasing number of participants in the world economy. As the developing markets continue to liberalize their trade policies and economies, their participation in world trade is expected to continue the upward trend that it has shown since the 1980s.

SUMMARY

International trade theories attempt to explain motives for trade, underlying trade patterns, and the ultimate benefits of trade. The western European notion of mercantilism theorized that nations, not individuals, should be involved in the transfer of goods between countries in order to increase the wealth of home countries, specifically through the accumulation of gold. The classical theories of absolute and comparative advantage looked at cost efficiencies of production as motivators of trade. Weaknesses in their basic assumptions led to the development of the factor endowment theory, which explains trade among nations on the basis of factors, or inputs, used in production, such as land, labor, capital, technology, facilities, and distribution networks.

Recent theorists have found that individuals, rather than nations, initiate and conduct trade. Further, traditional theories ignore the importance of technology and marketing and management skills. The international life cycle theory offers different motivations for trade based on the four stages of a product: innovation, growth, maturity, and decline. Other modern theories explain foreign investment as a natural competitive response through which firms seek to optimize market opportunities offering production advantages, economies of scale, and favorable capital markets, or as firms reacting to the investment decisions of competitors by following the leader.

Economic development theories attempt to explain the transition from an underdeveloped economy to a developed, manufacturing-oriented economy. Classical economic theory limited a nation's development and economic growth to its supply of land and labor and discounted any effects of technological improvements that might create greater efficiencies. Rostow's theory of economic growth attempted to relate economic development to changes within society and identified five stages of development: traditional society, preconditions for takeoff, takeoff, the drive to maturity, and the age of mass consumption. The big-push theories argued that only synchronized uses of capital to develop wide ranges of industries in combination with an overall popular effort would propel developing nations into more developed stages. Alternatively, Hirschman's strategy of unbalance advocated selective investment in developing countries to create backward and forward linkages. Economists such as John Kenneth Galbraith and Amartya Sen have also contributed to the understanding of developmental economics, and Sen has come up with a framework for development that is useful for governments deciding on policies in the developing world.

Political and economic systems run along a continuum that has democratic, free-market economies on one extreme and totalitarian, centrally planned economies on the other.

Nations have been divided into three categories: the first, second, and third worlds; these distinctions are based principally on gross national income per capita criteria. A *fourth world*, or *shadow world* exists where many transactions are not included in official GNI figures, leading to a significant understatement of real national wealth. Other social criteria influence categorization, such as life expectancy, infant mortality levels, literacy rates, and health and education standards.

Trading patterns have shifted away from industrialized countries toward less-developed and newly industrialized countries. Increasing competition from countries such as China and India are challenging the preeminence of the United States.

DISCUSSION QUESTIONS

1. What were the fallacies of the theory of mercantilism?

2. Briefly describe the differences between the theories of absolute and comparative advantage. What were the shortcomings of these theories?

3. Discuss the various stages of the international product life cycle. Give an example of a product that was introduced to various countries under this theory.

4. Discuss the differences between a free-market economy and a centrally planned economy. What type of economy exists in Japan?

5. Select a country from the first world and a country from the third world and compare the two in respect to:

    - GNI per capita
    - Annual export levels
    - Life expectancy
    - Literacy rates
    - Energy consumption levels
    - GNI growth rates

    What do you find similar? What do you find different?

6. What problems or concerns may exist when GNI per capita is used as an indicator to evaluate national economies and potential business opportunities? What other factors could be used?

NOTES

1. Galbraith, *Economics in Perspective*.
2. *The Wealth of Nations* has been reprinted by various publishers. For the specific references in this chapter, the Modern Library edition was used.
3. Ricardo, *Principals of Political Economy and Taxation*.
4. Mill, *Principals of Political Economy*, 1845.
5. Samuelson, "International Trade and the Equalization of Factor Prices"; Samuelson, "International Factor Price Equalization, Once Again."
6. Leontief, "Domestic Production and Foreign Trade."
7. Vernon, "International Investment and International Trade in the Product Life Cycle."
8. Rostow, *Stages of Economic Growth*.
9. Galbraith, *Nature of Mass Poverty*.
10. This discussion is taken primarily from three Amartya Sen books: *Poverty and Famines* (1981), *Inequality Reexamined* (1992), and *Development as Freedom* (1999).

11. *CIA World Fact Book.*

12. The World Bank changed the term "gross domestic product" (GDP) to "gross national income" (GNI), as the new term reflects goods and services as well as investment income. The text uses the terms GNI and GDP interchangeably.

13. This is calculated in *purchasing power parity (PPP)*, and is from the World Bank, *World Development Indicators,* September 2004.

14. For more on this point, refer to DeSoto, *The Mystery of Capital.*

15. World Bank, "Classification of Economies."

16. DeSoto, *The Mystery of Capital.*

BIBLIOGRAPHY

Berker, G.S., and R.J. Barro. "A Reformulation of the Economic Theory of Fertility." *Quarterly Journal of Economics,* February 1988, 1–25.

CIA World Fact Book, 2004, http://www.odci.gov/cia/publications/factbook/index.html.

DeSoto, Hernando. *The Mystery of Capital.* Basic Books, New York 2003.

Fardoust, Shahroukh, and A. Dhareshwar. *Long-Term Outlook for the World Economy Issues and Projections for the 1990s.* Edison, NJ: World Bank Publications, 1990.

Galbraith, John Kenneth. *The Nature of Mass Poverty.* Lincoln, Nebraska, 1979.

———. *Economics in Perspective: A Critical History.* Boston: Houghton Mifflin, 1987.

Gultekin, M.N., N.B. Gultekin, and A. Penati. "Capital Controls and International Capital Market Segmentation: The Evidence from the Japanese and American Stock Markets." *Journal of Finance,* September 1989, 849–69.

Heckscher, E. "The Effects of Foreign Trade on Distribution of Income." *Economisc Tidskrift,* 1919, 497–512.

Heller, H. Robert. *International Trade: Theory and Empirical Evidence.* 2nd ed. Englewood Cliffs, NJ: Prentice-Hall, 1973.

Leontief, W.W. "Domestic Production and Foreign Trade: The American Capital Position Re-examined." *Economia Internationale,* February 1954, 3–32.

McCarthy, F. Desmond. *Problems of Developing Countries in the 1990s.* Edison, NJ: World Bank Publications, 1990.

Mill, J.S. *Principals of Political Economy.* New York: D. Appleton, 1845.

Mundell, Robert. "International Trade and Factor Mobility." *American Economic Review,* June 1957, 321–35.

Officer, Laurence H., ed. *International Economics.* Boston: Kluwer Academic Publishers, 1987.

Ohlin, Bertil. *Inter-regional and International Trade.* Cambridge, MA: Harvard University Press, 1933.

Porter, Michael. "The Competitive Advantage of Nations" New York: Free Press, June 1, 1998.

Ricardo, David. *The Principals of Political Economy and Taxation.* New York: E.P. Dutton, 1948.

Rostow, W.W. *The Stages of Economic Growth: A Non-Communist Manifesto.* New York: Cambridge University Press, 1961.

Samuelson, R.A. "International Trade and the Equalization of Factor Prices." *Economic Journal,* June 1948, 186.

———. "International Factor Price Equalization, Once Again." *Economic Journal,* June 1949, 74.

Sen, Amartya. *Development as Freedom.* New York: Anchor, 2000.

Smith, Adam. *The Wealth of Nations.* New York: Modern Library, 1994.

Vernon, R. "International Investment and International Trade in the Product Life Cycle." *Quarterly Journal of Economics,* May 1966, 190–207.

World Bank. "Classification of Economies," http://www.worldbank.org/data/countryclass, October 9, 2004.

CHAPTER 4

International Monetary System and the Balance of Payments

CHAPTER OBJECTIVES

This chapter will:

- Define the important terms and concepts of the international monetary system.
- Provide a brief history of the development of the monetary system, from the gold standard to the establishment of the International Monetary Fund.
- Introduce the objectives, roles, and structure of the International Monetary Fund.
- Describe the origins, uses, and valuation methodology of the special drawing right.
- Explain the problems affecting the Bretton Woods system that resulted in development of the managed, or dirty, float.
- Identify areas of reform facing the international monetary system.

The U.S. dollar has fallen relative to the *euro* (and relative to the currency of many other countries) recently, which has helped improve the relative pricing of U.S. exports abroad. It has also made foreign imports into the United States relatively more expensive. Thus, in terms of purchasing power, having a weaker currency (as will be described in this chapter) helps domestic manufacturers at home and abroad.

INTERNATIONAL MONETARY TERMINOLOGY

To conduct international business or international trade, a well-organized and internationally accepted

system must exist to settle the financial transactions that arise out of trade payments. Moreover, this system has to be in step with the nature of the financial transactions that occur in international business and trade and must be flexible enough to accommodate the constant changes in the patterns, directions, volumes, and nature of the financial flows. This mechanism is broadly termed the *international monetary system*, or IMS. Although international trade dates back thousands of years, the use of money as a medium of settlement is relatively recent. Initially, barter was the primary trading mechanism. It was replaced by more formalized systems that relied on the use of gold as the basis for the settling of international transactions.

The settlement of transactions can be relatively easy when trade is carried on domestically, within the borders of individual countries, because the currency of the country is acceptable to all involved parties. Once more than one currency is involved, however, a need arises to develop an internationally acceptable basis to settle transactions.

HARD CURRENCIES

The first requirement for setting up an IMS is to arrive at an international agreement establishing the basis on which to settle transactions. Arriving at this basis is not easy, because it involves valuing the currency of one country against the currency of one or more other countries. Thus, if a currency forms the basis of the settlement, then it has to be accepted by everyone involved.

Currencies of certain countries have a fairly wide acceptance for the settlement of international obligations and are used as a medium in international transactions. These currencies are known as *hard currencies*. The U.S. dollar, British pound, Japanese yen, and euro are examples of hard currencies. Hard currencies can be used by two countries in settling their transactions even if that particular currency is not the home currency of either country. For example, trade transactions between Canada and Mexico can be settled in U.S. dollars, a currency acceptable to both countries even though it is not the home currency of either country. Another important feature of hard currencies is that there is usually a free and active market for them. In other words, if necessary, these currencies can be easily acquired and disposed of internationally in large quantities. There are also usually very few restrictions on the transfer of such currencies in and out of their home countries. Hard currencies, therefore, are an important basis on which to construct an international monetary system.

SOFT CURRENCIES

Soft currencies, on the other hand, are not widely accepted as a medium for settling international financial transactions. Usually there is no free market or foreign exchange for them. Thus, they are not easy to acquire, and disposal is even more difficult. Many soft currencies are subject to restrictions by monetary or governmental authorities on their transfer in and out of their countries. Examples of soft currencies are the Zimbabwe dollar, North Korean won, and Cuban peso.

CONVERTIBILITY

Linked to the notion of hard and soft currencies is the concept of *convertibility*, whereby one currency can be freely converted into another currency. Some countries impose restrictions on currencies so that they cannot be freely converted into the currencies of other countries. These restrictions usually exist in countries that have centrally controlled economies and where transactions outside the country can be made only with official approval. Convertibility implies the availability of a free and active market for a currency. While a currency may be unrestricted in terms of governmental regulations for conversion into other currencies, there may not be adequate demand for that currency by persons outside the country. Such currencies are also said to be lacking in convertibility. Therefore, hard currencies possess the characteristic of convertibility, while soft currencies do not.

When full convertibility of a currency is restricted, a black market often arises that operates outside the control of the government. Essentially, the black market is a free market that parallels the official market and provides full conversion into the local currency, but at a substantial premium over the official rate. The black market in developing countries often operates around parks, international hotels, or transportation stations. As an example of an inconvertible currency, the Zimbabwe dollar has an official exchange rate, but the actual rate in the market place is much higher relative to the foreign currency.

EXCHANGE RATE

When the currency of any one country is used as a medium of settlement for an international transaction, its value has to be fixed vis-à-vis the currency of the other country, either directly or in terms of a third currency. This fixing of a price or value of one currency in terms of another currency is known as the determination of the *exchange rate*. The exchange rate essentially indicates how many units of one currency can be exchanged for one unit of the other currency or vice versa. Exchange rates are not usually fixed permanently. The values of a currency may change upward or downward because of a variety of factors. The frequency with which the currency values change also depends on the type of exchange-rate arrangement of a currency. More fundamentally, however, it has to be understood that the movement of the value of a currency can be either up or down.

APPRECIATION

When the value of a currency is revised or changes upward, it is said to have appreciated.[1] Appreciation of a currency implies that it has become more expensive in terms of other currencies (that is, more units of other currencies will be needed to purchase the same amount of this currency, or fewer units of the appreciated currency will buy the same amount of the other currency). For example, the exchange rate of the pound sterling and the U.S. dollar is £1 = US$2. If, for example, the pound sterling appreciates by 50 percent, then £1 will be equal to US$3. More U.S. dollars can be purchased by the same amount of currency (that is, £1). Alternatively, in this example, before ap-

preciation US$2 could buy £1. After appreciation, US$3 will be needed to buy the same amount of the foreign currency, that is, £1.

DEPRECIATION

When the price of a currency is changed downward, it is said to have undergone *depreciation*. A currency, upon depreciation, becomes less expensive in terms of another currency. Fewer units of the other currency can be purchased with the same amount of the currency after its devaluation. Alternatively, more units of the depreciated currency are needed to purchase the same amount of foreign currency.

For example, at the current exchange rate, US$1 buys DKr6. After a hypothetical depreciation of the dollar, US$1 becomes equal to DKr4. In effect, after depreciation, US$1 now can buy only DKr4. Alternatively, it would take US$1.50 to buy DKr6 instead of only US$1, as was the case before depreciation.

A BRIEF HISTORY OF THE INTERNATIONAL MONETARY SYSTEM

The first form of an international monetary system emerged toward the latter half of the nineteenth century. In 1865 four European countries founded the Latin Monetary Union. Its monetary system rested on the use of bimetallic currencies that had international acceptability within member countries of the union. *Bimetallism* (using gold and silver) was the basis on which the values of the different currencies were determined.

THE GOLD STANDARD

The gold standard, which replaced the bimetallic standard as a system with wide international acceptance, lasted from its introduction in 1880 until the outbreak of World War I in 1914. The central feature of the gold standard was that exchange rates of different countries were fixed, and the parities, or values, were set in relation to gold.

Thus, gold served as the common basis for the determination of individual currency values. Each country adhering to the gold standard specified that one unit of its currency would be equal to a certain amount of gold. Thus, if country A's currency equaled two units of gold and country B's currency equaled four units of gold, the exchange rate of country A's currency against country B's currency would be one to two.

THE GOLD SPECIE STANDARD

The gold specie standard was a pure gold standard. The primary role of gold was as an internationally accepted means of settlement through an arrangement of corresponding debits and credits between different nations. At the same time, gold was in the form of coins, the primary means of settling domestic transactions. Therefore, the gold specie standard required that gold should be available through the monetary authorities in unlimited quantities at fixed prices. There could be no restraints on the import or export of gold, and anyone could have coins struck at the mint if he or she possessed the requisite amount of gold. In effect, this system meant that the face value of gold coins was the same as their exact intrinsic value. The amount of coins, and therefore currency, that a country could issue would be limited to the amount of gold in the possession of a country or its citizens.

THE GOLD BULLION STANDARD

Under the gold bullion standard, the direct link between gold and actual currency that a country could issue was eliminated. Currency could be in the form of either gold or paper, but the issuing authority of the currency would give a standing guarantee to redeem the currency it had issued in gold on demand at the announced price, which would be fixed. Gold was thus backing the issue, but the requirement to maintain exact proportions between the amount of gold in a country's possession and the amount of currency was eliminated, because the authority could reasonably expect that not all the paper currency that it had issued would come up for redemption at the same time. There was, however, a clear need to maintain a link between the amount of a currency in use and the amount of gold available in the depository of the issuing authority, because a certain proportion of gold backup had to be maintained to honor the estimated requested redemption.

The gold bullion standard was widely adopted in the late nineteenth century. Under the gold bullion standard, international transactions could be settled fairly easily, because each country had defined the value of its currency in terms of gold. Thus, a person with U.S. dollars could trade in those dollars for gold with the U.S. authorities and obtain British pounds in England with the gold.

On a country level, the gold standard proved an effective mechanism to settle overall international transactions. A country with a balance of payments deficit faced a situation in which it had to lose some of its gold to pay its debts to the country with the surplus. This led to a reduction in money supply (that was partially backed by gold) and a reduction in prices, which increased the country's export competitiveness and made imports costly. As a result, the balance of payments tended to move away from the deficit toward an equilibrium position because of increasing exports and declining imports. The effect was the opposite on the country with the surplus, which moved away from its surplus position to a position of overall balance of payments equilibrium.

A flaw of the gold standard was that it tended to exacerbate economic conditions between successful countries and those not so successful. For example, if Britain purchased goods from France, then gold would leave Britain and go to France under the gold standard. The continual outflow of gold led to fewer reserves, an increase of interest rates, a contraction of loans, a weakening of prices, and eventually cutbacks in output and employment. In France, the continual influx of gold would raise reserves, which would lead to more loans, higher prices, and higher employment. If these flows continued, depression would occur in Britain, and speculation in France.[2]

Exchange rates were fixed under the gold standard and could not fluctuate beyond upper and lower limits, known as the upper and lower gold points. This slight fluctuation was possible because of the costs involved in the physical movement of equilibrating gold flows from the deficit to the surplus country. If exchange rates went beyond the gold points, the physical transfer of gold would become more remunerative and push the price back within the gold points.

The gold standard worked fairly well during the period from 1880 to 1914. The supply of gold was reasonably steady, and the world economy continued to grow steadily, free from any major international financial crisis. The British Empire was at its zenith, and London was the center of international trade and finance. The central role played by the United Kingdom in general and the Bank of England in particular inspired confidence in the system, which became widely accepted.

The outbreak of World War I, however, radically changed the scenario for the gold standard. Pressures on the United Kingdom's finances because of war expenditures and the resultant gold outflows shook popular confidence in the system. During the war years, no universal system prevailed, most major currencies were in effect floating freely, and the war effort was financed by the creation of large amounts of money that was not backed by gold.

THE INTERWAR YEARS (1918–1939)

At the end of World War I, the IMS was in a state of disarray. Most currencies had undergone wide fluctuations, and the economies of several European countries were severely damaged by the war. Several attempts were made, primarily motivated by Great Britain, to return to the gold standard in the years immediately following the end of World War I. For Great Britain, perhaps, this was an attempt to restore its preeminent prewar position in the international monetary arena. Great Britain therefore announced a prewar exchange parity linked to gold. This was not a realistic exchange rate, however, and it was actually grossly overvalued, given the external balance situation at that time. As a result, Great Britain was forced to redeem substantial amounts of its currency in gold, which led to further outflows of gold and increased pressure on the UK monetary situation.

While Great Britain tried to maintain a strong currency, redeemable in gold, several other countries, eager to improve their international competitive position, began a rush of currency devaluations without any formal agreement with other countries on what a desirable and internationally acceptable value of their currencies should be vis-à-vis other currencies. Apart from the fact that most economies were damaged by war, different countries witnessed different rates of inflation, which upset their international competitive positions at their current level of exchange rates. In an effort to become more competitive, most countries ended up creating a devaluation race, with no formal boundaries or agreed-on set of rules. The position was clearly one of a nonsystem, in which the values of the currencies were determined by the arbitrary decisions of national authorities and the play of market forces.

The difficulties caused by the Great Depression, the problems Germany faced in financing its war reparations, the collapse of the Austrian banking system, and the introduction of *exchange controls* (restrictions on convertibility of currencies) were symptomatic of the chaos that afflicted the international monetary framework in the 1930s. The United States, having become the world's leading economic power as well as the major creditor, added to the general monetary difficulties by continuing to maintain a relatively undervalued exchange rate, despite having huge balance of payments surpluses.[3] Moreover, by acquiring substantial quantities of gold, which it financed by its balance of payment surpluses, the United States exerted further pressure on the economically beleaguered nations of Europe. Some countries, such as Great Britain and France, established strict exchange controls to ensure the availability of foreign exchange to meet essential imports. Currency blocs were also formed (for example, the Dollar Area Bloc and the Sterling Area Bloc). In each currency bloc, there were several member countries that had no exchange controls, but all collectively exercised exchange controls with countries outside the bloc.

THE BRETTON WOODS SYSTEM (1944–1973)

During World War II there was a general and increasing recognition of the futility of the arbitrary and antagonistic exchange-rate and monetary policies that had been followed by the major industrialized countries during the 1920s and 1930s.

It was realized that these policies had been largely counterproductive and had resulted in lower trade and employment levels in most countries. It was also found that these nonformal arrangements had led to a worldwide misallocation of resources that had retarded the efficiency of their utilization. As a result, in 1943 the United States and Great Britain took the initiative toward creating a stable and internationally acceptable monetary system. At the United Nations Monetary and Financial Conference at *Bretton Woods*, New Hampshire, in 1944, delegates of 44 countries, after considerable

negotiations, agreed to create a new international monetary arrangement.

The Bretton Woods Agreement adopted a *gold exchange standard*, primarily along the proposals made by the U.S. delegation, which was led by Harry Dexter White. The gold exchange standard got its basic logic from the gold standard because it sought to bring gold back into a position of international monetary preeminence and, at the same time, to revive the system of fixed exchange rates. The new system recognized the difficulties inherent in completely rigid exchange rates and made some provisions for flexibility.

Under the Bretton Woods system, participants agreed to stipulate a par value for their respective currencies, either directly in terms of gold or indirectly by linking the currency's par value to the gold content of the U.S. dollar. The exchange rates could fluctuate to the extent of 1 percent of the par value on either side. The par values themselves could not be changed except with the concurrence of the *International Monetary Fund (IMF)*, an institution set up by the Bretton Woods Agreement.[4] Usually, the fund would not object to changes of up to 10 percent in par values.

Thus, the U.S. dollar had a central role in the arrangement. The U.S. government guaranteed that it would be ready to buy or sell unlimited quantities of gold at US$35 per ounce in redemptions of the dollar. To maintain its par value in terms of the U.S. dollar, each participant in the system agreed to buy or sell its currency in requisite amounts against the U.S. dollar.

The dollar's convertibility into gold gave it the primary position in the system because member countries could hold either dollars or gold as their reserves. Many preferred to hold U.S. dollars, which had the advantage of interest income accruing on the reserves, which was not true of reserves held in the form of gold. Moreover, many *central banks* used the dollar as their *intervention currency* (that is, the currency they bought or sold to maintain the values of their own currencies within the par-value limits prescribed by the Bretton Woods arrangements). The dollar, being the reserve currency, also became the predominant currency for settlement of international trade and financial transactions.

THE INTERNATIONAL MONETARY FUND

AIMS

The Bretton Woods Conference created the International Monetary Fund to administer the exchange-rate arrangements and to secure orderly monetary conditions. More specifically, the five aims of the IMF, as laid out in its articles, are to achieve the following:

1. Promote international cooperation through consultation and collaboration by member countries on international monetary issues
2. Facilitate the expansion and balanced growth of international trade
3. Promote exchange-rate stability and orderly exchange-rate arrangements
4. Foster a multilateral system of international payments and seek elimination of exchange restrictions that hinder the growth of world trade
5. Try to reduce both the duration and the magnitude of imbalances in international payments by making its resources available (with adequate safeguards)

The IMF was asked to deal with three of these goals as a first priority. It was to administer the exchange-rate arrangements agreed on by the member countries, to provide member countries with financial resources to correct temporary payments imbalances, and to provide a forum in which the members could consult and collaborate on international monetary issues of common concern.

MEMBERSHIP

Initially the IMF had 44 member countries and now has 184. Growth in membership was particularly rapid in the 1960s, as newly independent nations of Asia and Africa became members. Most countries of the world are now members of the IMF. Isolationist nations such as North Korea and Cuba are examples of countries that have not yet joined the membership roll of this organization.

Membership in the fund is based on subscription to its resources in the form of a quota. A member's quota, being equal to its subscription to the fund, determines the member's voting power, as well as, to a considerable extent, its access to the fund's resources. Members' quotas are periodically adjusted to reflect changes in the underlying criteria that were used to establish them initially. Quota sizes are determined by a set formula that takes into account several factors, such as national income, gold and dollar balances, average imports, variability of exports, and so on. The method of computation has undergone several refinements and changes since its inception. There is now a greater emphasis on trade and trade variability as criteria for determining a country's quotas rather than on such criteria as GDP.

STRUCTURE

The highest decision-making body of the IMF is the board of governors, which consists of one governor appointed by each member of the fund. Generally, they are the ministers of finance or governors of central banks of the member countries. Day-to-day operations are overseen by the executive board, which consists of executive directors appointed by the countries with the largest quotas; in addition, groups of countries with smaller quotas jointly elect one executive director each. In 2006 there were 24 executive directors, 5 appointed by the largest quota holders[5] and 19 elected by the other members in groups of different countries.

The United States has the largest quota. Other large quota holders are Germany, France, Japan, the United Kingdom, and Saudi Arabia. Because major decisions require an 85 percent majority, the United States has an effective veto power over major decisions.

Operation of the fund is headed by a managing director, who is elected by the executive board for an initial term of five years. The managing director reports to the board of governors and participates in the deliberations of major committees of the fund. Traditionally, the managing director has been from one of the European member countries of the fund.

FORMS OF IMF ASSISTANCE

The IMF offers assistance to its member countries by making financial resources available to them through a wide range of sources. The primary purpose of IMF loans is to correct balance of payments imbalances.[6] The basic facility, known as a credit tranche drawing, permits a member country to borrow from the fund, in four tranches, or stages, funds equaling its total subscription to the fund or its quota. Each tranche constitutes 25 percent of the member country's quota. Loans under this facility are short-term and are repayable in eight quarterly installments, the last of which has to be within five years of the drawing. Credit tranche drawings were the most utilized facility during the initial years of the fund. Since 1980, funds borrowed through other special facilities have exceeded those made under the basic credit tranche facility.

EXTENDED FUND FACILITY

The extended fund facility was established in 1974 to provide member countries with financial resources for periods long enough to allow them to take corrective measures with respect to their balance of payments difficulties. The basic rationale of this facility is to allow the countries time to correct structural and policy distortions in their economies without having to bear the shocks of too rapid a transition. Moreover, the resources provided under the facility help the member countries tide over temporary balance of payments deficits that may occur in the course of corrective action. Assistance is provided on the basis of specific corrective programs proposed by the borrowing countries. These programs are usually spread over a period of three years. Borrowing up to 140 percent of the quota is permitted under the facility, subject to the upper limit of 165 percent of the quota not being exceeded when the borrowers' outstanding amounts in the credit tranche facility are also taken into account. Repayments are to be made on a longer schedule than in the credit tranche facility; the first installment begins after 4½ years, and the last is made 10 years after the funds are borrowed. Some countries that have benefited from this financing are Ukraine, Columbia, Pakistan, and Argentina.

COMPENSATORY FINANCING FACILITY

The compensatory financing facility was established in 1963 to provide financial assistance primarily to less-developed countries that were faced with balance of payments difficulties because of temporary export shortfalls that occurred because of factors beyond their control. Later, coverage of the facility was broadened to provide assistance to member countries facing balance of payments difficulties because of an increase in the cost of cereal imports. Since the facility is designed to finance the imbalances arising out of shortfalls in exports or because of an increase in the cost of cereal imports, computation of allowable drawings under this facility is based on the estimated shortfall in exports or increased import costs as measured against the median export performance and cereal import costs of the country. Repayments are normally made within three to five years after the funds are borrowed.

SUPPLEMENTARY FINANCING FACILITY AND ENLARGED ACCESS POLICY

The supplementary financing facility was created in 1979 to meet the needs of member countries whose imbalances in their balance of payments could not be financed from their normal quota allocations. Funds for this facility are raised by funds borrowed from countries with surpluses.

Under the enlarged access policy, the IMF was able to continue to finance payments imbalances of certain member countries, in excess of normal quota allocations. Access to the resources of the fund under the enlarged access policy was extended to a cumulative total of up to 300 percent of a member's quota, depending on the difficulty of the balance of payments situation and the nature of the efforts being made to remedy the situation by the borrower. In exceptional cases the IMF can allow a member to borrow even in excess of these limits. The repayment schedule is spread over a long period, with the last repayment installment due seven years after the borrowing date.

STRUCTURAL ADJUSTMENT FACILITIES

Structural adjustment facilities and enhanced structural adjustment facilities are relatively new facilities established by the IMF and are designed to provide financial assistance to member countries that are undertaking specific programs of structural adjustment within their economies.

Structural adjustment programs are essentially a set of policy measures designed to improve the overall efficiency and productive capacity of the economy, as well as to remove existing distortions or other operational deficiencies. Repayments under the facilities are spread over a longer term than are those of other facilities, and the borrower has to agree to a specific policy-change program, which it must treat as its own and not as one imposed by the IMF. Several countries of Africa, Asia, and Latin America will benefit from these new facilities.

IMF CONDITIONALITY

Conditionality is the technical term used to denote the policies that member countries who receive financial assistance from the IMF are expected to follow within their own economies in order to remedy their balance of payments problems. The basic rationale provided by the IMF for requiring conditionality to accompany its lending is the need to address the root causes of the problems and generate in the borrower the capacity to meet its own balance of payments shortfalls and to be able to repay the fund loans. Conditionality is, of course, different for different countries, because the reasons for balance of payments problems differ in varying situations.

There are, however, four conditions that are found in nearly all IMF lending programs:

1. The achievement of a realistic exchange rate that would improve the external competitiveness of the economy; this most often means a substantial devaluation of the currency for many countries
2. The elimination of subsidies and controls within the domestic economy in order to achieve a more efficient allocation of resources and to remove the impediments to enhancing the productivity of the economy

3. Reductions of tariff, trade, and exchange restrictions, thereby creating a relatively more open external sector

4. A reduction of public sector and government spending, which is intended to eliminate excess demand and its impact on the balance of payments

As the balance of payments problems have become increasingly difficult in terms of both their magnitude and their complexity, the conditionality of the IMF has tended to allow a longer time frame in which borrower countries can make the necessary policy adjustments. Moreover, IMF conditionality has tended to change from focusing almost exclusively on demand-side measures to focusing on policies that are aimed at stabilizing the supply conditions in borrowers' economies. Some of the policies that IMF conditionality requires in the area of supply-side stabilization are increases in real interest rates, economic pricing of public services, and tax reforms intended to expand manufacturing output and employment.

While providing financial assistance to member countries, the IMF receives from the borrowers specific policy programs that are to be followed during the period the member country is in receipt of assistance. These programs include specific targets for certain economic benchmarks, such as bank credit, budgetary deficits, external borrowings, and so on. The programs also contain official commitments not to increase restrictions on exchange rates. The IMF uses these targets as well as assurances as basic criteria to assess the performance of borrower countries. The performance of the borrowers in terms of their criteria is taken into account by the IMF while releasing further tranches of assistance. This practice allows the IMF to monitor and to some extent influence the policies of the countries utilizing its resources. Detailed guidelines have been laid down by the executive board of the IMF, under which the performance criteria are used to phase and control the financial assistance of the IMF to member countries.

In some cases there has been considerable resentment against the imposition of conditionality, both on grounds of its not being appropriate for the conditions prevalent in several borrower countries and on grounds that it is an infringement of a country's sovereign right to determine its economic policy. In some countries IMF conditionality has been blamed for causing considerable problems for the poorest sections of society and for taking a heavy social toll by its economic prescriptions. These fears, as well as some even less-founded ones, were the impetus for IMF protests at annual meetings in Seattle in 1999 and again in Washington, D.C., in 2002. Counterarguments hold that the IMF is often a scapegoat for economic ills that originated well before its establishment. Moreover, some politicians in the borrowing countries have found it convenient to pass on to the IMF the blame and responsibility for tough economic measures.

IMF conditionality, although basically remaining the same, has thus tended to be modified to take into account the realities in the borrowing countries and now stresses the role of the borrower countries in taking the primary responsibility for carrying out adjustment programs as a part of their own official policy and not as an outside prescription.

SPECIAL DRAWING RIGHTS

USING SPECIAL DRAWING RIGHTS

Special drawing rights (SDRs) were created as a reserve asset by the IMF in 1970. SDRs are essentially book entries that represent the right of the country holding them to access resources of equivalent value. SDRs owe their origin to the crisis in the IMS that began to emerge during the 1960s, when the volume of trade expanded much faster than the production of gold. Under the Bretton Woods arrangements, countries could hold reserves in the form of either gold or U.S. dollars. Reserves of U.S. dollars with other countries resulted in the United States' having to run ever-larger balance of payments deficits. It was feared that a serious liquidity crisis could result if the United States was not able to sustain and manage large deficits, or if the deficits themselves increased to a point at which they threatened the stability of the external balance of the United States. SDRs were therefore created as an additional reserve asset to complement existing reserves of U.S. dollars and gold.

Apart from being an international reserve asset, SDRs are the unit of accounting for all transactions between the IMF and its member countries. In addition, SDRs are used to settle international transactions between central banks of IMF member countries. SDRs are not, however, a privately used or traded international currency for commercial or other purposes. Certain international organizations, such as the Asian Development Bank, the Arab Monetary Fund, and the World Bank, have been permitted to hold SDRs.

SDRs are allocated to member countries by the IMF board of governors. Allocations of SDRs are made on the same basis as ordinary quotas to the funds of member countries. Holdings of SDRs constitute a part of the countries' international reserves in addition to gold, foreign exchange, and reserve assets with the IMF. Holding an SDR gives the bearer the option to acquire foreign exchange from the monetary authorities of another IMF member. In fact, the IMF intends the SDR to become the principal reserve asset of the international monetary system.

VALUATION OF SDRs

Originally, the value of the SDR was fixed in terms of gold, with 1 SDR being equivalent to 0.888671 grams of gold or 35 SDRs being equal to 1 troy ounce of gold. In 1974, this basis of SDR valuation was replaced by a system that utilized a weighted average of 16 currencies, called a basket. Under this arrangement, which lasted from 1974 to 1980, the value of the SDR was determined on a daily basis. The currencies in this basket were those of IMF member countries whose shares in world exports of goods and services exceeded 1 percent each during the years from 1967 to 1972. While this arrangement lasted, there were some changes made in the basket composition that were meant to reflect the changing proportions of world trade being handled by different countries whose currencies were in the basket and by those whose share increased over time, even though their currencies were not in the basket.

Despite the changes made to reflect the changing positions of the shares of different countries in the world's exports of goods and services, this arrangement continued to suffer from certain problems. For one, many of the currencies in the basket were not actively traded internationally, at least in the forward market, which made actual weighting extremely difficult. To remedy this situation and to simplify the calculation procedure, a new SDR basket was introduced in 2000 that comprised the currencies of the countries and areas that had the largest share in world exports of goods and services. The currency composition of the new SDR basket was as follows:

U.S. dollar	45%
Euro	29%
Japanese yen	15%
Pound sterling	11%

The value of the SDR is determined by the prevailing market value of the currencies adjusted according to their basket weights. Since the introduction of the euro in 2000, this currency has replaced that of the German mark and French franc in the basket. Overall, since the 1980 valuation, the respective shares of the U.S. dollar and the Japanese yen have increased at the expense of the others in the basket.

Although SDRs are meant as reserve assets and are to be used only to settle official transactions between the IMF and its members and between the members themselves, there have been commercial uses of SDRs. The commercial utility of SDRs derives from the relatively stable nature that comes from their basket composition, which evens out the wide fluctuations that are the bane of all major international currencies. As a result, many international borrowers have denominated their bonds and other borrowing instruments in SDRs. SDRs have also been used to denominate trade invoicing, even though settlement is ultimately made in one of the traditional currencies. Other users of SDRs in the past have included the International Air Transport Association for fixing international airfares, and the Republic of Egypt for denominating tolls for transit through the Suez Canal.

A major controversy surrounding SDRs is their use as a mechanism to create aid financing to meet the requirements of LDCs. LDCs hold that SDRs should be linked not to quotas but to the actual needs of IMF member countries. Several industrialized countries, however, including the United States, feel that this instrument is primarily meant for creating international reserves and liquidity, and its use as an aid-financing mechanism would distort the original intentions and result in excess liquidity in the international economy. It has also been argued that aid would be extremely difficult to monitor from the utilization point of view if it were channeled through the SDR mechanism.

Although it is intended to be a major reserve asset, the SDR comprises much less than 10 percent of the world's international resources. A greater role for the SDR, however, would be in the interest of both developed and developing countries.

DIFFICULTIES IN THE BRETTON WOODS SYSTEM

Because the U.S. dollar was a key international reserve currency under the Bretton Woods system, the deficit in the U.S. balance of payments was essential if the liquidity requirements of the IMS were to be fully met. If the U.S. dollar deficits grew larger and larger, however, the holders of dollars would tend to lose confidence in the currency as a reserve and in the capacity of the United States to honor its obligations. The economist Robert Triffin noted this problem in relying too heavily on the U.S. dollar. The *Triffin paradox* states that the more that foreigners relied on the U.S. dollar to expand trade, the less confidence they had in the United States' being able to honor its commitment of redeeming dollars for gold.

Signs of a future crisis became apparent in the late 1950s, when the United States started running extremely large balance of payments deficits. U.S. expansion and investment overseas, aid under the *Marshall Plan*, and a strong economic recovery by Europe were some of the factors that went into making the U.S. trade account into one of almost constant deficit. By the 1960s it was clear that many European and other countries were growing increasingly uncomfortable with their holdings of U.S. dollars as reserves, and many of them wanted to redeem them for gold at the officially announced price. Moreover, given the central role of the U.S. dollar in the system, it could not be devalued to improve the competitive position of the United States versus other countries.

The crisis of confidence was reflected in a run on gold, which pushed its market price well above the announced official price of US$35 per ounce. The central banks of various countries did manage to stabilize the price of gold, at least at the official level, by forming a gold pool and undertaking open-market operations. As a result, however, the gold market was split in two: the official and the unofficial, with U.S. authorities ready to redeem in gold U.S. dollars received only from official sources. Moreover, the U.S. government exerted pressure on European and other holders of dollar reserves not to press for redemptions into gold.

Another inherent defect in the system was that it passed on the effects of U.S. domestic monetary policies to other countries. If the United States followed expansionary policies, other countries were forced to follow a reverse policy to maintain exchange parity. Moreover, the U.S. rates of inflation continued to be higher than those of European countries. Further, the inability to neutralize the inflationary effects of U.S. dollar holdings irked many countries, which felt that they were losing control over their domestic monetary policies. Due to this problem, the German mark and Dutch guilder had to be revalued, and in 1968 the pound was substantially devalued.

By 1970 U.S. gold reserves had fallen to US$11 billion, while short-term official holdings of U.S. dollars were more than double this amount. The crisis came to a head in 1970, with a decline in U.S. interest rates that sparked a massive outflow of capital from the United States to Europe. The pressure on the value of the U.S. dollar continued unabated despite central bank support from many European countries. As a result, in May 1971, Switzerland and Austria revalued their currencies, and Germany and the Netherlands allowed the prices of their currencies to be determined by the market. A continued flight from the U.S. dollar strengthened doubts about the ability of the U.S. dollar to maintain convertibility into gold.

These doubts were confirmed on August 15, 1971, when President Richard Nixon announced the suspension of the convertibility of the U.S. dollar into gold. With the abandonment of dollar convertibility into gold, the underlying basis of the fixed exchange-rate arrangements of the Bretton Woods

system collapsed, and many other countries stopped fixing their exchange rates according to official parities, allowing them to be determined instead by the market.

An attempt was made to return to fixed parities in 1971, through the *Smithsonian Agreement*, under which the United States raised the official price of gold to US$38 per ounce, marking a 7.9 percent devaluation of the dollar. The bands within which currencies could fluctuate against each other were widened to a range of 2.25 percent on each side of the fixed rate, but the dollar was not made convertible into gold. Moreover, the movement of capital across countries continued to put pressure on exchange-rate parities. Faced with either heavy outflows or heavy inflows of foreign currencies, several countries were forced to abandon the freshly fixed parities and allow their currencies to float freely on the international markets. Despite raising the price of gold for a second time, to US$42.20 per ounce, the United States was not able to stem the outflow of dollars, and it became extremely difficult for European countries to maintain the value of their currencies against the U.S. dollar. By the end of the first quarter of 1973, most of the European countries had withdrawn from their participation in the system of parities established under the Smithsonian Agreement.

THE FLOATING-RATE ERA: 1973 TO THE PRESENT

The transition to a system of *floating exchange rates* was not the result of any formal agreement, such as the one that had created the system of fixed exchange rates. It occurred primarily because the earlier system broke down and there was no agreed-on formal arrangement to replace it. In fact, at this stage there was no universal agreement on an appropriate exchange-rate arrangement. Universal agreement continues to elude the international monetary community, and a variety of exchange-rate arrangements are followed by different groups of countries. The most important types of exchange-rate arrangements are different types of floating rates, pegging, crawling pegs, basket of currencies, and fixed rates.

PURE FLOATING RATES

Under the pure-floating-rate arrangement, the exchange rate of a country's currency is determined entirely by such market considerations as demand and supply. The government or the monetary authorities make no efforts to either fix or manipulate the exchange rate. Although many industrialized countries officially state that they follow a policy of floating for their exchange rates, most of them do intervene to influence the direction of the movement of their exchange rates.

MANAGED, OR DIRTY, FLOATING RATES

An important feature of the *managed-float* system is the necessity for the central bank or the monetary authorities to maintain a certain level of foreign exchange reserves. Foreign exchange reserves are needed because the authorities are required to buy or sell foreign currencies in the market to influence exchange-rate movements. On the other hand, under a free-floating-rate arrangement, these reserves are not necessary, because the exchange market is cleared by a free play of the forces of supply and demand, which fix a particular exchange rate that is the equilibrium rate at any given point of time.

PEGGING

Under a *pegging* arrangement, a country links the value of its currency to that of another currency, usually that of its major trading partner. Pegging to a particular currency implies that the value of the pegged currency moves along with the currency to

which it is pegged and does not really fluctuate. It does fluctuate, however, against all other currencies to the same extent as the currency to which it is pegged (for example, the currency of the Republic of Gabon, the CFA franc, has been pegged to the euro since 1999).[7]

CRAWLING PEGS

Under a *crawling-peg* arrangement, a country makes small periodic changes in the value of its currency with the intent to move it to a particular value over a period of time. The system, however, can be taken advantage of by currency speculators, who can make substantial profits by buying or selling the currency just before its revaluation or devaluation. The advantage of this system is that it enables a country to spread its exchange-rate adjustment over a longer period than pegging does, thereby avoiding the shocks that can be caused to the economy by sudden and steep revaluations or devaluations.

BASKET OF CURRENCIES

Many countries, particularly LDCs, are increasingly fixing the rates of their currencies in terms of a basket of currencies. The arrangement is similar to that used for valuation of SDRs. The basic advantage of the system is that it imparts a degree of stability to the currency of a country as the movements in currencies that comprise the basket counterbalance one another. The selection of the currencies that are to be included in the basket is generally determined by their importance in financing the trade of a particular country. In most currency baskets, different currencies are assigned different weights, in accordance with their relative importance to the country. Thus, a basket of currencies for a country may comprise different currencies with different weights. The actual method of computation of the exchange rate from the basket is relatively similar worldwide but may have individual variations. Some countries, although fixing their exchange rate in terms of a basket of currencies, may choose to conduct most of their official transactions in one or two currencies, which are known as the intervention currencies.

FIXED RATES

Under a fixed-rate arrangement, a country announces a specific exchange rate for its currency and maintains this rate by agreeing to buy or sell foreign exchange in unlimited quantities at this rate. At present, however, there are hardly any countries that still follow a completely rigid system of exchange rates. Some of the countries of the former socialist bloc do have fixed exchange rates that are announced from time to time and that are used for all official transactions, particularly with countries with which they have bilateral trade arrangements.

EUROPEAN MONETARY SYSTEM

Several European countries that were members of the *European Economic Community (EEC)*, concerned by the collapse of the Bretton Woods arrangements, decided in 1979 to enter into an exchange-rate arrangement that would regulate movements in their currencies with respect to one another. The currencies of these countries, with respect to the U.S. dollar, were to float jointly. Limits for variations of currencies within the member-country group were fixed at a 2.5 percent range, while as a group, the currencies would vary within a range of 4.5 percent against the U.S. dollar. These arrangements were also a part of the general scheme to achieve significant economic and monetary integration among the member countries of the EEC. One way of achieving greater monetary integration was to reduce the level of fluctuation from their parity values of currencies of different countries within the EEC. The lower range of 2.5 percent prescribed for intracommunity fluctuation was termed the *snake*, while the broader range of

4.5 percent fluctuation as a group against the U.S. dollar was called the *tunnel*.

International monetary cooperation was, however, not so easy to come by in practice, because different member countries were subject to their own individual constraints and found that keeping up with the limits imposed by the "snake" arrangements did not serve their best economic interests. As a result, France, Great Britain, and Italy withdrew their participation from this arrangement within two years of its inception.

Violent fluctuations in exchange rates in the international markets and renewed interest in achieving greater economic and monetary integration within the members of the EEC prompted efforts to reconsider the establishment of a system of fixed parities, with a limited amount of flexibility, for the exchange rates of member countries. In pursuit of these objectives, the *European Monetary System (EMS)* was established by nine member countries of the EEC in 1979. In some ways, it was a successor to the erstwhile "snake" arrangement and reflected the experience gained with that system. This system was later replaced with the *European Monetary Union (EMU)* in 1992.

DIFFICULTIES IN THE FLOATING-RATE ERA

Exchange rates in the floating-rate era have been marked by violent fluctuations that have been prompted by a variety of factors. There were periodic crises in the international monetary system, which were reflected in the extreme fluctuations of exchange rates.

The first major crisis to affect the IMS after the breakdown of the Bretton Woods arrangements was the oil crisis that began in 1973, when OPEC placed an embargo on its members' oil exports, which by 1974 resulted in a fourfold increase in oil prices. For some nations, such as the United States and Japan, this meant a sudden and substantial increase in the volume of their import payments, which put pressure on their balance of payments. The industrialized countries were able to meet this crisis by adjusting their economies to a lower level of oil consumption and more aggressive export policies that increased foreign exchange earnings. The oil-exporting countries, on the other hand, accumulated substantial balance of payments surpluses, which were denominated in U.S. dollars. In 1974 the United States lifted capital controls on the international movements of dollars, making them freely transferable across the globe. As long as the dollar remained the primary currency for holding and recycling the dollars held by OPEC countries (also known as *petrodollars*), the value of the dollar continued to be strong, despite a virtually continuous trade deficit.

The continuous trade deficits, however, and policies that encouraged capital outflows, caused confidence in the dollar to weaken, leading to a sharp fall in its price in 1978. Further, this decline of confidence in the dollar was exacerbated by the difficulties the United States faced in Iran because of its revolution, as well as the problems created by the second oil crisis, of 1979, when the OPEC countries indulged in yet another round of dramatic price increases. The attractiveness of the dollar was enhanced yet again, very quickly, as U.S. authorities decided on a monetary policy that would result in higher U.S. interest rates, which in turn would attract overseas demand for the dollar and raise the exchange rate.

The changed monetary policy also helped to maintain international confidence in the U.S. dollar in the face of the second oil shock as well as the unsettled conditions in Iran, especially in light of the general freeze on Iranian assets held in the United States. A major factor in this new confidence was the expectation that inflation would remain at a lower level in the United States than in other countries. Therefore, investments made in the United States seemed attractive. To invest in the United States meant that the overseas investors had to acquire U.S. dollars, which increased the demand and strengthened the exchange rate of the currency. Although the United States ran huge balance of payments deficits from 1981 to 1985, the dollar's value continued to appreciate. Apart from the high interest rates and low inflation, U.S. investments were attractive because of the strong performance of the U.S. economy, which continued to enjoy a virtually uninterrupted expansion. Moreover, the United States seemed to be the safest haven for investors, as political crises affected many parts of the world and threatened to spread to many more. Other factors that strengthened the U.S. dollar in this period were the decline in the price of oil, the reinvestment of funds by major commercial banks in the U.S. market, and speculative actions of investors in the foreign exchange markets, who kept pushing the value of the dollar even higher by making speculative purchases and increasing demand.

FLUCTUATIONS IN THE U.S. DOLLAR: THE PLAZA AND LOUVRE ACCORDS

Continued appreciation of the dollar had by early 1985 caused enough economic problems for the United States to precipitate active government action to arrest this trend. The high price of the dollar had made U.S. exports expensive and imports cheap, which led to a decline in the former and a steep rise in the latter, creating a huge deficit in the U.S. trade account. Moreover, most of this deficit was financed not by internal resources but by external borrowings. As a result, the United States decided to follow policies that would reduce the attractiveness of overseas investments in dollar assets and improve the budgetary and trade deficit position. The most important of these policies were an attempt to reduce

U.S. interest rates, a reduction of the budget deficit, and coordinated action to bring down the value of the dollar, an action to be taken by the monetary authorities of the major industrialized countries.

The third policy was initiated in September 1985, when finance ministers of the United States, Japan, France, the then West Germany, and the United Kingdom, as well as their central bank governors, met at the Plaza Hotel in New York City and reached an agreement on coordinated action to be taken to bring down the value of the U.S. dollar. The agreement, known as the *Plaza Accord*, prompted a dramatic decline in the already depreciating dollar, which continued to fall steadily over the next year and a half. By the end of the first quarter of 1987, the value of the dollar had fallen so much that it was considered too weak. Therefore, in 1987 the group of six industrialized countries (the United States, the United Kingdom, West Germany, France, Canada, and Italy) agreed during their annual summit, held that year in Paris, to arrest the decline in the value of the dollar. The agreement, known as the *Louvre Accord*, did not have such a dramatic and immediate impact in achieving its objective as the Plaza Accord, because the dollar continued to decline for a while. By 1988, however, the dollar had recovered some of its strength.

The Plaza Accord was successful primarily because it was in a relatively better position to achieve its objectives, with the dollar already on a downward path. On the other hand, the Louvre Accord had a much more difficult agenda: to reverse the trend in the international foreign exchange markets. Moreover, the Louvre Accord required a relatively consistent and long-term policy-coordination effort that was not so likely to come to pass, given the individual economic imperatives and policies of signatories.

European Monetary Union

In keeping with the goal of achieving greater monetary integration in Europe, the *European Monetary Union* came into effect in 1992. This agreement was part of the general agreement concerning the European Union, which also came into effect that year. The European Union originally consisted of 15 member nations; its membership was expanded by an additional 10 countries in May 2004, as is shown in Table 4.1.

The primary focus of the European Union was to create one marketplace throughout the continent of Europe to compete with that of the United States. The European Union was created as an economic union with the primary aim of full integration of the aforementioned national economies into one united Europe. The European Union eliminated internal trade barriers among member nations, adopted common external trade policies, abolished restrictions on the mobility of the factors of production, and began to coordinate economic activities, such as monetary, fiscal, taxation, and social welfare programs, in an attempt to blend the nations into a single economic entity.

On January 1, 2002, the euro was launched in the 12 member states that opted into the EMU. Of the original 15 EU member states, all but 3 adopted the euro as the single currency.[8] Denmark, Sweden, and the United Kingdom opted to either not join or delay joining the EMU. Establishment of the new currency was not an isolated event, however. The European Union had to change thousands of national laws, product standards, and regulations to ensure that they were harmonized throughout the member nations. These changes were necessary to create a unified system that would permit the free flow of goods, services, labor, capital, and technology in Europe.

Maastricht Treaty

The Maastricht Treaty went into effect in November 1993. Its purpose was to lay the framework for the economic and political integration of the European Union. The treaty, named for the city in

Table 4.1

European Union Membership

The EU 15		2004 EU Additions	
Austria	Italy	Cyprus	Lithuania
Belgium	Luxembourg	Czech Republic	Malta
Denmark	Netherlands	Estonia	Poland
Finland	Portugal	Hungary	Slovakia
France	Spain	Latvia	Slovenia
Germany	Sweden		
Greece	United Kingdom		
Ireland			

the Netherlands where it was signed into law, rests on three pillars:

- A common foreign and defense policy
- Cooperation on police, judicial, and public safety matters
- New provisions to create an economic and monetary union among the member states

The final bullet point is the focus of the discussion here, and it consists of the creation of certain *convergence criteria* that the government of each member state must adhere to in order to qualify for participation in the common European currency. These rules were necessary because for an economic union among multiple sovereign nations to work, the member states must maintain similar monetary and fiscal policies (and results).

The convergence criteria for the European Union are itemized below:

- Government deficit must not exceed 3 percent of GDP
- Government debt must not exceed 60 percent of GDP
- Inflation and long-term interest rates must not exceed those of the three lowest EU member states by more than 2 percent

- Foreign exchange rate of currency must float within a range of 15 percent of those of the other member countries for a period of two years prior to the adoption of the euro

As you can see from the bullet points above, there is a combination of both fiscal and monetary policy requirements necessary for a country to qualify for inclusion in the EMU. Of the 12 original members of the EMU, all qualified for the single currency prior to its launch in January 2002. Italy and Greece had to make the biggest improvements (primarily in their inflation levels) in order to qualify. These same criteria were used in order to phase in the 10 member states that joined the European Union (and thus the EMU) in May 2004.

DENMARK'S CHALLENGE TO MONETARY UNION

While the success of the euro since its issue has exceeded initial expectations, three of the original 15 EU member states do not currently participate in the single currency. The first to buck the trend was Denmark. In the 1990s, and again on September 28, 2000, the citizens of Denmark voted to not participate in the euro, instead opting to keep the Danish krone intact. The "Euro-skeptics," or individuals that feared the spread of the European Union in the continent, twice defeated national referendums on adopting the euro. The Danes feared infringement on their national sovereignty due to its relative size. The European Parliament, which will eventually become the European Union's primary legislative body, has representation from each member nation according to the population of each country. Under the current arrangement, Denmark has only 14 members of European Parliament (MEPs) out of a total parliamentary body of 732. Thus, it is easy to see the fears of a small nation concerning its ability to manage its own internal affairs, and not having to encounter undue influence from the rest of Europe via the European Union's Brussels headquarters.

While Denmark does not participate in the euro, the small nation has opted to allow the krone to float against the euro within a range of 2.5 percent. This policy has worked so far due to the relative strength of the Danish economy, the country's current account surpluses, low unemployment relative to EU averages, sound public finances, and marginally higher interest rates relative to the *European Central Bank (ECB)*.[9] The ECB is essentially the central bank of the European Union and is responsible for implementing monetary policy for the European Union.

While Denmark's economy prospers, it is easy to see that the country can benefit from having its currency fixed to the euro, without having the political intrusion into its internal affairs that, so far, its citizens have voted against in public referendums. It will be interesting to see what happens should the economy falter in the future.

ASIAN FINANCIAL CRISIS

The 1997–98 *Asian financial crisis* provides another example of problems that can occur in the current international monetary system. The original cause of the problem was thought to be the unpegging of the Thai baht to the U.S. dollar. The Thailand

economy had grown by 9 percent over the period 1985–95, and massive speculation had ensued in the economy. Once the Thai government decided to allow the baht to float, the currency plummeted in value, losing more than 50 percent of its value in 1997.[10] Additionally, the Thai stock market crashed by 75 percent. Other countries, including the Philippines, South Korea, Malaysia, and Indonesia, all experienced currency attacks as investors attempted to sell the Thai baht on the world currency market. In Hong Kong, the Hang Seng stock market index fell by more than 23 percent in October, while the government raised interest rates from 8 percent to 23 percent over the period in an attempt to keep the currency pegged to the U.S. dollar.

While it is tempting to assign blame to currency failures for this financial episode, this crisis was merely a symptom and not the root cause of the problem. If currency was at the heart of the problem, you would expect to find budgets at high deficit levels, and high levels of inflation throughout Southeast Asia. While some of the affected countries had some of these symptoms, they were certainly not pervasive throughout the region. If there had been budget deficits, central banks would have printed money in an attempt to balance the budget, which would cause inflation and the desire to sell the inflated currency in favor of a more stable one.[11] Additionally, interest rates were not excessively high throughout the region either. Pegging an exchange rate to another currency (the U.S. dollar) requires raising interest rates in order to stop the flight of capital and propping up the value of the domestic currency by buying it (and selling U.S. dollars).

Root Cause of the Asian Financial Crisis

The primary problem was speculative bank lending due to government-guaranteed loans. The Thailand economy, as well as that of South Korea, had large amounts of nonperforming loans on the balance sheets of the nations' banks. Since the governments in the region had provided guarantees for loans, *moral hazard* was the result. Moral hazard ensues when there is no punishment for banks if loans are defaulted on, which creates an incentive for the banks to overlend. Once the first speculative loans go bad, the government has to step in to bail out the domestic banks. The bailout of the first bank creates a panic for the other banks, and the downward spiral begins. The banks of Southeast Asia were not regulated with regard to quantifying the risk of their loan portfolios, and since the domestic banks had overloaned on many speculative projects, the assets were overvalued.

Thus, the boom-and-bust cycle in the asset markets due to speculative lending by banks preceded the currency crises in all affected nations. In the aftermath of the Asian financial crisis, the IMF provided more than $120 billion to four countries in an effort to improve the performance of the once-strong economies. The majority of economists called for stricter regulation in the banking sector, and many banks in the region were closed. Large commercial banks have also recently agreed to an overall system of quantifying risk at major international banks, in a system called the *Basel Accord*. Under this system, the amount of capital held in the financial institutions must reflect the amount of risk in the loan portfolios. This calculation is done via a standardized bank credit-scoring system. Other suggestions for improvement include increased levels of financial reporting for companies (or "transparency guarantees," in the words of Amartya Sen).

ISSUES FOR REFORM

The violent fluctuations in exchange rates ever since the inception of the floating-rate era have raised serious questions about the efficiency and desirability of the present arrangements for settlement of international financial obligations. It is evident that the system has not proved to be perfect, and

there have been several adverse effects, especially for the less-developed nations of the world. Some of the main issues that have to be addressed in this context are:

1. International exchange-rate stability
2. Enhancement of international liquidity
3. A more equitable international monetary system from the point of view of the LDCs
4. Bank reform in national markets (as discussed in the Asian financial crisis section)

INTERNATIONAL EXCHANGE-RATE STABILITY

While there is general agreement that the current state of violent fluctuations in exchange rates is not desirable, there is no definite agreement on how this should be resolved, if such resolution is at all possible.

Some proponents of the extreme view seek a return to the gold standard, citing the stabilizing role of gold and the near-complete exchange stability the world enjoyed during the days of the gold standard. Conditions have since changed drastically, however, and it is hardly likely that there would be enough gold to back the enormous volume of international obligations now in circulation. Another proposal to restore international exchange-rate stability is to return to fixed exchange rates. It is argued that a return to fixed rates would reduce international currency volatility, which would improve international trading efficiency and remove the costs involved in avoiding possible losses because of currency fluctuation. Fixed rates are also claimed to have a moderating influence on domestic monetary and fiscal policies and engender a conservative approach that fosters macroeconomic stability. Moreover, fixed rates would allow a consistent approach toward domestic resource allocation, and the patterns of domestic resource allocation would not have to change to take into account major movements in exchange rate and competitive positions of different industries. Fixed exchange rates also do not permit speculation, which has caused serious disruption in the international markets and substantial losses to persons involved in international trade transactions.

Fixed exchange rates, however, do have downside risks. First, they hold domestic policies "ransom" to external conditions, as external conditions force changes in domestic policies if exchange rates have to be maintained at a predetermined level. Defending a particular exchange rate requires the maintenance of substantial foreign exchange reserves and incurring considerable losses on the foreign exchange markets during intervention operations. Large reserves tend to be a wasteful use of resources because they do not yield the highest possible rate of return, and return considerations are overshadowed by safety and liquidity requirements. Moreover, some countries, especially the less-developed ones, simply may not have access to sufficient amounts of foreign currencies to maintain the needed levels of exchange reserves.

As of now it is not likely that the IMS will revert to a system of fixed exchange rates, at least in the foreseeable future, but it does remain as an option at the back of the minds of a large number of international economists.

Target Zones

The target zone arrangement was perhaps the most actively and seriously discussed arrangement of the late 1980s, as an alternative to the present nonsystem.[12] The target zone system envisions the establishment of relative wide bands around certain parities, within which currencies of countries participating in the system can fluctuate with reference to one another. Once a currency approaches the limit at the edge of a band, the central banks would intervene in the exchange market to bring it back

into line. The major mechanism, however, would be the long-term coordination of national economic policies that would keep the values of participating currencies within the target zones so that frequent intervention by central banks would not be required. The target zone proposal has definite merit, inasmuch as it seeks to provide exchange-rate stability while making necessary provisions for flexibility, which is essential in the current international economic environment. Implementation of target zones, however, faces a number of hurdles. First, there must be agreement on what the range of permitted fluctuations should actually be, and, even before that is determined, the basic parity of exchange rates around this range should be established. Second, mechanisms have to be established to prevent speculation in the international foreign exchange markets taking advantage of the system. Third, if the system is to work, a serious commitment is needed from participating countries to coordinate their national economic policies. This commitment, even if made initially, is difficult to maintain, given the varied pressures that national governments face at home. Moreover, with changes in governments taking place periodically, there is no real guarantee that the policy commitments given by one government will be honored by the next.

International Liquidity

International liquidity depends on the amounts of internationally acceptable monetary reserves available to different countries. The importance of international liquidity clearly stems from its role in financing the external transactions of all countries. Through the 1980s the liquidity position of the developing countries tended to worsen because of a number of factors: lower export earnings, higher export costs, reduced access to external commercial borrowings because of the debt crisis, large debt-service requirements, and reductions in official development assistance in real terms, all of which have limited the capacity of these countries to continue to finance crucial imports needed for sustaining their ongoing developmental efforts and to give them the elbow room to make necessary adjustments in their economies.

As a result, many developing countries have been seeking an enhancement of international liquidity through greater access to IMF resources. This access is sought through attempts to increase the quota sizes allocated to different countries. The argument of the developing countries is that the quota sizes should be determined not by the existing criteria, but by assessing the financing requirements of individual countries. A link of SDR allocations to the aid requirements of developing countries has been strongly advocated for several years. This view is opposed by the developed countries, who feel that there is no real need to increase the present level of liquidity in the international economy. They feel that the resources of the IMF are meant for specific purposes, and the present procedures are designed to ensure their optimal utilization. According to the opponents, developmental assistance is best routed through the World Bank, because it is accompanied by serious appraisal and follow-up procedures. Discretionary use of the resources of the IMF could lead to excessive borrowing, which could prove counterproductive and promote a lax attitude toward the tough decisions needed to be taken by the developing countries to improve the efficiency and productivity of their economies. Moreover, according to the industrialized countries, enough resources are available to countries that can prove their creditworthiness to receive them.

A MORE EQUITABLE INTERNATIONAL MONETARY SYSTEM

Many developing countries have raised the issue that the international monetary system as it exists today is weighted heavily in favor of the industri-

alized countries. All key decisions of the IMF, for example, are subject to a veto by the United States, because an 85 percent majority is needed to make these decisions, and the United States holds 17.46 percent of the total votes. Moreover, although the developing countries comprise more than 70 percent of the world's population, their share of IMF votes is only 38 percent. One way for the LDCs to achieve a greater voice in the international monetary arena is an increase in their IMF votes to 50 percent. Little progress has been made in this direction. Another route that can be taken by developing countries is to reduce their reliance on the currencies and financial systems of industrial countries in settling transactions among themselves. As a result, several regional clearing arrangements have been established to promote the use of the currencies of developing countries. Most of them, however, have not been able to achieve any great success because of a number of different problems that have arisen since their introduction. Regional clearing arrangements have not been abandoned, however, and efforts are under way to find ways to make these systems more effective and beneficial to the developing countries. One example of such an arrangement is the Asian Clearing Union.

SUMMARY

The ability to properly value and exchange one currency for another is fundamental to conducting international business. Hard currencies, such as the U.S. dollar, the euro, and the British pound, are easily acquired and disposed of in a free and open market. Soft currencies are not easily exchanged because of government controls. The IMS serves as the basis for currency exchange by establishing the internationally accepted framework and methodologies of valuation.

The early forms of the IMS used gold as the basis for exchanging one currency for another. International events, such as World War I, large balance of payments deficits in the United Kingdom and Europe, and World War II, along with the emergence of the United States as the world's largest creditor, ultimately led to the development of the gold exchange standard at Bretton Woods. The International Monetary Fund was designed to administer and enforce the Bretton Woods Agreement by providing financial assistance for member countries with balance of payments problems through its facilities operations. Gaining IMF assistance, however, required implementation of conditionalities, which aimed at stabilizing the economies of borrowers.

Special drawing rights were created as reserve assets by the IMF when the United States began experiencing large balance of payments deficits and gold production could not keep pace with the increasing volume of international trade. Initially fixed in terms of gold, valuation of the SDR in 1974 was changed to a basket of 16 currencies and, in 2000, a basket of the developed world currencies (the U.S. dollar, the British pound, the euro, and the Japanese yen).

The U.S. dollar was the key component of the Bretton Woods Agreement and provided the liquidity required by the IMS. As U.S. deficits grew, however, confidence in the dollar as a reserve currency fell, requiring its devaluation. Two unsuccessful attempts in 1971 and 1974, along with the abandonment of rights to convert U.S. dollars into gold, resulted in the development of the modern IMS, the floating-rate era. A variety of exchange-rate methods have developed, including managed or dirty floats, crawling pegs, and fixed rates.

The floating-rate era has been harmed by extreme volatility caused by a variety of factors. These include the oil crises of the 1970s, the chronic fiscal and balance of payments deficits of the United States, and the appreciation of the U.S. dollar because of its relative political stability and position as a safe haven. In 1985 and 1987, the Plaza and Louvre agreements, respectively, implemented policies to bring down and then arrest the decline of the value of the U.S. dollar. In the 1990s, the Asian financial crisis exposed the problem of moral hazard in the banking sector in multiple Southeast Asian nations. The aftermath of this crisis was a concentrated effort toward improving the risk assessment of credit portfolios for internationally active banks via the Basel Accord.

The current monetary system has clear shortcomings, particularly for developing countries. Monetary system reformists are suggesting that new policies be implemented to increase international exchange-rate stability and enhance international liquidity.

DISCUSSION QUESTIONS

1. What is the difference between a hard currency and a soft currency?
2. What was the importance of gold in the early international monetary system? What problems arose under this system?
3. Describe the Bretton Woods Agreement. What position did gold hold in this system?
4. Outline the structure of the International Monetary Fund. What are its aims? What is conditionality?
5. What is a special drawing right?
6. Discuss the difficulties that occurred in the late 1960s and early 1970s that required the United States to abandon the gold exchange system.
7. What is the difference between a pure floating rate and a managed, or dirty, floating rate? Provide an example of currencies that are managed.
8. Why are international exchange-rate stability and liquidity important for conducting international business?

NOTES

1. If a currency is fixed against another currency, any formal upward adjustment of its value against the reference currency is termed a revaluation. Correspondingly, any formal downward adjustment is termed a devaluation.

2. Galbraith, "Money."

3. This echoes current complaints about China's keeping its currency value low by fixing its currency to the U.S. dollar. The primary difference is that the Chinese balance of payments is closer to equilibrium.

4. Another Bretton Woods institution, the World Bank, is discussed in detail in Chapter 6.

5. The largest quota holders as of 2006 are the United States, Japan, Germany, France, and the United Kingdom.

6. The World Bank, as is discussed in Chapter 6, provides loans for productive purposes (i.e., projects that improve sectors or industries within the borrowing country).

7. The Communauté Financière Africaine franc (CFAF) was formerly tied to the French franc.

8. The 10 additional member states in 2004 were not given the option of opting out of the currency union.

9. The Copenhagen Inter-Bank Offering Rate (CIBOR) typically has been 25 basis points higher than the ECB rate.

10. "Survey of Asian Finance."

11. Krugman, "What Happened in Asia?"

12. Some would call this a market-based system.

BIBLIOGRAPHY

Aliber, Robert Z. *The International Money Game.* 2nd ed. New York: Basic Books, 1976.

Deane, Marjorie. "At Quiet Bank-Fund Meetings: Thoughts of Monetary Reform." *Financier*, November 1988, 13–16.

Galbraith, John Kenneth. *Money: Whence It Came and Where It Went.* Boston: Houghton Mifflin, 1995.

Glascock, J.L., and D.J. Meyer. "Assessing the Regulatory Process in an International Context: Mixed Currency SDRs and U.S. Bank Equity Returns." *Atlantic Economic Journal*, March 1988, 39–46.

Heinonen, Kerstin. "The Role and Future of the SDR." *Kansallis-Osake-Pankki Economic Review*, July 1990, 567–77.

Hosefield, J.K. *The International Monetary Fund, 1945–1965.* Washington, DC: International Monetary Fund, 1969.

"IMS Survey." Washington, DC: International Monetary Fund (October 2004).

International Monetary Fund. *Annual Report.* Washington, DC: International Monetary Fund, 2005.

Krugman, Paul. "What Happened in Asia?" 1998. http://www.hartford-hwp.com/archives/50/010.html.

Pozo, Susan. "The ECU as International Money." *Journal of International Money and Finance*, June 1987, 195–206.

Saxena, R.B., and H.R. Bakshi. "IMF Conditionality—A Third World Perspective." *Journal of World Trade*, October 1988, 67–79.

Scammell, W.M. *The Stability of the International Monetary System.* Totowa, NJ: Rowman and Littlefield, 1987.

"Survey of Asian Finance," *Economist*, 2003.

Suzucki, Y., J. Miyake, and M. Okabe. *The Evolution of the International Monetary System: How Can Efficiency and Stability Be Attained?* Tokyo: University of Tokyo Press, 1990.

Tew, Brian. *The Evolution of the International Monetary System: 1945–1988.* London: Hutchinson Education, 1988.

Triffin, R. *Our International Monetary System: Yesterday, Today and Tomorrow.* New Haven, CT: Yale University Press, 1968.

Appendix 4.1
Balance of Payments

The *balance of payments (BOP)* is an accounting system for the financial transactions of a country with the rest of the world. The BOP shows trade inflows and outflows for a country and draws a picture of how the nation has financed its international economic and commercial activities. It measures the value of all export and import goods and services, capital flows, and gold exchanges between a home country and its trading partners. This accounting of the flows of goods and capital between nations provides crucial information in determining a nation's economic health. Thus, it becomes critical information for policy makers and officials on the domestic front and within supranational organizations, as well as for all international business people, especially potential investors of resources across national borders.

Identifying just how a nation finances its activities and what claims other countries hold on its assets provides one measure of its economic strength. In what type of position to meet claims against its assets does a country stand? How able is the country to purchase goods or services from other countries? The measures provided by the BOP system are not entirely instructive on an annual basis; what is more important are the displays it shows over time in trading patterns and aggregate annual flows of goods, capital, and reserves between nations.

Preliminary Definitions

To understand the BOP system, it is important to comprehend some of the terminology used in the process. First of all, the BOP is a system based on the double-entry accounting method. Thus, for each transaction, two entries are made: a debit and a credit. For example, if a country imports goods and services,

the value of the payment made for such imports will be debited in one account that records transactions relating to trade and credited in other accounts that record either the increase of assets of the country held by foreigners or the decrease in short-term foreign assets held by residents. For example, if the United States imported $50,000 of wines from the United Kingdom, the payment would be recorded as a debit in the current account, which records the transactions in goods and services, and as a credit in the capital account, which records inflows and outflows of financial assets from the country. The entry in a particular subhead of the capital account will depend on the manner in which payment is made for imports. If payment is made out of the foreign exchange reserves of the country, the account subhead for the decrease in short-term foreign assets is credited. On the other hand, if the payment is made in the local currency and the local currency continues to be held by the UK firm, then the account subhead credited is the increase in short-term domestic assets held by foreigners.

Because each entry in the BOP is matched by an equal and opposite entry, by definition the account has to balance. Table 4.1A, a complete BOP for the United States, illustrates the organization of information in a BOP. The trade flows are organized into four separate categories, or accounts: the current account, the capital account, financial account (the official reserves account,) and the statistical discrepancy (errors and omissions).

Information on the flow of goods in and out of a country is usually provided by customs information collected as merchandise crosses international borders. Information on service flows is generally estimated through the use of statistical sampling of actual expenditures. Information on payments made for exports and imports, as well as outflows and

Table 4.1A

Complete Balance of Payments for the United States

Type of Account	2003	2002
Current Account		
Exports		
Goods, balance of payments basis	$713,122	$681,874
Services	$307,381	$292,233
Income receipts	$294,385	$255,542
Exports of goods, services, and income receipts	$1,314,888	$1,229,649
Imports		
Goods, balance of payments basis	$(1,260,674)	$(1,164,746)
Services	$(256,337)	$(227,399)
Income payments	$(261,106)	$(251,108)
Imports of goods, services, and income payments	$(1,778,117)	$(1,651,657)
Unilateral transfers	$(67,439)	$(58,853)
Current Account Total	**$(530,668)**	**$(480,861)**
Capital and Financial Account		
Capital account transactions, net	$(3,079)	$(96,145)
U.S. official reserves, net	$1,523	$(3,681)
U.S. government assets, other than official reserves, net	$537	$(32)
U.S. private assets, net	$(285,474)	$(175,272)
Foreign-owned assets in the U.S., net	$248,573	$706,983
Other foreign assets in the U.S., net	$580,600	$94,860
Capital and Financial Account Total	**$542,680**	**$526,713**
Statistical discrepancy (errors and omissions)		
Statistical discrepancy	$(12,012)	$(45,852)

Source: International Monetary Fund, *Balance of Payments Statistics Yearbook 2004* (Washington, DC: International Monetary Fund, 2004).

inflows because of credit and capital flows, is provided by commercial banks. Financial institutions also provide information on capital and credit flows across the borders of a country. Finally, the monetary authority or central bank of each country reports official borrowings, and each country maintains its own accounts. In the United States, the Department of Commerce maintains the records of national accounts. The figures for each country are then synthesized by two agencies, the United Nations and the International Monetary Fund, into an aggregate global snapshot of flows between nations.

The position of a country in any of these accounts is in equilibrium when outflows equal inflows; it is in deficit when outflows of foreign exchange because of imports and other payments exceed inflows because of exports or other receipts. A country is in surplus when total foreign exchange inflows exceed total outflows. The final balance is done in an attempt to capture a history of all flows between nations, whether they are because of reserves of gold, currencies, foodstuffs, manufactured goods, investments of home-country funds abroad, the provision of insurance, travel facilities, or hotel accommodations or other services.

CURRENT ACCOUNT

The *current account* takes note of three separate types of flows between nations, similar to the concept of revenues (credits) and expenses (debits) in business operations. The first type of transfer is visibles: financial inflows and outflows arising out of actual exchanges of merchandise between countries through exporting and importing. Exports add to the account and imports subtract from the balance of the account. The net position of this section of the BOP is the *balance of trade (BOT)*.

Flows of imports and exports are evaluated not only according to volumes, but also according to a nation's terms of trade. Terms of trade refer to the ratio of the export prices of a country to its import prices. A rise in export prices in relation to import prices improves the BOT if the trade volumes remain constant. Generally, rising prices for exports will tend to eventually squeeze the volume of exports in relation to imports. Quantities of goods traded between nations tend to change slowly; thus, an initial rise in the terms of trade will improve a country's trade balance in the short term, with deleterious effects on the balance becoming apparent only in the long term.

The second category of transfers within the current account are *invisibles* and services between nations, including such items as transportation of people or goods, tourist services provided by other countries, supplying insurance for foreign policy buyers, international consulting services, and such financial and banking services as loans or fees for establishing lines of credit or acting as brokers in foreign exchange transactions. This category also includes the transfer of investment income from international investments overseas back to home-country residents and the remittance of profits back to parent corporations. These transfers are considered to be income resulting from the employment of production factors abroad, such as investment capital. The actual movement of the factors of production, that is, capital in the form of dollars going into plant and equipment overseas, is differentiated as a capital movement because the factor itself is moved across borders.

The third category within the current account keeps track of unilateral (or unrequited) transfers by countries to other countries, which is the flow of funds or goods for which no quid pro quo is expected. These items include aid provided by a government or private interests to other countries, which can be in the form of grants issued by the government, money sent home to their families by immigrants, and private funding and aid by foundations and international aid agencies, such as the Red Cross. Unrequited transfers can be private funding and aid by foundations and international aid agencies, such as the Red Cross, that provide financial and physical assistance in the event of national disasters. Unrequited transfers are made to institutions and private individuals alike.

The current account is considered the most important of the four BOP accounts because it measures all income-producing activity generated through foreign trade and is considered the prime indicator of the trading health of a nation. A BOT deficit, however, is not in itself a negative condition in certain instances, and it could be considered normal for a country as long as other services, transfers, and capital accounts can finance the deficit within the merchandise sector. Some countries, such as Switzerland, whose forte is the financial services sector, have chronic BOT deficits but are economically healthy because of their strength in other sectors. Other countries exhibit continuing deficits in their BOT because they are in the process of development.

The BOT and the current account are not the only indicators of the economic position of a country. The history and level of development of a nation must also be considered in assessing its relative health. Another important indicator in weighing national economic strength in relation to other countries is the BOP capital account.

CAPITAL ACCOUNT

The *capital account* of a nation measures its net changes in financial assets and liabilities abroad. It also chronicles the flow of investment funds across national borders. The capital account notes an inflow when residents of a country receive funds from foreign investors. These funds may be invested in stocks (equity) or bonds (debt) or any other financial assets that foreign owners hold and for which resident borrowers are liable for payment. The resident is then required to remit to the foreign financiers returns on the investment in the form of dividends or profits. Naturally, an outflow of funds occurs when a resident of the home country acquires assets abroad; the overseas counterpart then incurs an international liability.

The capital account is made up of three separate segments. The first is long-term capital movements, which can be in the form of either direct or portfolio investments. Direct investments are those made by individuals or multinational corporations in facilities or assets abroad, where the investor has control over the use and disposition of the assets. For BOP purposes, effective control is determined as that time when foreign owners from one country hold more than 50 percent of voting stock or when a single resident or an organized group from one country owns more than 25 percent of voting stock in a foreign company.

Long-term portfolio investments are those in which investors contribute capital to a foreign concern and invest their funds in stocks or bonds but do not control the facility or the assets of the enterprise. These investments are considered long-term if they are held for more than a year. Portfolio investments that mature in less than a year are considered short-term capital flows, the third segment of the capital account. Some short-term movements are considered compensatory, in that they finance other activities, such as those in the current account. Others represent autonomous international financial movements undertaken for their own sake in order to speculate on fluctuations in exchange and interest rates. Many of these actions consist of trading and hedging activity undertaken in international financial forward, futures, options, and swaps markets.

These capital outflows can have the effect of increasing aggregate demand overseas or of displacing exports from the home country. By the same token, however, investment outflows may also provide for returns from abroad in the form of dividends, profits, or increased equity.

OFFICIAL RESERVES ACCOUNT

The *official reserves account* exists for government use only, to account for the position of one government against others; that is, this account reflects the actual holdings of a country and what might be the equivalent of cash or near-cash assets for a corporate entity. This account reflects holdings of gold and foreign exchange. It also takes into account loans between governments and decreases and increases in liabilities to foreign central banks and the country's balance in special drawing rights with the International Monetary Fund.

NET STATISTICAL DISCREPANCY

In theory, the BOP should balance perfectly within the account of one single country and among all countries of the world as trade flows progress in an orderly fashion and as all nations of the world report those flows consistently and accurately. In actuality, this scenario is far from the truth, because of differences in accounting practices, mistakes, and unsanctioned transfers of funds between countries through *smuggling*, underground economic activity, and the sale of illegal items. Thus, the BOP includes a separate account that adjusts for these discrepancies, which can be sizable amounts. In 2003, for example, the *net statistical discrepancy* for the U.S. BOP reached $12 billion.[1]

PROBLEMS IN BOP

BOP problems occur when a country's external assets or liabilities increase beyond proportion, that is, when the BOP shows either a surplus or a deficit of external resources. Although surpluses and deficits in the BOP are normal features, they pose a problem when they are excessive and persistent to a point where they cannot be sustained. While surpluses also pose certain problems for a country, deficits present the real difficulties. Deficits generally occur when a country is not able to match the outflows of foreign exchange because of imports, debt service, or other payments with its export or other inflows. If the deficit remains persistent, a country is faced with several options. The country can

- borrow from other governments and multilateral institutions (for example, the IMF) to fill the gap between the inflows and outflows.
- draw down its level of foreign exchange reserves to meet the shortfall.
- devalue its currency in order to make exports attractive and imports unattractive, so that the gap between inflows and outflows is corrected.
- make fundamental adjustments in its economy to reduce the outflows and increase the inflows of foreign exchange, which could include reducing the level of nonessential imports, controlling local inflation, improving domestic

productivity and efficiency, and improving the allocative efficiency of the economy.

The issue of BOP problems has attracted considerable attention, especially after 1973, when the LDCs of the world faced huge increases in their oil bills, which increased their expenditures of foreign exchange and, by creating a recession in Western countries, reduced their foreign exchange earnings. BOP difficulties lead to problems in the domestic sector. When external creditors find that a country is not able to service its borrowings, they are reluctant to lend it additional money or tend to charge higher rates of interest for a perceived higher risk. The country facing the crisis loses access to external credit with which to finance essential imports for meeting developmental and consumer needs. Moreover, it is not easy to make fundamental economic adjustments. Many developing countries have large sections of the population at or below the poverty level, and any economic adjustment measures calling for reduction in government subsidies or assistance for these sections of the population are not likely to be politically acceptable. Moreover, there are entrenched vested interests in different sectors of the economy that are eager to maintain the status quo and even resort to disruptive activities to prevent their privileges from being disturbed.

The intention of the adjustment measures, however, has a reasonably sound theoretical basis. Devaluing the currency to bring it closer to its actual market value boosts exports and discourages imports by making them more expensive. Controlling inflation also increases export competitiveness, as does the increase in productivity and efficiency of the domestic industries. Reducing the demand for imports automatically reduces the outflows of foreign exchange.

Although the BOP problems can be resolved through these actions, there is considerable cost involved. Devaluation can lead to an increase in domestic inflation because import prices will be higher. Moreover, the advantage of devaluation is lost if the export sector of a country is using a large proportion of imported inputs. The terms of trade of a country also worsen with devaluation, as it is forced to part with a greater quantity of exports for the same quantity of imports. Reduction in import demand leads to economic slowdowns, which exacerbate existing problems of stagnant growth and high unemployment.

The policy makers of a country therefore have to tread very carefully and balance these diverse and often conflicting considerations while attempting to correct imbalances in the position of their external payments. Creditors, trading partners, and multilateral institutions play a vital role in determining the success of the efforts of a country to resolve BOP problems. If they follow supportive policies, a country can overcome its fundamental constraints and recover its external balance. Its problems can be exacerbated, however, if the creditors and trading partners follow a beggar-thy-neighbor policy, for example, by indulging in competitive devaluation or manipulating interest rates to attract foreign capital that might be needed by other countries in difficulty.

U.S. Trade Deficits

The historical position of the United States in world trade illustrates these problems. Some form of BOP statistics have been maintained by the U.S. government since 1790, when America had a deficit of $1 million in goods and services.[2] In the twentieth century, the United States had a positive balance in goods and services for more than six decades. During that period, some of the largest surpluses were during the war years of 1943 and 1944, when surpluses were $11.038 billion and $12.452 billion, respectively, reflecting U.S. exports directed toward the war effort. In 1947 the balance in goods and services also reflected U.S. efforts toward war-torn countries, and the surplus was $11.617 billion.[3]

In the late 1960s the U.S. BOP began to come under pressure and in the 1970s the current account began to show substantial deficits. A number of factors contributed to the trend reversal, including the huge increase in U.S. imports, the emergence of strong competition in world export markets from Europe and Japan, and the quadrupling of the price of oil.

In the 1980s the situation continued to worsen. Imports rose from $333 billion in 1980 to nearly $500 billion in 1986. On the other hand, exports remained relatively stagnant, growing only marginally, from $342 billion to $372 billion, over this period. The large gap between inflows and outflows because of exports and imports was financed primarily by private capital transfers into the United States. The effect of the private capital flows into the United States nullified the effect of the huge trade deficit on the U.S. currency, which continued to appreciate between 1980 and 1985.

The strength of the dollar, however, further weakened U.S. competitiveness in international markets and enabled Europe, Japan, and some of the Pacific Rim countries to build substantial market shares not only in overseas markets, but also in the U.S. domestic market. In fact, the years of an overvalued dollar had tended to make the deficit structural, or built-in, in character, which occurred because overseas manufacturers, taking advantage of the high dollar, were able to underprice their products and capture U.S. domestic market shares in such areas as consumer electronics and automobiles. Having achieved market penetration, overseas exporters used the long period of dollar overvaluation to consolidate and secure their gains by building dealer networks, after-sales service arrangements, and consumer brand loyalty. Thus, even though the dollar depreciated substantially after 1985, there was no significant drop in either the market shares covered by the overseas exporters or the overall volume of imports.

The widening of the current account deficit only worsened during the 1990s. The increased competition from China and Southeast Asia led to the movement of many manufacturing jobs from the United States to the Asian continent; and this led to the further decrease in the amount of manufacturing output in the United States during the 1990s and until the present. The United States has continued to maintain a surplus in the trade of invisibles (or services) with the rest of the world. The U.S. dollar has begun to depreciate heavily against the euro and the yen over the last few years, which has tended to make U.S. exports be priced more favorably abroad, and the imports to the United States be priced less favorably. It remains to be seen just how long the dollar will drop, and what effect this will have on the BOP of the United States in the coming years.

Given the size of the economy, however, the trade deficits do not create a calamity. While there is cause for concern and reason for remedial action, there is no reason for panic, both because of the size of the deficit and because of its nature.

Some analysts, such as economist Robert B. Reich, believe that attention should be focused on the reasons behind these deficits. For example, the United States currently runs a deficit with the four tigers: Hong Kong, South Korea, Singapore, and Taiwan. Some Americans worry about this situation, but Reich asks the questions, Exactly what are U.S. interests in world trade, and Who are "we"? He notes that while Americans are exporting less, they may not be selling fewer goods in world markets, because "these days about half of the total exports of American multinational corporations come from their factories in other countries," compared to a one-third equivalent 20 years ago.[4] Thus, he maintains that nearly a third of our imbalance with the Pacific Rim countries, for example, results from the multinationalization of industry and U.S. subsidiaries making prod-

ucts there and selling them back to Americans on domestic soil. He also notes that some U.S. companies are key export players in other market arenas. Many large U.S. companies, for example, have moved overseas in the past few years to capitalize on the low wage rates in countries such as India and China.

DISCUSSION QUESTIONS

1. What is the BOP?
2. What are the four basic accounts under the BOP?
3. Name a source for the U.S. BOP. What source(s) exist for international BOP?
4. Examine the U.S. BOP (Table 4.1A). What do you observe about the current account over time? Are U.S. exports greater or less than U.S. imports? Do services improve the merchandise import and export balance?

NOTES

1. U.S. Department of Commerce, 2003.
2. U.S. Department of Commerce, *Historical Statistics of the United States.*
3. Ibid.
4. Reich, "The Trade Gap."

BIBLIOGRAPHY

Asheghian, Parvis. "The Impact of Devaluation on the Balance of Payments of Less Developed Countries: A Monetary Approach." *Journal of Economic Development*, July 1985, 143–51.

Business Council for International Understanding. Descriptive brochure. Washington, DC, 2003.

Crook, Olive. "One Armed Policy Maker." *Economist*, September 1988, 51–57.

Gladwell, Malcolm. "Scientist Warns of U.S. Reliance on Foreigners." *Washington Post*, September 9, 1988, E1.

Gray, H.P., and G.E. Makinen. "Balance of Payments Contributions of Multinational Corporations." *Journal of Business*, July 1967, 339–43.

International Monetary Fund. *Balance of Payments Statistics Yearbook, 2003, 2004*. Washington, DC: International Monetary Fund (annual).

McGraw, Thomas K. *America Versus Japan*. Boston: Harvard Business School Press, 1986.

Nakamai, Tadashi. "Growth Matters More than Surpluses." *Euromoney*, February 1984, 101–3.

Obstfeld, Maurice. "Balance of Payments Crises and Devaluation." *Journal of Money, Banking and Credit*, May 1984, 208–17.

Reich, Robert B. "The Trade Gap: Myths and Crocodile Tears." *New York Times*, February 2, 1988, 34.

Solop, J., and E. Spitaller. "Why Does the Current Account Matter?" *International Monetary Fund Staff Papers*, March 1980, 101–34.

Striner, Herbert E. *Regaining the Lead: Polities for Economic Growth*. New York: Praeger, 1984.

U.S. Department of Commerce. *Historical Statistics of the United States: Colonial Times to 1970*, 1976.

World Bank. *The World Development Report, 2003*. Available at http://econ.worldbank.org (Access date is April 5, 2006).

Yoder, Stephen Kreider. "All Eyes Are on MITI Research Wish List." *Wall Street Journal*, April 29, 1988, 1, 24.

CASE STUDY 4.1
STRUCTURAL ADJUSTMENTS IN MASAWA

Masawa is a small country located in southwestern Africa, with an area of approximately 240,000 square miles and a population of approximately 60 million. The northern and western parts of the country are hilly terrain, while the southern and eastern areas are plains. Masawa has substantial natural resources: mineral deposits of manganese, copper, and tin in the northern hill areas and large tropical forests in the southeastern parts of the country. The eastern part has most of the cultivated land, and agricultural production, especially cereal crops, is concentrated there. There are some cocoa plantations in the western part of the country, and cocoa is an important commercial crop. The main exports of Masawa are copper, tin, and cocoa. Manganese deposits are too small to be commercially viable for export.

The country attained its independence from colonial rule in 1961 and since then has seen four political upheavals. Emorgue Watiza, a leader of the country's freedom movement, was the first president. He ruled Masawa for six years before being ousted by the military, which installed General Ramaza, who was assassinated in 1974 and replaced by another military ruler, Colonel Waniki. Colonel Waniki instituted a series of political reforms, and after 21 years of power, handed over the reins of government to Dr. Sabankwa, the winner of the country's first democratic election. Dr. Sabankwa brought excellent credentials to the presidency. He held a PhD in political science and government from the University of Paris and had been active in the movement for restoration of democracy in Masawa. He belonged to the Waldesi tribe, which comprised

30 percent of the population, and enjoyed almost total loyalty of his tribespeople. Waldesi, the largest single tribe in the ethnic composition of Masawa, includes 3 other major and 16 minor tribes. The 3 other major tribes are the Mokoti (18 percent), Lemata (15 percent), and Simoki (11 percent). The remaining 27 percent of the population is made up of members of the smaller tribes, none of which individually constitute more than 5 percent of the population.

Dr. Sabankwa enjoyed considerable support from the Simoki and several minor tribes at the time of his election. After eight years in office, however, that support has eroded, and rumblings of discontent have been heard, even from Sabankwa's own Waldesi tribespeople, especially those living in urban areas. Much of the discontent is clearly the result of the economic difficulties the country is facing, which in turn have led to considerable difficulties for both the urban and rural populations. Reactions, however, tend to be more pronounced in the densely populated and politically conscious urban areas.

Most of Masawa's economic difficulties began before the election of Dr. Sabankwa. The country had little in the way of industrial or technological development when it attained independence, and the annual per capita GNP was $160. Much of the agriculture was conducted along primitive lines and was largely dependent on seasonal rainfall, which tended to be fairly erratic. In the initial years of independence, Masawa's rulers sought to adopt a centralized planning approach to economic development, which assigned a key

continued

Case 4.1 (*continued*)

role to the government in nearly all aspects of economic activity. The public sector accounts for 90 percent of industrial production, and all key infrastructure projects are run by government agencies. Masawa has a large number of highly paid civil servants who administer the wide range of economic and other controls imposed by the government. Although private enterprise is officially permitted, there are a number of bureaucratic disincentives for entrepreneurship. A typical new venture in the private sector needs separate approvals from 32 different government agencies and departments.

As in many other countries of the developing world, the state-owned industrial enterprises of Masawa have had losses for a variety of reasons, including inefficient management, overstaffing, administered prices of products, and outmoded technology. The government has guaranteed most of the debt taken on by the enterprises and has had to resort to substantial deficit financing to make good on these obligations.

The government of Masawa has faced a major budget deficit every year for the past 11 years, and, for several reasons, the deficit has become a permanent feature of the government's finances. Government expenditures have been rising rapidly in five areas: defense, oil imports, administrative expenses of the government, subsidies to industrial enterprises, and price subsidies for essential consumption items, especially food. On the other hand, revenues have been stagnant, principally because of the absence of strong measures to secure better tax compliance by the vast majority of taxpayers. The government has, therefore, resorted to large-scale deficit financing, which has pushed the inflation rate progressively

higher every year. In 2005, Masawa experienced 93 percent inflation, and there were indications that this number would increase by another 40 percent in 2006.

Imports have been increasing steadily over the past seven years, while exports are stagnant, because the world market for Masawa's principal exports continues to be sluggish. The exchange rate of Masawa is overvalued by about 70 percent, and there is a large premium on the black market for foreign currencies. The country has suffered considerable flight of capital as wealthy industrialists lost faith in the political and economic stability of Masawa.

The external debt of Masawa, largely to official creditors, is well above the level considered dangerous for sustaining the debt-service schedule. The country has no access to the international capital market, having defaulted on the amortization of earlier loans, taken primarily by state-owned corporations. Foreign exchange reserves are at a dangerously low level and are sufficient to finance only two weeks of imports.

Dr. Sabankwa called a meeting of his cabinet to discuss the issue of accepting an International Monetary Fund structural adjustment loan, in order to tide the country over the immediate problems on the balance of payments front and to improve future prospects. Before a full meeting of the cabinet, the finance minister briefed Dr. Sabankwa on the pertinent issues, and, after a long, late-night conversation with the finance minister, Dr. Sabankwa realized that he had a difficult situation to resolve.

The IMF is willing to extend a $3 billion loan to Masawa under its structural adjustment lending program, but it wants Masawa to draw up a
continued

Case 4.1 (*continued*)

set of concrete economic measures to restructure the economy. Although several measures have been recommended by the IMF, five are the most important:

1. The level of imports should be reduced.
2. Masawa should devalue the exchange rate by 40 percent.
3. The government should initiate a phased reduction of official subsidies on food.
4. The government should take steps toward privatizing state-owned enterprises.
5. Administrative expenses of the government should be reduced by cutting the government staff and salaries.

While these measures seem sensible and useful, effective implementation of them would create many practical difficulties. First, cutting food subsidies would be an extremely unpopular measure and might spark civil disturbances, especially in the urban areas. Moreover, those most affected would be the urban poor, who are already under great economic hardship. Devaluing the exchange rate also has ominous implications. Politically, it might be viewed as a weakening of the economy and provide another reason for opposition groups to attack the government's handling of the economic situation. Further, the costs of imports would rise and contribute to an increase in the already high inflation rate. Privatization would also be difficult, since there are few people in Masawa with the managerial or technical expertise to take over the operations of these enterprises. Further, there was bound to be strong opposition from the trade unions to any move for privatization.

Reducing the level of imports would be a feasible option, but it would hurt the growth rate considerably, because imports of essential industrial equipment and machinery would have to be curtailed. Further, a very large cut in imports might not even be possible because of the inelastic level of defense and oil imports.

As he mulled over these issues, Dr. Sabankwa wondered whether a compromise solution could be found: Would these steps, if implemented, not generate political unrest that would lead to the fall of his government?

DISCUSSION QUESTIONS

1. What would be your position if you were a member of Dr. Sabankwa's cabinet?
2. Should Masawa accept the plan as it exists or should it insist on some modification? If modification is needed, what changes should be made? What arguments should be made to convince IMF officials to agree to these modifications in the structural adjustment plan?

Chapter 5

Foreign Exchange Markets

CHAPTER OBJECTIVES

This chapter will:

- Suggest the underlying need for foreign exchange markets.
- Introduce the terms and definitions used in the foreign exchange markets.
- Describe the structure and operations of the foreign exchange markets.
- Present the mathematical formulas used to compare currency movements in the foreign exchange markets.
- Discuss common techniques used to manage currency risk and exposure.
- Explain the need for and problems associated with forecasting foreign exchange rates.

BACKGROUND

Nearly all international business activity requires the transfer of money from one country to another. Trade transactions must be settled in monetary terms: Buyers in one country pay suppliers in another. Repatriation of dividends, profits, and royalties from overseas investments, contributions of equity, and other kinds of financial dealings from such investments also involve the transfer of funds across national borders. The transfer of funds poses problems quite different from those associated with the transfer of goods and services across national borders. Buyers and sellers are willing to accept and use goods and services from other countries quite routinely. For example, U.S. consumers are content to drive Japanese cars, such as Toyotas and Hondas, while the Japanese are quite willing to use U.S. operating systems or other hi-tech products.

This internationalization that applies to product usage is not found when it comes to accepting the currency of another country, however. While the U.S. importer is happy to receive Japanese products and the Japanese importer is glad to accept U.S. products, neither is normally in a position to accept the other's currency. A U.S. importer usually has to pay a Japanese exporter in Japanese yen, while a U.S. exporter will generally want to be paid in U.S. dollars. This is quite logical, since each country has its own currency, which is legal tender within its borders, and exporters are likely to prefer the currency that they can use at home for meeting costs and taking profits.

A U.S. importer who must pay a Japanese exporter has to acquire Japanese yen. To do so, he must exchange his own currency, dollars, into yen. Such an exchange of one currency for another is called a *foreign exchange* transaction.

For example, a German company invests in an electronics manufacturing facility in Australia. Therefore, it must convert its euros into Australian dollars to meet project costs in Australia. In another example, a U.S. multinational has a plant located in Great Britain. At the end of the financial year, it wants to repatriate its profits to corporate headquarters in the United States. Therefore, it will convert British pounds sterling—profits earned by the plant in Great Britain—into U.S. dollars. As another example, suppose a Japanese investor has a large stock holding on Wall Street. After a rally in which his holdings appreciate substantially, he wants to repatriate his profits to Japan. To do so, he would convert his U.S. dollar profits into Japanese yen.

How do the German company, the U.S. multinational, and the Japanese investor convert the currency in their possession into the currency they desire? The answer is provided by the foreign exchange markets.

THE STRUCTURE OF THE FOREIGN EXCHANGE MARKETS

The demand for conversion of one currency into another gives rise to the demand for foreign exchange transactions. The foreign exchange markets of the world serve as the mechanism through which these numerous and complex transactions are completed efficiently and almost instantaneously.

The main intermediaries in the foreign exchange markets are major banks worldwide that deal in foreign exchange. These banks are linked together by a very advanced and sophisticated telecommu-

nications network that connects them with major clients and other banks around the world. There is no physical contact between the dealers of various banks in the foreign exchange markets, unlike in the stock exchanges or the futures markets, which have specific trading floors or pits.

Some of the larger and more active banks have installed computer terminals called dealing screens in their trading rooms. Through these terminals, banks can execute trades and receive written confirmations on online printers. Telephone transactions are normally confirmed by an exchange of telex messages or transaction notes.

Banks that are active in foreign exchange operations set up extremely sophisticated facilities for their foreign exchange traders; these facilities are located in trading (or dealing) rooms, which are equipped with instantaneous telecommunication facilities.

A very important feature of modern trading rooms is their access to information about political, economic, and other current events as they unfold. A major source of this information is the British news agency Reuters, which furnishes subscribing banks with a dedicated communication system that provides on-screen information beamed from the central newsroom of the agency. There are also many services, including Reuters and Telerate, that provide up-to-the-second information on the prevailing exchange rates quoted by banks worldwide. Any changes in exchange rates anywhere in the world can be immediately brought to the notice of traders.

Exchange trading is an extremely specialized operation that puts enormous pressure on traders because rates change rapidly and there are chances to make huge profits or incur massive losses. Bank management continually monitors the activity and progress of its dealing rooms, while setting very clear guidelines in order to limit the level of risk the traders can take while trading currencies on behalf of the bank.

To relieve traders from the task of booking orders, trading rooms are supported by backup accounting departments that record the transactions made by the traders and that do the necessary computations to track the trading activity. They also supply the traders with background data and analytical reports to optimize the traders' strategy and performance. Such information is fed into electronic trading boards that are clearly visible to traders. Generally, this information includes the risk exposure of the bank in each currency and the current rates for different currencies, as well as a host of other information.

Exchange trading at a bank usually begins every day in the early morning with an in-house conference of traders and senior managers to discuss the currency expectations and the strategy for the day. Most trading is conducted during local business hours, but the ease of communication made possible by the latest technology enables banks to continue to trade with banks in other time zones after the local business day is over. Therefore, some major banks have a system of shifts, through which traders come in to trade in markets in different time zones. By using night trading desks, many major banks have been able to establish 24-hour trading operations.

There are two levels in the foreign exchange markets. One is the customer, or retail, market, in which individuals or institutions buy and sell foreign currencies to banks dealing in foreign exchange. For example, if IBM wishes to repatriate profits from its German subsidiary to the United States, it can approach a bank in Frankfurt with an offer to sell its euros in exchange for U.S. dollars. This type of transaction occurs in what is called the customer market.

Suppose the bank does not have a sufficient amount of U.S. dollars to exchange for the subsidiary's euros. In this situation the bank can approach other banks to acquire dollars in exchange for euros or some other currency. Such sales and purchases are termed interbank transactions and collectively constitute the interbank market. Interbank transactions are both local and international.

The interbank market is extremely active. Banks purchase currencies from and sell currencies to one another to meet shortages and reduce surpluses that result from transactions with their customers. Transactions in the interbank markets are almost always in large sums. Amounts less than US$250,000 are not traded in interbank markets. Values of interbank transactions usually range from US$1 million to US$10 million per transaction, although deals involving amounts above this range are also known to take place. A large proportion of the transactions in interbank markets arise from banks trading currencies to make profits from movements in exchange rates around the world.

It is important to note that in all this trading activity in foreign exchange markets, billions of dollars of international currency are exchanged without any physical transfer of money. How are the transactions settled? The answer lies in a system of mutual account maintenance. Banks in one country maintain accounts at banks in other countries. These accounts are generally denominated in the home currency of the bank with the account. In banking parlance these are called vostro accounts, which essentially means "your account with us," or nostro accounts, which means, literally, "our account with you." Thus, if Citigroup New York has a euro account with Dresdner Bank in Frankfurt, it will term the Dresdner account its nostro account. For Dresdner, this will be a vostro account. Similarly, Dresdner Bank would have a U.S. dollar account with Citibank or another bank in the United States. For Dresdner this will be a nostro account, while for the U.S. bank it will be a vostro account. Foreign exchange transactions are settled by debits or credits to nostro and vostro accounts.

MARKET PARTICIPANTS

The foreign exchange markets have many different types of participants. These participants differ not only in the scale of their operations but also in their objectives and methods of functioning.

Individuals

Individuals may participate in foreign exchange markets for personal as well as business needs. An example of a personal need would be sending a monetary gift to an overseas relative. To send the gift, the individual would utilize the market to obtain the currency of the relative's country. Individual business needs arise when a person is involved in international business. For example, individual importers use the foreign exchange markets to obtain the currencies needed to pay their overseas suppliers. Exporters, on the other hand, use the markets to convert the currencies received from their foreign buyers into domestic or other currencies. Business or leisure travelers also participate in the foreign exchange markets by buying and selling foreign and local currencies to meet expenses on their overseas trips.

Institutions

Institutions are very important participants in the foreign exchange markets because of their large and varied currency requirements. Multinational corporations typically are major participants in the foreign markets, continually transferring large sums of currencies across national borders, a process that usually requires the exchange of one currency for another. Financial institutions that have international investments are also important foreign exchange market participants. These institutions include pension funds, insurance companies, mutual funds, and investment banks. They need to switch their multicurrency investments quite often, generating substantial transaction volumes in the foreign exchange markets.

Apart from meeting their basic transaction needs, both the individual and institutional participants use the foreign exchange markets to reduce the risks they incur because of adverse fluctuations in exchange rates.

Banks

Banks are the largest and most active participants in the foreign exchange markets. Banks operate in the foreign exchange markets through their traders. (British banks and many others use the term "exchange dealer" rather than "exchange trader." These terms can be used interchangeably.) Exchange traders at banks buy and sell currencies, acting on the requests of their customers and on behalf of the bank itself.

Customer-requested transactions form a very small proportion of trading operations by banks in the foreign exchange markets. To a very large extent, banks treat foreign exchange market operations as an independent profit center. In fact, some major banks make substantial profits on the strength of their market expertise, information, trading skills, and ability to hold on to risky investments that would not be feasible for smaller participants. On occasion, banks can also incur substantial losses. As a result, foreign exchange operations are closely monitored by bank management teams.

Central Banks and Other Official Participants

Central banks enter the foreign exchange markets for a variety of reasons. They can buy substantial amounts of foreign currencies to either build up their foreign exchange reserves or bring down the value of their own currency, which in their opinion may be overvalued by the markets. They can enter the markets to sell large amounts of foreign currencies to shore up their own currencies. In the latter part of the 1980s, central banks and treasurers of the United States, Japan, and the then West Germany intervened quite often to correct the imbalances between the values of the yen and deutsche mark (then the currency of West Germany; the unified Germany now uses the euro) versus the U.S. dollar.

The main objective of central banks is not to profit from their foreign exchange operations or to avoid risks. It is to move their own and other important currencies in line with the values they consider appropriate for the best economic interest of their country.

Central banks of countries that have an official exchange rate for their currency must continually participate in the foreign exchange markets to ensure that their currency is available at the announced rate.

Speculators and Arbitragers

Participation by speculators and arbitragers in the foreign exchange markets is driven by pure profit motive. These traders seek to profit from the wide fluctuations that occur in foreign exchange markets.

In other words, they do not have any underlying commercial or business transactions that they seek to cover in the foreign exchange market. Typically, speculators buy large amounts of a currency when they believe it is undervalued and sell it when the price rises. *Arbitrage* occurs when investors try to exploit the differences in exchange rates between different markets. If the exchange rate for the pound is cheaper in London than in New York, they would buy pounds in London and sell them in New York, making a profit. Arbitrage opportunities are now increasingly rare, however, because instantaneous communications tend to equalize worldwide rates simultaneously.

A substantial part of the speculative and arbitrage transactions comes from exchange traders of commercial banks. Often these transactions represent a conscious effort to maximize profits with clearly defined profit objectives, loss limits, and risk-taking boundaries. In fact, the overwhelming proportion of foreign exchange market transactions today are driven by speculation.

Foreign Exchange Brokers

Foreign exchange brokers are intermediaries who bring together parties with opposite and matching requirements in the foreign exchange markets. They are in simultaneous contact through hotlines with scores of banks, and they attempt to match the buying requirements of some banks with the selling needs of others. They do not deal on their own account and are not a party to the actual transactions. For their services they charge an agreed-on fee, which is often called brokerage.

By bringing together various market participants with complementary needs, foreign exchange brokers contribute significantly to the "perfection of information," which makes the foreign exchange markets as efficient as they are. Apart from this, brokers also perform another important function. They preserve the confidentiality and anonymity of the participants. In a typical deal, the broker will not reveal the identity of the other party until the deal is sealed. This achieves a more uniform conduct of business as deals are decided purely on market considerations and are not influenced by other considerations that might be introduced if the parties' identities became known.

LOCATION OF FOREIGN EXCHANGE MARKETS

The foreign exchange markets are truly global, working around the clock and throughout the world. The very nature of foreign exchange trading, as well as the revolution in telecommunications, has resulted in a unified market in which distances and even time zones have been compressed. Traditionally, London and, later, New York were the main centers of foreign trading. Other centers, however, such as Tokyo, Hong Kong, Singapore, and Frankfurt, have become extremely active. Smaller but significant markets exist in many European and some Asian countries.

The individual foreign exchange trading centers are closely linked to form one global market. Trading spills over from one market to another and from one time zone to another. Price levels in one trading center immediately affect those in other centers. As the market closes in one time zone, others open in different time zones, taking cues from the activities of the earlier market in setting up trading and price trends. A continuous pattern is thus established, giving the impression of one unified market across the world.

JAPAN

Because of its geographical position, Japan can be considered the market where the world's trading day begins. The Japanese markets, led by Tokyo, are extremely active, with a very high daily turnover. Most of the deals are backed by customer-related requests to finance or settle international commercial transactions. Dollar-yen deals predominate in the market, because of the large share of U.S.-related business in the international transactions of Japan.

Since the deregulation of Japanese foreign exchanges, the element of speculative activity has increased considerably, especially in the Tokyo market. The volume of trading in the market has also increased as the securities and equity markets of Japan have opened up to foreign investment and some foreign investment banks have been allowed to operate in Japan. Brokers are extensively used in the Japanese markets, especially in transactions between banks located within the country. The market, however, closes at a set time in the afternoon, thus putting a limit on the volume of transactions that can take place. This system has inhibited somewhat the development of the Tokyo market, which would otherwise be significantly larger.

SINGAPORE AND HONG KONG

Singapore and Hong Kong are the next markets to open, about one hour after Tokyo. These markets are much less regulated, and in pursuit of their aim to become major international financial centers, both markets offer liberal access to overseas banks and commercial establishments. At the same time, the governmental authorities have attempted to create a friendly market environment to promote maximum trading activity. Market activity has increased considerably because several overseas banks, attracted by the incentives offered, have opened branches in both centers. Brokers are heavily involved in local transactions in Singapore, while international transactions are handled primarily through direct deals between banks. The trading activity of Hong Kong is a mix of direct deals and broker-intermediated transactions. Both of these markets have grown tremendously in the past few years.

BAHRAIN

The Bahrain market in the Middle East emerged as an important center of foreign exchange trading in the 1970s, as oil-linked commercial transactions grew considerably. Located in the middle of overlapping time zones, Bahrain is often used by traders in other markets to serve as a link in their global cycle. Bahrain provides a bridge between the closing of the Far Eastern and opening of the European markets because it is open during the time when the markets in those locations are closed.

EUROPEAN MARKETS

Europe, taken as a whole, is the largest foreign exchange market. Its main centers are London, Frankfurt, and Zurich. European banks have no set closing time for foreign exchange trading and are free to trade 24 hours a day, but they generally cease trading in the afternoon. Both direct and brokered deals are common in European trading. In the past, some of Europe's markets, such as that in Paris, have exhibited a unique feature: rate fixing. Once a day, representatives of the larger banks and the central banks met to fix the exchange rate of the U.S. dollar against local currencies and hence against one another. The fixed rate represented the balance of offers and bids and was close to what the rate would be internationally. There was sometimes a small discrepancy, however, which offered an opportunity for arbitrage. This opportunity, of course, existed for only a very short time, as market pressures quickly equalized the prices. The fixed rate was important primarily because it was considered to be the legal official rate and was often specified in contracts. This practice is less important in the European markets now, given that many of the countries are using the same currency (the euro).

U.S. MARKETS

The New York market opens next. It is one of the world's largest markets, and the top foreign exchange trading firms are headquartered there. The volume of business in New York has increased tremendously since deregulation of the banking system and the increasing presence of overseas banks. Both brokered as well as direct dealing are common in the New York exchange market. The West Coast markets are essentially tied to New York and closely follow the trading patterns that are established there.

MARKET VOLUMES

Foreign exchange markets are clearly located in the largest financial markets in the world. Their turnover exceeds several times that of securities, futures, options, and commodities markets. The actual turnover figures, however, are difficult to ascertain, because banks do not publish data on the volume of their transactions.

In 1979 one study estimated the daily turnover of the world foreign exchange market to be about US$200 billion.[1] A 1986 survey by the Federal Reserve Bank of New York put the daily turnover of U.S. banks at US$50 billion.[2] Today, the estimated turnover is as much as US$1.5 trillion per day on a global level. The currencies that predominate in foreign exchange trading activity on a worldwide basis are the U.S. dollar, the euro, the yen, the Swiss franc, the pound, the Canadian dollar, and the Australian dollar. Some other currencies of increasing importance in foreign exchange markets are the Swedish krona, the Indian rupee, and the Chinese yuan.

A daily turnover of US$1.5 trillion would amount to an annual figure of US$547.5 trillion. The enormity of this figure, which estimates the annual volume of global foreign exchange trading, can be appreciated if one compares it with the U.S. GNP, which was US$11.71 trillion in 2004.

USES OF THE FOREIGN EXCHANGE MARKET

The foreign exchange market provides the means by which different categories of individuals and institutions acquire foreign exchange to meet different needs, but it is important to understand the economic functions performed by the foreign exchange markets and their role in international trade in goods and services. Two basic functions are the avoidance of risk and the financing of international trade.

International trade transactions, which must be settled monetarily, carry significant risks both to the buyer and to the seller. If the transaction is invoiced in the currency of the seller, the seller stands to lose if the currency depreciates in the time lag between agreement on the price and the actual date of payment. Consider, for example, a British importer of U.S. computers. The importer agrees to buy the shipment of computers for US$150,000, and the current exchange rate is US$1.5 to £1. At this rate, the cost to the British importer is £100,000. Usually, in such instances payments are made after goods are shipped or received. In this example assume a lag of three months between the signing of the contract and the actual payment by the British importer.

Suppose that in this period the value of the U.S. dollar appreciates and US$1 becomes equal to £1. In this event, the British importer will have to part with £150,000 to purchase the US$150,000 needed to meet the contractual obligation. As a result, the importer stands to incur a substantial loss: £50,000. Although this is an exaggerated example, the risks are indeed real and can often wipe out the entire profit from a transaction.

Foreign exchange markets provide mechanisms to reduce this risk and assure a certain minimum return. Foreign exchange markets also provide the financing mechanism for international trade transactions. Financing is required to cover the costs of goods that are in transit. These costs are considerable if goods are sent by sea. At the same time, the risks are also high because the parties are in different countries, and, in the event of default, the recourse for the party defaulted against is limited. These problems are solved efficiently through the foreign exchange markets, specifically through the use of internationally accepted documentation procedures, the most important being letters of credit (which are discussed in chapter 12).

TYPES OF EXPOSURE IN FOREIGN EXCHANGE MARKETS

There are four major types of risks or exposure that a corporation faces in the course of its international business activity: transaction exposure, economic exposure, translation exposure, and tax exposure.

TRANSACTION EXPOSURE

Transaction exposure is the risk that a company's future cash flows will be disturbed by fluctuations in exchange rates. A company that is expecting inflows of foreign currency will be faced with transaction exposure to the extent that the value of these inflows can be affected by a change in the rate of the company's currency against the preferred currency for conversion. Exchange rates are extremely vola-

tile, and a sharp movement can adversely affect the real value of cash flows in the desired currency. A corporation can have both inflows and outflows in a currency. Moreover, it can have different amounts of inflows and outflows in different currencies. In this situation, the company nets out its exposure in each currency by matching a portion of its currency inflows and outflows. The net exposure in each currency is aggregated for all currencies to arrive at a measurement of the total transaction exposure for the company. The period over which the cash flows are considered for arriving at the figure for transaction exposure depends on the individual methods and views of the company. Organizations use a variety of methods to assess the degree to which their net exposed cash flows are at risk. These methods can center on the time lag between the initiation and completion of the transaction, the use of currency correlations, or statistical projections of exchange-rate volatility. Sophisticated strategies for assessing transaction exposure often include some element of all of these considerations.

ECONOMIC EXPOSURE

Economic exposure is a relatively broader conception of foreign exchange exposure. The prime feature of economic exposure is that it is essentially a long-term, multitransaction-oriented way of looking at the foreign exchange exposure of a firm involved in international business. The standard definition of economic exposure is the degree to which fluctuations in exchange rates will affect the net present value of the future cash flows of a company.

Economic exposure is a particularly serious problem for multinational corporations with operations in several different countries. Since currency fluctuations do not follow any set pattern, each operation is subject to a different degree and nature of economic exposure. Measuring the degree of economic exposure is even more difficult than measuring translation exposure. Economic exposure involves operational variables, such as costs, prices, sales, and profits, and each of these is also subject to fluctuation in value, independent of the exchange-rate movements. Many techniques are used to measure economic exposure. Most of these techniques rely on complex mathematical and statistical models that attempt to capture all the variables. Use of regression analysis and simulation of cash-flow positions under different exchange-rate scenarios are two examples of such techniques.

Managing economic exposure can involve extremely complex strategies and instruments, some of which are outside the foreign exchange market.

Translation Exposure

Translation exposure is the degree to which the consolidated financial statements and balance sheets of a company can be affected by exchange-rate fluctuations. It is also known as *accounting exposure*.

Translation exposure arises when the accounts of a subsidiary are consolidated at the head office at an exchange rate that differs from the rate in effect at the time of the transaction.

Tax Exposure

Tax exposure is the effect that changes in the gains or losses of a company because of exchange-rate fluctuations can have on its tax liability. An unexpected or large gain based solely on exchange-rate fluctuations could upset the tax planning of a multinational by causing an increased tax liability. Gains and losses from translation exposure generally have an effect on the tax liability of a company at the time they are actually realized.

Types of Foreign Exchange Markets

There are two main types of foreign exchange transactions that are often characterized as different markets—spot transactions and forward transactions. Often dealers specialize in one of three transaction categories: cash, tom, or spot.

The Spot Market

The spot market consists of transactions in foreign exchange that are ordinarily completed on the second working day of the deal being made. Within the spot market, there can be three types of transactions:

1. *Cash*, in which the payment of one currency and delivery of the other currency are completed on the same business day
2. *Tom* (short for "tomorrow"), in which the transaction deliveries are completed on the next working day
3. *Spot exchange*, in which the transaction deliveries are completed within the same day of the deal being struck

Price Quotation in Exchange Markets

The prices of currencies in the spot market can be expressed as direct quotes or indirect quotes. When the price of one currency is expressed as a direct quote, it reflects the number of units of home currency that are required to buy the foreign currency. A *direct quote* on the New York market would be US\$1.30 = €1. An *indirect quote* is the reverse; the home currency is expressed as a unit, and the price is shown by the number of units of foreign currency that are required to purchase one unit of the home currency. For example, in the New York market an indirect quote would be US\$1= €0.77 (to purchase one unit of the home currency, the U.S. dollar, €0.77 are needed).

An important feature of foreign exchange price quotation is the number of decimals used. Since large amounts are traded, quotes are usually given at least up to the fourth decimal, especially for such major currencies as the pound and the U.S. dollar. Thus, a quote for the pound would be £1 = US$1.7643.

Long and Short Positions

A bank can be in the spot market in three positions:

1. *Long*, when it buys more than it sells of a currency
2. *Short*, when it buys less than it sells of a currency
3. *Square*, when it buys and sells the same amount of currency

Whenever a bank is long or short in a currency, it is exposed to a certain amount of risk. The risk arises in a *long position* because the value of the bank's excess currency could depreciate if that currency falls in price. Thus, the market value of the assets of a bank would be lower than the cost price. In a short position, the bank agrees to sell more currency than it has in its possession. If the price of the currency in which the bank is short rises, the bank will experience a loss. The bank will have to acquire and deliver the currency at a higher price than the agreed-on selling price. Both long and short positions can also result in profits, if the currency in question appreciates or depreciates. Since large losses are possible, banks must carefully evaluate the amount of exposure they can withstand. Specific limits are laid down for long and short positions in each currency, as well as aggregate limits for all major currencies.

There are usually two types of trading strategy followed by banks in the spot market. One strategy is to determine whether the currency is going to appreciate or depreciate and then assume a long or short position, allowing the trader to profit from the currency movement. This strategy is often called running a position, or positions trading. The other strategy is to assume and liquidate long and short positions very quickly (often within minutes), as exchange rates fluctuate during the business day. This strategy is known as in-and-out trading.

THE FORWARD MARKET

The forward market consists of transactions that require delivery of currency at an agreed-on future date. The rate at which this forward transaction will be completed is determined at the time the parties agree on a contract to buy and sell. The time between the establishment of contracts and the actual exchange of currencies can range from two weeks to more than a year. The more common maturities for *forward contracts* are one, two, three, and six months. Some forward transactions are termed outright forwards, to distinguish them from swap transactions.

Forward transactions typically occur when exporters, importers, or others involved in the foreign exchange market must either pay or receive foreign currency amounts at a future date. In such situations there is an element of risk for the receiving party if the currency it is going to receive depreciates during the intervening period.

For the purposes of a quick example of this concept, assume that the owner of a small business wished to purchase an amount of softwood lumber from a Canadian company in June 2004. At that time, the Canadian dollar was worth US$0.74. If the purchase had been made in June, the total purchase of Can$3,000 would have cost the business owner US$2,220.00 (3,000 × 0.74). If for some reason the business owner had waited until November 2004 to purchase the softwood lumber from the Canadian company, the Canadian dollar would have risen to US$0.84 by that time. Thus, the same Can$3,000 purchase would have cost the business owner US$2,520.00 (or US$300 more than the same product would have cost in June!). The owner of the small business could have eliminated all or part of this risk by purchasing a forward currency contract over this period of time.

Table 5.1

Major Currency Cross Rates as of April 7, 2006

	U.S. Dollar	Yen	Euro	Canadian Dollar	British Pound	Australian Dollar	Swiss Franc
1 U.S. Dollar	1	118.325	0.8262	1.1463	0.5746	1.3739	1.3034
1 Yen	0.008451	1	0.006982	0.009687	0.004856	0.011611	0.011015
1 Euro	1.2104	143.2206	1	1.3874	0.6955	1.6630	1.5776
1 Canadian Dollar	0.8724	103.2279	0.7208	1	0.5013	1.1986	1.1371
1 British Pound	1.7403	205.9266	1.4378	1.9949	1	2.3911	2.2684
1 Australian Dollar	0.7278	86.1228	0.6013	0.8343	0.4182	1	0.9487
1 Swiss Franc	0.7672	90.7818	0.6339	0.8794	0.4408	1.0541	1

To fix a minimum value on the foreign exchange proceeds, these recipients can lock into a rate in advance by entering into a forward contract with a bank. Under such a contract, the bank is obligated to purchase the currency from the exporter at the agreed-on rate, regardless of the rate that prevails on the day when the foreign currency is actually delivered by the exporter. Banks in turn enter into contracts with other banks to offset these customer contracts, which gives rise to interbank transactions in the forward market.

The date on which the currencies are to be delivered under a forward contract is fixed in advance and is usually specific. In some customer contracts, however, the banks provide an option to the customers to deliver currencies within a certain time that can range up to 10, 20, or 30 days. The costs of such contracts are, naturally, higher than the cost of contracts with specific maturity dates, because banks have to incur additional costs and efforts to create offsetting contracts in the interbank market. Forward contracts are popular with customers who are not certain of the dates on which they will have to pay or receive foreign currency amounts and would therefore like some leeway in executing their contractual obligations.

FOREIGN EXCHANGE RATES

A foreign exchange rate can be defined as the price of one currency expressed in units of another currency. The price of pounds expressed in terms of U.S. dollars could be 1.8391. Therefore, 1.8391 would be the foreign exchange rate of the pound. Many journals and newspapers report foreign exchange rates either daily or periodically. Table 5.1 shows the major currency *cross rates* on April 7, 2006 as shown on Yahoo Finance. Notice that you can determine both the direct and the indirect exchange rates for each of the currencies listed in the table.

Since it is often confusing to decide whether a rate is an indirect or direct quote, a uniform standard of exchange-rate quotation was adopted in 1978. Under this standard, the U.S. dollar was to be the unit currency and other currencies were expressed as variable amounts relative to the U.S. dollar. This method, where foreign currency prices are quoted as US$1, is known as stating the price in *European terms*. The prices of some currencies, such as the British pound and Australian dollar, however, are quoted in terms of variable units of U.S. dollars per unit of their currency. Such quotations are known as *American terms*.

BID AND OFFER RATES

Rates in the foreign exchange market are quoted as bid and offer rates. A bid is the rate at which the bank is willing to buy a particular currency, and an offer is the rate at which it is willing to sell that currency. Banks in the market are generally required by convention and practice to quote their bid and offer prices for particular currencies simultaneously.

When quoting their bid and offer rates for a particularly currency, banks quote a price for buying the currency that is lower than the price they charge for selling it. The difference between the buying and selling price is called the *bid-offer spread*. In a typical spot market transaction a U.S. dollar–pound sterling quote would be 1.8410–1.8420. The quote on the left-hand side would be the bid rate, at which the bank would be willing to sell US$1.8410 in exchange for a pound. The quote on the right-hand side would be the offer rate, at which the bank would be willing to buy US$1.8420 for a pound. Notice that the selling rate is higher because the bank is prepared to sell fewer dollars for a pound (US$1.8410) than it is prepared to buy. The use of both American and European terms reverses the bid-offer order. Moreover, a bid quote for one currency is an offer quote for the other currency in the transaction. To avoid confusion, a useful rule of thumb is to remember that in its quote the bank will always part with smaller amounts of the currency it is selling than it will receive when it is buying. In the example, the bank is willing to part with US$1.8410 per unit of pound sterling when selling them, but it wants to receive US$1.8420 per unit of pound sterling when it is buying.

In practice, exchange traders quote only the last two decimals of the exchange rate, especially in the interbank market. The interbank quotations of bid-offer rates feature extremely fine spreads because transactions are in huge volumes and the competition is intense.

CROSS RATES

Exchange rates are quoted prices of one currency in terms of another currency. In practice, however, prices of all currencies are not always quoted in terms of all other currencies, which is particularly true of currencies for which there is no active market. For example, rate quotations for Malaysian ringgits in terms of Swedish krona are not easily available, but both currencies are quoted against the U.S. dollar. Their rates with reference to the dollar can be compared, and a rate can be determined between these two currencies. (See Table 5.1).

PREMIUMS AND DISCOUNTS

The spot price and forward price of a currency are invariably different. When the forward price of the currency is higher than the spot price, the currency is said to be at a *premium*. The difference between the spot price and forward price in this case is called the forward premium. When the forward rate of a currency is lower than the spot rate, the currency is said to be at a *discount*. The difference between the spot and forward rate in this case is called the forward discount. Some illustrations of forward premiums and discounts are:

Spot rate for U.S. dollar/Can. dollar = Can$1.19
Forward rate for U.S. dollar/Can. dollar = Can$1.29

Notice that in the forward rate, it will require Can$1.29 to buy US$1, while in the spot rate only Can$1.19 is required. The U.S. dollar is costlier in the forward quote than in the spot quote and is therefore at a premium against the Canadian dollar. The premium on forward quotes of the U.S. dollar is Can$0.10.

Now, assume the following exchange rates between the U.S. dollar and Canadian dollar:

Spot rate: Can$1.29 = US$1
Forward rate: Can$1.09 = US$1

In this case the spot rate for the U.S. dollar is more expensive, in terms of Canadian dollars, than the forward rate. In other words, the U.S. dollar is cheaper in the forward market, because only Can$1.09 is needed to buy US$1 forward, whereas Can$1.29 is needed to buy US$1 in the spot market. Thus, the U.S. dollar is at a discount of Can$0.20 in the forward market.

It is very important to recognize the type of quotation when considering forward premiums and discounts. When the quotes are indirect, that is, when the home currency is expressed as a unit and the foreign currency as a variable, forward premiums are subtracted from the spot rate to arrive at the forward rate. Similarly, forward discounts are added to the spot rate to get the forward rate. Following are examples showing premiums and discounts.

Premium:

Spot rate: US$1 = Can$1.29
Forward premium on Can$ = Can$0.010
Forward rate for US$/Can$ = Can$1.28

Discount:

Spot rate: US$1 = Can$1.29
Forward discount on Can$ = Can$0.020
Forward rate for US$/Can$ = Can$1.31

When the exchange rates are quoted as direct rates, that is, when the foreign currency is the unit, premiums are added to the spot rate to arrive at the forward rate; discounts are subtracted.

Consider a situation in which the pound sterling is at a premium:

Spot rate: £1 = US$1.78
Forward premium on £ = 0.10
Forward rate for £1/US$ = US$1.88

Consider a situation in which pound sterling is at a discount and direct quotations are used. The forward rates will be calculated as follows:

Spot: £1 = US$1.864
Forward discount: US$0.020
Forward rate: £1 = US$1.844

Notice that the method of arriving at the forward rate is reversed when moving from direct to indirect rates. Remember, however, that the basic rule applicable to all types of quotations is that a currency at a premium will buy more units of the other currency in the forward market than in the spot market, while the reverse will be the case when the currency is at a discount. Also, it is important to note that the premium and discount calculations will be applied at the variable currency, either in a direct or indirect quote. Thus, in the examples above, currencies that are at a premium or discount are the ones that are variable, that is, whose rates are not expressed as a unit.

Forward premiums and discounts arise when the exchange markets expect the future value of currencies to be either higher or lower. The amount of premium can and does vary quite often with the length of the forward quote, and banks often quote a series of exchange rates indicating the forward premium or discount over a range of forward deliveries. Table 5.2 illustrates a typical foreign exchange forward quotation.

In this quotation, the 30-day forward quote shows Canadian dollars at a premium of 10 points, while 60-day and 90-day premiums are at 20 and 30 points, respectively. Points here represent values in terms of the fourth decimal place of the exchange-rate quotation.

Table 5.2

Foreign Exchange Forward Quotation

Transaction	US$
Spot	1.6560
30-day forward	1.6550
60-day forward	1.6540
90-day forward	1.6530

Another important point to remember is that forward premiums and discounts are relative. When one currency is at a premium against another, the other currency is simultaneously at a discount against it. This is only natural, because the exchange rate is the value of one currency in terms of another currency. In one example, the Canadian dollar is at a 10-point premium against the U.S. dollar for 30-day forward rates. Therefore, the U.S. dollar is at a 10-point discount against the Canadian dollar for 30-day forward rates.

Forward Rates in Percentage Terms

Another way of expressing forward premiums and discounts is by quoting them as annualized percentages. There are two ways these can be calculated, one for indirect rates and the other for direct rates. The formula for computing forward rates when direct rates are used is as follows:

$$\text{Forward premium or discount} = \frac{\text{Forward rate} - \text{Spot rate}}{\text{Spot rate}} \times \frac{12}{n} \times 100$$

where n = number of months.

Consider a situation in which the U.S. dollar and pound sterling rates are quoted as follows:

A. Spot US\$/£ = US\$1.6420
   30-day forward US\$/£ = US\$1.6400

B. Spot US\$/£ = US\$1.7435
   30-day forward US\$/£ = US\$1.7455

Quotation A shows that the U.S. dollar is at a premium of 20 points for the 30-day forward rate against the pound sterling. This premium can be expressed in percentage terms using the following formula:

$$\frac{1.6400 - 1.6240}{1.6420} \times \frac{12}{1} \times 100 = -1.4616\%$$

Thus, the U.S. dollar is at a premium of 1.46 percent against the pound sterling.

Quotation B shows that the U.S. dollar is at a 20-point discount against the pound in a 30-day forward contract. This discount can be calculated as follows:

$$\frac{1.7455 - 1.7435}{1.7435} \times \frac{12}{1} \times 100 = +1.37\%$$

Thus, the U.S. dollar here is at a 1.37 percent discount against the pound.

Forward Premiums and Discounts Using Indirect Quotes

The formula for calculating forward rates as annual percentages using indirect quotes is:

Forward discount or premium as a forward rate percent per annum:

$$= \frac{\text{Spot rate} - \text{Forward rate}}{\text{Forward rate}} \times \frac{12}{n} \times 100$$

Suppose the following quotes are available in the New York interbank market:

A. Spot US$/Can$ = Can$1.5670
   3-month forward US$/Can$ = Can$1.5570
B. Spot US$/Can$ = Can$1.5670
   6-month forward US$/Can$ = Can$1.5520

These rates can be expressed in percentage-per-annum terms, using the formula for indirect quotes.

Quotation A shows that the U.S. dollar is at a 100-point discount against the Canadian dollar for a three-month forward contract. Expressing this as a percentage on an annual basis would work out as follows:

$$\frac{1.5670 - 1.5570}{1.5570} \times \frac{12}{3} \times 100 = +2.57\%$$

Thus, the U.S. dollar is at a 2.57 percent per annum discount against the Canadian dollar.

Quotation B shows that the U.S. dollar is at a discount of 150 points over the Canadian dollar for a six-month forward contract. In percentage terms on an annual basis, this is expressed as follows:

$$\frac{1.5670 - 1.5520}{1.5520} \times \frac{12}{6} \times 100 = +1.93\%$$

Thus, the U.S. dollar is at a discount of 1.93 percent per annum against the Canadian dollar for a six-month forward contract.

DEVALUATION AND REVALUATION OF EXCHANGE RATES

Exchange rates move up and down almost continuously in the exchange market. A downward movement is a *devaluation*, while an upward movement is termed a *revaluation*. Devaluation has a specific meaning in the context of exchange-rate policy, where a country lowers the officially fixed value of its currency. We are using the term to mean a

downward movement in the currency. Similarly, revaluation has a specific meaning, which is the reverse of devaluation, but in this section it is used to mean upward movements in currency prices. Both devaluation and revaluation are considered on a spot basis. It is important to measure these changes in exchange rates to compute the actual implications they have for foreign exchange transactions. The formulas for calculating the changes are different for direct and indirect quotes. The formula for calculating direct quotes is as follows:

Percent devaluation or revaluation =
$$\frac{\text{Ending rate} - \text{Beginning rate}}{\text{Beginning rate}} \times 100$$

For example, suppose the following quotes for pound sterling are available on September 1, 2006, for spot transactions in the New York interbank market:

A. 10:00 A.M. £/US$ = US$1.6800
   12:00 A.M. £/US$ = US$1.6400
B. 12:30 P.M. £/US$ = US$1.6700
   2:30 P.M. £/US$ = US$1.6900

In example A, the U.S. dollar has seen a revaluation of 400 points against the pound. This revaluation expressed in percentage terms is calculated as follows:

$$\frac{1.6400 - 1.6800}{1.6800} \times 100 = 2.38\%$$

Thus, the dollar rose 2.38 percent against the pound.

In example B, the pound has been revalued against the U.S. dollar by 200 points. Expressed in percentage terms, this revaluation is calculated as follows:

$$\frac{1.6900 - 1.6700 \times 100 = 1.19\%}{1.6700}$$

Thus, the pound sterling appreciated or was revalued by 1.19 percent against the U.S. dollar. The formula for measuring changes in spot rates when indirect quotes are used is as follows:

Percentage change in spot rate =

$$\frac{\text{Beginning rate} - \text{Ending rate} \times 100}{\text{Ending rate}}$$

For example, suppose the following quotations are available in the New York interbank market for spot rates on September 1, 2006, and September 3, 2006:

A. 10:00 A.M. US$/ € = €1.2530
   12:00 A.M. US$/ € = €1.2030
B. 10:00 A.M. US$/ € = €1.2700
   12:00 P.M. US$/€ = €1.2150

In example A, the U.S. dollar has suffered a depreciation of 500 points against the euro. This depreciation (devaluation) expressed in percentage terms is calculated as follows:

$$\frac{1.2530 - 1.2030 \times 100 = 4.16\%}{1.2030}$$

Thus, the U.S. dollar has fallen 4.16 percent against the euro.

In example B, the U.S. dollar has seen a devaluation (depreciation) of 550 points against the euro. This depreciation is expressed in percentage per annum terms as follows:

$$\frac{1.2700 - 1.2150 \times 100 = 4.53\%}{1.2150}$$

Thus, the U.S. dollar has been devalued (depreciated) 4.53 percent against the euro.

TRIANGULAR ARBITRAGE

Occasionally, prices of one currency can vary from one market to another. A currency may be cheaper in New York than it is in London. If such a situation arises, it provides an opportunity for market participants to buy the currency in New York and sell it in London. This activity is known as *triangular arbitrage*, or intermarket arbitrage (see Figure 5.1). Whether such arbitrage is possible is indicated by comparing a currency's actual price in one market and its price in another market, using cross-rate quotations. There are several steps an arbitrager must take to profit from such an opportunity. For example, assume that the following exchange rates are quoted in the interbank market:

New York: £/US$ = £1.8300
             €/US$ = €1.2700

Paris: £/€ = £1.42

The euro and the pound sterling are quoted against the U.S. dollar in New York and against each other in Paris, but we can also compute the exchange rate of the euro against the pound in the New York market through the mechanism of cross rates:

$$\frac{£1.83 = £1.44}{€1.27}$$

It is evident that the two rates for pounds in terms of euros in New York and Paris are not the same. It would be profitable, therefore, to buy pounds in New York and sell them in Paris. Thus, a U.S. arbitrager can get £183,000 in the New York market for US$100,000, and then sell these in Paris for €128,873. The euros can then be sold in the

Figure 5.1   **Triangular Arbitrage**

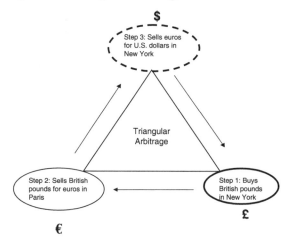

New York market and bring US$101,474.99. The arbitrager can make a clean profit of US$1,474.99 without incurring any risk.

Arbitrage opportunities exist for a very short time in the interbank markets, because market movements quickly bring the rates back into line. (Refer to the steps in Figure 5.1.)

If such an opportunity were indeed present in the interbank market, there would be an enormous number of arbitragers acting on the same strategy. Thus, the first step, selling U.S. dollars and acquiring British pounds, would push up the demand for British pounds and decrease the demand for U.S. dollars. As a result, there would be upward pressure on the price of British pounds in the New York market. The second step, the sale of British pounds acquired in New York for euros in Paris, would lead to enormous selling pressure on British pounds and buying pressure on euros. This would push down the price of British pounds and push up the price of euros in this market. Large quantities of euros would be unloaded in the New York market for U.S. dollars, again pushing down the price of euros and increasing the price of U.S. dollars. The net effect of these pressures would be an increase in the price of British pounds in New

York, while the price of British pounds in Paris would go down.

The converse movement would soon be enough to equalize prices in the two markets and eliminate the arbitrage opportunity. In fact, with modem information and computing technology, arbitrage opportunities hardly ever exist. If they arise momentarily, they are almost instantaneously eliminated as exchange traders are able to spot them simultaneously and execute transactions that move the rates back into proper alignment, in other words, the cross rates and quoted rates for currencies in different markets quickly become the same.

COVERED INTEREST ARBITRAGE

Covered interest arbitrage is a technique used to exploit the misalignment between the forward exchange rates of two currencies and their interest rates for the corresponding period. Usually, the differences in the interest rates of two countries for securities of similar risk and maturity should be equal but opposite in sign to the forward exchange premiums or discounts of their respective currencies, if transaction costs are ignored. This proposition is known as the theory of interest-rate parity. For example, assume that the following are U.S. dollar and Canadian dollar exchange and interest rates:

US$/Can$ spot = US$1/Can$1.2750
US$ 3-month forward rate = US$1/Can$1.2758

3-month U.S. treasury bill rate = 1.75%
3-month Bank of Canada treasury bill rate = 2.00%

A U.S. investor could invest US$100,000 in three-month treasury bills (T-bills) and earn 1.75 percent interest. At the end of three months, he would earn US$438 and end up with a total cash balance of US$100,438. If he chose to invest in three-month Bank of Canada Treasury bills, he would first convert his US$100,000 into Canadian dollars at the prevailing rate of US$1 to Can $1.2750. He would receive Can$127,500, which he would invest in Bank of Canada treasury bills with a three-month interest rate of 2 percent. He would receive Can$128,138 at the end of three months as principal and interest. This sum would be convertible to U.S. dollars at a forward rate of 1.2758, which would yield US$100,438. Thus, the investor would receive the same return regardless of the country in which he invests. The higher interest rate of the United States is compensated by the higher premium of the Canadian dollars. Thus, there is no transnational flow of investment funds between the two countries.

When these conditions are not present, that is, if the interest rate parity does not hold, an opportunity arises for arbitrage. This type of arbitrage takes advantage of the disequilibrium between the interests rates and forward exchange premiums and discounts between two currencies. The basic strategy is to invest in another country and cover the exchange risk at favorable terms, so that the profits being made are completely riskless. Moreover, arbitragers need not even invest their own funds. They can borrow funds and return them after taking their profits at the maturity of the transactions.

For example, assume that the following are the interest rates and spot and forward exchange rates for U.S. dollars and pounds sterling:

US$/£ spot = US$1.7840 = £1
US$/£ forward = US$1.7850 = £1
US 3-month prime rate = 3% per annum
UK 3-month prime rate = 6% per annum

The arbitrager makes six steps:

1. The arbitrager borrows US$100,000 in the United States at a prime rate of 0.75 percent (3%/4).
2. He exchanges the dollars for pounds at the spot rate of £1 = US$1.7840, which yields £56,053.812.
3. The pounds are invested in three-month deposits in the United Kingdom at a rate of 1.50 (6%/4) percent, which yields £56,264.28 at the end of the three months.
4. The maturity proceeds of the UK deposit (interest and principal) are covered by a forward contract for reconversion into U.S. dollars at the prevailing fund rate of £1 = $1.7720. The investor locks in 1.7850 × £56,264.28, or US$100,431.74.
5. The arbitrager repays the U.S. loan taken at 0.75 percent, US$100,187.62.
6. The arbitrager takes a profit of US$244.12.

Thus, the arbitrager has made a completely riskless profit of US$244.12, without even investing any of his own funds. Again, such opportunities arise only rarely, and if they do, they are quickly eliminated by market movements. If the situation described arises, there will be huge borrowings in the U.S. dollar, conversions into pound sterling, investments in sterling deposits, and reconversion into U.S. dollars. This situation will tend to raise U.S. interest rates, appreciate the spot rate of pounds sterling, depress UK interest rates, and reduce the forward premium that the U.S. dollar enjoys over the British pound. All these changes will make it less profitable to borrow funds in the U.S. and convert them to pounds sterling for deposit in the United Kingdom and then reconvert back into U.S. dollars. The arbitrage opportunity, therefore, is eliminated, and the interest rate and forward premiums and discounts move back into line.

CURRENCY FUTURES MARKETS

Currency futures are standard value-forward contracts that obligate the parties to exchange a particular currency on a specific date at a predetermined exchange rate. Currency futures are traded at the International Money Market Division (IMM) of the Chicago Mercantile Exchange (CME). These futures were introduced in 1972 because in the new environment of floating exchange rates, it was believed that the interbank market would not be able to provide foreign exchange services to small investors or corporations that wanted to speculate in currency fluctuations through a daily trading strategy. Speculators are the main participants in the currency futures market, which has a daily turnover in excess of US$40 billion. More recently, commercial banks have begun to deal in currency futures through arbitrage companies, which grew out of the IMM operations. The activity of the IMM adds liquidity to the interbank market.

DIFFERENCES BETWEEN FUTURES AND FORWARD MARKETS

Although futures are similar to forward contracts, in that they allow market participants to fix their forward liability by locking into a future exchange rate, there are important differences between the two.

One of the most important differences is that while forward contracts can be of any size, futures contracts are of specific sizes (for example, Can$50,000 or SFr125,000). Thus, if a company wishes to buy a Swiss franc currency future, it will have to enter into a contract for at least SFr125,000. Larger contracts will be in multiples of this amount. Forward contracts are available in a variety of currencies, including some that are not actively traded. Currency futures contracts are available only in specific currencies, usually the currencies of the industrialized countries.

Futures contracts have standardized maturity dates that are regulated by the exchange authorities, while forward contracts have a relatively wide range of maturities. The element of standardization also affects the future margin requirements. (Margins are

deposits paid by persons entering into contracts as security for ensuring compliance with contractual obligations.) Futures contracts stipulate specific initial and maintenance margins, but forward contract margins are negotiable between banks and their clients. The futures markets are highly regulated, and brokers can charge only fixed commissions. Regulation in forward markets is almost nonexistent, and commissions can vary.

Futures markets are highly speculative in nature, and rate movements are more volatile than in the forward market. In fact, this extreme volatility has resulted in the fixing of maximum price changes that are permissible on a particular trading day. Similarly, standards of minimum movements in rates have been fixed to affect a change in futures quotes. Operationally, perhaps the greatest difference between the two markets is the facility to exit or liquidate a position in the futures market, which is not available in the forward market. In the futures market, corporations or individuals can liquidate their existing position before the settlement date by selling an equivalent futures contract. This facility makes it easier for the speculators and hedgers in the futures markets to cut their losses or take their profits without having to wait for the contract period to expire.

FOREIGN CURRENCY OPTIONS

Foreign currency *options* are contracts that give the buyer the right, but not the obligation, to buy or sell a specified amount of foreign exchange at a set price for an agreed-on period.

For example, a U.S. corporation enters into an option contract to buy SFr100,000 within a two-month period at a rate of SFr3.6 per US$1. If the rate of the Swiss francs appreciates against the U.S. dollar to a point at which each Swiss franc is equal to one U.S. dollar, the corporation can exercise the option and acquire the foreign currency at the previous rate and not the prevailing rate. On the other hand, if the

Swiss franc depreciates to, say, four Swiss francs to the dollar, then it would not be economical for the corporation to utilize the contract at the fixed rate of 3.6 francs to the dollar. Thus, the corporation would choose to buy its Swiss francs off the market and let the option go unexercised.

There are two types of options. A *call option* allows the option purchaser to buy the underlying foreign currency. A *put option* allows the option buyer to sell the underlying currency.

OPTION TERMINOLOGY

Options markets are characterized by their unique terminology, which describes essential features of the contracts. Eight of the important terms are:

1. *Writer:* A person who confers the right but not the obligation to another person to buy or sell the foreign currency.
2. *Strike price* or *exercise price:* The rate at which the option can be exercised, that is, the rate at which the writer of the option will buy or sell the underlying foreign currency to the purchaser in the event the latter exercises his or her option.
3. *At-the-money option:* An option whose exercise, or strike, price is the same as the prevailing spot exchange rate.
4. *In-the-money option:* An option whose exercise price is better, at the time of contract writing, than the spot price for the relative currency.
5. *Out-of-the-money option:* A currency option whose exercise price is worse for the purchaser than the prevailing spot price.
6. *American option:* An option that can be exercised at any date between the initiation of the contract and the maturity date.
7. *European option:* An option that can be exercised only on the maturity date.
8. *Option premium:* The price paid by the purchaser of the option to its writer. The option premium is higher for in-the-money options and lower for out-of-the-money options. Option premiums are higher than the prevailing forward premiums in the interbank markets for contracts of similar maturities.

FORECASTING FOREIGN EXCHANGE RATES

Forecasting exchange rates is often vital to the successful conduct of international business. Inaccurate foreign exchange forecasts or projections can eliminate entire profits from international transactions or result in enormous cost overruns that could threaten the viability of overseas operations. Exchange rates must be forecast for any decision that involves the transfer of funds from one currency to another over a period time. For example, when companies approach foreign markets to borrow or invest foreign currencies, they must project future exchange rates to compute even roughly their possible costs and returns. If a British company is borrowing Japanese yen, it will have to forecast the long-term pound-yen rate to compute what its repayment liabilities are going to be over the life of the loan and amortization period. Similarly, decisions involving both financial and nonfinancial investments overseas require foreign exchange forecasts to calculate the returns profile, because it depends considerably on the rate at which the foreign currency is going to be acquired for investment and the rate at which earnings will eventually be repatriated. Even when it is simply a question of *hedging* foreign exchange risks, currency forecasts are important. Only when a corporation has a clear view of what it believes the future direction of exchange-rate movements will be can it make a proper hedging decision and decide which hedging strategy or instrument is best for its purposes.

PROBLEMS IN FORECASTING FOREIGN EXCHANGE RATES

It is generally recognized that there is no perfect foreign exchange forecast or even a perfect methodology to forecast foreign exchange rates. There is no accurate and precise explanation for the manner in which exchange rates move. Movements of exchange rates depend on the simultaneous interaction of a variety of factors. How these factors influence one another and how they influence exchange-rate movements is impossible to quantify or predict. Exchange rates have been known to react violently to single, unexpected events, which have thrown many forecasts and theories completely off balance for that period.

Participants in foreign exchange markets, especially corporate treasurers, grapple with uncertainty and use a variety of techniques to develop some sense of what exchange rates are going to do in the future.

FUNDAMENTAL FORECASTING

Fundamental forecasting is a technique that attempts to predict future exchange rates by examining the influence of major macroeconomic variables on the foreign exchange markets. The main macroeconomic variables that are used in this analysis are inflation rates, interest rates, the balance of payments situation, economic growth trends, unemployment trends, and industrial and other major economic activities. These variables are quantified through comprehensive models that build relationships between the different factors with various statistical techniques, especially regression analysis.

A major problem with fundamental forecasting is that the timing of the events that influence exchange rates, and the gap between the occurrence of these events and their impact on exchange rates, is very difficult to measure. The latest data to make precise quantitative estimates of the relevant macroeconom-

ic variables are seldom readily available. Perhaps the greatest weakness of fundamental analysis in forecasting exchange rates is that it takes into account only some of the factors that influence the movement of rates in the foreign exchange markets. There are several other noneconomic, nontangible factors, such as market sentiment, investor fears, speculative intentions, and political events, that have an enormous influence on exchange rates and can override, at least in the short run, other fundamental considerations and factors.

TECHNICAL FORECASTING

Technical forecasting relies on past exchange-rate data to develop quantitative models and charts that can be used to predict future exchange rates. Technical analysts try to see historical patterns in the previous exchange-rate movements and attempt to build future patterns on that basis. This approach relies more on personal views and perceptions than on strong economic analysis. There are other technical models that use economic techniques to forecast exchange rates. These models try to capture as many variables as possible and incorporate them into complex models, ascribing to each variable a certain level of influence in the overall computation of the future exchange-rate movements.

Technical models have been found to be of questionable use in practice. Studies conducted over the past few years have shown that technical models have not proved to be accurate predictors of future exchange-rate movements, but their widespread adoption by many market participants has given them a unique influence as factors in forecasting exchange-rate movements. Because a large number of market participants using similar models will tend to behave in a similar manner, moving the exchange rate in the direction indicated by their model is a sort of a self-fulfilling prophesy. Usually, technical models concentrate on the near term and are favored by participants who have an interest in short-term trading and speculation in the exchange markets. Many companies, however, use technical models to provide a way of looking at foreign exchange possibilities, and if they are in agreement with the corporate view, they could serve to reinforce that view.

Assessing Market Sentiments

Another forecasting technique is the assessment of market sentiment, as reflected in the spot and forward rates of currencies. If the spot and forward rates of currencies are expected to appreciate, there would be buying pressure from speculators, which would push the exchange rate up to the expected level. Thus, the spot and forward rates that prevail can be seen as the realized expectations of future movements of currency. Some market participants base their forecasts on this logic, especially for future rates, and treat the forward rate as an unbiased estimator of the future spot rate.

Forecasting Strategy

As is evident, no one technique is truly adequate for forecasting future movements in the exchange rate. Usually, corporate participants base their expectations on a combination of techniques and their individual experience and expertise in the area. The importance given to each type of forecasting technique will depend on the views of the individual firm. It is important that a comprehensive and broad-based view be taken when making foreign exchange-rate projections. These projections should be constantly reviewed and updated.

Summary

The foreign exchange markets act as the intermediary through which complex transactions between different currencies are completed. Individuals and institutions, such as multinational corporations, pension funds, commercial banks, central banks, arbi-

tragers, speculators, and foreign exchange brokers, all participate in the markets to varying degrees, with the large international banks being the most active. Located in major business centers around the world (London, New York, and Tokyo are the largest), the foreign exchange markets have three basic functions: settlement of trade transactions, avoidance of risk because of currency fluctuations, and the financing of international trade.

The three major transactions in the foreign exchange markets are the spot, forward, and swap transactions. Based on the prices of currencies and using various formulas, traders attempt to take advantage of momentary disequilibriums in the prices of currencies, or currency and interest disparities, by trading in different locations or markets. They also try to minimize losses associated with unanticipated changes in currency values. Some of the techniques used are triangular arbitrage, covered interest arbitrage, and hedges.

Forward contracts, which are generally used by large international banks and MNCs, can be tailor-made for any contract size or currency, but they require execution of the transaction on the date of contract maturity. Futures contracts differ from forward contracts by offering standardized, regulated contracts of smaller sizes, which can be easily liquidated. Options are yet another form of currency contract, which, like futures contracts, are standardized and can be easily liquidated. Options offer the right, not the obligation, to buy or sell a foreign currency at a set price up to an agreed date.

Corporations face four major types of risk or exposure in their international activities: transaction exposure, economic exposure, translation exposure, and tax exposure. Forecasting foreign exchange rates is often vital to conducting international business, but generating accurate forecasts is extremely difficult. Fundamental forecasting examines macroeconomic variables, such as balance of payments, inflation rates, and unemployment trends, to predict future exchange rates, while technical forecasting relies on historical exchange-rate data to predict future currency exchange rates.

DISCUSSION QUESTIONS

1. Why does international business need a foreign exchange market?
2. Who are the participants in foreign exchange transactions?
3. Where are foreign exchange markets located? Where are the main centers of foreign trading?
4. Discuss the four types of risk facing multinational corporations.
5. What is the difference between the spot and the forward markets?
6. You currently hold US$1 million and are interested in exchanging U.S. dollars for Swiss francs. The current spot rate of US$1 = SFr1.475 is a direct quote. True or false?
7. What is a long position? Short position? Square position?
8. What is the bid-offer spread for a US$/£ quote of US$1.8410–$1.8420?
9. What is covered interest arbitrage?
10. What is the difference between the futures and forward markets?
11. What is an option?
12. What is the difference between fundamental forecasting and technical forecasting?

NOTES

1. Federal Reserve Bank of New York, *Summary Results of U.S. Foreign Exchange Markets Survey Conducted in March 1986* (New York: Federal Reserve Bank of New York, 1986).

2. Ibid.

BIBLIOGRAPHY

Aliber, Robert Z. *The International Money Game*. 2nd ed. New York: Basic Books, 1976.

Black, Fisher, and Martin Scholes. "The Pricing of Options and Corporate Liabilities." *Journal of Political Economy*, May–June 1973, 637–59.

Buckley, Adrian. "Multinational Finance: The Risks of FX." *Accountancy*, February 1987, 80–82.

Choi, J.J. "Diversification, Exchange Risk and Corporate Risk." *International Business Studies,* Spring 1989, 145–55.

Dornbusch, R. "Equilibrium and Disequilibrium Exchange Rates." *Zeitschrift fir Wirtschafts und Sozialwissenshaften* 102 (1983): 573–99.

Dufey, G., and I. Giddy. "Forecasting Exchange Rates in a Floating World." *Euromoney*, November 1975, 28–35.

Ensig, Paul. *The Theory of Forward Exchange*. London: Macmillan, 1937.

Griffiths, Susan H., and P.S. Greenfield. "Foreign Currency Management: Part I—Currency Hedging Strategies." *Journal of Cash Management*, July–August 1989, 141.

Kwok, Chuck. "Hedging Foreign Exchange Exposures: Independent Versus Integrative Approaches." *Journal of International Business Studies*, Summer 1987, 33–52.

Ma, Christopher K., and G.W. Kao. "On Exchange Rate Changes and Stock Price Reactions." *Journal of Business Finance and Accounting*, Summer 1990, 441–49.

Madura, Jeff. *International Financial Management*. 2nd ed. St. Paul, MN: West Publishing, 1989.

Mckinnon, Ronald I. "Interest Rate Volatility and Exchange Risk: New Rates for a Common Monetary Standard." *Contemporary Policy Issues*, April 1990, 1–17.

Soenen, L.A., and R. Aggarwal. "Corporate Foreign Exchange and Cash Management Practices." *Journal of Cash Management*, March–April 1987, 62–64.

Sweeney, R.J. "Beating the Foreign Exchange Market." *Journal of Finance*, March 1986, 163–82.

Taylor, Mark P. "Covered Interest Arbitrage and Market Turbulence." *Economic Journal*, June 1989, 376–91.

Walsh, Carl E. "Interest Rates and Exchange Rates." *FRBSF Weekly Letter*, June 5, 1987, 41.

Woo, Wing Thye. "Some Evidence of Speculative Bubbles in the Foreign Exchange Market." *Journal of Money, Credit, and Banking*, November 1987, 499–514.

Yahoo Finance. "International Currency Tables." April 7, 2006. http://finance.yahoo.com/currency, accessed on April 7, 2006.

CASE STUDY 5.1
GLOBAL BANK CORPORATION

Global Bank Corporation is a major international bank headquartered in New York City, with branches in 11 other countries: Canada, Germany, Brazil, Great Britain, Japan, France, Australia, Netherlands, Singapore, Hong Kong, and Dubai. Total assets in 2005 were $90 billion, and the bank was among the top 500 banks in the world. The bank is organized into three main divisions: retail banking, institutional banking, and investment banking. Global retail banking undertakes transactions with individual customers, for example, savings accounts, checking and money market accounts, issuance of certificates of deposit, operation of automated teller machines, loans to individual customers for different purchases, funds transfer facilities, and so on. The institutional banking division carries out business with the bank's institutional and corporate customers: the trusts of major companies and other large clients. Much of the work of the institutional banking division is concerned with devising comprehensive financing arrangements for its clients. The investment banking division of Global has three main functional areas:

1. The capital markets group, which provides a wide range of services to companies seeking to raise funds in the international financial markets.
2. The private banking group, which provides fund management and advisory services to large-net-worth clients.
3. The foreign exchange division, which carries out exchange trading and handles foreign exchange transactions and provides advisory services.

The foreign exchange trading function of the bank is decentralized to levels of operation for each country and further to each individual trading operation. Each level of decentralization, however, has to operate within established trading and exposure limits that are laid down by the bank's corporate risk management committee, which meets every month at the headquarters in New York City. A typical trading operation at Global Bank Corporation is divided into two main areas: interbank exchange market trading and customer-based trading. The former is primarily a speculative operation aimed at generating substantial profits for the bank from interbank trading, while the latter operation is intended to serve customers by providing them with a wide range of foreign exchange services, ranging from risk management to a simple sale or purchase of foreign currency. The interbank trading division has been fairly successful in the past four years and has consistently made profits, although the level of profits has varied over the years. The main focus of the trading activity is the Tokyo, New York, and London markets. At other centers, the trading operations of the bank are more oriented toward meeting the foreign exchange needs of customers.

In the past 15 years, the Singapore and Hong Kong markets have become extremely active and a large number of international banks have set up trading operations to generate profits from the booming interbank market. The investment banking division is planning to set up new operations in this area. Both markets have an environment

continued

Case 5.1 (*continued*)

relatively free of regulation and excellent communication and other infrastructural facilities for establishing trading operations. Singapore seems to be a more stable alternative because the probusiness climate in Hong Kong could eventually be hindered by decisions of the Chinese government. While the Chinese government has said that Hong Kong will remain as it has historically been, there were recent protests in Hong Kong concerning the fear that free speech would be taken away by new regulations out of the mainland. While this has not occurred as of this time, business professionals in Hong Kong remain skeptical.

Despite the advantages, establishing a new interbank trading center in Singapore has given rise to some doubts. The bank has not opened a new trading center for the past seven years and will have to hire a new team. Some senior investment banking division executives feel that while interbank trading is a good source of profit and helps to strengthen the company's bottom line, it is also risky. Having a fourth interbank trading operation will increase the overall exposure of the bank and will make controls more difficult to enforce. Other executives feel that because the exchange market is an around-the-clock operation,

a presence in the Singapore market will allow the bank to have an active presence in all time zones and increase the effectiveness of overall global trading operations. At present, there is a time lag between the closing of the Tokyo market and the opening of the London market; during this time, the bank has no presence in the market. Further, the proponents of the Singapore trading location argue that once this trading location has been stabilized, a fifth location can be opened somewhere in the Middle East, for example, in Bahrain. The profits from the Singapore trading center in the interbank market could be used for aggressive pricing of corporate foreign exchange products to later capture increased market share.

DISCUSSION QUESTIONS

1. Should Global Bank Corporation set up a new foreign exchange operation in Singapore? If so, what should be given priority (for example, interbank trading or customer telex sources)?
2. What additional information would you consider relevant in evaluating a proposal to set up a new foreign exchange trading operation?

CASE STUDY 5.2

CHEMTECH, INC.

As he walked into his office in downtown Frankfurt one Tuesday morning, Jorge Muller, corporate treasurer of Chemtech, smiled at his secretary. "Good morning, Marita," he said. "Anything important happen while I was away?" he continued, referring to his short trip to Paris that had spilled over from the weekend to Monday. "Nothing much," replied Marita, "except there was a call from Mr. Carl Volten of Hamburg Bank. He wants you to call him as soon as possible." "Thanks," Muller replied as he sat down to begin work on what he knew would be a critical week.

Chemtech, Inc., is a leading pharmaceutical manufacturer in Germany and had total sales of more than $26 billion in 2005. The company had been founded just after World War II and had established a strong market presence in both the German domestic market and several international markets. The emphasis of the company has always been to push ahead in the export markets of the industrialized countries, because opportunities to sell its sophisticated and fairly high-priced products in markets of less-developed countries were limited. Total export sales come from the following countries:

United States	$6 billion
United Kingdom	2 billion
France	2 billion
Italy	1.50 billion
Canada	.75 billion
Sweden	.70 billion
Japan	1.20 billion
Total	$14.15 billion

While Chemtech has enjoyed great success in its export markets, and sales have grown at an average of 11 percent over the past seven years, profits from exports have not grown at the same pace. International competition has intensified in most markets due to U.S. and Swiss pharmaceutical manufacturers, and the firm has been forced to give greater discounts to retain market share. Although productivity has risen, it has not risen enough to offset increasing production costs, especially the higher labor costs that Chemtech encountered over the past three years following a settlement with the labor unions. One of the most important problems, however, has been the continued appreciation of the euro against the U.S. dollar and pound sterling, which has reduced export profits considerably. The problem has been particularly acute in the past eight months, because a continuously weakening dollar has hurt export revenues and therefore profitability by as much as 9 percent.

Muller was asked by Chemtech's director of finance to come up with a strategy to guard against foreign exchange fluctuation losses. Muller called his friend and long-time adviser Karl Volten, vice president of corporate foreign exchange services at Hamburg Bank, for suggestions.

Volten was a foreign exchange expert with many years of top-level experience in advising large corporations on managing their foreign exchange exposures. He had an MBA in finance from a major U.S. university and had worked as an exchange trader in the New York branch of

continued

Case 5.2 (*continued*)

the Hamburg Bank for six years. He had been assistant vice president of corporate foreign exchange advisory services for three years and has held his current position for the past two and a half years.

Volten felt that Chemtech should buy US$/ call options on the IMM exchange through the New York branch office of the Hamburg Bank. By purchasing an option, the company could lock in a minimum euro price for the dollar revenues it earns from U.S. operations, and if the euro weakens before maturity of the contract, the company could choose not to exercise the option. As a matter of policy, Chemtech repatriated U.S. dollar profits every six months, and options could be bought for six-month maturities. Options could also be sold off before the due date.

For example, the ruling U.S.$/€ rate today was U.S.$1 = €2.5. It is expected that the euro will be strengthened further, although no one can predict by how much. Chemtech can lock in a particular level of exchange rate by buying a euro call option for the strike price of €2.3 per dollar. There would be an up-front cost for the option of €0.3 for every dollar of the contract amount. The company would therefore be locking into an effective rate of €2 = $1.

The strategy has several advantages. For one, the company is covered against excess depreciation of the dollar. If the dollar appreciates beyond €2.3, the company could simply forgo the option and buy euros in the open market. In fact, if the dollar goes beyond €2.6, the company can recover its entire hedging cost of €0.3 per dollar

and actually profit from the option transaction. If, on the other hand, the dollar weakens beyond €2.3, the company can exercise the option and buy the euros at this price. Hedging costs will be fully recovered if the dollar weakens to €2 = $1, and any further weakening of the dollar will mean additional profits for Chemtech.

The strategy appeared extremely attractive to Muller. "We win on both sides," he figured, "since we are saved from any excess strengthening of the euro and still have the opportunity of making substantial gains on any large weakening of the currency. It's a lot better than going for the plain old forward contract for €2.2 per dollar. True, we lock in our price at €2.2 and we are saved against any depreciation of the dollar beyond that, but if the dollar strengthens against the euro, we would be locked out of the opportunity to profit from it. I think I will prepare a report for the treasurer," he decided.

DISCUSSION QUESTIONS

1. Is the suggested options strategy completely risk free?
2. If you were the treasurer, what would you think of this proposal? Are there any reasons for rejecting this strategy in favor of forward contracts?
3. Under what circumstances would a forward contract be a better alternative to achieve the objectives of the company?

CHAPTER 6

Supranational Organizations and International Institutions

CHAPTER OBJECTIVES

This chapter will:

- Identify major international trade organizations, such as the World Trade Organization and the United Nations Conference on Trade and Development, and the roles they play in shaping and molding the international business environment.
- Describe the major financial institutions, such as the International Monetary Fund, the World Bank, and the International Finance Corporation, and the assistance they provide in channeling financial resources to developing countries.
- Review the growth of regional financial institutions and their important positions as providers of financial resources.

BACKGROUND

Increasing economic, financial, and commercial interdependence among nations of the world after World War II created a need to coordinate international action and policies to secure the smooth flow of trade. Apart from regular, periodic meetings of officials and businesspersons from different countries, these nations recognized a need for the establishment of permanent organizations to provide stability and continuity to the process of international economic interchange. Some supranational bodies were set up in the period immediately following World War II, while more were established in the following decades. Two major categories of international organizations can be identified as those having a global focus and those set up to meet the needs of particular regions.

GENERAL AGREEMENT ON TARIFFS AND TRADE

The *General Agreement on Tariffs and Trade (GATT)* was established initially as a temporary measure to reduce trade barriers among its founding members. Since its inception in 1947, GATT has evolved into a permanent body to include most industrial and developing countries, excluding those of the socialist bloc.

GATT was originally established to avoid the kind of competitive protectionism that had plagued international trade in the period between the two world wars, which was reflected in high tariff barriers and a major slump in trade volumes. The objectives of GATT—liberalization of the international trade restrictions and the lowering of tariff barriers—were to be achieved by multilateral negotiations and voluntarily agreed-upon rules of conduct. As a permanent international body, GATT was to provide the forum for the conduct of these negotiations and the development of necessary ground rules for liberalizing the international trade environment. GATT was also intended to serve as an agency for mediation and settlement of trade disputes.

One of the main tenets of GATT regulations is the requirement for its members to comply with the most-favored-nation clause, which obligates all member countries to give the same tariff concessions to all GATT countries that they give to any one member country. For example, if Germany reduces the import duty on Japanese television sets from 40 percent to 10 percent, then it must level the same rate of duty on television sets from other countries.

There are, however, important exceptions to the most-favored-nation clause, which recognize the need for preferential treatment to be given to the less-developed countries (LDCs), which without special treatment are not able to compete on a one-to-one basis with the industrialized countries. The developing countries thus have preferential access to the markets of developed countries for some of their products under the generalized system of preferences.

The second major exception relates to the establishment of regional trading alliances: members of regional trade agreements can extend trade concessions to one another without extending these concessions to countries that are not members of the alliance. Regional trade agreements, such as the European Union (EU), the North American Free Trade Agreement (NAFTA), and the Association of South East Asian Nations (ASEAN), are three examples. To ease the problem of dealing with tariffs and duties on individual products, most negotiations concern making generalized reductions in tariff rates for a large number of products in certain categories.

In the eight rounds, or negotiating sessions, under GATT,[1] significant changes were made. The average tariffs on industrial products, levied by the developed countries, came down significantly. GATT countries have accounted for 85 percent of world trade since its inception. This trend has only improved since the creation of the World Trade Organization in 1995.

There were still several problems with GATT, however, such as an increasing emphasis on protectionism, not only from the developing countries, but also from the industrialized world. The use of nontariff barriers to discriminate against imports from other countries has enabled many member countries to negate the intended effects of the tariff reductions agreed to under the GATT rules of conduct. Further, GATT regulations were imprecise, and many signatory states found loopholes to evade the requirements, almost on a routine basis. Many trade issues arose in the 1970s and 1980s that had not been foreseen by earlier negotiations, and provisions for regulating them were not included in the agreements. There are also substantial difficulties between major trading partners, as relative economic and competitive strengths change and new arrangements and terms are sought by old trading partners. In the mid-1990s, the increasing importance of both the service sector and intellectual property rights led to the need for a fundamental change in GATT. In 1994, at the end of the Uruguay Round of trade talks, the decision was made to expand GATT into a new organization known as the *World Trade Organization (WTO).*[2]

WORLD TRADE ORGANIZATION

Since GATT had been successful in reducing tariffs worldwide since 1948, and given the increasing importance of the service sector and intellectual property rights in the modern economy, the members of GATT formed the World Trade Organization in January of 1995 to increase the scope of the trade agreements beyond manufactured products. The WTO currently has 149 member nations that participate in trade discussions. The WTO is both a forum for resolving trade disputes and an arena for agreeing on the rules of operation for international trade. Since we have already outlined GATT, we will next focus on providing a brief description of the other two primary areas of the WTO, the General Agreement on Trade in Services and the Agreement on Trade-Related Aspects of Intellectual Property Rights.

General Agreement on Trade in Services

The *General Agreement on Trade in Services (GATS)* is the first and only set of multilateral rules governing international trade in services. The inclusion of services was negotiated in the Uruguay Round and was developed primarily due to the increase in importance of the service sector in the developed world, and also due to the greater potential for trading services brought about by the advancement in communications technology over the past few decades. All services are covered under GATS, and the most-favored-nation treatment applies to all services as well.[3] GATS identifies four ways of trading services:

1. *Cross-border supply:* services supplied from one country to another
2. *Consumption abroad:* consumers or firms making use of a service in another country (i.e., tourism)

3. *Commercial presence:* foreign company setting up a branch or subsidiary in another country
4. *Presence of natural persons:* individuals traveling to another country to supply services

The reason that these definitions are necessary is that the trade in services is a much more diverse area than the trade in manufactured goods. The business models of service sector industries such as financial services, telecommunications, tourism, and even restaurants are very different. These varied industries under the service sector umbrella perform their operations in very different ways.

GATS requires member governments to regulate their services reasonably, objectively, and impartially, and the agreement does not require that any service be deregulated. As you will recall from the discussion concerning the Asian financial crisis, the lack of effective regulation in the banking sector was at the heart of the problem. Thus, if GATS had required deregulation of the service sector by its member nations, the problem of moral hazard could not have been improved.

Another important tenet of GATS is *transparency*. GATS specifies that all governments should adequately publish all laws and regulations that deal with the service sector. This will provide for easy access to the domestic service regulations for foreign companies and governments wishing to conduct business in another country. The guiding principle of these transparency rules is *nondiscrimination*, or the treatment of foreign enterprises on the same basis as domestic enterprises. The industrialized countries are likely to press for progressive liberalization of trade in services, while the developing countries may demand greater shares in the international services market and greater mobility of their workforces to move to the developed countries as a part of the liberalization of rules regarding manpower services.

AGREEMENT ON TRADE-RELATED ASPECTS OF INTELLECTUAL PROPERTY RIGHTS

Another creation of the Uruguay Round was the *Agreement on Trade-Related Aspects of Intellectual Property Rights*, or *TRIPS*. The purpose of TRIPS is to allow for the creation of domestic laws that concern the protection of intellectual property rights, as well as the enforcement of such laws in violating countries. TRIPS established minimum levels of protection that each WTO member government must provide to the intellectual property of fellow WTO member states. TRIPS covers the following types of intellectual property[4]:

- Copyrights
- Trademarks (including service marks)
- Geographical indications: such as "Champagne," "Scotch," and "Tequila"
- Industrial designs
- Patents
- Layout designs of integrated circuits
- Undisclosed information, including trade secrets

TRIPS provides guidelines for how basic principles of the trading system and other international intellectual property rights agreements should be applied. It also spells out how various WTO member governments must provide adequate protection of intellectual property rights in their domestic laws, and sets rules for how countries should enforce intellectual property rights within their own borders. TRIPS also provides a means of settling disputes regarding intellectual property between members of the WTO.

When the WTO came into being in January 1995, the developed countries of the world were given one year to harmonize (or equalize) their intellectual property laws so that they were in compliance with the specifications required by TRIPS. Some developing countries were given until the year 2000 to ensure that their laws and practices conform to the TRIPS agreement. LDCs were provided 11 years (until 2006) to meet these requirements.[5]

The TRIPS agreement has been a point of contention for many years between the developed world and the developing nations. The developed world sees the need for strict intellectual property rights enforcement as a way of recouping their research and development costs for products such as pharmaceutical drugs. The LDCs see these same protections as trade restrictions. In the case of pharmaceutical drugs, the LDCs argue that in lieu of intellectual property restrictions, much cheaper versions of the drugs could be provided for a greater number of people. This is similar to the *utilitarian* viewpoint made famous by such philosophers as Jeremy Bentham, who argued that moral values are reflected in policies that provide the greatest happiness to the greatest number of people. These same arguments have been made by students around the globe recently concerning online music sharing. High school and college students have found it reasonable to argue that music provided online by such providers as Napster or via the Apple iTunes Music store should be provided either without cost or at a much-reduced cost. Thus, very similar arguments are being made by developing countries with regard to pharmaceutical drugs and those in the developed world with regard to online music sharing. While the arguments are the same, the impact that the result of these policies have for the affected citizens is of no comparison. Discussions like these will only continue with the increased integration of world markets and with the continued importance of the TRIPS for all WTO-member nations.

THE DOHA AGENDA

In November 2001, at a WTO conference in Doha, Qatar, the member nations of the WTO agreed to launch a new round of trade negotiations. One of the primary thrusts of the new trade round concerns the problems that the developing countries are having implementing some of the changes decided upon in the Uruguay Round (TRIPS, for example). Another important area for reform is agricultural trade barriers. The countries of the developing world claim that agricultural protectionism by the countries of the developed world (such as the United States, Canada, and the members of the European Union) leaves them without the ability to sell their agricultural products to the most developed nations. Thus, their primary avenue for income growth has been closed. At the start of the Doha trade round, both developed and developing nations made promises to improve market access for agricultural and other products via reductions in export subsidies, quotas, and tariffs.

UNITED NATIONS CONFERENCE ON TRADE AND DEVELOPMENT

The *United Nations Conference on Trade and Development (UNCTAD)* was established in 1964 to address concerns of developing nations regarding issues of international trade that affected their economic development. The main concern of most developing countries was that under the old system, unequal players were asked to play on a level playing field. The LDCs, which were extremely weak economically and industrially backward, had no way of competing with the industrialized nations in the world market on the same terms. Moreover, they argued, given the structure of the international economy, they were parting with more of their goods as exports than they were receiving as imports. In effect, the prices of their exports were not rising as did the prices of their imports. This feature is conceptu-

alized in economics as the terms of trade argument. Further, LDCs' exports suffered from low demand and price elasticities, which meant that they could not raise export prices by reducing supplies. On the other hand, their imports were critical for them and their supplies were controlled by large monopolistic entities that could charge exorbitant prices.

UNCTAD was established to provide a forum for the developing countries to communicate their views on international trade issues to the industrialized countries and to seek trade concessions from them. After considerable and sustained pressure from the developing countries, the developed countries agreed to an across-the-board reduction of tariffs for developing countries under an arrangement known as the generalized system of preferences (GSP). The GSP tariff reductions, however, were for only limited amounts of imports from developing countries and did not create any significant niches for developing-country exporters in the markets of industrialized countries. Moreover, since the liberalization in tariffs was only for manufactured goods, many developing countries with little industrial activity cannot benefit from the reduced tariffs.

Membership of the UNCTAD rose from 119 in 1964 to 192 countries in 2006. Although the deliberations and resolutions of UNCTAD have not solved the problems faced by developing countries in the international trade area, they have had important positive effects on the international trade environment in general. UNCTAD conferences have resulted in a better and more informed understanding of the respective positions on various issues of the developed and developing countries. In the October 2004 meeting of the Trade and Development Board in Geneva, issues concerning trade between the *developed countries* (the North) and the *developing countries* (the South) were discussed. UNCTAD is committed to studying the factors that have led to many African nations being left behind in terms of participation in the benefits of globalization. The

UNCTAD participants agreed that it is the moral responsibility of the organization as well as other supranational organizations previously discussed to find ways of improving the performance of LDCs in the world economy.

A number of permanent working committees have been formed, such as the Commission on Trade in Goods, Services, and Commodities, the Commission on Investment, Technology, and Related Financial Issues, and the Commission on Enterprise, Business Facilitation, and Development. These commissions continue to deal with major issues and analyze in depth complex problems, thereby contributing to an increase in the level of understanding of the problems by representatives and officials of different countries. Thus, UNCTAD has become a permanent international organization that focuses global attention on the trade development problems of LDCs and actively investigates issues in all their complexity and implications. UNCTAD also has emerged as an important source of suggestions for solving these problems, especially because of the broad knowledge base it has created over the years. At the time of its inception, the creation of UNCTAD was hailed as one of the most important events since the establishment of the United Nations. Although the concrete impact of the organization has been limited, it has kept alive the dialogue between the industrial and developing world and is likely to continue to promote better understanding between them.

REGIONAL TRADE GROUPINGS

Regional trade groupings have emerged in the past two decades as major forces shaping the pattern of international trade. These arrangements have enabled countries located in different geographic locations to pool their resources and lower restrictions on trade among themselves in order to achieve greater economic growth.

Regional groupings offer several advantages over global trade arrangements to their members. Because there are fewer countries involved, and their state of economic development is relatively homogenous, it is easier to find commonality of interest and arrive at a workable agreement on the basis of voluntary adherence by member countries.

Regional groupings offer the additional advantage of cultural, geographical, and historical homogeneity, which provides an environment conducive to the spirit of mutual cooperation. Even with all the positive factors, however, regional groupings can still face severe internal dissension among member states, especially if the general economic situation is poor and countries follow restrictive, inward-looking policies. The experience of regional groupings in international trade has therefore varied considerably. While the European Union and the Association of South East Asian Nations are notable successes, trade arrangements in Africa and Latin America have not achieved many significant benefits for their member countries.

FORMS OF REGIONAL INTEGRATION

Many nations have entered into *bilateral agreements* (involving two countries) or *multilateral agreements* (involving more than two countries) in the attempt to increase trade between member states. There are five different forms of regional economic integration. Some of these forms of economic integration also include some degree of political integration. Some have been around for many years, while others are relatively new. These forms of regional economic integration are listed in increasing order of integration as follows:

- Free trade area
- Customs union
- Common market
- Economic union
- Political union

FREE TRADE AREA

The first form of regional economic integration is the *free trade area*. The United States has entered into many of these bilateral agreements recently. Over the last few years, the United States has signed bilateral free trade agreements with countries as diverse as Singapore, Chile, Vietnam, and Jordan. These agreements are between just the United States and the designated bilateral partner (Chile, for example). The agreements reached between these two countries pertain only to them. Some argue that these agreements are really not free trade agreements at all, just reduced trade barriers for specific goods and services, with those items not addressed still being protected.

The most commonly known multilateral free trade agreement is the North American Free Trade Agreement (NAFTA). NAFTA came into effect in 1994 and is a free trade agreement of the United States, Canada, and Mexico. NAFTA has been successful in increasing the volume of trade between its member nations, but critics cite the movement of jobs from the United States to Mexico as an example of a flawed system. Mexican companies have formed *maquiladoras*, or manufacturing facilities located in the northern part of Mexico, in an attempt to capitalize on the southern movement of manufacturing plants from the United States.

Free trade areas eliminate trade barriers among their members (at least the barriers agreed to in the free trade agreement), but members can set their own trade policies with nonmembers. Thus, the United States is able to negotiate bilateral agreements with countries such as Chile and Vietnam, but Canada does not have to honor these agreements. In fact, Canada has signed its own separate free trade agreement with Chile.

A weakness of free trade agreements is that they are vulnerable to *trade deflection*, a process in which nonmember nations reroute their exports to member nations with the lowest external trade barriers. Thus, free trade areas require *rules of origin* specifications to clarify what actually constitutes member goods and services within the free trade agreement. As an example, if Mexico had the lowest external trade barriers when compared with Canada and the United States, a country that is not a member of NAFTA (such as Brazil) could attempt to access the U.S. and Canadian markets more cheaply by sending goods to Mexico for reexport into the United States or Canada. Another weakness of free trade areas is that they are vulnerable to *trade diversion*. This occurs when member nations stop importing from lower-cost nonmember nations in favor of member states. Since the goal of a free trade area is the reduction in the prices that consumers pay for products via the reduction of protective trade barriers, such trade diversion would seem to be counterproductive.

CUSTOMS UNION

The second form of regional economic integration, *customs union* agreements, combine the elimination of internal trade barriers among member nations with the adoption of common external trade policies toward nonmembers. Thus, a customs union is a free trade area with a common external trade policy. This eliminates the trade deflection problem that is associated with free trade areas. The most well-known customs union is the *Mercosur Accord*, an agreement between Argentina, Brazil, Paraguay, and Uruguay. These nations agreed to form a customs union in 1995. Peru joined Mercosur in 2003. The Mercosur Accord covers 209 million people, with a combined annual GDP of $656 billion. Within three years of the formation of the customs union, the trade between the member nations doubled. The Mercosur Accord nations have recently been talking with European Union officials about forming the world's largest free trade area. Thus far, talks have not produced a new agreement. This idea came about from the existing example of a customs union between the European Union and Turkey.

Another example of a customs union is the *Andean Community*, an agreement signed by five Latin American countries—Bolivia, Chile, Colombia, Ecuador, and Peru—in 1969, in effect creating a subregional trading arrangement. An important motivation for the creation of the Andean Community was a growing dissatisfaction among several Latin American countries about restrictions on trade in goods and services. The Andean Community works through a secretariat that handles all administrative and executive matters. The decisions of the community are made through a commission made up of a representative from each member country. Disputes between members on the interpretation of the pact's statutes are heard and settled by the Court of Justice of the Andean Community. Although progress has been relatively slow, some important steps toward regional integration have been taken by the Andean Community countries. The community covers 1.8 million square miles (4.7 million sq km) and 120 million people.

Under the industry sectoral programs, a number of industry sectors are selected for the implementation of coordinated or rationalized development plans that aim to achieve the best utilization of competitive advantages available in different countries in the region. Thus, the country having a competitive advantage in a particular industrial product will concentrate on the production of that product, while other products related to that industry will be manufactured by other member countries. Countries exchange their allocated products among other member states on a tariff-free basis. At present, sectoral cooperation in industrial activity encompasses petrochemicals, automotive products, and metals.

The members of the Andean Community have been able to establish coordinated policies to promote and control foreign direct investments, with the goal of achieving a certain similarity of restrictions in all member countries in order to develop leverage in negotiating investment permissions with overseas investors. At the same time, by creating intraregional competition to attract foreign investment flows, the community aims to prevent the possibility of the investors gaining unfair advantages by playing one country of the region against another. Chile, however, wanted to attract greater levels of foreign direct investments and left the Andean Community (at the time called the Andean Pact) in 1976, because it could not hope to do so under the community's restrictive provisions.

The Andean Community has made little progress in tariff reduction among its member countries. Further regional cooperation in Latin America has been limited because most countries have been beset by serious internal economic problems following debt crises.

COMMON MARKET

The third form of economic integration, the *common market*, increases the agreements in place for a customs union to include the elimination of barriers that inhibit the movement of the factors of production. The member nations involved in a common market agree that labor, capital, and technology are able to move across borders without any barriers. Many of the countries engaged in customs unions have the eventual goal of becoming common markets.

Another group that has formed a common market is in Central America. The Central American Common Market was formed by a 1960 treaty signed by Guatemala, Honduras, Nicaragua, and El Salvador. Costa Rica later joined the common market. Additionally, the Caribbean Community and Common Market (CARICOM) was formed in 1973. This group includes many island nations in the Caribbean including Jamaica, the Bahamas, Saint Lucia, Belize, Haiti, and Trinidad and Tobago, to name just a few.

The most famous example of a common market is the *European Economic Area (EEA)*. This group

Table 6.1

Norway's Current Account Surplus
(US$ millions)

1998	1999	2000	2001	2002	2003
72	8,511	26,002	26,153	24,560	28,419

Source: World Trade Organization, "Trade Policy Review: Norway," September 2004. http://www.wto.org, accessed October 15, 2004.

includes the European Union plus Norway, Iceland, and Liechtenstein. The three countries outside of the European Union decided to keep the common market status that they had prior to increased integration experienced in the European Union in 1992. The common market status of the EEA allows these three countries to participate in the internal market of the European Union, but not in the full integration of the 25 nations that currently make up the European Union. One weakness of this approach for EEA members is that they must accept the regulations and laws of the European Union without influencing the vote in the European Parliament.

Each of the non-EU members of the EEA has its own economic reasons for not joining the European Union in its entirety. Norway and Iceland have historically depended on the fisheries industry and have objected to some of the provisions of the European Union's *common agricultural policy (CAP)*. While the fisheries industry represents less than 1 percent of Norway's GDP, it remains its most protected industry.[7] Additionally, Norway has a large current account surplus due in large part to the export of oil and gas. Norway's current account surplus has trended upward since 1998, as is shown in Table 6.1.

Since 1990, Norway has saved the surplus in its annual government accounts into the State Petroleum Fund. The existence of this fund may also shed some light on why Norway has thus far not

been interested in pursuing further European Union integration, as many citizens in Norway fear that this fund could be used to fund problem areas of other nations in an integrated Europe. The fund is projected to grow from its current level of 54 percent of GDP to about 90 percent by the end of 2010.[8]

Liechtenstein has not integrated further than the EEA with the European Union given the country's high level of integration with Switzerland. Liechtenstein has had a customs union with Switzerland since 1924, has the same currency as the Swiss, and relies on the Swiss for defense. Since the Swiss failed to ratify the EEA amendment in 1992, any further integration by Liechtenstein with the European Union has been stalled.

ECONOMIC UNION

The fourth level of economic integration, economic union, involves eliminating internal trade barriers, adopting common external trade policies, abolishing restrictions on the mobility of the factors of production, and coordinating economic activities. As discussed in Chapter 4, the European Union (EU) is the primary example of this form of integration. The original 15 EU member states agreed to coordinate their monetary, fiscal, taxation, and social welfare programs in an attempt to blend these formerly sovereign nations into a single economic entity. Nations such as Denmark have voiced their concern that the continued march toward economic integration is not palatable for a small country and have opted out of the European Monetary Union. Others such as Norway have opted to not officially join the European Union, as was just discussed. Chapter 4 itemizes the various methods used to converge the various member states into one economic entity. The European Central Bank (ECB) was created to serve as the central bank for all members of the European Monetary Union and is based in Brussels, Belgium. While the ECB formulates monetary policy for the European Union, the European Commission and the European Parliament are in charge of the European Union's fiscal policy. Managing the fiscal and monetary integration of the EU member states has proven to be challenging. How the European Union is able to handle either the defection of a large member state or the failure of a large member state to meet the annual economic convergence criteria will provide useful information as to the future success of the EU integration efforts.

POLITICAL UNION

The fifth and final level of economic integration is that of *political union*. This represents the complete political and economic integration of all member states, in essence making them one unified country. Many Euro-skeptics believe that this will be the eventual result of the integration process of the European Union, although it remains to be seen how successful the current level of economic integration will be over the long term. The primary example of a successful political union was the Articles of Confederation, which made the 13 separate colonies into the United States of America. The founding fathers of the United States assembled for the Second Continental Congress and agreed to the formation of the union in 1776, but it was not without compromise. The member states retained freedom in all matters that were not expressly delegated to the Congress, and the politically divisive issue of how to handle slavery was eliminated from the discussions so that the union could be formed expeditiously.[9]

ASSOCIATION OF SOUTH EAST ASIAN NATIONS

The Association of South East Asian Nations (ASEAN) was founded in 1967 by Singapore, Thailand, Malaysia, Indonesia, and the Philippines. Brunei joined the organization when it attained its independence in 1984. The association has been expanded over the years to include Cambodia, Laos, Vietnam, and Myanmar.

Over the past 20 years, ASEAN has made significant progress. Preferential trading arrangements have been established under which special, lower tariffs are levied on the import of goods from member states. Members have cooperated on the coordinated development of industry in the region through the industrial project scheme, whereby member states select a particular project for establishment in a country and in which every other member state holds equity. To counter the problem of food shortages in some parts of the region, member states have created the food security reserve scheme, under which a common stockpile of rice is maintained for supplementing the needs of any member country experiencing a shortfall.

Several other coordinated projects have proved that this regional arrangement has worked. An ASEAN finance corporation has been established to finance joint ventures, and agreements have been reached between central banks of member countries to reduce exchange-rate fluctuations and exchange imbalances by using currency exchange arrangements among themselves. ASEAN has fostered regional cooperation in other areas, such as projects for education, population control, and cultural exchanges among member states.

ASEAN has enabled the member states to represent their region as a collective body and improve their bargaining position with nonmember states, especially the industrialized countries. The aura of political stability and regional amity engendered by the body has also been a major factor in attracting overseas investment in several member countries. In recent years, the region has been one of the leading recipients of foreign direct investment, trailing only China and India.

Active cooperation between members is supported by a small secretariat located in Jakarta, Indonesia. Among the other notable achievements of ASEAN in the nearly four decades of its existence are:

- An emergency sharing scheme on crude oil and oil products
- Joint approaches to problems in international commodity trade
- A program for cooperation on the development and utilization of mineral resources
- A planning center for agricultural development
- A center for development of forest tree seeds
- A program for tourism cooperation
- A plant quarantine training center
- An agreement to align national standards with international standards (such as the International Organization for Standardization)

ASEAN has not been an unqualified success, however, and progress has been slow, particularly in coordinated industrial development, because of several constraints. The level of complementarity between the member states is low, and many of them have competitive economic structures, especially because industrial output in most countries tends to be quite similar. Unlike the members of the European Union, ASEAN members are under significant financial stress, and large resources have to be mobilized to fund their ambitious development programs and government expenditures. Because import duties comprise a major source of revenue for the ASEAN countries, tariffs can be reduced only to the extent that members are able to absorb the resulting revenue loss. The lack of financial resources also constrains the development of joint industrial projects. The issues of equitable distribution of benefits from jointly owned or jointly run projects and of tariff preferences are difficult to resolve, given their complex implications.

In 1992, the *ASEAN Free Trade Area (AFTA)* was established. The goal was to integrate the ASEAN economies into a single production base in order to create a regional market of 500 million people. This agreement requires that tariff rates levied on a wide range of products traded within the region be reduced to no more than 5 percent by 2008.[10] The free trade area covers all manufactured and agricultural products, but 1.09 percent of products are not included in the agreement. These are listed in the General Exception List and are typically excluded for reasons of national security and the protection of human, animal, or plant life and health, and in order to protect things of artistic, historic, or archeological value. The eventual goal of AFTA is the elimination of all import duties for the five original members of ASEAN by 2010, and by 2015 for the new members.

On balance, however, ASEAN has been a significant success. Trade among ASEAN countries has grown from US$44.2 billion in 1993 to US$95.2 billion in 2000. This represents an annual increase of 11.60 percent.[11] After a decline in total exports for the region in 2001 due to the economic slowdown of the United States, Europe, and Japan, ASEAN exports recovered in 2002 and 2003.[12] If a continued political will on the part of member countries to sustain the progress of cooperation is forthcoming, there is no doubt that the arrangement will bring greater economic and political coordination to the region, which has already emerged as an important economic zone, even by global standards. The leaders of ASEAN have begun negotiations with China in order to establish an ASEAN-China free trade area by 2010. This could increase ASEAN's exports to China by 48 percent, and China's exports to ASEAN by 55 percent. Similar discussions have also taken place with Japan, Korea, India, and Australia. The group is also interested in forging trade alliances outside of the Asia-Pacific region and has been discussing possible agreements with the European Union, the United States, and Canada as well.

ASIA-PACIFIC ECONOMIC COOPERATION FORUM

In response to the growing interdependence among the economies of the Asia-Pacific region, APEC was established in 1989. APEC, which now has 21 members, has become the primary regional vehicle for promoting open trade and economic cooperation. The goal of APEC is to advance Asia-Pacific economic dynamism and the sense of community among the member economies. The members of APEC, which include nations such as the ASEAN member countries, the member countries of NAF-TA, the People's Republic of China, the Republic of Korea, Peru, Russia, and New Zealand, total more than 2.5 billion people with a combined GDP of $19 trillion. The nations of APEC comprise 47 percent of world trade. To effectively promote the goals of the organization, a 10-year moratorium on new members to APEC was put in place in 1997.

In 1994, the leaders of APEC agreed on the future vision of APEC at their annual meeting in Bogor, Indonesia. The "Bogor Goals" include three areas of cooperation, which are known as the "three pillars" of APEC. The three key areas of cooperation are shown below:

1. Trade and investment liberalization
2. Business facilitation
3. Economic and technical cooperation

These goals would seem to be complimentary to those of the WTO. Unlike the WTO, APEC does not require any treaty obligations of its participants. APEC is the only intergovernmental group in the world that operates on the basis of nonbinding commitments, open dialogue, and the equal respect for the views of all participants.[13] The decisions made in APEC are reached via consensus, and the commitments are undertaken voluntarily by the member economies.

FINANCIAL ORGANIZATIONS

INTERNATIONAL MONETARY FUND

The role of the International Monetary Fund (IMF) as a supranational organization is discussed in considerable detail in Chapter 4. It is useful to recall, however, that the role of the IMF as a supranational organization has been expanding in recent years with its efforts to coordinate the response of the financial world to the debt crisis in Latin America during the 1980s as well as the financial crisis in Asia in the 1990s, and exert its own efforts in this regard. The other important role of the IMF is providing loans for structural adjustment in economies facing severe macroeconomic instability and distortions. There is an increasing emphasis on coordination of lending activities between the IMF and other supranational lenders, as well as on assessing the social impact of IMF programs for structural adjustment in developing countries.

WORLD BANK

The *World Bank* was created (along with the IMF) at the Bretton Woods Conference in New Hampshire in July 1944, and it officially came into existence on December 27, 1945. The initial objective of the World Bank was to make financial resources available to European countries to rebuild their war-shattered economies and later to provide critically needed external financing to developing countries at affordable rates of interest. The creation of the World Bank, together with the IMF, was also intended to strengthen the structure and encourage the development and efficiency of international financial markets. The World Bank consists of four main agencies:

1. International Bank for Reconstruction and Development (IBRD, generally known as the World Bank)

2. International Development Association (IDA)
3. International Finance Corporation (IFC)
4. Multilateral Investment Guarantee Agency (MIGA)

International Bank for Reconstruction and Development

The main objective of the World Bank today is to support social and economic progress in developing countries by promoting better productivity and utilization of resources so that their citizens may live better and fuller lives. The World Bank seeks to achieve its objectives by making financial assistance available to developing countries, especially for specific economically sound infrastructural projects, for example, in the areas of power and transport. The basic rationale for the emphasis on such projects is that a good infrastructure is necessary for the developing countries to carry out programs of social and economic development. In the 1970s World Bank loans were also given to promote the development of the social services sectors of borrowing countries: education, water supply and sanitation, urban housing, and so on. Loans were also provided for the development of indigenous energy resources, such as oil and natural gas. Since the early 1980s much World Bank lending has been policy based; that is, it has aimed to support economic adjustment measures by borrowing countries, particularly those faced with heavy external debt-service requirements. Policy-based lending, sector-policy lending, and structural-adjustment lending programs of the World Bank provide critically needed financial assistance to countries attempting to alter the current orientation of their economies to enhance productivity and efficiency in the allocation of resources, improving external competitiveness, reducing overburdening subsidies, and repairing other economic distortions that prevent a higher rate of growth and create macroeconomic instability.

Another important aspect of financial assistance provided by the World Bank is loan guarantees. The World Bank helps member developing countries to obtain increased access at better terms to international financial markets by guaranteeing repayment of loans. This form of assistance has been increasingly used to improve resource flows from private creditors to the highly indebted developing countries. The use of guarantees is also being considered by the World Bank in order to help member-country borrowers issue securities in the international financial markets.

World Bank Lending

There are five major categories of World Bank loans:

1. *Specific investment loans* are loans made for specific projects in the areas of agricultural and rural development, urban development, energy, and so on. They have a maturity ranging from 5 to 10 years.
2. *Sector operations loans* comprise about a third of the World Bank's lending and are aimed at financing development of particular sectors of a country's economy such as oil, energy, or agriculture. Loans under this category are also provided to the borrower's financial institutions, which then lend the funds to actual users in a particular sector of the economy.
3. *Structural adjustment and program loans* are targeted at providing the financial support needed by member countries that are undertaking comprehensive institutional and policy reforms to remove imbalances in the external sector. These loans, therefore, support entire programs of structural adjustment and are not specific to any particular project or sector of the economy.

4. ***Technical assistance loans*** are provided to member countries that need to strengthen their technical capacity to plan their development strategies and design and implement specific projects.

5. ***Emergency reconstruction loans*** are provided to member countries whose economies, especially the infrastructure, have experienced sudden and severe damage because of natural disasters, such as earthquakes or floods. The emphasis of these loans, apart from restoring the disrupted infrastructural facilities, is also on strengthening the capacity of borrower countries to handle future events of this type.

Since 1982 World Bank loans have been made at variable rates of interest that are adjusted twice a year and are based on a spread of 0.75 percent on the average cost of the outstanding borrowings of the bank.[14] Apart from interest, World Bank borrowers have to pay a front-end fee and a commitment fee on their borrowings. Repayment terms, including grace periods and final maturity, are determined on the basis of the per capita income of the borrowing country. Final maturity can range up to 20 years for countries with the lowest per capita income. In 2004, the World Bank loaned US$20.1 billion in support of 245 projects in 95 countries. The total outstanding loan commitments by the bank surpassed US$109 billion in 2004.[15]

Fund-Raising by the World Bank

The primary capital resources of the World Bank come from contributions made by its 184 member countries, but nearly all loan funds are raised by borrowings in international financial markets. The bank enjoys a credit rating of AAA in the world's financial markets, which enables it to obtain easy access to funds and excellent borrowing terms in its chosen markets. Funds borrowed by the bank had surpassed US$100 billion by the end of 2003. Bor-

rowings are made in a variety of major international currencies that reflect the nature of the bank's loan portfolio. Approximately 20 different currencies have been used by the bank to raise funds in the international markets. The World Bank typically borrows at variable interest rates, which are adjusted twice a year. Fixed-spread loans were introduced by the bank in 2000; these loans have a fixed spread over the *London Inter-Bank Offered Rate (LIBOR)* for the life of the loan.

The World Bank has played a pioneering role in the development of the currency swap market, whereby it improves its access and terms to preferred markets or adjusts its borrowing currency mix with the lending currency mix. The bank also uses *interest-rate swaps* to adjust mismatches in its borrowing and lending portfolios and improve the management of interest-rate risk.

The bank has made significant profits on its operations over the years, even though it charges a relatively low spread to its borrowers. As a matter of policy, all profits are transferred to the general reserve, which is maintained as a safeguard against the contingencies of loan or other financial losses.

Organizational Structure

Each World Bank member country subscribes to a certain proportion of the total paid-in capital of the bank. The subscription of each country differs and depends generally on its international economic importance. The member countries are, in effect, the shareholders of the bank and the ultimate guarantors of its financial obligations. The United States has the largest share of paid-in capital (28.9 percent) and is, therefore, the largest shareholder of the bank. Major industrialized countries, such as Japan, Germany, United Kingdom, and France, are among the other important shareholders.

The board of governors of the bank is the highest policy-making body, and each member state appoints one representative to the board, usually either its finance minister or the governor of its central bank. Each country also appoints an alternate member to the board of governors. The board of governors makes only major policy decisions about the functioning of the bank, such as capital increases, major changes in lending emphasis, and the creation of new affiliates, which are approved at its annual meetings.

Day-to-day administration of the bank's work is entrusted to the president of the bank, who is traditionally from the United States. The president is supported by a 24-member board of executive directors, who are appointed by member governments. The major industrial countries, Saudi Arabia, and China have their own executive directors, while other member states, with lesser shares, form regional groupings to appoint executive directors. The bank has four major administrative divisions:

- The *operations division*, which is essentially responsible for World Bank lending
- The *financial operations division*, which is responsible for raising and managing the financial resources of the bank
- The *policy, planning, and research division*, which is concerned with in-depth economic studies, analysis, and planning to support the objectives of the bank
- The *administration and personnel division*

World Bank headquarters are in Washington, DC, and there are regional representative offices in many developing countries. The World Bank's staff, which at the end of 2004 numbered 9,300, consists of personnel drawn from more than 100 nationalities and represents a wide variety of professional skills.

International Development Association

The *International Development Association (IDA)* was established in 1960 to provide long-term

funds at concessionary rates to the poorest member countries of the bank. This affiliate does not have a separate organizational structure, and its operations are conducted by the staff of the World Bank. The president of the World Bank is also the president of the IDA. The basic objective of the association is to provide long-term financing to those members who cannot afford to borrow on normal World Bank terms. IDA funds are used to promote long-term, long-gestation development projects. As of 2006, the IDA had 165 member nations.

As member countries grow economically and their per capita income increases beyond a particular level,[16] they graduate from IDA assistance and become eligible for World Bank loans under its various lending programs.

IDA loans have long maturities, sometimes as long as 40 years with a 10-year grace period for the repayment of principal. Historically, a nominal service charge of 0.75 percent per annum has been levied, and a commitment fee of 0.5 percent has been charged on approved but nondispersed credits. IDA funds are raised from member-country subscriptions, repayments of outstanding credits, and allocations from the income of the bank. IDA funds are periodically replenished by member countries.

In fiscal 2005, IDA provided US$8.7 billion in financing for 160 projects in 64 low-income countries. The five largest recipients of IDA credits are India, Vietnam, Bangladesh, Pakistan, and Ethiopia. Although in recent years IDA replenishments have led to a certain amount of debate on the amount of contributions to be made by the industrialized countries, there is no doubt that the role of the IDA is critical in providing sorely needed external assistance to many countries with large populations that are at the lowest rung of the global economic ladder.

International Finance Corporation

The *International Finance Corporation (IFC)* was established in 1956 with the objective of promoting the development of private enterprises in member countries. As of 2006, the IFC had 178 member nations. The IFC operates primarily through its own staff, but it is overseen by the World Bank's board of executive directors. The president of the World Bank is also the president of the IFC.

The IFC makes equity investments and extends loans to private enterprises in developing countries. In accordance with its mandate, the IFC cannot accept government guarantees of its loans. The primary role of the IFC, however, is not providing financial assistance alone. It serves as a catalyst to promote private capital flows to the private sector in developing countries. The IFC is never the sole financier in any particular transaction, and its contribution is usually a minor proportion of the total mobilized amount. The corporation also does not accept management positions or seats on the boards of directors of the organizations to which it lends funds. In addition, the IFC provides financial, technical, and legal advice to the companies in which it invests. Advisory services are also provided to companies who do not borrow directly from the IFC.

As a matter of policy, the IFC exits from companies in which it has invested as they develop and mature, usually selling its interests to local parties. The importance of the activities of the IFC has grown in recent years, with increasing emphasis on the development of the private sector by the industrialized countries and its growing acceptance by many developing countries, which are increasingly disillusioned by the lackluster performance of parastatal enterprises in their countries.

Apart from its traditional investment activities, the IFC has also played an important role in strengthening the financial infrastructure of developing countries through its capital markets department. The department provides needed technical and legal assistance to many developing countries to strengthen their financial markets. The IFC provides assistance in this area for such issues as framing legal statutes to regulate securities markets and the development of financial institutions, such as leasing companies, venture capital companies, commercial banks, credit-rating agencies, and export-import financing institutions.

The IFC also plays an important catalyzing role in setting up depository institutions; establishing trading, disclosure, and market practice standards; and directing external flows toward developing countries by helping to establish and develop capital markets and financial institutions and by participating in and promoting international investment efforts through pooled investment vehicles, such as country funds.

Although in the past the IFC had funded its investments from its own capital and borrowings from the World Bank, it has also raised substantial amounts on its own by directly borrowing in the international capital markets. The IFC is rated a AAA borrower by major U.S. credit-rating agencies.

Multilateral Investment Guarantee Agency

The Multilateral Investment Guarantee Agency (MIGA) was established in 1988 and currently has 167 members. Its main objective is to promote overseas direct investment flows into developing countries by providing guarantees against noncommercial risks that investors face in most economies. Noncommercial risks are generally risks arising out of political actions by most governments, such as confiscation, expropriation, and nationalization of the assets of the overseas enterprise. Other noncommercial risks covered by MIGA include risks arising out of such unforeseen circumstances as wars and civil disturbances.

The Future Role of the World Bank Group

The role of the World Bank group has constantly evolved ever since its inception. The next few decades pose several major challenges to the organization, as it pursues its fundamental objectives of improving the living standards of people in poor countries by catalyzing greater economic growth and sustainable development. In the past decade, the World Bank has had to deal with a whole new set of issues created by the Asian financial crisis and the flow of much-needed external capital to industrial countries instead of the developing world. Given the significant gaps in the demand and supply of external resources for the developing countries as a whole, the bank will have to make additional efforts to meet the enhanced requirements of its member countries. Further, it will be required to increasingly collaborate with other multilateral institutions, such as the IMF, on the important issue of providing economic and institutional resources to many developing countries with a view to improving their levels of productivity and efficiency. The bank may also increasingly adopt a regional approach to solving difficult problems that need a broader geographical approach than do specific country operations.

Along with the main objective of fighting poverty in many countries across the world, the World Bank is likely to pay increasing attention to the question of the fragile environment and the global ecosystems and their interrelationships with the consequences of development, particularly in the context of the environmental impact of bank-financed projects. Another new direction for the World Bank is the increasing association with the work of nongovernmental voluntary organizations in developing countries. The World Bank has become increasingly involved in the support of organizations such as the *International Centre for Settlement of Investment Disputes (ICSID)*, which has assisted in mediation or conciliation of over 160 investment disputes between governments and private foreign investors since its inception in 1966. The number of cases submitted to this organization has increased in recent years; the group saw 30 cases in 2004 alone.

Internally, there is likely to be an ever-greater need for political and financial support to the bank from member governments, especially those of the industrialized countries.

INTER-AMERICAN DEVELOPMENT BANK

The *Inter-American Development Bank (IADB)* was established in 1959 with the primary objective of promoting social and economic development in Latin America. The bank, headquartered in Washington, DC, has 46 member countries, including 20 that only provide capital and have voting representation, which are known as nonborrowing members.

The main operations of the IADB are focused on providing long-term public financing to member countries. The main areas for which loans are extended include agriculture and rural development, transport, communications, and mining. Since the onset of the debt crisis in the 1980s in Latin America, the IADB has adopted special lending programs that aim to direct financing where it is most urgently needed. Loans are made on a project basis, with proposals being initiated by borrowing countries and examined and approved by the bank. The bank also provides technical assistance to the member countries for the preparation of project proposals and their implementation.

Unlike the World Bank, the IADB obtains a significant portion of its funding from member contributions to the paid-in capital of the bank. The United States has the largest contribution of paid-in capital (30 percent), followed by Brazil and Argentina. Loans are made only to Latin American and Caribbean countries, however, and only to governments. In 2005, the bank made over US$7 billion in loans to 26 countries in Latin America and the Caribbean. The announced policy of the IADB is to stop lending to a country whose account falls in arrears. In recent years the IADB has borrowed substantial funds in the international financial markets to supplement its resources for financing development in member countries. It continues to be well regarded in the international capital markets, despite the debt crisis faced by many of its member nations in the 1980s.

The role of the bank has been expanded to undertake financing of social projects, such as health, education, and rural development. Moreover, the smaller and economically weaker countries of Latin America have been given the highest priority in the extension of loans. Loans typically have a maturity period of between 30 and 40 years. In addition, the IADB assists member states in mobilizing resources in their internal markets, especially through cofinancing arrangements.

ASIAN DEVELOPMENT BANK

The *Asian Development Bank (ADB)* was founded in 1966 with the objective of promoting economic growth and cooperation in Asia and the Far East, including the South Pacific region. Although membership is primarily concentrated among countries of the region, major industrialized countries, such as Japan, the United States, Canada, and Germany, are also members in the capacity of donors. The bank currently has 64 member nations. Traditionally, the president of the bank has been Japanese. Indonesia has been the largest borrower from the bank historically, but India and China were granted the most loans in 2004, taking up 48 percent of the total for the year. The ADB approved 80 loans totaling US$5.3 billion in 2004, for the purposes of 64 projects.[17]

The ADB provides different types of financial and technical assistance to member countries in the region, including guarantees, investment loans, and direct technical assistance. The important areas that receive ADB assistance are agriculture, industry, energy development, transport and communications, development of finance institutions, water supply, sanitation, and urban development.

Most ADB loans are long-term, and maturities range from 10 to 30 years. Loans carry a fixed rate of interest that varies according to the prevailing rates in the international financial markets at the time of the extension of the loan, although in recent years the ADB has also started to lend at variable rates, like the World Bank. Repayment and grace periods vary, depending on the per capita income of the borrowing country. Grace periods range from two to seven years.

The ADB has a *soft-loans* facility known as the Asian Development Fund, in which concessional terms are granted to borrowing countries. This facility is funded by member-country contributions. Loans from this facility are provided free of commitment fees and require a nominal service charge of 1 percent per annum.[18] Repayments are spread over a 32-year period, including a grace period of eight years.

AFRICAN DEVELOPMENT BANK

The *African Development Bank (AfDB)* was established in 1963 with the primary objective of accelerating the development process and improving socioeconomic conditions in the newly independent countries of Africa. The bank is headquartered in Abidjan, Ivory Coast. An important characteristic of the AfDB is its strong emphasis on maintaining its fundamentally African character and orientation. In fact, until 1982 non-African countries were not permitted to become members of the bank. Non-African countries are now allowed to become members only with certain specific safeguards aimed at preserving the unique African orientation and identity of the bank. Currently, the bank has 53 members from Africa and 24 non-African members, including the United States, Canada, France, China, and the United Kingdom. The bank is organized into three different affiliates, the largest entity being the bank itself, which lends to the more economically advanced member states and charges rates of interest at a spread over the cost of its own borrowed funds. The second affiliate is a soft-loan window, known as the African Development Fund (ADF), which channels concessional assistance to poorer member countries. There is no interest on this assistance, and historically there has been only a nominal service charge of 0.75 percent per year. The ADF receives its resources from the non-African countries, including several industrialized countries. The third affiliate is the Nigeria Trust Fund (NTF), which lends funds at rates and maturities that are between those charged by the AfDB and those charged by the ADF. The NTF, set up in 1976, is funded entirely by the Nigerian government. The bank raises its resources from paid-in capital by member countries, concessional loans from governments of industrialized countries, and, more recently, significant borrowings in the international financial markets that have been supported by the excellent credit ratings earned by the bank from major U.S. credit-rating agencies.

The AfDB's strategic plan for the years 2003–2007 included some new methods for reducing the level of poverty on the continent, and ways of improving the governance, environmental protection, and treatment of women in Africa. This included the creation of the Central Micro-finance Unit. Micro-finance, or lending small amounts to the poorest individuals on an unsecured basis for the creation of small businesses, has been successful in other areas of the world and is seen as an avenue of great opportunity for improvement in Africa.

EUROPEAN INVESTMENT BANK

The *European Investment Bank (EIB)* was established in 1957 by the Treaty of Rome, in conjunction with the creation of the European Economic Community. Although the bank is a separate legal entity, it is intimately connected with current EU activities and pursues four objectives:[19]

- Regional development and economic and social cohesion within the European Union
- Environmental protection and improving the quality of life in the region
- Preparing the accession countries for EU membership
- Community development aid and cooperation policy among member countries

The EIB attempts to implement these objectives by promoting funds for investment in projects that serve these ends. The EIB raises its resources both from paid-in subscriptions by member states and from borrowings in the international markets. Loans are made to finance projects in individual member countries and projects that serve the interest of the community as a whole, for example, projects to develop energy resources or infrastructural facilities that benefit all member states.

Germany, France, Italy, and the United Kingdom are the four largest shareholders of the EIB, and all EU member nations are also members of the EIB. Many of the EIB lending operations are for long-term loans at fixed rates of interest, with maturities varying from 7 to 20 years. The bank is operated on a purely nonprofit basis, although it does generate income internally to meet its operating expenses and to build up a general reserve, which is prescribed as being equal to 10 percent of its subscribed capital.

Another important feature of the EIB is its policy to lend to developing countries that are not members of the European Union. For example, the EIB recently approved a loan to Mexico for the expansion and modernization of a Volkswagen production facility in Puebla, Mexico. Although such lending has fluctuated in recent years, significant amounts have been channeled to developing countries by the bank over the past two decades.

Support to developing countries is complemented by the operations of the European Development Fund (EDF), which is funded out of allocations made from the budgetary resources of the European Union.

JAPAN BANK FOR INTERNATIONAL COOPERATION

Formerly known as the Overseas Economic Co-operation Fund, the *Japan Bank for International Cooperation (JBIC)* is a development bank established and funded by the government of Japan, with the objective of providing financial assistance to developing countries. Although JBIC assistance is provided to developing countries across the world, the main recipients have been Asian countries. Most of the assistance is on concessional terms. Borrowers are usually required to bid for the assistance in terms of the interest rates they are willing to pay. Given the recession in Japan over the past few years, the expansion of the JBIC has not been as significant as expected, but the bank is still a viable source of financing for development projects for Asia.

EUROPEAN BANK FOR RECONSTRUCTION AND DEVELOPMENT

The *European Bank for Reconstruction and Development (EBRD)* was established in 1991 to promote development in eastern and central Europe following the collapse of communism. The bank uses investment and influence to transition formerly centrally planned economies to market-based democratic systems. In 2004, the EBRD invested €4.1billion in 129 projects in 27 countries. The bank is headquartered in London and is owned by 60 countries worldwide, the European Investment Bank, and the European Union. Some examples of EBRD loans include funds for the improvement of the national railway system in Poland, and a loan to the Riga Water Company in Latvia for the purposes of improving municipal water and wastewater sys-

tems.[20] Other loan purposes include environmental improvement associated with the operations of the Hungarian oil and gas firm MOL, and a loan to the Serbia and Montenegro pharmaceutical company Hemopharm in order to improve its efficiency in producing non-brand-name drugs.

SUMMARY

The increasing interdependence of the nations of the world has increased the need to coordinate international actions and policies. Since World War II, permanent international institutions, or supranational organizations, have been formed to serve the vital role of providing economic stability and continuity in the world economy. Some institutions have a global focus, while others are designed to meet more specific regional needs.

The General Agreement on Tariffs and Trade, charged with liberalizing international trade restrictions, offers the most-favored-nation clause to member organizations. Eight rounds of GATT meetings were held, resulting in significant reductions in tariffs on industrial products. After the creation of the World Trade Organization in 1995, the Doha round focused on the improvement of the economic performance of the developing countries. The GATT and WTO rounds highlight the differences in perspective that exist between developed and developing countries, as negotiators attempt to establish a coordinated, nonprotectionist global trade policy that serves the common interests of all parties.

In contrast to the WTO, the United Nations Conference on Trade and Development is a forum for developing countries to communicate their international trade perspectives as a group to the industrialized countries. Although limited in impact, UNCTAD has served to improve the dialogue between the developing and developed countries.

Groups such as the European Union, ASEAN, and the Andean Community have been established to coordinate regional trade policy, with the European Union and ASEAN being the most successful. There are five different levels of economic integration: free trade area, customs union, common market, economic union, and political union.

The IMF and the World Bank are international lending institutions, each performing specialized roles in the international monetary system. While the IMF focuses primarily on lending for structural adjustments because of balance of payments problems, the World Bank, comprised of four main agencies (IBRD, IDA, IFC, and MIGA), provides external financing to developing countries at affordable rates of interest. The IBRD's main objective is to support social and economic progress in developing countries and offers five major types of loans: specific investment loans, sector operations loans, structural adjustment and program loans, technical assistance loans, and emergency reconstruction loans. The IDA provides long-term funds (loans with maturities of 50 years with 10-year grace periods) to the poorest member countries in order to promote long-term development projects. The IFC promotes the development of private enterprises by making equity investments and providing loans. Operating as a catalyst, the IFC exits from the enterprise as it develops and matures. MIGA promotes overseas direct investment in developing countries by providing guarantees against noncommercial risks.

Other development banks, such as the IADB, the ADB, and the AfDB, have been formed to provide regional assistance in the Western Hemisphere, Asia, and Africa, respectively. The European Investment Bank and the European Bank for Reconstruction and Development promote investments in the European Union and in eastern Europe, while the JBIC, established and funded by Japan, is a viable source of financing for third world developing-country projects.

DISCUSSION QUESTIONS

1. Discuss the WTO and its role in international trade.
2. What is the most-favored-nation clause?
3. What trading organization represents the international trade objectives of developing countries? How do the concerns of developing countries differ from those of the industrialized, developed countries?
4. What is a regional trade group? What are the advantages provided by these groups?
5. Describe the structure at the World Bank and the services of its four main agencies.
6. What types of loans does the World Bank provide? How are these different from loans provided by the IMF?
7. What will the role of the World Bank be in the future?
8. Identify three regional financial institutions and outline their financial services.

NOTES

1. The ninth round, the Doha Development Agenda, was undertaken under the auspices of the World Trade Organization.
2. World Trade Organization, "Understanding the WTO."
3. There have been some temporary exemptions in cases in which preferential agreements had been signed prior to GATS. These exemptions cannot last longer than 10 years, and new exemptions cannot be added or extended.
4. Specific forms of intellectual property are discussed further in Chapter 8.
5. The least-developed countries were provided an extension until 2016 for conforming with TRIPS (primarily for pharmaceutical patents).
6. In fact, the name "Mercosur" implies the eventual goal. It stands for Mercado Común del Sur, or "Common Market of the South."
7. World Trade Organization, "Trade Policy Review: Norway."
8. Ibid.
9. Ellis, *Founding Brothers.*
10. Association of South East Asian Nations, "Southeast Asia: A Free Trade Area."

11. Ibid. Prior to the Asian Financial Crisis, growth in the region was increasing by 29.6 percent annually.

12. Association of South East Asian Nations, *ASEAN Annual Report 2003–4.*

13. APEC.

14. Prior to July 31, 1998, the spread was 0.50 percent.

15. World Bank, *Annual Report 2004.*

16. In fiscal 2004, countries with annual per capita GNI of up to $865 were eligible for IDA assistance.

17. Asian Development Bank.

18. This charge is effective during the grace period, the interest moves to 1.5 percent during the amortization period as of December 1998.

19. European Investment Bank.

20. European Bank for Reconstruction and Development.

BIBLIOGRAPHY

African Development Bank. "Strategic Plan 2003–2007." http://www.afdb.org/en/publications/new_titles/adb_strategic_plan, accessed October 15, 2004.

Asia-Pacific Economic Cooperation. http://www.apec.org.

Association of South East Asian Nations (ASEAN). Secretariat. http://www.aseansec.org.

———. *Annual Report 2003–4.*, Chapter 2, "Economic Integration and Cooperation."

———. "Southeast Asia: A Free Trade Area.," Brochure. http://www.aseansec.org.

Asian Development Bank. http://www.adb.org. Accessed October 15, 2004. http://www.iadb.org. Accessed on April 7, 2006.

Ellis, Joseph J. *Founding Brothers: The Revolutionary Generation.* New York: Vintage, 2002.

European Bank for Reconstruction and Development. Brochure.http://www.ebrd.com/pubs/general/6388a.pdf, accessed April 7, 2006.

European Investment Bank. http://www.eig.org.

Inter-American Development Bank, Annual Report 2005, http://www.iadb.org/exr/ar2005, accessed April 7, 2006.

World Bank. *Annual Report, 2004.*

World Trade Organization. "Trade Policy Review: Norway.," September 2004.

———. "Understanding the WTO." Brochure. http://www.wto.org.

PART III

ENVIRONMENTAL
CONSTRAINTS
IN INTERNATIONAL BUSINESS

CHAPTER 7

Analyzing National Economies

CHAPTER OBJECTIVES

This chapter will:

- Describe the importance of national economic analysis and identify the major indicators used in this analysis.
- Describe the sources of data and research tools that can be incorporated in national economic analysis.
- Discuss the results of analysis as inputs to developing an international marketing strategy.

THE PURPOSE AND METHODOLOGY OF COUNTRY ANALYSIS

Targeting a new country either as a market or as a manufacturing location must be preceded by a detailed analysis of the country's past, present, and future economic situation. This analysis is extremely important for a multinational corporation, because the nature and state of an economy's development are crucial factors in determining a country's suitability as a new market or manufacturing location. Emerging trends also must be analyzed to develop an estimate of how the corporation should respond.

Country analysis takes many forms, depending on the type of information sought, the objectives, the required depth and detail, the time frame being considered, and so on. In general, four broad categories serve as starting points:

1. Leading economic indicators at a particular point in time
2. Trends in different economic indicators
3. Trends in various specific sectors
4. Analysis of specific areas or sectors of the economy

The methodology for analysis of a country's economic prospects and its potential varies according to the purpose of the analysis and the MNC's situation. If the MNC has a local subsidiary in the country and the object of the analysis is to plan for further expansion or diversification into new industries, a two-tier analysis is carried out. At the first tier, the local subsidiary gathers and processes all the available local data and passes on the resulting information, along with its own assessment of the situation and prospects, to the home office abroad. The home office, which is the second tier, then examines the information and the subsidiary's recommendation and makes its own assessment, keeping in mind its global corporate and strategic goals, as well as the opportunities and constraints available worldwide. The management of the local subsidiary is often closely consulted while the home office views are being formulated, because some strategic considerations may not be put on paper for security and confidentiality reasons. The home office usually has an independent economic research division or economic analysts to generate independent information that is compared with and used to support or contest that supplied by the subsidiary.

If a country is totally new to an MNC, the methodology is different. Some corporations hire consultants who are experts on a particular country to do a comprehensive economic analysis. Information is also gleaned from the materials available publicly, such as government publications, country studies, commercial publications, and so on. Local consultants are sometimes employed by MNCs because of their deeper understanding of the local environment and better access to relevant information. Another option is the use of international consultants who utilize local associates. The local associates provide vital contacts and sources of information, while the international consultants integrate and analyze the data and prepare the formal report on the country being studied.

PRELIMINARY ECONOMIC INDICATORS

Regardless of the methodology employed by the MNC in its economic analysis of a country's potential as a location for industrial production or as a market for its products or services, there are certain general economic criteria that are almost invariably considered. A discussion of the more important of these criteria follows.

SIZE OF THE ECONOMY

The size of the economy is a basic measure of a country's potential as a market for an MNC's products. It is generally measured by the gross national income, which is the sum total of goods and services produced in an economy, including the net transactions it has with the external (foreign) sector. The GNI is an important measure because it shows the total level of economic activity in a country. An alternative measure is the *gross domestic product (GDP)*, which indicates the gross amount of goods and services produced within the country. The GDP does not take into account the contribution of the external sector to the economy.

INCOME LEVELS

Income levels of the citizens of a country are a very important economic indicator for an MNC. To a significant extent, the prevailing income levels influence the nature of the potential a country offers as a market for different types of goods. The broadest measure of the income levels enjoyed by a population is per capita GNI. Per capita GNI is determined by dividing the total GNI by the total population.

Per capita GNI varies greatly from country to country. Industrialized countries that have a high gross national product and relatively small populations tend to have a high per capita GNI. On the other hand, less-developed countries have a low GNI but relatively larger populations, which results in a very low per capita GNI.

The World Bank has formulated four categories of countries based on their per capita GNI:

1. *Low-income* countries, with a per capita GNI of US$765 or less
2. *Lower-middle-income* developing countries, with a per capita GNI between US$765 and US$3,035
3. *Upper-middle-income* countries, with a per capita GNI between US$3,036 and US$9,385
4. *Developed* countries, with a per capita GNI exceeding US$9,386

Countries with a low per capita GNI would not have a very large potential as a market for such goods as automobiles and air conditioners, which are considered necessities in developed countries but are luxuries in developing countries. On the other hand, countries with a low per capita income are likely to have lower labor costs and could prove attractive to MNCs as sites for manufacturing facilities.

INCOME DISTRIBUTION

Although the per capita GNI statistics provide a broad indication of the income levels of different countries of the world, this information is by no means adequate for assessment of a country as a potential market. GNI per capita is actually a very broad measure that does not take into account the distribution of income within a country. Moreover, it provides no information on the size of market segments that would be potential targets for an MNC marketing effort. For example, a small country such as Kuwait has a very large per capita GNI because of a high GNI and a very small population, but it is not a very large market for automobiles because of the limited number of people who would purchase autos. On the other hand, a very low per capita GNI of a country might mask the significant purchasing power of a particular segment of its citizens.

In most developing countries there are sharp inequalities of wealth, and a large percentage of the country's total wealth is concentrated in the hands of a fairly small percentage of the population. This segment has significant purchasing power and offers considerable potential for different types of goods and services marketed by MNCs. This situation is particularly true in countries where the low per capita GNI occurs because of a very large low-income population. Thus, a country may have a large GNI, but its per capita GNI is low because of its large population.

In countries where there is substantial purchasing power in the hands of a small percentage of the population, it should be kept in mind that the absolute size of this wealthy segment may be considerable because it is a percentage of a very large absolute number. Thus, if a country has a population of 400 million and only 5 percent of its citizens are wealthy enough to qualify as a potential market segment for an MNC, the total market would still be 20 million people, which is the size of the entire population of some industrialized countries.

The degree of income distribution also provides other important clues to the economy in general and different market segments within it in particular. A more even income distribution would generally be found in the developed or industrialized countries, which would offer large potential for standardized mass-consumption products. The size of the very-high-income group in the total population would reveal the country's potential as a market for luxury goods, such as designer clothes and accessories, luxury automobiles, and so on.

Less-developed countries would show a very large percentage of very-low-income groups that usually would not offer an immediate market for most products promoted by MNCs. The size of the wealthy segments, on the other hand, would be a factor in determining the market size.

Another important indicator of market potential is the size of the middle-income groups within the overall income distribution. In the developed countries, the middle-income groups are usually the largest proportion of the population, which implies the existence of big markets for a wide range of mass-produced consumer products. The middle class is relatively small in most less-developed economies, which limits their potential as a market for a wide variety of consumer goods.

Trends and income distributions tend to move relatively slowly because they reflect basic socio-economic structures and patterns that are fairly resistant to change. In less-developed countries, however, these patterns have been changing at a relatively rapid pace over the past four or five decades. An important trend has been the emergence of a large middle class with substantial purchasing power and a positive attitude toward utilizing that power for the purchase of consumer goods.

PERSONAL CONSUMPTION

In addition to the income distribution patterns prevalent in a country, the prevailing consumption patterns influence a country's potential as a market. While income distribution statistics provide information on how and to whom income accrues, data on personal consumption indicate how this income is spent on goods and services. Personal-consumption data indicate the buying habits of the citizens of a particular country: what they buy, in what quantities, in which parts of a country, and so on. This information is vital for an MNC because it indicates patterns of consumer behavior and therefore sets parameters for marketing efforts. Thus, a country where the consumers spend a large proportion of their income on food and shelter offers no potential market for luxury goods such as VCRs. On the other hand, the same country may provide markets for inexpensive goods that meet the basic necessities of life. Although characterized by low consumption levels, a country may have substantial market segments comprised of persons with considerable discretionary income. Many MNCs develop marketing strategies on the basis of consumption patterns. Thus, patterns of consumption give important clues to an MNC regarding the possibilities for marketing different types of goods in a particular country.

GROWTH AND STABILITY PATTERNS

The size of the economy, income levels and distribution, and personal consumption are static indicators, inasmuch as they represent the position of a country at a particular point in time. An MNC contemplat-

ing long-term involvement in a country either as an exporter to that country or as a direct investor must also concern itself with a country's prior, current, and projected economic trends.

The growth rate of a country's economy, for example, must be watched carefully. Past growth trends show how the economy has been moving and the rate at which it is contracting or expanding. Projected growth rates indicate how it may do in the future. The growth trends generally have a direct relation to the market size for different products and services in a country. A faster growth rate would indicate more rapid industrial development.

Countries that seek rapid rates of growth aim to achieve this largely through an increase in the level of their industrialization and modernization of existing industries by the introduction of modern technologies and new industries. Such countries are likely to welcome MNCs as direct investors in production facilities. Moreover, countries that have achieved a rapid growth rate over the past few years are usually the ones that have opened up their economies to external technologies, have pushed their export efforts, and have increased the competitiveness and efficiency of their domestic economies. Such countries are likely to prove to be potential winners as markets for MNCs because they would be expected to have increased levels of income.

Rapidly growing economies are also characterized by the development of a professional middle class, which evens out the distribution of income relative to that in previous years and provides a market base for an MNC's consumer products.

Growing economies also offer enhanced markets for capital goods, technology, and related services. Therefore, MNCs closely monitor future growth trends to identify potential countries for export marketing and direct investment activities. The absolute growth rate and the growth rate per capita are related in this context. The absolute growth rate indicates the overall level of economic activity and gives the broadest indication of its enhancement to a country's market potential. Growth rate per capita indicates achievement not only on the economic front but also, indirectly, on the population front. If the growth per capita is rapid, the country can be considered to have surmounted one of the most important economic problems that afflict most developing countries: overpopulation.

Actually, per capita GNI is also an important indicator because of its future implications. A higher per capita GNI would imply an increased availability of resources to invest that could be further deployed for accelerating economic growth and improving the living standards of the population, which would represent a real change in the economic profile of the country as a market for goods and services and as a location for overseas production. If the growth rate is matched or exceeded by the population growth, the economic benefits of progress would be lost.

POPULATION

The population of a country represents an important economic statistic. It is an important factor in influencing the size of market potential for a large number of goods and services, especially goods for personal consumption.

Population density (the number of persons living per square mile) is a particularly relevant factor. A high population density could have both negative and positive implications. On one hand, it may imply overcrowding, overpopulation, and pressure on the resource base of a country. On the other hand, it may also imply reduced transportation costs in marketing products, availability of large numbers of consumers, and an easily accessible pool of labor.

Geographical distribution of the population is also important. Areas of high population concentration within a country generally offer wider market potential and greater possibilities of servicing the labor requirements for an overseas manufacturing facility.

The educational level of the population is also extremely important. Consumption patterns, living standards, and so on vary considerably with level of literacy. A country with a high level of literacy is likely to offer greater potential for an MNC's products because individuals are likely to have a broader outlook on the types of products they consume and would, in general, be willing to accept new products and services that an MNC might offer. For some types of products (books and other intellectual media, software, and so on), literacy levels are critical factors. Moreover, they also determine what sort of advertising strategy the MNC should pursue to promote its products locally. Literacy levels also indicate the potential of finding local skilled labor and local managers for a company's operations.

In general, literacy levels directly correlate with levels of per capita income. While developed countries have high literacy levels, ranging from 95 percent to 100 percent, less-developed countries have levels that range from 5 percent to 40 percent.

The rate of population growth is another trend worth watching. A growing population indicates an expanding market in countries where the density of population is low and per capita incomes are rising. A high population growth rate in countries already overpopulated indicates growing economic difficulties that could be manifested in severe shortages of available resources, heavy pressures on the infrastructure and services system of a country, fiscal difficulties for the government, shortages of capital for investments, increasing numbers of people living in poverty, and ever-increasing prices.

The age structure of a population should also be considered. In developed countries, larger proportions of the population tend to be over the age of eighteen, and there are a sizable number of people in the over-sixty age-group. Less-developed countries, however, are characterized by fairly young populations, where persons younger than eighteen are the dominant segment. Relatively young populations imply possibilities for higher population growth over the next few years, particularly in countries where birth control is not practiced widely. Moreover, such countries are also characterized by high dependency burdens, where the income-earning members of the population have to support a large number of nonearning members on a per capita basis. Dependency burdens have important economic implications, inasmuch as they affect the amount of discretionary income people may or may not have after taking care of the essential needs of their dependents and themselves. Most countries with high dependency burdens have lower levels of discretionary income, which limits their potential as markets for an MNC's products.

SECTOR ANALYSIS

It is also important to analyze different sectors of the country's economy, to identify the particular areas that could offer business opportunities. The state of development of a particular sector of the economy can provide clues to its product needs and the possibilities of providing necessary imports and support for the establishment of a manufacturing operation by an overseas corporation. For example, an MNC contemplating the establishment of an automobile plant in a developing country would have to assess the engineering sector in general and the automotive industry in particular, to determine the degree and availability of local support by way of ancillary and spare parts manufacturers, skilled labor, and locally trained production personnel.

On a broader level, sector analysis suggests the state of a country's overall economic development. From a macroeconomic standpoint, economic activity is divided into three broad categories: the primary, secondary, and tertiary sectors.

The *primary sector* incorporates traditional economic activities, such as agriculture. The *secondary sector* comprises primarily manufacturing and industrial activity. The *tertiary sector* refers to services and related industries.

Industrialized and developed countries are characterized by a high proportion of their economic activity in the secondary and tertiary sectors. For example, in 2002 agriculture contributed less than 2 percent of the GNI of the United States, Great Britain, Sweden, and Switzerland, and contributed only 2.5 percent of the GNI of Canada. In contrast, the contribution of agriculture to the GNI of developing countries was extremely high, for example, 40 percent for Nepal, 41 percent for Ethiopia, and 37 percent for Malawi.[1] A high concentration of economic activity in agriculture implies that the country is overdependent on one type of economic activity, has little industrial development, and is likely to have low levels of per capita income, relatively high rates of unemployment, and an unsteady economic performance. For an MNC, such data suggest that these countries do not offer good potential for expensive products but may prove reasonably good locations for setting up processing plants for raw materials and agricultural produce, because costs of material inputs and labor would be quite low. On the other hand, they may lack the infrastructural facilities required for large-scale industrial plants.

A highly developed country would have its economy dominated by the industrial and services sector. For an MNC, this economy would provide opportunities to market a wide range of industrial products and allow the establishment of almost any type of manufacturing operation. At the same time, such economies are likely to be characterized by strong competition from both domestic and international corporations.

INFLATIONARY TRENDS

Local inflationary trends must also be closely watched. *Inflation* is the increase in prices over time measured against a certain benchmark, usually known as the base year. Different indices, consisting of different commodities at different market levels, are constructed to gauge the overall degree of price increases in a country. High inflation can have severe economic consequences. Generally, income levels do not keep pace with inflation, which reduces the purchasing power of consumers and erodes their potential as a market segment, especially for products that have relatively high income elasticities, such as nonessential goods and services. High inflation would also have severe implications for local manufacturing operations, because prices of inputs would increase and pressures would rise to increase wage levels.

Increased inflation in a particular overseas manufacturing location would also have serious effects on the competitiveness of the products produced in that location if they were to be exported to overseas markets. Moreover, in real terms, local inflation would devalue the local currency against the MNC's home currency (if the local rate of inflation exceeds that prevailing in the MNC's home country). As a result, the value of the profits to be repatriated to the home country would go down in home currency terms. High inflation in overseas locations also could prompt restrictive measures by the government, which could result in hampered operations of the MNC or erosion of their profitability.

In recent years, especially in the 1980s and 1990s, many countries have experienced *hyperinflation*, a situation in which inflation occurs in hundreds of percent or even thousands of percent per year. A number of Latin American countries, such as Brazil, Argentina, and Bolivia, have experienced hyperinflation. More recent examples include countries such as Zimbabwe, where recent inflation levels hit 600 percent during 2004.[2] In such situations, MNCs have to be extremely cautious in initiating new ventures and managing existing ones in order to avoid losing their profits.

EXTERNAL FINANCIAL POSITION: EXTENT OF DEBT

The external financial sector of a country is another extremely important variable that has to be considered very carefully by MNCs while they are evaluating the country as a site for potential investment or marketing efforts.

The primary indicator of the strength of a country's external sector is its balance of payments position. The balance of payments (BOP), as was discussed in Chapter 4, is an annual record of all the external transactions of a country. A strong BOP position implies that a country can meet its external obligations. Such countries are ideally suited for investment by MNCs. They are not likely to have substantial import controls, because they are in a position to pay for imports with their current earnings of foreign exchange. A strong BOP position is also likely to foster a lenient policy toward foreign direct investment, because the country is able to generate the necessary foreign currency resources to permit conversion of local currencies into foreign currencies for repatriation of MNC profits.

A country facing BOP difficulties, in contrast, is likely to impose restrictions on imports in order to conserve foreign exchange resources. In such countries the chances of greater restrictions on repatriation of profits by MNCs could also be high. As a result, an MNC may find it more difficult to do business there.

Analysis of current and future trends is perhaps more important in this area than in any other, as the balance of payments scenario changes quite rapidly. All too often a country that had an excellent BOP position and was encouraging foreign investment and imports has its external position deteriorate within a few years to such an extent that it is compelled to clamp down on imports and restrict foreign investment. Obviously, plans of many MNCs involved in such countries would be completely upset by such a policy reversal. It is therefore extremely important that an MNC keep an ongoing watch on the emerging trends in the BOP and make timely adjustments if the MNC foresees major changes in this area.

The volatility of the BOP of a country is generally higher if the composition of its exports is not diversified. It is imperative that the composition of exports of the potential investee country be analyzed closely. Countries that depend on the exports of one commodity are generally prone to greater instability in their export revenues, because a decline in the prices and demand for that commodity in the international markets could jeopardize the whole BOP. This situation occurred in oil-exporting countries such as Mexico and Venezuela when oil prices dropped steeply in the early 1980s. Over the last decade, this problem has also hindered the development efforts of the African nation of Ghana, which has attempted to diversify its export base away from cocoa, timber, and gold but has experienced BOP problems over this same time period.

EXCHANGE-RATE LEVELS AND POLICIES

Exchange-rate trends are another vital consideration for MNCs contemplating overseas direct investment. An appreciation of the exchange rates in the country under consideration would increase the home currency value of the revenues generated in that country by the MNC. In contrast, a depreciation of the currency of the investee country would have the opposite effect. The MNC must carefully monitor the direction of the future movements of exchange rates, but forecasting exchange rates is an extremely difficult proposition because a large number of factors are involved. For many countries, however, an estimate of the future trends can be attempted on the basis of such economic fundamentals as BOP prospects, import and export trends, levels of overseas borrowings, debt service burden, local trends, and trends in inflation.

In many countries, especially LDCs, exchange rates are controlled and administered by authorities under various types of official arrangements. While some countries allow free conversion of their currency to other nations' currencies, others have their rates determined on the basis of a currency basket (see Chapter 4). Many countries also have dual or multiple exchange rates that are prescribed according to the type of transaction. Some countries also have different rates for repatriating profits out of the country. MNCs must be very careful in evaluating the exchange-rate arrangements and regulations of the potential investee country and should assess how they are likely to impact the translation of revenues from the local currency to the home currency.

Many countries also follow preset exchange-rate policies that, by administrative actions, are aimed to bring the exchange rate to the level desired by the monetary authorities. On other occasions, the policy could maintain the exchange rate within a certain bandwidth. For example, the Chinese government has purchased large amounts of U.S. dollars in the effort to keep the yuan floating within a narrow band relative to the dollar in recent years.[3] Policies to attain exchange-rate objectives may or may not be announced. When they are not announced, they must be estimated and appropriate action taken. The MNC must seek the assistance of its own or external experts to gauge the policy direction from the prevailing trends over a certain time period.

BANKING AND FINANCIAL MARKETS

Finance is a crucial resource to any business operation, and MNCs must carefully evaluate the banking and financial market structure of the target country. The banking sector must be well developed and able to provide the needed working capital and term financing for meeting the MNC's operational requirements within the investee country. Moreover, the financial market structure must provide opportunities for raising funds to meet the cost of operations. The MNC must also evaluate the costs of funds in local markets and assess whether it would be cheaper to raise funds locally or to bring them in from abroad. The host country, however, may have regulations that prohibit, restrict, or require the sourcing of funds from abroad or the local market.

COMPARISON OF SIMILAR ECONOMIES

Typically, an MNC has a global perspective and will analyze several countries as potential sites of direct investment or export marketing. Choosing the best option involves many considerations, including a comparison of the economic structure and performance of different countries. There are several difficulties, however, in comparing economic data across countries. For one, each country publishes data in its own currency, which must be translated into a standard international currency to permit any sort of comparison, and straight translation into an international currency may not yield accurate figures. Exchange rates of one country could be officially fixed at a value much higher than the actual market rate, which could artificially inflate certain crucial country data and provide misleading information. This has been the case in Zimbabwe for the past few years.

Moreover, data standards vary greatly across countries in breadth and coverage. Some countries, especially the industrialized ones, have sophisticated data-collection and processing systems at their disposal, while many developing countries may not be able to gather even the basic data. The data also vary considerably in their timing. At a particular point in time, data for the same period may not be available for a set of countries to be compared. The reliability of data is also not always certain. Political leaders in certain countries sometimes manipulate official data to present a better picture of the economy than is actually the case, in order to preserve their own support at home and abroad. Some data often are not comparable at all. If the basis of the computation

for personal income or the definition of the level of income differs across two countries, for example, then the numbers for these two indicators cannot be compared accurately. Because the computational basis does differ, any comparative analysis has to make the necessary adjustments in the nominal figures published by the sources of each country.

TAX SYSTEMS

A very important constituent of the analysis is the prevailing tax system. Taxation levels have a crucial effect on MNC operations, because high tax rates can take a substantial proportion of MNC earnings in overseas locations. Complicated and cumbersome tax procedures and systems also can make it extremely difficult for an MNC to organize and manage its international accounting system.

Tax systems and tax rates vary considerably across the world. Some countries have taxes on production levels, which are based on the quantity of goods produced by the company; such taxes are known as "excise duties" and are collected at the production site of goods. In other countries, industries are taxed by the system of value addition.

Countries often indicate their attitudes toward foreign investment and economic activity by the design of tax provisions that concern foreign business entities. Some countries eager to attract foreign investments have liberal tax requirements and often provide incentives for foreign investors that lower their tax rates below those of domestic industries, but many other countries tax overseas business entities at differential rates that are higher than those levied on domestic business entities. Additional taxes often are levied in some countries on the repatriation of profits by overseas investors.

The tax consideration, therefore, weighs quite heavily in any economic analysis by an MNC on a targeted country. Some countries may have a *double taxation avoidance treaty* with an MNC's home country, which is a treaty whereby an MNC's revenues would not be taxed in the overseas location in return for the same tax treatment for the overseas country's companies in the MNC's home country. Such countries would obviously provide the best tax environment for an MNC's operations.

FISCAL AND MONETARY POLICY SITUATIONS

The fiscal and monetary situation of any country is a key indicator of its economic health and the direction of future economic trends. The fiscal situation generally refers to the position of the finances of a government, whether it is able to match its expenditures with the revenues it generates, how those revenues are generated, and the effects of the fiscal policy on the country's general economic situation. The monetary situation, on the other hand, refers to the picture of the economy as seen from the perspective of the money supply and other monetary aggregates and their influence on the general economic situation.

There is considerable debate on what constitutes a good local fiscal and monetary situation and what an appropriate fiscal policy is. Generally, the debate revolves around the size of the budget deficit or surplus and how a deficit is financed. It can be safely argued, however, that a stable fiscal policy and situation would imply a scenario in which the government is able to incur sufficient expenditures to maintain a desirable rate of growth in the economy without building up too much public debt or fueling inflationary expectations. Countries with large budget deficits that are financed by the creation of more money tend to be inflationary and could disrupt the real rate of economic growth. A country with large fiscal deficits financed by government borrowings could be a dangerous place to invest. The size of the deficit and the level of government borrowing must be examined in the context of the total size of the GNI. A large absolute deficit may be disastrous for one country but manageable for another.

Any analysis has to bear in mind the current and indicative future effects of the continued deficits of a country. The economies of some countries may already be stretched, and a slight increase in the fiscal deficit may trigger immediate inflationary trends. On the other hand, there could be larger economies in which deficits would not make such a large, immediate difference. Large deficits may also signal higher taxes, lower subsidies, and lower government expenditures, which could slow down the economy, depress prices, and possibly shrink the market for the MNC. Not only is it important for an MNC to watch the level of the fiscal deficit; it is also important that the MNC consider how the government has been handling the situation and what economic consequences have emerged out of the effort.

The monetary situation is reflected to a large extent in the level of the money supply in relation to the total size of the economy. An excessive money supply in theory, and to some economists in practice, pushes up prices, as too much money chases too few goods. Inflation, therefore, is often attributed to an excess money supply.

Central banks generally take this view and often try to control the level of inflation in a country by adjusting the level of money supply through a series of monetary measures, some of which have a direct bearing on an MNC's profitability. For example, if a central bank fears that there is excess liquidity in the economy, it may decide to raise the level of interest rates in the banking system, making it more expensive to borrow money from banks and thus eliminating the incentive for loans. Central banks in some countries even place restrictions on the volume and purposes for which credit can be extended by banks to their customers. When the authorities choose to follow a tight monetary policy, the MNC may find itself squeezed for liquidity to finance its operations. Interest-rate hikes also tend to slow down economic activity, which could adversely affect export sales or the sales of local manufacturers being contemplated by an MNC. These fears can be abated as the diversity of the MNC's operating areas increases.

Fiscal and monetary policies also interact in a number of ways with the external payments situation and the exchange rates. Trends in fiscal and monetary policies also provide clues, although no definitive answers, to the future movements of exchange rates between countries. Thus, an MNC must also careful analyze the fiscal and monetary situations and the policy stances taken in this context by the authorities.

ECONOMIC PLANNING: IDEOLOGY AND PRACTICES

After the fall of communism in eastern Europe, the importance of central economic planning decreased. But it is helpful to discuss this type of economic planning, as there are countries in the world that still cling to this form of economic governance. In countries such as these, the economy is expected to be directed by the government through a central planning authority, which formulates broad plans for the entire economy over the medium to long term. Typically, the length of an economic plan is five years. In most countries where economic planning is used, the nation's entire economic development is strongly influenced by what is decided by the planners. For example, plans dictate which areas of industry, agriculture, or services will be emphasized or what the level of government expenditures will be on each of these sectors. Some plans even spell out specific projects in the public or government sectors that will begin during a particular plan period.

The development expenditures to be incurred are laid out for different areas or provinces of a country. Thus, the plans provide a blueprint of the overall economy. Although in several instances plans are not adhered to fully, there is no doubt that they provide ex-

cellent insights into the direction an economy is likely to take, the activities that are likely to be encouraged, and the host government's economic priorities.

The MNC considering investment in a planned economy has to place some importance on the plan in order to position itself at the best strategic point, where it maximizes its own objectives and fits in best with the host country's economic priorities. Thus, a country targeting to double the production of steel in a particular plan period, that does not have the capability or the know-how to do so on its own, presents an excellent opportunity for MNCs who are in the business of setting up steel plants or other activities that are spin-offs of such projects.

COMPETITION

The element of competition is ever present in most countries, and if they are open to one multinational corporation, they are open to others. The strengths of the competing multinationals; their marketing, production, and management strategies; their shares of the market; and the history of their emergence in the local markets must be analyzed, both to draw lessons and to prepare a competitive strategy to enter and penetrate the overseas market. Competition can also arise from local manufacturers as well as state-owned entities. In fact, local competitors often have considerable influence with the host governments and are able to carve out privileges for themselves to secure their own market position. This is particularly true where the local competition happens to be government-owned enterprises.

MARKET DEMAND FORECASTING

PURPOSES

Market demand forecasting is usually a secondary stage in the analysis of a country as a potential market and is attempted after the overall macroeconomic environment and business climate are found conducive to a marketing effort. The basic objective is to obtain reliable, current information to fashion a successful marketing program. This data can also be used to weigh the costs of exporting products to foreign countries against the prospective benefits of manufacturing these goods in those markets.

The methodology in gathering data is to first estimate the demand for potential sales of a type of product an MNC wants to sell in the country in its entirety, then to estimate its potential share of that market. Through such a process, the firm will be better able to predict the costs, sales, and profits associated with marketing the product in the new area.

Data are gathered and processed in several stages. At the first level, there can be surveys of existing information regarding market size and historic demand within an individual country market. Next, the company might expand its research to in-depth study, in order to identify specific demand, supply, and consumer characteristics within the market. Third, the company must evaluate this data to develop the most appropriate match of its resources within the network of existing opportunities. It can also use this information in its ongoing operations to change strategies in existing markets to develop, design, package, and promote products in future markets, and to control operations by giving the company a measure of potential market share.

DATA COLLECTION AND SOURCES

The market researcher will first attempt to gather information or data from existing published sources, which is the least expensive method of gathering demand data. Sources of such information are numerous. In the United States, the Department of Commerce and the International Trade Administration provide a great deal of information regarding markets in other countries. The Department of Commerce also provides a series of marketing publications. One of these, *Foreign Economic Trends and Their Implications for the United States*, is prepared by U.S. embassies abroad, identifies key economic indicators within each country, and describes the country's current economic situation, including inflation, consumption, investment trends, and debt levels. It also discusses attitudes in each country toward U.S. investments and the implications these trends and attitudes have for U.S. investors.

Another series is *Overseas Business Reports*, which provides information on marketing in individual countries. These pamphlets give marketers key information on all aspects of the marketing environment within a country, such as population, consumer and demographic trends, and information on the logistics of doing business in the country, such as specific regulations or procedures for marketing within its borders.

Organizations such as the World Bank, the Export-Import Bank of the United States, and the International Monetary Fund provide other sources of data. The *Organisation for Economic Cooperation and Development (OECD)* publishes information on a full range of economic trends, providing data on production and productivity by industry classification, the structure and composition of the labor force, market consumption patterns, economic divisions within the country according to industrial sectors, relative profit shares and price structures in industries, costs of wages and labor, and financial indicators, inflation, and interest rates. In addition, the OECD provides a full range of information regarding each country's level and composition of foreign trade and official levels of reserves. The range and depth of these statistics are impressive, and they provide a great deal of valuable information for the market analyst. They are limited, however, to the OECD countries, which generally have highly developed statistical bases. Additional information regarding market behavior can be obtained from international trade associations, business groups, service organizations, chambers of commerce of individual countries, foreign groups, and the governments of other countries. Much of this information is available on the Internet free of charge.

Many governments publish such data in annual statistical yearbooks, and some private firms make a business of providing such information services to companies or individuals requesting information about specific countries. These companies provide information on a large number of indicators, such as population, GNI, export composition, basic goods and energy production, balance of payments information, media availability and usage, plus information on history, problems, and the nuts and bolts of doing business in these countries.

Other firms develop and publish indexes of market potential by identifying possible markets in three forms: according to size as a percentage of world consumption, according to intensity or degree to which consumers hold purchasing power, and according to historic growth patterns with a concentration on the past five years to identify past and potential trends. The objective is for the marketer to be able to see recent patterns in growth and make predictions about future growth areas by correlating the market characteristics and factors with detailed data on consumer and buying behavior. Thus, the next level of involvement in marketing research is a detailed country investigation of existing data gathered by others.

PRIMARY RESEARCH

A firm may decide to conduct its own primary research either through its own resources or through the services of an agent, consultant, or specialty firm. While collecting detailed data on consumer demand levels is arduous, this process is even more difficult in overseas markets for a number of reasons.

First, the physical distance between countries makes it difficult to conduct research on site. Second, collecting takes more time abroad than it does at home, thus creating time lags and reducing the currency of the information.

Gathering information from consumers in foreign locales is also fraught with problems based on cultural differences. For example, U.S. consumers think nothing of responding to surveys regarding buying behavior, habits, preferences, and use of goods. There may be cultural barriers in other countries to participating in such personal question-and-answer sessions, especially with interviewers of the opposite sex.

In addition, barriers frequently arise in the form of language and comprehension problems, where translations are either inaccurate or inappropriate or literacy levels are low. Similarly, researchers may encounter difficulty in developing a sample that is significantly representative of the population. For example, in many less-developed countries, the telephone is not as ubiquitous as it is in industrialized countries; fewer families own phones, and telephone books, when published, are often inaccurate. For this reason, researchers cannot use random samples gleaned from phone directories or the Internet, as they do in the United States.

Consequently, when researchers evaluate primary data, they must be sure to regard those results with a healthy amount of skepticism and within a cultural framework or perspective similar to that of the target country. They must also have an open mind in analyzing the results of such research and consider all possible explanations for buyer behavior.

AREAS OF RESEARCH

To evaluate total market potential, international marketers use a number of forecasting methods, which fall into four categories, depending on their types and treatment of data. Some methods analyze existing consumption patterns within the country under scrutiny; others look at historical market data regarding past market activities; others use data from comparable countries; and some attempt to find correlations between a number of descriptive factors and market demand.

All these methods suffer from some basic shortcomings in many potential market areas, generally the less-industrialized countries of the world. Difficulties arise for the following reasons:

- Sales data are often sparse; therefore, the forecaster has no actual data on which to base projections of potential market share and must use other arbitrary determinations of demand, such as apparent consumption, which is a measure of local production plus imports adjusted for exports and domestic inventory variations.
- Data may be available for some but not all variables being used in market demand analysis models, so the researcher may not have information on enough variables to construct or use a viable computer model.
- Data availability may vary among countries; that is, some or all data may not be available for each country under consideration.
- Existing data may be out of date.

Given these caveats, marketers still find that the tools they have developed to estimate market demand are effective in assisting firms in the decision-making process.

TRADE ACTIVITIES

Market analysts look at existing patterns of consumption of goods and services to get a feel for prospective sales of their goods within that market, as well as its basic need levels. Some of this information can be gleaned from a look at the composition of the home country's exports to the target market. In the United States, for example, information regarding estimated U.S. market shares in foreign markets according to product types is published by the Department of Commerce. Alternately, or in

addition to looking at export competition within its own sphere, the firm also examines the total composition of imports for the foreign market from all world competitors. This international information, organized according to *standard industrial codes* (*SIC*), is available from supranational organizations, such as the United Nations and the OECD.

These kinds of import-export analyses are not, however, definitive, because they present a static historical perspective. The company has no assurance that the target country:

- Will continue to import the same levels or types of goods
- Will not mount efforts to increase its own local or nationalized production and displace imports or foreign subsidiary production
- Will not have political, economic, social, or legal problems in its future that lead to the imposition of trade barriers or limits on imports

INPUT-OUTPUT TABLES

Another method of looking at current consumption of goods and products in foreign markets is through the construction of input-output tables, which systematically organize usage flows of countries' input and output goods. These complex tables are constructed so that all industrial sectors are displayed along the vertical and horizontal axes. In these tables, output or production for one industry becomes input or demand for another. For example, in the manufacturing of cars or trucks, the vehicles are outputs for the automobile manufacturer, but require inputs from such basic sectors as steel or aluminum. Similarly, construction output of houses, roads, and buildings requires inputs of concrete, lumber, hardware, and other basic building materials. These tables show the relationships among volumes of goods sold among sectors and their interdependence or their independence from one another. If this information is analyzed in light of expectations regarding future economic trends in the nation, the forecaster can make some judgments about potential changes in demand for goods in that country. Input-output tables are particularly helpful if the analyst predicts a period of economic growth for the nation, in which case the analyst can attempt to predict in which sectors that growth will translate into market demand.

Most developed, industrial countries publish input-output tables as a matter of course. Increasing numbers of developing countries are publishing such tables as an aid to promoting growth in their economies through accurate prediction of demand in appropriate sectors. While they are useful tools, these tables suffer from several limitations. One problem has to do with the reliability, breadth, and comparability of data among countries. Not every country has a complete and accurate set of data about production inputs and outputs. Another problem is that of dated information.

Input-output tables also suffer from their assumption of fixed relationships between two industries. Thus, they give a static picture of interactions between industries and use fixed coefficients to account for increases in demand for inputs from increases in production. They also do not take into account increases in production efficiencies, the use of new production processes, or other possible dynamics, such as new technological developments.

HISTORICAL TRENDS

Another basic method of examining and predicting market trends in a potential market is based on an analysis of past activity within the country. It is crucial in methods based on past usage that the data used are complete, broad, and reliable. The data set should include accurate figures for local production and inventory levels and for the country's imports and exports. Thus, an analyst can determine the country's apparent consumption or market demand, which is figured from local production plus imports,

total goods adjusted for exports, and fluctuations in inventory levels.

The analyst then determines the historical trends revealed by this information and extrapolates through a time series analysis to determine future trends. The crucial assumption made in this analysis is that past trends will continue to be in effect in the future and that consumer behavior, values, and buying activity will continue as they have in the past. This method is sometimes used in conjunction with a comparison of historical trends experienced by other, comparable nations in tandem with growth predictions for the target market country's GNI or levels of production.

COUNTRY COMPARISONS: ANALYSIS BY ANALOGY

The use of data from one country to predict market demand patterns for another country is referred to as analysis by analogy. This process makes a crucial assumption that products in new markets move along a universal path according to a country's level of development. Using this method, analysts identify comparable countries as those that are reasonably similar in market and in economic, political, and developmental structures and stages. The market researcher then looks at the consumption patterns for the product in relation to changes in the country's growth. For example, the researcher might plot consumption with changes in personal income and increasing development in one country and then ascribe this predicted relationship to the fortunes of another country and make predictions about product use based on expectations of increases in personal income.

Analysis by analogy must also be used with caution. The use of blind, absolute analogy is dangerous because no two countries are exactly similar. They differ according to nonquantifiable but significant factors, such as cultural traditions, values, and tastes.

They may also differ in levels of technology, the path their developmental growth takes, and the pricing of goods. Another key problem is the assumption that demand relates to a specific variable, such as personal income or aggregate GNI within a nation. In fact, other variables, such as pricing, may have as much as or even more of an effect on market demand for the product. This method also explains a static, not dynamic, relationship between demand behavior and the economic situation and cannot account for changes to be expected in the countries under comparison.

REGRESSION ANALYSIS

To deal with the need to account for the potential effects of a number of variables on market demand, some analysts use a statistical technique called regression analysis to identify significant relationships between market demand and other variables, such as economic or population indicators. This method uses data collected from several countries on a historical basis for market demand levels and one or several other economic indicators, such as growth or price levels. One of the most widely used indicators is that of economic growth as calculated by GNI. In regression analysis the relationship between the variables is characterized as a formula, $Y = a + bx$, where Y represents total market potential, a is equal to actual use, and bx is a function of consumer use of the product times the selected indicator. For example, statisticians may find a correlation between increases in GNI or country wealth (b) and purchases (a) of luxury or non-necessities, such as appliances, designer clothing, automobiles, or leisure items.

While this linear method is helpful and can examine the relationship of several variables at once through expansion of the formula (for example, $Y = a + bx1 + bx2 \ldots bxn$), it is also not without its limitations. For example, while it uses specific indicators as variables, these do not account for consumer differences in tastes or for product changes. This is also a situation that uses static information to provide a snapshot of the existing situation. The regression model also does not account for the achievement of a saturation level where demand increases to a point, then levels out.

INCOME ELASTICITY

The most common and most frequently used variable affecting market demand is (not surprisingly) personal income levels. Thus, the forecasting method that uses income elasticities looks at the relationship between two crucial variables: demand for a specific product and individual income levels. It analyzes the relationship between changes in the levels of both demand and income, which is accomplished by dividing the percentage change in product demand by the percentage change in income. If there is an increase or decrease in demand, the demand is considered to be elastic, and the ratio of the two is equal to or greater than one.

If a change in income yields less than an equal change in demand for a product, it is said to be inelastic and the value of the ratio is less than one. Frequently, elasticities follow the dictates of common sense. Food, for example, is a basic necessity and therefore demand is generally inelastic for food products; that is, regardless of changes in income, consumers maintain an even level of demand for food products. On the other hand, items that are considered luxuries are often highly elastic, and a correlation would be found between increases in demand for items such as televisions or radios and increases in income levels.

For example, sales of a luxury item such as a CD player are likely to be highly elastic, perhaps reaching 2.5. Such an elasticity would mean that for every unit of increase in average individual income, demand for CD players would rise two and a half times. This demand elasticity will eventually level out, however, once a certain income level is reached and the market for CD players becomes saturated.

For a market researcher to use income elasticity analysis in forecasting foreign market demand, the researcher must be able to accurately determine current demand levels for a given product in a country and develop reasonable expectations of forecasts of average per capita income changes in that country. Then, using elasticities found for the same items in similar countries, the researcher can estimate foreign demand as a function of the foreign increase in income plus the elasticity for the product, as seen previously. Thus, an expectation of a foreign increase in income of one quarter (0.25) multiplied by a high elasticity given for a product (such as 2) will yield an expectation of an increase in demand of 0.5, or 50 percent, in the foreign market.

Income elasticities, as with other market estimation procedures, raise warnings. Again, the method holds the relationship out as being static; elasticity is represented as a constant value and does not allow for the dynamics of the market.

The methodology also does not account for the importance of prices in the demand equation, even though they can have a direct effect on demand, in that lowered prices often lead to increased demand or higher prices to lowered demand because of shifts of consumer purchases to lower-priced substitutes. The formula also does not account for differences in individual tastes for products and the proportion of demand generated by these preferences. Those using income elasticity analysis should keep in mind that high elasticity does not equal high demand volumes. It merely signifies the relationship between income and demand for goods. Generally speaking, goods with high elasticities would be more likely to be low-volume, high-priced goods, while high-sales-volume products are often those that are income inelastic.

METHODS OF ESTIMATING MARKET SIZE AND SHARE

Once the market researcher develops suitable market data, there are a number of methods available to estimate market size and probable share of that market. Three of these methods are the market buildup, chain ratio, and analogy methods.

MARKET BUILDUP

In the market buildup method, the marketing firm gathers data from a number of small separate segments within the overall market and estimates their potential market sales in each segment. These estimates are added to develop an aggregate market total. In evaluating market potential, the marketer must take into consideration differences between segments in consumer tastes, demographics, and competition and must be careful not to assume that similar market segment sizes provide similar market opportunities.

CHAIN RATIO

The chain ratio method is used for consumer products. It consists of a string of estimates regarding target market size and attributes. It is rough, and it varies according to the accuracy of the assumptions, data, and variables used. Still, if a firm knows its markets well and has high-quality data, this method can be useful in predicting sales levels.

As an example, assume that a U.S. brewing company, such as Rolling Rock, decides to market its beer, brewed in glass-lined tanks in Latrobe, Pennsylvania, to a particular target market in Canada. Rolling Rock would use the chain ratio method of estimating sales as follows: First, it would multiply the number of people in the target market by the estimated percentage of people who drink beer. This number would then be multiplied by the number of beer drinkers who drink imported beer times the estimated number of bottles of beer drunk per week by the average Canadian beer drinker. This number, multiplied by 52 weeks per year, divided by 24 bottles per case, yields a case volume, which is multiplied by the price per case of beer to yield a total dollar volume of imported beer sales in the Canadian target market. In this way, Rolling Rock would have an estimate of the total imported beer market in Canada and the challenge that faces it in penetrating that market.

ANALOGY WITH KNOWN DATA

Another method used to estimate market size and share works through analogy with known data from existing markets. The analogy method relates hard data about market size and penetration in one country to unknown information in another. Assume, for example, that Rolling Rock believes that its market share in the United States would correlate to possible market share in Canada according to the variable of total population. (It could also use another market indicator, such as per capita income.) If MUS = market demand in the United States, MC = market demand in Canada, VUS = population of the United States, and VC = population of Canada, the formula that would yield an estimate of Rolling Rock's market share in Canada would be:

$$\text{If } \frac{MUS}{VUS} = \frac{MC}{VC}$$

$$\text{Then } MC = \frac{MUSVC}{VUS}$$

If the countries are dissimilar but the marketer has a fair estimation of relative proportion of the total population fitting the buying criteria, the marketer can adjust the formula to reflect that proportion by multiplying the ratio against his or her total.

DESIGNING INITIAL MARKET STRATEGY

Firms use the tools and procedures for identifying economic trends and market demand for developing an overall marketing plan, which incorporates the firm's objectives into a strategy for approaching new markets successfully or for evaluating existing operations in foreign markets. One method of viewing the existing situation in foreign markets is to compare estimates of market demand and company share with actual company performance. Through such a comparison, the firm can identify competitive gaps in the market between its potential and actual shares of markets, which it can actively attempt to narrow through increases in sales and expanded market coverage.

If sales are lower than estimated potentials, the company may be missing competitive opportunities because of underuse of its products by consumers, limitations in the product line, or gaps in the coverage of the entire market, either by being too thinly spread across the market or by not focusing intensively enough on the most lucrative market segments or geographic areas. The company also may be missing an opportunity to increase market share at the expense of its competitors. By aggressively targeting the portion of the market covered by weak competitors, it may be able to increase its market share to its full potential.

In sum, through judicious use of these forecasting techniques, the company should be able to develop, hone, and coordinate its overall marketing plan to maximize opportunities that exist in new markets, develop and implement effective operating strategies, penetrate new markets, and gain market share. Market researchers must be sure, however, not to use such techniques blindly or alone. Instead, they must be tempered with common sense and should be utilized in concert with other sources of information or analysis, such as expert opinions, field visits, and in-depth research to verify initial findings.

If the company is absolutely intent on marketing in the new country and expects to reap large benefits in terms of increased sales and profits, it might be wise to spend resources to conduct primary research in that market area, to be more certain of consumer tastes, preferences, and buying behavior. Conducting this research, however, is difficult and expensive. These costs must be balanced against expectations of high demand and growth of markets and market share.

All this market information must be integrated into the company's overall strategic marketing plan for all markets in all countries. At this stage, the company must decide on the level of standardization that it will find most appropriate among the marketing programs. Through standardization, the company can realize economies of scale by using similar strategies for penetrating geographically diverse markets. This is often referred to as the geocentric approach. This approach implements the strategy that best fits the various markets in which a company operates. In other situations or with other aspects of the *marketing mix*, the company may prefer to adapt its marketing program to the cultural and market differences specific to the separate marketing environments. This is often referred to as the polycentric approach. This strategy is typically more costly given the customization to each different target market in which a company serves. Sometimes, companies opt for the ethnocentric approach, which uses the same methods developed in the home market for each subsequent foreign market the company enters.

Similarly, the company must make sure that its collection process for market data takes place on an ongoing basis and is coordinated in a systematic, timely, and centralized way. For this reason, many international marketing firms develop and maintain extensive marketing information systems, which contain the economic models used by market planners in the company and different levels of available market data obtained from a variety of sources, especially the field-level offices in different countries. The key to the effectiveness of the system lies in continuous updating of all market information, so that the information is accurate, relevant, cost-effective, and convenient to use. An effective marketing information system provides the marketing firm with the tools to develop a comprehensive strategic global marketing plan that not only identifies which markets hold the greatest potential for the firm but also gives the firm a perspective on the best methods of entering the new markets.

The information provided by a company's marketing information system and the strategic plans devised on that basis are essential not only to MNCs' continued growth and expansion but also to their very survival. International markets are becoming increasingly competitive, and often the quality of information a particular company has is likely to determine whether it is a winner or a loser.

SUMMARY

Country analysis must be viewed as a prerequisite for making decisions about expanding operations internationally, regardless of whether the planned venture is simply exporting or establishing a new manufacturing location. To assess the suitability of a new target country, a company needs analysis of general economic data, such as country size, current stage of development, income distribution levels, personal consumption patterns, economic growth, and country stability. Understanding the target country's composition and mix of primary (agriculture), secondary (manufacturing), and tertiary (services) sectors is important in determining whether the country has sufficient skills and resources to support the new venture. Inflation trends, balance of payments, and foreign exchange rates and policies are also important factors for determining the suitability of a country. Special consideration also must be given to the tax structure of the targeted country. After performing this type of analysis on numerous countries, the MNC can select the location that best serves its project.

The fiscal and monetary policies of a country provide key information on the general health of the national economy. Also, economic plans developed by the central government help to identify the country's future growth directions. The presence of multinationals and the current level of competition provide further information about the target country's suitability for expansion.

Market demand forecasts must be prepared using secondary data, which comes, for example, from the Department of Commerce, world organizations such as the World Bank and the International Monetary Fund, or the target country itself. Primary data such as consumer surveys gathered by the MNC itself may also be considered when developing market demand forecasts. Four general methods are used to develop total market potential: analysis of existing consumption methods, use of historical data from past market activities, use of data from comparable countries, and development of correlations between a number of descriptive factors and market demand. Market size and share can be estimated by using market buildup, chain ratio, and analogy methods.

The quality of information and the strategic decisions developed from that information are critical to the MNC's survival and expansion.

DISCUSSION QUESTIONS

1. Why is country analysis important to the international businessperson?
2. If you are a manufacturer of toys interested in beginning export operations, which economic indicators would you choose to analyze country opportunities? How would these indicators change if you were considering building a computer manufacturing and assembly plant overseas?
3. What information results from a market demand forecast? Describe the general process of forecasting market demand.
4. What data problems occur when conducting a forecast?
5. Discuss alternative analysis techniques that can be used to estimate market demand.

NOTES

1. World Bank Group, "Country Profiles."
2. Anyadike Obinna, "Zimbabwe: Pensioners Hurt by Record Inflation," http://www.IRINnews.org (accessed December 6, 2004).
3. Yahoo Finance, "Currency Converter," http://finance.yahoo.com/currency (accessed April 14, 2006).

BIBLIOGRAPHY

Cateora, Phillip R. *International Marketing*. Homewood, IL: Irwin, 1987.
International Monetary Fund. *International Financial Statistics*. July 2003.
———. *World Economic Outlook*. April 2003.
Obinna, Anyadike. "Zimbabwe: Pensioners Hurt by Record Inflation." http://www.IRINnews.org (accessed December 6, 2004). http://www.irinnews.org/report.asp?ReportID= 38601&SelectRegion=Southern_Africa&SelectCountry =ZIMBABWE
Organization for Economic Cooperation and Development. *Historical Statistics, 1960–2003*. Washington, DC: World Bank, 2004.
World Development Report. New York: Oxford University Press, 2004.
World Bank Group. "Country Profiles." 2004. http://web. worldbank.org/WBSITE/EXTERNAL/COUNTRIES/ 0,,pagePK:180619~theSitePK:136917,00.html
Yahoo Finance. "Currency Converter." http://finance.yahoo. com/currency (accessed April 14, 2006).

APPENDIX 7.1

A STEP-BY-STEP APPROACH TO MARKET RESEARCH

U.S. companies may find the following approach useful:[1]

SCREEN POTENTIAL MARKETS

Step 1. Obtain export statistics that indicate product exports to various countries. Export Statistics Profiles (ESPs) from the Department of Commerce can provide this information. If ESPs are not available for a certain product, the firm should consult the *Custom Statistical Service* (Department of Commerce), *Foreign Trade Report* (Census Bureau), *Export Information* System *Data Reports* (Small Business Administration), or *Annual Worldwide Industry Reviews* (Department of Commerce).

Step 2. Identify between 5 and 10 large and fast-growing markets for the firm's product. Look at these over time (the past three to five years). Has market growth been consistent year to year? Did import growth occur even during periods of economic recession? If not, did growth resume with economic recovery?

Step 3. Identify some smaller but fast-emerging markets that may provide ground floor opportunities. If the market is just beginning to open up, there may be fewer competitors there than in established markets. Growth rates should be substantially higher in these countries to qualify as up-and-coming markets, given the lower starting point.

Step 4. Target between 3 and 5 of the most statistically promising markets for further assessment. Consult with a Department of Commerce Export Assistance Center, business associates, freight forwarders, and others to help refine targeted markets.

ASSESS TARGETED MARKETS

Step 1. Examine trends for company products, as well as trends regarding related products that could influence demand. Calculate overall consumption of the product and the amount accounted for by imports. The National Trade Data Bank (NTDB) and the National Technical Information Service (NTIS) offer *Industry Sector Analyses* (ISAs), *Country Commercial Guides* (CCGs), and other reports that give economic backgrounds and market trends for each country. Demographic information (such as population and age) can be obtained from world population information (Census Bureau) and from the *Statistical Yearbook* (United Nations).

Step 2. Ascertain the sources of competition, including the extent of domestic industry production and the major foreign countries the firm is competing against in each targeted market by using ISAs and competitive assessments. This information is available from the NTDB and the NTIS. Look at each competitor's U.S. market share.

Step 3. Analyze factors affecting marketing and use of the product in each market, such as end-user sectors, channels of distribution, cultural idiosyncrasies, and business practices. Again, the ISAs and Customized Market Analyses (CMAs) offered by the Department of Commerce are useful.

Step 4. Identify any foreign barriers (tariff or nontariff) for the product being imported into the country. Identify any U.S. barriers (such as export controls) affecting exports to the country.

Step 5. Identify any U.S. or foreign government incentives to promote exporting the product or service.

DRAW CONCLUSIONS

After analyzing the data, the company may conclude that its marketing resources would be better used if applied to a few countries. In general, company efforts should be directed to fewer than 10 markets if the firm is new to exporting; one or two countries may be enough to start with. The company's internal resources should help determine its level of effort.

NOTE

1. This information is drawn from U.S. Department of Commerce, *A Basic Guide to Exporting*, http://www.unzco.com/basicguide, accessed April 14, 2006.

CASE STUDY 7.1

THE REPUBLIC OF MAZUWA

It was only 8 A.M., but nearly all the top managers were already in at McBride and Mackers corporate headquarters in Minneapolis, Minnesota. The company was a leading consulting organization specializing in market research, especially in the area of international marketing. Founded in 1965, the company had established an enviable track record in international marketing research and counted a number of top corporate names among its clients.

The company was founded by Walter McBride, a graduate of Columbia University, where he received an MBA with a major in marketing. Three years after establishing his firm, McBride was joined by Jim Mackers, a practicing management consultant with one of the large accounting firms. The firm grew steadily over the years, and by 2006 total billings were approximately $4 million.

In the 1960s and most of the 1970s, much of the company's business involved doing marketing research for companies looking for business opportunities in Latin America, especially Brazil, Chile, and Argentina. In the 1970s, as the focus shifted to the Middle East, the company earned substantial revenue from undertaking consulting contracts for business opportunities in that region.

The company has just won a contract for doing a market study for a large diversified manufacturer of consumer goods that was looking at the Republic of Mazuwa as a potential export market. McBride and Mackers had little experience with Africa, and its only connections were

some minor research projects done for North African countries in conjunction with studies on Middle Eastern markets. It had won the contract primarily on the basis of its excellent record in other markets and its competitive bids.

Having received the contract, the company had to come up with a strategy to analyze the Mazuwan economy. As a first step, a preliminary study team was sent to Mazuwa to get a sense of the situation there and to report back to headquarters with its recommendations on the best possible way to look at the country's economy and study it as a possible market for export of the client's products. In the meanwhile, back at the head office, a preliminary fact sheet on the essential features of Mazuwa had been put together by other members of the project team (see Table 7.1).

The study mission returned after a four-day stay in Silvata, the main business center and port of Mazuwa. They also visited the capital city of Kilbanga and met with government officials in the Ministries of Finance and Trade and the Bureau of Statistics. Shortly after their return, they prepared a brief but well-documented summary of their findings, which was circulated to the members of the policy committee, which comprised all the top managers of the company. McBride called an urgent meeting to discuss the findings and to make a decision on the best strategy to adopt.

Five top managers attended the meeting; McBride, as president of the company, is in charge

continued

Case 1.1 (*continued*)

Table 7.1

Essential Features of the Republic of Mazuwa

Country Data Sheet

Country	Republic of Mazuwa
Population	38 million
Area	267,000 square miles
Per capita GNP (annual)	US$450
Ratio of urban/ rural population	60% rural; 40% urban
Foreign debt (commercial credits)	US$3 billion
Debt service rate (debt service/exports)	42%
Main exports	Copper, coffee, unfinished leather
Main imports	Petroleum and petroleum products, fertilizers, arms
Main industries	Agroprocessing, mineral extraction, small industrial goods
Balance of payments	Average debt of US$410 million over the past three years
Total export volume	US$740 million (2003)
Total import volume	US$1,190 million (2003)
Form of government	Military dictatorship with provincial councils headed by presidential appointees

of corporate policy and overall management of the company; Mackers is executive vice president and in charge of day-to-day operations, with personal responsibility for the management consulting division; John Waters, an MBA from Stanford and head of the marketing research division, with the title of senior vice president; Gilbert Harris, head of financial advisory services, a CPA by profession and a senior vice president; and Robert Ponsford, senior vice president and head of the management information systems consulting division.

Jacob Peters, vice president of the marketing research division, and Charles Seidman,

assistant vice president in the division that had done the preliminary study, have also been invited to attend. The meeting began at 8:30 A.M., and McBride called it to order and began the discussion.

McBride: Good morning and welcome to the meeting. It's nice to see all of us together at once. Most of you are usually several thousand miles apart for most of the time. You have already had a look at the preliminary report by Jacob and Charles. It is a good job; thanks to both of you. We will do this as quickly and smoothly as pos-
continued

Case 7.1 (*continued*)

sible. I'll shoot off any comments to begin with, and then everyone can make his own comments in turn. We'll give Jacob and Charles time to respond to the comments and answer any questions. I'll conclude by summarizing the issues, and we'll make a decision once Charles and Jacob have given their responses to our questions.

As you have read in the summary, Mazuwa is, by any standards, a difficult country to do research in, in the best of circumstances. Most of the data are available only through government sources, and most of the official figures are fairly unreliable. Further, whatever data we get are dated, and by the time we do the numbers at our end, I am not sure we'll be able to make much of a contribution to the client's marketing plans. I am therefore forced to rethink the whole project and am inclined to tell our clients quite clearly that there is little we can do for them in Mazuwa, at least at this stage. I am being pessimistic, but the picture drawn by Charlie and Jacob does not appear to be too encouraging.

Mackers: Walter, I think you are really being overcautious. We have created marketing plans for new countries in the past and made a success of it. In the Middle East we had all kinds of cultural and language problems, not to mention dealing with the arbitrary system of administration. I know Mazuwa's data are dated and extremely difficult to gather, and some of the data could be pretty much unreliable. However, I think we should make a go of it and tell our client that this analysis is based on this type of data and must therefore be treated with that amount of caution. Anyway, if we don't go ahead with this project, I am sure someone else will, since Peitra, our client, is interested quite seriously in expanding into Africa. I know there is a risk of us spending a lot of time

and effort on this and not being able to come up with any useful information at all, but then we are in this business, and having gone international, there are some risks we have to take.

Waters: I have been rolling this around in my head ever since Peitra, approached us the first time around. The more I think about it, the more convinced I get of the feasibility of this project. All we really have to do is to put enough effort and commitment into the exercise. What I propose is that we send three of our best analysts down to Silvata and Kilbanga and have them pick up these data firsthand from the government and the chamber of commerce. Their presence will allow for a thorough recording, analysis, cross-referencing, and verification of the data. While they are there, any doubts and discrepancies can be discussed with local officials, who, on the first visits, were quite helpful and open, much to our surprise. I am aware that nearly all the records are maintained manually and that computers are few and far between, but with our analysts on the spot, we can overcome these problems and come out with a good information set that we can use to put together what I would call a pioneering marketing research effort for our client.

Harris: I agree with John that the project is doable and that we can come out with a fairly decent report on the business possibilities for Peitra in Mazuwa, but I think we need to take a different approach to doing this. Putting a team of three of our best analysts in this area is really going to add up to enormous costs, and we will have a hard time justifying the expense to our clients. Moreover, our people are needed in other, much higher-value contracts, and taking them away for an extended

continued

Case 7.1 (*continued*)

period of time could hurt business at that end. My thought in this matter would be to get hold of a local research firm. I know there are a couple of good business consulting groups in neighboring Dolawi, who could gather the data and send them to us for less than half the cost. Obviously, we will not have the quality and reliability of the data that our own analysts would generate, but then, that's the trade-off we will have to make.

Peters: As the person who has been down at the field level, I can only testify that the difficulties are real and challenging but are not insurmountable. What will be critical is the strategy we adopt. Perhaps we can look at a few country studies done on other, similarly placed African countries and see how such situations have been approached before. There must be some information available from secondary services. There have been a number of World Bank loans to Mazuwa, and I am sure there must be considerable economic data available at the major international development institutions. Our preliminary findings would certainly benefit from access to this type of information.

McBride: Thanks, Jacob. There have been a number of different views on this, and I am of the opinion that most of us really want to do this. The only question, and a very important one, is how. I believe that this is in principle worth taking a crack at. However, while devising a strategy on how to do this project, I want the following to be kept in mind. First, we don't want to be seen giving wrong information to our clients. Second, the project shouldn't cost us more to do than we are being paid; loss leaders are okay but not at this point in the company's financial situation. Third, I do not want this project delayed. We have built a reputation for timely delivery after years of sustained efforts; let's keep it that way.

DISCUSSION QUESTIONS

1. If you were present at the meeting, what would be your position?
2. Prepare a strategy for doing a study for the client, keeping in mind the considerations established by Walter McBride.

CHAPTER 8

International Law

CHAPTER OBJECTIVES

This chapter will:

- Briefly describe how legal systems differ between countries.
- Discuss the legal concepts that are important in the international business environment.
- Identify current U.S. laws that specifically affect international trade and multinational corporations.
- Examine the importance of intellectual and industrial property rights.
- Define the methods for resolving international business conflicts and the legal organizations that are available in the international arena.

PUBLIC AND PRIVATE LAW

International transactions are complex and tend to be risky. Consequently, disputes often arise between business partners. To the international businessperson, however, the normal recourse to national law is not always available, because host-country laws often discriminate in favor of their citizens. Moreover, there is no international body of law that governs international transactions. Thus, when people refer to the study or the conducting of *international law*, they are merely referring to the laws that govern the activity of nations in their relationships with one another. These laws collectively are referred to as the public law of nations, which reflects individual countries' methods for dealing with other nations of the world. Public law is based not only

on written law but also on unwritten customs and conventions.

Public law, that is, the manner in which nations interact according to a legal framework, differs from private law. *Private law* applies not to nation-states but to individuals within those nation-states. These parties enter into agreements called contracts in order to establish a set of rules and regulations regarding their mutual interests and interactions. Their contracts stipulate the terms of their agreements regarding what is to be exchanged, when, where, and for what price in what currency. This private law is still affected, however, by the rules and regulations emanating from public law—overall stipulations regarding permissible behavior between the contracting parties. For example, despite having contracts to the contrary, private citizens may be prohibited by the laws of their countries from buying goods that a nation has barred for importation, because of public policy or national economic goals.

Different Legal Systems

The legal systems of different countries are based in one of four legal traditions or foundations: civil, common, bureaucratic, and religious law. *Civil law* traces its origins from ancient Roman law and, more recently, the Napoleonic Code and is practiced in most European nations and the former colonies of those countries. Civil law is a body of law that is written essentially in the form of statutes and is constructed and administered by judicial experts in government. A hybrid of civil law is practiced, for example, in Japan. Under the hybrid systems, government experts are involved in the development of new statutes, but before even being proposed, these potential laws generally achieve political consensus. Law is seldom modified or amended in civil law systems.

Common law, which is practiced in Great Britain and its former colonies, for example, the United States, is more susceptible to challenge, change, and amendment. The common law system is based not on federal administration but on judicial interpretation of the law as well as on customs or usages existing within the nation. Under common law, decisions made by the court are based on preceding judicial judgments rendered by prior courts.

Bureaucratic law, which is practiced in many communist countries as well as dictatorships, is law that is set by the country's current leadership. This law is subject to change rapidly, when regimes change. In the summer of 2003, the citizens of Hong Kong feared that the Chinese government would impose an antisubversion law on the island, as is in place on the mainland. This law, which could be used to quell future protests in Hong Kong, contradicted the concept of "one nation, two systems" that

has existed between China and Hong Kong since China took over possession of the island from Great Britain in 1997. While the Chinese government eventually backed off on its implementation of an antisubversion law in Hong Kong, this is an example of how bureaucratic law can suddenly change the operating environment in a formerly open society.

The countries that adhere to *religious law* are primarily Muslim. In these nations, religious law is generally mixed to an extent with other forms of law, such as civil or common law. In some countries, such as Saudi Arabia, religious precepts referred to as the sharia (one translation of which is "way to follow") govern all behavior and are administered by the government and Islamic judges. A system such as this is also known as a *theocracy*.

International Treaties Framework

These legal traditions and systems provide each nation with its own public law and a framework for conducting both its relationships with other countries and its citizens' relations with private citizens from other nations. This framework, a law of nations, is formalized for individual countries through their agreements, which are developed either individually or within a block with other nations. These agreements outline rules and regulations to be observed by the parties with regard to economic and commercial matters. The more important of such accords are treaties; those that are considered less important are called protocols, acts, agreements, or conventions.

These agreements are binding on the parties that enter into them. If there are only two nations involved, the agreement is termed a bilateral treaty; if there are more than two nations involved, the agreement is termed a multilateral treaty. Treaties are entered into primarily to facilitate the conduct of commerce between nations. They determine the rules to be followed, define the rights and obligations of each party, and provide for the enforcement of judgments when the terms of the treaties are violated.

There are many different kinds of treaties entered into by nation-states. The most fundamental provide the basis for conducting business between nations by allowing the citizens of the counterpart country to participate in business activity in the home country through trading, investing, or operating or owning a business. Such treaties are known as treaties of friendship, commerce, and navigation and stipulate fundamental parameters to be observed by citizens within each nation while interacting with those from the other and establish guidelines for doing business across borders. Thus, they address such issues as the entry of people, goods, ships, cargoes, and capital into countries. They also establish guidelines regarding the acquisition of property by foreign nationals, as well as the protection of their own citizens and their property abroad. Similarly, they address flows of resources between countries in the transfer of funds or currencies between the two nations.

Tax treaties allow for countries to establish criteria for determining who has jurisdiction over income earned, how double taxation is to be avoided, and how the countries can cooperate to reduce the evasion of taxes by each other's citizenry.

LEGAL CONCEPTS RELATING TO INTERNATIONAL BUSINESS

SOVEREIGNTY

Even casual examination of international law requires the definition of the concept of *sovereignty*, which is the principle that individual nations have absolute power over the governing of their populaces and the activities that occur within their borders. To be considered a sovereign entity, a nation must be independent, have a permanent population and well-defined boundaries, possess a working economy and government, and have the capacity to conduct foreign relations. To be sovereign and conduct relations with other nations, the country must be recognized as such by those other nations. Recognition is the official political action taken by the countries of the world to accept the status of a country as a legal entity and a full-fledged member of the political and economic system of the world. One example of a nation *not* recognized as sovereign is Northern Cyprus, which Turkish-Cypriots have occupied since 1974, and which is officially recognized as a nation only by the Republic of Turkey.

SOVEREIGN IMMUNITY

Sovereignty implies that a nation can impose laws and restrictions, levy taxes, and circumscribe business activities. A manifestation of this sovereign power is the doctrine of *sovereign immunity*, which is the principle that a sovereign state enjoys immunity from being held under the jurisdiction of local courts when it is party to a suit unless the state itself consents to be a party to that suit. Therefore, courts have no jurisdiction to hear claims against a sovereign nation.

To deal with this problem, the United States passed the Foreign Sovereign Immunity Act (FSIA) in 1977 in an attempt to clarify the situation. This law stipulated that, in the eyes of the United States, a foreign nation waives its right to sovereign immunity when it or its agency engages in a commercial activity. The FSIA focuses on the nature and the purpose of commercial activity undertaken and covers business activities that take place in the United States, are performed in the United States but involve activities elsewhere, or have a direct effect on the United States, even if performed outside the country's borders.

ACT OF STATE

The *act of state doctrine* is a legal principle that refers to claims made by foreign parties whose assets or belongings have been taken by the state in public actions. This doctrine holds that sovereign nations can act within their proper scope in confiscating these assets. To be an act of state, however, the activity must satisfy several conditions. It must be an exercise of foreign power, conducted within a country's own territory, with a degree of consequence calculated to affect a foreign investor or party, and it must be an action that is taken by the state in the public interest.

Because acts of state are considered to be within the rights of sovereign entities, judicial bodies in other countries have no standing to consider the legality of such actions. The biggest issue in these actions arises in regard to foreign owners being compensated adequately for the loss of these assets. Although international law and convention require that owners be paid appropriately for their confiscated or nationalized assets, the definition of "appropriate" varies according to each party's opinion and judgment. This problem is a major concern when investments are expropriated by developing nations, especially because some of these countries have repudiated the classical principles of compensation for expropriation, citing the country's overriding development goals.

EXTRATERRITORIALITY

Extraterritoriality refers to the application of one country's laws to activities outside its borders. Such a transnational reach across borders comes into play when a government seeks to restrict, limit, or direct business activities, such as monopolistic practices, the collection of taxes, or allowable payments for corrupt practices. The United States, in particular, attempts to extend its regulatory and legal reach across national borders in all these areas, although it is not always successful. One such attempt by the United States began in the early 1980s, when President Ronald Reagan decided to impose economic sanctions on the Soviet Union

to protest Soviet pressure on Polish officials to impose martial law and crack down on leaders of the Solidarity trade union.

The sanctions prohibited American companies and their foreign subsidiaries and affiliates using U.S. licenses from selling equipment or technology to the Soviet Union for the transmission or refining of oil and gas. The sanctions were targeted at the Soviet Union's construction of a 2,600-mile natural gas pipeline from Siberia to western Europe and raised a storm of controversy in the United States and Europe. At the center of the controversy were technological licenses issued by General Electric to foreign affiliates in Scotland, France, Italy, and Germany, which the U.S. government forced General Electric to cancel. Protests by the licensees were made on the grounds that the sanctions violated international legal principles of the sanctity of valid contracts between parties and on the impropriety of the U.S. attempt to use extraterritoriality. Licensees appealed to their national governments, and European leaders rejected the sanctions out of hand, arguing that President Reagan had no right to extend U.S. laws beyond U.S. territory, and instructed the licensees to continue their operation.[1]

AREAS OF CONCERN TO MULTINATIONAL CORPORATIONS

U.S. TRADE LAWS

One area in which nations use their legal systems to affect international commerce is trade law. One aspect of this legal jurisdiction is the granting of licenses allowing U.S. concerns to export goods. Through the issuing of such licenses, national governments control how and to what degree national resources will be allocated to foreign users through the export of commodities, services, and technology. Other methods of controlling trade are the imposition of tariffs in the form of customs duties on imports and exports, and nontariff barriers that slow exchanges of goods and services by increasing the complexities of international commerce.

In addition to these controls on trade and international trading agreement participation under the World Trade Organization (WTO), the United States also has specific trade laws designed to protect U.S. citizens from the unfair trade practices of other nations, which include subsidies and pricing practices with countervailing and antidumping laws.

COUNTERVAILING DUTY

Countervailing duty (CVD) law is designed to provide for the imposition of tariffs to equalize prices of imports that are low because of subsidies provided by home governments to encourage trade. These subsidies can include financial help from a government, such as loans with special interest rates; providing input goods, raw materials, or services at preferential rates; forgiveness of debt; and assuming costs of industry manufacturing, production, or distribution.

Before countervailing duties are levied, many legal steps must be taken. The legal proceedings follow two paths: determination of injury to an industry or firm, and findings that imported goods have been subsidized. In the first situation, the U.S. government, through the efforts of the International Trade Commission (ITC), must decide that the existing or potential domestic industry has been injured by the practices of foreign exporters. Proceedings can be initiated by the government itself or through the petition of private parties (usually the injured industry).

After an action is initiated and a case is brought before the ITC, efforts are mounted along the second path to determine whether or not the goods being imported into the United States are subsidized. If it is found that prima facie subsidization exists, sales of those goods by the foreign interest are suspended

in the United States, and the party must post a bond for the amount of the estimated subsidy. Within 75 days after a determination is made, the administering authority makes a final decision regarding the existence and the amount of the subsidy.

Following the finding of a subsidy, the ITC makes its final determination of injury. If both authorities rule affirmatively regarding subsidies and injury, then a countervailing duty is levied on goods brought into the United States in the amount of the subsidization. The conduct of such cases is a lengthy, arduous, and expensive process that involves many teams of lawyers representing the domestic industry and the countries in question.

ANTIDUMPING LAWS

U.S. *antidumping laws* also protect American industries and companies against the unfair practices of parties in other nations as they relate to pricing practices, specifically, *predatory pricing*. Through such a practice, a foreign competitor attempts to capture a large share of a target market by cutting prices below those charged locally. Once such a share is attained and domestic competition is eliminated, the exporter can freely raise prices to prior or even higher levels. This practice is considered predatory if the seller is charging a price that does not reflect the fair value of the goods and is counterbalanced by higher prices charged in domestic or other markets.

The legal process of imposing duties on such dumped goods is similar to that in countervailing duty cases. The initiation of the case is the same, and the ITC is charged with determining both preliminary and final findings of injury to the domestic industry. Meanwhile, the administrative agency attempts to determine whether or not the goods are being sold for less than their fair market value. If the final findings of both determinations are affirmative, dumping duties equal to the amount of actual fair market value above the price charged in the U.S. market are assessed on the foreign goods in question. The duty remains in effect only as long as and to the extent that the dumping practice continues.

ANTITRUST LAWS

One special area of legal concern for practitioners of international business is the application of antitrust laws by the United States to the activities of those engaging in international commerce. U.S. antitrust laws are based on free-market economic principles of competition. Thus, antitrust laws in the United States were enacted to prevent businesses from engaging in anticompetitive activities and to challenge the growth of monopoly power in industries.

The United States is noted in the international legal community for strict enforcement of these laws and for transnational application of these restrictions. The United States attempts to enforce antitrust statutes through the use of extraterritoriality and the imposition of its laws on the activities of U.S. business concerns in other nations. U.S. justification for such activity is that the United States rightly has extraterritorial reach if the action being disputed or acted against has the effect of materially affecting commerce in the United States.

The two main U.S. laws covering the antitrust area are the Sherman Act and the Clayton Act. The *Sherman Act* was instituted in 1890 with the goal of preserving competition in both U.S. domestic and export markets. It prohibits anticompetitive or monopolistic activities by business entities. Some such anticompetitive practices are trust building, agreements to fix prices or allocate markets by industry participants, and agreements to engage in monopolistic activities in the United States or with foreign nations.

The antitrust purview was extended by the adoption of the *Clayton Act*, which prohibits the acquisition of the stock or assets of another firm if the effect of that acquisition is the reduction of competition within the industry or the creation of a monopoly. This law has been interpreted by U.S. courts to affect activity in international markets, because it requires only that the effect of the acquisition or merger be felt in the U.S. market; there are no geographic constraints as to the physical locale where these acquisitions were made. Thus, the statute would cover horizontal mergers between industry competitors, vertical mergers between producers and suppliers or distributors, and mergers that have the effect of eliminating potential competition in markets.

The *Webb-Pomerene Act* of 1918 allows some American firms to seek exemptions from the application of these antitrust laws if they join together to gain access to foreign markets by exporting their goods. Under the Webb-Pomerene Act, firms are given specific exemptions from antitrust law and are allowed to join together to agree on prices and market allocations if such activity does not have the effect of reducing competition within the United States. Similarly, in 1982 Congress passed the Export Trading Company Act, which provided some guidance for these companies to facilitate international trade by acting as middlemen between potential buyers and sellers of export goods. Frequently, these *export-trading companies (ETCs)* trade simultaneously in products that compete against each other and represent competing firms. The purpose of the 1982 law was to provide an exemption from antitrust law so that U.S. firms could combine resources in pursuing these export activities, as long as competitiveness in domestic U.S. trade remained unaffected.

FOREIGN CORRUPT PRACTICES

In the 1970s questions about and interest in unethical behavior mushroomed as the events of Watergate unfolded. This interest was magnified with revelations that the Lockheed aerospace firm had made enormous payoffs to Japanese premier Kakui Tanaka for his help in security contracts. It appeared also that other firms in such industries as construction, arms, aerospace, and pharmaceuticals routinely made payments to facilitate contract awards, sales orders, or project clearance by foreign regulatory agencies. In response to these revelations, the *Foreign Corrupt Practices Act (FCPA)* was enacted in 1977 to deal with payments abroad.

The FCPA contains three major provisions regarding the payment of bribes and payoffs. First, it sets standards for accounting for all businesses, so that enterprises keep accurate books and records and maintain internal controls on their accounting procedures and systems. Second, it prohibits the use of corrupt business practices, such as making gifts, payments, or even offers of payments to foreign officials, political parties, or political candidates, if the purpose of the payments is to get the recipient to act (or not act) in the interests of the firm and its business dealings. Third, it establishes sanctions or punishments for such behavior. Violation of the accounting standards of the law could lead to fines of up to US$10,000, imprisonment of up to five years, or both. Violation of the corrupt practices sections of the act could result in fines of up to US$1 million.

Under the terms of the act, the word "corrupt" is used to denote activity in which it is clear that the payment or offer is being made with the purpose of inducing a public official to use his or her power wrongly in providing business for a firm or in obtaining special legislative or regulatory treatment for a company. The act also differentiates between bribes and payments made to facilitate international business by exempting payments made to minor officials in foreign bureaucracies. These payments, often called "grease," are routinely paid to smooth the path of business for international firms. For example, a payment may provide for faster service or red-tape clearance. These payments are considered a legitimate cost of doing business but must be accounted for appropriately. There are those who oppose making such payments illegal and defend them as being a reasonable cost of doing business, especially in foreign environments with different cultural patterns, values, and mores. They criticize

the law for being expensive in its compliance and reporting requirements and cite difficulties in making the necessary distinctions between facilitative payments and customary business expenses, such as entertainment of potential customers. These critics also believe that the law has worked to the detriment of American business by causing the loss of enormous volumes of business, especially to firms from other countries in which such payments are considered routine and ordinary operational costs.

The position of the United States and its laws regarding these payments differs from that of many other countries of the world, where such practices as making payoffs and paying bribes are considered ordinary costs of doing business in international settings. Historically in Germany, such payments have been considered customary and have been accounted for as tax-deductible special expenses, just as they have been in the United Kingdom. Similarly, France and Japan have had no restrictions on making such payments to facilitate the development of business. The question remains, however, as to whether or not these allowances for such payments put French, Japanese, German, and British firms at a competitive advantage over American firms.

TAX TREATIES

An area of particular interest for sovereign nations that affects international firms and their operations is that of taxation. Tax procedures and policies can have significant effects on the well-being and health of firms. They can discourage growth, investment, and the pursuit of profits by being onerous, or they can stimulate economic development and growth by providing incentives for firms and individuals. Taxation policies and laws differ around the world; rates vary considerably, as do types of taxes. Some countries, for example, allow for a lower tax on capital gains than on regular gains, to provide incentives for long-term savings and investment, while others tax all gains at the same rate.

In general, income taxes are assessed in a progressive manner, termed *progressive taxation*; that is, the larger one's income, the higher the tax rate. European countries levy a *value-added tax (VAT)* only on the value that is added to products as they progress from raw materials to consumer goods. The VAT has the benefits of being relatively easy to collect and administer as well as being easily raised or lowered according to the country's economic needs, but it has the disadvantage of not being progressive. Consequently, both low- and high-income members of society are taxed at the same rate because their total tax obligations may differ only according to their purchases, not according to their levels of income.

Taxes are levied not only to produce income or revenue for nations but also to affect public policy. For example, some taxes are intended to discourage the consumption of certain items. These so-called *sin taxes* are often levied on such goods as alcoholic beverages and tobacco products. Other tax policies provide incentives for firms to engage in particular activities. One such incentive in the United States encourages export activities by providing tax breaks for companies exporting as foreign sales corporations.

Countries differ greatly in the focus, provisions, regulations, levels of compliance, and enforcement of their tax policies. These differences can lead to significant problems for the multinational firm conducting business across the boundaries of different taxing authorities that vary in their determination of who is taxed on what property, what income, and at what rate. The question then becomes to which taxing authority must a multinational firm or an employee of that multinational firm remit taxes. The solution is one that recognizes both the concept that all sovereign nations have the authority to tax and the concept that corporations and individuals should be spared from having undue or double tax liabilities.

In consequence, nations around the world enter into tax treaties that generally provide for credits in the home country for taxes paid in the host country by corporations or individuals. Thus, the entity is not taxed twice on the same income or property. For example, the United States taxes personal income not according to the residence or site where the income was earned but according to the nationality of the taxpayer. Therefore, expatriates working abroad are liable for taxes on income earned in those foreign settings. Tax law, however, provides a break for these individuals by allowing them exemptions from taxes for housing allowances for foreign residences and income tax relief on a portion of their income earned abroad. As of 2006, the maximum exemption for foreign-earned income per year was US$80,000.

Tax conventions or treaties between nations define the basis for taxation, such as the site of the official residence of a firm or person or the location of operations for that firm. The agreements also define what constitutes taxable income and provide for the mutual exchange of information and assistance to increase compliance with and enforcement of tax laws in order to decrease tax evasion.

INTELLECTUAL AND INDUSTRIAL PROPERTY RIGHTS

Another crucial area of concern for multinational firms involved in R & D and advanced technology is the protection of such intangible assets as know-how, processes, trademarks, trade names, and trade secrets. These assets generally find protection under legal systems that provide for the creation of patents and copyrights. The dangers involved with such assets are that they could be stolen, used, copied, and sold without proper authority or compensation. As is discussed in Chapter 6, the Trade-Related Aspects of Intellectual Property Rights (TRIPS) was signed during the Uruguay Round of trade negotiations and is a part of the World Trade Organization's basic framework. Following are a more detailed discussion of intellectual property and highlights of some of the major agreements of the past concerning this topic.

Patents are rights granted by governments to the inventors of products or processes for exclusive manufacturing, production, sale, and use of those products or processes. Patents are the equivalent of the legal ceding of monopolistic power over the subject matter of the patent. They are intended to stimulate the creation of new technology and inventions by providing creators with assurances of gain from the potential benefit from their endeavors. Patents protect the subject from infringement of rights only in the country in which they are registered. Consequently, a multinational firm marketing its products or processes in a number of countries must make sure that its patents are protected in all existing as well as potential market areas.

TRADEMARKS AND TRADE NAMES

Trademarks and *trade names* are designs, logos, and names used by manufacturers to differentiate and identify their goods with customers. They are considered an integral part of the total product, which is the entire image and package surrounding the product being marketed. Trademarks and trade names have an indefinite life and can be licensed to others, as long as they retain their brand distinction and do not pass into generic descriptive use, as happened, for example, with aspirin. Goods that use false trademarks are *counterfeit* products, and producers and sellers of such goods are subject to prosecution under trademark laws of individual countries. Trademarks are generally not considered infringed on when they are imitated ("knocked off"), as long as they are not characterized as the original merchandise.

The inappropriate use of trade names and trademarks creates legal conflicts around the world.

Recently, Rap star Missy Elliott's clothing line ran into trouble in Denmark. The logo on the clothes was too similar to that of the country's queen. The shoes, bags, and shirts in the collection carry a logo that consists of a crown on the top of the word "respect," and Missy Elliott's initials, "M.E." Queen Margrethe II's logo consists of a crown on top of the characters "M-2-R," with the "R" standing for the Latin word for queen (*regina*). Clothing maker Adidas-Salomon AG was forced to withdraw the line from Danish stores after the royal court said that the logo infringed on the queen's copyright. Even though copyright laws are global, Adidas does not plan to remove the collection from store shelves outside Denmark.[2]

PATENT LAWS AND ACCORDS

Different countries around the world have different criteria for the proper registration and granting of patents. A multinational firm must take care to comply with the different requirements of each country. For example, the lifetime of a patent may vary from country to country; nations may have different requirements about products or processes having published descriptions, whether they worked or were used prior to patent application, and whether a product is substantially different from previously patented goods. The countries may also differ in the procedures used to resolve conflicts when more than one inventor claims the rights to the same patent. Consequently, ensuring protection of patents can be a complex, lengthy, involved, and expensive process for firms engaged in commerce in a multitude of markets.

The United States, for example, has a *first to invent* patent-granting policy that requires that any new patent filing be new, useful, and unobvious. Interestingly, what is at first deemed obvious is overturned in 30 to 40 percent of the cases.[3] Japan, on the other hand, allows patents for minor modifications. This policy has tended to flood Japan's patent office with new filings. This large amount of patent filings delays the process for getting new patents approved and could also prove detrimental to the level of innovation in the country.

These complexities and intricacies have led to the emergence of international agreements regarding the mutual recognition of patents on goods and processes of member countries. The largest of these is the *Paris Convention*, which provides for the protection of patents and trademarks. This convention, also called the Paris Union, was established in 1883. Under its terms, members agree to recognize and protect the patents and trademarks of member countries and allow for expedited (that is, a six-month priority period) registration for enterprises having filed in home countries that are members of the union. Similar patent agreements exist between the United States and Latin American countries in the Pan American Convention of 1929 and in subregional groups, such as the European Community and Sweden and Switzerland. In these nations, filing for patents in one of the member countries automatically confers protection in all member countries.

Trademarks are generally used without consent when a product with a worldwide reputation is not registered in all potential markets. Thus, with its reputation at stake, a multinational firm is faced in such situations with either having to litigate to regain use of its trademark or trade name or having to buy back that identifying symbol or name. While registration of all trademarks and trade names prevents these problems, such action becomes very expensive, especially if the firm markets several product lines in many markets where registration requirements differ substantially. For example, in some countries trademarks are registered only after they have been used, while in others, they cannot be used until they are registered.

To deal with these problems, cooperating international entities have made attempts to synchronize registration processes in recent years. The *Madrid Agreement of 1991* provides for the protection of trademarks in a centralized bureau in Geneva, the International Bureau for the Protection of Industrial Patents, which is a part of the *World Intellectual Property Organization (WIPO)*. Currently, 181 countries are members of WIPO. Registrations under this agreement have the benefit of being effective in many nations and potentially all members of the Madrid Agreement. Once the trademark is properly registered in its home country, an application may be made for international registration, at which point the trademark is published by the international bureau and communicated to the member countries where a firm is seeking patent protection. It is then up to the member countries to decide within twelve months whether or not they wish to refuse acceptance of the mark, and, in that case, they must outline the grounds for such refusal.

COPYRIGHTS

Copyrights give exclusive rights to authors, composers, singers, musicians, and artists to publish, dispose of, or release their work as they see fit. The people in the music business face problems with the illegal use of their material—*piracy*, which is the unlawful duplication of copyrighted material including sound recordings to make bootleg tapes and records. A major area in which copyrights are routinely infringed is computer software. Many developing countries are known to illegally copy computer software and sell it at reduced prices in the local markets. This was a primary reason for the inclusion of intellectual property protection in trade agreements under the WTO.

Copyright protection is sought by creators of works of art, literature, and music to ensure that no one wrongly reaps the benefit of their creative efforts through the sale, use, or licensing of those works. Copyright protection is divided into two categories: that which protects the right of a creator to economic benefits or returns from his or her work and that which protects the creator's moral right to claim title to the work and to prevent its being altered without consent or published without permission.

International copyright protection is covered under the *Berne Convention of 1886* for the Protection of Literary and Artistic Works, which has 150 signatory countries. To be covered under the Berne Convention, material must be published or generally made available in a member country. The author or artist need not be a citizen of that member country to be afforded copyright protection. Thus, artists from nonmember countries, such as the United States, gain coverage by publishing simultaneously at home and abroad.

A similar agreement that also provides for international copyright protection is the *Universal Copyright Convention (UCC) of 1952*, sponsored and administered by the *United Nations Educational, Scientific, and Cultural Organization (UNESCO).* Members of the UCC are accorded national status within each other's borders; that is, citizens holding copyrights are entitled to the same protection against copyright infringement as national citizens. Many members of the Berne convention are also signatories of the UCC.

OPERATIONAL CONCERNS OF MULTINATIONAL CORPORATIONS

WHICH NATIONALITY?

In the world of international commerce, there is no such entity as an international corporation; rather, the multinational firm consists of connected groups of individual operating units organized to operate within a variety of nations. The nationality of each corporation depends not on its own choice or determination but on the laws within the nation of operation. In some countries, a corporation need

only be incorporated within the national boundaries; in others, it must have a registered office on domestic soil; in still others, it must be managed and operated within the country. Some nations allow for corporate dual citizenship.

The determination of nationality is a crucial matter, because it has the potential to affect all business operations. For example, multinational corporations may seek protection or assistance from their national governments or domestic courts of law in disputes with host countries. Nationality also determines tax liability and entitlement to government-sponsored incentive programs and tax breaks, as well as the degree of liability carried by the directors of a corporation. The determination of what constitutes a corporation also tends to differ among countries. All these factors imply that the multinational concern must seriously consider the form of organization it wishes to adopt in a particular country. The choice of form will depend on the strategic objectives of the corporation in a particular country and how the corporation believes it can best serve those objectives.

LOCAL LAWS

Local laws affect the welfare and day-to-day operations of a firm. The labor laws of a nation, for example, affect the multinational corporation's use of labor. Some of these laws stipulate minimum wages, standards for working conditions, requirements for levels and types of fringe benefits, and timing and duration of holidays and vacations. In some countries management is considered fully liable for worker safety and faces possible criminal prosecution for worker injuries or deaths suffered on the job.

Some nations have requirements that multinational firms employ certain percentages of local labor within their operating and managerial classes of employees and stipulate hiring and firing procedures and levels of severance pay when employees are terminated. All nations have national policies regarding contributions to the labor pool through immigration. They regulate or place limits on the number of foreigners or *guest workers* and the length of employment and sometimes the types of jobs or positions they are allowed to hold.

Individual nations also impose standards on product safety and put into place testing requirements and compulsory regulatory processes for gaining product approval. In the United States, the Consumer Product Safety Commission evaluates the safety of various products and sometimes recommends that unsafe products be taken off the market. Similarly, the Federal Drug Administration tests and evaluates new pharmaceutical products to determine whether or not they are safe to be used by the public. Internationally, more and more attention is being paid to the development, enforcement, and standardization of product safety laws. In recent years, businesses, politicians, and trade groups in the developed world have requested that these standards be included in trade agreements, and they have sometimes been successful.

Local laws also affect the operations of multinational firms when they involve controls on wages, prices, or currency transactions. Wage and price controls are generally imposed as part of efforts to encourage and stimulate economic development by keeping the incomes of workers up (through minimum wages) or their costs down (through limits on prices). Such controls are also used to bring down inflation, lower import volumes, and raise exports to bring the balance of payments into equilibrium.

Similarly, some countries put limits on currency exchanges because they wish to increase their store of hard currency. These nations often set limits on the amounts of local currency that can be exchanged for hard currency and on amounts paid for goods or profits that can be repatriated by multinational firms.

Resolving Business Conflicts

The problem of business conflicts is particularly complex in the arena of international business, primarily for three reasons. First, the contracting parties are generally not as familiar with each other as are parties from the same country, and they are subject to the jurisdiction of their own countries and laws. Thus, an injured party cannot claim redress in his domestic courts against the defaulting party if the latter is based in a foreign country.

Second, international transactions operate in a relatively uncertain environment and face the risks of fluctuations in prices and exchange rates, changes in laws and regulations, transit risks, and so on. The possibilities of transactions not being completed to the satisfaction of both parties are higher than in a domestic environment.

Third, business ethics, practices, and cultures vary considerably across countries. Language is often a barrier, and there is always a distinct possibility of a misunderstanding because of a communications gap between the two parties. Communications are also hampered by the fact that the parties can be at a great distance from each other during the life of the transaction.

Contracts

It is essential that conflicts in international business be avoided to the extent possible. One of the best ways to avoid conflicts in international business is to have a clearly drafted contract, with all terms and conditions well understood by both parties. A contract is defined as a promise or set of promises, for the breach of which the law gives a remedy, or the performance of which the law in some way recognizes as a duty. An international commercial contract spells out the details of the transactions, the obligations of the two parties, the consideration involved, and so on.

The international businessperson must be aware of the possibility of conflict. Therefore, five specific steps should be taken when signing contracts with overseas parties:

1. The contract provisions must be unambiguous and clear and cover every relevant aspect of the transaction.
2. The applicable law used in the contract should be understood by the company.
3. The contract should stipulate the relevant jurisdiction where the potential disputes will be settled. This is known as the *choice of forum.*
4. Risk transfer must be clearly outlined in the contract, especially where the contract involves sale and purchase of goods. The contract should state clearly the stage at which the risk of loss of the goods passes from the seller to the buyer.
5. The contract should contain some provisions for dispute resolution without resorting to arbitration or litigation.

RESOLVING DISPUTES

Despite the insertion of all precautionary clauses into a contract, disputes may emerge. Usually, the method adopted to deal with such situations is either arbitration or litigation, but there are some interim dispute resolution methods that are quicker and less expensive: adaptation, renegotiation, and mediation.

Adaptation

Provisions can be inserted into a contract to enable the agreement to be adapted to changing circumstances over the life of the transaction, which is particularly important when the contract involves a long-term commitment by both parties. There are several issues for which the adaptability of a contract is desirable so that both parties enjoy some flexibility in the performance of their respective obligations. Typically, in long-term contracts, flexibility is sought in such issues as prices and delivery schedules. Most contracts contain a *force majeure clause*, which absolves the parties of their obligations under the contract if they are prevented from carrying them out by circumstances beyond their control.

Renegotiation

If a dispute arises during the life of the contract over some provisions, the two involved parties can renegotiate the contract. In certain instances, the contract itself contains a proviso to the effect that under certain circumstances, if the parties differ, they will renegotiate certain parts of the contract. Renegotiation has obvious advantages. Apart from saving court fees and other charges involved in formal dispute-resolution procedures, renegotiation can be an ongoing process that need not disrupt the continued progress of business under the contract.

Mediation

Mediation is a method of dispute resolution using the offices of a third party known as the mediator. The actual mediation proceedings are generally less formal and rigid than arbitration, but the nature of individual mediation proceedings does vary. Mediation, if carried out in a nonconfrontational and relatively cooperative manner, can be an effective way to resolve commercial disputes without resorting to the long and relatively difficult methods of arbitration and litigation. What is important is the cooperation of the two parties in the mediation proceedings, because they are not bound by the verdict of the mediator, whose role is essentially to moderate and balance the discussion and suggest ways to reach a common ground on a mutually agreeable basis. Of course, mediation can become a long and tedious process if both parties adopt a confrontational approach and especially if the issues involved are complex and the mediator is relatively unfamiliar with them at the outset.

In summary, the international businessperson operating in overseas environments is faced with a multitude of complex, differing, and sometimes conflicting bodies of law regarding allowable forms of ownership and business activities. Thus, it is crucial that the firm ensure adequate coverage by its own legal staff or by retaining effective local counsel. In doing so, the company can take the greatest amount of precaution to avoid problems that can arise in international legal disputes.

LOCAL COURTS, LOCAL REMEDIES

If disputes are not resolved by the informal methods, parties to the contracts have at least two possible paths of dispute resolution to pursue, commercial litigation and international arbitration, which assume that other methods of dispute resolution have been ineffective. Before these methods can be used, another established rule of international law holds that recourse to international legal forms is pursued only once the parties have exhausted local possibilities for achieving relief. These local remedies include the use of local courts or action by national governmental and administrative bodies. This rule applies only to actions between private parties, however, and not to those between states and individuals, because a state cannot be said to have local remedies to exhaust. The exhaustion rule protects the interests of both the foreign national and a host state. By respecting the sovereignty of states and the primacy of national jurisdiction in international disputes, the rule gives the states the necessary flexibility to regulate their internal affairs. At the same time, the rule requires states to recognize their international responsibility to offer justice to foreign nationals. Thus, the rule protects the interest of the multinational by promising

either effective local remedies or a remedy in an international form.

THE PRINCIPLE OF COMITY

The principle of sovereignty provides for international etiquette in the form of countries' reciprocal respect for each other's laws and powers regarding the actions of citizens abroad. This is the *principle of comity*, under which each nation defers to another's sovereignty in the protection of the rights of foreign citizens under their own legislative, executive, and judicial systems. The provision of comity is discretionary for each government and stems not from law but from tradition and good faith. It accounts for the international convention that provides immunity from the laws of the visited country for another nation's diplomats. The expectation is that in *reciprocity* the governments of foreign nations will similarly provide for diplomatic corps members working abroad.

LITIGATION

The litigation of international disputes involves the use of courts to apply both domestic and international law to resolve conflicts between parties. In the event that litigation is necessary, parties look to the courts of the host country, the home country, or even a third country for a resolution.

Litigation through court systems has the disadvantage of being a lengthy and involved process that can use a vast amount of a firm's resources in the form of time and expenses. For example, obtaining evidence from one country while in another is an intricate process involving *letters rogatory*, which provide the means for courts of different countries to communicate with one another. Domestic lawyers obtain letters rogatory by petitioning the district court where the action is pending to issue letters to the appropriate judicial counterpart in the foreign country. The letters, couched in standard polite language, request the provision of certain evidence necessary to try the case in home courts. Generally, under the principle of comity, courts will grant such requests. Obstacles and refusals do arise in foreign environments when national interests or principles are involved, as is the case when U.S. courts seek evidence in antitrust suits intended to extend judicial extraterritoriality.

Another problem with litigation is that even if a party receives a judgment in its favor, it may have difficulty enforcing that judgment, particularly if the court used for settlement of the dispute does not have jurisdiction over the losing party. *Jurisdiction* is the capacity of a nation to prescribe a course of conduct for its citizens and to enforce a rule of law on its citizens. To enforce any legal rule, both jurisdiction to prescribe and jurisdiction to enforce that rule must be present. Because of these complexities and in the interest of expediency, those involved in disputes of an international nature often turn to arbitration, a quicker and easier method of resolving such conflicts.

An example of the problems of jurisdiction is evident in the case of a major U.S. international bank, Bankers Trust Company, and Libya. In January 1986, in an effort to deter Libya from supporting the activities of terrorists in the Middle East and Europe, President Ronald Reagan instructed all Americans to leave Libya and placed a total ban on the conduct of trade between the two countries. In conjunction with the trade ban, and in order to protect U.S. companies with assets in Libya against retaliation, Reagan ordered a freeze on all Libyan assets located in the United States or held by U.S. banks. Officials estimated that the freeze involved several hundred million dollars, primarily in cash and other liquid assets.[4]

At the time of the freeze, the Libyan government had deposits with Bankers Trust of nearly $300 million, with $161 million on deposit in the London branch and $131 million in New York; all

of which was frozen. Subsequently, the Libyan Arab Foreign Bank sued in British courts for the return of its funds on the grounds that a freeze of assets by the United States was not enforceable overseas. The lawyer for the Libyan bank asserted that British law governed deposits in that country and that the policies and actions of other nations should not interfere. The "writ of the United States does not run in this country," he said.[5]

Bankers Trust argued the other side of the issue, asserting that it could repay foreign currency deposits only in the currency concerned. Thus, to repay Libya it would have to use dollars in London and would therefore be breaking U.S. sanction law by releasing the funds denominated in dollars.

The British court ruled in favor of Libya on the grounds that U.S. law had no jurisdiction over English banking activities.

INTERNATIONAL ARBITRATION

In arbitration, parties to a dispute agree to take their case to a third party in the form of an agency of independent arbitration. They submit whatever documents of evidence they feel are relevant and agree to accept the judgment of the arbitrators, waiving their rights to appeal through court systems.

Arbitration has several advantages over litigation. It is a speedier process than court procedures; the parties have a say in the choice of expert arbitrators, as compared to arbitrary judicial assignments; and the parties can have private adjudication. Results are achieved faster and less expensively in arbitration, because the proceedings are less complex and less formal than in litigation. The main drawback of international arbitration is that its use precludes further appeals, because there is no parallel in arbitration to appellate courts within judicial systems.

The use of arbitration by international parties is backed by laws and governmental treaties that allow for the recognition and enforcement of awards made through arbitration. The United States is a signatory to many treaties providing for the recognition of arbitration, including the multinational treaties on arbitration in the New York Convention of 1958, the Inter-American Arbitration Convention of 1975, and the New York Convention on the Recognition and Enforcement of Foreign Arbitral Awards of 1970. This last treaty was signed by more than 60 countries, and it lends uniformity and credibility to the practice of international arbitration and provides for each country's recognition of arbitration awards and agreements. It also prevents the parties from adjudicating disputes that they agreed to arbitrate.

To provide for arbitration rather than litigation of potential disputes between parties to an international contract, the terms of the contract must include a clause regarding the arbitration of potential disagreements. Arbitration clauses in international contracts must cover several important points of agreement between the parties, including the following:

- The determination of the scope of the arbitration
- The nature of potential disputes to be covered
- Whether the arbitration findings are protected by national treaties
- The language to be used in the conduct of the arbitration

More important, arbitration clauses in contracts between international parties include a choice of law under which to conduct the arbitration. Because each party usually prefers the procedural and substantive law of its own country to govern the proceedings, frequently the law of a third country is chosen as a compromise. Similarly, the contract clause often includes a choice of forum for the arbitration, which might be stipulated as an existing institutional framework, such as a major international arbitration center. One such center is the *London Court of International Arbitration*,

which has dealt with disputes regarding private international commercial transactions since 1982. As of April 2006, the organization had in excess of 1,500 members from 80 countries.

Other alternatives in the choice of arbitration forums are available. The parties can designate the use of a specific private commercial arbitration firm or the creation of a commission to arbitrate the dispute. Many public entities choose the latter course because the commissions are composed of an equal number of arbitrators chosen by each side, to ensure proper airing of each party's position. Stipulating the choice of forum often has the advantage of simultaneously ensuring a choice of law under which there are minimal amounts of judicial interference prior to, during, and after the proceedings and few complex procedural requirements for conducting the arbitration. In England and France, for example, there have historically been statutes covering arbitration laws that allowed for judicial intervention in the process. These laws also have allowed for very narrow scopes of discovery and limited powers ceded to the arbitrator to force the production of evidence.

INTERNATIONAL CENTRE FOR SETTLEMENT OF INVESTMENT DISPUTES

When the contract being disputed involves investments in foreign countries, the parties can seek adjudication through the International Centre for Settlement of Investment Disputes (ICSID), which is affiliated with the World Bank, as is briefly discussed in Chapter 6. This forum was established in 1967 through an international convention to settle disagreements arising between states and foreign investors, especially in cases of acts of state that result in the nationalization or expropriation of investors' assets.

The role of the ICSID is not to develop rules

and regulations regarding host country–investor relationships but to establish a methodology and forum for disputing parties to resolve their differences. To use the ICSID, all parties must agree to refer their dispute to it and accept that forum's ruling as final and binding. In addition, all signatory countries to the convention must accept the decision as binding. Signatories to the ICSID convention include most industrialized countries and many less-developed nations.

Most Latin American countries, however, do not subscribe to the ICSID, believing that its provisions infringe on their sovereign rights. These nations subscribe to the *Calvo doctrine*,[6] which is the belief that when foreign interests choose to enter a nation and conduct business within that country, they are implicitly agreeing to be treated as if they were nationals and thus are subject to the laws and decisions of the sovereign nation and have no legal recourse outside that nation.

Disputes between states can be submitted for adjudication to the international court associated with the United Nations, the *International Court of Justice* at the Hague. All members of the United Nations by definition have access to this international court. The purpose of the court is to make judgments about disputes between nations that have chosen to submit to its jurisdiction. Problems or disagreements experienced by private individuals or corporate entities can be brought before the court only if they are sponsored or put forward by one of the court's member states. As with arbitration, the parties in the action must agree to submit to the jurisdiction of the court, but once a judgment is reached, there is no overriding international method of providing for the enforcement of that decision, save through sanctions imposed by individual nations or other international pressures brought to bear on the transgressing party.

In the European Union, members can seek redress of disputes through the *European Court of Justice*, which not only rules on the constitutionality of EU administrative activities but also provides recourse for legal questions referred to it by any court in a member country. The judgments of the European Court of Justice have the force of law in the EU and are binding on individuals, corporations, and governments. The purpose of the court is to provide for uniformity in the development of a legal process within the entire community. There are 15 judges at the European Court of Justice, who serve six-year terms.

Dispute settlement under trade agreements is generally achieved through consultations and negotiations between the parties. If terms cannot be reached, the disputes are sometimes taken to councils for consideration. Under the auspices of the WTO, such a council can be appointed to hear disputes and render an advisory opinion. Should one of the parties choose to ignore that advice, the complaining country is allowed to suspend its trade obligations with the other party of the suit.

SUMMARY

The operations, profit, and welfare of the modern multinational corporation can be profoundly affected by differences in international legal systems or even the imposition of domestic laws on the operations of a firm in a foreign environment. These laws can be in the areas of antitrust activity, protection of intangible property rights, taxation, corrupt practices, and all aspects of ongoing business operations for the multinational firm.

While treaties, trade agreements, and conventions among countries provide some international framework for a legal system, disputes continue to arise between parties in commerce. Some of these disputes can be avoided through the judicious writing of clear, unambiguous contracts that provide for these potential pitfalls. Some conflicts still occur between private parties, between nations, or between nations and individual interests. The resolution of these conflicts involves the answering of questions regarding legal jurisdiction, statutory interpretation, and the enforcement of judgments by judiciaries or third-party arbitrators in either national or international forums.

DISCUSSION QUESTIONS

1. Is there a single body of international law that governs all countries in the world?
2. What are the differences among civil law, common law, and religious law?
3. Why are international treaties important to conducting international business?
4. What is the doctrine of sovereign immunity?
5. What is extraterritoriality?
6. What is predatory pricing?
7. How do antidumping laws protect domestic manufacturers?
8. What are antitrust laws?
9. What U.S. law was enacted to control bribery and payoffs in international business? Why were bribes being paid? How do other countries view the practice of bribery?
10. What techniques can be used to resolve business disputes rather than resorting to litigation?
11. How is arbitration similar to or different from litigation?
12. What is the International Court of Justice?

NOTES

1. Felton, "Congress May Weigh Limits on President's Authority to Impose Trade Restrictions."
2. Yahoo News, "Missy Elliott's Line Hits Snag."
3. "Monopolies of the Mind."
4. Felton, "Reagan Tightens Economic Sanctions on Libya."
5. Duffy, "Libyan Bank Sues Bankers Trust."
6. Named after Argentine diplomat Carlos Calvo (1824–1906).

BIBLIOGRAPHY

Boston.com. "Missy Elliott's Line Hits Snag." February 13, 2005. http://www.boston.com/ae/music/articles/2005/02/12/missy_elliotts_line_hits_snag?mode=PF

Brand, Ronald A. "Private Parties and GATT Dispute Resolution: Implications of the Panel Report on Section 337 of the U.S. Tariff Act of 1930." *Journal of World Trade,* June 1990, 5–30.

Brown, Jeffrey A. "Extraterritoriality: Current Policy of the United States." *Syracuse Journal of International Law & Commerce,* Spring 1986, 493–519.

Carroll, Eileen P. "Are We Ready for ADR in Europe?" *International Financial Law Review,* December 1989, 11–14.

Chard, J.S., and C.J. Mellor. "Intellectual Property Rights and Parallel Imports." *World Economy,* March 1989, 69–83.

David, R., and J. Brierley. *Major Legal Systems in the World Today.* 3rd ed. New York: Macmillan, 1978.

Duffy, John. "Libyan Bank Sues Bankers Trust." *American Banker,* June 1987, 2.

Felton, John. "Congress May Weigh Limits on President's Authority to Impose Trade Restrictions." *Congressional Quarterly,* November 1982, 2882–84.

———. "Reagan Tightens Economic Sanctions on Libya." *Congressional Quarterly,* January 1986, 59–60.

Fox, W.F. *International Commercial Agreements.* Netherlands: Kluwer Law and Taxation Publishers, 1988.

Getz, Kathleen A. "International Codes of Conduct: An Analysis of Ethical Reasoning." *Journal of Business Ethics,* July 1990, 567–77.

Greer, Thomas V. "Product Liability in the European Economic Community: The New Situation." *Journal of International Business Studies,* Summer 1989, 337–48.

Kruckenberg, Dean. "The Need for an International Code of Ethics." *Public Relations Review,* Summer 1989, 6–18.

Litka, Michael. *International Dimensions of the Legal Environment of Business.* Boston: PWS-Kent Publishing Company, 1988.

Mcgraw, Thomas K. *America versus Japan.* Boston: Harvard Business School Press, 1986.

"Monopolies of the Mind." *Economist,* November 11, 2004.

CASE STUDY 8.1
COMPUSOFT SYSTEMS, INC.

It was a fairly thorough and well-drafted international sales and service agreement that CompuSoft Systems, Inc., of Palo Alto, California, had entered into with Los Santos Services, a large computer software reseller in the Latin American country of Cartunja. As Ken Rossi, marketing director of CompuSoft, read the fax message from Dom Simoes, executive vice president of Los Santos, he regretted the decision to sell to Cartunja, even though the agreement had been hailed three years ago, upon its signing, as a major step forward in international market expansion in Latin America. "It's time to call in the attorneys," thought Rossi as he reread the fax to let the implications of its contents sink in fully.

CompuSoft Systems began in 1991 as a small venture-capital enterprise, put together by a group of four young, technically qualified professionals. Mitch Holland had a PhD in electrical engineering and had worked for four years with a large software development company in California's Silicon Valley. Tom Heilbroner held an MS degree in electronics and systems development from the University of Stanford and had been with the management information systems division of a New York City–based multinational corporation for three years, where he developed specialized software and networking systems for the internal use of the company. Peter Daniels was a certified public accountant, had worked in the consulting division of a large accounting firm for three years, and had specialized in the development of computer-based accounting systems. Ken Rossi had a master's in business

administration in accounting from Yale and also held an electrical engineering degree from Virginia Tech.

Like many Silicon Valley firms, CompuSoft had done extremely well. It had grown rapidly, and by 1999 sales had reached $640 million. The company was able to carve a small but significant niche in the accounting software market, and its wide range of accounting software applications packages had gained acceptance with a large number of U.S. companies. CompuSoft's products were known for their reliability and quality, but further market expansion seemed difficult, given the growing intensity of competition especially from the larger and financially stronger software companies who offered aggressively priced products. Further, the market for accounting software in the United States appeared limited, and overall market growth was leveling off.

In the face of these circumstances, CompuSoft concluded that the time was ripe for a shift in its strategy, and in 2000, the company decided to go international. None of the senior management had any international business experience, and initially there were some doubts about the wisdom of this move. It was felt, however, that the company need not take on the responsibility of marketing its products overseas itself and that this could be easily done through a local agent in a foreign country with whom the company would enter into a comprehensive agreement that would include all promises necessary to protect it from difficulties in the future.

continued

Case 8.1 (*continued*)

Latin America was chosen as the first region for the international marketing effort of Compu-Soft, and agreements were signed with three local software retailing companies in three countries, including Cartunja. The company hired a top San Francisco law firm specializing in such agreements to draft and negotiate the contracts with the local selling agents.

Under these contracts the local selling agents were to market CompuSoft's software packages in sealed covers, supplied in a fully finished form by the company. The agents were not permitted to make any alterations, modifications, or changes in either the contents of the software or the external packaging. Another important provision of these agreements was that the reseller would advise each buyer in writing of the copyright to the software, and a statement of the restrictions on the use of the software was printed on the external cover of the software package. In addition, another leaflet defining the rights and obligations of the holder of the copyright (CompuSoft) was included in the package. The local agents also agreed to make all efforts to ensure that the copyrights of CompuSoft Systems were not violated in their respective countries.

For the first two years, things appeared to go well. The company had made considerable effort to adapt its accounting software to the needs of Latin American corporate customers, and the programs were an immediate success with local companies. The local agents also pushed the products because they were keen to maximize the attractive benefits of the graduated commission system put together by Rossi.

The first hint of problems came up in January 2003, when Simoes called Rossi to say that they would be lowering the estimates of sales to Peseta National Bank, a leading state-owned bank in Cartunja, which had 274 branches in 13 cities and townships all over Cartunja. Similarly, the estimated sales to 11 other state-owned banks were down by 60 percent. No reasons for the declines were given, except that the bank officials had informed Los Santos that their original interest in this software was only of a preliminary nature, and, on closer examination, they found that they were not ready to computerize their accounting systems using such sophisticated programs. The news came as a setback to CompuSoft, and, on closer analysis, it was felt that the reason given by the banks was not the real one. There was no competing product in Cartunja, and the banks badly needed to computerize their systems, having come under considerable criticism from the finance ministry and external auditors for having large arrears in the reconciliation of accounts between different branches and the corporate head offices. Further, Peseta National had already acquired the package from Los Santos, and it had been installed and running smoothly for the past four months. CompuSoft had also conducted a six-week training program, free of cost, for the accounting and systems personnel of Peseta National. The personnel were quite comfortable with the software and reported no problems. Therefore, in February 2003, Rossi called Simoes and asked him to dig further and find out what was really happening.

In the first week of March, Simoes came back with a startling answer; it appeared that the management information systems division of Peseta National had copied the software and was busy installing it at 70 of its other branches. Further, he learned that Peseta was likely to pass

continued

Case 8.1 (*continued*)

the program on, along with installation services, to 11 state-owned banks. It was a clear violation of the copyright. CompuSoft's top management was, expectedly, disturbed. They called Simoes and asked him to take every possible step to stop Peseta National Bank from further infringing the copyright.

The fax on Rossi's desk was a reply from Simoes. In effect, it said that Peseta National Bank and the 11 other banks in question are 100 percent state-owned institutions, and any legal action against them would be tantamount to legal action against the government. Further, if Los Santos instituted a suit against Peseta National, it might lose substantial orders that it was negotiating with other state-owned enterprises. Given the power of the government, a suit would hurt Los Santos in its other lines of business and build an adversarial relationship with the government. It would therefore be better if CompuSoft would initiate action against the Peseta National Bank directly.

"This is a real big one," thought Rossi. "If we do go ahead and fight it out, the government may ban our products from official purchases. If we don't, everybody in Cartunja and everywhere else in Latin America will merely copy our software, and our entire international expansion effort there would come to naught."

DISCUSSION QUESTIONS

1. What should CompuSoft Systems, Inc., do in this situation and why?
2. Suggest a strategy to deal with the situation, keeping in mind the possible international legal issues.

CHAPTER 9

Sociocultural Factors

CHAPTER OBJECTIVES

This chapter will:

- Define the term "sociocultural" as a combination of societal, political, and cultural norms and responses and discuss its influence in international business.
- Discuss how attitudes and beliefs influence human behavior, especially attitudes toward time, achievement, work, change, and occupational status.
- Present the influence of aesthetics and material culture within different societies.
- Examine how communication, both verbal and nonverbal, may serve as a barrier to international business operations.
- Investigate the importance of social status and the family within different cultures and their effect on the business environment.
- Identify the role of multinational corporations as agents of change in the international community.

SOCIOCULTURAL FACTORS AND INTERNATIONAL BUSINESS

Multinational corporations operate in different host countries around the world and have to deal with a wide variety of political, economic, geographical, technological, and business situations. Moreover, each host country has its own society and culture, which are different in many important ways from almost every other society and culture, although there are some commonalities. Although society and culture do not appear to be a part of business situations, they are actually key elements in shaping

how business is conducted, from what goods are produced, and how and through what means they are sold, to the establishment of industrial and management patterns and the determination of the success or failure of a local subsidiary or affiliate.

Society and culture influence every aspect of an MNC's overseas business, and a successful MNC operation, whether it involves marketing, finance, operations, information systems, or human resources, has to be acutely aware of the predominant attitudes, feelings, and opinions in the local environment. Differences in values and attitudes between the management at the parent offices and expatriate managers at the subsidiary or affiliate level, on one hand, and local managers and employees, on the other, can lead to serious operational and functional problems, which arise not because there are individual problems but because of the important differences between the societies and cultures. Society and culture often mold general attitudes toward fundamental aspects of life, such as time, money, productivity, and achievement, all of which can differ widely across countries and lead to differing expectations between the management in the home office and local employees of subsidiaries and affiliates.

While some sociocultural differences are obvious, others are relatively subtle though equally important. It is often difficult for an international manager to catch on to these subtle differences if he or she has not lived or worked in cultures other than that of the home country. Sometimes, the cultural differences can be large, but if some attempt is made to understand these cultural differences, expatriate managers can ensure that these gaps do not materially affect the performance of business.

MNCs have realized, sometimes through costly blunders, that sociocultural factors are vital ingredients that make up the overall business environment and that it is essential to appreciate these differences and their influences on business before an attempt is made to set up an operation in a host country.

SOCIETY, CULTURE, AND SOCIOCULTURAL FORCES

There are many definitions of culture. In general, *culture* can be defined as the entire set of social norms and responses that dominates the behavior of a population, which makes each social environment different. Culture is the conglomeration of beliefs, rules, techniques, institutions, and artifacts that characterize human population. It consists of the learned patterns of behavior common to members of a given society—the unique lifestyle of a particular group of people.

The various aspects of culture are interrelated; culture influences individual and group behavior and determines how things are done. Features of culture include religion, education, caste structure, politics, language differences, and production.

Society refers to a political and social entity that is defined geographically. To understand society and culture we must relate one to the other, hence the term "*sociocultural.*" To be successful in their relationships with people in other countries, international managers must study and understand the various aspects of culture.

How should one begin? With as broad a concept as culture, it is necessary to utilize some type of classification scheme as a guide to studying or comparing cultures. Table 9.1 outlines Murdock's list of 70 *cultural universals* that occur in all cultures.[1] While this schematic is limited by its one-dimensional approach, it provides an initial guide and checklist for the international firm and manager. For example, the international firm selling contraceptives must be aware that it is dealing with the family customs, population policy, and sexual restrictions of different cultures. Since many individuals base their decisions regarding contraception on religious beliefs, the seller must also consider this aspect of various cultures in the plan.

ELEMENTS OF CULTURE

The number of human variables and different types of business functions preclude an exhaustive discussion of culture here. Instead, we have broken down the broad area of culture into some major topics to facilitate study.

ATTITUDES AND BELIEFS

In every society there are norms of behavior based on the attitudes, values, and beliefs that constitute a part of its culture. The attitudes and beliefs of a culture, which vary from country to country, influence nearly all aspects of human behavior, provid-

Table 9.1

Murdock's List of 70 Cultural Universals

Age grading	Food taboos	Music
Athletic sports	Funeral rites	Mythology
Bodily adornment	Games	Numerals
Calendar	Gestures	Obstetrics
Cleanliness training	Gift giving	Penal sanctions
Community organization	Government	Personal names
Cooking	Greetings	Population policy
Cooperative labor	Hairstyles	Postnatal care
Cosmology	Hospitality	Pregnancy usages
Courtship	Housing hygiene	Property rights
Dancing	Incest taboos	Propitiation of sins
Decorative art	Inheritance rules	Puberty customs
Divination	Joking	Religious rituals
Division of labor	Kin groups	Residence rules
Dream interpretation	Kinship nomenclature	Sexual restrictions
Education	Language	Soul concepts
Ethics	Law	Status differentiation
Ethnobotany	Luck/superstitions	Supernatural beings
Etiquette	Magic	Surgery
Faith healing	Marriage	Toolmaking
Family	Mealtimes	Trade
Feasting	Medicine	Visiting
Fire making	Modesty concerning natural functions	Weaning
Folklore	Mourning	Weather control

Source: George P. Murdock, "The Common Denominator of Cultures," in *The Science of Man in the World Crises,* ed. Ralph Linton, pp. 123–42 (New York: Columbia University Press, 1945).

ing guidelines and organization to a society and its individuals. Identifying the attitudes and beliefs of a society, and how or whether they differ from one's own culture, will help the businessperson more easily understand people's behavior.

ATTITUDES TOWARD TIME

Everywhere in the world people use time to communicate with one another. In international business, attitudes toward time are displayed in behavior regarding punctuality, responses to business communications, responses to deadlines, and the amounts of time that are spent waiting in an outer office for an appointment. For example, while Americans are known to be punctual, few other cultures give the same importance to being on time as Americans. In terms of business communications, Japanese companies may not respond immediately to an offer from a foreign company. What a foreign company may see as rejection of an offer or disinterest may simply be the lengthy time the Japanese company takes to review the details of a deal. In fact, the U.S. emphasis on speed and deadlines is often used against Americans in foreign business dealings where local business managers have their own schedules.

ATTITUDES TOWARD WORK AND LEISURE

Most people in industrial societies work many more hours than is necessary to satisfy their basic needs for food, clothing, and shelter. Their attitudes toward work and achievement are indicative of their view toward wealth and material gain. These attitudes affect the types, qualities, and numbers of individuals who pursue entrepreneurial and management careers as well as the way workers respond to material incentives.

Many industrial psychologists have conducted research in this area to determine what motivates people to work more than is necessary to provide for their basic needs. One explanation is the *Protestant ethic*, which has its basis in the Reformation, when work was viewed as a means of salvation and people preferred to transform productivity gains into additional output rather than additional leisure. Europeans and Americans are typically considered to adhere to this work ethic because they generally view work as a moral virtue and look unfavorably on the idle. In comparison, in places where work is considered necessary only to obtain the essentials for survival, people may stop working once they obtain the essentials.

Today, few other societies hold to this strict basic concept of work for work's sake, and leisure is viewed more highly in some societies than in others. It has been argued that many Asian economies are characterized by limited economic needs that reflect their culture. Therefore, it is expected that if incomes start to rise, workers would tend to reduce their ef-

forts so that personal income remains unchanged. The promise of overtime pay may fail to keep workers on the job, and raising employee salaries could result in their working less, a phenomenon that economists have called the *backward-bending labor supply curve*. In contrast, the pursuit of leisure activities may have to be a learned process. After a long period of sustained work activity with little time for leisure, people may have problems in deciding what to do with additional free time.

These attitudes, however, can change. The demonstration effect of seeing others with higher incomes and better standards of living has motivated workers in such cultures to put in longer hours to improve their own financial status and material well-being. Additionally, attitudes toward work are shaped by the perceived rewards and punishments of the amount of work. In cultures where both rewards for greater amounts of work and punishments for lesser amounts of work are low, there is little incentive for people to work harder than absolutely necessary. Moreover, when the outcome of a particular work cycle is certain, there is little enthusiasm for the work itself. Where high uncertainty of success is combined with some probability of a very positive reward for success, one finds the greatest enthusiasm for work.

ATTITUDES TOWARD ACHIEVEMENT

Cultural differences in the general attitude toward work are also accompanied by significant national differences in achievement motivation. In some cultures, particularly those with highly stratified and hierarchical societies, there is a tendency to avoid personal responsibility and to work according to precise instructions, followed to the letter, that are received from supervisors. In many societies, especially where social security is low and jobs are prized, there is both a tendency to avoid taking risk and little innovation in work or production processes. In such cultures, the prospect of higher achievement is not considered attractive enough to warrant taking avoidable risks. In many industrial societies, however, attitudes toward personal achievement are quite different. Personal responsibility and the ability to take risk for potential gain are considered valuable instruments in achieving higher goals. In fact, in many cultures the societal pressure on achievement is so intense that individuals are automatically driven toward attempting ambitious goals.

Attitudes among workers and managers often influence the types of management that has to be utilized to achieve corporate goals. In a culture that emphasizes risk taking, greater responsibility, and individual decision making, a decentralized management system would be more appropriate. In a culture where there is a tendency to put in only adequate amounts of work and where achievement is not a valued personal attribute, the company will follow a more centralized management system, with only limited delegation of decision-making authority.

ATTITUDES TOWARD CHANGE

The international manager must understand what aspects of a culture resist change, how those areas of resistance differ among cultures, how the process of change takes place in different cultures, and how long it will take to implement change. There are two conflicting forces within a culture regarding change. People attempt to protect and preserve their culture with an elaborate set of sanctions and laws invoked against those who deviate from their norms. Differences are perceived in light of the belief that "my method is right; thus, the other method must be wrong."

This contradictory force is one in which the public is aware that the cultural environment is continually changing and that a culture must change in order to ensure its own continuity. In other words, to balance these attitudes, the manager must remember

that the closer a new idea can be related to a traditional one when illustrating its relative advantage, the greater the acceptance of that new concept. Usually cultures with centuries-old traditions that have remained closed to outside influences are more resistant to change than other cultures. The level of education in a society and the exposure of its people to knowledge and the experience of other cultures is an extremely important determinant of its attitude toward change. The influence and nature of religious beliefs in a society also influence attitudes toward change.

ATTITUDES TOWARD JOBS

The type of job that is considered most desirable or prestigious varies greatly across different cultures. Thus, while the medical and legal professions are considered extremely prestigious in the United States, civil service is considered the most prestigious occupation in several developing countries. The importance of a particular profession in a culture is an important determinant of the number and quality of people who seek to join that profession. Thus, in a country where business is regarded as a prestigious occupation, the MNC will be able to tap a large, well-qualified pool of local managers. On the other hand, if business is not considered an important profession, much of the country's talent will be focused elsewhere.

There is great emphasis in some countries on being one's own boss, and the idea of working for someone, even if that happens to be a prestigious organization, tends to be frowned on. In many countries, however, MNCs are able to counter the lower prestige of business as a profession by offering high salaries and other forms of compensation. Some, in fact, succeeded in luring some of the best local talent away from jobs that are traditionally considered the most prestigious in those countries. In most cultures, there are some types of work that are considered more prestigious than others, and certain occupations carry a perception of greater rewards than others, which may be because of economic, social, or traditional factors.

DOES RELIGION AFFECT COMMERCE?

International business is affected by religious beliefs in many ways, because religion can provide the spiritual foundation of a culture. Business can bring about modernization that disrupts religious traditions, and international business can conflict with holy days and religious holidays. Cultural conflicts in the area of religion can be quite serious. For example, a MNC would have problems with a subsidiary where employees traditionally enjoy a month-long religious holiday.

Religion can also impose moral norms on culture. It may insist on limits, particularly the subordination of impulse to moral conduct. Another example of business conflicting with religion is the development of a promotional campaign for contraceptives in any of the predominantly Roman Catholic countries.

In certain countries, religion may require its followers to dress in a particular manner or maintain a certain type of physical appearance, which may conflict with the MNC's appearance and presentation norms. Certain products manufactured by the MNC or some ingredients used in manufacturing may be taboo in some religions. For example, beef and tallow are taboo in the Hindu religion and cannot be used as ingredients in soap manufacturing in India. Similarly, pork products cannot be sold or used in manufacture in Muslim countries because pork is religiously impure according to the tenets of Islam.

In many religions, the general philosophy of life is completely different from that in the Western world. Within some Asian religions, for example, the notion exists that nothing is permanent and therefore the world is an illusion. To followers of such beliefs, time is cyclical—from birth to death to reincarnation—and the goal of salvation is to escape the cycle and move into a state of eternal bliss (nirvana). These religious beliefs directly affect how and why people work, as in the Buddhist and Hindu religions, where people are supposed to eliminate all desires and therefore may have little motivation for achievement and the acquisition of material goods.

AESTHETICS

Aesthetics pertains to the sense of beauty and good taste of a culture and includes myths, tales, dramatization of legends, and more modern expressions of the arts: drama, music, painting, sculpture, architecture, and so on. Like language, art serves as a means of communication. Color and form are of particular interest to international business because in most cultures these elements are used as symbols that convey specific meanings. Green is a popular color in many Muslim countries but is often associated with disease in countries with dense, green jungles. In France, the Netherlands, and Sweden, green is associated with cosmetics. Similarly, different colors represent death in different cultures. In the United States and many European countries, black represents death, while in Japan and many other Asian countries, white signifies death.

In many countries physical contact in public by persons of opposite sexes is not considered proper, and exposure of the human body is treated as obscene. MNCs must be exceptionally careful in designing their advertising programs, the packaging of their products, and the content of their verbal messages to ensure that they do not offend the aesthetic sensibilities of the country they are operating in.

MATERIAL CULTURE

Material culture refers to the things people use and enjoy and includes all human-made objects.

Its study is concerned with technology and economics. Material cultures differ very significantly because of tradition, climate, economic status, and a host of other factors. Material culture is an extremely important issue to be considered by an MNC. Almost everything a society consumes, or, in other words, whatever the MNC sells or hopes to sell, is determined by the material culture of the population. For example, selling humidifiers in a tropical country would be a failure because they are not needed by the local people and are simply not a part of the material culture. Alternatively, selling American-style barbecues would be a failure in parts of the world where outdoor cookery is not a part of popular material culture.

Technology is an important factor that affects the material culture of a society. As more and more new products and processes are made available by technology, and if they are sufficiently used by the people, they ultimately become a part of the material culture. One example is the personal computer, which has become an integral part of the material culture of most industrialized societies. Therefore, a U.S. multinational might target France or Australia as a major market for selling computer peripherals. There would not, however, be a market for this product in the nations of sub-Saharan Africa, at least at present, because computers are not a part of the material culture in these countries.

Tradition also determines material culture to a considerable extent. The French, for example, prefer drinking wine, while Germans prefer drinking beer, the distinction being largely traditional, but critical for a company aiming to establish a market for alcoholic beverages in these countries.

A country's particular physical and geographic circumstances also play an important part in influencing its material culture. Space limitations in Japan prevent the use of large domestic appliances, such as large-capacity deep freezers or refrigerators, and preclude a real estate market featuring rambling

suburban homes, even though the economy may be prosperous enough to pay for these luxuries. Thus, suburban homeowner living is not a part of the material culture of Japan, and this affects the type of products the Japanese middle class will or will not buy. For example, sales of lawn mowers, backyard pools, and home security systems are likely to be extremely low in Japan, while those of compact, sophisticated appliances and luxuries that can be accommodated in small apartments are likely to be very high.

LITERACY RATE

The literacy rate of a potential overseas market or facility is used by many areas of the international business firm. The marketer uses it to determine the types and sophistication of advertising to employ. The personnel manager uses it as a guide in estimating the types of people available for staffing the operation. Literacy rate numbers, however, rarely provide any information about the quality of education.

Countries with low literacy rates are less likely to provide the MNC with all the qualified personnel it needs to staff its local operation and will necessitate the transfer of a large number of expatriate managers. Literacy rates must be used with caution, however, because they often hide the fact that a country with a low literacy rate but a very large population may have a large number of qualified professionals, who as a percentage of the population may be very small but form a fairly large absolute number by themselves. Literacy rates generally have a more direct bearing on the general level of education and abilities of the workers at the lower levels, because much of the population that suffers from illiteracy is at the lowest economic level in society.

EDUCATION MIX

When considering education as an aspect of culture, an MNC not only should look at literacy rates and levels of education but also should try to understand the education mix of a certain society; that is, which areas are considered important for concentrated education? For example, a combination of factors caused a proliferation of European business schools patterned on American models. First, increased competition in the European Union resulted in a demand for better-trained managers. Second, Europeans began establishing their own business schools after they were educated at American business schools and returned home. Third, the establishment of American-type schools with faculty from the United States was frequently accomplished with the assistance of American universities.

This trend toward specialized business education is slower in less-developed countries. Historically, higher education in LDCs has focused on the humanities, law, and medicine; engineering has not been popular, with the exception of architectural and civil engineering, because there were few job opportunities in that field, and business careers have lacked prestige.

Brain Drain

Brain drain is a phenomenon experienced by many developing nations, especially China and India. Because governments overinvested in higher education in relation to demand, developing nations have seen rising unemployment among the educated. These unemployed professionals must immigrate to industrialized nations to find appropriate work, which effectively represents a loss to the country that has spent substantial amounts of scarce public resources to finance professional education.

Communication and Language

Communication and language are closely related to culture because each culture reflects what the society values in its language. Culture determines to a large extent the use of spoken language—specific words,

phrases, and intonations used to communicate people's thoughts and needs. These verbal patterns are reinforced by unspoken language—gestures, body positions, and symbolic aids.

Spoken language becomes a cultural barrier between different countries and regions. In one country, verbal language can consist of many dialects and different colloquialisms and may be totally different from the written language. There is no way to learn a language so that the nuances, double meanings, and slang are immediately understood, unless one also learns other aspects of the culture.

Languages delineate culture. In some European countries there is more than one language and, hence, more than one culture. Belgium and Switzerland are two such examples, with French and Dutch spoken in the former, and German, Italian, French, and Romansh officially spoken in the latter. Different cultures exist within each country. One cannot conclude, however, that where only one language exists, there will be only one culture. The people of both the United States and Great Britain speak English, but each country has its own culture. An example of the problems facing an international firm that must respond to the language aspects of a culture involves the sort of computer hardware marketed in Canada.

Canada's heated debate about its official language may affect computer users. After several years of study, a joint government-industry committee has come up with Canada's first national standard for computer keyboards with both English and accented French letters.

Although the Canadian government is officially bilingual, English remains the dominant language. Many English speakers resent the government's move to promote French, which is dominant only in Quebec. Hence, selling keyboards with both English and accented French letters could prove to be an obstacle in the English-speaking provinces of Canada.

Where many spoken languages exist in a single country, one language usually serves as the principal vehicle for communication across cultures. This is true for many countries that were once colonies, such as India, which uses English. Although they serve as national languages, these foreign substitutes are not the first language of the populace and are therefore less effective than native tongues for reaching mass markets or for day-to-day conversations between managers and workers. In many situations, managers try to ease these communication difficulties by separating the workforce according to origin. The preferred solution is to teach managers the language of their workers.

When communication involves translation from one language to another, the problems of ascertaining meanings that arise in different cultures are multiplied many times. Translation is not just the matching of words in one language with words of identical meanings in another language. It involves interpretation of the cultural patterns and concepts of one country into the terms of those of another. It is often difficult to translate directly from one language to another. Many international managers have been unpleasantly surprised to learn that the nodding and yes responses of their Japanese counterparts did not mean that the deal was closed or that they agreed, because the word for yes, *hai*, can also simply mean "it is understood" or "I hear you." In fact, it is typical of the Japanese to avoid saying anything disagreeable to a listener.

Many international business consultants advise the manager in a foreign country to use two translations by two different translators. The manager's words are first translated by a non-native speaker; then a native speaker translates the first translator's words back into the original language. Unless translators have a special knowledge of the industry, they often go to a dictionary for a literal translation that frequently makes no sense or is erroneous.

Nonverbal language is another form of communication. Silent communication can take several forms, such as body language, space, and language of things. Body talk is a universal form of language that may have different meanings from country to country. Usually, it involves facial expressions, postures, gestures, handshakes, eye contact, color or symbols, and time (punctuality). The language of space includes such things as conversational distance between people, closed office doors, or office size. Each of these has a different connotation and appropriateness in different cultures. The language of things includes money and possessions.

GROUPS: FAMILIES AND FRIENDS

All populations of men, women, and children are commonly divided into groups, and individuals are members of more than one group. Affiliations determined by birth, known as *ascribed group memberships*, are based on sex, family, age, caste, and ethnic, racial, or national origin. Those affiliations not determined by birth are called *acquired group memberships* and are based on religious, political, and other associations. Acquired group membership often reflects one's place in the social structure. Employment, manners, dress, and expectations are often dictated by each culture to its members. Group rituals, such as marriage, funerals, and graduations, also form a part of the societal organization.

In some societies, acceptance of people for jobs and promotion is based primarily on their performance capabilities. In others, competence is of secondary importance. Whatever factor is given primary importance (seniority, sex, and so on) will determine to a great extent who is eligible to fill certain positions and what their compensation is. The more egalitarian or open a society, the less difference ascribed group membership will make.

Three types of international contrasts indicate how widespread the differences in group memberships are and how important they are as business considerations. These contrasts involve sex, age, and family. Differences in attitudes toward males and females are especially apparent from country to country. The level of rigidity of expected behavior because of one's gender is indicative of cultural differences. Often, these differences are clearly reflected in education statistics, although many countries have instituted or have plans to institute additional educational opportunities for females.

In many countries age and wisdom are correlated. Where this is so, advancement has usually been based on seniority. In the past, this has been a common practice in Japan. Contrary to this, in many countries retirement at a particular age is mandatory and relative youthfulness may be an advantage in moving up in an organization. Barriers to employment on the basis of age or sex are undergoing substantial changes around the world, and data collected about these trends that are even only a few years old are not considered reliable.

Kinship, or family associations, may play a more active role as an element of culture in some societies than in others. An individual may be accepted or rejected based on the social status of his or her family. Because family ties are so strong, there is a compulsion to cooperate closely within the family but to be distrustful of links involving others outside the family.

In some countries, the word "family" may have very different connotations. In the United States, we have come to depend on the nuclear family—mother, father, and children—as the definition of family. In other societies, the extended family may be the norm. A vertically extended family includes grandparents and possibly great-grandparents as part of a single family, while horizontally extended families include aunts, uncles, and cousins.

The impact of the extended family on the foreign firm derives from the fact that it is a source of employees and business connections. Responsibility to a family is often a cause of high absenteeism in developing countries where workers are called to help with the harvest. Motivation to work also may be affected in cultures where workers are responsible for the welfare of their extended families. When additional income means additional mouths to feed and further responsibility, workers may reduce output if they are given an increase in salary.

The international firm may be directly affected by the cultural aspect of group and social organizations. Even if individuals have qualifications for certain positions, and there are no legal barriers for hiring them, social obstacles may make the international firm think twice about employing them. Class structures can also be so rigid within one type of group that they are difficult to overcome in other contexts. For example, in a society where caste structures are deeply ingrained, serious problems could arise if these caste levels are not considered in determining work groups, supervisor roles, and managerial promotions; if individuals in a lower caste are placed higher within the corporate hierarchy than members of higher-caste groups, internal tensions may arise.

GIFT GIVING AND BRIBERY

Gift giving is a custom that has great value within a business environment. It is important not only to remember to bring a gift, but also to make certain that the gift you have chosen is appropriate. In some cultures, gift giving is not expected or encouraged, and the international businessperson must be familiar with the appropriate behavior in each environment.

Gift giving is viewed as a different and separate activity from *bribery*, at least in the United States. During the 1970s many large international companies were faced with serious problems after they were caught paying bribes to government officials to obtain large contracts from foreign business firms. While much of the criticism has been vented against multinational companies, especially those from the United States, it is important to note that the practice was widespread. In 1977, however, the United States passed the Foreign Corrupt Practices Act, making illegal certain payments by U.S. executives of publicly traded firms to foreign officials. The legislation has been controversial and often called inconsistent. One such inconsistency is that it is clearly legal to make payments to people to expedite their compliance with the law, but illegal to make payments to other government officials who are not directly responsible for carrying out the law. It is important for the international business executive to identify the thin line between complying with foreign expectations and bribery and corruption.

OTHER THEORIES OF CULTURE

CULTURAL CLUSTER APPROACH

Some theorists have attempted to group cultural patterns based on geographical similarities. One such theory is the *cultural cluster approach*. This approach groups cultures together based on where people are located in the world as follows:

- Nordic countries—Denmark, Finland, Norway, Sweden
- Germanic countries—Austria, Germany, Switzerland
- Anglo countries—Australia, Canada, United States, United Kingdom, Ireland, South Africa
- Latin American countries—Argentina, Chile, Columbia, Mexico, Peru
- Arab countries—Saudi Arabia, Bahrain, Kuwait, Oman
- Far Eastern countries—China, Hong Kong, Indonesia, Philippines

A quick glance at the groupings above reveals many differences among the groups themselves, and there are certainly differences within individual

countries as well. Few academic cultural theorists would agree that all of the citizens of the United States are culturally the same, so attempting to classify the members of other countries in this manner would appear to be problematic at best. These types of classifications are often too general and have little practical use in a business environment.

Other cultural classifications have moved away from geography and have looked at factors that are present for individuals rather than trying to classify large groups of people in the same manner. Two other theories discussed here are Hall's low-context, high-context approach and Hofstede's five dimensions of culture.

EDWARD HALL'S LOW-CONTEXT, HIGH-CONTEXT APPROACH

Edward Hall's low-context, high-context approach categorizes individuals (and societies) in terms of how they communicate and what is required in order to successfully communicate in a given society. In a *low-context culture*, the words used by the speaker explicitly convey the speaker's message to the listener. This is similar to interacting with a computer. If information is not explicitly stated, the meaning can be distorted. In low-context cultures, behavior and beliefs may need to be spelled out clearly, and the society in question is very rule oriented. In codified systems such as this, knowledge is easier to transfer between individuals and groups, as there are written directions for what is expected in a given situation. Some examples of societies or groups where low-context communication is more prevalent are groups that have been together for a short period of time and might also be engaged in only small or specific tasks. The communication among employees at large corporations typically exhibits low-context communication, as does that within sports groups, where the rules of engagement are clearly laid out. In terms of national societies, the United States has historically been the example of the low-context approach to communication. In low-context cultures, the information content in advertising should be higher than that in high-context cultures.

The second societal grouping is the *high-context culture*. In these groups, the context in which a conversation occurs is just as important as the words that are actually spoken. To be successful in this form of communication, an individual or company must understand certain cultural clues that are being communicated along with the spoken words. Groups exhibiting the high-context approach typically have been together for a long period of time, and there is more internalized understanding of what is being communicated than in low-context cultures. Much of the knowledge in these settings is situational, and thus there is less written or formal communication. In high-context cultures, it is harder to transfer knowledge outside of the group, given the lack of codified rules of engagement. Some examples of high-context cultures include family gatherings, small religious congregations, or a party with friends. On a national level, prior studies have shown that the citizens of Japan and France typically exhibit behavior that is closer to the high-context approach. In terms of marketing strategies, the information content is less for high-context cultures than for low-context cultures, as less information needs to be conveyed.

To date, there has not been much statistical evidence in support of national cultures clearly exhibiting one approach or the other, but there has been some validation of this theory at the individual or situational level. In other words, the context with which specific communication takes place depends on the group that is involved, and it is hard to apply this theory at the national level.

GEERT HOFSTEDE'S FIVE DIMENSIONS OF CULTURE

Other theories of culture better lend themselves to comparison across cultures than does Edward Hall's theory. *Hofstede's five dimensions of culture* is one example of such a theory. The five dimensions of culture as theorized by Hofstede are as follows:

- *Social orientation:* individual versus collective
- *Power orientation:* power tolerant versus power respect
- *Uncertainty orientation:* acceptance versus avoidance
- *Goal orientation:* aggressive versus passive
- *Time orientation:* long-term versus short-term

These dimensions, as well as the extremes for each, are discussed below.

Social Orientation

The first of Hofstede's five dimensions is social orientation. This orientation reflects a person's beliefs about the relative importance of the individual and the groups to which that person belongs. One extreme is individualism. This form of social orientation is exhibited primarily by Western societies and others that follow a free-market-based system. Individualistic people or countries tend to put themselves ahead of the group as a whole. The other extreme is collectivism. This form of society prefers group consensus rather than individual effort or decision making. Many of the former communist countries tend to exhibit this form of social orientation.

Power Orientation

The next of the five dimensions is that of power orientation. This dimension refers to the beliefs that people tend to hold about the appropriateness of power and authority differences in hierarchies such as business organizations. One extreme of this dimension is power respect. Individuals in these cultures tend to accept power based on the position and do not question authority as much as do individuals in other cultures. Some examples of power-respect cultures are France, Spain, Italy, Brazil, and Japan. Other societies tend to be power-tolerant cultures. These cultures are more often willing to question authority. Some examples of power-tolerant cultures are the United States, the United Kingdom, Denmark, and Israel.

Uncertainty Orientation

The third of Hofstede's cultural dimensions, uncertainty orientation, refers to the feelings that people tend to have regarding uncertain and ambiguous situations. Some cultures exhibit uncertainty acceptance. These cultures tend to not be bothered by change. Some examples of societies that typically represent this category are the United States, Canada, and Denmark. The other extreme in the uncertainty-orientation category is uncertainty avoidance. Societies that are more hierarchical tend to exhibit an avoidance of uncertainty and thus embrace rigid rules-based systems. Recent studies have shown that former Soviet bloc countries, where employment was certain in a centrally planned system, have yet to completely accept the ambiguity that comes with a free-market economy, and these countries tend to avoid uncertainty.[2]

Goal Orientation

Another of Hofstede's five dimensions, goal orientation, deals with the manner in which people are motivated to work toward different goals. Sometimes in the developed world, we tend to think that all societies have similar aggressive goals regarding achieving material possessions. This aggressive goal behavior is seen countries such as the United States, Germany, and Japan. Other countries exhibit passive

goal behavior and tend to place a higher value on social relationships and the quality of life. Many of the Nordic countries exhibit these passive goal beliefs. In a recent study comparing the quality of life in different countries in the world, all of the Nordic countries (Sweden, Norway, Finland, Iceland, and Denmark) were in the top ten in this category.[3]

Time Orientation

The final of Hofstede's five cultural dimensions is time orientation. This category deals with the extent to which members of a culture adopt a long-term outlook versus a short-term outlook regarding life, work, and other issues. Some cultures tend to exhibit a future-oriented viewpoint, and individuals within these cultures value things such as dedication and perseverance, while other cultures tend to have a shorter-term outlook. Some examples of long-term-oriented cultures are Japan and China. Short-term-oriented societies tend to look to the past and the present more than to the future, and individuals within these cultures have a respect for traditions. Some examples of short-term-oriented cultures are Pakistan and parts of Western Africa.

One benefit of Hofstede's approach is that numerous studies have been undertaken to validate his findings. Hofstede's original study was of IBM employees between the ages of 30 and 34, and subsequent studies have been implemented via behavior-oriented questionnaires designed to determine where individuals rank on each of these five cultural dimensions. What is apparent is that few cultural theories have proved to be effective over entire populations within a specific country. It is helpful, however, to be aware of these approaches in a multinational business environment, as they could aid the successful business manager in managing day-to-day employee issues.

The goal of cultural studies in a business environment is to achieve something called cultural convergence. This is where a business leader avoids using only self-reference criteria when making judgments involving businesses or individuals in different countries. A successful manager for a multinational firm not only will make an attempt to understand the foreign culture where the business is involved, but also will modify and adapt his or her behavior to become more compatible with the local culture. This process is known as *acculturation* and calls to mind the old adage "When in Rome, do as the Romans do." As the Danish philosopher Søren Kierkegaard has said, "The first thing to understand is that you do not understand." Prior to entering a foreign market, multinational corporations must first realize that the cultural norms observed in other markets may not be the same as those observed in the multinational firm's home country. Thus, understanding these cultural differences is a requirement for successful entry into a foreign market.

MANAGEMENT OF CULTURAL CHANGE

Managers must understand what aspects of a culture will resist change, how those aspects will differ among cultures, how the process of change takes place in different cultures, and how long it will take to implement changes. They must also consider that change may occur in different ways: Their organization may act as an agent of change, influencing the foreign culture; it may be somewhat changed itself; or it may both create change and be changed at the same time.

In deciding how much change an organization will assume and how an organization may attempt to influence its host environment, a manager must consider the value system of the organization and its strategic mission, goals, and objectives. In addition, the costs and benefits of change need to be outlined, because the costs of change may far outweigh the benefits reaped from change.

If it is determined that some change is necessary in the foreign locale, the international manager should remember that resistance to change is low if the amount of change is not too great. If too much change is perceived by individuals within a certain culture at the outset, resistance will be stronger. In the same vein, individuals will be more apt to allow and accept change if they are involved in the decision and participate in the change process. Also, people are more likely to support change when they see personal or reference group rewards.

To ease the problems associated with change, the international manager must find opinion leaders and try to convince those who can influence others. The international firm should also time the implementation of change wisely. Change should be planned for a time when there is the least likelihood of resistance. When considering timing, all elements should be considered to avoid conflict, such as political disturbances or religious holidays. Moreover, the international manager needs to look toward the home office for possible areas for change that will improve the potential for acceptance and success within the foreign environment.

SUMMARY

When businesses cross national borders, they face a diversity of societies and cultures quite different from their own. "Society" refers to a political and social entity that is geographically defined and is composed of people and their culture. "Culture" is a set of social norms and responses that conditions the behavior of a population. The term "sociocultural" describes how society and culture relate to each other.

In the study of culture, the major topics are attitudes, beliefs, religion, aesthetics, material culture, education, language, and society organizations. Attitudes and beliefs influence human behavior by providing a set of rules and guidelines including attitudes toward time, achievement and work, change, and the importance of occupation. Religion provides the spiritual basis for a society by imposing moral norms and appropriate behavior. Aesthetics include various forms of artistic expression. Material culture refers to objects and possessions and focuses on technology, while nonmaterial culture covers a set of intangibles. Communication and language can be silent, as well as spoken or written, and may be a barrier to an international organization. Silent language includes body language, gestures, color, and symbols.

Societal organizations may take a number of different forms and indicate the level of social stratification within a society. Social groups may be either ascribed (determined by birth) or acquired.

Business customers may differ from one country to another and must be understood before an MNC begins any negotiations or business dealings outside its own culture. Understanding the importance of gifts and how they differ from bribes can be critical to international business relations.

Cultural theories that pertain to the discussion of an MNC's international dealings include the cultural cluster approach; Hall's low-context, high-context culture; and Hofstede's five dimensions of culture. These theories all exhibit strengths and weaknesses in their attempts to categorize individuals and societies based on certain cultural beliefs.

The international organization must understand cultural differences when attempting to initiate change in a foreign location. Change prompted by an MNC must be carefully planned, and an MNC must clearly identify the costs and benefits of that change before proceeding.

DISCUSSION QUESTIONS

1. Define the term "sociocultural." Why should international business managers be aware of this term when making their everyday decisions?

2. What are the elements of culture?
3. What is the typical American and European attitude toward work? Do you personally hold this attitude toward work?
4. How can religious beliefs affect international business decisions in the Middle East?
5. You have found out that your competitor is paying bribes to generate new business. Should you also pay them? Explain.
6. How can nonverbal communication affect a business relationship?
7. How might family groups and extended families affect the decisions of an international manager?
8. Why might multinational corporations act as agents of change? Provide some examples.
9. How can managers of a multinational firm get their local employees to accept new ideas?

NOTES

1. In George P. Murdock, "The Common Denominator of Cultures," in *The Science of Man in the World Crises*, ed. Ralph Linton, pp. 123–42 (New York: Columbia University Press, 1945).

2. "Cross-Cultural Differences in Central Europe," *Journal of Managerial Psychology*, January 2003.

3. *Economist*, "Human Development Index," 30.

BIBLIOGRAPHY

"All in Favor of Bribery, Please Stand Up." *Across the Board*, June 1984, 3–5.

"A People Problem." *The Economist*, November 25, 1988, 49–50.

Commission of the European Community. *The European Community and Education*. Brussels: Commission of the European Community, 1985.

Dienes, Elizabeth, Geert Hofstede, Ludek Kolman and Niels G. Noorderhaven, "Cross-Cultural Differences in Central Europe." *Journal of Managerial Psychology*, Volume 18, 76–88 January 2003.

Culture at Work. "High and Low Context." http://www. culture-at-work.com/highlow.html.

Economist. "Human Development Index." *Pocket World in Figures.* Profile Books, Ltd., London, 2005 edition, 30.

Fatemi, Khosrow. "Multinational Corporations, Developing Countries, and Transfer of Technology: A Cultural Perspective." *Issues in International Business*, Summer–Fall 1985, 1–6.

"Islam for Beginners." *Economist*, March 18, 1989, 95–96.

Jacoby, N.H., P. Nehemkis, and Richard Eells. *Bribery and Extortion in World Business.* New York: Macmillan, 1977.

Kim, W. Chan, and R.A. Mauborgne. "Cross-Cultural Strategies." *The Journal of Business Strategy*, Spring 1987, 28–35.

Reardon, Kathleen. *International Business and Gift-Giving Customs.* Janesville, WI: Parker Pen, 1981.

"Some Guidelines on Dealing with Graft in Korean Operations." *Business International*, February 25, 1983, 62.

Terpstra, Vern, and K. David. *The Cultural Environment of International Business.* 2nd ed. Cincinnati, OH: South-Western Publishing, 1985.

CASE STUDY 9.1
DELIS FOODS CORPORATION

The year 2005 was a very good one for Delis Foods Corporation, a San Francisco–based food conglomerate. Its domestic sales were $24 billion and its international sales were $7 billion, making it one of the largest companies in the processed-foods business. Innovative product development and strong marketing strategies were two of the main reasons for its success. Its international operations were directed out of San Francisco by William Schaefer, an executive with almost 18 years of experience in international marketing, the last 10 of which had been in the marketing of food products. Schaefer was proud of the 2005 performance, in which his division had registered a worldwide sales increase of 12 percent over the previous year. Despite the overall results, however, there were two areas that continued to trouble him. Both were in the Asian country of Dikorma.

Dikorma, a small country in Southeast Asia with a population of about 60 million, is a nation that is fast industrializing, and the per capita GNP has risen to $6,600 per annum from a level of only $2,400 per annum 12 years ago. It is viewed by Delis Foods as an important target market that presents excellent opportunities. There is a large middle class that is fairly cosmopolitan and sophisticated. The country has a relatively free export-import market and the balance of trade is maintained comfortably. Retail distribution is well developed, and necessary ancillary services—transportation, banking, and commercial codes—are also not a problem. The initial experience of Delis Foods with its large-scale marketing of instant noodles in Dikorma had

been a great success. Delis soon became a household brand name, and it was able to penetrate the market quite successfully with other products, such as ketchup, instant coffee, and nondairy creamers.

Following up on its success, Delis Foods decided to make a bid for a segment of the huge cold-drink market. Dikorma is a tropical country and temperatures remain above 80 degrees for 11 months of the year. There is a large urban middle class, which provides a steady market for cold drinks. Delis Foods decided to introduce instant iced tea into this market. The product idea was fairly simple. The company would market iced tea in concentrated liquid form, and the consumer would only have to add water and ice to get a cool drink. There was no other iced tea brand available in Dikorma, and Delis Foods would have a monopoly. Moreover, Dikorma's middle class had proved receptive to new ideas in the past; the case of instant noodles was clear evidence.

The company decided on a hard-sell campaign across the country, utilizing all major media, including television, radio, newspapers, magazines, and roadside signs. The main theme was simple: "Beat the heat with Velima Iced Tea." A number of promotions were carried out, and the distributors and retailers were given attractive discounts to push the product.

Despite the initial effort, sales did not take off, and three months after the product launch, it began to become increasingly clear that the company had a loser on its hands. Schaefer was

continued

Case 9.1 (*continued*)

extremely annoyed and placed the blame on the marketing staff who designed and implemented the campaign. He asked them to find the reasons the product had not taken off and to modify the campaign accordingly.

The marketing group in Dikorma analyzed the entire project quite intensively, but it came up with little that could be called a mistake in the campaign. Moreover, there was apparently no dissatisfaction with the quality of the product. True, the coverage of the product had been limited to the urban centers, but that was because it was relatively highly priced and the rural market could not afford a sophisticated product such as instant iced tea. The product was retested, but it was found to conform to all standard requirements and there were no quality problems.

Confident that they had corrected the few errors in the campaign and assured that the product had no quality problems, the local marketing group of Delis Foods launched another, bigger campaign, promoting the product much more aggressively than in the previous campaign. This time attractive consumer incentives were offered, such as a free crystal glass with the purchase of every bottle of iced tea. The results were somewhat better. Attracted by the offer of free glasses and by the glittering campaign, consumers reacted positively and sales started to improve. The marketing group heaved a sigh of relief, but not for long.

Within the next six months, for what appeared to completely inexplicable reasons, sales began to drop off again. The company had not increased the price, nor were the initial incentives withdrawn, although it was proving quite expensive to the company to maintain these incentives. The drop in sales continued and began to become more accentuated each month. The marketing group and Schaefer were perplexed. They seemed to have done everything right, but all of a sudden, everything seemed to go wrong.

After eight months of the second promotion, sales were so low that the company started to lose money on the product. The retailers also became nervous and stopped ordering. Some then complained that they were having trouble disposing of their inventories. Schaefer had to make a painful decision: to admit that the product had failed and to withdraw it from the market. He did so in July 2006, and Velima Iced Tea was taken off the shelves in Dikorma. The chairman of Delis Foods, Peter Sanderson, was quite philosophical about the issue and told Schaefer not to be too hard on himself. "We all learn from our mistakes," he told Schaefer and asked him to find out why the product had failed.

Thinking over this issue, Schaefer realized that it might be a good idea to get an external view of the problem. After all, in-company analysis, however sharp and intense, still has its limitations. Moreover, in this case the limitations were exposed beyond doubt. Delis Foods had tried to think of all the reasons its iced tea failed but did not come up with any that would explain, in concrete form, why an excellent product failed in an excellent market despite a great campaign and all other positive circumstances. He called MacArthur & Associates in Jakarta and asked for Gayle Johnston. Johnston was the chief marketing consultant at MacArthur & Associates and was an expert on Southeast Asia markets. "He should be able to tell us what really went wrong," thought Schaefer as he noted his appointment with Johnston for the following Thursday in San Francisco.

continued

Case 9.1 (*continued*)

The meeting with Johnston was quite illuminating. Johnston brought to bear a whole new line of thinking. According to him, it was a sociocultural asymmetry that caused problems for Delis Foods in Dikorma. As Johnston explained, there was no way an iced tea product could have succeeded in Dikorma, because it clashed very strongly with ingrained sociocultural values. People in Dikorma, Johnston pointed out, do not drink tea without milk. In Dikorma iced tea, by definition, would be consumed with milk, but the entire campaign showed the beverage as being essentially sweetened black tea with ice. The other cultural barrier, Johnston continued, was that tea in Dikorma was viewed as a hot drink, not a cold one. Dikormans have been drinking hot tea for hundreds of years and were not likely to see it as a cold drink. Cold milk, yes, even perhaps cold coffee, but certainly not iced tea.

Schaefer protested that Dikormans had reacted positively to instant noodles, and they had never had those before. They also had adopted several other new products: ready-baked cakes, frozen pizzas, and so on. Why this hostility toward iced tea? "That is simple," replied Johnston. He explained that Dikormans did not have pizza or cake ingrained in them as a part of their traditional culture. These were new products and they accepted them as such. What was not

new but was ingrained in their culture was tea. It is general experience that ingrained dietary habits are quite difficult to change, especially if the change is dramatically in opposition to the existing culture.

"Perhaps you are right," Schaefer said. "At least the market has proved that you are. In the future we should do better. How about doing a study of the sociocultural traits of Dikorma and of our products to suggest which products we should try to keep out of this market?" "That will be no problem. Only please make sure that you tie in the recommendations of my study with those of your marketing group," concluded Johnston.

DISCUSSION QUESTIONS

1. What kind of strategy would you advise Delis Foods Corporation to adopt to avoid this kind of situation in the future? Analyze the sociocultural traits of a select country and devise a food product strategy that suits the cultural environment.

2. Suggest a list of typical processed food items that would in your opinion not be successful in a country with a tropical climate and explain why.

CHAPTER 10

Foreign Investment: Researching Risk

CHAPTER OBJECTIVES

This chapter will:

- Look at the forces and opportunities that support foreign investment by multinational corporations.
- Discuss the role political risk plays in counterbalancing the benefits or opportunities of investing abroad.
- Describe the various ways host governments control foreign investment.
- Present management techniques that can be used to reduce political risk when investing abroad.

WHY INVEST ABROAD?

Every firm that considers investing abroad must weigh the potential advantages against the potential risks. To do that, in-house analysis must identify and evaluate key factors. There are several reasons to consider initially as to why firms should invest abroad, and a few general factors can be linked to the overall level of risk a particular host country holds for an MNC making a foreign direct investment. These factors include the attitude of the host country's government, the political system in place, the level of public discontent or satisfaction, the unification or fragmentation of the local society on cultural and religious lines, the kind of internal and external pressures faced by the government, and the history of the country in the past few decades. In the pages that follow, we address each of these concerns in turn.

A recent publication by the *Economist* ranked the countries of the world in terms of the friendliness of the business environment. The rankings reflect the opportunities for, and the hindrances to, the conduct of business, as measured by the countries' rankings in 10 categories, including market potential, tax and labor market policies, infrastructure, skills, and the political environment.[1] The top 20 countries are listed in Table 10.1.

BIGGER MARKETS

Many international firms decide to invest overseas to tap larger foreign markets. To keep growing, a firm must increase its sales, which may not always be possible in the domestic market. Domestic markets, however large, are limited to a particular size and rate of growth and are the target of competition

Table 10.1

Most Business Friendly Environments

1	Canada	12	France
2	Netherlands	13	Germany
3	Finland	14	Belgium
4	United States	15	Norway
5	Singapore	16	Taiwan
6	United Kingdom		
7	Hong Kong	17	Australia
8	Denmark	18	New Zealand
9	Switzerland	19	Chile
10/11	Ireland/Sweden (tied)	20	Austria

Source: Economist. "Business Environment Rankings." *Pocket World in Figures,* 2005 edition, 59. Profile Books, Ltd., London.

from other domestic firms with similar products and marketing capabilities. In such situations, a move overseas is a logical step for a company wanting to tap a larger market. Apart from the fact that the existence of a new, larger customer base would help boost sales, overseas markets often confer additional advantages to the firm. For example, these markets may not have products that are similar to or of the same quality as those of the firm going overseas, and the competition from overseas markets may not be as strong as domestic competition.

HOST-NATION DEMANDS

Occasionally firms must invest overseas to tap international markets because host-country government restrictions require that the firm's products be manufactured locally. Such restrictions are generally imposed to boost the local economy and general domestic production and employment. Thus, the MNC that wants to tap an overseas market has to invest in overseas plants that are run by domestic managers, in local subordinates, or through some other arrangement.

ECONOMIES OF SCALE

A firm accessing an overseas market might want to invest there if it finds that it is cheaper to manufacture goods locally, rather than manufacturing them at home and exporting them. When the local market is large and the demand is consistent enough to justify investment in the plant and equipment needed to set up a manufacturing operation, production economies can occur through other factors. For example, the labor costs may be lower in the overseas location, the sources of raw materials may be closer to the plant in the overseas location, and the costs of shipping and marketing the products may be lower than those of home-based operations. Another important factor is the location of the firm. An overseas plant location may also be better suited to serve a third-country market.

COMPETITIVE MOTIVES

Often firms operate in head-on competition with other domestic and international firms. This type of competition is particularly severe in oligopolistic industries, where only a few large firms dominate the market. In such an environment, the moves of one firm are quickly duplicated and challenged by the others. Thus, if one firm moves abroad, its competitors make similar moves. One obvious motive for the move is to keep pace with the first firm in new markets and overall level of sales. The other motive is the need to match the overseas strategy of competitors, because if that is not done, the competition could acquire additional strength from its overseas operation, which could be leveraged in the domestic market, too. Competition often occurs between firms of different countries who dominate parts of the same industry (for example, Caterpillar Company of the United States and Komatsu of Japan dominate the earthmoving machinery industry). If one company invades the home-country market of another, it is very likely that the competitor will be motivated to retaliate by accessing its competition's domestic market. An example of this occurred in the 1990s, when Kodak decided to enter the Japanese market to counter Fuji's market share gains in the United States.

TECHNOLOGY AND QUALITY CONTROL

Many firms feel that if they license their technology to a company in the overseas location, their technology might be leaked to competitors. In fact, many companies, especially in the high-technology area, hold on to their know-how so closely that they do not license it as a matter of policy. The practice of retaining information within the company is often referred to as *internalization*. Some companies feel that licensing their technology may result in the licensee producing a product of inferior quality, which may be damaging to the product image. To obviate such possibilities, companies prefer to set up their own overseas manufacturing operations. Having their own operations also provides some companies with greater assurance of regular supply, better maintenance, and after-sales services for their products, which are crucial to retaining customer loyalty in a highly competitive international environment.

RAW MATERIALS

Many firms rely on raw materials imported from abroad, a reliance that can stem from both availability and cost considerations. The raw materials may not be available in the home country, or, alternatively, it may be more economical to access raw materials from overseas than domestically if the price differences exceed the additional transportation costs. If a firm decides to rely on overseas raw materials, it often becomes dependent on a regular supply at predictable and relatively stable prices. Long-term contracts with overseas suppliers are one way of achieving predictable and stable prices. In

some cases, however, companies are not willing to take the risk of the supplier's reneging on the contract and decide to invest in extractive mining and other such raw materials sourcing operations overseas. Sometimes such investments are motivated by the consideration that the necessary technology is not available in the source country and therefore must be provided by the corporation interested in extracting the materials. Often permission from the governments of the countries where raw materials are available is centered on the type of technology the overseas corporation is able to bring to use in the extractive processes.

FORWARD INTEGRATION

Many companies wish to eliminate middlemen from their operations and forward integrate the different stages involved in the manufacture of their products and their sales to the consumer. For example, a firm may be producing soft-drink concentrate and selling it to a local bottler overseas that bottles and sells it in foreign markets. The profits from the revenues generated from the sales of the soft drink would be shared by the company producing the soft drink concentrate and the local bottler. If the company selling the concentrate had its own bottling plant in the foreign country, it would be able to control the entire operation and eliminate sharing its profits with the intermediary agent. This motivation may prompt the company manufacturing the concentrate to set up its own bottling operation overseas.

TECHNOLOGY ACQUISITION

Multinational corporations often invest in other countries to gain access to new technologies that are not developed in the home country. Access to new technology is often sought by the outright acquisition of new firms possessing such knowledge. These new technologies are generally intended for integration with the entire global corporate strategy of the MNC

Table 10.2

Conflicting Objectives between Developing Countries and Multinational Corporations

Developing Countries	Multinational Corporations
Promote local ownership	Maintain global controls and efficiency
Increase local ownership and control	Minimize costs of technology and capital
Reduce duration of contracts and change payment, characteristics	Receive reasonable returns for risk
Separate technology from private investment	Provide technology as part of long-term production and market development
Eliminate restrictive business clauses in technology and investment agreements	Maintain ability to affect the use of capital, technology, and associated products
Minimize proprietary rights of suppliers	Protect rights for profit from private investments
Reduce contract security	Use contracts to create stable business environment; to develop trust
Encourage technology and R & D transfer to host country	Maintain control of technology and R & D paid for by the company
Develop suitable products for host country	Gain global economies of scale to lower costs of products

that acquires them. Often, the company that acquires a new technology through an overseas acquisition sets up an overseas facility, which enhances the existing operations by adding the managerial, financial, and technological strengths of the parent company.

ASSESSING POLITICAL RISK

Political risk for multinational corporations includes adverse actions that may be taken by host-country governments against the firms. These actions can include changes in the operating conditions of foreign enterprises that arise out of the political process, either directly through war, insurrection, or political violence, or through changes in government that affect the behavior, ownership, physical assets, personnel, or operations of the firm.

Political risk does not necessarily arise out of an upheaval in the political climate of the host country. Perceptions often change within the same government, and, as a result, decisions detrimental to the interests of the firm can be made. Moreover, because

policies can and do change, some degree of political risk is present in nearly all countries.

Factors responsible for political risk can be grouped into two categories: inherent and circumstantial. Inherent factors are conditions that are present constantly around the world that generate a certain danger of adverse action by host governments from the point of view of the multinational corporation (such as terrorism). Circumstantial factors are those conditions that can arise out of particular events in different countries.

INHERENT CAUSES OF POLITICAL RISK

Different Economic Objectives

The motivations and goals of a U.S. MNC are often at variance with those of the host government (see Table 10.2). A primary example is in the area of balance of payments considerations. A host country may be facing difficulties with its balance of payments and therefore might seek to conserve its resources by maximizing the inflows and minimizing the outflows. It may also try to optimize the use of the available foreign exchange resources, which could lead to restrictions on repatriation of profits, dividends, and royalties by a multinational corporation to its home country. It may also result in government restrictions on the time lag permitted for import and export payments, which could interfere with the internal leading and lagging strategy of a company, which is devised to manage its finances and avoid exchange- and interest-rate risks.

Monetary and Fiscal Policies

The monetary and fiscal policies of a host government may be at variance with an MNC's desires. For example, a host country that is faced with impending inflationary conditions might want to raise the interest rates on bank lending, which may be detrimental to the interests of an MNC, whose costs of funds, and therefore of production, would go up correspondingly. The banks may also be directed to maintain quantitative ceilings on lending to prevent excessive increases in the money supply of the host country. The MNC, on the other hand, would be keen to retain its financing sources according to its own requirements and attempt to circumvent these ceilings, which may further incur the displeasure of the host government and result in the risk of further punitive action.

Similarly, fiscal policies followed by host governments may not be in the MNC's interests. The interest of the host government is invariably to maximize revenues, while that of the MNC is to minimize its tax liability. Increasing taxes is a major inherent risk that an MNC faces while operating overseas. Moreover, most countries levy a heavier tax on the repatriable portions of an MNC's profits, which is often in addition to the normal corporate taxes paid by a local company. Sometimes under these

regimes, separate exchange rates are specified for different transactions. The goal of the host country might be to defend a particular level of the exchange rate that it deems appropriate in the pursuit of its best economic interest. For the MNC, however, this might mean that there is an artificial distortion in the amount of funds it is able to repatriate, which adversely affects its overall profitability.

Economic Development and Industrial Policies

The industrial and economic development policies of a host country can often pose a risk for an MNC. For example, countries may want to promote certain backward geographical regions where infrastructural facilities are low and might therefore require the expansion of MNCs to such regions even though investment there may not be economically feasible. Many host countries want to promote domestic industry and, particularly, small and medium-size enterprises. To do so, host countries tend to provide subsidies or other fiscal incentives or reserve the production of certain goods for such industries. Another promotion mechanism is the purchase policy of the government.

In many host countries, especially less-developed countries, the government is the largest buyer of goods and services. Exclusion from government contracts, therefore, affects the sales of an MNC's products significantly. Also, in many of the core and sensitive industries (for example, defense and infrastructure-oriented industries), MNC participation is simply prohibited. The risk arises from the possibility that some industries in which an MNC is active might be declared core industries, or sensitive industries, and MNC operations may be expropriated or forcibly sold to local parties. The rationale behind the exclusion of MNCs from key industries is apparently apprehension in the minds of host governments that MNC control of key industries might endanger national security and hamper the ability of the government to conduct an independent foreign policy. Such policies are similar to what Vladimir Lenin referred to as the *commanding heights* of the economy. The commanding heights were key industries required to effectively control an economy. In the early 1900s, such industries included railroads, steel, and heavy industry. Based on many of the current barriers to foreign control, the modern-day commanding heights of the economy would appear to be banking, telecommunications, broadcasting, and other such service sector industries.

Colonial Heritage

Many host countries are former colonies that have gained their independence. The colonial era was marked by complete political domination by foreign powers and economic domination by foreign companies. Most of the foreign companies in that era used their privileged, often monopolistic, positions to exploit local resources, markets, and labor to maximize their profits. As a result, they were seen to be a drain on the economies of the colonies, which left a sense of distrust of MNCs in the minds of host-country governments, who fear that MNCs may still exploit their economies. As a result, they are extra careful in scrutinizing proposals for foreign direct investment by multinationals and monitor MNCs' activities closely. These concerns also explain to some extent why such stringent controls are placed on MNC activities. This fundamental apprehension does not permit MNCs to operate freely and creates a constant risk of adverse action by host governments.

Sociocultural Differences

To a degree, political risk arises out of the sociocultural differences between a host country and an MNC. Social codes of conduct in certain countries contrast sharply with those of the MNCs. While in a host country, an MNC's executives face the risk of offending local sensibilities over crucial sociocultural issues. Moreover, some basic behavioral trends and norms followed by an MNC as a part of its usual way of functioning may prove offensive to the government or the clientele. For example, Western companies often have female executives representing them in meetings and negotiations, which might offend host officials or clients in Middle Eastern countries because women there are not expected to play such roles. Even relatively simple things, such as greetings, gift giving, and hospitality, can become serious issues if they offend a key government official or a client in a host country. An MNC must always do its homework and adapt itself to local culture if it wants to avoid political risk.

CIRCUMSTANTIAL CAUSES OF POLITICAL RISK

Change of Government

A change of government is a major political risk faced by MNCs. In many countries political opponents have economic policy positions different from those of the government in office, and a new government is often keen to reverse the policies of its predecessors. Thus, an MNC that might have excellent relations with a host government may find its assets under the threat of expropriation because of a change in government. In addition to having a different economic policy, a new host government may be hostile toward an MNC if the company is perceived as a supporter of its political opponents.

Political risk is particularly high in countries that are in the midst of a transition from one type of political system to another, such as from a capitalist to a socialist society. In the past, in many countries that shifted from capitalist to socialist systems, entire assets of MNCs were expropriated, some with compensation, but some without.

Political Difficulties of Host Governments

In many countries where economic and social conditions are fairly unstable, it is often difficult for a government to manage the resulting public discontent. Many governments, in an attempt to shift blame for economic ills, target MNCs as the cause of those problems. The politicians in power often play on the inherent mistrust that the general public has of these foreign, wealthy, and powerful firms.

Political Action Brought on by Other Groups

MNCs also face the risk of adverse political activity from opposition parties seeking an issue about which to criticize the government. A host government's support for an MNC provides opposition parties with an ideal issue to manipulate nationalist feelings by propagating the line that the country is exploited by the MNC and that this exploitation is supported by the incumbent party. Sociopolitical activists and environmental groups are another source of political risk. Many MNCs have large investments in factories and extractive industries, which easily attract attention. Therefore, many consumer, labor, and environmental groups can attack the safety and pollution standards of MNCs, even though those standards may be better than those of domestic corporations in the same industry. Moreover, such attacks are likely to evoke a more active response from host governments, such as penalizing the MNC more heavily than a domestic industry for similar offenses.

Bilateral Relations Between the Host and Home Governments

The attitude of a host government toward an MNC is dependent on the bilateral relations between the host government and the MNC's home government. If the MNC's home government comes into conflict with the host government, it is likely that the latter will take direct or indirect action against the MNC. In several instances, when hostilities have broken out between two countries, the assets of MNCs have been confiscated without compensation. Even when the conflict falls short of outright war, adverse action against MNCs can result. For example, if one country faces a ban on some of its exports to an MNC's home country, it may retaliate by blocking the repatriation of the MNC's profits. Occasionally, action has been taken against MNCs to settle political scores. For example, if an MNC's home country takes an opposing stance at international forums or indirectly supports the host country's enemies, the host country can retaliate by taking action against the MNC within its jurisdiction.

Local Vested Interest

MNCs also face the possibility of adverse action from the lobbying efforts of local vested interests. As a rule, MNCs have considerable competitive power because they enjoy many advantages. They introduce a dynamic competitive force into local economies that upsets the entrenched positions of local businesspeople by capturing market share and reducing local firms' ability to skim off the market by charging higher prices for their products. Moreover, by introducing new products of superior quality at relatively competitive prices, an MNC is often able to expose the weaknesses of local businesses and force them to improve their own economic and operating efficiencies to regain their competitiveness in the marketplace.

While some local businesses respond to the MNC challenge in this way, many do not. These businesses try to fight the MNC's intrusion by pressuring the government to impose restrictions on the MNC, to increase its costs and reduce its ability to compete. In some cases, local vested interests lobby the government to prohibit the MNC's entry into the country or attempt to have regulations introduced that prohibit the MNC from doing certain kinds of business. The local interest groups are thus a serious political risk in many countries.

Social Unrest and Disorder

Fundamental and deep-rooted tensions in some countries fragment the local social order. Either on their own or at the manipulation of political interests, these tensions occasionally erupt into riots and other acts of public violence. In such situations, the law enforcement machinery of local governments may be inadequate to protect public property against destruction and looting. MNC assets have sometimes become the targets of arsonists and looters, especially if they are instigated by vested interests. As recent political uprisings in Haiti and in Ukraine illustrate, political protest comes in many forms, both violent and nonviolent, but in either case, the rules of engagement for a multinational corporation could change very quickly.

TYPES OF HOST-NATION CONTROL

Host governments impose different types of controls on the activities of MNCs, ranging from limits on the repatriation of profits to labor controls.

LIMITS ON REPATRIATION OF PROFITS

Many host governments place limits and conditions on the repatriation of profits, dividends, royalties, technical know-how fees, and other such revenue. Some governments impose an absolute ceiling on the amount of dividends that can be repatriated each year, and in some cases, these ceilings are subject to additional conditions that stipulate a maximum percentage of profits that can be repatriated. Moreover, corporations may also be asked to meet certain financial standards, such as debt-equity ratios, before

permitting any repatriation of profits or dividends. Other countries have a hierarchal approval process. Remittances of small amounts of profits are allowed freely, but higher amounts need the approval of the authorities, which could be the central bank or the government itself.

Certain countries facing severe balance of payments problems place time restrictions on the repatriation of dividends and profits, which means that regulations are introduced whereby corporations have to retain their entire earnings in the host country for a certain time period, which can vary from a few months to several years. In countries faced with a shortage of foreign exchange, a time constraint can appear without a specific regulation to this effect. This constraint occurs when each request for repatriation must be approved by the central bank and only a limited number of requests can be approved each year. As a result, requests are rated sequentially, and repatriation must wait, sometimes several years in countries in the midst of a serious and prolonged balance of payments crisis.

CURBING TRANSFER PRICING

Many host governments are alert to the practice of transfer pricing by MNCs. To eliminate the outflow of profits through this mechanism, they establish regulations that reduce the MNC's ability to move funds by manipulating the company pricing structure. Normally such regulations enable host-country authorities to disregard the internal prices charged by the parent to the subsidiary and to assess the company using an independent calculation that is based on standard international prices for that commodity instead of that shown on the books of the company. These regulations enable the host government to assess an MNC's tax and tariff liabilities independently and reduce the advantages that an MNC tries to achieve through transfer pricing.

PRICE CONTROLS

Many host governments have highly controlled economies. One of the important features of such an economy is the presence of price controls. An MNC entering such a country may be forced to sell its goods at the controlled prices, even though they may be well below the planned prices. In some instances, host governments require specific margins over costs. Additional controls may also be imposed, usually in situations of shortages, impending inflation, or potential or active social discontent over prices.

OWNERSHIP RESTRICTIONS

Many governments restrict foreign ownership of MNCs to a certain percentage, which means that the remaining portion must be owned by local partners or offered as a public issue in the local stock market. In such situations, the company often cannot exercise total control over operations, and limits are placed on the amount of profits it can repatriate. When total ownership is in the hands of the company, a very high dividend can be declared to transfer profits and capital out of the country. If the company is partly owned by local nationals, this manipulation is not possible because local shareholders can question company policies. Moreover, the company cannot declare an unduly high dividend because the same level of dividend would have to be paid to local shareholders. In addition, once ownership is diluted, an MNC faces a takeover threat, because local interests can hold enough shares to acquire the local subsidiary and oust the management.

JOINT VENTURES

Some countries require that MNCs come into their country only as a partner in a joint venture with a local company. The motive of the host government is to secure monitoring and control leverage over the MNC through its local joint-venture partner and to promote domestic industrial capabilities by associating local companies with international corporations. These joint ventures can sometimes work to an MNC's detriment, because a suitable joint-venture partner may not be available or the one chosen may not perform its share of obligations. Additionally, sometimes joint-venture partners may have differing goals, which hinders the success of the combined effort. Moreover, some MNCs are wary of joint ventures with local companies because they fear the leakage of closely held advanced technical knowledge.

PERSONNEL RESTRICTIONS

Some host governments require that local nationals be placed on the board of directors of an MNC's local subsidiary. In many instances conditions of an MNC's entry into a foreign country stipulate that a certain number of top positions be filled by local nationals. Quite often this regulation is implemented by making a reverse condition, such as limiting the number of expatriate employees or managers a company can bring into its operations in the host country. These restrictions are made even more severe by stringent approval procedures for the issue of expatriate visas by home governments, and very often maximum salaries payable to overseas executives are subject to ceilings and higher tax rates.

IMPORT CONTENT

One of the primary concerns of many host governments is that MNCs are a drain on the foreign exchange resources of the country because they generate profits in local currencies and repatriate them in foreign currencies. To ensure that this foreign exchange drain is minimized, many host countries place restrictions on the amount of imports used for manufacturing products locally. The same objective is often achieved by specifying that a certain percentage of local inputs is used in the MNC's product. Some MNCs that rely largely on imported inputs for the domestic market and, therefore, cannot meet the import content requirements, must make up the foreign exchange loss by exporting either a certain percentage or a certain amount of their production. In other words, some sort of balance sheet of the foreign exchange inflows and outflows is often drawn up and the size of the export obligation is decided on the basis of projected foreign exchange outflows of an MNC's operations. Such restrictions can pose difficult problems for MNCs whose strategy is to basically produce and sell in the domestic market of the host country and whose products are designed for this purpose.

DISCRIMINATION IN GOVERNMENT BUSINESS

Industrial policies followed by host governments are a major source of risk for MNCs. Discrimination in allocating government business is a major restriction on the scope and potential of MNC business opportunities in countries where the government plays a powerful economic role. Government purchases usually are made from domestic corporations. If such corporations happen to be the competitors of the MNC, then the former gains a major competitive edge through its access to an exclusive market. Moreover, government purchases are generally high in volume and result in substantial profits for companies who get that business.

LABOR CONTROLS

Some countries impose fairly comprehensive labor and social controls on MNCs. The stipulation can be targeted at ensuring that the labor for the firm will be recruited only through a government agency that screens all potential employees, which enables the government to influence the production of the company by controlling the supply of labor. The

compensation paid to employees is also often regulated by host governments. Some host governments stipulate that the wage rates of local employees be higher than the rates paid by domestic corporations to workers performing comparable tasks. The host governments also sometimes require additional benefits for local employees, such as health insurance, various allowances, and arbitrary levels of bonuses.

ASSESSING THE RISK

Assessing political risk is a two-stage process. In the first stage an assessment is made of the riskiness of the host country as a place to do business. In the second stage an MNC considers the risks involved in making a particular investment. An investment should be made only if the level of risk at both stages is found to be acceptable.

ASSESSING COUNTRY RISK

Country risk is a very broad measure that focuses on the riskiness of the country as a whole as a place for MNCs to conduct business. One prime consideration is the level of current and future political stability of the country. A stable country obviously provides a better investment climate. An assessment of political conditions is made by gathering relevant information from several sources: national and international media, diplomatic assessments, or professional agencies that specialize in monitoring developments in certain countries.

Some of these professionals develop their own ratings for the different degrees of risk in various countries with regard to foreign direct investment by MNCs. These ratings are developed by assigning weights to different political, social, and economic factors that could lead to political instability and disorder. These weights are then added and averaged according to a particular formula to arrive at a final rating of a country's level of risk. Because different factors are included and the exercise of assigning risk weights is arbitrary, there is a strong element of subjectivity in this analysis. In general, Western industrialized countries carry low levels of risk for MNCs. Risks seem to increase in inverse proportion to the income of the countries, with the low-income countries posing higher risk. There are, however, important exceptions, because some middle-income countries prone to sociopolitical turmoil carry an even greater risk than some of the lower-income countries.

ASSESSING INVESTMENT RISK

One starting point in assessing the risk attached to making investments is to investigate the attitude and actions of the host government with regard to similar investments made by other MNCs. The existence of local lobbies and the influence they exert on the government is also a useful indicator of investment-specific risk. Powerful local lobbies in a particular industry imply higher risk.

Tax structures, industry standards, government discrimination, ownership and management requirements, repatriation conditions, export obligations, and location constraints should also be considered.

MANAGING RISK

REJECTING INVESTMENT

Many MNCs find that the risks in potential countries are too great in comparison to the expected returns. Therefore, they reject the potential investment. Rejection may also occur when the initial negotiation of terms between the host country and the MNC do not result in an agreement. Because the host country is eager to attract overseas investment, the MNC rejection may sometimes prompt the host government to relax some of the conditions.

LONG-TERM AGREEMENTS

Many MNCs find that one way to reduce political risk is to negotiate long-term commitments from the host government on the regulation of the firm. Negotiating these safeguards requires skill and foresight. A balance must be struck between achieving the safest possible terms for the company and recognizing the current national policies of the host government. The limitation of these safeguards, however, is that there is no practical way to enforce them in the event that the host government reneges on its part of the contractual obligations. A government is less likely to take any adverse actions if it is bound by a written agreement not to do so, as compared to a situation in which it has not given any such assurances.

LOBBYING

Many MNCs resort to lobbying politicians and officials of host governments to influence the direction of policies and decisions that affect them, because much political risk arises from the potential actions that can be taken by host governments. *Direct lobbying* is done by establishing a liaison or representative office in the capital city of the host country. The representative of the company establishes direct contacts with local officials and politicians and lobbies them to maintain favorable policies for the MNC. At other times, a local liaison agent is used to lobby local officials, especially in those countries where the domestic political and official structure is complex and not easily understood by outsiders.

Indirect lobbying is favored by many MNCs in countries where local officials are averse to dealing directly with foreigners. Lobbying can also take the form of influence buying, bribing the officials and politicians who are important players in the shaping of official policy and attitudes of the home government toward MNCs. Although many multinationals do not admit offering such bribes, for obvious reasons, it is a common practice in many countries.

LEGAL ACTION

If threatened, MNCs can resort to legal action, but this approach is useful only in countries where there is an efficient legal system and independent judiciary. Recourse to the law would be warranted when a MNC is of the opinion that a new decision or regulation of the host government is illegal under the laws of the country or is in violation of any initial agreements made with the host government. Legal action, however, is a last resort, taken only when there is no other option. Moreover, such actions are usually taken only by those companies that have decided to divest their investments in the host countries, because bringing a legal suit against the host government is likely to bring forth retaliation.

HOME-COUNTRY PRESSURE

Many MNCs, when faced with an adverse position taken by the host government, seek the intervention of their home governments, generally through diplomatic channels. The foreign office of the home country generally exerts informal pressure on the government of the host country to alter its attitude toward the MNCs. If the issue is important, this intervention can take place even at very high levels, such as heads of state. Apart from the general threat of deterioration of bilateral relations, home governments also occasionally hold out thinly veiled threats of retaliation against the corporations of the host country in the jurisdiction of the home country or threaten to erect trade or other barriers. This channel is effective when relations with the MNC's home country are particularly important to the host country.

JOINT VENTURES AND INCREASED SHAREHOLDING

Many MNCs decide to invest in host countries as joint-venture partners with local corporations; such ventures reduce the political risk. Once a local company is partnered with an MNC, any adverse government decision against the MNC also affects the local partner. A local partner would clearly exert a restraining influence on a government contemplating any such action. Moreover, the local partner, in all likelihood, would have significant contacts in the appropriate quarters of the host government that could be used for intensive lobbying on the MNC's behalf. Moreover, many host governments would take a more indulgent approach to the MNC operating as a joint venture because it would be perceived as sharing its profits and technical know-how with a local company and the traditional exploitative image of MNCs would be mitigated.

Many companies achieve similar objectives by using a slightly different route. Instead of taking on a local company as a joint-venture partner, they increase the level of local shareholding. In many instances the increase in local shareholding is effected at the behest of the host government, which imposes the increase as a condition for the MNC's continued operation in its jurisdiction.

Increased local shareholding increases the benefits for the host country in many ways. The amount of profits to be repatriated abroad is immediately reduced when the local shareholders receive their dividends and other revenue in local currency. The foreign exchange liability arising out of share appreciation is also reduced because the basic foreign shareholding is replaced to some extent by domestic shareholding. With a large amount of local shareholding, the policies and operations of the corporation are more open to public and government scrutiny, and, therefore, control. The possibility is also reduced that the MNC can indulge in financial and business transactions detrimental to the country.

PROMOTING HOST GOALS

To gain the host country's acceptance of its operations, an MNC may, as a strategic move, attempt to promote host-country objectives, for example, by maximizing foreign exchange earnings. MNCs try to contribute to this objective by promoting exports of either their own products or the products of other local manufacturers. The action is strategic in that it is taken to prevent future problems and does not form a part of the normal business operations and objectives of the company. Once export earnings have been generated by the MNC for the host country, it becomes fairly difficult for the host government to justify adverse action, because the drain on foreign exchange resources is removed.

RISK INSURANCE

Many countries have agencies that offer insurance coverage against the political risks faced by MNCs based in their countries. In the United States, the *Overseas Private Investment Corporation (OPIC)* guarantees risks faced by MNCs in developing countries. OPIC provides coverage against various eventualities that can adversely affect the MNC in a host country, such as expropriation, blocking of repatriation of funds by a host government, and problems created by the breakdown of law and order.

The World Bank, in an effort to promote private investment in developing countries, has an agency that protects corporations that invest in such countries from different forms of political risk. This agency, which began operation in 1989, is the Multilateral Investment Guarantee Agency (MIGA). Risk coverage through MIGA is intended to allay fears of political risk that prevent many MNCs from investing in developing countries, even if the latter are open to overseas investment. This agency is also discussed in Chapter 6.

CONTINGENCY PLANNING

Despite whatever measures a company may adopt and however good its relations with a host govern-

ment might be, there always remains a definite element of political risk of nationalization, expropriation, or some other unacceptable form of regulatory imposition or control. To guard against such an eventuality, most MNCs have a contingency plan, which may or may not be in the form of a formal document. Some contingency planning is done when the investment is first made in the host country. If a country is considered risky in terms of possible expropriation, companies try to reduce the value of their physical investment and rely more on the supply of expertise and know-how that is paid for on a short-term basis. A country also may be considered dangerous because of technology leakage. In such a situation, the MNC would probably retain the know-how at its headquarters and supply intermediate products to its subsidiary for the final stages of processing or manufacturing.

SUMMARY

Investment in international business requires a cost-benefits analysis of the benefits gained versus the risks encountered by the investing firm. Influencing the decision to expand internationally are the opportunities to tap larger markets, host-country regulations requiring local production, achieving economies of scale, competition, implementing quality controls, raw materials sourcing, forward integration to eliminate middlemen, and the acquisition of new types of technologies.

Counterbalancing these factors are the political risks MNCs face from unilateral actions or expropriation by host-country governments. Political risks increase when the MNC and the host country have different economic objectives or conflicting fiscal and industrial policies. Circumstantial political risks may occur when the host government changes and the policies of the preceding government are reversed, or when the current government facing political difficulties or social unrest must amend its prior policies to the detriment of the MNC.

Host governments may also impose a variety of national controls on MNCs' activities, including limitation on the repatriation of profits and dividends, efforts to curb transfer pricing, implementation of price controls, restrictions on foreign ownership, local staffing and management requirements, import content rules, and labor and social controls.

Assessing political risk involves first assessing the riskiness of the host country as a place to conduct operations and then identifying the level of risk assumed by the MNC for making a particular investment. Political risk cannot be eliminated completely, but management techniques can help reduce the level of political risk. Such techniques include not investing in particular countries, establishing long-term agreements with host-country governments, lobbying, legal action where a well-developed legal system exists within the host country, obtaining political pressure and assistance from the MNC's home-country government, providing for local ownership or joint venturing, promoting host-government objectives, developing contingency plans, and purchasing insurance coverage for political risk.

DISCUSSION QUESTIONS

1. Discuss the various factors that cause multinational firms to invest abroad.
2. What role does political risk assessment have in shaping an MNC's foreign investment decisions?
3. Is political risk assessment an exact science? Explain.
4. How do host governments try to control the activities of MNCs within their own countries?
5. Which of the following businesses are most and least vulnerable to expropriation?
   - Agriculture
   - Automobile manufacturing
   - Mining
   - Accounting

   - Heavy equipment manufacturing
   - Hotels
   - Restaurants
   - Oil fields
   - Personal electronic goods manufacturing
   - Banks
6. Identify techniques that MNCs use to manage country risk.

NOTE

1. *Economist*, "Business Environment Rankings," 59.

BIBLIOGRAPHY

Austin, J.E., and D.B. Yoffie. "Political Forecasting as a Management Tool." *Journal of Forecasting* 3 (1984): 395–408.

Blanden, Michael. "Of Tin Hats and Crystal Balls." *Banker,* July 1988, 44, 46.

De La Torre, J., and D.H. Neckar. "Forecasting Political Risk." In *The Handbook of Forecasting: A Manager's Guide,* ed. Sypors Makridakis and Steven C. Wheelwright. 2nd ed. New York: John Wiley, 1987.

Economist. "Business Environment Rankings." *Pocket World in Figures,* Profile Books, Ltd., London, 2005 edition, 59.

Encarnation, D.J., and S. Vachim. "Foreign Ownership: When Hosts Change the Rules." *Harvard Business Review,* September–October 1985, 152–60.

Erol, Cengiz. "An Exploratory Model of Political Risk Assessment and the Decision Process of Foreign Direct Investment." *International Studies of Management and Organization,* Summer 1985, 75–79.

Fatehi-Sedah, K., and M.H. Safizadeh. "The Association Between Political Instability and Flow of Foreign Direct Investment." *Management International Review,* Fourth Quarter 1989, 244.

Friedmann, Roberto, and J. Kim. "Political Risk and International Marketing." *Columbia Journal of World Business,* Winter 1988, 63–74.

Ghadar, F., and T.H. Moran, eds. *International Political Risk Management: New Dimensions.* Washington, DC: Ghadar and Associates, 1984.

Globerman, Steven. "Government Policies Toward Foreign Direct Investment: Has a New Era Dawned?" *Columbia Journal of World Business,* Fall 1988, 41–49.

Goddard, Scott. "Political Risk in International Capital Budgeting." *Managerial Finance* 16 (1990): 7–12.

Lichfield, John. "Trans-Atlantic Company Acquisitions Gain Momentum." *Europe,* April 1989, 24–25.

Miller, Van V. "Managing in Volatile Environments." *Baylor Business Review,* Fall 1988, 12–15.

Perlitz, Manfred. "Country-Portfolio Analysis: Assessing Country Risk and Opportunity." *Long Range Planning,* August 1985, 11–26.

Rice, Gillian, and Essam Mahmoud. "A Managerial Procedure for Political Risk Forecasting." *Management International Review,* Fourth Quarter 1986, 12–21.

Schmidt, David A. "Analyzing Political Risk." *Business Horizons,* July–August 1986, 43–50.

Sethi, S.P., and K.A.N. Luther. "Political Risk Analysis and Direct Foreign Investment: Some Problems of Definition and Measurement." *California Management Review,* Winter 1986, 57–68.

Stanley, Marjorie T. "Ethical Perspectives on the Foreign Direct Investment Decision." *Journal of Business Ethics,* January 1990, 1–10.

Terpstra, V., and K. David. *The Cultural Environment of International Business.* 3rd ed. Cincinnati, OH: South-Western, 1991.

CASE STUDY 10.1
AMALGAMATED POLYMERS, INC.

Martha Sanders was quite relaxed as she went on a round of the executive offices, distributing copies of the briefing papers for Monday's investment committee meeting. She would have a nice weekend, after all the hectic preparation and redrafting that had taken place during the week and at times had threatened to spill over into Saturday. Now, with her work done, she could go home on time.

While Martha Sanders was looking forward to the weekend, James Hyman was growing increasingly tense. Martha was his secretary and had typed the briefs, several times, and now they were perfect documents and she could go home. The briefs contained a proposal for his company to take an equity stake in Gulf Plastics, a medium-size company producing a wide variety of plastics in Mazirban, a small but wealthy Arab country in the Persian Gulf. The proposal had been prepared by Hyman after almost six months of preliminary groundwork, and on Monday the members of the investment committee, which comprised the entire senior management of the company, were going to take their first look at it.

There were a number of reasons the proposal made sense. Hyman's company, Amalgamated Polymers, Inc., was a leader in the production of plastics and similar petrochemical by-products. It was based in Edinburgh, Scotland, and had plants in Great Britain, the Netherlands, and Turkey. The company had its own in-house R & D facility, which had helped Amalgamated become one of the important forces in plastics technology during the past 15 years. Its patented product, Amalite, was in great demand by household

goods manufacturers for making such kitchen items as storage jars and plastic cutlery. Much of the company's sales of Amalite were concentrated in Europe and North America, but competition in these markets was growing, and there was a need to expand sales in other areas. While Amalgamated Polymers had considerable international marketing skills and sales contacts, it was essentially handicapped by a limited production capacity. To export to other markets, especially in developing countries, would mean an expansion of production capacity in the existing plants or establishment of new plants. Expanding capacity in the existing plants would have been difficult and expensive. The Netherlands and Edinburgh plants faced severe environmental constraints and had come under pressure from local authorities, and particularly from environmental groups, because of their pollution-creating effects. The company had been forced to install very expensive equipment to reduce the harmful content of the emissions from its plants. Expanding capacity would no doubt give rise to pressures from local governments and other groups to install even stricter emissions-control equipment. Further, given the high labor and production costs in Great Britain and the Netherlands, it did not make sense for the company to increase production at these plants in order to make sales in new markets, where prices had to be extremely competitive. Similar problems were confronting the company in connection with opening new plants in Great Britain and the Netherlands. High costs, environmental concerns, and high wages ruled

continued

Case 10.1 (*continued*)

out a move to invest in new plants. Further, the company was already highly leveraged and did not want to take on additional debt to finance new operations. There were other problems in Turkey. The company had received a license to establish and open one plant under a liberal foreign investment policy adopted by the government then in power, but another government had taken over and reversed that policy, and the chances of getting a license for a second plant were almost zero.

The scenario had prompted Amalgamated Polymers to look for other options. One option was to establish a new plant in a low-cost location that would be closer to potential markets. There were several countries that offered themselves as potential sites for this option. The company actively considered the opening of a new plant in a developing country because some of the constraints they faced in the developed countries were not present. The issue of overleveraging the firm, however, by taking on excessive debt to finance an entirely new operation continued to dog this option. Further, setting up a new plant in a developing country would require a time lag that was incompatible with the need of the company to penetrate quickly into new markets and take advantage of its technological edge in certain areas. The issue of timing was particularly important, because other companies also had major technological research plans and could catch up very soon, eliminating the advantage enjoyed by Amalgamated.

These considerations had led to the idea of taking an equity participation in an ongoing company in a middle-income or low-income country. The strategy was to infuse new technical and management capability into the company to make it internationally competitive. Once this was achieved, its products could be exported to other, new markets. The option of a joint venture with an ongoing company in plastics manufacturing seemed to address all the fundamental concerns, at least in principle. To acquire an equity stake significant enough for the company to be able to influence the management of the joint venture, Amalgamated would not be pressed too hard financially. Further, since it was supplying technology and management know-how, its contribution could be capitalized to offset a significant part of the total equity contribution it had to make under the proposed joint venture. Because the existing company already had the basic infrastructure set up and would be sharing other costs, the total costs of capacity expansion would not be too high. There also would be no difficulty in directing some of the company's existing production capacity to the targeted markets, because the government of the company with which the joint venture was being contemplated was keen to earn foreign exchange. The costs would be further reduced because it would not be necessary, at least in the initial stages, to expand production capacity by too much.

Mazirban had offered an ideal opportunity to implement the joint-venture approach. The country was a large producer and exporter of crude oil and natural gas, which were its main sources of revenue, but, like many other states in the Persian Gulf, the government was eager to diversify the economy and invest the surplus oil revenues in new industries employing high technology. Petrochemicals were a natural choice, because the raw materials, crude oil and natural gas, were plentiful and available at minimal cost. With

continued

Case 10.1 (*continued*)

the collaboration of major multinational firms, the government had established several petrochemical and oil-refining complexes. To attract additional foreign investments, it had established a liberal investment policy that placed virtually no constraints on overseas parties to joint ventures in Mazirban. The only important conditions were that any overseas venture in Mazirban had to be established jointly with a local party and that the terms of this venture had to be approved by the government.

Amalgamated Polymers found a potentially ideal partner in Gulf Plastics Ltd, a major plastics company owned by members of the ruling family and based in Ochran, the main port of Mazirban. Gulf Plastics was established in 1997 and for the past nine years had concentrated on the manufacture of basic plastic products, which it marketed primarily within the country. Gulf Plastics had been established with the help of a Japanese petrochemical company that also helped to run the company for the first five years. A few Japanese technicians still held key positions in the manufacturing operations division of the company. Gulf Plastics had been looking for a technical and management partner to upgrade its technology and help it move overseas. Amalgamated Polymers, which had compatible interests and strategies, appeared to be an ideal partner.

The terms of the collaboration would also not present a problem; they were fairly standard in the petrochemical industry, and the details could be taken care of easily.

Despite all these positives, there were a number of questions that Hyman felt the executive committee would raise on Monday. He would have to spend the weekend in virtual self-isolation to think of what questions were likely to be raised and what responses he should have ready to justify this investment. After all, it was very important to him. If the project was approved, he would be placed in charge of his company's side of the venture, and eventually it would mean a senior position at the plant in Mazirban, boosting his career prospects. On the other hand, if the proposal was rejected by the committee, six months of work would come to naught, and he would face the additional embarrassment of giving the news to the Mazirban government and to Gulf Plastics, who were not likely to hide their feelings.

DISCUSSION QUESTION

1. Assume you are in James Hyman's position and prepare a list of possible questions that the investment committee might raise about the proposal and your responses to them.

PART IV

FUNCTIONAL OPERATIONS IN INTERNATIONAL BUSINESS

CHAPTER 11

International Marketing

CHAPTER OBJECTIVES

This chapter will:

- Review the key elements in creating and maintaining a viable marketing mix in the international business arena.
- Contrast the views of product standardization and product differentiation, and discuss which types of products best benefit from local adaptation.
- Discuss the issues surrounding the question of centralized versus decentralized marketing management in a worldwide market.
- Discuss the major marketing-mix decisions—product, promotion, pricing, and distribution—within the international business context.

WHAT MUST BE DONE: THE INTERNATIONAL MARKETER'S DILEMMA

Marketing is one of the most important areas of operation for multinational corporations. With the internationalization of business, MNCs face increased competition at home from both foreign and domestic competitors and internationally as they seek to enter new markets. In developing a competitive strategy, firms utilize the marketing process to identify, create, and deliver products or services that are in demand at prices that customers are willing to pay. When it is performed successfully, the marketing process identifies profitable areas in which resources should be fo-

cused, increases sales revenues, generates profits, and creates a long-term, sustainable, competitive advantage for the MNC. When it is performed inadequately, the results can be disastrous. Please refer to Appendix 11.1 for a checklist of questions to consider in order to achieve an effective export marketing program.

The basic marketing-mix decisions consist of four separate but interconnected functions. These are the *four Ps of marketing: product, price, promotion, and placement*. Companies satisfy consumer needs by developing and manufacturing the goods desired in that market, educating potential clientele regarding the existence and qualities of those products, assuring that product cost is balanced between quality and price, and ensuring that adequate volumes of products are distributed to sales outlets or customers in a timely fashion.

While these marketing subfunctions are complex enough on the domestic level, internationalization significantly increases their complexity. Foreign markets not only are physically removed but also differ culturally. Specific cost structures in the foreign market may dictate special pricing, distribution channels found in the domestic environment may be unavailable in the foreign market, portions of the product may need to be modified to meet local tastes, and promotional methods may need to be adjusted to local media. Thus, every single function of the marketing mix may require modification, or at least fine-tuning, for the MNC to do business in the foreign locale.

International marketing entails operating simultaneously in different environments, coordinating these international activities, and learning from the experiences gained in one country to make marketing decisions in other countries. The international marketing firm must make important strategic global decisions about what to sell in which markets. Thus, the company requires huge amounts of accurate and timely information on the nature, economic condition, and consumer needs of the foreign market. The company must understand the conditions of the foreign market and the competitive movements of other firms operating in that environment. As a result, the MNC must rely heavily on conducting appropriate and accurate assessments to determine whether these potential markets will prove profitable despite the added costs.

To Centralize or Decentralize: The First Key Decisions

In developing a successful international marketing program, a firm must make several key decisions about its prospective strategy in world markets. Two crucial questions an MNC must ask are:

1. Whether or not the marketing program can or should be standardized across all markets or adapted individually to each separate market.
2. Whether marketing should be centralized in company headquarters or decentralized to individual market locations or foreign manufacturing subsidiaries.

It may be human nature that prompts management to attempt to standardize the marketing function throughout the world, because standardization greatly simplifies the complexity of marketing and probably provides significant cost benefits to a firm. Selling the same product throughout the world achieves greater efficiencies and scale economies in many areas of operation. Production runs can be longer, thus lowering unit costs. Research and development expenses normally required to adapt the product to each foreign market can be eliminated. Specific creative work required for adapting advertising and promotional campaigns for the foreign market are not required, nor are specialized sales-training programs. Pricing standardization obviates the need for calculating different prices in individual markets.

The major drawback of standardization involves the risk of market loss by not being attuned to individual differences in consumer tastes or local behavior. This cost is difficult to assess, and it is only through definitive, exhaustive market research that a firm can determine whether its standardized marketing program is losing customers.

In general, the question of standardization or adaptation is related to the nature of the product or service. Industrial products sold to other firms or businesses or to governments can be sold relatively unchanged throughout the world. Dynamic random access memory chips (DRAMs), for example, are an important part of the personal computer and are in standard use in the manufacture of computers in the United States, Europe, Japan, and Southeast Asia. In contrast, consumer goods, including such items as automobiles, furniture, and clothing, are tied intricately to personal taste preferences or fads and require more adaptation.

The degree of standardization also relates to the degree of comparative differences between the two environments in their cultures, physical attributes, institutional infrastructure, and political and economic composition. The greater the degree of difference between a foreign market and the domestic marketers, the more likely it is that the attributes or promotion of a product are inappropriate. For example, although there are distinctive differences between markets in the United States and those in Canada, products would be more likely to pass unchanged from one to the other; this would be far less true if the two cultures differed significantly, as do those of the United States and Nigeria.

Similarly, firms must make decisions about the planning, implementation, and control processes involved in their world marketing programs. Should programs be created, developed, and implemented from headquarters, or from on-site subsidiary locations, where personnel are aware of and understand the differences between marketing environments? Proponents of decentralized marketing functions would argue that the advantages of subsidiary involvement in the process are that the local personnel are more familiar with the characteristics and problems of the local target markets and would be better suited to adjusting the marketing mix to suit those necessities and to solve problems. Detractors of this recommendation point out that the MNC, by having a decentralized program, would lose control of the program and that overall corporate costs would be increased through replication of activity in various subsidiary markets.

The pattern that generally emerges is somewhere between these two extremes. Most multinationals have a combination of marketing programs that are, to some degree, both centralized and decentralized, which ensures that the company has control over activities within the subsidiary and the ability to formulate a global marketing program where warranted. It can also pinpoint those areas where it is possible to standardize portions of its marketing program across markets. By the same token, however, input from subsidiaries is crucial if the firm is to develop effective marketing programs in individual foreign target markets.

The organizational structure that evolves finds the headquarters of a multinational enterprise taking responsibility for developing the company's philosophy and overall strategy, developing products and product strategies, name brands, and packaging. The foreign subsidiary, on the other hand, takes advantage of invaluable on-site experience and information to tailor the promotion, distribution, and pricing of the product so that it meets the needs or characteristics of the market. When such an intertwining of responsibilities between the headquarters and the subsidiary is created, it is crucial that there be ongoing communication between the two parties. In this way, the MNC can maintain control over its subsidiary's operations and institutionalize efficiencies between headquarters and subsidiaries as well as among the subsidiaries themselves.

Typically, organizations decide among three alternatives regarding their marketing plans: ethnocentric, polycentric, and geocentric. The ethnocentric approach is exhibited when a firm markets its goods and services in foreign markets using the same marketing mix that is used in the domestic markets. This strategy is more often successful when there is very little cultural difference between the home and foreign markets. While this is the least costly of the three alternatives, this approach is risky in markets where there are large cultural differences between the foreign and home markets. Sometimes, firms attempt the polycentric approach in their marketing mix. These firms attempt to customize the marketing mix in each market in an attempt to meet specific needs of customers in each market. While this strategy could be successful if the company competes in foreign markets with varied cultures, it is the most costly approach of the three alternatives given the customization in each market. The third alternative. the geocentric approach, entails the standardization of the marketing mix, which allows a given firm to offer the same product or service in different markets, and to use essentially the same marketing approach to sell the product or service globally. The difference between this approach and the ethnocentric approach is that the standardized model used in all markets may not necessarily be the same as the model used in the home market. This approach, which is followed by such companies as Coca-Cola, creates huge economies of scale. But the approach is not without some risk: If the wrong choices are made in the process of standardizing the marketing approach, the effect of the marketing campaign could be lower than if some customization was offered throughout the areas where the MNC competes.

PRODUCT DECISIONS

When most people think of products, they think of things or services for sale by companies. The physical product as we know it, however, is actually only part of the total product. The total product is the entire package of the physical product and includes its type and form, brand name, instructions for use, accessories, and even the level of after-sales service. These attributes of the total product help determine the image that the product develops among consumers and the value it provides to purchasers.

Desired product attributes vary among users in different cultures or countries. For example, one classic study conducted on consumer attitudes regarding product attributes of soft drinks found that French, Brazilian, and Indian college students found it important that the drinks not contain any artificial ingredients, while students in the United States ranked taste and availability through vending machines as more important.[1]

There are two general classes of products marketed domestically and internationally: industrial products and consumer goods. Industrial products are goods sold to manufacturing firms, businesses, or governments and include such durables as steel, hardware, machinery, parts, electronic components, and other equipment. Industrial goods tend to be more universal in specifications and are consequently far more frequently standardized than consumer products. Consumer goods, on the other hand, are purchased by a large number of individuals who may vary drastically in their needs and tastes. These goods are frequently mass-merchandise items, including clothing, luxury goods, food products, appliances, and automobiles. Because of differences in taste, such goods far more often require adaptation to personal preferences, differences in culture, education levels, or even fads or fashions within countries than do industrial products.

PRODUCT-POSITIONING DECISIONS

The decisions regarding the positioning or development of a product in different markets depend on three crucial factors: the individual characteristics of each market and the environment in which the product will be sold; the functional need for the product (or the use to which it will be put) in the market; and a company's financial requirements and its competitive position in that foreign market.

The environment of each market can have a profound effect on the optimal product characteristics in that locale. The type of product marketed can be affected by the legal, economic, social, cultural, and physical forces of the targeted market. For example, types of products sold are definitely affected by a country's physical characteristics, such as geography, terrain, and climate. Automobiles sold in tropical climates, for example, would be less likely to require rustproofing than those in snowy climates where roads are salted.

Economic forces similarly help determine which products are appropriately marketed in foreign markets, especially if they are tied to levels of economic development. For example, it would be foolish to attempt to market electric-powered products in countries that do not have sufficient or reliable sources of power. Relative income levels and standards of living in each market determine, to a very large extent, the nature of consumer needs in that country, as well as the consumers' definition of appropriate price and product quality. Thus, a marketer must be sure to correctly identify those needs so that the product is not overly sophisticated or mismatched in other attributes. For example, products such as snack foods, which enjoy high-volume sales in industrialized countries, might be considered luxury goods in a less-developed country and would not find a ready market.

Cultural or sociological forces also have a profound effect on the appropriateness of products in different cultures. In a country with high illiteracy rates, it would, for example, be unwise to package products so that the goods could not be determined easily from photographs on the labels, but care must be taken not to confuse individuals with these illustrations. Take, for example, the experience of a baby food manufacturer that attempted to sell its product in an African nation by using the same label it used in other markets. The label showed a picture of a baby with the type of food spelled out on the jar. Sales were, of course, abysmal, because local consumers interpreted the labels to mean that the jars contained ground-up babies.[2]

Other products are affected by different traditions. For example, package sizes must be smaller in markets in which there is little refrigeration and shopping is done on a daily basis. Some products literally do not suit foreign tastes and must be made saltier or sweeter or offered with different condiments. French fries, for example, in the United States are served with ketchup; in Great Britain, "chips" are served with vinegar. Similarly, brand names may be affected. In Asian markets, such as Taiwan, a very popular brand of toothpaste used to be named "Darkie," but such a brand name would definitely find disfavor in American markets, where consumers are conscious of the use of any sort of racial stereotyping.

Even colors hold different meanings in different cultures and must be considered for suitability in product designs. Red, for example, connotes richness or wealth in some countries but may be considered blasphemous in some African countries. While black symbolizes death or mourning for Americans and Europeans, white has the same connotation in Japan and other Asian nations.[3]

Many products are evaluated by consumers in light of their country of origin. Indeed a great deal of research has been conducted on this topic by a number of marketers. This research has shown that products from eastern Europe, for example, are seldom rated as being stylish, whereas products from France or Germany are expected to be well designed.

Different markets have different legal criteria and standards for products. Some of these are standards for safety and content purity. Others have differing requirements regarding labeling. For example, in some countries all contents must be indicated on the package or the source of the contents must be delineated. Other countries may have limits on the types or sources of goods imported into the country, or restrictions regarding the use of brand names or the recognition of copyrights from other countries.

Through an exhaustive analysis of these attributes of foreign market environments, the marketing program can determine the appropriate mix of products for each foreign market. This mix is the variety or assortment of products offered at each level of quality and price. Thus, a firm might have several established lines that it markets in different locations according to the local needs and desires.

In determining the appropriate product line, a firm also takes into consideration the position of the product in its life cycle. For example, a consumer good in the stage of maturity for domestic home markets may be ripe for introduction into a new market that lags behind home markets in development, but would be expected to behave similarly over time.

PRODUCT STRATEGIES

A multinational corporation has three different alternatives in targeting the foreign market. It can either extend its product line, adapt the product line, or create an entirely new line of products for the market.

In *product extension*, a firm markets the same products abroad as it does at home, in the expectation that tastes and demands are similar enough to guarantee consumer acceptance. This product strategy is generally used when research determines that crucial characteristics of the domestic and international target markets are similar.

In *product adaptation*, a firm modifies its existing product line to take into account the cultural, legal, or economic differences between domestic and foreign markets. For example, product colors might be switched, electrical specifications might be modified to accommodate different voltages, or measurements might be changed to the metric system. Automobiles sold in countries where motorists drive on the left side of the road, such as England and Japan, must be adapted to a right-hand drive.

The third product strategy is to create a new product specifically for a targeted international market. The product might be within a firm's area of expertise but not included in its existing product line. For

An example of a moke.

example, a form of transportation used in Barbados and other Caribbean nations and tropical locales is the moke,[4] a vehicle that resembles a cross between a Jeep and a golf cart. This gasoline-powered vehicle is open to the elements but is smaller than conventional vehicles, seats four, and is perfectly suited to the needs of tourists for transportation over short distances on narrow island roads.

Once a firm has made the crucial decisions regarding the appropriate product mix, it needs to decide what message should be communicated about that product and how it should be delivered in its new markets. A firm has many alternatives regarding the content of its promotion message. It can either extend its message from existing markets or adapt its message to the target market, which yields a scenario of five different overall product and promotion strategies for the international enterprise.[5] Their use depends on the features of the product, its expected benefits for buyers, its expected functional use, and its competitive position against other products. These five methods are product extension–message extension, product extension–message adaptation, product adaptation–message extension, product adaptation–message adaptation, and new product.

The easiest method is marketing the same product with the same message. This method of product extension–message extension works well when there are few differences between domestic and foreign markets and the product is used for the same purposes in both markets. It is also the most profitable, because no additional expenses are incurred for adaptations to individual market areas. Examples of this type of strategy are those used by soft drink manufacturers in world markets who are marketing the same product, a nonalcoholic beverage, which is used for the same purposes, quenching thirst.

In some instances, a firm might market the same product in a foreign target market, but that product may be used for a different function or purpose, and the message regarding its attributes must be adapted for the target market. In such a product extension–message adaptation strategy, a company merely changes the message communicated to its consumers. For example, goods that might be considered luxury items used to pursue leisure activities in one market might be necessities in another. For example, bicycles, motor scooters, and cross-country skis might be touted for leisure use in one country but for basic transportation in another.

In product adaptation–message extension, the product is changed but the message is extended. This strategy is effective in markets where the product serves the same functional use but under different environmental conditions, where products must be slightly adapted to suit local tastes. Examples are fast foods that require different menus or recipes, or vehicles with different tires designed to suit the physical conditions of roads in different markets. This strategy has the advantage of establishing a consistent product image across markets and standardization of the communication message with its associated cost savings.

In product adaptation–message adaptation, both the product and the message are changed to meet conditions in foreign target markets where both the characteristics of the market and the use of the product differ from those in domestic spheres. Because the product is put to a different use in the foreign market, it follows that its message differs from that used at home. Under this strategy, however, the firm may still realize some cost benefit in using the same basic R & D or production costs if several of the product attributes are similar.

Developing a new product specifically for new markets generally requires communications designed specifically to suit the international market. Sometimes, however, the firm may be able to extend a message if the product developed is serving a slightly different function but one similar to that of its domestic product line. While this new product strategy is the most expensive to follow, it may ultimately yield success in the form of high sales because the firm has developed a product that meets the needs of customers in the target market.

PROMOTION DECISIONS

As with product decisions, the development of appropriate promotional efforts raises the question of standardization or adaptation. Promotion involves reaching potential consumers and providing them with information on the product's existence and attributes and the needs it satisfies. The promotional mix, which includes advertising, personal selling, and sales promotions, must create a relationship between a firm and its customers, as well as enhance long-term sales potential and consumer confidence in the product and the firm. Naturally, the more this promotional program can be standardized, the greater the potential savings to the firm because of achieved efficiencies.

Once a firm has established its target market and defined its characteristics, it then decides on its communications message and which promotional tools and media will be most effective in communicating that message. Great care must be taken to ensure that the content of the message is appropriate to different cultures. Mistakes in this area, such as inappropriate brand names or advertising copy, are very expensive, embarrassing, and unfortunately, all too frequent. For example, General Motors attempted to market its Nova (literally "star") automobile in Mexico without considering that the name when spoken could be interpreted as "*no va*," which means "it doesn't go" in Spanish. Similarly, Coca-Cola experienced difficulties in China in attempts to market its product under a brand name designed to be the equivalent of the English pronunciation of "Coca-Cola," but the Chinese characters translated literally into "bite the wax tadpole."[6]

Promotional Tools

The tools used in promotion include advertising, personal selling, sales promotions, publicity, and public relations.

Advertising methods are similar around the world, primarily because they are based on those developed in the advertising industry in the United States and focus on print, television, and radio advertising. The actual advertising programs may differ, however, because they are directly connected to reaching consumers by addressing their specific cultural values and needs. Where possible, international firms attempt to standardize their advertising in order to achieve savings. Some companies, for example, create a logo that is used internationally, such as McDonald's golden arches.

While companies may wish to develop an advertising program that can be carried across borders, they must be attuned to differences between cultures in order to reach the proper market and deliver the appropriate message. In Japan, for example, earthier advertisements have been permitted than in the United States, and television and print advertisements include bathroom humor and sexual frankness, such as topless models. Similarly, products banned from being advertised in the United States are advertised in Japan. Imagine the shock of a Westerner encountering explicit ads for such products as tampons, laxatives, hemorrhoid medicines, toilet bowl cleaners, and condoms.

Similarly, an international promotion planner must be apprised of the availability of different types of media in each market. A television campaign suitable for markets in developed countries, where many people own sets, would not reach many potential consumers in poor, developing countries where television sets are rare. Countries also vary in the availability of their print advertising sources and radio programming and the number of stations. Thus, advertising programs must be developed with the assistance of someone knowledgeable about the available advertising channels in the overseas market. This person helps to identify appropriate media for use in each country and avoid potential problems and mistakes because of cultural insensitivity to the meaning of colors, symbols, and nonverbal and verbal messages being delivered to the buying public or to the use of media. For example, in India owls do not connote wisdom as they do in the United States; they indicate bad luck. In land-poor, urban Hong Kong, consumers could not identify with the Marlboro man's riding the range on horseback. Adaptation of the copy showing him as a stylized urban cowboy with a pick-up truck was found to be far more relevant to consumers.

On-site resources can also prevent companies from choosing inappropriate media. For example, billboards cannot be used in parts of the Middle East, not because of cultural considerations but merely because under local weather conditions an outdoor advertisement would last less than two weeks.[7]

Personal Selling

Another promotion tool used by international marketers is that of personal selling, in which individual salespeople communicate the qualities and characteristics of the products to prospective customers. The use of personal selling by firms depends on a number of factors. One of these is product type. Generally personal selling is used more for industrial products, which are purchased by agents for companies or governmental concerns in larger numbers, than for consumer products, which rely on mass merchandizing to stimulate high volumes of sales. An exception is Avon, which has successfully used its own version of personal selling to promote the sale of its lines of cosmetics, fragrances, jewelry, and gifts to customers around the world.

The use of personal selling also depends on the resource characteristics of the target country. In some nations where the costs of labor are low, firms might find it more cost-effective to employ hundreds of sales representatives than to buy expensive and limited airtime on a federally controlled television station or attempt to reach a highly illiterate consumer population through media advertising. Still, the use of personal selling may be difficult or impossible in other countries, where street addresses or doorbells are not to be found or where such intrusive hard-sell methods are not welcome.

Even with personal selling, firms attempt to standardize their programs by using the same training programs and recruiting for their sales forces around the world. Indeed, some firms attempt to establish an international sales force in the hope of achieving strategic advantages over competitors. For example, Steelcase, Inc., a multinational firm and distributor of office furniture headquartered in Grand Rapids, Michigan, has trained its global sales force using the same basic program with only slight modifications to accommodate differences between countries. The company believes that this training provides for a uniform sales culture and the generation of additional business opportunities, such as approaching sales prospects working for multinational firms at several locations at the same time. For example, if a sales representative for Steelcase meets with a multinational's purchasing officer for the domestic location, the representative's counterpart can be meeting simultaneously with equipment buyers for the firm's foreign subsidiaries in overseas locations. An added benefit to the firm is that a consistent training program allows Steelcase

to integrate its sales approaches and strategies and coordinate sales activity around the globe.[8]

SALES PROMOTIONS

Sales promotions are those activities pursued by a firm in an attempt to generate interest in the company's products, greater levels of sales, and enhanced distributor effectiveness. Some of the most popular promotional efforts are those that involve contests or sweepstakes. Other promotions include company sponsorship of sporting or cultural events or participation in trade shows. Sales promotions also come in the form of cents-off coupons on company products, in-store samples and demonstrations of products, and point-of-purchase displays designed to catch shoppers' attention.

As with the other tools of the promotional mix, these efforts may be constrained by foreign legal requirements, such as limitations on premium amounts and prior government approval of discounts. Some countries may not allow companies to give gifts. Other constraints may come from the sociocultural aspects of the target market. For example, it may not be worth a company's effort to attempt to stage store demonstrations if the product is sold to consumers in small rural markets rather than in supermarkets. Still, sales promotions may be effective in those markets that have limited opportunities for utilization of the other promotion tools.

PUBLICITY AND PUBLIC RELATIONS

Publicity and public relations refer to a firm's relationship with entities in its markets other than the buyers of its product, which include nonconsuming members of society as well as agents from the various arms of government. Public relations programs are put in place to allow the company a method of communicating about itself, not merely about its products. Thus, public relations departments generally communicate with the press about the activities of the firm, including work with consumer groups and corporate charitable programs, such as scholarship programs or contributions to local charities.

PRICING DECISIONS

Pricing is crucial to the success of any marketing program. An overpriced product may fail to attract customers, and an underpriced product may lower profitability. Pricing must therefore be carefully balanced to achieve the optimum level of sales and revenue. The optimum level can, of course, depend on the corporate objective, which can vary from maximizing profit to maximizing market share.

Thus, a company may wish to lower prices in order to achieve maximum competitiveness or market share in individual markets, or it may wish to see high prices and, in turn, higher sales revenue figures on its balance sheet. In other situations, a company might be concerned about the relationship between prices charged and taxes payable in high-tax countries. Therefore, an international corporation must review and establish its pricing policies in light of overall short-term and long-term strategic objectives. Consequently, price setting is customarily carried out at corporate headquarters.

Pricing is a difficult part of the international marketing mix to administer because of its complexities. While a firm may prefer to charge the same price for its goods in all markets, the differences between these markets frequently indicate a need to set different prices in different locales. For example, a company determines an appropriate price for its goods as they are exported across borders. This price would not be appropriate, however, for goods produced by offshore subsidiaries because of differences in relative costs of labor and resources, competitive forces, governmental regulations, and even market strategies. A firm, therefore, would pursue a course in which goods are priced according to the exigencies of the local markets, not on an international basis.

PRICING METHODS

An international marketer considers several crucial factors in determining appropriate price structure. These factors fall into three general categories: the strategic objectives of the firm, the costs involved in the production of goods, and the competitive forces interacting in the market in relation to consumer demand. The goal of the multinational firm is to develop a competitive pricing structure that will provide for both short-term and long-term profitability, as well as for some flexibility to allow for differences between markets.

Cost-Based Pricing Methods

Some pricing methods begin with production costs as a determination point. In *cost-plus pricing*, an amount is added to the cost of production to determine appropriate pricing at the next level of distribution. The cost-plus method has the advantage of being simply administered once all related costs of production are identified. It does not, however, take into account the competitive environment in which the goods are to be sold.

Determination of costs is often also achieved through the use of *average cost pricing*, in which the firm identifies both the variable and fixed costs of production. *Variable costs* are those that vary with the levels of production. For example, labor or raw materials used in the manufacture of goods are variable costs, while fixed costs are those that do not change regardless of production levels. Some fixed costs are rent, plant and equipment, and basic overhead costs. Through an examination of its cost structure, a firm can determine its average variable costs and average fixed costs to determine a total cost figure on which prices can be based according to expected levels of production.

Another easy method of price setting is using *target return levels* in setting prices. In this method, a company wants to achieve a specific return level in relation to costs or to the original investment. Thus, a fixed percentage or level of monetary return is added to the total costs of the product to determine its ultimate price.

The pricing of goods produced for export must also take into account added costs from their being produced in one country and transported to another. Price escalation in the context of exports refers to the additional costs associated with the movement of the goods from the domestic manufacturer to the foreign consumer, which involves several intermediaries. The escalation occurs because at each level a percentage markup is taken against not only the original factory price but the aggregate of all markups as well.

These cost-based pricing methods have the distinct drawbacks of being focused on short-term objectives and of being inflexible. They are often not integrated into a strategic plan and may or may not provide for a company's long-term benefit by providing for future expenses. For example, cost-based pricing may cover R & D prior to a product's introduction, but it may be insufficient to fund ongoing research essential to the future strength of the company. In addition, such a pricing program may not allow the firm or subsidiary the flexibility necessary to meet the demand or competition in the market.

Demand is, in fact, an important determinant of appropriate prices to be charged in various markets because in market economies, especially for interchangeable commodities, it is the market that ultimately sets the price or value of consumer goods. Elasticities of demand in relation to income are an important characteristic of markets. Similarly, demand is affected by the prices charged for goods. Some products are highly sensitive to price, and an increase can result in an equal or larger decrease in demand. Other products are not price sensitive and experience no changes in demand regardless of price shifts. It is important, therefore, for interna-

tional marketers to have a feel for the competitive relationship between prices and demand in foreign marketing environments to determine appropriate price levels.

Many firms price their goods entirely in relation to the prices charged within the market by competitors, which is especially true for smaller companies that follow the moves of the market leaders in oligopolistic markets, where a few large firms hold the largest portion of the market for certain goods or products. Other firms meet competitive challenges by using factors other than prices, such as offering exemplary service or stressing other attributes of the total product package.

Some firms use pricing to achieve strategic or marketing objectives, de-emphasizing the importance of production costs in setting prices. For example, some firms attempt to reap high profits from their markets; they set high prices for new products to cash in on their novelty value and the fact that competitive products are not yet available. Alternatively, the firm may use pricing to gain market penetration at the expense of profits. In this method, the firm intentionally keeps prices low in order to capture large portions of the market, allowing room for increasing prices once its position is firmly entrenched in the foreign market. Care must be taken in using this approach to avoid being charged with trade actions based on accusations of dumping or predatory pricing.

Dumping, which is considered an unfair trade practice, occurs when exporting nations purposefully underprice their goods for foreign markets only to displace domestic competition and gain market share, with the ultimate objective of raising prices when that position is well established. Dumping pricing differs from market-penetration pricing in that it is lower than the price the exporter charges for the same goods in its own markets or is less than the costs of production.

Transfer Pricing

Transfer pricing is a specific concern of multinational firms with production facilities and subsidiaries in many different parts of the world; it is the determination of appropriate prices to be charged between different branches of the same firm that are conducting business with each other. The basic problem with these intracompany transfers is one of conflicting objectives by supplier subsidiaries and recipient subsidiary branches. The supplier wishes to charge the branch operations the same price it charges other purchasers in order to boost sales revenues and profit determinations on its balance sheet. By the same token, manufacturing subsidiaries receiving the goods also wish to put their balance sheet in the best light and look for the lowest possible cost for input resources or goods, and greater flexibility in using costs to determine competitive prices in local markets.

Four typical methods of assessing costs in transfer pricing are:

1. Charging the subsidiary buyer for the direct manufacturing costs in order to cover all production costs for the transferred goods.
2. Charging the subsidiary buyer cost plus expenses to adjust for production and fixed costs in the manufacture of the goods.
3. Charging prices in accordance with those the subsidiary buyer would pay for the same goods in local markets.
4. Charging the subsidiary buyer according to *arm's length*; that is, quoting the subsidiary buyer the same price as for all customers. This method has the advantage of dispelling any suspicions that a firm is using pricing policies for any purposes other than accounting properly for the transfer of goods and materials between different operating units of the same enterprise.

The objectives of the individual operating units in transfer pricing must also be considered in light of overall multinational corporate objectives. For example, a firm might want to support operations in specific locales by holding costs down until a certain level of market coverage or penetration is reached. In this case, a firm would direct that the transfer prices to the subsidiary be held to a minimum. Transfer pricing may also be used to achieve other objectives, such as shifting revenues from countries with high taxes to those with low taxes. For example, if a parent company in a high-tax country charged low prices on input goods for a subsidiary in a low-tax country, it could realize higher income in the second country and pay less tax, while keeping expenses high in the country with high tax rates. This practice may be illegal in some countries, as in the United States, where suspicion of the use of transfer pricing for tax evasion can lead to the Internal Revenue Service challenging a company's tax returns and determining tax liability using arm's-length pricing.

Transfer pricing also can be used to circumvent restrictions by foreign governments on the repatriation of profits to the multinational parent or on the convertibility of currencies into the currency of the home country. In these situations, the parent artificially hikes the prices of transferred goods for the subsidiaries, and their payment of these "costs" is happily received by a third arm of the company in a different location. Similarly, transfer pricing can be used to lower profits to avoid government pressure to reduce prices. Profits can be lowered to avoid concessions to the demands of labor to share in company profits.

International pricing is also affected by other factors in world markets. One major force is governmental power over pricing that is exercised to achieve national or economic objectives. To achieve goals such as economic or production growth, nations sometimes intervene in the pricing process by levying duties or tariffs on goods and services entering their country and, in turn, raising their cost to importers. For example, in Canada, tobacco products are heavily taxed in an effort to curb consumption. Canadian government figures conclude that 70 percent of the price of a carton of cigarettes in Canada is due to the taxation of the product. The Tobacco Act of 1997 mandates that wherever cigarettes are sold, there must be information on the packaging that clearly describes the hazards associated with the use and the emissions from the product. This is typically done via graphic pictures on the package and the store displays.[9]

Producers of goods within countries also might face government intervention in pricing through the establishment of price freezes, price subsidies, floors or ceilings on prices, or artificial limits for goods considered as satisfying basic or fundamental needs of the populace.

A second problem encountered by firms that vary their pricing procedures according to prices set by differing markets is that of *gray-market exports*, which are situations where individuals take advantage of a firm's pricing policies that account for market variations in demand and acceptable prices. With gray-market exports, goods are legally imported from the producing country into another country, and then are reexported to a third country where higher prices are charged for the same goods. Thus, because of the original firm's pricing differences, the exporters of the second country can compete successfully with the MNC in selling its own goods in foreign markets. These gray markets exist in many industrialized countries where currencies are strong and markets for goods are large. In the United States, for example, gray markets flourish in foreign-made consumer goods, such as watches and cameras.

Setting prices can also be affected by legal constraints in individual countries. In the United States, under the terms of antitrust laws, *price fixing* or the administration of prices is illegal, but legal restrictions in other nations may differ on prices administered nationally or internationally.

PLACEMENT DECISIONS: DISTRIBUTION OF PRODUCTS

THE IMPORTANCE OF PLACEMENT

The marketing function of distribution involves the critical process of ensuring that a firm's products reach the proper location for sale at the proper time and in the proper quantity. Breaks in the distribution flow can have critical ramifications, in the form of disgruntled customers, spoiled or damaged goods, excessive costs, and lost sales.

The type of product being transported determines the appropriate method of distribution and choice of channel. For example, one of the companies of United Technologies manufactures refrigerated transportation containers for fresh produce in which temperatures must remain constant, or importers are faced with receiving, say, instead of bananas, a shipment of brown mush.

Distribution decisions are also of critical importance because they are often long-term in nature, involving the signing of contracts with transporters or equipment leasers or the development of expensive capital equipment or infrastructures, such as rail lines, wharfs, ports, docks, and loading facilities.

This process, difficult in domestic markets, grows more complicated in international environments because it has two stages. First, the international exporter must transport goods from the domestic production site to the foreign market; then they must establish methods of distribution for the goods within the foreign country.

Numerous players within distribution systems are required to get goods to market. The distribution chain begins with the producer of the goods and then generally flows through an intermediary in the form of a wholesaler or distributor, who in turn provides the retailer with the goods for sale. Other services provided in the distribution of goods are storage facilities; transportation to markets via rail, truck, barge, or plane; and insurance services for those goods being carried between nations.

This relatively simple scenario becomes much more complicated with the addition of the international component, at which point other people enter the act to facilitate these exchanges. There are freight forwarders, who see to the details of international transportation, and exporters and importers, who conduct their international trading as either agents or brokers. Sometimes these individuals take title to the goods and trade them on their own behalf (merchant middlemen); alternatively, they represent the firm's interests and arrange for the distribution of goods for a fee (agent middlemen). Other players in the distribution game are resident buyers, who work in foreign markets to acquire goods, and foreign sales agents, who sell a product line in international markets. These classifications are augmented by such entrants in the process as *export management companies*, which provide distribution services for firms under contract; buyers for exports, who actively seek merchandise for purchase by the principals they represent; and selling groups, such as those established in the United States under the terms of the Webb-Pomerene Act, to promote trade. Some agents specialize and focus primarily on barter or countertrade agreements with non–market economy countries. Further down the chain, key players are those who deal directly with customers, such as a sales force, door-to-door salespersons, individual merchants, and the customers themselves.

FACTORS INVOLVED IN DISTRIBUTION DECISIONS

Distribution choices depend on several factors. One is the nature of the product. Is it perishable or fragile,

or is it a product that will require after-sales service? Might it be better distributed by an authorized company dealer? Another consideration is the degree of control over distribution. Greater control over the distribution process requires greater involvement by a firm in terms of time, money, and energy.

Another factor is costs. Whatever mix a firm wishes to employ may be constrained by the availability of middlemen or channels of distribution, by physical limitations imposed by the characteristics of the country, or by infrastructural deficiencies in the country, which limit types and methods of usable distribution modes. In some countries foreign firms do not have access to all distribution modes, as in Japan, where the distribution system is controlled predominantly by *sogo shosha*, enormous general trading companies that control much of the import and export trade.

The choice of a distribution program is also constrained or defined by the nature of the outlets for goods or services, and nations differ quite extensively in these frameworks. While some countries, such as the United States, have a variety of small and large retail outlets, other countries, such as Japan, have an enormous number of mom-and-pop retail outlets, which provide Japanese customers with individualized service. In France, a U.S. cosmetics company made a strategic mistake by assuming that its products would be appropriately distributed through a chain store's sole rights to distributorship. Its assumption was wrong, because in France cosmetics are traditionally distributed by perfumers, small retailers who specialize in cosmetics and are considered the ultimate arbiters of fashion.

A nation's developmental level also affects its distribution resources and networks. A lack of refrigerated methods of transportation will limit the marketing for frozen goods or fresh produce. Similarly, income levels might support the air-freight delivery of live lobsters in rich countries, while poorer countries rely on slow delivery by boat of less-exotic foodstuffs.

Distribution decisions can be even more complex in less-developed countries where distribution channels are dominated by specific ethnic groups within the country. This control, called *ethnodomination*, means that a multinational firm must be aware of and gain access to the members of the distribution channel to get its goods to retail outlets. Examples of ethnodomination are the Chinese ethnic groups who control the wholesale trade of vanilla and cloves in Madagascar, rice distribution and milling in Vietnam, retail trade in the Philippines and Cambodia, and poultry and pineapple production in Malaya.

The standardization debate on international marketing strategies was raised in the 1960s among members of the marketing community who claimed that the world was developing into an enormous global market where few differences existed among consumers from various countries in their tastes, standards of living, and buying behavior. Others discovered, however, that crucial differences between countries militated against such globalization of markets and the standardization of the marketing function. Table 11.1 outlines obstacles to standardization in world markets.

Indeed, many firms have found that standardization efforts are foiled primarily by the vast diversities among consumers in world markets. In fact, there may be a class of world consumers that consists of well-traveled and sophisticated people who are receptive to universal advertising and global themes.[10] Still, this group of consumers is very small. The majority of consumers, internationally, vary enormously in their national identities, tastes, preferences, languages, and cultural environments. Thus, all facets of the marketing function are susceptible to failure because of improper attention to the differences between markets that are caused by differences between cultures.

SUMMARY

The basic marketing functions of the four *P*s—product, pricing, promotion, and place (distribution)—are similar for both domestic and international marketing. Because of the complexities and differences of cultural, legal, and political environments, international marketing becomes much more complicated. Two crucial decisions facing the international marketer are the extent to which products are standardized or adapted to meet the needs and wants of the local consumer, and whether international marketing programs should be centralized or decentralized. Industrial products are more easily standardized, while consumer products generally require adaptation to meet local preferences. Management of international marketing programs tends to rely on corporate headquarters for overall strategy, R & D, brand names, and packaging, with the foreign subsidiary developing locally sensitive pricing, promotion, and distribution strategies. Extensive ongoing communication between headquarters and the foreign subsidiary, however, is crucial to effective coordination of the marketing program.

Five product-promotion strategies can be adopted to market the same product, an adapted product, or a totally new product using the same message or an adapted message specially designed for the foreign market.

While advertising methods are relatively similar throughout the world, actual promotional campaigns must be adapted to meet the product characteristics, cultural environment, and media availability in foreign markets. Personal selling programs may be standardized, however, while other promotion tools, such as sales promotion and publicity, require adaptation to the local environment and must be responsive to legal constraints.

Various pricing methods, such as cost-plus and target-return, can be used, but consideration of MNCs' long-term strategic objectives and applicable

Table 11.1

Obstacles to Standardization in International Marketing Strategies

Elements of Marketing Program

Factors limiting standardization	Product design	Pricing	Distribution	Sales force	Ads and promotion, branding and packaging
Market characteristics					
Physical environment	Climate Product use conditions		Customer mobility	Dispersion of customers	Access to media Climate
Stage of economic and industrial development	Income levels Labor costs in relation to capital costs	Income levels	Consumer shopping patterns	Wage levels, availability of manpower	Need for convenience rather than economy Purchase quantities
Cultural factors	Customs and tradition Attitudes toward foreign goods	Attitudes toward bargaining	Consumer shopping patterns	Attitudes toward selling	Language, literacy Symbolism
Industry conditions					
Stage of product life cycle in each market	Extent of product differentiation	Elasticity of demand	Availability of outlets Desirability of private brands	Need for missionary sales effort	Awareness, experience with products
Competition	Quality levels	Local costs Prices of substitutes	Competitors' control of outlets	Competitors' sales forces	Competitive expenditures messages
Marketing institutions					
Distributive system	Availability of outlets	Prevailing margins	Number and variety of outlets available Ability to "force" distribution	Number, size, dispersion of outlets	Extent of self-service
Advertising media and agencies				Effectiveness of advertising, need for substitutes	Media availability, costs, overlaps
Legal restrictions	Product standards Patent laws Tariffs and taxes	Tariffs and taxes Antitrust laws Resale price maintenance	Restrictions on product lines Resale price maintenance	General employment restrictions Specific restrictions on selling	Specific restrictions on messages, costs Trademark laws

governmental regulations should also be included in the development of an international pricing strategy. Distribution channels, their availability and limitations in different locations, and the extent to which the marketed product requires follow-up servicing and support can create a wide degree of variability in an MNC's international distribution policy.

DISCUSSION QUESTIONS

1. What are the four Ps of marketing?
2. How does international marketing differ from solely domestic marketing?
3. What are the advantages of a standardized marketing strategy? What are the disadvantages?
4. What types of products are best suited to standardization?
5. How does the total product differ from the physical product?
6. Discuss the basic strategies through which multinationals introduce and promote products in a foreign market.
7. Discuss the four major tools used in promotion. What are the types of concerns an advertising manager in the MNC home office might have when developing a promotion strategy?
8. What is cost-plus pricing? What is average cost pricing?
9. How can transfer-pricing costs be assessed within a multinational corporation?
10. What factors should be considered when making distribution decisions?

NOTES

1. Green, Cunningham, and Cunningham, "The Effectiveness of Standardized Global Advertising."
2. Ricks, *Big Business Blunders.*
3. Ibid.
4. Mini Moke Club, photograph, http://mokeclub.org., accessed April 24, 2006.
5. Keegan, "Multinational Product Planning."
6. Ricks, *Big Business Blunders.*
7. Ibid.
8. Flynn, "The Challenges of Multinational Sales Training."
9. Health Canada, http://www.hc-sc.gc.ca/hecs-sesc/tobacco/legislation/index.html, accessed April 24, 2006.
10. Ryans, "Is It Too Soon to Put a Tiger in Every Tank?"

BIBLIOGRAPHY

Buzzell, Robert D. "Can You Standardize Multinational Marketing?" *Harvard Business Review*, November–December 1968, 74.

Darlin, Damon. "Japanese Ads Take Earthiness to Levels Out of This World." *Wall Street Journal*, August 30, 1980, 11.

Douglas, S.P., and Yoram Wind. "The Myth of Globalization." *Columbia Journal of World Business*, Winter 1987, 19–29.

Flynn, Brian H. "The Challenges of Multinational Sales Training." *Training and Development Journal*, November 1987, 54–55.

Foxman, Ellen R., Patriya S. Tansuhaj, and John K. Wong. "Evaluating Cross-National Sales Promotion Strategy." *International Marketing Review*, Winter 1988, 7–15.

Green, Robert T., W.H. Cunningham, and Isabella C. Cunningham. "The Effectiveness of Standardized Global Advertising." *Journal of Advertising* 4 (1975): 25–30.

Jain, Subhash C. *International Marketing Management.* 3rd ed. Boston: Kent, 1990.

———. "Standardization of International Marketing Strategy: Some Research Hypotheses." *Journal of Marketing*, January 1989, 70–79.

Jain, Subhash C., and Lewis R. Tucker Jr. *International Marketing: Managerial Perspectives.* 2nd ed. Boston: Kent, 1986.

Kahler, Ruel. *International Marketing.* 5th ed. Cincinnati, OH: South-Western, 1983.

Keegan, Warren J. "Multinational Product Planning: Strategic Alternatives." *Journal of Marketing*, January 1969, 58–62.

Leavitt, Theodore. "The Globalization of Markets." *Harvard Business Review*, May–June 1983, 92–102.

Muskie, Edmund S., and Daniel J. Greenwood III. "The Nestle Infant Formula Audit Commission as a Model." *Journal of Business Strategy*, Spring 1988, 19–23.

Nagashima, Akira. "A Comparison of Japanese and U.S. Attitudes Toward Foreign Products." *Journal of Marketing*, January 1970, 68–74.

———. "A Comparitive 'Made-In' Product Image Survey Among Japanese Businessmen." *Journal of Marketing*, July 1977, 41 (3), 95–100.

Peebles, D.M., and J.K. Ryans. *Management of International Advertising: A Marketing Approach.* Newton, MA: Allyn and Bacon, 1984.

Quelch, John A., and Edward J. Hoff. "Customizing Global Marketing." *Harvard Business Review*, May–June 1986, 59–68.

Reierson, Curtis. "Attitude Changes Toward Foreign Products." *Journal of Marketing Research*, November 1967, 385–87.

Ricks, David A. *Big Business Blunders: Mistakes in Multinational Marketing.* Homewood, IL: Dow Jones-Irwin, 1983.

Ryans, John K., Jr. "Is It Too Soon to Put a Tiger in Every Tank?" *Columbia Journal of World Business*, March–April 1969, 69–75.

Samiee, Saeed. "Pricing in Market Strategies of U.S. and Foreign-Based Companies." *Journal of Business Research*, February 1987, 17–30.

Simmonds, Kenneth. "Global Strategy: Achieving the Geocentric Ideal." *International Marketing Review*, Spring 1985, 8–17.

Simon-Miller, Francoise, "World Marketing: Going Global or Acting Local? Five Expert Viewpoints." *Journal of Consumer Marketing*, v. 3, n. 2, March 1986, 5–15.

Terpstra, Vern. *International Dimensions of Marketing.* 2nd ed. Boston: Kent, 1985.

APPENDIX 11.1
A CHECKLIST FOR EXPORT MARKETING

Market Potential	
Segmentation	1. Are the ultimate consumers American tourists or foreign citizens?
	2. Are we tapping the burgeoning middle class in industrialized nations?
	3. Are our customers the wealthy elite in the underdeveloped countries?
	4. Are our buyers affiliates of our company?
Size of market	1. How long is the sales potential?
	2. What volume could be sold at higher or lower prices?
	3. What sales potential do we estimate for the next few years?
Special opportunities	1. Would differential pricing be noticed, and would it be objectionable?
	2. Do prices abroad fluctuate seasonally?
	3. Could some particular price policy foster trust and long-term relations?
	4. How does the delivered price relate to other elements of the marketing mix?
Marketing Mix	
Individualizing and adaptation	1. Should our product be modified (simplified or embellished) to increase its suitability for foreign markets?
	2. How should we position our product to gain for it the appropriate level of price perception?
	3. Could special packing or packaging enhance the value of our product?
	4. Would freight, customs duty, and so on be substantially lower for separate components to be assembled abroad?
	5. Is assembly abroad less expensive than in the United States?
Reducing the buyer's risk	1. Does our price include warranty service?
	2. How quickly and assuredly are spare parts available?
	3. Might feasibility studies cause our product to be specified?
	4. In the country of destination, at what stage of the product life cycle is our offering?
Buyer-seller relationship	1. How closely can we estimate what the buyer is willing to pay?
	2. What is our reputation for quality and commercial integrity?
	3. Have we avoided misunderstandings about measurement units such as "ton" and commercial terms such as cost, insurance, and freight (or "CIF")?
	4. Should our quotation include a cushion for later price concessions?
Channel	1. At what point in the distribution process is our price compared with those of competitors?
	2. How many middle agents are in the distribution chain, and what functions do they perform?
	3. Can we reduce the cost of distribution?

continued

Apendix 11.1 (*continued*)

Foreign Market Environment	
Degree of market control	1. Is the price of our commodity determined through market institutions?
	2. How closely do we control the availabilities and prices of our line at the point of final sale?
Foreign attitudes	1. How important is price in the purchasing decision?
	2. Is the prevalent business philosophy "low turnover, big markup"?
	3. Are high-priced goods subject to special tariff surcharges?
	4. What is the business culture with respect to haggling, price fixing, and boycotting the price cutters?
	5. Are price deals effective?
	6. In what ways are we affected by any foreign laws in margins, prices, price changes, intercompany pricing, and the "most favored customer clause"?
Competition	1. In our line, how active is worldwide competition?
	2. Are the competitors' quotations valid?
	3. Is our price level encouraging foreign imitators?
Some alternatives	1. What do we learn from foreign competitors' prices about manufacturing opportunities abroad?
	2. Have we considered licensing as an alternative to selling?
	3. Could multilateral transactions in foreign exchange of foreign merchandise make our product's final price more attractive?

Cost Considerations	
Commercial risks	1. What are the costs and risks of submitting a foreign quotation?
	2. Could our exported merchandise be shipped back to the United States and interfere with our domestic marketing?
Incremental costs	1. Are foreign orders absorbing idle capacity?
	2. Are we disposing of excess inventory?
	3. Does potential foreign business warrant expansion that captures economies of scale?
	4. Are we pricing a product line, a single product, or a onetime opportunity?
	5. Have we separated our variable and fixed costs?
	6. Do foreign orders require special production changes, extra shifts, or other costly adjustments?
	7. What are the differential marketing and administrative costs of selling abroad?
	8. What is the total impact of export sales on our costs?
	9. How closely does the country of destination enforce its antidumping laws?
Special risks and opportunities	1. Have we costed out all possible modes of transportation?
	2. Do our costs include insurance on our goods until we receive payment, even if the purchaser insists on insurance coverage?
	3. Do our credit terms reflect various risks: (a) commercial, (b) inflation, (c) currency exchange rate, (d) blocking of remittances, (e) expropriation, (f) interest-rate fluctuations?
	4. Do export sales offer any tax advantages?
	5. What is our profitability mix between original equipment and spare parts, initial order and reorder?

continued

Apendix 11.1 (*continued*)

Administrative Considerations	
Internal organization	1. What are our objectives in international business?
	2. What are our specific goals with respect to the present quotation?
	3. Who (title and location) is authorized to quote a binding price?
	4. What intrafirm conflicting interests regarding international marketing must be resolved?
	5. Do our affiliates in different countries compete against one another?
Price policy	1. What is our basic price policy (such as same freight on board, or "FOB," factory price to everyone)?
	2. What is our stance toward competition: price higher, same, lower, ignored?
	3. How flexible are we to accommodate good customers, meet competition, and offset new duties or changes in currency values?
	4. How important is foreign business for us?
	5. Could our foreign involvement harm our image domestically?
Procedures	1. Have we ensured compliance with applicable U.S. laws?
	2. Do we use standard forms for preparing quotations?
	3. Do our quotations have a time limit?
	4. Do we formally review quotations accepted and rejected?
Intracompany policy	1. Is pricing a legal means of repatriating earnings?
	2. Are we permitted to avoid foreign customs duties through high prices on raw materials and low prices on finished goods?
	3. What is the influence of our intracompany pricing on income taxes in the United States and in the country of destination?
	4. Are we quoting arm's-length prices to our affiliates?

Source: S.C. Jain, *International Marketing Management*, 3rd ed. (Boston: Plus-Kent, 1990). Reprinted by permission.

CASE STUDY 11.1
EUROMANAGÉ, INC.

Euromanagé, Inc., was established in Lyons, France, in 1957 by the Picard brothers, Alain and Michel, as a manufacturer of high-quality baked products that were sold to gourmet shops throughout France, especially in the major cities. As the company grew in strength financially, it expanded its product line to include soft drinks (both bottled and powdered), snack foods, and breakfast cereals. By 2006 the company was a leading processed-food and soft drink manufacturer in France and had established its presence in Switzerland, West Germany, Austria, and the Netherlands.

Having gained considerable international experience in Europe, the company had made the decision in 2005 to expand into Latin America, starting with Massilia, one of the largest countries in Latin America, with a per capita income of US$6,800 a year, nearly the highest among all countries of the region. Although under considerable Spanish and Portuguese influence because of its heritage, Massilia had a large middle-class population that was increasingly open to international products of different categories. Premarketing research had shown that there was a substantial market for the high-quality, upper-end soft drinks and processed-cheese products of Euromanagé. Estimated sales for the first year were US$40 million.

Massilia had a mixed retail system for soft drinks and processed foods. Soft drinks were sold primarily through individually owned small stores that also sold other types of groceries. Large supermarkets in the major cities were also a major source of soft drink sales (about 15

percent). The balance was sold through a variety of outlets, including automatic vending machines (11 percent), restaurants and similar establishments (6 percent), and miscellaneous outlets (8 percent). The large international soft drink manufacturers dominated the market and had established their own bottling plants in four key regions and set up a comprehensive distribution system operated through local distributors, who had signed agreements with the franchisees.

Euromanagé considered several strategies to break into the market and reached the conclusion that it could achieve maximum penetration by attacking the high end of the market and carving a niche in the mineral water, fruit juice, and fruit drink markets. Much of this market was concentrated in the urban areas, where the professional class was located. With a well-designed marketing plan, Euromanagé hoped to put forth an image of the aesthetic social superiority of its products that would appeal instantly to the upwardly mobile and the ambitious sections of Massilia's middle class.

It was also evident that the initial marketing arrangement would be made with the large supermarkets, where most of the higher-income middle-class customers in urban areas did their shopping. Although in some areas there were high-end individually owned stores, the supermarkets controlled as much as 70 percent of the middle- to higher-income retail market in the urban areas. Further, the supermarkets also stocked a wide variety of imported foods, and they could also carry Euromanagé processed-cheese prod-
continued

Case 11.1 (*continued*)

ucts. Further, at some point in the future, the supermarkets could carry more items from the Euromanagé product line. Initial surveys had shown that customers at the major supermarkets welcomed the availability of high-quality French soft drinks and cheeses. Although this issue was settled fairly quickly, the international marketing strategy for Massilia became bogged down in indecision on a choice of a distribution system. Massilia was located on a different continent, and the company's experience in establishing distribution networks in Europe could not be easily duplicated. Considerable effort, including on-the-spot studies of the distribution system in Massilia, enabled the company to narrow down the options to two. The first was to establish a company distribution office in Mardoe, the major port city and capital of Massilia. Under this arrangement an executive of Euromanagé would be placed in overall charge of the Massilia distribution operation and would be assisted by a small locally recruited staff. The office would maintain direct contact with all the supermarkets selling Euromanagé products and coordinate imports and local transportation to various supermarket locations. Letters of credit for imports would be opened by the distribution office on receipt of the supermarket purchase orders. The local office would also be in charge of collections and assist the supermarkets in efficient inventory control of Euromanagé products.

The proposal seemed to offer many advantages. Euromanagé was entering into a fairly competitive market with well-entrenched competition. Pricing was a key factor and the existence of an in-house distribution arrangement would save considerably on the middleman's commission. Further, the distribution office could keep in close touch with the supermarket and offer the company excellent feedback on the market response to Euromanagé products. Further, the executive in charge of the distribution center could actively follow up the promotion of Euromanagé in the new markets.

The second distribution option was to appoint a local agent in Mardoe as the company's sole distributor of soft drinks and processed-cheese products. The distributor would import the products after receiving and consolidating orders from the supermarkets. All transportation, collection, and other arrangements would be made by the distributor, who would also provide periodic market feedback to Euromanagé. The latter would, at the same time, be free to talk directly to supermarkets on such issues as the market response to new products, needed changes in product quality and varieties, nature of store-level promotions, and so on. The distributor would charge a commission on a graduated scale, depending on the level of sales achieved each year, over a given base. There would, however, be a minimum fixed amount of commission payable to the distributor to cover fixed costs.

There were considerable advantages in this proposal, too. The wholesaler would obviously have a better knowledge of the local market and arrive at arrangements with the local supermarkets more easily than would be possible for Euromanagé to accomplish directly. Further, with local experience, the wholesale distributor would be able to smooth out routine problems with the supermarkets more effectively. Because letters of credit would be opened for the account of the wholesaler, Euromanagé would be safe from the credit risk involved in collecting payments from

continued

Case 11.1 (*continued*)

the supermarket outlets. At the same time, the company would also be relieved of the difficult job of handling collections in a foreign country. The wholesaler already had an office and the necessary facilities in Massilia and would not need additional investments. Moreover, the distributor would have considerable experience and business contacts within the local distribution system and would easily be able to route Euromanagé products to the supermarkets.

Pierre Goulet, vice president of international marketing for Euromanagé, was perplexed. Both options seemed to have great advantages, but each also had several disadvantages, and what might have worked in Europe might not work in Latin America. Goulet wrote an informal interoffice memo to his marketing manager of the Western Hemisphere, Guy Lassalles, asking him to evaluate the difficulties and risks in each alternative from the long-term perspectives of the company, before the executive committee had to make a decision the following week.

DISCUSSION QUESTION

1. Assume you are Guy Lassalles and draft an interoffice memo providing the analysis sought by Goulet.

CHAPTER 12

International Finance

CHAPTER OBJECTIVES

This chapter will:

- Emphasize the importance of managing working capital within the multinational corporation.
- Outline the development of the international capital markets, the Euromarkets, and the international equities markets.
- Describe techniques for dealing with inflation, taxes, and blocked funds.
- Present sources of capital for financing MNC operations.

FINANCING INTERNATIONAL BUSINESS

The financing of international business operations is a far more complex, tricky, and challenging task than managing the finances of a domestic business. Several additional considerations and factors that affect finances come into play when a business goes international. Many of these factors are positive ones, for example, newer, larger, and more flexible sources of financing and access to a greater variety of financial instruments for more efficient use of financial resources. On the other hand, financial operations become subject to a variety of new constraints and risks. The task of financial managers in international business, therefore, becomes a twofold operation: minimizing the risks to the finances of a company and maximizing the utilization of the new opportunities presented by the international environment.

WORKING CAPITAL MANAGEMENT

In an international business, the management of working capital has several imperatives in addition to the traditional requirements. In domestic selling, optimal working capital management requires the following: the availability of liquid resources in adequate amounts to meet due obligations; management of the timing of the flow of financial resources, accelerating the inflow of receivables and lagging the outflow of payables; and maintaining an optimum level of liquid cash to minimize the occurrence of idle balances.

Maintaining an effective amount of working capital is essential for companies of all sizes but may be even more important for small, growing companies participating in the international arena. Table 12.1 illustrates the effects that management

Table 12.1

Effect of Trade Account Movements on Working Capital Needs for a Small Business

Paradorn, LLC

	Year 1	Year 2	Year 3	Year 4	Year 5
Cash conversion cycle (days)	37	72	145	13	6
		All Rise	Stale Inventory	Lead A/R	Lag A/P
YE sales	$1,500,000	$1,500,000	$1,500,000	$1,500,000	$1,500,000
Daily sales	$4,167	$4,167	$4,167	$4,167	$4,167
YE COGS	$750,000	$750,000	$750,000	$750,000	$750,000
Daily COGS	$2,083	$2,083	$2,083	$2,083	$2,083
Inventory	$125,000	$200,000	$350,000	$125,000	$125,000
YE accounts receivables	$175,000	$250,000	$175,000	$75,000	$175,000
YE accounts payables	$135,000	$175,000	$135,000	$135,000	$200,000
Inventory days (COGS)	60	96	168	60	60
Accounts receivable days (sales)	42	60	42	18	42
Accounts payable days (COGS)	65	84	65	65	96
Required working capital	$77,500	$150,000	$302,500	$27,500	$12,500

of the trade accounts (accounts receivable, accounts payable, and inventory) can have on the working capital needs of a hypothetical small business.

As you can see from Table 12.1, the hypothetical example maintains the same levels of annual revenues and annual cost of goods sold, so the effect of the cash conversion cycle can be illustrated. The *cash conversion cycle* for a business is the length of time (usually expressed in days) between the purchasing of raw materials and the receipt of cash after the finished goods have been sold. The length of days in the cash conversion cycle is calculated as follows: inventory days on hand + accounts receivable days on hand – accounts payable days on hand. The shorter the length of the cash conversion cycle, the less working capital needs to be financed from outside the company's operations (and the

more working capital can be generated internally). In the example above, the required working capital for each year is determined by multiplying the daily amount of cost of goods sold by the number of days in the cash cycle. So the required working capital for year 1 is calculated as: $2,083 \times 37 = $77,071$ (which is rounded up to $77,500). In the second year, the required working capital almost doubles when the cash conversion cycle increases from 37 days to 72 days. The required working capital more than doubles from year 2 to year 3, as the cash conversion cycle increases from an average of 72 days to an average of 145 days. Year 4 is an example of how accelerating the inflow of accounts receivable can significantly reduce the required working capital borrowing need, while year 5 is an example of how lagging the outflow of payables can achieve similar benefits in terms of the amount of working capital that is required to be financed outside the operations of the business (this of course assumes that the creditors of Paradorn, LLC, do not sever their business relationship with this small company!).

In addition to these basic factors, several other considerations come into play when an MNC's working capital requirements spread across several countries. The first factor is the availability of the appropriate currency. Unlike a purely domestic business, an MNC can have short-term financial obligations falling due in several currencies at its different locations around the globe. The financial manager, therefore, must decide between maintaining liquid reserves of the needed foreign currencies or moving the currencies in the spot exchange market, or, if it is available, making necessary arrangements through the forward exchange market.

The requirements of financing in different currencies to meet short-term obligations can also be met by borrowing locally in the different money and financial markets. These options generate the consideration of whether the option of borrowing locally is better than taking a covered position in the forward exchange market. In other words, a choice has to be made between a money market hedge and an exchange market hedge. The decision will depend on several factors, primarily the expected rates of exchange fluctuation and the interest-rate differentials and their expected reliability.

The presence of *exchange risk* and the policy of the international corporation are other crucial variables that impact the management of working capital across national boundaries. Exchange risk will depend on the firm's foreign currency liabilities that are not matched by offsetting transactions. How a firm chooses to determine its level of tolerable exposure and how it deals with it depend largely on the internal policy of the firm. Attitudes vary considerably in this respect. Several firms spend considerable time, effort, and money to minimize their exposure to currency fluctuations. Other firms

prefer to take the risk exposure and hope to profit from favorable currency movements.

The necessity to manage working capital over a wide geographical base is another major challenge faced by international financial managers. In a multifaceted organization with financial centers located in different cities, MNCs need to coordinate the financial position of different offices, which is vital to secure the optimal utilization of company funds and avoid unnecessary costs because of idle funds or short-term borrowing.

Management of working capital in different countries also implies the necessity of ensuring a relatively smooth transfer of funds, both within and outside the corporation. There are distinct possibilities that unexpected hurdles may arise because of government restrictions, exchange controls, or other political risk–related factors that may prevent funds from reaching their destination on time. Moreover, these considerations also influence fundamental financing decisions, such as whether to use funds from the home country or a third country or to raise resources locally. Although modern technology has made almost instantaneous transfer of funds around the world fairly easy, problems are still possible because of inaccurate messages, incorrect codes, and transit system failures. It is clearly more difficult to ensure the reliability of international financial technology in a wide range of countries, many of which are not technologically advanced.

Another challenge that confronts international managers is taxation. Taxation laws vary among countries and are often fairly complex. Moreover, in several countries there are frequent major changes in tax laws that could adversely affect the management of working capital, which is run on a fairly tight basis and which has little room for maneuvering. Moreover, different tax laws often require that transactions be structured to minimize tax liability and achieve the lowest possible post-tax financing costs.

Intracompany Pooling

Intracompany pooling is a financing technique that seeks to optimize the total availability of resources on a worldwide or area-group basis. A multinational corporation is likely to have several offices, each of which generates income and incurs expenditures and, therefore, has either operational surpluses or shortages of financial resources at any given time. The advantages of this technique are obvious. The surplus funds held with one office or subsidiary of a company would essentially be idle, because they are not utilized products. If intracompany pooling is effective, the corporate financial headquarters or regional control centers will know the exact locations of surpluses and shortages. With this knowledge available at a centralized point, instructions can be sent to move funds from the surplus to the deficit locations, which evens out the imbalances. Considerable cost savings are achieved because the idling of funds is avoided and the need to borrow funds at high interest is obviated. Consider an example of a company with one branch in Manila, the Philippines, and another in Cairo, Egypt. The corporate headquarters of the company, located in Phoenix, Arizona, keeps a constant eye on the funds position of the overseas offices. In the course of business, it is possible that one of the branches, say, Manila, is saddled with surplus funds of $300,000, while the Cairo branch finds itself confronted with a short-term deficit of $250,000. In the absence of intracompany pooling, the Manila funds would be idle for perhaps a month, while the Cairo branch would have to borrow $250,000 for a month, which could be at a rate of 10 percent per annum, or as much as $2,083 in interest charges. If, however, the Phoenix headquarters can monitor this situation, they can arrange for the Manila branch to remit $250,000 to the Cairo branch, reducing the former's idle funds and saving the interest charges of the Cairo branch.

Another strategy that corporate headquarters can devise, at the corporate level or at that of a regional center especially designated for this purpose, is a policy that requires that the surplus balances of all the company's branches and offices be maintained at a particular central office. Several benefits accrue from such a strategy. First, the various locations minimize the size of their resources and are in fact saved from the effort involved in utilizing them productively. Moreover, adequate opportunities for remunerative investments of short-term funds may not be available in many branch locations.

Centralized pooling of additional resources, therefore, can be located at centers where there are extensive opportunities for short-term investments at competitive terms. Such centers would have the necessary liquidity for absorbing sizable investments without any significant effect on market conditions. Pooling of surplus balances at one location also creates personnel economies because when this task is consolidated at one point, it can be managed more efficiently with fewer staff than if it was managed at several locations. Further, expertise in funds management can be concentrated at one point and used effectively, and funds from many branches would contribute toward sizable volume at the central location, reducing transaction costs and increasing the possibility of securing better returns on short-term investments.

Centralizing the management of funds reduces to some extent the political risk associated with assets held in overseas locations. The MNC is able to move funds to a safe location before a restriction comes into effect. As a result, the total volume of funds exposed to an impending or even possible government restriction on repatriation is substantially reduced. The centralized management of funds makes it possible for the corporation to devise and implement a global financial strategy that ties in to the overall strategy for achieving the global corporate objectives.

Global coordination and pooling of intracompany

transactions is not free from problems, however. The transfer of funds out of certain countries is subject to exchange and capital controls and therefore may not be possible at all. Moreover, many countries have laws that could levy a tax on even the temporary repatriation of funds. Also, devising and installing an efficient and versatile global electronic communication and funds-transfer system, generally through a multinational financial institution, is quite expensive, in terms of both initial and recurring costs (service, rental, and maintenance). A corporation has to clearly weigh the expenses against the potential benefits of such an arrangement. Usually only large companies with locations in different parts of the world find it economically viable to establish intracompany funds-transfer and management systems.

Even those companies that find the establishment of an intracompany funds-transfer system viable must take several other measures to make the system cost-effective. Costs involved in intracompany transactions can be considerable, and reducing them can add significantly to the company's bottom line. Minimizing transaction costs can be achieved by reducing the number of individual transactions through the consolidation of small transactions. Alternatively, offsetting arrangements can be made for different branches of the company, and only residual balances need to be actually transferred through the system. Transaction costs can also be reduced by using more efficient and cost-effective means of funds transfer, such as online transfers through major banks.

HEDGING AGAINST INFLATION

Dealing with inflation in different countries calls for active working capital management policies. High inflation tends to erode the value of receivables but also lessens the burden of payables in real terms. When inflation is expected to rise, plans are made for local receivables to be delivered at the earliest possible date. *Leading* is the technical term for the early receipt of goods. Conversely, an MNC would tend to delay its payables. The policy of creating deliberate delays with respect to outflows or inflows is called *lagging*. Centralized cash management systems also help in corporate efforts to minimize the inflationary erosion of liquid assets by permitting their transfer to locations where there are lower inflation rates and expectations.

MANAGING BLOCKED FUNDS

Blocked funds are generally those resources of overseas entities that host governments do not allow to be repatriated, at least temporarily. Funds blocking can take place for a number of reasons. A government may face difficulties in its balance of payments, which would reduce the available foreign exchange resources. To optimize the use of limited resources, a government may block overseas entities' repatriable funds and limit foreign exchange to financing essential imports and other payments. Occasionally a change of government can lead to an across-the-board blocking of funds usually repatriable by overseas entities, which could be motivated by political considerations—discrediting the former government or overturning its policies, for example. In specific cases, blocking may occur if a particular overseas corporation fails to comply with certain local regulations or requirements or is considered politically to be working against the best interests of the host nation.

Blocking can take various forms. For example, the host currency is deemed nonconvertible and repatriation of any funds is ruled out. Other forms of blocking involve repatriation of only a portion of the funds, repatriation only after a certain time lag, a combination of restrictions on the percentage of assets to be repatriated and the time constraints, absolute ceilings on the total amount of funds that can be repatriated over a certain time period, preapproval requirements for repatriation of funds, and special conditions placed on companies seeking repatriation.

Techniques for Dealing with Blocked Funds

Export Orientation for Multinationals.

Because the basic rationale for nearly all decisions and regulations that block funds is the shortage of foreign exchange, many MNCs seek to address host-country concerns by developing an export orientation that creates foreign exchange inflows that offset the outflows caused by asset repatriation. Thus, many MNCs whose primary business is production, sales, or services for the domestic market tend to divert some of their production to other foreign markets, thereby earning foreign exchange for the host country. In some instances, MNCs who do not produce exportable goods in the host country use their international marketing prowess, through their branches and affiliates abroad, to market goods produced by other manufacturers in the host country. Some MNCs, in fact, go so far as to start new export-oriented product lines either through their existing company or through another local subsidiary. The export earnings achieved are surrendered to the national authorities, who, in turn, unblock MNC funds, which can be repatriated.

Substitution of Fresh Investments.

Many MNCs substitute blocked funds for fresh investments from abroad. If an MNC is not permitted to repatriate funds, it often uses them to meet local expenses connected with fresh investments, either in new projects or in the expansion of existing ones. These funds are used in some instances to defray the ongoing expenses that arise in the course of day-to-day operations. This utilization is tantamount to repatriation, inasmuch as funds for this purpose would not be required to be remitted from the head office. In some countries, such adjustments are prohibited and firms must bring in additional resources of foreign exchange from abroad

if they wish to make new investments in startups or expansions. In the case of investments for which the company is bringing advanced and new technology to the country, however, authorities tend to take a more lenient view and permit such arrangements. Such companies usually face fewer restrictions on repatriation of their funds.

Nonformal Techniques

MNCs very often use informal means to secure repatriation of blocked funds. One important way is the exertion of pressure on the host government through diplomatic channels. At other times pressure is exerted by the parent company's home government on the host government. Occasionally, MNCs seek to influence host governments through their own governments at a time of negotiations for aid programs or other economic agreements from which the host country is expected to benefit substantially.

Direct attempts to influence government decisions are not uncommon. The frequency of such attempts and the degree of their success varies from country to country. In some countries attempts to bribe government officials are taken as almost routine, and several instances have been reported in the international press where multinationals have sought to directly influence government officials to obtain repatriation approvals. In some situations, however, such attempts backfire. For example, an MNC may become extremely influential with a particular host government and secure favorable terms. In the event this particular government is removed from office, the ties with the ousted government can be held against the MNC, and it may face an extremely hostile attitude from the new government, including jeopardizing the repatriation of its funds.

Financial Techniques.

Blocked funds take the form of idle balances when they cannot be repatriated, invested in new projects or expansions, or be used to meet the operating expenses of the company. In this eventuality, MNCs attempt to use these funds directly in the local financial markets and indirectly in the international financial markets. In the local financial markets, corporations attempt to invest the blocked funds in instruments whose maturities are similar to the expected duration of blocking. Of course, an ideal match is not always available because of the relatively undeveloped financial markets of many countries and the fact that the exact duration the funds will remain blocked is rarely known.

Accessing the international markets for utilizing blocked funds is not straightforward, however, and in most cases involves either circumvention of host-country regulations or, at a minimum, exploitation of certain loopholes. One way this is done is to place the blocked funds as security or collateral with multinational banks located in the host country for loans taken abroad by branches in other countries. It is extremely difficult for authorities in host countries to monitor all such deals and prove the precise links between a particular deposit locally and a loan extended overseas.

Parallel or *back-to-back loans* are another technique employed by MNCs to use blocked funds productively through the international markets. Under this arrangement, blocked funds are lent out to a local company, which arranges an equivalent loan to the parent company overseas.

Transfer Pricing

Transfer pricing is one of the most controversial issues surrounding the overseas operation of MNCs. The term itself refers to the pricing arrangements made among different units of a multinational corporation. Transfer pricing is discussed in the context of international marketing in Chapter 11; the discussion in this chapter focuses on the financial implications of this technique. In any MNC, affiliates receive from one another a wide array of

raw materials, intermediate products, semifinished goods, services, technical know-how, patents, and so on, which must be paid for. Because both parties in these transactions belong to the same organization, the main determinant of prices is corporate policy. Actually, the pricing decision in this instance is not derived so much economically as administratively or strategically. It is inherently difficult in this situation to ensure a fair price. First, the definition of a fair price varies depending on who's perspective is taken: the host government's, the MNC's, or that of the MNC's home government. Second, given this leverage, an MNC is bound to use it to offset constraints in other areas of its operation. It is treated, in fact, as a fund management technique by MNCs, because it offers considerable flexibility in moving funds from one subsidiary to another, avoiding taxes, dodging tariffs, and financing imbalances in different operational locations.

Capital Budgeting and Financial Structure of an MNC

The financial analysis needed to make decisions about investments in different countries must go beyond the exercise used for domestic investments and incorporate several additional factors and variables that influence project performance and returns.

Exchange Control Restrictions on Remittances

A project may be financially stable in terms of the revenue it generates in the country where it is located, but government restrictions may not allow the profits to be either partially or fully repatriated or may place time constraints on the repatriation. From the point of view of the parent company, this project would not be financially viable because the actual returns on investment would not meet acceptable standards.

POLITICAL RISKS

Political risks are connected to the issue of government restrictions on remittances. Such risks arise from the possibility of new or more stringent regulations being imposed by the host government. Such regulations could be imposed not only on the remittance of profits but also on the type of activities an MNC can perform or on the manner in which it conducts its business. Political risk also incorporates the possibility of expropriation of assets, and the risk becomes an important factor in new investment decisions, because it raises the kind of uncertainty that would affect future returns on investments. Although it is difficult to quantify political risk because of several subjective considerations, methods have been devised to provide a numerical grading of the different levels of political risk attached by overseas investors to different countries. The basis of most of these methods is a relative weighting scale of comparative risks in different countries. There is some justification to this approach, because in many instances the investment decision for an MNC involves choosing in which of several countries to locate the investment.

TAX CONSIDERATIONS

Tax regimes vary greatly in different countries, with respect to both statutes and implementation procedures and practices. In evaluating an investment decision in an overseas location, an MNC's financial analyst must factor in the implications of the host country's tax regulations. In most countries overseas entities' income on investments is taxed at special or different rates, which may be higher in cases of repatriation of funds.

SOURCES OF FUNDS

Any financial analysis preceding an investment decision must consider the sources of funds used to finance overseas investments. A corporation may have access to cheaper local financing or to a greater volume of financing because of its credit rating in the overseas market. It may be able to raise funds in third-country markets. At the same time, it may face funding constraints because local regulations prohibit overseas borrowings for host-country projects. Local financing may be accompanied by special disclosure, operating, and reporting requirements. Also, local restrictions may be placed on overseas entities receiving funds from particular sources.

Credit ratings help large, publicly traded companies access equity markets. But not all the participants in the international business arena are large enough to obtain a credit rating from a reputable credit agency such as Moody's Investors Service or Standard & Poor's. These smaller, often private, companies must fine additional methods of accessing capital.

Some local governments provide assistance to smaller companies that are attempting to enter the exporting market. In the United States, for example, the *Export-Import Bank of the United States (Ex-Im Bank)* provides working capital financing that enables U.S. exporters to obtain loans to produce or buy goods or services for export. These working capital loans are made by commercial banks but are backed by the guarantee of the Ex-Im Bank. For eligible exporters, the Ex-Im Bank has assumed up to 90 percent of the bank loan, which means that if the exporter fails to pay back the commercial lender, the Ex-Im Bank will cover up to 90 percent of the outstanding principal and interest at the time the borrower defaults on the loan. Ex-Im Bank requirements include that the company be located in the United States, have at least one year of operating history, and have a positive company net worth. An additional program to benefit small exporting companies in the United States is currently available via the Small Business Administration (SBA). The SBA Export Express program, its Export Working

Capital program, and its International Trade Loan program are examples of government-sponsored assistance programs to aid small businesses in entering the export market. Many of the SBA programs do not necessarily require an extensive amount of exporting experience. But these programs do have requirements for successful domestic operation over a reasonable period of time. As with the Ex-Im Bank guarantee program, obtaining an SBA loan also involves getting credit approval from a commercial bank.

CURRENCY OF BORROWING INVESTMENTS

In overseas investments the commitment of an MNC's own or borrowed resources has to be made in a particular foreign currency. When the MNC makes its investment decision, it must be aware of the different currency options available. The wrong choice of currency for borrowing could lead to substantial financial losses because of adverse fluctuations in exchange rates over the life of the loan.

DIFFERENT INFLATION RATES

Inflation rates are an extremely important consideration in evaluating investment decisions; the entire profitability of a project could be eliminated by inflation losses. Inflation rates became particularly important in the 1980s because many developing countries where MNCs of industrialized countries have substantial investments experienced hyperinflationary rates. When making a decision to invest in a country where inflation rates are expected to be high, the financial manager has to realistically assess the impact of inflation on net returns to the parent company and devise inflation-adjusting mechanisms in the financing strategy, so that the returns can be made to the greatest extent possible, immune from inflationary conditions in the host country.

LETTERS OF CREDIT IN INTERNATIONAL TRADE

Another important aspect of international finance is how an international transaction takes place between the seller of a good (the exporter) and the buyer of a good (the importer). Sometimes firms enter into agreements with their local banks to provide assistance in facilitating an international trade. One example of such an agreement is a draft. A *draft* is a demand for payment from the buyer at a specified time. Two primary types of drafts are sight drafts and time drafts. The *sight draft* requires payment when the importer receives the goods, while a *time draft* extends credit to an importer for a specified period of time. When the bank is involved in processing and accepting a time draft, the collection process is simplified for the exporter. The bank agrees to accept the time draft for a fee, and the exporter holds the *banker's acceptance* until it comes due. Once the time draft is accepted, it is referred to as a trade acceptance, which is legally enforceable once the word "accepted" is written on the draft. Problems can arise with this form of payment. If an importer refuses shipment for some reason (it could have found a better deal for example), the exporter will incur legal fees in an attempt to receive payment. The exporter might also incur *demurrage fees*, which are fees for storage of the exporter's goods at the foreign loading dock.

To remove the exporter's concern that the importer will refuse to pay for the shipment of goods, a more effective process is the letter of credit. A *letter of credit* is a written commitment by a bank, made at the request of a customer (the buyer), to effect payment or honor drafts of the seller, if the seller complies with certain specific conditions. Thus, a letter of credit can be issued by a bank that promises to pay an exporter once the exporter has fulfilled its part of the bargain. The letter of credit details conditions under which an importer shall pay the exporter for goods. *Clean letters of credit* do not require the presentation of any documentation, other than the *bill of exchange*, to obtain payment. Most letters of credit are *documentary letters of credit;* when presented with these, the bank will require the presentation of documentation to obtain payment, for example, the invoice, customs documents, proof of insurance, a *packing list*, an export license (from the exporter's home country), the certification of product origin (to assess tariffs and quotas), an inspection certificate (to see whether the goods meet quality standards), and a bill of lading. A *bill of lading* is a receipt given by the carrier to the shipper acknowledging receipt of the goods being shipped, and specifying the terms of the delivery. The bill of lading is the most important document in a letter of credit, and it is also the document that has historically raised the most controversies during international transactions. The bill of lading is a receipt for the goods being shipped, a document of title for the property included in the shipment, and evidence of the contract of carriage, and it is a negotiable document.

There are many different forms of letters of credit. A *revocable letter of credit* can be modified or revoked by the issuing bank without notice or consent from the *beneficiary* (seller or exporter). An *irrevocable letter of credit* can be modified or revoked only with the consent of the beneficiary. Similarly, letters of credit can be either confirmed or unconfirmed. Under a *confirmed letter of credit,* the *advising bank* is committed to honor the payment of the credit, provided that the beneficiary meets the terms and conditions of the credit. The advising bank is a bank that is typically in the home country of the exporter. This is an important distinction, as the advising bank is the bank that is known to the seller. Having a confirmed letter of credit is particularly important when an exporter is dealing with a buyer from a country that is politically or economically unstable. The safest form of letter of

credit for an exporter is a confirmed, irrevocable letter of credit.

There are times when an exporter may want to have a transferable letter of credit. The beneficiary (exporter) can request that the letter of credit be transferred to another beneficiary for execution. If the same parties are undertaking multiple transactions, a revolving letter of credit can be established. This establishes a credit exactly the same as the original letter of credit but with shorter periods for shipment, and the ability to substitute documents specific to the current transaction.

The final form of letter of credit addressed here is the stand-by letter of credit. This is a bank guarantee, by which the beneficiary (seller or exporter) can claim payment if the principal (buyer or importer) does not fulfill its obligations. The bank will require proof of default, and the only time that the beneficiary obtains payment from the bank is when the principal fails to pay for the shipment of goods. The bank charges associated with this form of letter of credit are less than for the other types, as the utilization of the stand-by letter of credit is the exception rather than the rule. There are many different forms of letters of credit, and this section highlights only some of the more typical forms. The utilization of a letter of credit can reduce the risk of nonpayment for the exporter and can facilitate trade in some areas of the world that otherwise would be too risky to sell goods in without this form of protection.

INTERNATIONAL CAPITAL MARKETS

International capital markets have become increasingly important as a source of financing for the operations of MNCs, not only because of the decline in bank financing, but also largely because of several developments that have increased the competitiveness, size, and sophistication of the financial markets themselves. "International capital markets" and "international financial markets" are terms used to describe the three basic types of markets in which MNCs can raise money: national financial markets, Euromarkets, and national stock markets.

It should be noted, however, that both national financial markets and national stock markets are international in the sense that, although they are located in a particular country and are subject to that country's laws and regulations, they are open to foreign borrowers and investors. The degree to which they are internationalized varies, of course, but in general the financial and equity markets of nearly all the industrialized countries are open to foreign borrowers.

An essential difference between borrowing funds from a bank and raising funds from a financial market is that when a corporation borrows from a bank, the bank takes on the risk, and the depositors who place funds with the bank are not in any way responsible. Because the bank is taking the risk and going through the effort of pooling depositors' funds, it receives a certain remuneration, which can be quite high. Borrowing in a financial market implies that a corporation is reaching the investing public directly, without using the intermediary services provided by the bank. The corporation has to make the necessary arrangements on its own to inform the investors that it is in the market to raise funds and to convince them of its creditworthiness. Some banks, especially investment banks, do play a role in such transactions, but it is marginal in the sense that they provide only certain types of services, for which they receive fees. Generally, therefore, corporations find it cheaper to raise funds through the international capital markets because they are able to save the intermediary costs involved in bank financing.

Another important reason that MNCs would use this option is the sheer size of the resources that can be raised in these markets. There are limits on which banks can lend funds; not all banks have such large resources at their disposal and are willing to take excessive risks.

Financial markets provide a wide variety of financial instruments that can be combined and tailored to serve individual financing needs. Almost every aspect of a financing transaction can be custom designed to serve the purpose of an MNC: the maturity, currency, dates of transaction, repayment schedule, and types of interest-rate arrangement.

THE EMERGENCE OF INTERNATIONAL CAPITAL MARKETS

Bank lending dominated the international financial arena through the 1970s, although signs of strains had become evident toward the end of the decade. The international debt crisis, which became publicly known in 1982, signaled a formal end to the domination of bank lending as the main source of international finance.

Through the 1970s and the 1980s, several developments had prepared the financial markets of the world to literally take off. One important step in this direction was financial deregulation in many industrialized countries. The United States, Great Britain, France, and Japan introduced, at different stages, legislation that to a significant extent eliminated restrictions on the free flow of funds across their countries. The deregulation measures also improved the access to overseas markets for borrowers from these and other countries. Unfortunately, the improvement in the movement of capital was not accompanied by the improvement of many commercial lenders' ability to adequately quantify the risk in their loan portfolios. The Asian financial crisis in the late 1990s brought this need to the forefront. While commercial banks are currently in the process of developing similar risk rating systems for their credit portfolios via the Basel Accord, the need for enhanced control on the movement of currencies in some parts of the world remains.

Dramatic improvements in information and tele-communication technology has enabled the transfer of funds and market information around the world almost instantaneously, which gives the financial community the power to deal in several markets simultaneously. Effectively, the communications and information revolution integrated the international markets to a much higher degree. The widespread use and application of computer technology has enabled financial managers to create a wide array of highly complex financial instruments that can be fine-tuned to client requirements.

The distinction between domestic and international markets has become blurred with the rapid mobility of capital and almost instantaneous communication. What has emerged is a truly international market that offers a wide range of financing options to MNCs.

NATIONAL FINANCIAL MARKETS

The major national financial markets that serve as international financial centers are New York, Tokyo, and London. Other important national markets that are open to foreign borrowers as well as investors are Geneva, Hong Kong, Paris, Frankfurt, and Singapore.

These markets are generally free from government control as far as day-to-day operations are concerned. There are few, if any, restrictions on the inflow and outflow of funds from these markets to and from other financial centers. All these markets have excellent communications and other infrastructural facilities necessary for the smooth operation and execution of a very large volume of transactions on a daily basis. As can be expected, most of the major international financial players—commercial banks, investment banks, and securities and brokerage houses—have a presence in nearly all these markets. Most of the borrowing in national markets by foreign borrowers is done in the form of bond issues and commercial paper. Bonds are fixed-term

promissory notes, usually issued at a discount from face value, which is equal to the rate of interest received by the investor of the bond until maturity. A corporation that wants to raise funds through a bond issue usually hires an investment bank or securities brokerage house to underwrite and actually make the transaction. The lead underwriter or lead manager generally organizes a syndicate of other similar financial institutions that agree to underwrite some part of the issue for a share in the fees. The actual arrangements can vary considerably, depending on the kind of services performed by the underwriter or lead manager. Often the underwriter or lead manager, along with the syndicate, buys the entire issue of bonds from the borrowers and then sells or places them with investors. The difference between the price at which the lead manager and syndicate buy the bonds and the price at which they sell them constitutes their spread, or profit margin. In addition, the lead manager gets a separate fee for bringing together the syndicate and arranging the various services required for a bond issue. Alternatively, the bonds can be sold directly to investors with the underwriters agreeing, for a certain fee, to buy on their own account any bonds that are not sold.

Bonds issued by a foreign party in a national market require the services of a local underwriter or lead manager who is familiar with local regulations and market conditions and who has the necessary connections in the financial and investment community to successfully launch and sell the bonds. Because the bonds represent an unsecured loan to a particular company that is not located within the sovereign jurisdiction of the country, investors have to be absolutely certain of the creditworthiness of the foreign issuer. Moreover, the regulatory authorities of certain countries, especially the United States, impose stringent disclosure requirements on foreign issuers before they can float their bonds. In addition to disclosure, in most instances a foreign issuer must obtain a report on its creditworthiness from a leading rating agency. The two leading agencies are Moody's Investors Service and Standard & Poors, both located in New York. The rating given a particular corporation or other borrower determines not only whether it will be able to issue bonds in a particular market but also the rate of interest it will have to pay on the bonds. A company that receives a better credit rating will be able to borrow at a lower interest rate because investors will be willing to accept a lower return in exchange for a better risk.

Despite their openness, national bond markets are somewhat restricted for overseas borrowers with respect to taxes and the amounts that can be issued.

Foreign bond issues in different markets are known by individual market names. Those issued in the United States are known as *yankee bonds*, in Japan as *samurai bonds*, and in Great Britain as *bulldog bonds*.

EUROMARKETS

Euromarkets include three main types of financial markets—Eurocurrency markets, Eurobond markets, and Euroequities markets—that emerged in the 1970s and 1980s; they are named according to how they dominate the financial arena. The prefix "Euro" does not imply that the currency, bond, or equity is that of a European country (or the European Union). A *Eurocurrency*, in effect, is any freely convertible currency (including the U.S. dollar) that is held in a bank outside the country of its origin. For example, U.S. dollars deposited with Natwest Bank London, are termed Eurodollars. It is not necessary that the bank be a foreign one. The important factor here is that the bank be located outside the country of the relevant currency. If U.S. dollars were held in the Paris branch of Citibank, they would still be Eurodollars. The crucial feature in the creation of Eurocurrency is the shifting of its ownership outside the country of its origin. The dollars deposited with Citibank Paris or Natwest London will be credited

to the bank's account in dollars, which will be maintained in the United States. Thus, there would be no outflow of actual dollars from the United States, but from the U.S. standpoint, these funds would become deposits held by overseas entities. Eurodollar deposits can be created in a number of ways. For example, an Austrian company sells chemicals to a U.S. importer and receives payments in U.S. dollars and wants to reclaim its earnings in dollars. It can either deposit these dollars with a bank in the United States or a bank elsewhere. If it takes the latter option and deposits the dollars with a bank in, say Frankfurt, it would create a Eurodollar deposit. The Frankfurt bank, which now holds the funds, can lend them to another bank or borrower, and then lend the funds to additional banks. Borrowers using the funds to finance purchases can lead to the creation of further Eurodollar deposits, because their suppliers could again redeposit the funds with a bank outside the United States. Thus, the Eurodollar volume can increase in multiples of the original through this sequence of deposits and loans. In fact, the Euromarkets have grown tremendously over the years, especially during the 1980s and 1990s. This growth was not only because of the process of multiple deposit-loan creations. Several additional factors were responsible for their explosive increase in size, activity, and depth.

Origins and Development of the Euromarkets

Although as far back as the 1920s, European banks took deposits in the currencies of countries other than the ones in which they were located, Euromarkets as they exist today began to emerge only after World War II.

Postwar tension between the United States and the Soviet bloc countries generated the fear of a general freeze on Soviet dollar assets held in the United States. To preempt such an eventuality, these countries moved their dollar assets from banks in the

United States to banks in Europe. A large proportion of these dollar funds were deposited with two western European branches of two Russian-owned banks: the Banque Commerciale pour l'Europe du Nord, in Paris, and the London branch of Moscow Nardony Bank. The funds were channeled into other European-based banks, primarily in London.

This initial impetus to hold U.S. dollars outside the United States was encouraged by a series of U.S. government regulations that made holding Eurodollars a profitable proposition. Interest-rate ceilings were imposed by the U.S. government under Regulation Q in 1966, which led U.S. depositors to place their funds with European banks to take advantage of the prevailing higher interest rates. The demand for U.S. dollars based outside the country also arose simultaneously, because heavy taxes were levied on foreign borrowers raising funds in U.S. markets. Dollar funds could be raised at lower costs in Europe, where the European banks could lend their dollar assets without borrowers having to pay high U.S. taxes. The difficulties of the U.S. dollar in the Bretton Woods system had become quite apparent by the late 1960s. In 1968 the U.S. government, keen to slow down the buildup of external obligations in U.S. dollars, restricted U.S. corporations from exporting domestic capital (that is, dollars) to finance their overseas expansion. This move created an enormous demand for non-U.S.-based dollar funding, which was met to a great extent by the Euromarkets.

Apart from U.S. government restrictions, the international monetary developments under the Bretton Woods arrangements also helped create the Eurodollar market. Under the Bretton Woods arrangements, the U.S. dollar became, in addition to gold, one of the major forms in which the world's central banks held international reserves, which led to an accumulation of dollar assets held outside the United States, in effect creating a huge supply of Eurodollars. Added to this basic accumulation were

the commercial banks and other financial institutions in Europe who had dollar balances to their credit. They found that holding dollars outside the United States gave them greater operational flexibility and, for the most part, offered a better return than dollars held in the United States.

The increase in the supply of U.S. dollars was matched by an increase in demand for non-U.S.-based dollar loans. The imposition of exchange controls on the lending of pound sterling funds to nonresidents of the United Kingdom also stimulated the demand for the lending of U.S. dollars by London banks, who now could not make loans in their own currency.

Apart from these historical factors, there are some general factors that attracted both borrowers and investors to the Euromarket. For one, the markets are decidedly more efficient than the traditional banking markets. This efficiency translates into a lower spread or interest differential between the borrowing and lending rates. The lower spread implies that intermediation costs are lower, and both borrowers and investors benefit. Borrowers can raise funds at a lower interest rate, while investors get a higher rate of return.

There are several reasons that interest-rate spreads are lower in the Euromarkets. First, the banks do not have to maintain any specified reserves of Eurocurrencies and are not subject to central bank regulatory requirements, which lowers the costs for the bankers because a greater proportion of the funds can be now utilized for lending and do not have to be held as required reserves.

Second, funds held by banks outside the country of their origin are also cheaper to hold, because they are not covered under any federal deposit insurance scheme and no premium has to be paid for the purpose. The savings can be passed on, in part, to the depositors by allowing them a higher rate of interest on deposits of the same maturity in the domestic market.

Transactions in the Euromarket are usually for very large amounts. Moreover, there is acute competition for business among major international banks. The huge size of the transactions brings in economies of scale, thereby reducing costs. Costs are pared still further by competition, because banks try to underprice competitive offers in an effort to obtain huge volumes of business, which is very profitable because of the overall turnover. Transactions in the international capital markets generally involve a direct deal between a corporation (issuer) and the investing public, and therefore only companies with excellent credit ratings can expect to access these markets for any sizable amounts. Therefore, nearly all participants in the Euromarkets are entities with high credit ratings and are generally known internationally. Such companies usually demand and receive the best rates for their transactions, which reduces the overall average cost of funds raised in the Euromarkets.

The Euromarket, in effect, is a wholesale market where transactions generally range in multiples of millions of dollars and the value of the smallest deals is about US$500,000. The large transaction size introduces economies of scale because the overhead costs incurred by financial institutions (which are primarily fixed costs) can be spread over the transaction.

There are, however, certain risks attached to Euromarket operations. Deposits and investments are not guaranteed by any central bank, and if one party reneges on a contract, the other party has no recourse to the monetary authorities of the reneging party's country. Also, because the market consists of funds held in countries other than those from which they originate, there is no lender of last resort, which means that in the event of a financial panic, such as a market crash, there is no safety net that can prevent the bottom of the market from falling out. Thus, if a crash occurs, instability and chaos can be expected, because there is no authority, such as a central hank, in charge of restoring orderly conditions.

Another danger that has emerged from the rapid development of Euromarkets is the possibility of taking high and unwarranted risks. These markets are free from regulatory controls, which leaves the participants free to determine their own degree of risk exposure. In the absence of regulatory control and in the face of the possibility of extremely high profits, it is quite possible that many participants might be tempted to take unwarranted risks and destabilize the entire market, or at least parts of it if they find their gambles failing. The lack of disclosure requirements in the markets, as well as the fact that many Euromarket accounts do not show up on the balance sheets of financial institutions, increases the possibility of a buildup of hidden risks that could overwhelm participating institutions without a warning. The absence of such activities from balance sheets also prevents regulators in the home countries of Euromarket participants to effectively monitor and supervise their activities.

NATIONAL STOCK MARKETS

Raising funds by listing and selling corporate stocks on exchanges outside a home country has become an important source of financing for corporations involved in international business. During the 1990s many stock markets of the world showed impressive performances and registered substantial gains. Many investors and multinational corporations realized that listing in the world's different stock exchanges could lead to a better diversification of risks because many stock markets do not move in tandem. Thus, losses in one market can be offset by gains in another, which would add to the financial stability of an overall portfolio.

Many of the world's stock markets also grew considerably in size and depth over this period, as more and more companies listed their shares and there was an increase in trading volume. An important factor that encouraged this trend was the deregulation of some of the major stock exchanges, which widened the scope for international participation. The major stock markets of the world are located in Tokyo, New York, London, Taiwan, Hong Kong, Frankfurt, and Paris.

Many companies are finding overseas listings attractive because they increase the overall demand for the companies' shares, which pushes up their values. The international character of a company is also firmly established with an internationally listed equity. In addition, a company is able to lower the cost of the capital, because it is able to raise equity instead of obtaining high-cost debt financing. In addition, the option of listing internationally opens up a whole new avenue of raising capital.

Listing on an international stock exchange can be done by either a Euroequity issue or a dual-equity issue. In a *Euroequity issue*, shares are sold solely outside the country of the issuer. In contrast, a *dual-equity issue* is split into two parts, one sold domestically and the other overseas.

Usually, the markets of the industrialized countries permit the listing of foreign stocks and their purchase, as well as the purchase of local stocks by foreign investors. Some newly industrialized countries permit overseas listings, while others permit limited investment by overseas investors.

New York

New York is the world's largest securities market. Generally, the shares of larger and well-established companies are listed on the New York exchange. There are various types of memberships in the stock exchange, which provide the right to perform different types of stock market activities. For example, commission brokers execute orders on behalf of customers and convey them to floor brokers, who do the actual trading on the floor of the exchange. The New York Stock Exchange, like all other exchanges in the United

States, is controlled by a federal authority, the Securities and Exchange Commission (SEC). The SEC guidelines and supervisory activities are intended to ensure smooth operation of stock market activities and prevent any fraudulent or unethical trading practices or transactions. The main indicator of the overall price movements on the New York Stock Exchange is the Dow Jones Industrial Average. The Standard & Poor's 500 Index is another widely published and accepted index. As of December 31, 2005, the total *market capitalization* (the value of total stocks outstanding at a particular point in time) of the NYSE stood at US$13.3 trillion.

Tokyo

The Tokyo stock exchange one of the largest in the world in terms of market capitalization. The Tokyo market is extremely active and has generally been characterized by upward movement, so that it has an extremely high price-earnings ratio (the ratio of the prices of listed companies' shares to their earnings). Nominal prices are kept extremely low, and tradable amounts are denominated in units of 1,000 shares. The Nikkei 225 is now one of the leading performance indicators in international economics, and the market is still essentially dominated by four major securities houses: Nomura, Nikko, Daiwa, and Yaimaichi. Market capitalization of the Tokyo stock exchange as of December 31, 2005, stood at US$4.6 trillion.

London

London is a truly international stock exchange, with more than three hundred overseas companies listed, representing more than fifty countries. Two main types of stocks are available: ordinary and preferred. *Ordinary shares* confer voting rights, while *preferred shares* give the first right to holders on the assets of the company. The most commonly quoted index is the Financial Times (FT) Index. After 1986, many regulations that limited activity on the London Stock Exchange were removed, and banks were permitted to undertake securities transactions by acquiring securities houses. This reform also removed the distinction between different types of stock market functionaries: brokers and jobbers. Since the 1986 reforms, which were known as the "big bang," London has grown to be a major center for the listing and trading of international stocks. In 2001, the two hundredth anniversary of the modern stock exchange was celebrated. As of December 31, 2005, the total market capitalization of the London Stock Exchange stood at US$3.1 trillion.

Euronext

The Paris stock market has been liberalized considerably in recent years, and a large number of international stocks are listed there. Although in absolute size the Paris market is considerable, it is relatively small in relation to the industrial size of France because of several historical reasons, chiefly the tendency of French companies to rely on debt rather than equity financing to meet their needs. The market has historically been organized in two sections: spot and forward. Special procedures apply in the Paris market for the trading of stocks. Prices are set at periodic fixings, usually twice a day. The price established at the fixing is the official price, although other market-determined prices can prevail with respect to the orders executed between the fixings. The forward market operates on the basis of a call-over method, in which stocks are traded as they are called up. Securities of small companies are traded on an over-the-counter market located within the exchange and operated by stockbrokers who are members of the exchange.

Given the increasing financial integration in the continent of Europe, the Paris stock market merged with the exchanges of Amsterdam and Brussels in September 2000 to create the *Euronext*. In 2002,

the Euronext merged with the Portuguese exchange and also acquired London's futures and options market. Over the last few years, steps have been taken to merge these formerly separate exchanges into one large continental market. Thus, investors located in these EU countries have the ability to invest in securities in multiple countries. Currently, 1,400 companies are listed on the Euronext, and the Euronext is one of the largest derivative exchanges in the world. Recently, the Euronext has expressed an interest in merging with the New York Stock Exchange in an effort to further expand its reach in Europe. As of December 31, 2005, the market capitalization of the Euronext was $2.7 trillion.

NOREX Alliance

In 1998, the Copenhagen stock exchange and the Stockholm stock exchange established the *NOREX Alliance*. Since that time the stock exchanges of Norway, Iceland, Finland, Estonia, and Latvia have also joined the alliance. This was the first stock exchange in the world to implement a common system for share trading and to harmonize the trading and membership rules and regulations for exchanges in different countries. As yet another example of the increasing integration of global financial markets, the NOREX Alliance includes the shares of approximately 900 companies and had a total market capitalization of US$1.1 trillion as of December 2005.

Deutsche Borse

The Deutsch Borse is another major European stock market; it had a market capitalization of US$1.2 trillion as of December 31, 2005. Regulation of the Frankfurt Stock Exchange (which is the primary trading center for the Deutsche Borse) is somewhat more stringent than that of the exchanges of other industrialized countries. Trading has historically been limited on the Frankfurt exchange because many German companies are closely held. In addition, German shareholders tend to take a long-term view of their equity investments and to hold on to shares even if the companies are not performing up to the expected level at a particular point in time. Moreover, high listing costs and availability of other financing services have discouraged several German companies from using the stock exchange to mobilize resources. Shares are usually not registered, and there are no limits placed on foreign ownership of equity in German companies. The Frankfurt Stock Exchange uses the trading post system, in which transactions in specified securities are conducted at a particular place on the trading floor. Frankfurt is the main stock exchange of Germany. Open-market operations of the European Central Bank (ECB) are also conducted through Frankfurt.

Hong Kong

Hong Kong is one of the most important stock exchanges in the Far East. It has extremely active primary and secondary markets. A large percentage of companies on the Hong Kong exchange are real estate firms, reflecting the importance of this business for Hong Kong. The Hong Kong exchange is under the supervision of the China Securities Regulatory Commission for general regulatory purposes, but day-to-day transactions are unfettered by government regulations. Trading volume generally tends to be very high, and the market offers excellent liquidity. The total market capitalization as of December 31, 2005 was US$1.05 trillion.

EMERGING MARKETS

In the late 1970s and 1980s, several newly industrialized countries (NICs) and the stock markets of developing countries were opened to foreign investors to varying degrees. The most important of these are Taiwan, Malaysia, and South Korea. The Taiwanese market is dominated by a few very large companies whose individual market capitalizations are in excess of US$1 billion. In 2003, the requirements for foreign institutional investors were deregulated somewhat to allow for an increase in foreign investment. Mainland China has also seen a rapid increase in the performance of its stock markets. Since their inception in 1990, the Shenzhen and Shanghai stock markets have grown to include more than 1,250 listed companies and more than 60 million investor accounts. The mainland continues its integration with Hong Kong, as each year hundreds of *red-chip stocks* are issued on the Hong Kong stock exchange but are controlled by the mainland.

The Malaysian stock markets are also considerably well developed, especially by developing-country standards. A number of Singapore and British stocks are listed on the Kuala Lumpur exchange, which has had considerable activity since its inauguration in 1973, which is attributed largely to greater demand from the investing public. Several public brokerage firms perform brokerage services. Stocks on the Kuala Lumpur exchange also can be bought through the Singapore exchange. To list its shares on the Kuala Lumpur stock exchange, a company has to meet certain requirements set by the Malaysian authorities. The Singapore exchange is another increasingly important stock market in the Asia-Pacific region. The country, which has benefited by having free-trade agreements with many countries in the world, has seen rapid growth in its economy and stock market over the last few years. The Singapore exchange has also teamed up recently with the American Stock Exchange (AMEX), the Australian Stock Exchange (ASX), and others in an effort to provide investment alternatives to its investors.

The South Korean equity market grew rapidly over the last three decades. There are certain restrictions on foreign ownership of South Korean stocks, but there are special channels, such as country funds, through which overseas investors can participate in the South Korean stock market. Other stock markets, such as the National Stock Exchange of India, have seen large increases in market capitalization following the reduction of regulation in the financial sector.

It is expected that along with the general economic development, newly industrializing countries and other more advanced developing countries will witness an increase in the size, sophistication, and activity of their capital markets. These markets are expected to open up in a phased manner, first to overseas investors and then to borrowers. Once this occurs, it will be possible for multinational corporations to raise equity capital in local markets and diversify the composition of their international asset holdings by including in them stocks listed on the exchanges of various developing countries.

SUMMARY

In addition to the maintenance of liquid resources, management of the timing of cash flows, and minimization of idle cash balances required by domestic finance operations, international finance requires the management of currency exchange risks, transfer of funds between countries, and international tax issues. Intracompany pooling optimizes the total availability of capital resources on a global basis; surplus funds from operations in one location are used to offset shortages in another location. International financial managers must consider host-country foreign exchange and capital repatriation controls, as well as taxation laws, in determining whether to centralize or decentralize working capital funds.

Leading and lagging techniques in receivables and payables serve to offset the effects of high inflation in the host country. To deal with blocked funds, MNCs may develop various strategies: develop an export orientation, use the blocked funds for investments in the host country, exert pressure on the host government through diplomatic channels, or invest in financial instruments in the local financial market. Transfer pricing is a technique that MNCs use to avoid taxation and tariffs and improve their competitive positions.

MNCs must constantly manage foreign exchange and transaction exposure. Parallel loans, timing of funds transfers, centers for fund transfers, and credit and currency swaps are useful techniques. Debt-equity decisions, local ownership laws, and host-government attitudes affect the financial structure of MNC subsidiaries and affiliates. External sources of funds for investments are the large commercial banks and international capital markets, such as the Eurocurrency markets and national capital and stock markets. Eurocurrency markets offer a variety of financial instruments in hard currencies held outside the national borders of the currency, including Eurocredits, certificates of deposit, Eurobonds, swaps, note issuance facilities, and Eurocommercial paper. In addition to the Tokyo, New York, and London stock exchanges, other stock markets, such as Paris, Frankfurt, Hong Kong, Taiwan, Malaysia, and South Korea, are playing increasingly important roles as external sources of capital.

DISCUSSION QUESTIONS

1. What are the two major tasks of the international financial manager?
2. What is intracompany pooling?
3. What is leading and lagging? How can these techniques benefit the MNC?
4. How can a multinational utilize funds in a foreign subsidiary that have been blocked by the host government?
5. What are some of the additional factors that must be included in a financial analysis when an MNC is making an international rather than a domestic investment decision?
6. What are the advantages of raising capital in the financial markets rather than through a bank? What are the disadvantages?

7. Discuss the services investment banks provide. What is a lead underwriter? What is a syndicate?

8. What are Euromarkets? Where are they located?

9. Where are the primary international equity markets located?

BIBLIOGRAPHY

Argy, Victor E. *Exchange Rate Management in Theory and Practice.* Princeton, NJ: International Finance Section, Department of Economics, Princeton University, 1982.

Babbel, David F. "Determining the Optimum Strategy for Hedging Currency Exposure." *Journal of International Business Studies,* Spring–Summer 1983, 133–39.

Cha, Laura M. "The Future of China's Capital Markets and the Role of Corporate Governance." China Securities Regulatory Commission. 2001. http://www.csrc.gov.cn. Accessed 11/15/04.

Griffith, V., and H. Southworth. "Chaos Theory." *Banker,* January 1990, 51, 54.

Herring, Richard J., ed. *Managing Foreign Exchange Risk: Essays Commissioned in Honor of the Centenary of the Wharton School, University of Pennsylvania.* New York: Cambridge University Press, 1983.

Kenyon, Alfred. *Currency Risk Management.* New York: John Wiley and Sons, 1981.

Kettell, Brian. *The Finance of International Business.* Westport, CT: Quorum Books, 1981.

Madura, Jeff. *International Financial Management.* 2nd ed. St. Paul, MN: West Publishing, 1989.

———. Development and Evaluation of International Financing Models." *Management International Review,* 25, no. 4, 1985, 17–27.

Meek, G.K., and S.J. Gray. "Globalization of Stock Markets and Foreign Listing Requirements: Voluntary Disclosures by Continental European Companies Listed on the London Stock Exchange." *Journal of International Business Studies,* Summer 1989, 315–36.

Parrott, M., S. Kanji, D. Lane, and E. Cohen. "European Stock Markets: A Bad Hangover." *Banker,* January 1988, 25–32.

Rodriquez, Rita M. *Foreign Exchange Management in U.S. Multinationals.* Lexington, MA: Lexington Books, 1980.

Tyan, Salim V. T&D Mideast Ltd. 2006. http://www.dsuper.net/~styan/rice.htm.

Vinson, Joseph D. "Financial Planning for the Multinational Corporation with Multiple Goals." *Journal of International Business Studies,* Winter 1952, 43–58.

Warren, Geoffrey. "Latest in Currency Hedging Methods." *Euromoney,* May 1987, 245–64.

CASE STUDY 12.1

SCRINTON TECHNOLOGIES

The party at the banquet hall of Grosvenor House Hotel in London was a glittering affair. A large number of top bankers, CEOs of industrial companies, and important government officials were attending the formal celebration marking the commissioning of Scrinton Technologies' new plant in Southampton, England, which would be manufacturing a small range of state-of-the-art medical diagnostic equipment, including computer-enhanced imagery and hi-tech scanning systems. Scrinton was a world leader in diagnostic equipment, and the new plant represented the most advanced manufacturing facility of its type in the world. Only Scrinton's own plant in Sacramento, California, was anywhere near this facility in terms of technical sophistication and advancement of production equipment and processes.

The Southampton plant was a major commitment for Scrinton, involving an outlay of US$110 million. Scrinton's top management had viewed this project as a strategic move, to have a manufacturing facility in Europe before further European Union expansion. At the same time, it was considered essential that only the highest technology and processes be used in the plant to ensure products of futuristic sophistication and unquestioned quality and reliability. The European market was large and growing but at the same time was highly sophisticated and competitive. Competition was particularly strong from German and Swiss companies, many of which had been supplying hospital equipment to medical centers all over Europe for several decades. Although it lacked the long-standing relationships

of its competitors, Scrinton was confident that, with its edge in technology, it would be able to catch up with the competition and successfully wrest market share. Some European hospitals and clinics were already using Scrinton's equipment and were appreciative of the quality and reliability of its products. The need to keep a distinct technological edge over the competition, now and in the future, meant that the company had to find considerable resources to finance an ambitious and extremely expensive venture.

Scrinton had decided to go ahead with the Southampton plant. The financing was raised from five sources:

1. Syndicated Euromarket loan: €40 million
2. Bond issue in the U.S. market repayable in seven years: US$38 million
3. Long-term loan from a consortium of major main commercial banks: US$16 million
4. Equity issue on Wall Street: US$12 million
5. Internal resources: US$4 million

The project took three years to complete, and the debt service schedule of Scrinton UK, a wholly owned subsidiary that had taken the loans and made the equity and bond issues, was repayment of the bank loan in five years, repayment of the syndicated loan in seven years, and redemption of the bond issue in seven years.

Revenues of the company were going to be
continued

Case 12.1 (*continued*)

principally in three currencies: pounds sterling, euros, and Swiss francs. It was decided not to invoice products in other currencies, and as a matter of policy, all attempts would be made to invoice in only these currencies. Exceptions would be made only in rare cases, generally when a particular sale was of strategic or critical importance to the company.

The company expected to make substantial sales and generate adequate revenue to cover its entire amortization schedule (see opposite) without any need to draw on the resources of the parent company, but a major issue was the possible fluctuation of interest and exchange rates over the life of the repayment plan. The company was exposed because its syndicated loan in the Euromarket was at variable rates, and its liability could increase substantially if interest rates went up. Further, although its revenues were going to be denominated in three European currencies, it had substantial liabilities in U.S. dollars, and any major appreciation of the dollar against the European currencies would place the entire debt servicing of the project in serious jeopardy.

Bill Smythe, finance director of Scrinton UK, was concerned about these issues as he made small talk with a London investment banker at the party. "I'll deal with this in the morning," he thought, forcing the problem away and beginning to pay more attention to his companion, who had moved away from the subject of a possible minicrash on the stock market in the next three months to the more timely subject of the latest rumors on the activities of the younger members of the British royal family.

The next morning, Bill Smythe looked over the projection of estimated revenues for each year. The pound liability was apparently no problem from an exchange-risk point of view, because the pound revenues of the company were sufficient to cover the liability. The syndicated loan, however was at a variable rate of 0.25 percent over the London inter-bank offered rate (LIBOR). If LIBOR moved up, the value of the pound liability could increase considerably and significantly increase the company's debt service costs.

The dollar borrowings presented a bigger problem. Both exchange- and interest-rate exposure was present because the repayment obligations were denominated in dollars. Further, the long-term loan from the consortium of banks was at a variable rate of 0.5 percent over the prime rate.

"There are so many options available to hedge these risks," thought Smythe, "but should we? After all, there is going to be a substantial hedging cost and I wonder whether it will be worth it."

DISCUSSION QUESTIONS

1. What could be the main options for dealing with the company's exposure?
2. Under what circumstances would the company suffer the greatest loss if its exposure were left completely uncovered?

continued

Amortization Schedule

Syndicated Euro-market Loan

Year	Principal	(in Millions of U.S. Dollars) Interest	Total
1	5	0.6	5.6
2	5	0.6	5.6
Y	5	0.5	5.5
4	5	0.5	5.5
5	5	0.4	5.4
6	5	0.3	5.3
7	10	0.3	10.2

Long-Term Consortium Loan

	Principal	(in Millions of U.S. Dollars) Interest	Total
1	2	0.25	2.25
2	2	0.25	2.25
3	2	0.25	3.25
4	2	0.25	3.25
5	6	0.25	6.25

Bond Issue

	Principal	(in Millions of U.S. Dollars) Interest	Total
1	0.4		0.4
2	0.4		0.4
3	0.4		0.4
4	0.4		0.4
5	0.4		0.4
6	0.4		0.4
7	0.4	38	38.4

Total Dollar Liability

Year	Amount (in millions)
1	2.65
2	2.65
3	3.65
4	3.65
5	6.65
6	0.40
7	38.40

Estimated Revenues

Year	(in millions) Euro	Swiss Franc	Pound
1	35.00	30.00	15.00
2	38.50	33.60	17.83
3	42.50	37.60	19.83
4	46.50	42.10	22.80
5	51.00	47.00	26.22
6	56.10	52.60	30.15
7	61.71	58.90	

CHAPTER 13

International Accounting

CHAPTER OBJECTIVES

This chapter will:

- Present the role and importance of accounting information to internal and external users.
- Describe the differences in accounting conventions and disclosure requirements as practiced around the world.
- Discuss the current efforts toward harmonization of accounting standards in the United States and the rest of the world.
- Identify special accounting problems affecting multinational corporations.
- Examine the accounting functions of planning, control, and auditing within a multinational context.

WHAT IS ACCOUNTING?

Accounting is essentially the recording and interpretation of financial information related to the functioning of a business. Accounting systems provide valuable information about the financial activity and position of a firm, which is subject to various interpretations by different users. Information users can be divided into two categories: external and internal. Information users in each category require different types of accounting information, and their needs are met by two different types of accounting functions: managerial accounting and financial accounting.

Managerial accounting is concerned with the information needs of the internal users of an enterprise, who require detailed information on all the firm's business activities. Financial accounting is oriented toward external users and is concerned with providing relevant information about the activities of the enterprise.

External users can be classified by how they use financial information. Potential investors want detailed information on past sales, earnings performance, and present strength. With such information, they can formulate expectations of a firm's future performance and potential returns and make appropriate decisions.

Creditors are also interested in the future performance of a firm but more in relation to evaluating its creditworthiness. Thus, banks making loans or suppliers providing credit need to determine the ability of a business to meet its obligations.

Government representatives also use financial information, not only as potential creditors or customers of the firm, but also as regulators who monitor an enterprise's activities to ensure that they are within the bounds of law. Customers and employees require information about a firm to make decisions about what products to buy, who to do business with, and where to seek employment.

To meet the financial information needs of all interested parties, business enterprises must maintain and provide data on the firms' activities from a number of perspectives and in a number of forms.

The task of meeting the financial information needs of internal and external users becomes extremely complex when an enterprise takes its business activities across borders. Additional problems arise not only from transactions between countries, such as the buying and selling of goods, but also because multinational operations are conducted in the sovereign jurisdiction of other countries. A firm must first recognize and respond to the accounting practices, conventions, reporting requirements, and currencies of different nations. Then it faces the problem of integrating the accounts of subsidiaries prepared in accordance with local conventions and regulations with the consolidated accounts of the entire corporation.

DIFFERENCES IN ACCOUNTING PRACTICES AMONG COUNTRIES

FACTORS AFFECTING ACCOUNTING SYSTEMS

Differences in accounting practices, standards, and conventions among different countries exist because of diverse economic, legal, political, and sociocultural environments. The level of development in each country is directly related to the degree of sophistication required by the accounting system. For example, nations with highly developed manufacturing and service sectors and a great deal of international trading activity require more detailed accounting and recording systems than countries with limited economic activity.

The nature of business activities in each nation also contributes to the molding of accounting systems. Systems are developed to cater to particular types of business activities. For example, countries with a concentration of large corporations and complex business structures are likely to have more advanced accounting systems than countries with simple business organizations.

Accounting systems in different countries are also directly affected by legal considerations. In some countries accounting practices are determined almost entirely by legal constraints.[1] In other countries, such as the United States, accounting practices develop through a mixture of law and standards set by members of the accounting profession.

The accounting system of a nation is also determined, in part, by its political orientation and the level of government involvement in business activity. For example, in a market-based economic system, the financial reporting function is geared toward information disclosure for several interested parties: investors, creditors, regulators, employees, and customers. Thus, the reports are varied in their form and content. In contrast, in a nonmarket economy, where the government owns and runs large portions of business operations, accounting systems are oriented not to external users but to the internal users, that is, the government. Thus, the emphasis of such systems would be on standardization and uniformity of information to facilitate centralized state control. Between these two extremes exist nations that have mixed political systems and correspondingly hybrid accounting systems.

The development and nature of accounting systems in different countries are also affected by sociocultural factors. For example, in a country where the virtues of trust and honor are highly prized, such as Japan, it would be considered offensive to ask for proof or documentation of business activities in an audit. Similarly, other sociocultural attributes, such as conservatism and fatalism, affect the nature and development of accounting conventions. Conservatism might evidence itself in larger estimates of bad debt reserves or smaller projections for sales estimates. Planning and budgeting for the future are likely to hold little importance or credence among members of a fatalistic society.

Notions of time affect not only the frequency of reporting but also the long-term and short-term views. What might be considered short-term or current in one accounting system might be considered long-term in another.

The educational, training, and learning characteristics of a nation also affect the type and level of accounting systems used, because relative levels of literacy and sophistication of the workforce affect the applicability or utility of information.

An accounting system is also affected by attitudes commonly held within a country regarding business operations and the nature of the accounting profession. If business is considered a force that is to be mistrusted, then an enterprise would expect to be under more pressure to have a larger and fuller disclosure of operations. Similarly, if business is esteemed and trusted, one would expect to see less public scrutiny of operations. In countries where the accounting system is not well developed, there is less interest and credence placed in accounting practices.

What Types of Differences Emerge?

The practice of holding reserves is one of the most important differences encountered in the accounting practices of different countries. In general, reserves are held by firms to protect against special situations, such as expectations that all the debts of a firm will not be repaid. In some countries, however, reserves are used much more extensively for situations that some consider the normal ups and downs of business operations. In these cases, reserves are used to smooth incomes and taxes from year to year. In profitable years, funds are moved to reserve accounts and thus escape taxation; in less profitable years, the firm can draw on this cushion to boost flagging income. Reserves are used to stabilize income by a majority of firms in Switzerland, about half of Italian companies, and in at least a dozen other countries.[2] This practice, however, has the effect of reducing the significance of a firm's income statements to such users as investors or creditors.

Other differences are found in definitions, terminology, and formats. For example, in the United States, long-term investments, assets, and liabilities are defined as those held for more than one year. In other countries, this definition may provide for longer holding periods, such as three years or more. The meaning of "*turnover*" varies even in English-speaking countries. In the United Kingdom, "turnover" is another term for sales, while in the United States, it refers to the renewal or replenishment of inventory stock.

Differences in Valuation

Differences also emerge in the way firms measure the value of assets and the way they determine income. These differences become apparent in a number of procedural areas, such as accounting for leases, carrying long-term debt, assigning value to shares of a company's own stock, R & D expenses, depreciation, and inventory valuing techniques.[3] For example, in the United States depreciation is calculated according to the normal life of an asset. The value of the asset, however, is adjusted for the amount of money expected to be gained when that asset is ultimately sold. This eventual sales price is referred to as the salvage value. While U.S. firms are allowed to depreciate only assets minus salvage value, in other countries the final asset is depreciated according to its full purchase price.

Other valuation and income differences emerge when countries do not agree on the use of the matching concept of accounting, a term that refers to the cash method of accounting, in which a business attempts to match expenses to the revenues associated with the incurring of those expenses, despite any differences in timing. Still more differences occur when it is accepted practice to keep certain business items off the balance sheet and out of the public or regulatory eye. In recent years, for example, there has been some debate in accounting circles about how to account for stock options on a company's financial statements.

Occasionally, off-the-balance-sheet items derive from the pursuit of illegal activities (for example, illegal payments or bribery) by businesses in countries with little regulatory supervision. The United States, for example, imposes strict requirements on accounting for legal facilitative payments made to low-level foreign officials to smooth the progress of business in foreign countries. Payments or gifts made to high-level government officials are illegal. In other countries, these practices are considered to be ordinary expenses of doing business abroad and are deductible for tax purposes.

THE IMPACT OF ACCOUNTING DIFFERENCES

The existence of accounting differences creates difficulties for financial analysts who try to compare the financial information of companies around the world. For example, ratios customarily used to evaluate performance, such as return on income or equity, are not comparable. Thus, statements from foreign firms and the financial data they contain must be evaluated in light of relevant differences, and the analyst of an international firm must be aware of likely differences and make necessary adjustments.

The main differences in accounting practices and conventions can be summarized as follows:

- The availability and the reliability of financial information vary from country to country.
- Financial statements and reports differ in language and terminology.
- Financial statements from different countries may include the same information but present it in different formats.
- Currencies used in the statements will generally differ.
- The amounts and types of information disclosed on financial statements are different from country to country.

All these differences must be considered by any financial analyst before making judgments about the strength or prospects of a firm. Foreign firms should be evaluated in the perspective of their own country and industry, not according to a home-country reference point.

DIFFERENCES IN DISCLOSURE

Information disclosure varies considerably across different countries. Disclosure requirements are a measure of public scrutiny of business enterprises within a country. Greater disclosure implies that the internal strengths and weaknesses of a company are made known to the general public. The differences lie not only in the level of detail but also in the types of disclosed business activities. The amounts and types of disclosure required are determined by several factors: social pressures, legal requirements, and the forces of industry competitors and external users of accounting information.

In the United States, for example, all firms that issue securities (publicly held companies) must file regular, detailed, and extensive reports with the Securities and Exchange Commission (SEC) regarding their business activities. Access to these reports is available to anyone who visits the SEC's public information office in Washington, DC, or subscribes to an information service that, for a fee, will provide copies of corporate filings. Company annual filings with the SEC are also available to download via Internet sites such as Edgarscan.

Pressure for extensive disclosure is sometimes encouraged by private interests, such as consumer groups. Corporations, on the other hand, tend to minimize the extent of information they must distribute. Corporate reluctance to part with information can be attributed to the desire to protect strategic advantages over competitors.

The type of disclosure required in the United States contrasts with that required in other countries, such as Switzerland, where secrecy is the norm. In Switzerland, which is known for supremely confidential bank accounts, little if any financial information is provided in annual reports, and no information is provided on the derivation of that information. The United States, on the other hand, has recently increased the standards that are now deemed acceptable in financial reporting. The *Sarbanes-Oxley Act* of 2002 requires that the board members of corporations be "financially literate," and that at least two of the board members hold the certified public accountant (CPA) designation (or have held it in the past). Additionally, the chief executive officer and chief financial officer are required to certify the financial results for each reporting year. The penalties for corporate fraud were also increased in the wake of the various corporate reporting scandals over the last few years.[4] Patterns of disclosure therefore vary around the nations of the world, with some countries requiring even greater disclosure than the United States and others requiring very little.

SEGMENTATION OF ACCOUNTING

In the United States, firms are required to report their results according to segments of business activities;[5] that is, they are required to disclose in their public reports where large percentages of their business are concentrated (for example, in industry lines, foreign operations, export sales, or to single customers, such as governments). Segments that comprise more than 10 percent of world revenues, total profits or losses, or total assets of a company must be reported separately.

Once these individual segments are identified, the firm must disclose revenues, operating results, and identifiable assets associated with each segment. The company, however, does have discretion in its segmentation criteria for sales abroad. While many companies segment foreign sales separately as a whole, others segment according to geographic operating areas, such as Europe and North America. The choice of definitional criteria can disguise critical information from the eyes of competitors. For example, a firm might hide its enormous sales in a central African country by treating sales for the entire continent as one segment.

The most recent annual reports of Sony Corporation segment sales by area and product group. The areas used are Japan, the United States, Europe, and "other areas," even though sales to other areas in 2004 represented more than 18 percent of the firm's total sales. Product groups were divided into seven areas: audio, video, televisions, information and communications, semiconductors, components, and other products (see Table 13.1).

The segmentation at Nestlé is also extensive. The company's annual report for 2003 shows sales in millions of Swiss francs and as percentages for Europe, the Americas, and Asia, Africa, and Oceania, as well as sales in main country markets for that year. The report also provides prior-year information regarding sales in those segment areas. The Swiss firm also segments sales according to all main product groups, from beverages, comprising 26.7 percent, to pharmaceutical products, providing 5.7 percent of sales for the year (see Tables 13.2 and 13.3).

Table 13.1

Sony and Subsidiaries Composition of Net Sales by Area and Product Group

| | Yen in Millions | | | | | |
| | Year End March 31 | | | | | |
Sales by Area	2002	%	2003	%	2004	%
Japan	2,248,115	29.7	2,093,880	28.0	2,220,747	29.6
United States	2,461,523	32.5	2,403,946	32.2	2,121,110	28.3
Europe	1,609,111	21.2	1,665,976	22.3	1,765,053	23.6
Other	1,259,509	16.6	1,309,831	17.5	1,389,481	18.5

Sales by Product Group	2002	%	2003	%	2004	%
Audio	747,469	15.7	682,517	15.0	623,582	13.1
Video	847,311	17.8	851,064	18.8	948,111	19.9
Televisions	984,290	20.6	950,166	20.9	917,207	19.3
Information and communications	998,773	20.9	836,724	18.4	834,757	17.6
Semiconductors	182,276	3.8	204,710	4.5	253,237	5.3
Components	511,579	10.7	527,782	11.6	623,799	13.1
Other	500,852	10.5	490,350	10.8	557,707	11.7

Source: Sony, *Annual Report 2004.*

Table 13.2

Nestlé Sales by Product Group (SFr millions)

Product	2003	%	2002	%
Beverages	23,520	26.7	23,325	26.2
Milk, nutrition, and ice cream	23,283	26.5	23,376	26.2
Prepared dishes and cooking aids	16,068	18.2	15,834	17.8
Pet care	9,816	11.1	10,719	12.0
Chocolate, confectionary, and biscuits	10,240	11.6	10,774	12.1
Pharmaceutical products	5,052	5.7	5,132	5.7

Source: Nestlé. *Annual Report 2003.*

Table 13.3

Nestlé Sales Percentages, 2003

Zone Europe	32.5
Zone Americas	31.4
Zone Asia, Oceania, and Africa	16.4
Nestlé Waters	9.2
Other Activities	10.5

Source: Nestlé, *Annual Report 2003.*

Research conducted by Frederick D.S. Choi and V.B. Bavishi on comparative requirements across countries of geographic disclosure by multinational firms in Europe, North America, and Japan shows that nearly all firms report foreign sales in general and by geographic area. Disclosure falls off, however, in reporting more sensitive data, such as income generated by foreign operations, assets held in foreign geographic areas, and exports and capital expenditures by foreign sources and geographic areas.

Social Reporting

One area in which reporting requirements for firms operating in different environments differ substantially is in the area of social reporting in financial reports, which goes far beyond the disclosure of such items on a balance sheet and income statement as assets, sales, earnings per share, and taxes. Social reports answer questions raised about the socioeconomic effects of a firm's operations on a nation's quality of life or economic status. According to one classification, these special impact reports take three forms: environmental quality, the effect a company has on its employees and the community, and national income accounting.[6]

The topics covered by special reports include controlling or correcting environmental pollution and ensuring product safety; assuring employee welfare in terms of equal opportunity, safe working conditions, and personnel practices; community involvement and contributions; and corporate morals, as embodied in codes of conduct and ethical guidelines. In some countries firms must attempt to identify the extent of their contribution to the national economic situation, both directly, as a result of investment and operations, and indirectly, by way of their contribution to increased employment. Historically in France, any firm with 300 or more employees has had to prepare a *bilan social,* or social balance sheet. A similar kind of report, the *social jaareslag,* has been required in the Netherlands, as has a *social bilanz* in Germany.

The trend toward requiring firms to be accountable for the social effects of their operations is growing worldwide. An MNC must take this aspect into consideration when devising accounting procedures and practices for an overseas subsidiary. Necessary expertise must be created to generate such reports, and the company's operations must be sensitive to these concerns. The result is that accountants in these nations and those responsible for reporting from a multinational perspective must enlarge their views and take these reporting requirements into consideration and develop expertise in new areas.

Policy Formation and Harmonization

Determining Policy

The determination of accounting policy—the setting of objectives, standards, and practices used by accounting professionals in each nation of the world—derives from two sources. Policy either emanates from national laws and the codification of practices, or it has been developed by members of the accounting profession itself, who represent their entire national membership and agree on standards to be observed by all practitioners.

The legal requirements of, or restrictions on, accounting practices come either from regulations imposed by government users of accounting information, such as tax authorities, or from planning agencies or national legislators. The relative importance of the roles played by these entities in the determination of accounting policy depends on two major determinants: the status and size of the accounting profession in each nation and the degree to which each government seeks to control or monitor business activity. Thus, it is not surprising that government forces are exceedingly strong in setting accounting policy in nations with planned economic systems and that they are far weaker and less intrusive in market economies.

POLICY MAKING IN THE UNITED STATES

Accounting policy in the United States is determined primarily by members of its highly sophisticated and well-regulated accounting profession. These members create policy by working together to develop a set of generally accepted accounting principles. The main policy-setting body in the United States is the Financial Accounting Standards Board (FASB), which determines accounting policy and promulgates such determinations through its publication of statements on issues of concern. The policies and statements are accepted by the American Institute of Certified Public Accountants (AICPA), another independent body of professionals, which sets auditing standards for external accounting requirements. Accounting practices are also delineated by law in the United States and are primarily requirements established by the SEC for all companies that issue securities to the public and by federal tax law, as set forth in the federal tax code.

POLICY MAKING IN OTHER COUNTRIES

Policy making in other countries varies along a continuum, because all countries include some combination of accounting policy set by legislation and accounting policy set by professional practice. The differences in policy come from differences in political orientation, levels of professionalism, the development of the accounting profession in each country, and the nature and depth of business within each country.

Some countries that rely more on legislation than on practice are those with strong governmental intervention in economic activity, such as France, Germany, Egypt, and Brazil. Other nations, such as England, have a greater combination of law and professional involvement in standard setting, while others, such as the Netherlands and Switzerland, experience minimal influence from legislative efforts.

Some nations, such as Japan, have only recently developed accounting standards and have patterned their systems on those of other nations; in Japan's case, the United States and Germany. Some countries, particularly less-developed nations, have adopted the principles of their former colonial governments and rely on legislation to set standards, because the membership of the accounting profession is small and not well regarded.

HARMONIZATION

Divergences have always existed among accounting systems around the world. These differences lead to complications that are intensified with the increase in international business activity. To combat these problems, efforts have been mounted to standardize accounting functions to some degree on a regional and international basis. Such efforts are generally known as *harmonization* among accounting executives, practices, and standards.

Three different methods of attempting to establish harmony among accounting methods that differ according to the requirements of users or circumstances have been identified: absolute uniformity, circumstantial uniformity, and purposive uniformity.[7] *Absolute uniformity* proposes that accounting methods be standardized regardless of users' different circumstances. This model has been criticized as being too inflexible and too radical, although it would, theoretically, be easier to administer than other models.

Circumstantial uniformity would use different practices according to the variations in the circumstances of economic facts and conditions. Once these circumstances are identified, accounting practices can be put into place to deal with them on a consistent basis. *Purposive uniformity* would vary the determination of accounting practices and standards according to both diversity of users and circumstances. This model has the advantage of providing flexibility for differing environmental situations and purposes and is embodied in U.S. regulatory practices.

The greatest effort to bring the postulates and practices of accounting into harmony in the international accounting arena is the *International Accounting Standards Board (IASB)*, which consisted of accounting professionals representing 65 countries and over 100 accounting organizations as of 2006. The purpose of the IASB is to provide a forum through which members of professional accounting groups can attempt to develop international standards that can be used in domestic operations. The representatives of the IASB are hampered, however, in that they have no authority to enforce any decisions and can only promise to promote such standards in the publication of financial statements, with policy-setting organizations, and with government or regulatory officials. The hope is that each nation will adopt the IASB's standards and resolutions, either as professional standards or as national law.

Another international organization is the *International Federation of Accountants (IFAC)*, which was formed in 1977 to succeed the International Coordination Committee for the Accounting Profession. The objective of the IFAC is to provide a forum through which members of the world's accounting profession can meet to establish international standards and principles for auditing practices, as well as standards for the training, education, and codes of ethics of accountants. The IFAC consists of members from more than 100 countries and represents more than 80 professional accounting groups.[8]

REGIONAL HARMONIZATION EFFORTS

Regional efforts at harmonization often fall in line with historical economic or political groupings of nations. Some of the regional national accounting associations are the Inter-American Accounting Association (IAA), the Union of European Accountants (UEC), and the Confederation of Asian and Pacific Accountants (CAPA). The problem with these groups is that although they can meet and attempt to harmonize standards, they are generally comprised of practitioners who have no authority behind their decision making to promote standardization. They can, however, use their influence to affect policy setting in individual countries and among their own national professional associations.

One regional grouping where the force of law is brought to bear on the practice of accounting, however, is the European Union. In the European Union, accounting standards are developed through the issuance of directives developed by its council of ministers. The European Union's progress toward harmonization of accounting practices has led to mandates for member countries to bring their laws into harmonization on selected topics.

SPECIAL ACCOUNTING PROBLEMS

Despite efforts to harmonize accounting practices and standards around the world, the managers of enterprises with operations in multiple foreign settings face formidable difficulties. Four specific problems faced by multinational firms are (1) accounting for differences in gains and losses because of differences in currency exchange rates, (2) the question of consolidating returns, (3) accounting under conditions of inflation, and (4) attempting to establish appropriate prices and costs for a multinational's products around the world and between units.

DIFFERENCES IN CURRENCY EXCHANGE RATES

One of the most crucial problems that international firms face is accounting for a transaction that is conducted in a foreign currency. How is such a transaction to be recorded on the books or reported to management in a consistent manner?

Differences in exchange rates between currencies cause two separate problems for the international business firm. The first is that of accounting for business transactions and gains and losses from currency-rate differentials that arise during such business activity. The second problem is interpreting financial results of transactions conducted in different currencies or devising translations of currencies to yield comparable and measurable results.

Accounting procedures designed to treat these transactions follow either the one-step transaction or the two-step transaction approach, both of which provide methods for recording business transactions in a home currency.

The *one-step method* records the transaction using the spot rate in effect on that day for the foreign currency. Assume, for example, that Bob of Bob's Lawn and Garden Store wants to acquire lawn ornaments from a German supplier to round out his inventory in anticipation of heavy summer sales. Thus, on January 1, Bob buys 10,000 gross of pink flamingos for €60,000 payable by February 1. On the first of January the euro is trading for $0.50 (that is, each dollar is worth €2). Consequently, under the one-step method Bob's ledger entries would be as follows:

Purchases:

Pink Flamingos	$30,000
Accounts Payable	$30,000 (€ @ $0.50)

If, however, exchange rates change between the time Bob places his order, records it in his books, and pays his account with the German flamingo maker, he will need to change his records to record the facts and the rate of exchange when the transaction is completed or actually settled. For example, if the value of the dollar falls and it takes $0.75 to buy €1, Bob's costs for his pink flamingos will rise

and must be accounted for as an adjustment to the original cost of the flamingos. The entries he must make are:

Purchases:

Pink Flamingos	$30,000
Accounts Payable	$15,000
Cash	$45,000 (€ @ $0.75)

The *two-step method* of accounting for gains or losses in transactions separates business activity and currency exchanges. The key difference from the one-step method is that gains or losses from the transaction do not affect the value of the asset acquired but are treated separately, as a result of assuming risk in engaging in the activity and opening the firm to fluctuations in exchange rates. Consequently, under this method our transaction above would be noted as follows:

Accounts Payable	$30,000
Exchange	
Adjustment: Loss	$15,000
Cash	$45,000 (€ @ $0.75)

In this method, the pink flamingos retain their value of $30,000 on Bob's books, and the difference between the agreed-on price or costs and the actual amount paid is noted in an exchange adjustment account that is eventually netted and applied as an adjustment to shareholder equity.

Some countries require the use of the one-step method, while others employ the two-step method. The United States has historically employed the two-step method and has required the immediate recognition of gains or losses from foreign currency transactions. In other countries it is common accounting practice to defer gains and losses from accounts payable and receivable until the transactions are completed, and these results are not included in the income statement.

These accounting steps become far more involved when firms engage in hedging to protect themselves from fluctuations in rates of exchange between countries. It must be remembered, however, that such complications arise only when the transaction is denominated in a foreign currency. Bob could have asked to pay his bill in dollars, in which case, he would have no risk because of changes in the rate of exchange between euros and dollars. Instead, the German manufacturer would take the currency risk and account for any changes in the dollar's value.

Problems arise for multinational firms with business operations that are carried out in different locales and reported in different currencies. When MNCs are required to translate local currency accounts into home currency at the close of the financial year, what criteria does an MNC use to report and compare its operations in different environments? These problems are not ones of valuation (determining appropriate values for assets in terms of other currencies) or of converting currencies from foreign currencies to a uniform home currency, but are those involved in restating operational results. The objective is for results to be integrated so that they can be analyzed by management and reported to regulatory authorities. The process of restating financial statements into a uniform currency is called *translation*. When the financial statements from all operating units of an MNC are combined, they are said to be consolidated.

Foreign statement translation is a two-step process for the controller of an MNC. First, the accounts must be made consistent by being restated according to the same accounting principles, such as those for valuing inventories and assets and determining depreciation. After the basis of the accounts has been adjusted to provide for consistency, the foreign currency amounts represented in the results can be translated into the reporting or home currency. Translation must not be confused with conversion. Translating is merely the restating of currencies,

while conversion refers to the actual physical trade or exchange of units of one currency for another.

Accountants use four different methods of translating statements from local currencies to the reporting or home currency: the current-rate method, the *temporal method*, the monetary-nonmonetary method, and the current-noncurrent method (see Table 13.4).

Statement 52 of the FASB introduced some new definitional concepts to the translation of foreign exchange accounts. The first is the use of a *functional currency*, which is defined as the "currency of the primary economic environment in which the entity operates."[9] It is differentiated from the reporting currency, which is the currency that the parent company uses in their consolidated financial statements. The determination of a functional currency is tricky for some subsidiaries. It could be the local currency if most of the subsidiary's business of buying, selling, or manufacturing is conducted using the local currency. The parent company's reporting currency could also be the functional currency, if the subsidiary's operations consist mostly of selling goods to the parent, or it could even be the currency of a third country, if the bulk of the entity's business is conducted in a third country.

The responsibility for choosing the functional currency rests with each firm, based on operational criteria regarding currencies involved in cash flows, prices, sales market, expenses, financing, and intercompany indicators. Functional currencies can change, but only if there is a change in the initial underlying operational criteria, a stipulation imposed by the FASB to prevent arbitrary changes in functional currencies that aggressive accountants might make to put financial statements in the best possible light.

Once the functional currency is determined, a firm can begin its process of translating statements under FASB 52 and consolidating, or combining, the results of disparate operations. The use of either the current or the temporal rate is determined by the location of operations and resulting functional

Table 13.4

Exchange Rates Employed in Different Translation Methods for Specific Balance Sheet Items

	Current	Current-Noncurrent	Monetary-Nonmonetary	Temporal
Cash	C	C	C	C
Accounts receivable	C	C	C	C
Inventory				
Cost	C	C	H	H
Market	C	C	H	C
Investments				
Cost	C	H	H	H
Market	C	H	H	C
Fixed assets	C	H	H	H
Other assets	C	H	H	H
Accounts payable	C	C	C	C
Long-term debt	C	H	C	C
Common stock	H	H	H	H
Retained earnings	*	*	*	*

Note: C = current rate; H = historical rate; and * = residual, balancing figure representing a composite of successive current rates.

currency. If the books and records are kept in the currency of the parent, no restatement is necessary. If, however, the books and records are kept in a local currency, the subsidiary has three different translation routes, depending on the functional currency.

If the functional currency is the local currency of the subsidiary, the parent merely translates the statements into U.S. dollars using the current-rate method. This situation holds unless the functional currency is a local currency in a high-inflation country, in which case the firm must use the temporal method of translation. High-inflation countries are defined as those with inflation rates greater than 100 percent for three consecutive years.

If the functional currency is the parents' home currency, even if the books are kept in the local currency, the firm uses the temporal method to re-

measure results. If the functional currency is a third currency, the firm remeasures from the local to the functional currency using the temporal method and then translates the result into the home currency using the current-rate method. Figure 13.1 provides a graphic description of this process.

CONSOLIDATION PROBLEMS

The results of these financial machinations are then integrated into a firm's comprehensive reckoning of operations and results. This consolidation process raises some special considerations for an MNC and questions about a firm's organizational and investment decisions. For example, what operations should be consolidated into the firm's overall operations? Some countries require only that the parent report the results of its operations and do not require the integra-

Figure 13.1 **Translating a Firm's Functional Currency into a Reporting Currency**

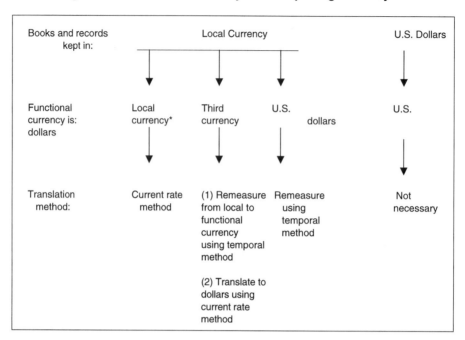

* In the case of a highly inflationary economy, the local currency may be the functional currency from an operating standpoint, but the dollar is considered the functional currency from a translation standpoint.

tion of the results of subsidiary or affiliated arms. In the United States, for example, tax laws require that firms consolidate their operations globally, because firms are taxed on worldwide income (although they are given credit for taxes paid to other governments). Some other issues raised are: What if a parent corporation owns only part interest in a subsidiary? What level of investment determines ownership or control? What distinction is made between having an investment in another concern and that concern's being an integral part of the parent corporation's network?

Consolidation Rules in the United States

In the United States the questions about whether or not a parent consolidates the results of subsidiary operations into its own depends on the level and type of involvement of the parent in the activities of the subsidiary. There are three different ways an investment in another enterprise can be handled under accounting rules: the cost method, the equity method, and consolidation. The *cost method* is employed when the parent firm holds an unsubstantial investment in the subsidiary. Under this method, the parent carries the investment as such and only reports income from the subsidiary when the subsidiary declares a dividend to the parent. Typically, the cost method is used in the United States when the parent owns less than 20 percent of the voting stock of the affiliate and that stock was acquired initially through purchasing. Monies flowing back to the parent are treated as dividends and do not change the level of the investment account of the parent.

If the parent owns a substantial portion of the stock of the subsidiary, from 20 percent to 50 percent, it uses the *equity method,* reporting income from the subsidiary as it is earned, not as it is received. The investment is carried on the parent's books at original cost and is adjusted according to earnings or dividends received from the subsidiary. Income from the foreign subsidiary increases the value of the parent's investment (whether it is received or not), and thus the value of the holding is adjusted upward to reflect an increase in the share of profits. Any dividends received by the parent from its holdings in the subsidiary have the effect of reducing the investment's book value, because it is considered to have the effect of lowering the profits of the subsidiary.

If the parent owns more than 50 percent of the subsidiary, it has a controlling interest in the foreign affiliate and must consolidate the results of the affiliate into its own reports. The consolidation process is carried out line by line to agree with the financial statements of the parent. Thus, before the two sets of figures are aggregated, they must be adjusted to agree according to the accounting principles used, and foreign currencies must be translated into the reporting currency. The parent and the affiliate must also adjust their books to correct for their intercorporate transactions and profits that have resulted from business dealings between the two entities.

INFLATION

Companies doing business in high-inflation countries must develop special procedures for dealing with the effects of inflation on the valuation of assets. Inflation also raises problems for MNCs in their attempts to evaluate and predict purchasing power for foreign operations and in evaluating their financial reports. As long as there are few changes in prices in a country, MNCs attempting to value their assets can use historical costs for those assets as appropriate measures. When inflation is significant, however, the value of those assets stated in historical terms inaccurately represents the wealth of the firm.

There are basically two responses when dealing with inflation. One can either reestablish a new basis for historical values that reflects the effects of inflation, or one can put into place a system that constantly corrects for changes in prices. In practice, under the first model, all financial statements are adjusted at a single point in time, and these adjusted costs become the new historical basis; under the second model, values are indexed on a continual basis according to changes in prices.

In accounting practice the use of models depends on the objectives of the financial reports. The two accounting methods for handling inflation are constant-dollar (or general-purchasing-power) accounting and current-cost accounting.

The goal of *constant-dollar accounting* is to report assets, liabilities, expenses, and revenues in terms of the same purchasing power. The original basis of the valuations, the historical costs, does not change under this accounting method. Instead, nonfinancial items are restated to reflect the purchasing power in effect on the date of the balance sheet. Financial items on the statements, such as cash, receivables, and payables, would not be restated, because their monetary valuation would already reflect the purchasing power of the currency on the date of the report.

In *current-cost accounting,* the emphasis is not on the loss of purchasing power associated with a specific currency but on the amount of money it would take to replace assets because of price increases. Thus, under current-cost accounting, historical costs are supplanted by new, adjusted costs, such as replacement costs. This method's objective is to account for the effects of inflation as it relates to the increases in the costs of specific assets and not overall prices.

The treatment of inflation in the presentation

of accounting records differs around the world. In the United States, firms are required to continue to use the historical cost standard as their basis for reporting financial results, but they are also required to disclose supplementary information regarding both price level and current-cost accounting. Other countries have different requirements. In Great Britain, current-cost balance sheets and income statements must be presented, and such financial statements may be presented as supplements to or in place of historical costs financial statements.[10] Some high-inflation countries require that firms adjust their statements to reflect the enormous rates of inflation and require the use of an inflation index and a monetary correction system.

The result of these different methods of accounting for inflation is that the MNC operating in a multitude of foreign environments must often keep multiple sets of books to adhere to the reporting requirements of each jurisdiction and the parent firm's home authorities.

TRANSFER PRICING AND COSTING

The international nature of the business of MNCs introduces a number of factors that have to be accounted for in determining the costs of their products around the world. Although multinational firms use the same methods as domestic enterprises for determining costs, their efforts are greatly complicated by the nature of operations in a global environment. For example, products and raw materials are affected not only by domestic forces, such as inflation and availability, but also by such international forces as changes in exchange rates, transportation fees, insurance costs, customs duties, and facilitating payments. Similarly, costs involved in conducting international trade are often influenced by government subsidies that are intended to promote exports sales.

Such costing and pricing problems are significant for exported products manufactured domestically; they are even worse for firms that have raw material and parts sources in several parts of the world. The complications become enormous, as accountants attempt to allocate costs to different products and operating units within different countries.

Transfers within an MNC's various affiliated arms, especially transfer pricing for goods and services between different parts of the company, create complex accounting issues. MNCs can use transfer pricing to achieve a variety of corporate objectives, such as reducing overall tax burden, avoiding restrictions on repatriation of earnings, or the exchange of local for home-country currencies. Thus, transfer prices set by MNCs not only concern the strategic decision makers in the company, but also often come under the scrutiny of external government officials. An MNC can deal with this problem to some extent by adjusting its performance measures for the subsidiary to focus on different criteria, such as achieving production efficiencies and maintaining low costs.

Companies have three ways of valuing goods and services that pass between arms or branches of the same corporation. They can use a cost-plus method, where they take actual costs of production and add a fixed monetary amount or percentage. Alternately, they can use the market price, less a certain percentage discount. Under arm's-length pricing they can charge the same price to affiliates or parents as they do to third-party buyers. While cost-based transfer pricing has the advantage of providing the firm with flexibility, most governments prefer that MNCs use the easily determined and monitored market-based pricing systems. The United States requires that firms use arm's-length prices, unless they can justify why different prices based on costs are more reasonable than those based on market prices.

OTHER INTERNATIONAL ACCOUNTING ISSUES

ACCOUNTING FOR EXPROPRIATION

One potential problem for any firm conducting business in a foreign environment is the political risk that its assets will be taken over by the government through expropriation or nationalization. When a firm is remunerated by a country for expropriated assets, many questions arise about determining the appropriate value of those assets in relation to the monies received. Book or historical values are not usually representative of true, current value, because they may not reflect what it would cost to replace the assets or what monies would actually be received if those assets were sold on the open market. The determination of value is generally arbitrary, not market oriented, because expropriation usually results from political action. Similarly, there are seldom comparable sales of similar assets or replacement assets in the country on which to base an estimation of value for the expropriated assets.

Consequently, to determine its position regarding gain or loss on the disposition of the assets, an MNC in such a situation must use an adjusted asset book value that accounts for increases in economic value over time. Thus, values placed on expropriated property are highly subjective. Once these values are estimated and compared to payments made by the expropriating government, the firm must deal with its gain or loss on the property. Such gains and losses shown as operating items do not affect the financial results of the firm in the United States, where losses because of expropriation are reported net of tax effects and are classified as extraordinary items. Most other countries allow such losses to be taken as direct write-offs against owners' equity or equity reserve accounts.[11]

PLANNING AND CONTROL

One of the biggest problems faced by MNCs in the implementation of international accounting methods and systems is the sheer multitude and variety of players, reporting sites, requirements, and forms. Thus, it is crucial that the international firm have a well-organized and comprehensive system of financial reporting and control in place to generate accurate, timely, and usable information. Many firms often take their existing domestic systems abroad, but these systems may need to be adjusted for local needs and different accounting requirements and conventions. For example, employees at a foreign site may find systems designed for the home environment too sophisticated for their levels of expertise, training, or abilities.

Ideally, MNCs should develop reporting functions and formats that can be used by all members of the network. Information supplied by all parts of the operating system must be uniform. Therefore, an MNC must decide beforehand on common formats, language, and currencies, as well as on a set of procedures to be followed. Similarly, care must be taken in the development of budgets, goals, and objectives for MNC subsidiaries and affiliates. An MNC must take into account different operating environments in setting goals and in evaluating relative performance.

AUDITING

Once an accounting system is in place and operational, its efficiency must be continually monitored by auditing. There are two types of auditing in a corporation. Internal audits assess whether or not the firm has proper operational and financial controls to assure the security of its assets and the compliance of individual employees in the operation of the system. External audits look objectively at the ledgers of a firm and provide an opinion as to whether or not the information recorded is valid, reliable, and accurate. This is the attest function of accounting. External auditors base their judgments on standards developed by the accounting profession; they are accounting professionals who have no affiliation with the corporation. Conducting external, independent audits provides a large portion of the business of the major accounting firms in the United States.

For internal audits conducted at a foreign subsidiary level, a firm has the choice of using local auditors or bringing in personnel from headquarters. The use of both types of auditors presents problems. Local auditors might facilitate the auditing process in keeping expenses down and avoiding language and cultural differences. Problems might arise, however, in terms of the rigorousness of corporate standards applied by local personnel because of their potential lack of familiarity with corporate requirements. Whereas auditors from headquarters could better examine subsidiary procedural lapses, they would run up against problems of their being unfamiliar with the language, the people, and the business practices accepted in the foreign environment.

SUMMARY

International business transactions present several accounting problems and raise many accounting issues because they encompass different environments, currencies, reporting requirements, and forms. The challenge of satisfying these financial and managerial accounting information needs must be met with an eye to developing uniform systems of reporting information in a manner that provides for its efficient integration and utilization by all users. Effective and accurate reporting of business transactions is required to present an accurate picture of the economic situation of the firm to both internal and external users.

DISCUSSION QUESTIONS

1. Who are the users of accounting information?
2. What factors influence the development of international accounting systems?
3. What is financial disclosure? Can it vary between countries? Explain.
4. What are the main differences in accounting conventions?
5. What is social reporting?
6. What role does the FASB have in setting accounting policy? Explain in terms of its domestic and international roles.
7. What regional international accounting organizations are trying to harmonize accounting practices? Discuss.
8. What is the difference between functional currency and reporting currency?
9. What are the four main accounting problems faced by multinationals?
10. How do multinationals account for losses due to expropriation?
11. Why are planning, control, and auditing important accounting functions?

NOTES

1. Arpan and Radebaugh, *International Accounting and Multinational Enterprises.*
2. Ibid.
3. Arpan and Al-Hashim, *International Dimensions of Accounting.*
4. AICPA, "The Enron Crisis."
5. Financial Accounting Standards Board, Statement 14, "Financial Reporting for Segments of a Business Enterprise," November, 1977.
6. Arpan and Radebaugh, *International Accounting and Multinational Enterprises.*
7. Ibid.
8. Ibid.
9. Financial Accounting Standards Board 1981.
10. Arpan and Radebaugh, *International Accounting and Multinational Enterprises.*
11. Choi and Mueller, *International Accounting.*

BIBLIOGRAPHY

AICPA. "The Enron Crisis: The AICPA, The Profession, and the Public Interest: Summary of Sarbanes-Oxley Act of 2002." http://www.aicpa.org/info/sarbanes_oxley_summary.htm, accessed April 25, 2006.

Arpan, Jeffrey S., and Dhia D. Al-Hashim. *International Dimensions of Accounting*. Boston: Kent Publishing, 1984.

Arpan, J.S., and L.H. Radebaugh. *International Accounting and Multinational Enterprises*. 2nd ed. New York: John Wiley and Sons, 1985.

Buckley, Adrian. "Does FX Exposure Matter?" *Accountancy,* March 1987, 116–18.

Cairns, David. "IASC's Blueprint for the Future." *Accountancy,* December 1989, 80–82.

Carsberg, B. "FASB #52: Measuring the Performance of Foreign Operations." *Midland Corporate Finance Journal* 1 (1983): 47–55.

Choi, Frederick D.S. "Multinational Challenges for Managerial Accountants." *Journal of Contemporary Business,* Autumn 1975, 51–68.

Choi, Frederick D.S., and Vinod B. Bavishi. "A Cross-National Assessment of Management's Geographic Disclosure." Paper presented at the Fourth Annual Meeting of the European Accounting Association, Barcelona, 1981.

———. "Diversity in Multinational Accounting." *Financial Executive,* August 1982, 45–49.

Choi, Frederick D.S., and G.G. Mueller. *An Introduction to Multinational Accounting*. Englewood Cliffs, NJ: Prentice-Hall, 1987.

———. *International Accounting*. Englewood Cliffs, NJ: Prentice-Hall, 1984.

Financial Accounting Standards Board. *Statement of Financial Accounting Standards. No. 52: Foreign Currency Translation*. Stamford, CT: Financial Accounting Standards Board, 1977.

CHAPTER 14

International Taxation

"Taxes are what we pay for a civilized society."
Oliver Wendell Holmes

CHAPTER OBJECTIVES

This chapter will:

- Present a rationale for the role and purpose of tax policy in modem society.
- Discuss the major forms of taxation employed by governments, including income, transaction, excise, severance, and tariff taxes, and the differences in compliance and enforcement of tax laws among countries.
- Describe special tax problems, treaties, and credits that may influence site selection for multinational operations.
- Review the advantages offered by international tax havens.
- Examine the types of incentives governments offer to corporations and to foreign nationals to promote international business.

WHY TAXES?

Taxes paid to governing bodies represent the contributions that all individual citizens and businesses make to public coffers. These funds finance most public services, including public education, state and federal government systems, local police and national defense forces, highway and waterway systems, protection of the environment, maintenance of state and federal parks and wilderness areas, and social programs that provide for the less fortunate by establishing housing, education, health care, and nutritional services.

The societal expectation underlying the principle that all wage earners should make a contribution to society is that it be a fair or equitable share. Every corporation or citizen in the same economic or business situation should thus be required to pay the same level of taxes. While the notion of equity underlies most national tax systems, it is not "fair" because every citizen does not pay the same proportion of wages in taxes. Therefore, most tax systems are progressive, and the more a person or corporation earns, the higher the tax bill because these entities are considered to be better able to pay a larger share.

In addition to the fairness or equity principle, tax systems are frequently based on the notion of neutrality, which means that business decisions and economic activities should not be prejudiced or directed by the consequences of tax policy. The rationale is that economic efficiency dictates that funds or capital should flow to the most efficient use. In practice, however, nations use tax policy to achieve other objectives, often at the expense of reducing economic efficiency of capital resources.

Governments may, for example, assess taxes to discourage consumption of scarce or unhealthy goods, such as alcohol and tobacco. Taxes may be applied to imports to raise their prices, discourage their purchase, and increase the relative attractiveness of domestic goods. Similarly, tax breaks may be instituted to encourage investment in specific industries, such as developing new sources of energy.

Policy objectives differ around the world, as do systems of taxation. These differences create problems for MNCs, which seek to minimize their multinational tax burden while optimizing the use of their financial and other resources in several countries.

Unfortunately, taxes often have a major impact on operational decisions. What international activities should be pursued? In which countries should they be pursued? How should activities be financed? Tax considerations are also involved in decisions concerning the form taken by an MNC's different subsidiaries and how prices will be determined between various segments and corporate headquarters.

Tax law is generally complex. In recent years, the U.S. tax code has consisted of 17,000 pages of tax regulations, and some estimates put the total number of pages of the current tax code at 55,000 (up from only 400 pages in 1913).[1] Further explanations of the law and accompanying regulations constitute many thousands more pages of text. In 1988 the Internal Revenue Service (IRS) found that the tasks of record keeping, learning about the law, and filing the basic 1040 tax return took longer than an average day's work (nine hours and five minutes). The addition of other schedules, such as Schedule A for itemized deductions or Schedule B for interest and dividend income, was estimated to require an additional four and a half and one and a half hours, respectively.

Multiply such complexity by extensive business technicalities and information, as well as by the number of international environments in which modern MNCs operate, and you have an idea of the difficulties involved in managing the tax function of a multinational enterprise. These complications also increase managers' difficulty in factoring all relevant tax consequences into business decision making.

TYPES OF TAXES

INCOME TAXES

There are many different types of taxes levied throughout the world. Income taxes are those levied by nation-states on individuals' and businesses' earnings or other inflows of money. Such taxes are generally levied in a progressive manner; the more one earns, the higher one is taxed. Income taxes are determined according to a person or firm's taxable income, that is, income that has been adjusted or reduced by deductions allowed by law.

Tax deductions account for expenses incurred by businesses or individuals and are subtracted from the taxpayer's total income. Tax deductions for individuals may be itemized or may take the form of a standardized allowable sum, the standard deduction. For individuals, such items as medical expenses, charitable contributions, mortgage interest, and losses from disaster or theft can be itemized and deducted from income before taxes are levied. Alternatively, individuals can take standard deductions, which, under the 2006 U.S. law, range from $5,150 for individuals to $10,300 for married couples filing together or surviving spouses. In addition, income can be adjusted for family size and special circumstances through the allowance of exemptions, each worth $3,100 in deductions from income. Deductions from income yield savings in taxes at the applicable tax rate, not in a dollar-for-dollar manner, because they reduce the income on which taxes are levied. Thus, if the tax rate applied to one's income is 33 percent, each dollar's worth of tax deductions yields a savings of $0.33.

Once taxable income is determined, taxes are calculated according to that amount. Adjustments to (reductions in) the amount of taxes due are characterized as tax credits. Because these credits reduce the actual tax liability, they yield tax savings on a dollar-per-dollar basis. Credits are allowed for individuals in the United States for such items as care for children, dependents, or disabled people; contributions to political parties; taxes paid to foreign governments; and general business expenses.

Companies are allowed such credits against their tax bills as expenses for general business; taxes paid to U.S. possessions or foreign governments; and the production of orphan drugs or energy from nonconventional sources. These credits show some of the social considerations taken into account in the development of tax policy. Orphan drugs for example, are those produced in very small quantities and used by very small groups of consumers. Consequently, they may be considered economically inefficient to produce by large drug-manufacturing concerns. To compensate drug companies for providing this service, a tax credit gives companies an incentive to provide for the medical needs of these citizens. Similarly, a credit for the production of energy from nonconventional sources (such as hydrogen, wind, or solar power) provides incentives for citizens to look for new energy sources and to reduce reliance on fossil fuels.

TRANSACTION TAXES

Another method of assessing taxes is that applied to transactions. *Transaction taxes* are levied at the time a transaction occurs or an exchange takes place. The most common transaction taxes encountered by citizens of the United States are state and local sales taxes, which are paid when items are purchased. Sales or transaction taxes are not progressive and do not discriminate in their application. All people are taxed at the same rate on their purchases, regardless of their individual wealth.

VALUE-ADDED TAXES

One variation of the transaction tax that is widely used in European countries is the value-added tax or VAT. The VAT was first put into effect in France in 1954 and takes the place of income taxes in some countries. It is a tax that is assessed only on the value added to products at each level of production. Take, for example, a French boutique that sells high-fashion clothing at the retail level. The VAT tax in France is assumed to be 10 percent. The first stage in the process of producing these items comes with the purchase of material to make the garments; thus, €200 million worth of fabric is bought from suppliers. The VAT tax on the purchase is €20 million (10% × €200 million).

At the next stage, the garment pieces are cut and assembled. This production work doubles their value; thus, they sell at the wholesale level for €400 million and the VAT connected with the sale is €20 million (10% × [€400 million − €200 million]). Finally, the finished suits sell to the boutique owner for €500 million, and the VAT generated at this stage is €10 million (10% × the value added of €100 million). Thus, the total VAT collected is €50 million on the total value of €500 (see Table 14.1).

In practice, at each stage the buyer pays the VAT on the entire amount and the seller forwards the tax to the country's treasury department. In our

Table 14.1

Example of the Application of a VAT
(in Millions of Euros)

Production-Value Stage of Product	Total Value	Prior Taxable Value	Taxable Value	VAT Generated
Raw material	200	0	200	20
Manufacturing	400	200	200	20
Retail	500	400	100	10
Total VAT				**50**

example, the first buyer is the manufacturer, who buys fabric for €200 million plus €20 million in VAT. The manufacturer's supplier remits the tax to the appropriate tax authorities. The manufacturer then sells the fabric as garments to the retailer for €400 million plus €40 million in VAT. The manufacturer sends the VAT to the government, but applies for a refund of the VAT withheld by the original supplier. In this way the manufacturer is assessed only on the value it added to the raw materials through the production efforts of cutting and assembly ([€400 million – €200 million] × 10% = €20 million).

The VAT is generally passed through to consumers as an indirect tax; it can, however, be absorbed by the producer. If the product is taken out of the country as an export, the VAT is not applied and is rebated entirely to the exporter. Such rebates create incentives to export because prices for export goods are cheaper than those for domestic goods. These rebates on goods exported from European countries have created controversy among members of the international community, who claim that rebating VAT for exports yields incentives that are unfair under the terms of the World Trade Organization.

In general, VAT taxes have the advantage of being easily administered; they can be raised or lowered easily. They have the disadvantage of not being progressive in that rich and poor people alike make the same contribution to taxes by the purchase of goods, regardless of the type of goods.

EXCISE TAXES

Another type of tax, the excise tax, is imposed on the manufacture, sale, or use of goods or on an activity or occupation. Excise taxes are frequently levied on luxury commodities, such as tobacco or liquor products (in which case they are often referred to as sin taxes), on such basic commodities as gasoline, or on services, such as entertainment. Excise taxes have the advantage of being applicable in specific situations for specific products to achieve policy objectives. Some of these objectives may be to limit the use of unhealthy or socially undesirable products, to ration scarce resources, or to regulate the use of specific products. In Canada, for example, a pack of cigarettes now costs CAD$8.00, and a carton now costs CAD$65.00. A large portion of this price is based on the amount of taxes associated with the purchase of cigarettes. This example of an excise tax is based on the desires of the Health Ministry of Canada to curb the consumption of this harmful product. As is typical when there are arbitrary differences in the price of a product in one country relative to another, the Canadian government makes sure that both visitors to and citizens of Canada are not bringing in cigarettes for resale in Canada from countries such as the United States, where the price of cigarettes is not nearly as high.

EXTRACTION TAXES

Another type of selective and special tax is a *severance* or *extraction tax*. This type of tax is levied on producers of mined, extracted, or harvested resources, such as minerals, ores, timber, and fuel products. The severance tax serves to reimburse the local or national community for the depletion of its natural resources. It may be assessed on a per-ton basis for ores or as a stumpage fee for timber depletion.

Tariffs (Border Taxes)

Taxes imposed at the borders of a country are generally characterized as tariffs. These border taxes not only allow governments to derive revenue from the entry of goods into the country but also serve to discourage the sale of imports by raising prices in the home market. Tariffs, therefore, encourage or support internal domestic production and the entry of foreign producers to build production facilities in the host country. Thus, tariffs are used by countries to achieve economic objectives of growth and domestic production.

Tax Compliance and Tax Enforcement

In addition to this formidable array of tax types, national governments impose many other types of taxes. Some are taxes on personal property, gifts received by individuals, estates of those who die, and employment taxes to fund various types of social programs. The relative frequency of use of these taxes in different nations is determined by the objectives of the government. In less-developed countries, for example, it is difficult to impose an income tax because income levels are low, and it is difficult to enforce tax compliance. Therefore, in LDCs it would make sense to impose excise taxes on luxury goods (paid by those who can most afford them) and severance taxes on extraction activities to fund the operation of government and government programs.

If the types of taxes imposed vary among countries, so does the level of compliance by corporate and individual citizens and the level of enforcement by national officials. Some nations, such as Italy, have historically been considered to be lax, while others, such as Germany and the United States, have been considered strict. U.S. tax law makes extensive provisions for the assessment of penalties, fines, and interest payments for failure to file, for a substantial understatement of tax liability and income,

for failure to pay taxes due, and for failure to pay estimated taxes. Nevertheless, many Americans continue to engage in tax evasion by attempting to hide income or by conducting business covertly and using cash transactions. Failure to comply with tax laws, however, may include criminal penalties, if the taxpayer intends to defraud the government. Thus, tax laws have been successfully used to prosecute criminals who profit from illegal activities, such as selling drugs or illegal gambling.

Some believe that the level of tax compliance in a country depends not as much on enforcement as on whether or not the public perceives the tax system to be fair. These perceptions explain the foundations of the massive reform effort mounted in the mid-1980s to change U.S. tax law. The belief among some policy makers was that making the law more equitable would induce Americans to pay their fair share. There has been much discussion more recently of reducing the tax liability for upper-income citizens, and others such as Steve Forbes have advocated moving to a flat tax. Still, the United States is actually at the low end of the tax scale. Countries that levy much higher taxes include Sweden and France, which have extensive social welfare systems. In comparison, tax rates are lower in countries that are more oriented toward free-market capitalism, such as Japan and the United States, which also do not have as extensive a net of social welfare programs to support the populace.

International Taxation
Taxes: MNCs

Multinational corporations begin to encounter serious tax problems when they establish operations overseas, because they must operate under a new tax code, with its own provisions and compliance procedures. Sales of goods through exports do not significantly affect an MNC's tax management. Sales made from domestic shores are simply included in total domestic sales. Thus, the source of taxable income is unchanged, as is the taxation jurisdiction of the company. Once an MNC establishes operations abroad, however, issues arise over the tax treatment of earnings made overseas by the tax authorities of the parent country. In its tax treatment of arms of parent corporations, the United States differentiates tax treatment by the form of the overseas affiliate, that is, between *branch offices* and *subsidiaries*.

Foreign branches are integral parts of MNCs and are treated as if they were merely domestic branches. Thus, income from overseas branches is added to the parent's domestic income, and taxes are assessed on that amount. As with domestic branches of a parent corporation, income from a foreign branch is taxed as it is earned, not as it is received. The advantage to an MNC of forming a branch overseas is that any losses in operations from that branch can immediately be offset against domestic earnings. The disadvantage is that taxes are immediately payable and cannot be deferred (postponed) because they are applied to income earned by the branch, not as profits are received.

Foreign affiliates of parent corporations formed as subsidiaries receive different tax treatment because they are incorporated within the borders of a different nation. Thus, they operate under the corporate laws of the country where they are located and which has taxing jurisdiction. Subsidiaries are liable for taxes paid to the foreign (host) government. Income sent to the parent is considered taxable when actually remitted as dividends, not when earned. Thus, through the reinvestment of profits or holding off on declared dividends, the parent is able to defer home-country taxes on certain portions of the income from the subsidiary.

Besides deferral of taxes, subsidiaries have other advantages, such as avoiding border taxes or import duties by manufacturing or producing within the country. They sometimes enjoy lower tax rates in the country of incorporation (host country) than in their home country. From a tax perspective, the drawbacks of using a subsidiary form of organization are that losses cannot be used against parental income and the foreign government may impose withholding taxes on the remittance of dividend income to the parent. In some overseas locations, local taxes may be higher than in the home country, and the tax procedures could be more cumbersome.

TAXES: U.S.-CONTROLLED FOREIGN CORPORATIONS

Because income generated from the operation of subsidiaries can enjoy deferral of taxes by being reinvested, U.S. tax authorities were faced with the problems created by the establishment of paper corporations abroad by U.S. taxpayers to shelter earnings from taxation. Thus, tax law was amended to provide for taxation of income earned overseas but not remitted to owners.

Under amendments to tax law enacted in 1975, limits were set on the deferral of income for U.S.-controlled foreign corporations (CFCs). Controlled foreign corporations are defined as those in which more than 50 percent of the voting stock, or more than 50 percent of the value of the outstanding stock of the foreign corporation, is owned by U.S. shareholders of any type: individual citizens, partnerships, trusts, or corporations. Therefore, a foreign corporation would be a CFC if five or more entities hold at least 10 percent ownership each, but not if 20 shareholders each own a 2 percent interest.

If the corporation is defined as a CFC, the owners cannot defer taxes on income, which is defined as Subpart F. Subpart F is a section of the 1962 Revenue Act that contains provisions for taxation of income accruing to U.S. shareholders in foreign incorporated affiliates of U.S. companies, provided such affiliates are deemed to be controlled foreign corporations. Specifically, income arising out of intracorporate deals, known as Subpart F income, is subject to tax under this provision.

Classification of Subpart F income of a U.S. affiliate that is also a CFC is a complex process because there are several exceptions and connected regulations that must be considered. Once income is classified as belonging to Subpart F, however, it becomes taxable by U.S. authorities at the time it is earned, regardless of whether it is remitted or not from the overseas affiliate to the U.S. shareholders. Typically, income that is taxable under Subpart F arises out of investment returns by way of dividends, royalties, interest, and so on.

DOUBLE TAXATION

A major problem that occurs for an MNC with overseas operations is that its existence in a multitude of environments subjects it to the jurisdiction of different taxing authorities and to double taxation on the same income. Thus, income earned by an MNC may be taxed when it is earned in the foreign location and again when it is remitted to and realized by the parent corporation. This situation also exists for individuals who earn income abroad. They are taxed on the income earned within the foreign country and by the U.S. government on their worldwide income.

Such double taxation is a clear violation of the U.S. tax principles of equity and fairness. Thus, in order to provide fair treatment of such income, U.S. law provides for a credit against U.S. tax liabilities that can be taken by both corporations and individuals for taxes paid on income to a foreign taxing authority.

TAX TREATIES

Bilateral and multilateral *tax treaties* provide a basis for reciprocal recognition of taxes paid to other nations and each nation's allowance of credits for taxes paid the other's jurisdiction. These treaties also often include provisions for reciprocal reductions in foreign withholding taxes on income earned on licenses, stocks, interest, royalties, and copyrights. They also establish the allocation of certain types of income to certain countries and allow tax audits to take place between countries. Tax treaties frequently also provide for the reciprocal exchange of tax information between nations, which is very important for enforcement of tax laws.

At present, the U.S. is signatory to more than fifty tax treaties with foreign nations, many of which are intricate and complicated. For example, the tax treaty with Canada is more than 11,000 pages long.

FOREIGN TAX CREDITS FOR U.S. CORPORATIONS

Foreign tax credits accorded to U.S. taxpayers are based on income taxes paid by a U.S. taxpaying entity to another country's treasury department or revenue service, which means that U.S. taxpayers are not given credits for the payment of value-added, sales, excise, or any other taxes paid to foreign concerns.

The purpose of foreign tax credits is to ensure that taxpayers are not penalized for engaging in foreign operations and that their tax bills abroad do not exceed domestic liabilities. Thus, if the rate paid on income abroad is less than the home or U.S. rate, taxpayers will be liable to the U.S. Treasury Department for the difference. In this way, they take care of their liability and pay their due share, but they are not unduly taxed on the same income.

For example, assume that a U.S. firm has a majority ownership in a subsidiary in Zimbabwe, where the tax rate is appreciably higher at 60 percent than the U.S. tax rate of 34 percent. If the subsidiary declares earnings of Z$100 million in Zimbabwe, it is assessed, and must pay (in Zimbabwean dollars) Z$60 million in taxes. If that income is also declared in the United States, the parent is liable for Z$34 million. The payment of Z$60 million to Zimbabwe, however, not only satisfies that liability but generates an additional foreign tax credit of Z$26 million (Z$60 million minus Z$34 million), which the firm can apply against its total U.S. income tax bill.[2]

If Zimbabwe's tax rate is lower than that of the United States, say 20 percent, the parent corporation is given credit for Z$20 million paid to tax authorities in Zimbabwe but must pay Z$14 million in U.S. taxes to satisfy the domestic tax bill of Z$34 million on the same Z$100 million of income taxed at a rate of 34 percent.

The key to determining whether or not U.S. firms can use foreign tax credits on taxes paid to foreign governments depends on whether or not an MNC declares the same income that was taxed abroad on its U.S. tax return. Thus, to take the credit for taxes paid abroad, the firm must recognize the income at home.

Foreign tax credits for corporations can be either direct or indirect, depending on the tax imposed by the foreign government. *Direct taxes* are those that are charged directly to the taxpayer, and, in this instance, would consist of foreign taxes on an MNC's branch income or foreign withholding taxes on remittances to a parent or U.S. investors. Under U.S. tax law, credits against U.S. tax liability may be taken in the amount of these paid taxes.

The code also provides a tax credit for *indirect taxes* paid by different segments of an MNC. These taxes come about when a subsidiary is taxed on income earned in the foreign site and then the parent is taxed again on dividends it receives from the subsidiary. Thus, the code provides for an indirect foreign tax credit that can be taken in addition to the direct foreign tax credit. Parent corporations are allowed to make use of the indirect foreign tax credit when they own 10 percent or more of the voting stock of the foreign subsidiary. This credit is called a *deemed paid credit* and is based on the dividends

paid by the subsidiary and the amount of foreign income taxes paid. The formula for determining the deemed paid credit is as follows:

$$\frac{\text{dividend (including withholding tax)}}{\text{earnings net of (minus) foreign income taxes}} \times$$

$$\text{foreign tax} = \text{deemed paid credit}$$

Thus, many international corporations are not penalized for doing business in different international operating environments because they receive credit for direct and indirect income taxes paid to foreign governments. The use of foreign tax credits is, however, subject to limits and does raise some issues in taxation.

Limits and Issues in Allocation of Foreign Tax Credit

The use of the foreign tax credit is subject to two major limitations. The first is that credit can be taken only against income taxes paid to foreign tax authorities, not against sales, value-added, or excise taxes. This limitation is a special concern for subsidiaries operating in countries where the government relies more on the use of a VAT or other transaction tax than on income tax.

The second major limitation is that foreign tax credits can be used to offset taxes only to the full extent of a person's or a company's U.S. tax liability. (Exceeding such liability would give the taxpayer a negative tax bill and entitle him to a rebate from the government.) Thus, a situation can arise for multinational firms where they develop credits for foreign taxes paid in excess of domestic liabilities. U.S. law provides relief for these individuals and allows tax credits to be carried back and forward by the taxpayer. The carryback is allowed for two years and is utilized by filing amended tax returns for prior years. Excess tax credits can be carried forward for five years. If the taxpayer does not have enough tax liability to use these credits within the carryback and carryforward periods, they are lost.

Beyond these limitations, concerns also arise in relation to issues regarding the administration and determination of foreign tax credits used against U.S. liabilities. Two such issues are the determination of taxable income and the allocation of deductions according to foreign-based and home-based income. Because taxable income (not gross income or sales) determines the amount of foreign taxes paid and resultant foreign tax credits, differences in accounting and tax practices between countries can lead to controversy in the determination of taxes and tax credits. Remember, gross income figures are reduced by deductions for the costs and expenses of doing business to arrive at an adjusted figure representing taxable income.

What may be considered an allowable deduction under the accounting practices of one country may not suffice under the tax law of another. Such differences often lead to disputes between MNCs and the tax authorities of the countries involved over what expenses are allowable in the conduct of business. Frequently, even if the corporations and the tax authorities agree about the method used to determine the firm's expenses and income, they may disagree on the allocation of that income to the expenses incurred in its generation among worldwide locations.

U.S. accounting conventions hold that expenses are matched to income for appropriate characterization of financial flows. In the operation of a global company, the question arises as to how to allocate deductible expenses. For example, what if a multinational firm is organized so that all international functions and operations are coordinated from a central headquarters? What portion of the company's general and administrative expenses for operating its headquarters should be applied to foreign income earned? The same problem arises in the allocation of R & D expenses for products marketed in a mul-

titude of locations. To satisfy these questions, the Internal Revenue Service issued stricter regulations in 1977 regarding the allocation of administrative and research expenses of multinationals to foreign-source income.

A problem remained, however, in that the resultant allocation of expenses is not always reciprocally recognized by foreign tax officials and does not always lead to a reduction of the related foreign-source taxable income. Foreign governments could tax the MNC on an amount that the U.S. government considers to be expenses (and, therefore, nontaxable). Thus, the MNC could wind up paying more in foreign taxes than they are required to pay by U.S. authorities, which creates a foreign tax credit. The solution pursued by multinationals is to create additional Subpart F income, from which they can generate and use more foreign tax credits.

SPECIAL ISSUES AND PROBLEMS IN INTERNATIONAL TAXATION

TAX HAVENS

Despite extensive nets cast by U.S. tax authorities to capture taxes owed, many individuals and corporations attempt to avoid being taxed on their income earned abroad. Although this activity has been limited by the imposition of regulations and taxes on unremitted earnings, crafty financiers continue to attempt to shelter income. One method of accomplishing that objective is to keep income overseas (and, thus, off domestic books) in countries without tax treaties with the MNC's home government. These countries provide sanctuary for foreign-earned income and impose few or no taxes at all and are termed "*tax havens.*" Monies deposited in these nations are safe from taxation until the subsidiary declares a dividend to the parent, at which time the remittance becomes taxable by the home tax authority.

To be efficient sanctuaries for a corporation's

worldwide income, tax havens must satisfy several criteria:

- They must not have a tax treaty with the corporation's domestic government that allows for the reciprocal tax treatment of income. Such a treaty would entail the sharing of earnings information and data.
- These nations must have low or no taxes on foreign-source funds. (Some tax haven countries do not provide equivalent tax amnesty for earnings within their own countries.)
- The countries must provide stable political and economic environments, so that funds deposited there will remain safe.
- The nations must allow for the free convertibility of currencies and have few if any restrictions on the inflow and outflow of currencies.
- The policies of the nations must be centered on a positive attitude toward businesses and their activities and, thus, have liberal incorporation laws.
- To accommodate financial flows, the countries must have well-developed banking systems with some degree of banking secrecy.
- The countries must also have infrastructures that support and facilitate general business operations, including such amenities as dependable telecommunications and transportation systems. A tax haven's close physical proximity to the home country makes it easier for depositors, who may then use the same lines or systems of communication and be in the same time zones.

Tax havens vary in their structure. Some countries, such as Caribbean tax havens, have very low or zero taxes on foreign or domestic income. These tax haven countries include the Bahamas, the Cayman Islands, Bermuda, the British Virgin Islands, and the Netherlands Antilles and are often used by U.S. nationals and corporations.

Other nations, such as Panama and Liechtenstein, provide sanctuary for foreign sources of funds but tax domestically produced income. Still other countries provide havens from taxation only for specific purposes or industries. These countries are primarily those that encourage investment within their boundaries by providing for tax exemptions for certain periods of time to promote industrial development. Two such countries that provide tax holidays are Ireland and Singapore, which provide tax incentives or lowered tax rates for the establishment of facilities in specific regions or zones.

TRANSFER PRICING

Multinational firms use the pricing of goods and services between their different operating arms to achieve a number of objectives, such as increasing rates of return in specific operating locations, lowering product prices in specific markets, circumventing restrictions regarding repatriation of parent-company profits, and getting around inconvertibility of host-country currencies. In addition, the uses of transfer pricing in intracompany transactions can also provide a method for MNCs to manage their international tax liability.

By shifting costs to countries with high tax rates, an MNC can enjoy savings on its tax bills, because by raising the costs of goods sold, a company can lower its taxable income, shifting profits to countries where tax rates on corporate profits are lower. U.S. companies usually attempt to shift deductible costs to themselves or to a parent corporation's accounts from the books of the affiliates. Thus, the costs of such items as intracompany loans, the sale of inventory and machinery, and the transfer of intangible property and their associated deductibility are transferred to high-tax-rate environments.

Such practices have come under intense scrutiny both by host governments and by the U.S. Internal Revenue Service, and the IRS can now challenge prices set by MNCs. Under certain circumstances, the IRS has the authority to recalculate those prices and assess tax liabilities according to prices set at arm's length—those prices that would have been reached if two independent parties engaged in the same transaction.

UNITARY TAXES

A special problem that has emerged in international taxation is the issue of applying *unitary taxes*, taxes imposed by a specific state on the basis of an MNC's multistate or worldwide profits, not merely those profits generated by operations in that state. This practice, originally developed in California, includes the assessment of a tax on the firm's total domestic or worldwide earnings based on a specific percentage figure. This percentage is derived from the proportion of the company's in-state sales, property, and personnel payroll in relation to its total national or global figures for sales, property held, and payroll. A rationale for the levying of such taxes by states is that doing so keeps corporations from using transfer pricing within different branches to shift income and tax bills to states that impose lower tax rates.

The use of unitary taxation has come under a great deal of criticism from all sides. U.S. multinational firms and the Treasury Department and foreign MNCs and their governments have protested loudly against the practice of levying unitary taxes and the method of income allocation. In the past, severe criticism has emerged from U.S. trading partners, such as Great Britain and Japan.

This pressure from foreign multinational corporations has given rise to a solution called *water's edge taxation*, which limits states to taxing only income from operations within the United States, not from global sales. It is more likely that changes in unitary taxation policy by individual states will come from opposition by MNCs and their decisions to disinvest in such states and move to states that do not apply the unitary tax concept. The state of California in the United States has been implementing a form of water's edge taxation since 1986. Given the state's fiscal crisis in recent years, there have been calls for further modifying the tax code to allow for more taxation of the foreign activities of multinationals headquartered in California.

TAX INCENTIVES FOR INTERNATIONAL BUSINESS

Not only are governments concerned with garnering tax income from the operations of international firms, but they also use taxation policy as a tool to promote international trade. Countries that impose value-added taxes frequently rebate those taxes on exported goods to encourage exports. Similarly, the United States promotes exports of U.S. goods through tax policy. At one time, the United States had six different incentive programs to encourage international trade by U.S. companies. Each involved the formation of special corporate entities for conducting such trade to keep it segregated from normal operations.

FOREIGN SALES CORPORATIONS

At present, the only existing incentive programs are *foreign sales corporations (FSCs)* and possessions corporations, which operate within possessions of the United States.

Foreign sales corporations were established to encourage and support the sale of U.S. goods and services abroad. These corporations must be established outside the United States in a possession or country that has a tax treaty (and that exchanges financial information) with the United States. FSCs (pronounced "fisks") act as sales agents for U.S. goods in foreign markets. The products sold are then exported from U.S. suppliers to foreign buyers. The advantages to forming a FSC is that a U.S. business receives favorable tax treatment of qualified foreign-source income, and its member companies receive full deductibility of qualified dividend distribution from the FSC. This tax treatment is, however, subject to many rules and stipulations.

The FSC, for example, must generate foreign gross sales receipts to qualify for special tax treatment. It must have no more than 25 members, a board of directors that includes at least one non-U.S. resident, no affiliation with an established domestic industrial sales corporation, and no preferred stock. It must also meet specific requirements regarding foreign management and foreign economic process requirements to generate its foreign receipts. Income from sales generated by the FSC is segregated according to IRS rules into exempt and nonexempt portions. The exempt portions receive favorable tax treatment, while nonexempt portions are not accorded such privileges.

Tax law includes provisions for slightly less involved legal requirements for the establishment of a small FSC, which does not have to meet the foreign management or economic process requirements of a larger FSC and enjoys the same tax benefits, but only up to $5 million per year of foreign gross trading receipts. Small U.S. businesses are also taking advantage of FSC law by joining together in a net tax-saving vehicle called a shared foreign sales corporation.

Small businesses can profit by using these vehicles to generate reductions on tax bills through FSC exempted income. They can afford to comply with the regulations by using management firms to coordinate much of the record-keeping and managerial work of the corporations. These management firms are beginning to set up shared FSCs to allow small businesses access to the tax incentive program, while eliminating the need to deal with the complicated workings of the law. Small business owners must, however, maintain some records to ensure that only products produced in the United States (not imports from other countries, such as Canada) are shipped overseas. They must also be sure to calculate profits according to special FSC rules regarding marginal costing and transfer pricing of products.

DOMESTIC INTERNATIONAL SALES CORPORATIONS

FSCs were established in 1984 to replace export promotion programs called *DISCs: domestic international sales corporations*, which were similarly organized in the interest of promoting U.S. export trade. If a firm organized as a DISC met the requirements set by law that 95 percent of the assets and 95 percent of the corporation's sales were export related, it was allowed to defer 50 percent of its tax liability from such activity either permanently or until it no longer met the 95 percent requirements. At such a time, all the deferred taxes were due. The DISC program was eliminated after major U.S. trading partners, particularly Japan and Canada, complained that DISCs constituted an unfair export subsidy in terms of the General Agreement on Tariffs and Trade (GATT). Consequently, FSCs were established, and DISCs were given five years in which to establish FSCs outside the United States. The law did provide, however, an escape clause for DISCs, which qualified tax-free income as $10 million worth of export receipts.

The escape clause exempted small DISCs, which could continue to operate if they met the stipulations of the law. They differ, however, from original DISCs in that even though they can permanently defer taxes on eligible income, they must pay interest to the IRS on the amount of deferred tax. Thus, the primary benefit accorded small DISCs is the financing of export sales. Thus, such DISCs are properly referred to as interest-charge DISCs.

U.S. POSSESSIONS CORPORATIONS

If a domestic operation derives at least 80 percent of its income from a U.S. possession (excluding the Virgin Islands) and generates at least 75 percent of its gross income from active trade, it may be able to take advantage of tax benefits established for U.S. possessions corporations. If these conditions are met for three years prior to the establishment of the corporation, it has the advantage of limitations on taxation of income from outside the United States, tax-free repatriation of earnings to the United States, liberal interpretation of transfer prices, and possible exemption from Puerto Rican taxation if it operates manufacturing facilities in certain areas of Puerto Rico.

INFLUENCE OF U.S. TAX LAW ON CORPORATE OPERATIONS

Clearly, managing the international tax function for a major MNC involves many different facets that relate directly to managerial decision making. The effects of taxation on the future operations of a corporation play a large role in determining where activities are carried out and in what type of legal form (branch, subsidiary, or export arm). Taxes must be factored into prices set for external and internal intracompany purchases and must be considered in determining appropriate cash levels, flows, and locations among worldwide operations. The international taxation situation is so complex that many MNCs use complex computer programs that can determine the tax effects of various managerial decisions regarding international financing, cash flows, and operations.

TAXATION OF INDIVIDUAL FOREIGN SOURCE INCOME

The existence of business operations in a multitude of environments and of a far-flung management staff involves the compensation of employees in foreign tax jurisdictions and subsequent taxation complications. In some countries, the principle of juridic domicile is strictly applied; that is, the citizen's income is not taxed by his or her home country if it is not earned or received within that country. The United States,

however, differs greatly in this approach. Under the Sixteenth Amendment to the U.S. Constitution, U.S. citizens are taxed on all of their income regardless of where it is sourced or earned in the world.

Naturally, the application of this principle could result in problems for U.S. citizens working in and being taxed by a host government, especially the problem of double taxation of the same income. Consequently, tax law provides relief for the U.S. expatriate who is earning income abroad and for the U.S. investor receiving income from foreign sources. These situations provide for a distinction in foreign income determination between that which is earned and that which is unearned.

Foreign earned income consists of all monies employees receive as payment for services rendered and includes wages, salaries, and commissions. Earned income does not include wages or salaries received in return for services rendered by employees of the U.S. government. *Foreign unearned income* is that which is derived from an individual's overseas investments. These sources of income include interest on investments, dividends, pensions, annuities, and even gambling winnings.

To provide for equity in the tax treatment of U.S. expatriates and to encourage citizens to work abroad, tax law provides for alternate forms of relief from taxes on foreign earned income and from double taxation by home and host governments. A U.S. citizen qualifies for special treatment if he or she satisfies the requirements of overseas employment either by being a bona fide resident of the foreign country or by being away at least 330 days during any 12 consecutive months.

An employee on foreign soil has two ways to treat foreign earned income. First, a portion of foreign earned income can be excluded up to a limit of US$80,000 per year. If the minimum 330-day residency requirement is met, but was less than a year, the allowance is prorated proportionately to provide for a new maximum exclusion. Married employees may each use the exclusion if they satisfy the other requirements of the relief provision.

The second alternative open to expatriate employees in handling foreign earned income is to include it in their income bases but claim foreign tax credits on their returns for taxes paid abroad on those earnings or wages. Generally, most expatriates, especially those in low-tax foreign countries, use the income exclusion provisions of tax law. Thus, if the tax abroad is lower than the tax at home, employees pay less tax because they do not have to make up the difference between taxes paid to the host government and taxes paid to the home government.

Alternatively, individuals use the foreign tax credit when their earnings or wages far exceed the amount of the exclusion and their foreign taxes paid far exceed comparable U.S. tax on the excluded amount. Expatriates also might choose to use the foreign tax credit rather than the exclusions, if the tax rate in the host country is much higher than that in the United States. In such a case, the international employee would use a credit to eliminate U.S. taxes for the existing year and in years ahead under carryforward provisions. Once an expatriate elects to use the foreign tax credit, however, it must be applied to all subsequent years unless it is actively revoked. A revocation is then effective not only for the year of change but also for four subsequent years.

As for corporations, the foreign tax credit of individuals is subject to limitations. For example, it can be calculated only according to foreign taxes paid on income, and the United States uses its own criteria in determining whether or not the tax paid is an income tax. Consequently, sales, value-added, property, severance, and excise taxes are not included in determining the credit. Some of these, however, may be deductible as a state, local, or personal property tax under Section 164 of the Internal Revenue Code. Also, according to the alternative minimum tax provisions of U.S. tax law, foreign tax credits cannot be used to reduce tax liability by more than 90 percent.

EXPENSES OF U.S. EXPATRIATES

U.S. tax law also takes into account the rigors and additional costs involved in overseas assignments and provides relief for expenses incurred abroad in securing scarce housing or paying a higher cost of living in a more expensive economy. Thus, the law provides relief for the expatriate who receives reimbursement for housing costs, which are deemed to include rent, insurance, and utilities. They do not include interest or taxes paid on housing, because these costs are deductible under other provisions of law. Under the provisions, the employee may exclude from income an amount in addition to basic exclusion to compensate for these additional costs.

SUMMARY

The management of the international tax function for a multinational enterprise is very involved and complicated and can have a profound effect on the welfare and profitability of a firm. The effects of taxation policies in home and foreign operating environments frequently determine managerial decisions regarding choice of international operations, the legal forms of such operations, price setting between branches of the enterprise and with the public, and the financing and cash flows of international operations around the world.

Individual nations vary in the types of taxes they levy and in assessment rates. All countries provide relief for taxpayers from being doubly taxed on the same income, and to facilitate international trade and investment flows, nations join in agreements regarding taxation of their citizens and reciprocal recognition of taxes paid within their jurisdictions. These tax treaties also frequently provide for the mutual exchange of information regarding business operations of multinational firms and facilitate enforcement of tax laws. Some countries purposefully avoid entering into such agreements to provide sanctuaries for foreign earned income so that it can find a safe haven from the long arms of domestic tax authorities.

Nations of the world use taxation as an arm of policy making to achieve social, economic, and political objectives, as well as to raise revenues. Most countries have as one such objective the increase of export trade from their borders. Consequently, they use tax incentive programs to promote such trade. Nevertheless, objectives, policies, and tax structures differ widely around the world. Thus, the tax manager of an international concern is faced with the formidable task of managing the multinational tax function to provide for the minimization of taxes in the pursuit of maximization of operational efficiencies and worldwide profitability.

DISCUSSION QUESTIONS

1. Why do governments levy taxes? What services do they fund?
2. What is tax equity?
3. How can taxes encourage or discourage certain activities? Explain.
4. What types of taxes may be levied other than income taxes?
5. What is a VAT?
6. What is double taxation? How can individuals or corporations avoid double taxation?
7. What is a tax haven? Identify five countries that qualify as tax havens.
8. What are FSCs? What are DISCs?
9. Why must MNCs concern themselves with taxes?
10. Does U.S. tax policy provide any incentives to U.S. citizens to work overseas?

NOTES

1. Cato Institute, "Cato Scholar Cites 10 Surprising Things About the Income Tax," www.cato.org, accessed April 13, 2004.

2. These examples ignore exchange-rate effects, as they are only for illustrative purposes.

BIBLIOGRAPHY

Bische, Jon E. *Fundamentals of International Taxation.* 2nd ed. New York: Practicing Law Institute, 1985.

Bond, Eric W., and L. Samuelson. "Strategic Behavior and the Rules for International Taxation of Capital." *Economic Journal,* December 1989, 1099–1111.

Borsack, Scott P. "Choosing to Do Business Through a Foreign Branch or a Foreign Subsidiary. A Tax Analysis." *Case Western Reserve Journal of International Law,* Summer 1987, 393–419.

Chambost, E. *Bank Accounts: A World Guide to Confidentiality.* New York: John Wiley and Sons, 1983.

Commerce Clearing House. *Internal Revenue Code of 1986.* Chicago: Commerce Clearing House, 1988.

Doernberg, Richard L. *International Taxation in a Nutshell.* St. Paul, MN: West Publishing Company, 1989.

Granell, A.W., B. Hirsh, and D.R. Milton. "Worldwide Unitary Tax: Is It Invalid Under Treaties of Friendship, Commerce and Navigation?" *Tax & Policy in International Business* 18 (1986): 695–758.

Gutfeld, Rose. "It Seems Like Days, but IRS Estimates Tax Filing Takes Only About Nine Hours." *Wall Street Journal,* September 1, 1988, 23.

Hoffman, William H., Jr., and Eugene Willis. *West's Federal Taxation: Comprehensive Volume.* St. Paul, MN: West Publishing Company, 1988.

Miller, Richard Bradford. *Tax Haven Investing: A Guide to Offshore Banking and Investment Opportunities.* Chicago: Probus Publishing Company, 1988.

Nutter, Sarah E. "U.S. Possessions Corporations Returns, 1997 and 1999." Internal Revenue Service. http://www.irs.gov/pub/irssoi/99posart.pdf., accessed November 15, 2004.

Rothschild, Leonard W., Jr. "Worldwide Unitary Taxation: The End Is in Sight." *Journal of Accountancy,* December 1986, 178–85.

Shapiro, Alan. *Multinational Financial Management.* Newton, MA: Allyn and Bacon, 1986.

Sinn, Hans-Werner, and R.J. Patrick Jr. "U.S. Tax Reform 1981 and 1986: Impact on International Capital Markets and Capital Flows." *National Tax Journal,* September 1988, 71.

Sinning, Kathleen E., ed. *Comparative International Taxation.* Sarasota, FL: International Accounting Association of the American Accounting Association, 1986.

U.S. Department of the Treasury, Internal Revenue Service. *Explanation of Tax Reform Act of 1986 for Individuals.* Publication 920. 1986.

U.S. Department of the Treasury, Internal Revenue Service. *Tax Guide for U.S. Citizens and Resident Aliens Abroad.* Publication 54. 2004.

U.S. Department of the Treasury, Internal Revenue Service. *Foreign Tax Credit for Individuals,* Publication 514, 2004.

CASE STUDY 14.1
SKYTRACK INSTRUMENTATION

Jerry Turner and William McKensie were in good spirits. Having finished a round of golf at the Green Holes Country Club in Quintacera, a resort town north of Divotia, the main business center in the Latin American nation of Celida, they headed for the clubhouse for a couple of drinks before lunch and an afternoon meeting with José Cervantes, their main consultant on government regulations. Turner and McKensie were president and chief financial officer of Skytrack Instrumentation, a British-based multinational specializing in air traffic control instruments for civilian aircraft. Their annual sales were approximately US$6 billion, spread over 45 countries on four continents. Skytrack Instrumentation Celida was established as a wholly owned subsidiary in 2004. The company had set up a highly automated manufacturing facility in a small industrial park just outside Divotia that had been created by the government of Celida to attract investment from overseas. With considerable cooperation from the government and the availability of many infrastructural facilities in Celida, Skytrack was able to set up the plant within two years, and production was expected to begin within the next three weeks. Turner and McKensie were taking a well-deserved vacation before the commencement of operations. Meanwhile, McKensie also had to start charting the tax strategy of the company, something he had not yet done. A preliminary meeting with Cervantes, a leading expert on government regulations for multinational enterprises in Celida, seemed to be a good first step.

Cervantes was well prepared for the discussion. He pulled out two separate briefs, detailing comprehensive outlines for two approaches that Skytrack could take to minimize its tax liability in Celida.

One of the approaches was based on the technique of transfer pricing, which the brief euphemistically called the "price adjustment approach." There was considerable scope with this technique because the subsidiary was importing nearly every component of its products from Great Britain and assembling them in Celida. In fact, the cost of components was almost 50 percent of the total costs of goods to be sold in Celida, according to early projections made by the company's accountants. If the import price was raised, the profit margins would be lowered and so would the tax liability. The tax rates on overseas corporations in Celida were as follows:

35% corporate income tax	Computed on earnings, including interest earnings, for the financial year
15% withholding tax	Computed on the amount of profits sought to be repatriated by the company

Projected sales of Skytrack Celida for the first year were approximately £160 million (calculated at the day's exchange rate of £1 for 34 Celidan pesos). The estimated costs of goods sold, selling expenses, interest expenses, and other costs were in aggregate £130 million. Net profit before taxes was estimated to be £30 million; of this, 35 percent, that is, £10.5 million, was to be paid as corporate income tax, which would leave the company with £19.5 million in profits. According to the local regulations,

continued

Case 14.1 (*continued*)

overseas companies were allowed to repatriate 75 percent of their post-tax profits each year. Under this provision, Skytrack could repatriate £14 million to Great Britain. There would be, however, a withholding tax of 15 percent on this amount, or £2.2 million. The total tax liability of Celida would be approximately £12.69 million on a profit of £30 million, or approximately 42.3 percent.

If, however, Skytrack UK could increase the price of components sold to Skytrack Celida by 15 percent (on a total annual sales of approximately 85 percent), the tax liability could be reduced substantially. Cervantes showed them the computation (in millions of pounds):

Original cost of sales	130
Increase in equipment prices	12.75 (15% of £85)
New cost of sales	142.75
Profit	17.25
Corporate income tax	6.0375
Net profit	11.21
Repatriated amount (75%)	8.40
Tax on repatriated amount	1.26
Total tax	7.296
Tax savings	5.40
Increase in headquarters tax liability on account of increase in income	3.2
Net tax savings	**2.2**

The other approach suggested by Cervantes was to use a tax haven, where the tax savings would be even greater. Skytrack could ship components, on paper, to Skytrack Cayman Islands, at the same price it would be shipping to Skytrack Celida. Thus, there would be no increase in Skytrack UK income because of higher prices, but Skytrack Cayman Islands would notionally resell these components to Skytrack Celida at a markup of 15 percent and in the process make a "profit" of £12.75 million, on which there would be no tax liability because the Cayman Islands is a tax haven. At the same time, Skytrack Celida would have a reduced tax liability of £5.4 million. The net savings would be £3.2 million over the direct approach.

The tax haven approach, however, was more complex. It required documentation to be routed through the Cayman Islands and increased the risk of making Celidan authorities suspicious. On the other hand, £3.2 million a year was a large sum, even for a company of Skytrack's size, and the use of tax havens was quite common.

DISCUSSION QUESTION

1. Which of the following options would you choose if you were McKensie? Explain your reasons for accepting or rejecting each option.
   A. No transfer pricing
   B. Transfer pricing
   C. Transfer pricing and using a tax haven
   D. Are there other alternatives? If so, what are their advantages and disadvantages?

CHAPTER 15

International Staffing and Labor Issues

CHAPTER OBJECTIVES

This chapter will:

- Identify common organizational structures used by multinational corporations.
- Discuss how MNCs recruit, select, train, and motivate management staffs.
- Describe the cultural and economic forces that influence the international manager's performance.
- Consider the problems of repatriating international managers and other ethical issues.
- Identify the trade-offs between localized and centralized management of labor.
- Discuss the major labor issues of wages and benefits, job security, and productivity as they relate to MNC operations.
- Present how international labor movements and codetermination are influencing MNC operations.

ORGANIZING A MULTINATIONAL CORPORATION

International firms can organize their operations in a number of different ways. Four of the most common organizing strategies are the functional structure, the regional structure, the product structure, and the matrix structure.

FUNCTIONAL STRUCTURE

Under the functional structure organization, responsibilities at headquarters are divided according to function, for example, marketing and finance, and the head of each division is responsible for the conduct of that function internationally. This strategy is efficient if there is a standardized product line; it permits coordination of all aspects of a function in one department. On the downside, this strategy encourages a narrow viewpoint, is inflexible, and can be time-consuming. It is hard to adapt this centralized approach to changing local conditions, and overall international integration of the various functions is very difficult to achieve.

REGIONAL STRUCTURE

In an MNC that uses the regional structure organizing strategy, headquarters retains responsibility for overall global strategy and control, but area managers have responsibility for all the operations and functions of their assigned regions. The regions should be organized on the basis of similar characteristics with less emphasis on functional categories. This structure integrates the separate functions very well throughout each region, but its drawback is that each function must be standardized in order to integrate across all the regions.

PRODUCT STRUCTURE

As with the regional structure, under the product structure organizing strategy, corporate headquarters has control of overall global strategy. Within the guidelines established by headquarters, a manager has international control over all the operations related to a single product. A major advantage of this structure is that all functions relating to a single product are integrated and perform as a whole internationally. The major drawback is that it is difficult to coordinate policies and strategies across product lines.

MATRIX STRUCTURE

The matrix structure involves dual lines of authority in which managers may report to two or more superiors. For example, they may have to report to the head of the product line and to the chief of a geographical region. This structure provides for coordination of the various departments, while still recognizing differences, leads to standardization of functions and overall control, and imparts flexibility to respond to environmental differences.

INTERNATIONAL STAFFING

International staffing involves the four basic stages of recruitment, selection, training, and motiva-tion of the right person to fill a job available in a foreign setting.

RECRUITMENT

Recruitment is the process of attracting people to apply for job vacancies. There are two main sources of recruitment for international positions: internal and external. Internal sources consist of promotion from within the company and employee referrals. Promotion from within is a very low-cost method for the firm. It has the added benefit of increasing employee morale because employees are made aware of opportunities for advancement. Uncertainty about an applicant and training costs are reduced because employees are already familiar with the objectives and procedures of the firm. Employee referrals involve the recommendation by a present employee of a family member or friend. The benefits of an employee referral are the low cost to the firm and the fact that the referrals will probably be fairly well informed about the various aspects of the firm.

External sources of recruitment include newspaper, radio, and Internet advertising, trade schools, employment agencies, job fairs, and labor unions. There is a difference, however, between recruitment in industrialized countries and recruitment in the less-developed countries. In the less-developed countries, there is an over-abundance of unskilled workers because of high unemployment and deficiencies in education and training levels. Internet and newspaper advertising may not be effective in LDCs because much of the population may not have access to the Internet and may be illiterate, and there are usually very few employment agencies in these countries. In industrialized countries, the problems are reversed; there are too many skilled workers and too few unskilled workers.

SELECTION

Employee selection involves choosing from an available pool of applicants that the firm considers best able to meet the requirements of the position. In industrialized countries the firm considers people through standardized procedures, such as application forms, personal interviews, and possibly physical or psychological exams. The selection process in LDCs is less formal and involves less testing; such considerations as family ties, social status or caste, language, and common origin tend to influence the selection process.

TRAINING

For an MNC, training of its overseas employees is an extremely important issue. Employees in overseas locations come from a different society and culture, which means that they have varying attitudes toward work, conduct, and other behavioral aspects that may be quite different from the MNC's expectations and standards. It is therefore critical for an MNC to train its overseas employees regarding its work ethic, discipline, efficiency standards, operating procedures, and, of course, the necessary operational skills.

One major limitation in many countries is that adequate training resources, including instructors, experienced personnel, and training facilities, may not be available. Generally, MNCs fly in large numbers of key technical personnel, who lead training sessions for both theoretical and on-the-job training, to train newly hired employees in foreign locations. Some personnel in charge of sensitive and complex industrial operations have to remain at the overseas locations until the local trainees are considered adequately trained and have enough experience to run the operations themselves.

For lower-level employees, typically factory workers, language is another important barrier to overcome. Companies take different approaches to this problem. Interpreters are used where language is an intractable problem. Often companies train bilingual local employees, who in turn pass on the training to those local employees who do not understand the language used by the MNC. Because most workers at the plant-floor level are not involved in significant amounts of theoretical work, this problem is mitigated to a large extent as long as they are able to understand the operating instructions for their specific tasks.

MOTIVATION

Motivating overseas employees also presents complex problems. Employees, especially at the lower levels, are relatively ethnocentric in their views, and their priorities and goals often differ from those of their counterparts in Western countries. While mobility, compensation, challenges in the work environment, and independence in functioning are important motivating factors for employees in Western industrialized countries, workers in LDCs tend to attach greater value to job security, number of holidays, working hours, social benefits, and the like. An MNC, therefore, must judge the local climate and expectations very carefully and come up with an appropriate mix of incentives to motivate employees without being unduly expensive.

Compare, for example, workers in a developed country and those in a developing country. The worker in the developed country is consumption oriented and wants compensation in terms of money. While vacation days are desirable, the employee tends to work more days of the year to increase the compensation package. The employee is interested in moving up the ladder to better jobs, but not necessarily in the same company.

A worker in a developing country, in contrast, wants job security because industrial jobs are scarce. If the worker loses his or her job, there may not be any other means of livelihood, especially because there is ordinarily no social security or unemployment insurance in developing countries.

There are a number of religious festivals in societies where the hold of traditional socioreligious practices is still strong, and workers in developing countries like to be certain that they have those days off. Historically, many workers in developing countries expect their employers to provide them with housing assistance or similar benefits that are not readily available to them. Thus, an MNC may have to create a compensation package that relies less on salary and more on other benefits for its workers in developing countries. Salary levels, however, also must be a little higher than the local going rate to guard against allegations that the MNC is exploiting local workers.

MANAGERIAL STAFFING

VALUE TO FIRM

Choosing a manager for an overseas operation is an important task because this choice can profoundly affect overseas growth and operations. The subsidiary manager will have a great deal of responsibility—more than a counterpart in a home production facility. The overseas manager must be multicultural and sensitive to business practices and customs of the host country, while being responsible for following the global objectives of the MNC and being able to put these objectives ahead of the local operation's well-being.

The success of its overseas managers is particularly important to MNCs for a number of reasons. A failure in the overseas assignment leads to large corporate costs in time and resources in the replacement of the expatriate, the lost productivity of the manager, and productivity slowdowns at the overseas plant. Bereft of skillful management, the overseas operation is more likely to experience such problems as increases in labor strikes, employee problems, government relations problems, and legal suits, because backup management resources may not be easily forthcoming.

To motivate their overseas managers, MNCs provide huge employment incentives in the form of large increases in salary and benefits, and most as-

signments carry the glamour of widening horizons, enriching experiences, and an excitingly different lifestyle.[1] Nevertheless, one out of every three expatriate workers from the United States finds that the assignment has gone wrong. In a study by Rosalie Tung, it was found that "incidences where expatriates had to be recalled to corporate headquarters or dismissed from the company because of their inability to perform effectively in a foreign country were numerous."[2] More than half of the 80 companies Tung surveyed reported failure rates between 10 and 20 percent. Some estimates hold that failure rates for poorly trained expatriate managers and personnel, based on location, are more in the range of 33 to 66 percent.[3]

The solution to minimizing failures in deploying personnel abroad lies in planning the management of a global corporation and carefully selecting and training these global managers. Managers with the aptitude, ability, and willingness to serve in international assignments must be identified by the corporation and trained extensively. Appropriate financial and career incentives have to be created to attract managers to international assignments and to reward those who accept them.

BRANCH MANAGER VERSUS HOME OFFICE: WHO IS IN CHARGE?

Overseas managers of MNCs face several challenges that arise from their unique position not only between two parts of a company (the parent corporation and the subsidiary) but also between two countries and two cultures. In addition, there is always a considerable physical distance between overseas managers and the corporate office. Consequently, overseas managers have a much greater degree of autonomy than their peers at the corporate office. As heads of local operations, they are fully responsible for their performance and must make a variety of executive decisions. Greater decision-making authority devolves both by design and by circumstance. The costs and delays associated with overseas communication encourage the parent corporation to give substantial leeway to the local manager. Even in areas where the decision making is reserved by the parent office, the local manager may have to exercise discretionary authority in emergency situations, when there is a breakdown in the communication channels, especially when decisions are needed immediately and cannot wait for a response from the head office.

Many parent offices delegate substantial authority to on-the-spot local managers in the belief that they will be able to make better-informed decisions. Generally, day-to-day operational decisions are vested with the local managers, while the overall global strategic decisions are made by the corporate office. Overseas managers have to adjust their decision making to corporate policy and maintain the fine balance needed for exercising just the right degree of discretionary authority at the local level.

Overseas managers have the effective responsibilities, in many ways, of corporate CEOs. Therefore, they must have an overall perspective of their operations, the internal and external environments, and the trends in the local political and economic situations, and a clear perception of the opportunities for and threats to the local operations. As the head of a local operation, the overseas manager represents the MNC to the local government, other firms, customers, and suppliers. It is essential that the manager deal effectively with each of these entities, all of whom are important for the success of any business operation.

Adaptability is probably one of the most important qualities required of an overseas manager. Managers sent to different countries land in professional and cultural environments completely different from their own. In addition, there are the problems of adjustment by spouses and families, which have to be addressed. A large number of expatriate managers have failed in their assignments because their families had difficulty adjusting to the new environment.

Thus, the adaptability of both manager and family is crucial to success in an overseas assignment.

BRANCH MANAGERS: WHOM SHOULD FIRMS CHOOSE?

A major issue for an MNC in staffing overseas facilities is whether to use a home-country national, a host-country national, or a third-country national.

Home-country nationals are citizens of the country where the headquarters are located. Home-country nationals who live and work in foreign countries are called expatriates. *Host-country nationals* are citizens of the country where the subsidiary is. They are local employees. *Third-country nationals* are citizens of neither the country of the subsidiary nor the country of the headquarters. For example, a German working in Brazil for a U.S.-based company is a third-country national.

Home-country nationals offer several advantages as overseas managers of a foreign subsidiary. Home-country managers are well trained and familiar with the company's operating requirements and practices. Thus, they have a better perception of corporate goals, policies, and strategies and can design their local operations accordingly. Overseas assignments broaden the perspectives of home-country managers, and these managers can begin to factor in the worldwide implications of their decisions, which is essential for all the firm's top executives. The overseas assignment of home-country executives thus provides valuable training for the company's future senior management. A home-country national in an overseas location provides headquarters with a presence in the foreign environment and enables the firm to stay abreast of developments firsthand. A home-country national also can represent the firm's interests with the host government more easily than a host-country national, who might encounter a conflict if asked to handle a confrontation with the host government.

Host-country nationals also have several advantages

as local managers. They know the local language, the culture, and the customs and may have valuable contacts in the local business world. Costs associated with hiring a local manager are usually lower because there are no relocation costs. Training costs can sometimes be higher, because the manager may need to be trained in the home country, but, in the long run, these costs generally are not significant. Hiring a host-country national may ease tensions with the host government and may in fact serve to comply with local requirements. The local manager may also be able to deal better with local employees, and especially with unions.

There are also disadvantages in using host-country nationals. These managers may be unfamiliar with home-country cultures and the MNC's policies and practices and may have attitudes and values different from those of the people at headquarters. Occasionally, these employees are hired away from the MNC by local competitors after the MNC has spent considerable time and money in training, and local mangers may experience conflicts in loyalty between their country and the MNC.

Third-country nationals may be hired for several reasons. They may possess skills lacking in both home- and host-country nationals. They may be more familiar with the language and culture of the host country than a home-country national, and they may appease the host government by being a third-country national. Many times there is the natural progression from one post to another. For example, a French national in charge of a French subsidiary may be relocated to head a Mexican subsidiary.

CHOOSING BRANCH MANAGERS: SELECTION CRITERIA

LABOR POOL

The labor pool has a direct effect on the MNC's choice of a manager. The availability, quality, and technical competence of managers in the host country are important factors in deciding on the overseas assignment. If the local labor pool is unable to provide managers with the required qualifications, a home-country national will have to be sent abroad.

CORPORATE POLICIES

The corporate objectives and policies of a firm affect its choice of an overseas manager. If the firm wants to maintain a high level of control of the subsidiary operations and ensure that they are run strictly according to the policies of headquarters, it will choose to send home-country nationals to overseas posts. Also, the MNC may want to promote management development of headquarters personnel by expanding their perspectives to include global considerations and exposing them to the overall corporate system.

Environmental constraints, costs, and the legal and cultural environments of the host country also affect the courses of action available to the firm. If the cost of relocating and compensating a headquarters employee is prohibitive, a host-country national may be chosen. Also, there may be legal restrictions requiring the use of host-country nationals or restricting the number of foreign personnel allowed into the country. If foreign personnel are allowed into the country, permission from the host government may be slow and difficult to obtain.

DESIRED LOCAL IMAGE

The type of local image the firm portrays is very important. Most MNCs want to have a favorable local image to attract and retain employees and to smooth governmental relations. Choosing a host-country national may reduce tensions with the host government and can result in considerable goodwill that may be of use later. In addition, the image of the firm with the local population may be enhanced, which may increase sales and employee morale.

LOCAL EMPLOYEE INCENTIVES

The hiring of host-country nationals for management positions may give current local employees an incentive to remain with the firm and to work harder because they can see a possible future with the firm through advancement. For this reason, the multinational enterprise may limit the management positions filled by expatriates.

EXISTING METHODS OF SELECTION

An MNC may find personnel for overseas assignments through a number of methods. If it acquires a local, ongoing business, the MNC may select managers for the local operation from the personnel resources of the acquired entity. If the local operation is in the form of a joint venture, the partner in the venture may contribute management expertise and personnel to the project. This may not always be the best alternative, however, because the partner's personnel may lack the necessary technical knowledge, be unfamiliar with the parent firm's practices, and be difficult to control because of an allegiance to the MNC's partner and not the MNC itself.

Home-country records can be used as a tool in selecting management personnel. Personnel records for each employee can include information on technical knowledge, language abilities, willingness to relocate, and the results of any adaptability tests. It is extremely important to consider the spouse of a potential candidate, because it is usually more stressful for an employee's spouse to relocate to a foreign country than it is for an employee.

POTENTIAL FOR CULTURE SHOCK

Culture shock is a pronounced reaction to the psychological disorientation caused by moving to a totally different environment. When a person is relocated to a different country, an initial phase of excitement and enchantment with the new culture is often followed by a period of disillusionment and negative feelings toward the culture. This disillusionment may be because of the employee's inability to adapt or, alternatively, because of a firm's lack of knowledge of a situation and the employee's resulting lack of preparedness for possible difficulties. Culture shock can result in extreme bitterness toward the foreign country and its culture, and even in physical illness. There may also be reverse culture shock when an expatriate is repatriated to the home culture.

Two factors may help to lessen the effects of culture shock: empathy and the avoidance of stereotypes. Empathy is the ability to understand what another person is feeling; in essence, to be able to see the world through another person's eyes. If the expatriate is able to expand this ability to encompass the whole culture, to achieve cultural empathy, that person will go a long way to understanding the views and actions of the members of the foreign culture. Stereotypes can be avoided by thoroughly researching the foreign country prior to relocating in the area. There are various online sources that help educate future expatriates concerning differences that they might encounter while working abroad. There are also books that help ease the transition, such as the *Culture Shock!* series of books, which discuss cultural characteristics in specific countries such as France, Denmark, New Zealand, Argentina, Morocco, the United States, and many others.

TRAINING BRANCH MANAGERS

ALTERNATIVE MODELS

Training is necessary to avoid problems in sending people to work abroad and to ensure project completion. In general, the depth of cross-cultural training for an overseas manager ranges from reading up on the assignment locale to ad hoc corporate training and in-depth immersion programs. A variety of resources are available for training, from how-to books for conducting business abroad to videotapes and orientation programs. The effectiveness of this training correlates with the amount of preparation engaged in prior to a manager's departure for an overseas assignment. The highest degree of expatriate success is experienced by managers who have had individual training tailored to their assignment in a specific country.

One categorization of cross-cultural training programs lists four different training models.[4] The intellectual model consists of readings and lectures about the host culture and assumes that an exchange of information about another culture is effective preparation for living or working in that culture. The area simulation model is a culture-specific training program based on the belief that an individual must be prepared and trained to enter a specific culture. It involves the simulation of future experiences and practice functioning in the new culture.

The self-awareness model is based on the assumption that understanding and accepting oneself is critical to understanding a person from another culture. Sensitivity training is a main component of this method. The cultural awareness model, which is practiced in current progressive training programs, assumes that to function successfully in another culture, an individual must learn the principles of behavior that exist across cultures. Understanding intercultural communication by recognizing that one's own culture influences personal values, behaviors, and cognitions is expected to result in an enhancement of a person's skill at diagnosing difficulties in intercultural communication.

BUSINESS COUNCIL FOR INTERNATIONAL UNDERSTANDING

One example of a comprehensive cross-cultural training program for overseas managers and their families is the program given by the Business Council for International Understanding (BCIU).

The objective of the BCIU Institute is not to just brief managers and family members but to provide them with the tools to ensure their ability to adapt to, or cope with, difficulties encountered abroad. The orientation strives to portray the situation as realistically as possible, which means discussing the negative as well as the positive aspects of overseas assignments.

The program at the institute includes five specific components: language studies, intercultural communications, area and country studies, practical training tailored to the specific country and the manager's functional area, and addressing spousal and family needs.

While the global manager learns some of the practicalities of doing business in the assignment country, family members receive concurrent training on problems to be expected and on alternatives to their current lifestyles. For example, spouses of managers going abroad may have to deal with the issue of trying to find employment in the foreign country or coping with a change from working outside to working inside the home. In some Middle Eastern countries, for example, female spouses are not allowed to work officially but can find jobs through informal channels. Other issues dealt with include managing a domestic staff, raising a family abroad, and transferring activities and interests to a new environment.

COMPENSATING BRANCH MANAGERS

WAGES

There are many problems associated with deciding on the amount of compensation to be given to an overseas manager. The local rate may be above or below the person's current salary, thus causing pay differentials between home- and host-country nationals performing the same job. An expatriate is usually paid an allowance and bonuses above the local rate. Problems arise when a person is transferred to another post or back to headquarters. What salary does the firm pay? Does the firm lower the salary to the old level or keep it elevated? There is also the problem of which currency to use to pay a salary because of fluctuating exchange rates. Compensation is usually paid in some combination of both currencies, thereby allowing tax breaks as well as the ability to save money in the home country.

Allowances are paid to cover the additional costs of living overseas. They are meant to keep the manager's standard of living approximately the same in the foreign country as it was in the home country. Allowances cover the differing costs of housing, food, utilities, transportation, clothing, personal and medical services, and education for any children. In addition, the firm always covers the cost of additional taxes incurred in a foreign country.

Bonuses, though rare, are paid to compensate an employee for any hardships, sacrifices, and inconveniences incurred as a result of the move. Bonuses are usually given only if the manager is assigned to a particularly underdeveloped, violent, or dangerous country.

In addition to allowances and bonuses, a firm usually provides home leaves for expatriates and their families and pay for periodic trips home. Home travel is considered essential for expatriate managers and their families to alleviate the pressures and tensions of overseas assignments.

TAXES

Tax laws vary greatly from country to country. In some countries, foreign workers are taxed only on the income they receive in the country. In the United States, current tax law allows a U.S. citizen to exempt the first US$80,000 of income earned abroad from U.S. taxes. The rest is taxed at the regular rate. If the United States has a tax treaty with the foreign country in question, the amount of foreign taxes paid on unearned income (interest, dividends)

can be credited against the amount of owed U.S. taxes. To get a foreign tax credit on earned income (salaries), expatriates must prove that they have been residents in a foreign country for at least a year and that the assignment to the foreign location is for at least two years.

REPATRIATING BRANCH MANAGERS
REVERSE CULTURE SHOCK

There are three problem areas associated with the repatriation of employees: personal finances, readjustment to home-country corporate structure, and reacclimatization to life in the home country. On reentry into the home country, an expatriate loses all the allowances and bonuses that make foreign assignments appealing. For many, this means a substantial decrease in salary. Also, repatriated employees may find that consumer prices and housing costs have greatly increased during their time abroad.

Once back at headquarters, managers may find that peers have been promoted and that they have less decision-making autonomy and fewer responsibilities. A manager also may feel left out of the corporate information loop. To attract candidates, the corporation should make foreign assignments as prestigious and important as possible in the corporate framework, which will help to ease the transition back into the corporate scheme by increasing the esteem a manager is given at headquarters by his or her peers.

The family of an expatriate may find that their comparative social status has dropped when they return to their home country. In many countries, subsidiary managers are thought of as corporate big wheels representing the entire company and, as such, receive club memberships and invitations to important government and social functions. Once at home, however, the situation changes and they are no longer the center of such attention. Children must adjust to new schools and lifestyles, and spouses who have grown accustomed to domestic help may find themselves on their own again.

To help with the problems associated with repatriation, several steps can be taken while an employee is still at the overseas assignment. The earlier the employee is notified of his or her return, the longer he or she has for adjustment. Headquarters should provide the expatriate with the maximum amount of information available about the new job to allay fears of a demotion. The firm also should bring the employee back to headquarters periodically so that the employee will not feel isolated and forgotten. A mentor might also be assigned to look out for the interests of the expatriate and to help with readjustment. The firm can also provide housing assistance and an orientation program once the family is back.

ETHICAL ISSUES

FEMALE MANAGERS OVERSEAS

There is a definite lack of consideration of women as candidates for expatriate assignments. According to a classic study by Nancy Adler of McGill University, only 3 percent of expatriate managers from 686 North American firms were women.[5] Adler attributes this scarcity to three beliefs held by MNC executives:

1. Women do not want foreign assignments.
2. Corporations resist sending women abroad.
3. Women would not be effective because of the prejudices of foreigners.

Adler refutes the first point, having found that there is no difference between men and women MBAs in attitudes toward overseas assignments. Rather than differences, she found that males and females showed equal interest in pursuing international careers.

Adler found confirmation of the second belief that corporations are indeed hesitant to assign women overseas. The reasons cited by respondents in her study were the prejudices of foreigners, dual-career marriages, a scarcity of women willing to go abroad, and concerns regarding the possible dangers to personnel based overseas from isolation and hardship. In addressing the third point, that corporations assume that women will have reduced effectiveness overseas because of the prejudice of foreigners against women in the work world, Adler asserts that while there "are genuine barriers in many Middle Eastern nations, most countries make a distinction between American women professionals and local women." Since this study was first published, there has been progress in the area of gender equality in the workplace, but there is still room for improvement.

OVERSEAS ASSIGNMENTS AS DUMPING GROUNDS

One important issue that an MNC faces in making decisions on selecting personnel for overseas assignments is the possible use of these assignments to remove undesirable or inefficient executives. This is a dangerous trend, however, that could harm the interests of the corporation in the long run. For example, the demands of an overseas assignment are usually much more complex and intense than those of a domestic assignment, and an executive who is regarded as a failure in a home country could be an even bigger failure overseas. The failure of local operations in one country may not affect the overall bottom line of a large MNC significantly, but it could prove damaging to its global image. Another problem associated with this approach is that the company is not likely to find good personnel in the future willing to take overseas assignments, once it is known within the corporation that these postings have been used to ease out inefficient or difficult personnel.

International Labor Issues

International labor issues are important considerations for multinational corporations operating manufacturing or service facilities in different countries. Managing a labor force that comprises different nationalities, has different work ethics and cultures, is governed by a variety of local laws, and has different traditions of union activities is an extremely complex and often a very difficult proposition.

Managing an International Workforce

Given the differences in union-management relations around the world and the need to maintain a uniform industrial relations policy throughout a corporation, MNCs are invariably faced with the decision of to whom to give the responsibility for handling overall industrial relations. The approach that an MNC takes generally depends on its worldview, whether it is ethnocentric, polycentric, or geocentric. Although MNCs are found to be widely different in their overall management policies from these three standpoints, some do take an ethnocentric view, where the parent office exercises substantial control over the local subsidiaries. When it comes to dealing with industrial relations in different countries, however, most companies give substantial freedom to their local managers to deal with local industrial relations problems.

Different social and political structures, different local laws, varying labor psychology, and unique traditions that influence industrial relations are the primary factors that help to justify this policy, which places substantial responsibility on local managers to deal with industrial relations problems as they arise. Moreover, the active and continuous involvement of local managers in handling local issues provides them with the opportunity to develop an ongoing relationship with workers and union representatives, which is essential to the smooth functioning of any operation and for the building of a basic understanding between management and labor.

Most corporations, however, do insist on a certain level of control by the parent company over the industrial relations policies subsidiaries follow. On most occasions, however, this control simply takes the form of coordination, in which the overall policy is determined by the parent office and local issues are left to the subsidiary managers.

Some major corporations have a tendency to create an industrial relations arrangement in which unions are not a part of the scene. While this could work in certain countries, it may not in others. It is clear that while coordination is workable, central control is not practical in organizing and managing industrial relations in a multinational corporation. Some multinationals use their multiple sourcing and labor-transfer capabilities to exercise leverage against unions in particular countries. For example, if a plant in one country is closed by striking union members, an MNC can shift production to a plant in a different country and maintain its stance against the striking workers in the first country.

Wages and Benefits

Wages and benefits vary around the world. The differences in the levels of wages and benefits workers enjoy are particularly pronounced when those of industrialized countries are compared with those of developing countries. There are also substantial differences within the industrial countries and developing countries themselves.

There are several reasons for these important differences. First, wages are determined by the local cost of living, which may be determined by a comparative index. This general determination is influenced by the existing wages in some industries or comparative industry sectors for comparative jobs. Government legislation or intervention is also a determinant. Many countries have minimum-wage legislation, and some have legislation on maximum wages. Tax issues also influence wage levels, because in high-tax countries companies must pay higher wages or provide additional benefits to offset the impact of higher taxation levels. The level and militancy of union organizations and the capacity for collective bargaining are often important determinants of wage levels.

Patterns of fringe benefits also differ widely. In countries with a strong welfare or socialist sociopolitical orientation, greater emphasis is placed on fringe benefits as a part of the overall compensation package, unlike some industrial nations, where compensation is almost entirely in the form of monetary income. In many countries companies are required by government legislation to pay certain fringe benefits. Thus, the percentage of fringe benefits in the total compensation package varies considerably in different countries.

Workers in Europe have historically received additional compensation according to the number of family members they support, or if they work in unpleasant conditions. In Belgium and the Netherlands, commuting costs have also been reimbursed to workers. One of the most comprehensive fringe benefits systems is in Japan, under which Japanese workers have received a family allowance, housing subsidies, free lunches, free education for their children, and subsidized vacations.

Procedures for increasing levels of compensation also vary considerably. In the United States, the number of union workers has dropped precipitously over the last two decades. Where unions exist, wages are governed usually by labor-management contracts that have a particular life span, customarily three years, after which they have to be renegotiated. Increases are often determined on the basis of a mutually agreed formula that links wage increases to a cost-of-living index. There is room within the general formula for individual wage increases on the basis of performance

during a particular time period, typically a year. In Japan a certain group of unions, which are seen as role models for a particular industry, lead the way for wage negotiation, which takes into account, among other things, the increase in the cost of living since the last wage settlement.

Once agreements have been reached with the leading unions in a particular industry, other unions in the same industry come to an agreement with their managements, more or less on the same basis. Wage increases in Great Britain are somewhat less stable and can be demanded by individual groups of workers within a particular company, and the demands often may not be related to the compensation being paid to workers in different companies in the same industry, or, for that matter, other groups of workers within the same company. Industrywide wages are generally standard in Germany, however, and strikes that demand wage increases outside the scope of industrywide agreements are not recognized. In most developing countries, *collective bargaining* by unions and intervention by the government are the main determinants of wage increases.

Usually MNCs have to pay a relatively higher wage to their employees in developing countries, in comparison to wages being paid for similar work in the industry by domestic companies. This differential wage policy is necessitated by the need for an MNC to counter and prevent criticism from the host government, local politicians, the media, and trade union organizations that it is an agent of foreign exploitation of the country. Foreign exploitation is a particularly sensitive issue in most newly independent developing countries, given these countries' colonial legacy during which they were subjected to substantial economic exploitation by their rulers and by companies from the ruling countries.

JOB SECURITY AND LAYOFFS

Emphasis on job security varies widely from country to country, and MNCs must take into consideration local laws, practices, and socioeconomic conditions while formulating policies and procedures for layoffs, suspensions, and termination of employee services. The emphasis on job security is perhaps the highest in developing countries, where jobs are scarce and there is no system of social security to take care of employees who cannot find other employment. In such countries, layoffs and retrenchments are difficult to implement, because both union and government pressures tend to be strongly against them. Moreover, industry practices in developing countries do not permit layoffs, especially of the type witnessed in the United States, where companies routinely lay off thousands of employees to improve profitability, to restructure the organization, or because demand for the products has fallen off. In fact, to prevent worker hardship, many governments have in the past nationalized operations of MNCs that have decided to lay off large numbers of workers. In developed countries job security is important, although not quite to the same extent as in developing countries. Among the industrialized countries, Japan and Germany place a particularly strong emphasis on job security. Japanese industry has been long noted for its tradition of lifetime employment. Although this is no longer true of a large number of companies in Japan, substantial benefits are available to Japanese workers who lose their jobs, especially because of corporate policies. These benefits include salary payments, retraining, assistance in finding alternative employment, and relocation assistance. Similarly, in Germany assistance is provided to workers who lose their jobs because of corporate decisions. In many instances companies must seek approval from the government and come to an understanding with unions before effecting any significant employee layoffs.

Labor Productivity

Labor productivity is a critical issue for MNCs. It determines, to a significant degree, the level of com-

petitiveness an enterprise can hope to achieve in the local and international markets. Labor productivity varies greatly in different countries, but this variance is not only because of differences in labor quality. In fact, eight factors that are crucial to improvement of labor productivity can be identified:

1. *Government's active role. Laissez-faire* attitudes tend to keep productivity at current levels rather than increasing it.
2. *Worker quality and skills.* The labor force must be constantly upgraded through training in the latest methods and technologies.
3. *Research and development.* A high level of R & D is needed to remain abreast of and preferably ahead of the competition. New products and information must continue in a steady stream.
4. *Business savings and investment* are a major source of capital, R & D, and training.
5. *Personal savings and investment* provide a pool of funds to be used for investments by commercial banks, which in turn stimulate the economy's growth.
6. *Natural resource development and substitution.* Obviously, there is a limit on the amount of natural resources that can be utilized. Thus, new sources must be developed to provide for the needs of business.
7. *Production techniques and systems must be constantly upgraded* and changed because of the high rate of obsolescence. The personal computer industry is a good example.
8. *Management techniques and philosophy.* Management must take a long-term view of the future. Short-term goals have proved to be ineffective and costly, and productivity can be increased only over the long term.

Table 15.1

Manufacturing Productivity, Compensation, Unit Labor Costs, and Unemployment Rate
(average annual rates of change)

	Productivity			Labor Compensation (U.S. dollar basis)		
	1973–87	**1982–87**	**1993–2003**	**1973–87**	**1982–87**	**1993–2003**
United States	2.5	4.5	5.0	7.4	3.5	4.3
Canada	2.1	4.3	2.6	7.2	3.3	1.3
Japan	5.3	4.8	3.5	12.9	15.2	3.3
France	3.9	3.0	4.3	10.5	9.2	2.7
Germany	3.3	3.3	2.7	10.2	11.4	3.2
United Kingdom	3.2	5.5	2.7	10.8	6.0	3.8
	Unit Labor Costs (U.S. dollar basis)			Unemployment Rate (in percent annually)		
	1973–87	**1982–87**	**1993–2003**	**1983**	**1993**	**2003**
United States	4.8	−1.0	−0.7	9.6	6.9	6.0
Canada	5.0	−1.0	1.3	11.5	10.8	6.9
Japan	7.3	10.0	0.3	2.7	2.5	5.3
France	6.4	6.0	−1.4	8.6	11.3	9.3
Germany	6.7	7.8	0.5	6.9	8.0	9.3
United Kingdom	7.4	0.5	1.1	11.8	10.4	5.0

Source: U.S. Department of Labor, Bureau of Labor Statistics.

Table 15.1 provides indexes of manufacturing productivity and other measures for some of the industrialized countries.[6]

TECHNOLOGY

Of the many issues that affect labor productivity, technology is one of the most important and presents major problems to MNCs seeking overseas locations for their plants. Many LDCs have major unemployment problems and are eager to develop industries that are labor intensive and provide maximum job opportunities. Modern technology is often capital intensive, however, and relies on reducing the role of human effort in accomplishing production goals with minimum costs and maximum efficiency.

As a result, in many instances MNCs have to use technology that is relatively less advanced to meet host-country requirements of providing greater job opportunities. Thus, a certain amount of productivity and efficiency has to be sacrificed to gain entry into a new market.

LABOR UNIONS

The concept of collective bargaining is central to the functioning of labor unions. After a union is certified by workers and recognized by management, it is the sole representative of those workers. It represents all the workers collectively when negotiating with management for compensation and working conditions, and signs agreements into legally binding labor contracts. The contracts cover such issues as wages, fringe benefits, holidays, vacations, promotion policies, layoff policies, job-security provisions, stipulations regarding working conditions and safety, administration of the contract, and grievance and dispute settlement.

In the end, the future of trade unions rests largely in their own hands. A few pioneers, notably in the Netherlands, have shown that a willingness to address their own organizational weaknesses (and an acceptance that some social reforms are inevitable) can translate into a much greater degree of influence. Noisy, colorful demonstrations attract media attention and raise the unions' profile. But they are not symptomatic of what influential unions do today, or of what they want to do tomorrow.

United States

Labor-management relations in the United States are relatively nonpolitical, in that the government is not a part of the collective bargaining process, but legislation does establish and enforce rules regarding the framework of collective bargaining (for example, both parties must bargain in good faith). The labor contract is enforceable through the courts, and either side can be sued for any breach of contract. For the most part, collective bargaining takes place at the company or plant level, that is, on a company-by-company basis. Some exceptions include the trucking and construction industries, which have regional contracts, and the steel industry, which has a national contract.

The contract agreed on is usually very extensive and covers almost every contingency. Its terms apply to all workers in the bargaining units, and individual workers cannot negotiate individually with management to obtain better terms. During the life of the contract, strikes and lockouts are usually banned, but if an old contract expires and a new one is still being negotiated, strikes and lockouts are allowed. *Strikes* occur when the workers walk out and refuse

to work. *Lockouts* occur when the employer closes or locks the plant and bars workers from entering. Fans of professional hockey will recall the lockout during the 2004–5 season, when the owners and the players could not agree on an appropriate salary cap; the entire season was canceled. Strikes are generally more frequent than lockouts. A *wildcat strike* occurs when workers strike during the life of an existing contract and give little or no notice. There are relatively few strikes in the United States, but they tend to last a long time. The emphasis in labor relations in the United States is on keeping the firm operating and profitable.

Great Britain

Labor-management relations in Great Britain are much more political and contentious than in the United States. Unions see the negotiation process as more of a class struggle and striking as an exercisable right. The unions are guided by the principle of *voluntarism*, which states that workers alone define and pursue their self-interest, which makes them militant and abrasive with authority, and they have very little regard for the welfare of the enterprise. They are also a powerful political force, in that a major political party, the Labor Party, espouses this class-struggle mentality, but the situation has been changing through the Tory Party, which is trying to institute legal restraints on the unions, based on the belief that too many strikes are destroying the very jobs they are trying to protect by forcing firms into bankruptcy. Great Britain's unions have been subject to new legal constraints and have lost much of their erstwhile unity, while membership has dwindled.

Another problem in Great Britain is the *dualism* of labor representation. Generally, unions are organized on a geographic basis, but there are also councils of stewards that represent only workers at a single company or plant, which results in serious conflicts between the union for the area and the steward's council. For example, the union may reject an agreement that has already been reached between the stewards and the management of a company. The problems resulting from dualism, coupled with the philosophy of voluntarism, lead to numerous strikes. Although unions and workers strike frequently, the strikes are usually not of very long duration.

Germany

In Germany union membership is purely voluntary. There is typically only one union for all workers in a single industry. Labor agreements cover only major issues such as wages. All the other issues, such as vacations and shifts, are negotiated at the plant level. Legally established work councils are able to codetermine issues involving safety and plant practices with management. Members of the work council are elected by the firm's workers. Strikes and lockouts during the life of an existing contract are illegal, regardless of the contract's provisions. They are legal when the existing contract has expired or is being renegotiated. A unique feature of German labor relations is that an individual worker can negotiate individually with management to try to obtain better terms.

Japan

Japanese unions are usually organized by enterprise. A union is made up of employees within a single company or single operational unit, regardless of occupation or position. Legislation in Japan determines minimum wages, working hours per week, overtime, vacation, sick leave, sanitary conditions, and layoff policies and procedures, which leaves little for collective bargaining to accomplish. Thus, negotiations are limited mostly to wages, but wages, positions, and promotions are usually determined through seniority. Every spring all the unions from every company embark on *shunto*, or the spring wage offensive, when the few negotiations take place. Unions want companies to remain profitable for the good of the

groups, so they never ask for too much. This attitude is diametrically opposed to the attitude of the unions in Great Britain. *Shunto* is an effort by the unions to raise wages across the country, so that no single firm becomes less competitive than another. There are very few strikes in Japan, and what strikes there are usually take place during *shunto*. The strikes are for very short periods of time, sometimes only half a day, and merely demonstrate worker support for the unions. Japanese union workers also promote a company's well-being and profitability because its success benefits the whole group.

Given the recession, deflation, and fall in union membership in Japan in recent years, the *shunto* has not been as successful in achieving wage increases on an annual basis. In fact, the recent focus has been on maintaining the existing structure and level of wages, rather than pushing for annual increases as has been done in the past.

MNC TACTICS

Over the past several years, the AFL-CIO has maintained that MNCs have several detrimental effects on U.S. industry. First, MNCs use capital resources for foreign investment that are needed for domestic investment and expansion. Second, MNCs export U.S. technology to other countries to take advantage of low-cost foreign labor, which denies American workers the rewards of using the technology. Third, MNCs replace U.S. exports with foreign-produced goods, which worsens the trade balance and decreases domestic employment. Fourth, MNCs use imports from their subsidiaries in low-wage countries instead of using domestically produced goods.[7] Finally, many MNCs have outsourced jobs to areas of the world with much lower wage rates, such as India and China.

Unions feel threatened by the rising power of MNCs and the advantages they have because of multiple production locales. When a firm decides to locate operations abroad, it is no longer dependent on only domestic plants, and the domestic union has no control over what happens half a world away. Most union concerns are in part because of the huge amount of resources MNCs have at their command. More important, an MNC's power and decision-making capabilities are exercised outside every country in which the MNC operates except the home country.[8] Some of the specific concerns unions have regarding MNCs include:

- MNCs' ability to relocate facilities if a contract is not agreeable to them.
- Restricted access to data by unions, especially financial data, to combat MNCs. For example, if an MNC says it is losing money on overseas operations and thus needs to cut labor costs, the union cannot confirm or deny this statement.
- An MNC's ability to choose where to locate and thus take advantage of differences in the amount and level of benefits they are required to provide by law.
- An MNC's ability to withstand strikes by threatening to close the facility and relocate. Because that factory is only one part of the corporation, the MNC is able to obtain cash and production from other plants.

Wal-Mart recently closed a store location in Quebec, Canada, when workers attempted to create the first unionized Wal-Mart store in North America.

COUNTERTACTICS BY LABOR

Unions only hope for competing with MNCs lies in international rules and regulations and international cooperation. Two main international labor organizations make efforts in this direction.

The International Labor Organization

The *International Labor Organization (ILO)* was established in 1919 under the Treaty of Versailles.

It is now affiliated with the United Nations and is composed of government, industry, and union representatives. Its premise is that the failure of any country to promote humane working conditions is an obstacle to nations that want to improve conditions in their own countries. The ILO tries to define and promote international standards regarding safety, health, and other working conditions.

Organisation for Economic Cooperation and Development

The Organisation for Economic Cooperation and Development (OECD) also consists of government, industry, and union representatives. It has developed a set of voluntary guidelines for MNCs and for host countries regarding labor conditions and fair practices. The organization is based in Paris but does not have any enforcement mechanisms in international jurisdictions.

The European Union

The European Union also attempts to coordinate the evolution of industrial relations standards within its member countries by issuing directives on issues of common concern. These directives are approved by the council of ministers before they become effective. Existing directives cover such issues as employee participation on company boards, the safeguarding of employee interests, and the right of employee representatives to information and consultation in the event of a change in the ownership of a business. Some of the EU directives, once accepted by the council of ministers, are incorporated into member states' national laws. The impact of EU directives on member states' national labor laws is increasing, especially as integration becomes closer.

INTERNATIONAL UNIONS

The prospect of international unions sounds very promising for solving many problems. International unions could employ transnational bargaining, which would mean a centralized and coordinated collective bargaining strategy between an employer and a union or group of unions for employees in facilities located in two or more nations.[9] In other words, one union could negotiate for all the plants that a single firm has around the world, thus guaranteeing equal treatment for all workers and restoring the power of the unions. In the real world, this is much easier said than done. The few international unions that exist are in similar countries, such as the United States and Canada.

CODETERMINATION

One final possibility of increasing the impact of workers on firms is the concept of codetermination. *Codetermination* means employee participation in management. An early example of codetermination was in the German coal and steel industries in 1951. By law, codetermination gave the representatives of workers and shareholders each 50 percent of the directorships, with one neutral director to break any ties. Codetermination has gained importance in many other countries as the emphasis of collective bargaining shifts, little by little, to agreements and counterbalancing of labor-management interests.

SUMMARY

The four most common structures used by MNCs to organize and manage operations are functional, regional, product line, and matrix structures. Staffing is crucial for MNCs because of technological advances, worldwide competition for skilled labor, and the constant need to increase productivity, reduce costs, and increase intracompany communication and information flows. International staffing involves recruitment, selection, training, and motivation and requires a bicultural sensitivity toward the host-country environment. High failure rates among expatriate managers have caused MNCs to carefully select and train global managers.

International staffing may involve filling the management position with expatriates, host-country nationals, or third-country nationals; each selection offers different advantages and disadvantages. Staff selection is affected by the availability of trained candidates in the host-country location, corporate policies regarding local versus corporate control, a candidate's knowledge of the local environment, the local image the MNC wants to project, and employment incentives. Also, the candidate's technical skills, language abilities, and adaptability must be evaluated. Adaptability assessment through an early-identification program test is important to minimize the effects of management, culture shock, and ineffectiveness on local operations. Cross-cultural training techniques are useful in reducing candidate failure rates and help ensure their success.

Specialized compensation arrangements for international managers make these positions very attractive. Income taxes and repatriation, however, can be problematic for an international manager. Gender biases in many countries may slow foreign assignments for female managers. The dumping of inefficient personnel in international positions may occur but can harm an MNC's long-term interests.

International managers are faced with a diversity of nationalities, languages, cultures, and work ethics, which can complicate motivation and management of the local labor force. To develop management-labor relations essential for efficient operations, local managers must have sufficient authority and flexibility. Centralized corporate control, through industrial relations policy, however, is required to achieve MNC-wide cohesion. Host-country laws and practices also may limit local management flexibility.

Wage and fringe benefit systems should reflect local costs of living and the extent of existing social welfare benefits. Further, to prevent criticism from host governments, local media, and trade unions, MNCs must be careful not to exploit lesser-developed countries in terms of wages and benefits. Policies and procedures for employee layoffs, suspensions, and terminations must also reflect the traditions and practices of the host country.

Labor productivity can vary in different countries. Improvements in productivity are a function of government support, worker quality and skill, research and development, innovation, business savings and investment, personal savings and investment, natural resources, production systems, and management techniques and philosophies. Because modern technology is capital intensive and may be unavailable in a host country, MNCs can sacrifice productivity and efficiency for low labor costs when expanding production into new markets. Labor relations and the role of unions also differ among nations, with some having a stronger union presence than others. International unions are seeking greater cooperation across national boundaries, but nationalistic attitudes, different goals, and physical distance may impede their growth. Codetermination is a recent development that attempts to increase worker influence and responsibilities in MNC operations.

DISCUSSION QUESTIONS

1. When staffing an MNC for positions outside the home country, what are some advantages and disadvantages of hiring host-country nationals? Expatriates?
2. What is a global manager?
3. Why do expatriate managers frequently receive additional compensation over their colleagues at equivalent positions in the corporate office? Why are these packages more complicated than packages provided to domestic employees?
4. What problems do expatriates face at the completion of their foreign assignments?
5. What obstacles do female executives encounter when seeking international positions?

6. Before investing in a production plant in a foreign country, what are some of the questions concerning labor management that an MNC should address?
7. What is collective bargaining? How does collective bargaining differ in the United States, Great Britain, Germany, and Japan?
8. How is productivity affected by a shortage of skilled labor?

NOTES

1. Harris and Moran, *Managing Cultural Differences.*
2. Tung, "Strategic Management of Human Resources in the Multinational Enterprise."
3. Harris and Moran, *Managing Cultural Differences.*
4. Ibid.
5. Adler, "Expecting International Success: Female Managers Overseas."
6. U.S. Department of Labor, Bureau of Labor Statistics.
7. Levine, "Labor Movements and the Multinational Corporation: A Future for Collective Bargaining?"
8. Ibid.
9. Ibid.

BIBLIOGRAPHY

Adler, Nancy. "Expecting International Success: Female Managers Overseas." *Columbia Journal of World Business*, Fall 1984, 82.

Campbell, Duncan C. "Multinational Labor Relations in the European Community." *ILR Report*, Fall 1989, 7–14.

Charnovitz, Steve. "The Influence of International Labor Standards on the World Trading Regime." *International Labor Review*, September–October 1987, 9–17.

Clarke, Christopher J., and K. Breenan. "Building Synergy in the Diversified Business." *Long Range Planning*, April 1990, 9–16.

Daniels, J.D. "Approaches to European Regional Management by Large U.S. Multinational Firms." *Management International Review*, Vol. 1, No. 2, 1986, 27–42.

Dowling, Peter J. "Human Resource Issues in International Business." *Syracuse Journal of International Law and Commerce*, Winter 1987, 255–71.

———. "Hot Issues Overseas." *Personnel Administrator*, January 1989, 66–72.

Duff, Mike. "Hands Across the Water." *Supermarket Business*, February 1985, 45, 47.

Fanning, W.R., and A.F. Arvin. "National or Global? Control Versus Flexibility." *Long Range Planning*, October 1986, 84–88.

Gellerman, Saul W. "In Organizations, As in Architecture, Form Follows Function." *Organizational Dynamics*, Winter 1990, 57–68.

Harris, Phillip R., and Robert T. Moran. *Managing Cultural Differences*. Houston, TX: Gulf Publishing Company, 1987.

Hogan, Gary W., and Jane R. Goodson. "The Key to Expatriate Success." *Training and Development*, January 1990, 50–52.

Leontiades, James. "Going Global—Global Strategies Versus National Strategies." *Long Range Planning*, December 1986, 96–104.

Levine, Marvin. "Labor Movements and the Multinational Corporation: A Future for Collective Bargaining?" *Employee Relations Law Journal*, Winter 1987–88, 47–57.

Morgenstern, Felice. "The Importance, in Practice, of Conflicts of Labor Law." *International Labor Review*, March–April 1985, 119–30.

Narasimhan, R., and J.R. Carter. "Organization, Communication and Coordination of International Sourcing." *International Marketing Review* 7 (1990): 6–20.

Ray, George F. "International Labor Costs in Manufacturing, 1960–88." *National Institute Economic Review*, May 1990, 67–70.

Savich, R.S., and W. Rodgers. "Assignment Overseas: Easing the Transition Before and After." *Personnel*, August 1988, 44–48.

Schultz, T. Paul. "Women's Changing Participation in the Labor Force: A World Perspective." *Economic Development and Cultural Change*, April 1990, 457–88.

Servais, J.M. "The Social Clause in Trade Agreements: Wishful Thinking or an Instrument of Social Progress?" *International Labor Review* 128 (1989): 423–32.

Staiger, Robert W. "Organized Labor and the Scope of International Specialization." *Journal of Political Economy*, October 1988, 1022–47.

Tung, Rosalie. "Strategic Management of Human Resources in the Multinational Enterprise." *Human Resource Management*, Summer 1984, 129.

U.S. Department of Labor, Bureau of Labor Statistics, http://stats.bls.gov/, accessed April 25, 2006.

Weisz, Morris. "A View of Labor Ministries in Other Nations." *Monthly Labor Review*, July 1988, 19–23.

CASE STUDY 15.1

REMAGEN BROTHERS LTD.

The protest meeting at the locked gates of Remagen Brothers Ltd. was getting increasingly turbulent. More than 2,000 unionized workers of the Weranpura factory were demanding a 26 percent increase in wages and an increase in the number of paid holidays to 21. The management's offer of a 9 percent pay increase led to a fairly quick breakdown in negotiations. The workers had gone on an indefinite strike that was now in its nineteenth day, with no chance of settlement.

Remagen's Weranpura plant had a history of troubled industrial relations from its outset. The plant was located in an industrial park set up by the government of Trivana, a small island country in South Asia. Remagen Brothers was a leading cosmetics, toiletries, and detergent manufacturer based in the Netherlands, with factories and other operations in 82 countries around the world. With sales revenues exceeding US$2 billion annually, Remagen was a leading multinational in the industry, and its products had a well-differentiated brand image and enjoyed considerable brand loyalty worldwide. Remagen's decision to invest in Weranpura was motivated primarily by the attractive incentives offered by the Trivanian government in the special industrial zone. Remagen was allowed to import all its plant equipment as well as raw materials and intermediate products free of customs duties. The government provided excellent infrastructural facilities to the company, including banking and financial services within the industrial park zone. Remagen's income from its Weranpura factory also was free from Trivanian taxes for five years and after that was to be taxed at a special rate. Profits and other remittances out of Trivana were freely allowed, although periodic reports had to be filed with the central bank.

Attracted by these incentives, Remagen's senior management had made the decision to establish a large plant to manufacture soaps and detergents to be marketed primarily in Southeast Asia. Trivana's labor costs were even lower than those of Southeast Asia, and Remagen's products were expected to have the edge needed to penetrate that highly competitive market.

Although Remagen's planners focused on the economics provided by Trivana's labor, other aspects of the local labor force were not studied in detail. Weranpura was located in the southeastern part of Trivana, which had a predominantly Marxist political orientation. All plants in the Weranpura industrial zone were unionized, and almost all the unions were affiliated with the People's Movement for Labor Rights (PMLR), an avowed Marxist labor federation that continually advocated militant action on the part of its affiliated unions to secure labor rights.

Remagen's managers began to sense the difficulties that lay ahead when the commissioning of the plant was delayed by a month because of a sudden strike by the workers of the plant's packaging unit. Top management, however, eager to start production, decided to lay off all the striking employees and hire new ones in their place. The view at that point was that the company should not be cowed by the union and should adopt a strong stance. This view was based on the fact

continued

Case 15.1 (*continued*)

that Remagen was paying at least 10 percent higher wages than any other employer in the Weranpura industrial zone and could hire new workers whenever it wanted.

This view did not prove to be an effective strategy in dealing with labor issues. Once the workers were fully unionized, it became difficult to terminate the services of employees.

The union provided excellent legal help for all its members, and an employee could involve the company in a long, fractious, and expensive litigation process. Labor laws in Trivana heavily favored employees over employers, and Remagen had no financial advantage it could leverage in the litigation process.

Further, the workers were now governed more by the orders of union leaders than by the edicts of the personnel department. The union's management was prone to ordering strikes even if a single employee was to be replaced.

During its first two years, the company had, therefore, adversarial industrial relations, and 87 workdays had been lost because of strikes. The management's policy continued to be based on maintaining a strong posture against the militant trade unions and refusing to give in to their demands. In the early strikes, although the company did lose workdays, the unions were not able to make much headway. The personnel department of Remagen's head office was pleased with the record of the Weranpura management, and the personnel manager had received two letters of commendation. This strike, however, was different. The workers and their leaders were apparently bent upon getting the company to agree to their demands. Further, it was also clear that the PMLR federation was providing financial support to the striking employees and

that with this support they could carry on the strike indefinitely.

The local manager of Remagen's personnel division, Vijaya Ratnapure, was of the opinion that this time the company should negotiate with the striking workers and raise the level of compensation it was willing to offer in order to bring it nearer to union demands. He reasoned that the company's image in Weranpura was at stake, and the PMLR had successfully carried out a campaign against it by branding Remagen a "foreign exploiter." The government, although somewhat centrist in its political inclinations, was sensitive to the views of the PMLR, because the next provincial elections were in six months, and there was talk of an alliance between the ruling party and the Marxists in this region. Therefore, if matters came to a head, Remagen could, at best, expect the government to be a mute bystander, caught between its political priorities and eagerness to attract overseas investment in special industrial zones. Perhaps it would be better, argued Ratnapure, to involve the leaders of the PMLR in the talks, as the union leaders had been demanding, which would be viewed as a major concession and perhaps could lead to a moderation of the worker demands on the compensation package.

Johann Michuft, the general manager of the plant, was initially taken aback by Ratnapure's suggestion, which seemed to go almost directly against the company's global industrial relations management policy. The company had a standard policy to make a firm and final offer, in line with industry wages (or better), in terms of compensation. Further, management's policy was not to negotiate with any party other than the bona fide representatives of the plant's unions.

continued

Case 15.1 (*continued*)

Talking to PMLR's representatives would clearly violate this policy. The company was doing quite well, and it could afford to give a raise to the workers that would be in line with what they were demanding, but that amount would be way ahead of the industry average in Weranpura (although much lower than wages paid to workers for similar jobs in the company's plants in Europe and North America). Further, dealing with the PMLR would be seen as a sign of weakness on the part of the company's management and could lead to another set of demands.

On the other hand, if the company did not negotiate with the unions and the representatives of the PMLR, it faced the possibility of a long-drawn-out strike that could result in the closure of this highly profitable plant. Moreover, the company's image as an employer would suffer in many countries of the region, where it was planning to establish other manufacturing facilities.

As he pondered these issues, Michuft typed a confidential memorandum to send to headquarters in the Netherlands, seeking instructions on whether company policy could be modified in Weranpura.

DISCUSSION QUESTION

1. What would be your instructions to Michuft if you were the director of international human resource management at Remagen's world headquarters in the Netherlands?

CASE STUDY 15.2
AIR AMERICA

Herbert Manning, general manager of Air America's Qamran office, had been with the company for 12 years. Manning had an undergraduate degree in economics and business and had worked for a leading travel agency in San Francisco, California, before joining Air America as a sales executive. With his earlier experience and his enthusiasm and energy on the job, Manning had made a favorable impression within the company very quickly. Within two years he had been promoted to the rank of area sales manager and had been elected vice president of Air America's worldwide sales club, having had the second highest amount of sales among all of Air America's sales executives worldwide. Manning continued to perform well as area sales manager, and three years later he was moved to the company's corporate headquarters in Dallas, Texas. His headquarters assignment was a major move upward; he was named vice president of international marketing and sales with responsibility for planning and implementing the company's marketing and sales strategies in the Middle East, Africa, and southern Asia. Air America, though a major international airline, was not very strong in these markets, which it perceived would become increasingly important in the future. Manning took up the challenge with his well-known drive and energy, and during the next three years, Air America succeeded in negotiating air route agreements with four countries in North Africa, three in the Middle East, and three in southern Asia. Qamran, a small sheikdom in the Middle East, was designated as the regional base for

this area and as a hub location for the airline. In three years, Manning's region had become an important source of revenue from international operations for Air America. Apart from an aggressive and well-targeted sales policy, overall increase in passenger traffic arising out of the oil price boom helped to boost ticket sales.

Toward the end of the third year, however, Air America, like many other airlines operating in the region, was suddenly hit with a sharp decline in demand as oil prices rose sharply and the world economy went into a deep recession. As the market shrank, competition intensified, and it became increasingly difficult to hold on to market share. By 2004 Air America's share of the Persian Gulf market had dropped by 7 percent and, combined with a sharp decline in overall market size, led to a steep reduction in total revenues.

Concerned with the difficult situation in the region, Air America's senior management decided that an aggressive strategy had to be adopted to recapture market share and rebuild the airline's image as a dominant force in the region. A key element of the strategy was to appoint Manning as the regional manager of the Middle East and North Africa.

It was a big promotion for Manning. Regional managers were considered to be senior management in the company and were responsible for participating in the formulation of global strategy. Moreover, Air America's corporate policy was one of considerable delegation and decentralization. Regional managers were, therefore almost completely independent in their local opera-

continued

Case 15.2 (*continued*)

tions and were primarily responsible for their own results. Manning was elated when his boss told him the news. He had wanted to go back to the field for some time now, and the position apparently offered all that he was looking for. In addition, relocation as a regional manager in Qamran meant that he would have several liberal fringe benefits given to Air America's expatriate managers: a large, furnished company house, a chauffeur-driven car, at least four servants, and additional allowances, including a large entertainment budget.

Manning's first year was extremely successful. He brought a new level of drive and enthusiasm to his job, which was infused throughout the local office, because he set a good example by his own untiring efforts. His years in the marketing division had provided him with considerable background knowledge of the operations, and he used that knowledge to seek and implement new ways to fight off Air America's competitors. Market share began to inch back upward and the revenue drop was reversed. Although the revenues were helped by a slight improvement in market conditions, there was no doubt that Manning's arrival had been a key factor in the reversal of Air America's fortunes in the region.

The second year was good, too, although not as good as the first. Market share increased, as did the revenues by smaller degrees. One significant explanation for the slowing of increases offered by Manning was that other airlines had initiated equally aggressive counterstrategies, and it was not possible to improve the rate of America's gains without seriously compromising profitability.

Results started to decline in the third year, however. Market share gains slid back by 2 percent and revenues showed a slight decline. Manning seemed to have lost the drive and initiative that had characterized his work just a few months before, and some of Manning's subordinates seemed unhappy with his behavior and left the company. Gilbert Wyles, Air America's senior vice president of human resources, was quick to guess that the problem was Manning and decided that a meeting would be useful to discuss the whole issue. Manning was after all a star performer, and if he was facing any problems the company was fully prepared to help him.

The meeting lasted three hours. Manning was initially hesitant to state the real problem and hedged around the issue, in vague terms, calling the difficulties personal matters. When asked to be more specific, however, and realizing that he had a sympathetic audience, Manning came out with it. The real problem, he said, was his wife's difficulties in adjusting to life in Qamran. Back in the United States, she was a client relations executive in a small advertising company. It was not a very high position, but it was important to her. She liked the job; it enabled her to keep busy and do something every day, and allowed her to use her skills at dealing with people constructively. She had developed a fairly close network of good friends and a large circle of pleasant acquaintances through her job. Her decision to leave the job and accompany Manning to Qamran had not been easy, but she had been sporting about it and had decided to make the best of a new lifestyle that awaited her in their new overseas home. She did make a sincere

continued

Case 15.2 (*continued*)

effort at adjustment, but Qamran's society was governed by strict Islamic tenets, which meant that social freedoms for women were severely restricted. Although the Mannings had a nice social life, with a number of social activities involving diplomats and other expatriates, there was nothing much she could do during the day. Women were not allowed to work in Qamran, and they were granted special work permits only in exceptional cases. Even then women had to dress in a particular fashion prescribed by the authorities.

After the first year, Mrs. Manning grew increasingly restless about her new situation. Her problems were accentuated by the long absences of her husband, who went on frequent business trips that were essential to the success of his assignment. Mrs. Manning thought of various solutions and different ways in which her life could be made more interesting, but nothing worked, and the mental discomfort of Mrs. Manning continued to increase. In the past few months, Mrs. Manning had had long periods of depression and was not responding very well to treatment, which caused Manning tremendous anxiety and had adversely affected his professional performance.

Gilbert Wyles suggested that Manning take a vacation quickly, at the place of his choice, and that by the time he returned the company would have an answer to his problem. Manning was somewhat relieved, but at the same time he was skeptical of the company's intentions. As he walked out of the corporate headquarters to catch a cab for his hotel, he wondered whether he had done the right thing.

Meanwhile, Wyles, in his well-appointed office, got busy, putting together a confidential memo to the international human resources policy group, a small set of top Air America executives in charge of framing company policies in international human resources management. The memo explained the background and circumstances of the situation and placed three options before the members:

1. The option suggested by Manning, to give Mrs. Manning a job in his office in Qamran as a public relations officer. This was possible, if the group were to modify the company policy on employment of spouses and enough pressure was exerted on the Qamran government.
2. Replace Manning with another expatriate executive, which could be easily done, but there might be similar problems for the replacement.
3. Appoint a local national as regional manager or bring in a third-country national from its other overseas offices.

DISCUSSION QUESTIONS

1. Which of the three options would you recommend to Air America and why? What would be the problems with the other options?
2. Is there a need for Air America to change its international staffing policies to avoid sending expatriate managers to overseas locations?

CHAPTER 16

Managing Operations and Technology

OPERATIONS, TECHNOLOGY, AND INTERNATIONAL COMPETITION

With increasing worldwide competition, the strategic implications of decisions concerning an MNC's choices for operations and technology become even more important than they normally are. These two elements influence where and how a company operates. Decisions regarding what an MNC will produce and in what location and to maintain a competitive edge are closely related to its technological and operational resources. Although some international business experts have chosen to treat technology and production in the international arena as separate factors, the two are interrelated issues because of the impact that technology has on international production decisions.

INTERNATIONAL PRODUCTION AND OPERATIONS

International management of operations and production may be very similar to the management of operations and production in a home country. Common to both are considerations regarding the efficient use of all the factors of production, productivity improvements, R & D, and the extent of horizontal or vertical integration, or both. The international environment, however, includes other considerations. Before making production decisions, an MNC must consider such additional factors as different wage rates, industrial relations, sources of financing, foreign exchange risk, international tax laws, control, the appropriate mix of capital and labor, access to suppliers, and the production-experience curve in each country. While many MNCs attempt to standardize their production systems on a worldwide basis by transferring production processes and procedures unchanged from the parent corporation, these environmental influences often make such standardization unsuccessful or at best difficult.

WORLDWIDE STANDARDIZATION

On one hand, there is strong justification for worldwide standardization. First, the capacity of management to develop a successful organization is improved, primarily by making it easier to carry out the home office management functions. Organization and staffing are simpler when overseas production facilities are replications of existing facilities, because future plants are reduced or enlarged versions of existing plants, and there are fewer labor hours and fewer costs involved with plant design. In addition, because technical-assistance workers are familiar with the standard plant design, the overseas technical staff can be smaller, and home-based technical workers can assist the foreign operation on an as-needed basis. Furthermore, production specifications are more easily maintained and updated. If

changes are necessary in production specifications, there is no need for a plant-by-plant evaluation to determine which operations are affected, which also implies cost savings in specifications maintenance for unified production processes.

SUPPLY

The second area that experiences direct benefits from standardization is supply. Increased profits are realized when all production facilities can be organized into one logistics system for supplies. This single system details the activities among suppliers, facilities, and consumers, and determines the corresponding requirements for raw materials and inventory (parts and finished products). In addition, with production processes standardized, machinery and parts necessary for the process are also standardized, allowing for interchangeable parts and machinery.

The option of using a production rationalization strategy is available if a company chooses to standardize product offerings, even if only regionally. Under *rationalization*, a subsidiary changes its purpose for production from manufacturing for its own market to manufacturing a limited number of component parts for use by several or all subsidiaries. This strategy has the advantage of production and engineering economies of scale and allows for higher-volume production with lower production costs than if the subsidiary manufactured for only end-product sales in its local market.

CONTROL

Control is also affected by worldwide standardization. When all manufacturing facilities are expected to adhere to the same standards, quality control is easier to monitor, with quicker response to variances in quality control reports. Similarly, while human and physical factors affect production and maintenance standards, machinery is expected to produce at the same rate of output and with the same frequency of maintenance service. It is possible to schedule maintenance of equipment based on historical records of similar equipment to avoid costly unexpected breakdowns.

Planning and design of production facilities under standardization strategies are also simpler and quicker to complete. Donald A. Ball and Wendell H. McCulloch Jr. list five steps in the process for planning a new plant based on a standardized system:[1]

1. Design engineers need only copy the drawings and lists of materials that they have in their files.
2. Vendors are requested to furnish equipment that they have supplied previously.
3. The technical department can send the current manufacturing specifications without alteration.
4. Labor trainers experienced in the operation of machinery can be sent to the new location without undergoing specialized training on new equipment.
5. Reasonably accurate forecasts of plant erection time and output can be made based on the experience with existing facilities.

With all of these advantages, it would appear that MNCs would strive for standardization, but environmental forces affect host-nation operations, resulting in a variety of sizes, equipment, and procedures for plant operations of the same company. In addition to the environmental forces, the plant designer must consider economic, cultural, and political forces that may limit or at least affect direct alternatives.

STRATEGIC CONTROL
Areas to Control

The control process involves continuous monitoring of the strategic plan to measure its effectiveness and to make corrections where necessary, either in the plan itself or in compliance.

Three major areas of importance to an MNC with regard to controlling international operations include control of foreign exchange risk, adjustments needed in routine control systems because of differences in various branch operating environments, and control of risks arising out of foreign operations, including relations with host governments.

Establishing systems of internal control is far more difficult in an MNC than in a domestic enterprise. The communication of goals, objectives, and corrections may be impeded by the distance between the parent company and its branch or subsidiary, as well as by differences in languages and operating procedures. The form of an operation may be such that a firm may have only partial ownership and thus may not have full authority to impose control measures. Similarly, the operating environment may have external forces that make the control measures unachievable. For example, an attempt to bring sales profitability levels up to corporate objectives by raising prices might be stymied in a foreign environment because of host-government controls on price levels.

Locating Decision Authority

The key factor in the control process for an MNC is the location of the decision-making authority between headquarters and subsidiaries. This problem is often referred to as centralization versus decentralization of control. Centralized decision making vests all important decisions with the headquarters of the firm, while decentralized decision making means that decisions are made entirely under the authority of subsidiary heads. These situations represent extreme ends of a continuum, but there is middle ground, where some decisions come from headquarters and others remain within the subsidiary.

The structuring of the locus of authority for

decision making includes a trade-off between the realization of different objectives. While centralized decision making provides for the overall integration of objectives and potential efficiencies for a firm in worldwide operations, it also distances subsidiary management from making valuable inputs to the process and adding their own expertise to provide for local operating efficiencies. Total decentralization of decision making may provide for local efficiencies, but it could also result in a loss of control by headquarters and in overall systemwide suboptimal operations.

The types of decisions involved include resource allocation, acquisition of capital equipment, employment of personnel, and use of liquid or capital assets. Other decisions involve the use of profits, determination of prices, reinvestment or repatriation of earnings, and determination of the sources and prices to be paid for raw materials or inventory goods. Decision authority regarding marketing and production, such as adaptations to products and product lines, markets served and methods of serving those markets, types of promotion and distribution, and channels to be utilized, must be allocated between the parent and the subsidiary or affiliate.

The degree of autonomy accorded to subsidiaries by MNCs depends on a number of factors, one of which is the mode of international operations. International activities, such as licensing and export functions, are usually carried out from corporate headquarters, but affiliates or subsidiaries based abroad require some degree of localized decision making to keep operations efficient.

Another factor is the nature of the industry and its technology. If a company's advantage is based in product development and the marketing of these products using the same technology worldwide, the firm is likely to have centralized decision making.

An MNC's size and maturity also help determine decision-making authority. An older, larger MNC might concentrate experienced personnel at headquarters and coordinate activities and decision making from that centralized location, while a younger, smaller operation might operate in an ad hoc manner and continue to locate decision-making authority in the subsidiary because the company lacks experienced personnel to run those functions from the central location.

The competence of subsidiary managerial staff plays a large part in the determination of whether decision-making authority should be placed there or not. If local personnel are of high quality with good experience and business judgment, they will be given more authority.

Similarly, centralization of decision making is affected by the local political environment and the sensitivity of an industry. An industry such as telecommunications is more sensitive to local political pressure because it is deemed essential to the welfare of the host country. Thus, local powers would impose pressure for more decentralized than centralized authority in the subsidiary.

In some countries the vesting of authority in local personnel may be an issue of political sensitivity with regard to the welfare of home-country nationals. In many situations, the host government feels that centralized authority and decision making by an MNC disenfranchises host-country nationals from authority, retarding their educational and career growth and, in turn, the development process overall.

If a decision needs to be made quickly, it is more likely to be made locally. Similarly, the importance or magnitude of a decision also influences its reference to headquarters or not. Generally, headquarters gets into the act of making decisions about large amounts of assets or strategic activities, such as the expansion of production capacity, the acquisition of capital assets, and the introduction or development of new products.

Branch Goals Versus Headquarters Goals

In addition to the factors that are characteristic of an industry, a subsidiary, and the decisions themselves, the locus of decision making is also affected by two potentially opposing forces: the objectives of the parent firm and those of the subsidiary. Subsidiary managers may, for example, be directed to set prices at certain levels or to allocate the results of production to other subsidiaries and not to high-profit markets. These decisions may benefit an MNC in the aggregate but reduce the subsidiary's performance. Thus, any benefits to the overall firm through the centralization of decision making may be negated by increasing frustration at the subsidiary level, which may lead to a lack of motivation or performance problems on the part of the subsidiary staff. The result of opposing pressure is a balancing act among the efficiencies to be achieved through centralization; the allocation of resources, assets, and profits among subsidiaries; the allocation of resources, assets, and profits between branches of a firm; and the operating integrity of the subsidiary. If an MNC truly operates from a global perspective, the overall coordination of the operations must be integrated in a worldwide system.

Other Control Concerns

Other control concerns arise in situations in which firms lack full ownership of a subsidiary and operate instead in a cooperative agreement or a joint venture. In these instances, an MNC may find its hands tied in efforts to centralize operations control of the affiliate.

An MNC must decide at the outset its minimum required level of control, but it must be realistic about limitations on its ability to control, and it must accept that it may not be able to make unfettered decisions regarding the allocation of production from the subsidiary or the repatriation or reinvestment of its resources.

Another control concern deals with the selection of a subsidiary's managerial staff. While an MNC can gain additional control from the use of expatriate corporate staff, it could lose access to the home-country operating environment. Thus, some firms make it a practice to use host-country nationals in subsidiaries but also provide training and exposure to operations in corporate headquarters to familiarize them with the corporate culture, objectives, policies, and procedures. The goal is to provide subsidiary executives a common basis with headquarters staff.

Evaluation of branch managers is a final important aspect of international control. The optimal situation is one that balances the objectives of an enterprise and its subsidiary in determining performance criteria. Thus, a subsidiary manager's performance should not be judged according to profits from sales if the MNC objective (as determined centrally) is to gain market share through lowered prices in the market served by the subsidiary, or if the central authorities determine that production should be allocated to other arms of the company. Instead, the manager's performance should be evaluated according to relevant criteria, which are both quantitative and qualitative. In this way, performance appraisal is divorced from operational profitability and is linked instead to criteria more relevant and appropriate to the situation.

DESIGNING THE LOCAL OPERATIONS SYSTEM

The local operational system will be somewhat reflective of the parent organization. For example, a foreign subsidiary is usually a smaller version of the parent company and has a similar organizational structure. If a parent company is structured according to functional divisions, for example, the foreign subsidiary will also be organized by functional departments. Furthermore, because the local operational system is most likely to be smaller than that of the parent company, it will not be integrated vertically or horizontally. Because of the increased investment necessary for vertical integration, it is often only conducted to the extent necessary to obtain scarce raw materials. Also, countries such as Mexico require foreign manufacturers to purchase inputs from local suppliers and legally restrict *vertical integration*, or expanding business into areas that are within the same production chain. As for *horizontal integration*, or expanding into related product lines, the subsidiary is unlikely to expand in such a way because it often becomes a conglomerate in its own right.

There are four elements in the design of a production system: plant location, plant layout, materials handling, and staffing. These elements, while directly applicable to the production of tangible goods, can also be applied to the design of a system for the production of services.

PLANT LOCATION

Factors affecting plant location include government incentives, land and labor costs, location of competition, employee preference, location of suppliers and infrastructure (such as ports), and conditions imposed by local authorities. Which particular factors will be most important depends to a great extent on the type of investment, such as market seeking, labor efficiency, or extraction mining. Because production and distribution costs are frequently in conflict, a plant designer often must choose between locating away from a major city because of government incentives and lower land and labor costs, on one hand, and locating near an urban center because of the availability of skilled labor, access to consumer markets, and a better infrastructure to support transportation, on the other.

PLANT LAYOUT

Plant layout should be determined before building construction. The plant not only will need to ac-

commodate current production needs for maximum utilization and return on investment, but also must include possibilities for future expansion. Accurate forecasts become crucial in terms of estimating future plant requirements, but plant layout may also be dictated occasionally by acquisition of an existing building.

MATERIALS HANDLING

Management may be able to achieve considerable production costs savings by careful planning for materials handling. Materials handling includes obtaining necessary inputs and maintaining appropriate inventories. If materials handling is inefficient, management may find surplus parts inventories at some sites, while other sites are shut down because of a lack of parts. The logistics of the production system, or coordination of the movements and storage of inputs and outputs, are an intricate part of the materials-handling function. The objectives of an MNC's logistics system are to minimize costs, secure supplies, and satisfy demand. For the ethnocentric MNC, logistics are confined to exporting with the least cost and in the least amount of time. Polycentric MNCs, on the other hand, have a tendency to de-emphasize logistics. The foreign subsidiary of such an MNC may not have rapid response to the introduction of new products by competitors or to excess demand or production shortfalls. The *geocentric* MNC will most likely maintain a separate logistics department that coordinates the activities among the markets, production location, and suppliers of its many subsidiaries.

STAFFING

The labor element is often overlooked in the design of a production system. The human factor, however, can be the key to the success of a production plant. Because temperature, lighting, noise level, and aesthetics in a plant can affect workers' productivity, these aspects of the work environment and their respective impact on workers must be evaluated. Decisions made in this regard are typically a function of host-country norms.

PRODUCTION AND OPERATIONS MANAGEMENT

There are two categories of activities inherent to production: productive activities and supportive activities. In terms of productive activities, given a period of introduction and orientation, managers of the productive activities expect the system to operate at a sufficient and prescribed level of output to meet demand. If the system fails to produce at such levels, managers, including the line personnel, must determine where and what the impediment is and how to correct it. Potential obstacles management must address are low output, inferior product quality, and excessive manufacturing costs.

PRODUCTIVE ACTIVITIES

First, management must verify supplies of raw materials. In addition to poor quality, vendors' failure to meet delivery dates or to supply materials according to specifications may cause disruptions in the production process. Although this is a problem in both developing and industrialized countries, it is often more common in developing countries, where the raw materials supply is a seller's market. When such a problem is identified, it is the responsibility of the purchasing department to educate suppliers, notifying them of exact standards and delivery date requirements and providing technical assistance when needed. It is often necessary to pay a higher price to obtain better service.

In addition to problems with outputs to the production system, management may find scheduling problems within the system itself. In a system of sequential steps, for example, poor scheduling will result in bottlenecks and excessive inventories in

some areas and work stoppages because of a lack of work in others. If back orders are a problem, a company may be running many short runs to fill these orders, thereby perpetuating the problem. This situation has been found to be an even greater problem in many cultures where long-term planning is frowned on culturally or socially. To rectify the situation, management may incorporate additional training for the scheduling staff, which includes stressing the importance of their work, providing additional supervision, or encouraging more cooperation between the marketing and production departments to avoid a back-order problem.

High absenteeism also may contribute to a low output. In many developing countries, production workers are often called away from work to assist in seasonal family business, such as helping with the harvest. Furthermore, where transportation systems are inadequate, it may be very difficult for workers to commute; management may need to organize its own transportation for workers. In addition, where absenteeism is caused by sickness, management may choose to provide in-house lunch programs to provide better nutrition, which, besides reducing the instances of absenteeism because of illness, also reduces the risk of work injuries. In a situation in which absenteeism is a result of low morale, management must again evaluate cultural factors. While some international production managers accept high absenteeism and low productivity as problems inherent in the foreign environment, others have found solutions to these problems by utilizing the same techniques found at home with modifications for their local environment.

Another obstacle to maintaining production standards designed for the foreign production system is that of inferior product quality. Because perceived quality is relative to the standards of a particular environment, it may be impossible to meet standards set by home-office managers. The marketing staff should evaluate the quality standards demanded by the market and then set the price-quality combination that reflects this demand, which would also include quality standards for inputs of raw materials. When a home office is concerned about global reputation for its name-brand quality standards, it may be possible for the foreign subsidiary to produce under a different name. The other alternative is for the home office to require the same level of quality produced abroad as is required in the home market.

Excessive manufacturing costs affect the ability of production management to meet the prescribed standards for the system. Anything that varies significantly from the projected budget is of concern. Again, low output may be the culprit, perhaps budget assumptions were completely out of line with the market, or poor inventory control of inputs and finished products may exist (imported supplies may be necessary because of the uncertainty or poor quality of supplies in the local market).

SUPPORTIVE ACTIVITIES

Supportive activities include quality control, inventory control, purchasing, maintenance, and technical functions.

Production depends on the purchasing department's obtaining raw materials, component parts, supplies, and machinery to produce a finished product. If a firm is unable to obtain these inputs, the production facility may experience costly shutdowns and lost sales. If such inputs are obtained at a higher cost than that paid by a competitor, a company must either charge more for its finished products or price competitively and realize a smaller profit. Purchasing agents must search for suppliers that will provide quality inputs and reliable service at the lowest possible price. If the quality of raw materials is low, the quality of the finished product will also be low. As the saying goes, garbage in, garbage out.

Purchasers must be able to locate vendors and, if necessary, be familiar with the processes and players associated with importing. A company that is

establishing a production facility in another country must decide between hiring purchasing staff from the home country and hiring within the host country. While natives have knowledge and acquaintance advantages, they may be susceptible to cultural influences, such as favoring family or extended-family members for sourcing supplies.

To prevent unexpected work stoppages caused by equipment failures, maintenance must be conducted on buildings and equipment. While preventive maintenance helps to avoid unexpected breakdowns, many less-developed countries are subject to cultural influences that often cause the attitude, "Why fix it if it isn't broken?" In addition, the maintenance team is under pressure from marketing and production to keep the machinery running constantly, which perpetuates a short-term view of the maintenance role.

The local environment may necessitate more frequent maintenance than that mandated by headquarters. Temperature and climate and the handling of equipment by less-experienced workers may cause unforeseen wear and tear not experienced in the home production plant.

The last element of the supportive function is technical assistance. The technical-assistance staff is responsible for providing production with manufacturing specifications and for checking the quality of the inputs and the finished products. Often, the technical staff must locate substitutes for hard-to-find raw materials or may be required to visit suppliers to educate or train them so that they can meet requirements and delivery dates.

JUST-IN-TIME SYSTEM

During the late 1980s and mid-1990s, some experts felt that the Japanese advantage existed due to culture (societal and corporate), quality circles, lifetime employment, or other sociocultural factors; today, more and more experts are identifying the abilities of Japanese companies to manage effectively as the key to their success. Some have stated that the Japanese advantage in production costs and product quality stems from the superior organization and administration of their production.[2]

One such element of superior organization and administration that has been implemented for the last decade in many American and European companies' production systems is the *kanban* or *just-in-time (JIT) inventory system*. JIT requires that externally sourced inputs never arrive at the production plant before they are needed. Parts arrive exactly when they are needed; suppliers know the production schedule, and parts arrive from suppliers several times a day. Although JIT schedules are frozen for a certain period, the system is still fairly flexible.[3] There are many benefits to such a system when it is carefully implemented, primarily because many costs are reduced as the work-in-process inventory and warehousing space requirements are greatly reduced. JIT works toward zero inventories, reducing warehousing, handling, and financing costs and time for tracking stocks and movements. Companies using JIT perceive buffer stocks as a hidden inefficiency that only adds costs to production.[4] Success in this type of system requires that the firm have a strong relationship with its suppliers.

INTERNATIONAL TECHNOLOGY

An integral part of any production system is the technology used in the manufacturing process. Technology also may be separate from the production system itself in the form of the end product or finished good. After World War II, government officials and experts believed that increasing capital inputs was the key to rapid economic growth, but the basis for this belief weakened as capital became more accessible and developments were not always successful. The importance of technology for stimulating expansion then became more important, and *technology transfer* became an issue in world economies. As a result, developing, exploiting,

and maintaining technological advantages became crucial issues for MNCs.

The question for an MNC and for a government official is, "How will we obtain the desired technology?" Often the choice for a firm is either through its own R & D efforts or by acquisition from another firm. For the government of a developing country, on the other hand, the choice is more limited. The technology usually must be transferred from sources other than those within the country. Within industrialized countries, the main focus is the protection of technology and the creation of new technologies. LDCs, however, must be concerned with the opposite: restrictions on transfers, royalty limitations, lack of patent protection, and other legal constraints. For LDCs international firms are responsible for a large share of technology transfers, but there are also noncommercial organizations that provide international transfers, such as development programs funded by other industrialized nations.

DEFINITION OF TECHNOLOGY

Technology has been defined as a perishable source comprising knowledge, skills, and means for using and controlling factors of production for the purpose of producing, delivering to users, and maintaining goods and services for which there is no economic or social demand.[5]

There are several elements of technology that can be used for classification purposes. First, there are three types of technology: *product technology*, which is knowledge used to make a product; *process technology*, which is knowledge used in the process of making a product, including the organizing of the inputs of machinery and equipment necessary for the production process; and *management technology*, which is knowledge used in running the business, including managerial skills that make the firm competitive.

A second level of classification within technology concerns the particular characteristics of the technology. These include hard and soft technology, proprietary and nonproprietary technology, front-end and obsolete technology and bundled and unbundled technology. *Hard technology* includes the physical hardware, capital goods, blueprints and specifications, and knowledge necessary to use the hardware, while *soft technology* encompasses the management, marketing, financial organization, and administrative techniques that can be combined with the hard technology to serve the needs of the user. Technology that is owned or controlled by an individual or organization is proprietary and may be either controlled as a trade secret or patented. An example of proprietary technology that is controlled as a trade secret is the formula developed by the Coca-Cola Company for the production of its soft drink of the same name. Nonproprietary technology is knowledge found in technical literature, hardware, and services that may be copied without infringing on proprietary rights. This reproduction often is achievable through reverse engineering, where the technology is broken down to learn how it was created. State-of-the-art technology is considered front-end, while old technology is termed obsolete. *Bundled technology* is another aspect of controlled technology, where the owner is willing to transfer it only as part of a package or system. *Unbundled technology* is available separate from the supplier's total technology system.

TECHNOLOGY DEVELOPMENT

There are three stages of technology development. Invention is the first stage. At this level, new knowledge is created that may be applied to business or industry. The next step is innovation, in which the new knowledge is introduced into the marketplace. It is not uncommon for a technology to complete the first stage and not reach the second or third stages. In fact, most inventions never reach the innovation stage. If they do, the next step is diffusion, or the spread of the new knowledge throughout the marketplace.

For example, telecommunications is well into the diffusion phase, but with developments in wireless technology, this industry is experiencing new invention and innovation stages, and diffusion is well under way in some other high-tech industries.

A technology advantage is an advantage held by a firm whose employees possess a superior business knowledge (product, process, or management) that is unknown to other firms. In the interest of maintaining this advantage, a firm may seek to protect its proprietary possession of the technology, usually through patents. Firms must continually develop new technology to perpetuate their advantages, because most patents are of limited duration.

Research and development is the prime source of a company's technology advantage. An MNC will often feel pressure from a host country to combine R and D facilities with production facilities. One motivation for establishing R & D facilities in a foreign country is that such facilities can aid in the transfer of technology by making easier product and process modifications for local markets and by strengthening the competitive stance of a subsidiary by offering local technical assistance to purchasers. Foreign R & D sites also allow subsidiaries to develop products in accordance with local market needs and to identify those needs that differ from those perceived by the home country. Local knowledge and skills can also be a benefit that is derived from locating R & D abroad. Before a company can complete its decision to locate an R & D function in a host country, an evaluation must be made of host-government controls and incentives. The ultimate question is whether or not such controls or incentives justify the economics of a research unit, in light of the availability of adequate universities, infrastructure, and local supply of technical skills.

TECHNOLOGY TRANSFER

Technology transfer is the process by which knowledge is diffused through learning from its place of origin into other world markets. Depending on the characteristics of the technology to be transferred, the time and expense involved will vary, and the choice of transfer method must incorporate such factors as the nature of the technology, the capabilities and objectives of the parties involved, and the elements of the sociocultural environment that enable the recipient country to assimilate and synthesize the technology. The transfer process also has distinct phases, from planning and product and facility design to personnel training, engineering for quality control, and technical support for local suppliers.

The transfer of technology may take place through market transactions, which creates issues for both governments and international managers. Host governments are concerned with obtaining up-to-date technology at low cost from MNCs, while companies are interested in protecting and realizing benefits from their technology.

Noncommercial ways of transferring technology usually involve foreign study in university programs, which enable foreign nationals to acquire knowledge and then bring the knowledge back to their own countries. There are also government-to-government agreements for technology transfers. Some examples are development aid programs for infrastructure, nuclear energy programs, and space research programs. Commercial methods for transferring technology are more varied, including foreign direct investment, turnkey projects, trade in goods and services, contracts and agreements, R & D programs located in foreign countries or through joint research efforts, migration of trained personnel or employment of local nationals by foreign firms, international tender offers, and industrial espionage.

In general, strategies for conducting technology transfers and exploiting technology advantages fall within two broad categories. Which strategy the firm chooses is determined by the type of business

and the type of technology. The first type of strategy involves extending the firm's own operation, which is known as internalizing. Internalizing requires a company to utilize foreign subsidiaries and affiliates in different markets to sell its products or services in local markets. In smaller markets, a company trying to internalize will attempt to meet demand through exports. This approach is best when:

- The firm makes new products that are not easily copied by others.
- Outside firms use the same technology and serve part of the market due to the large size of the market relative to the size of the firms.
- The firm depends greatly on the sale of the product or service that uses the technology.
- The firm is so small that it does not have the personnel to both use the technology internally and sell it to outsiders, or the firm is so large that it can easily exploit the technology through its own affiliates.
- The technology is more important to the firm than to potential buyers of the technology.
- The technology is costly to transfer from one firm to another.[6]

This strategy is the same as the approach for finding and exploiting other sources of competitive advantage, but another approach the firm might choose is that of externalizing. Using external markets has become increasingly important in light of the current wave of *outsourcing* to developing countries to capture significantly lower wage rates than are required in the developed world. Through this strategy, a company contracts with other firms to sell the technology itself, rather than sell the final product that results from such technology. Such contracts may be in the form of licensing agreements or management contracts.

There are two approaches, in particular, that have become more common external market strategies:

turnkey projects and licensing. Turnkey projects are contracted projects that encompass all elements of the project, usually including training. When the project is completed, the contractor turns the entire system over to the purchaser. A popular strategy in such industries as chemicals, petrochemicals, and petroleum refining, this method often includes an equity position for the contractor, which enables the firm to reap the benefits of its technology over a longer period of time.

The other external market strategy that has increased in practice is licensing. Table 16.1 explains the situations in which licensing would be considered the best strategy. For small companies that have inadequate capital or management expertise for international expansion via foreign direct investment, licensing is an advantageous option.

There are, however, several arguments against using licensing. The strongest argument is that a licensor may lose its competitive advantage to a licensee over time and, in the process, be prohibited from future direct investment in the market served by the licensee. If the licensor is a participant in the foreign venture, however, there is an infusion of protection against such an event. Furthermore, trademarks can be utilized as part of the licensing agreement, because trademarks remain the property of the licensor in perpetuity despite the fact that the license is for a limited time only.

In general, externalizing is best when:

- The firm's products are not central to its ability to survive in competition.
- The firm's skill is greater in creating the technology than in producing and marketing the final products.
- The firm's financial and personnel capabilities make it desirable to let another firm use the technology.
- The firm cannot protect its technology with a patent, and it could lose the benefits of that

technology unless it is compensated for the technology's use by rival firms.
- The firm's technology is not costly to transfer between firms.[7]

CHOICE OF PRODUCTION TECHNOLOGY

Once a company has decided to internalize, it often obtains its competitive advantage through overseas production facilities, and a company must choose the technology to implement in such plants. This issue becomes particularly controversial in developing countries, where many government officials are concerned that technology transferred by foreign firms for local production be appropriate to the resources of the country and not necessarily the same technology that is used in capital-rich countries with large markets or the home country of the foreign firm. In most instances, this results in pressure from host governments to establish smaller, more labor-intensive facilities. In other situations, however, host-country policies may invite capital-intensive production technologies to obtain state-of-the-art systems.

Before the choice is made, a firm must consider the availability of production technology alternatives that are, in reality, commercially feasible for operation. This may mean many more options in some industries than in others, depending on the nature of the product. Cost and availability of information concerning specific technologies also impact the decision. It is much easier to obtain information regarding capital-intensive equipment because information and technology flows are more likely to be from industrialized countries to developing countries than between developing countries.

Market sizes, which vary from one country to the next, also influence the plant design choice. Capital-intensive technology incorporates automated, high-output machinery but it is often severely limited in

Table 16.1

Licensing as a Preferred Strategy Under the Following Circumstances

Strategic Concept	Conditions
1. Product cycle standardization	Obsolescing products considered for licensing Imminent technology or model change Increasing competition in product market
2. Environmental constraints on FDI or FDI income	Government regulations restricting FDI to selected sectors only High political risk in nation Market uncertain or volatile, licensor lacking in requisite marketing abilities, or market too small for FDI
3. Constraints on imports into license nation	A high ratio for transport cost to value for item Tariff or nontariff barriers
4. Licensor firm size	Licensor firm too small to have financial, managerial, or marketing expertise for overseas investment Licensor firm too big (see item 12, below)
5. Research intensity	Licensor firm will remain technologically superior, so as to discount licensee competition in other markets
6. High rate of technological turnover	Change so rapid and technologies so perishable that even with equally proficient licensees, a design or a patent may be transferred with little fear of significant competition
7. Perpetuation of licensee dependency	Even without or beyond the licensing agreement, effective licensee dependency will be maintained by trademarks, required components, or licensee hunger for technical improvements
8. Product versus process technologies	Licensing opportunities are auxiliary processes (e.g., galvanizing in the steel industry, or anodizing aluminum) even if the basic product technologies are not licensed
9. Reciprocal exchanges of technology	Licensing as a valuable tool for obtaining technology of market rights in industries characterized by high R & D and market development costs and product diversity
10. "Choosing" competition	With a patent about to expire, licensing gives a head start to a licensee firm favored by the present patent holder (may be illegal in some countries)
11. Creation of auxiliary business	Even if direct royalty income is inadequate, margins on components to or from licensee can be handsome Other auxiliary business can be turnkey plants, joint bidding with licensee, and so forth
12. Diversification and product-line organization in licensor firm	Especially in large diversified firms, with dimensional attention focused on the "product imperative," a centralized examination of the product-country matrix reveals neglected market penetration possibilities via licensing (especially where considerable diversification puts a constraint on the financial and managerial resources available for equity ventures overseas)

flexibility regarding the production and size range of products. A capital-intensive system can produce in a few days what may amount to a year's supply in some markets. For these smaller markets, the design choice may be to install only one machine. Unfortunately, in some cases, the capacity of one such machine would still greatly overproduce for the demand in a particular market. Labor-intensive technology, on the other hand, employs more people and incorporates semiautomated general-purpose equipment with lower productive capacity.[8]

Labor and capital intensity are not the only contributing factors to the technology decision. The decision must include quality-control maintenance, waste minimization, response time to market demand fluctuations, training costs, labor relations, and the image or prestige factor of front-end equipment.

Until recently it was thought that a choice between labor and capital intensity was the only available option. There is a third alternative that, despite its high costs and high technological content, is starting to be utilized by industrialized nations. Such technology would create a mix of labor and capital and is known as hybrid plant design. In addition, when an MNC is faced with the need for a production design that incorporates both labor and capital requirements, intermediate technology and appropriate technology are options. Hybrid designs also offer solutions to the problem of choosing between labor- and capital-intensive production technologies. These designs are geared toward obtaining a certain product quality while ensuring a labor-intensive production method. In such a design, the production process includes both types of technology in distinct phases. Intermediate technology uses a combination throughout the process. It is not a question of using capital intensity in some steps of production and labor intensity in others; rather, it is the utilization of a less than fully automated process. In recent years, many LDCs have looked to intermediate technology as a means to create more jobs, use less capital, and still be able to produce the desired product quality. Although many governments are urging investors to implement intermediate technology, it is not easily accessed from industrial nations. There is often miscommunication between developed countries and the developing world regarding technological transfer. Industrialized nations often are looking for a place to sell their older technology, while developing nations are looking for the most up-to-date technology, which can allow for a more rapid industrialization. Moreover, there may be higher start-up costs associated with intermediate technology implementation than can be justified by the savings in reduced capital costs.

Appropriate technology considers the optimum technological mix by matching a country's markets with its resources and ability to produce certain components. Unlike an approach that would use intermediate technology, appropriate technology emphasizes applying the technology that is most appropriate to the immediate economic, sociocultural, and political variables. This approach may range from the most primitive of production processes to high-tech systems and takes into consideration that with some products the superiority in productivity and quality of a modern process is so significant as to make labor-intensive methods completely inappropriate. It is often the government that must choose between the use of less capital-intensive technologies to save scarce capital resources and create new jobs and more capital-intensive methods that will provide less-expensive products for its citizens.

PRICING TECHNOLOGY TRANSFERS

Unlike most free-market transactions, in which market demand and supply determine price, there is relatively little information available regarding pricing of technology transfers. In most instances, negotiating parties do not have access to data regarding previous sales or transfers of technology for similar products or between similar parties. Furthermore, because technology transfers may include many different types of services and, therefore, payments, even if price information were available, it would be difficult to discern what products, services, and prices would be comparable to the technology transfer negotiations currently under way.

Pricing of technology in recent years has become a controversial issue, especially for developing countries. Host-government intervention is common because it is frequently assumed that such transfers are overpriced to developing nations. Transfer pricing is also suspected when payments are made to parent companies by foreign affiliates.

Developing countries often see themselves in a vulnerable and weak negotiating position and assume that higher prices are set for their transactions than for similar technology transfers between industrial countries. In addition, there is a common belief that technology is protected by a patent monopoly that enables a seller to set excessive monopoly prices. It is the opinion of the governments of these developing countries that the prior costs of developing the technology have already been amortized over the home market sales and that international transfers do not need to compensate for much more than the incremental costs of the transfer.

To combat these host-government fears, there has been an increasing exchange of information among national agencies that are trying to better prepare a host country for negotiations. In defense against the patent monopoly claim, it is argued that this point confuses the concept of a patent as a monopoly with monopoly power in the marketplace. Despite the fact that the technology is patented, it still faces competition in the market from substitute technology. Furthermore, the claim that development costs have already been amortized does not consider the fact that several industrialized countries, including the United States, have tax agencies that instruct that such costs should be shared by all users of a technology to avoid the loss of income tax revenues that would result if companies expended all sunk costs within the home country. Companies involved in R & D plan for the pricing of currently available technology to cover sunk costs plus future R & D.

PROTECTING TECHNOLOGY

Different issues are embedded in the problem of protecting technology. Primary is the question of how an MNC can implement control measures for proprietary technology. Obtaining patents is one way to protect one's technology. In most countries, if the knowledge possessed by a firm is a manufacturing process and it produces a new product, that process and the product can be protected with a patent. Patents are usually held for limited periods of time. Copyrights are another tool available for protecting proprietary technology that covers knowledge embodied in text. Similarly, trademarks protect knowledge that is embodied in a product that can be sold. Trademarks usually imply a high standard of quality or expertise in services. There are other methods available, such as hiding the technology (e.g., the Coke secret formula), requiring key technical or R & D employees to sign agreements whereby they are prohibited from using new technology that they acquired outside the firm, and rapid exploitation of the technology, which would establish a large market share and discourage competitors from entering the market.

Despite these mechanisms for establishing and maintaining control, it is not uncommon for a firm to lose control. For example, companies in countries such as China have reputations for manufacturing branded copies of products that have been patented, copyrighted, or otherwise protected. Similarly, industrial espionage is almost considered merely a modern inconvenience, often depicted in television and screen productions as normal corporate behavior. Also, the mobility of employees makes it almost impossible to control 100 percent of a company's proprietary technology. Even in the absence of malice, an employee may unwittingly incorporate some of the learned technology in projects in development with other companies.

Protecting technology is an issue not only for an MNC but also for national governments. The private interests of the parties involved in buying and selling technology may not be compatible with a government's national interests. The home country or seller's country is concerned with the control of technology for national security reasons, while the host country becomes more active in monitoring international transfers as a guideline for future negotiations.

In reality, because of these issues, an international manager must constantly be aware that negotiations regarding technology transfer are between four players—the buyer, the seller, the home country, and the host country—without losing sight of the fact that this is not necessarily a win-lose situation. There may in fact be an arrangement that is mutually beneficial to all parties.

MANAGEMENT INFORMATION SYSTEMS

MIS IN AN MNC

The appropriate transfer and analysis of information regarding markets, operations, customers, and enterprise activities can be a crucial factor in the success or failure of a firm and its international activities. In the best of circumstances, the use of relevant information can provide a multinational concern with competitive advantages over its competitors by allowing it to develop a strategic position of strength.

On a more routine level, an MNC must manage its information flows from subsidiaries about operations, markets, and potential just to maintain its existing operating strengths in current markets

across the globe. This is a major challenge for an MNC, considering the distance involved, both physical and cultural, and the need to transfer data and information among a variety of environments. Moreover, information must be comparable and standardized if it is to be aggregated for analysis by an MNC.

CORPORATE REPORTS

One method of control MNCs use is the establishment of reporting requirements and procedures for staff and departments within the organization. These reports constitute a steady stream of information that flows to headquarters and is analyzed to provide input in senior management's strategic decision making about overall corporate resource allocation. Because written reports often represent the only formal presentation of information from the subsidiaries or operating branches regarding their activities, and because these reports often provide the basis for performance evaluation, it is crucial that subsidiary managers understand the reporting requirements, format, and purposes.

To be effective tools of control and decision making, reports from branches and arms of the firm must be timely, so that an MNC is able to respond with adjustments and corrections. Similarly, reports must contain complete information that is relevant to an MNC's needs in its evaluation of the subsidiary's performance. Information must be presented in an understandable, comparable format and include data that are usable by top management and strategic planners. Accuracy of data is critical because mistakes in reports from one region may upset calculations for the entire corporation.

Corporations require a variety of reports on activities in their worldwide operations, which fall into four categories: financial reports, operating reports, in-country reports, and market-based reports. Financial reports provide an MNC with information regarding the flow of funds within the subsidiary and between it and its suppliers and customers. They quantify the results of operations and provide information on the status of the on-site currency. These reports must be presented in an established form, use standardized currency conversions, and employ established conventions to permit comparison with the results of other corporate segments. This presentation of financial data may not be in the same format as that required by host-government regulatory standards. In many instances, therefore, it is necessary for a subsidiary to maintain a separate set of books for official reporting requirements in the host country.

Operations reports give management a view of subsidiaries' performance and an indication of such information as production volumes, inventory levels, supply contracts negotiated, and expended raw materials and energy. These reports frequently also note staffing changes, technological developments regarding operating procedures, and compliance with local laws, such as environmental or social welfare reporting requirements. The reports comprise the core of the information sent to headquarters; they chronicle the day-to-day achievements, problems, and status of an MNC's operating arms, and they give the MNC a basis of comparison from reporting period to reporting period. From formal operating reports and informal communication with branches, top management can keep its finger on the pulse of the enterprise and be aware of what resources are being utilized where, to what end, and how efficiently.

Subsidiaries also perform a valuable function by giving the managers at headquarters key information from the foreign operating environment. These in-country reports provide information on developments in the host country on economic, political, and social fronts. Such information provides a firm with timely data on which to base revisions of risk factors or decisions to limit or increase operations in the host country. They can also provide the firm

with an advantage in the event of potential crises, such as political or military upheavals, by providing top management with early warning signals, so that the loss of company assets and danger to company personnel can be minimized.

Subsidiaries also provide an MNC with information regarding activities in the market it serves. This information concerns the actions of a firm's competitors in existing market areas, consumer behavior, buying patterns, and demand and pricing structures. On-site personnel often also provide information to a firm about potential market development through the examination of new markets or the development of new products to satisfy different consumer needs in existing markets.

The information provided by these reports assists a firm in its efforts to develop and fine-tune its implementation of strategic and operating objectives. Consequently, to ensure that the information is interpreted and used correctly, it must be accurate, reliable, and consistent across all arms of a firm in terms of standards of measurement, accounting principles, and definitions.

Formal written reports are also supplemented with informal reports made in face-to-face contacts with subsidiary managers and through frequent telephone, voice over internet protocol (VoIP), and E-mail communications. These channels of informal reporting are important because they provide a subsidiary manager with methods for reporting on smaller occurrences that might not warrant formal reporting but may be significant. They also keep communication lines open in the event that there is need for further information on more important issues. To encourage this interaction (and to provide nontraditional support for expatriate or subsidiary managers), some firms assign managers a corporate mentor, who is charged with staying in touch with the manager so that he or she is involved in the headquarters-based activities of the firm.

Despite the care that is taken to ensure compara-

Figure 16.1   **Information Exchange Process Between a Parent and Single Subsidiary**

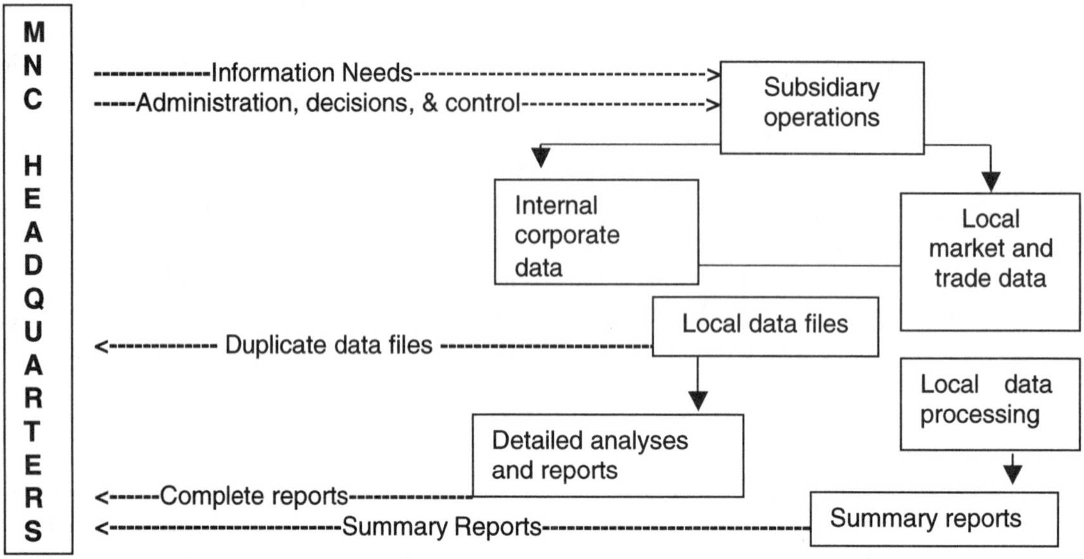

bility and compatibility of reports from all arms of an MNC, problems nevertheless arise in the management of information systems across international borders. Some firms assume that they can use the same reporting systems abroad as they do at home. This is not always the case because of differences in operating environments. For example, in some countries where computer skills are low, the use of computerized reports by overseas employees is not feasible. Similarly, if a system requires the use of computerized data collection or report transmittal, a myriad of compatibility problems may arise.

INTERNATIONAL DATA PROCESSING: INTEGRATION ISSUES

Information is constantly exchanged between the parent office and subsidiaries in every MNC operation. Figure 16.1 illustrates the process of information interchange between a parent and a single subsidiary. The interchange pattern becomes

vastly more complex when multiplied by a number of subsidiaries involved in the overall structure of an MNC.

The complexity of these networks and the involvement of the international component of information management raise several issues of concern to MNCs. These issues stem mostly from problems regarding compatibility of data-processing systems, the establishment of controls on data compilation and its transfer across national borders by host governments, and the risks involved in using multinational computer networks.

An MNC often has problems in sharing information with its subsidiaries because of differences in data-processing capabilities and system sophistication. While an MNC may have highly sophisticated computer systems, its subsidiaries may be equipped with much less sophisticated equipment, either because a subsidiary's information-management needs are less extensive or because the capabilities of the subsidiary's personnel do not allow for the efficient use of such equipment. In some cases, a subsidiary may have different software and hardware.

Another problem in integrating parent and subsidiary information systems is the high costs of centralization of information systems. Moreover, attempts by MNCs to impose tight controls on their branches with respect to data processing and transmittal lead to additional administrative costs, delays in information or data file transmission, the need for extensive and expensive computer systems, and the need to protect against loss of data during transmittal by piracy.

Through the decentralization of information management, an MNC can avoid these higher costs and allow subsidiaries to make their own decisions regarding computer systems. The trade-off, however, is a lack of corporate control over the management of the system. As with all aspects of the centralization versus decentralization debate, an MNC must balance these opposing outcomes in an effort to reach an appropriate level of managerial control over the information system for efficiency's sake without sacrificing subsidiary autonomy.

Another enormous problem for MNCs in the management of data and information is a result of forces in the external environment on the use of information systems. These are primarily the forces that emanate from political or governmental entities in host countries, which are concerned about national security, protection of economic forces, and, to some degree, cultural independence.

These concerns may lead to host-country union requirements regarding the employment of local data processors, and laws regarding privacy and the carrying of data across national borders. For example, some countries do not allow data to be transmitted across their borders for processing elsewhere. These restrictions are intended to retain employment in the country and to force firms to use local labor to satisfy the labor requirements of their data processing.

In some firms or businesses, this function can be a very large component of overall business activity. International banks are a prime example of a business that is based on the fast, reliable, and accurate use of computer systems to chronicle individual banking transactions. International banks frequently spend millions of dollars to establish data-processing systems and computer networks to facilitate the flow of information and data processing from branches around the world. In these instances, the speed of processing has a very real economic effect on business because the slow transfer of invested funds means losses in interest earned.

International firms can also be affected by government controls that deal with the issue of privacy of personal information. Such treatment usually includes limits on a firm's use of computer systems so that individuals have control over personal information, can correct it when necessary, and must give consent for it to be used by other parties. Such information could include personal data regarding sex, religion, race, or political orientation but could also include personal academic, criminal, and financial information.

Limits on the transmittal of such information affect an MNC's capacity to transmit personnel records to headquarters and can prevent an MNC from having complete records at centralized locations; an MNC may need additional resources to ensure compliance with local laws. In Norway, for example, a centralized data inspectorate must be notified each time personal information is sent abroad.

Governments use other methods to control transnational data flows. Some countries have attempted to limit the flows by imposing a tax on information leaving the country. Such taxation is difficult to implement because it is virtually impossible to objectively determine the value of economic information except on a case-by-case method. Other countries merely make it expensive to move data out of the country. In Japan, for example, Control Data

Corporation was forced to pay for its own private telephone line between Japan and the United States (at a cost of US$33,000 per month) and, because of governmental restrictions, can only use that line at 1 percent of its capacity.

Besides the additional costs and procedural problems involved in operating information systems in an international setting, MNCs also face a high level of risk in managing transnational information networks. The biggest problems a firm faces are maintaining the integrity of data through a control process that oversees data inputs to the system, and the management of the information at the local level to correspond to data needs at the corporate level. Other risks involved are the loss of data in transmission because of unreliable channels or through the piracy or theft of the data. Developing protection against such risks is very expensive and involves such measures as the establishment of a company's own computer network or the purchase of private communication lines.

The MNC's goal is to take advantage of its operation as an integrated system, of which the management of information is a major part, to minimize duplication of efforts and facilities, and to maximize operating efficiencies by coordinating information concerning operations and business opportunities around the world. Issues raised in the control of transnational data flows have the potential to adversely affect MNCs' pursuit of these objectives by placing limits on their ability to exchange and analyze this crucial information or by imposing additional operating costs through restrictions on the processing, location, and transmittal of data. These controls are a significant issue for the modern MNC that attempts to develop an information management system that strikes a balance between costs and benefits and has the capability of synthesizing data from worldwide operations while maintaining the appropriate technology at the subsidiary level.

SHOULD INTERNATIONAL FIRMS GO GLOBAL?

The process of controlling international operations is a formidable challenge for a firm attempting to make the best of its corporate strengths while remaining aware of its limitations. Some analysts believe, however, that the progressive firm should not content itself with an international focus but should adopt a global orientation toward operations and planning.

Some companies are merely international; they operate a variety of subsidiaries in a number of countries. In such a portfolio approach, individual operating arms or companies in a conglomerate are ranked according to criteria, such as their individual market strength and market growth, not as part of the global system, as are those within the Boston Consulting Group matrix of business units, which are categorized as "cash cows," "stars," "dogs," and "question marks." This focus and orientation is limited and leads to suboptimization of operations and resources, and to the company's missing opportunities to be exploited by integrating all operations worldwide. Rather than comparing individual units against one another in terms of a firm's entire portfolio of business activities, a firm would be better off if it looked at international factors from a global perspective to identify possibilities for operating synergies.

Similarly, a firm must consider worldwide competition in designing its strategy; for example, the forces of global competition may lead a firm toward the establishment of less-profitable business units as a defensive posture rather than toward an offensive move to profitability. Such a defensive action could be costly in the short term but pays dividends when viewed from a long-term, global perspective.

By accurately assessing the forces of global competition and a firm's relative advantages and strengths, an enterprise can devise a global strategy to become effective in world markets. Such a strategy may hinge on competing in all product lines, on competing in a product area that is protected from competition, on a global strategy area focusing on a specific market (global niche), or on a particular national or regional area market. Although the process of planning and subsequent implementation and control is highly complex because of the assimilation and analysis of information about a variety of operating and supply environments, it can provide incomparable strategic advantages for a corporation willing to take on such a global challenge.

SUMMARY

In the international business arena, production and technology can influence how and where a company operates. International production management for an MNC may in fact be very similar to production management in the home country. The international environment, however, includes other considerations. Before making production decisions, an MNC must consider such additional factors as wage rates, industrial relations, sources of financing, foreign exchange risk, international tax laws, control, and the production experience curve in each country. While many MNCs attempt to standardize their production systems on a worldwide basis, local environmental influences often make such standardization unsuccessful or at best difficult. The benefits of standardization are ease and simplification, which result in cost savings in organization and staffing, supply systems, options for rationalization, control, and planning. There are four elements in designing a local production facility—plant location, plant layout, materials handling, and the human factor. MNCs must determine whether to centralize or decentralize decision-making authority, which is influenced by the mode of international operations, the nature of industry and technology, the size and maturity of the MNC, the competence of the branch managerial staff, the local political environment,

the required speed of decision making, and the magnitude of the decision.

Operations management encompasses two categories of activities: productive activities and supportive activities. Productive activities require that deviations from expected output are investigated and corrected. Low output, which may be caused by inadequate raw materials, poor scheduling, inferior product quality, or excessive manufacturing costs, is an indication that corrective actions are necessary to achieve planned output objectives. Supportive activities include quality control, inventory control, purchasing, maintenance, and technical functions. The Japanese have been able to efficiently and effectively manage all elements of the production process, and this has led to such successful developments as the just-in-time system, the inventory control system first used by many Japanese companies.

Technology is knowledge that can be applied in a business environment. It is an integral part of any production system, although it may be separate from the production system itself in the form of the end product or finished good. Technology can be created through R & D or acquired with experience in business operations and transactions. In addition, technology may be purchased from the individuals or firms that have developed the technology, and it is often transferred between parties and across national boundaries for a cost. In terms of production technology, the choice of technology that is implemented in a foreign country depends on the cost-benefit evaluation of capital-intensive versus labor-intensive methods. Such evaluation must also consider the environmental (economic, political, and cultural) influences that affect technology. Information and data flows can be slowed by the incompatibility of hardware and software systems used in the corporate and branch offices as well as by political or governmental regulations.

Any MNC's competitive advantage is considerably dependent on technology advantages, whether they are a process, a product, or a management technology. An MNC must constantly be concerned with maintaining and improving this advantage. The perishability of technology requires that an MNC continue to make technology improvements. For an MNC, technological advances can be transferred among affiliates and subsidiaries in different countries.

Pricing of international technology transfers has become a major issue between the governments of developing countries and the owners of technology in industrialized countries. In the future, it is expected that such governments will share information regarding technology transfers and pricing among themselves to become better equipped to negotiate for such transfers.

For an MNC, control over proprietary technology is a difficult management task. Although there are protection measures and tools available to assist in control, there are also many instances where protection has been inadequate and a firm has lost its proprietary advantage. Because technology is closely associated with national security, governmental controls also affect an MNC and its ability to transfer technology.

DISCUSSION QUESTIONS

1. Why are production and technology so important to maintaining a multinational corporation's competitive edge?
2. Discuss the three key production issues as they relate to the following types of firms:
   - Truck manufacturer
   - Welding equipment manufacturer
   - Consumer electronics manufacturer (TVs, portable CD players)
   - Textiles manufacturer
3. You are the CEO of a U.S. automobile manufacturer who is interested in building a new production plant in eastern Europe. What factors should you review as you make your decision?
4. What advantages do manufacturers have when implementing a just-in-time system? How do you think suppliers respond to changes from their standard distribution approaches?
5. How can MIS make or break a multinational corporation?
6. What data problems might occur between the parent office and its subsidiaries?

NOTES

1. Ball and McCulloch, *International Business*.
2. Rugman, Lecraw, and Booth, *International Business*.
3. Hall, *Zero Inventories*.
4. Rugman, Lecraw, and Booth, *International Business*, 1985.
5. Robock and Simmonds, *International Business and Multinational Enterprises*.
6. Grosse and Kujawa, *International Business*.
7. Ibid.
8. Wells, "Don't Over-Automate Your Foreign Plant."

BIBLIOGRAPHY

Baden-Fuller, C., and J.M. Stopford. "Why Global Manufacturing?" *Multinational Business*, Spring 1988, 15–25.

Ball, Donald A., and W.H. McCulloch Jr. *International Business*. Plano, TX: Business Publications, 1988.

Carnoy, Martin. "High Technology and International Labor Markets." *International Labour Review*, November–December 1985, 643–59.

Contractor, F. "The Role of Licensing." *Columbia Journal of World Business*, Winter 1981, 76.

Davidson, W.H., and D.G. McFetridge. "Key Characteristics in the Choice of International Technology Transfer Mode." *Journal of International Business Studies*, Summer 1985, 5–21.

Dunning, J.H. *International Production and the Multinational Enterprise*. London: Allen and Unwin, 1981.

Goshal, S., and C.A. Bartlett. "Innovation Processes in Multinational Corporations: Proceedings of the Symposium on Managing Innovation in Large Complex Firms." INSEAD, September 1987.

———. "Creation, Adoption, and Diffusion of Innovations

by Subsidiaries of Multinational Corporations." *Journal of International Business Studies*, Fall 1988, 365–88.

Grosse, Robert, and D. Kujawa. *International Business*. Homewood, IL: Richard D. Irwin, 1988.

Hakanson, L., and U. Zander. *Managing International Research and Development*. Stockholm: Mekanforbund, 1986.

Hall, Robert. *Zero Inventories*. Homewood, IL: Dow Jones-Irwin, 1983.

Johanson, J., and L.G. Mattison. "Internationalization in Industrial Systems: A Network Approach." In *Strategies in Global Competition*, ed. V. Hood and J.E. Vahne. London: Croom Helm, 1987.

Keller, R.T., and R.R. Chinta. "International Transfer: Strategies for Success." *Academy of Management Executives*, May 1990, 33–43.

Munkirs, John R. 1988. "Technological Change: Disaggregation and Overseas Production." *Journal of Economic Issues*, June 1988, 469–75.

Porter, Michael, ed. *Competition in Global Industries*. Boston: Harvard Business School Press, 1986.

Rastogi, P.N. *Productivity, Innovation, Management, and Development: A Study in the Productivity Culture of Nations and System Renewal*. New Delhi: Sage Publications, 1988.

Robock, Stefan H., and Kenneth Simmonds. *International Business and Multinational Enterprises*. Homewood, IL: Richard D. Irwin, 1983.

Rugman, Alan H., D.J. Lecraw, and L.D. Booth. *International Business*. New York: McGraw-Hill, 1985.

Smith, Charles. "Two's Company: Mitsubishi and Benz Plan Wide Links." *Far Eastern Economic Review*, May 24, 1990, 67.

Stobaugh, R., and L.T. Wells Jr., eds. *Technology Crossing Borders: The Choice, Transfer, and Management of International Technology Flows*. Boston: Harvard Business School Press, 1984.

Wells, Louis T., Jr. "Don't Over-Automate Your Foreign Plant." *Harvard Business Review* January–February 1974, 84–97.

CASE STUDY 16.1

MILFORD PROCESSES, INC.

Kenneth Briggs, general manager of the technical division of Milford Processes, finished reading a long, well-prepared brief written by a task force he had put together to report on the severe quality-control problems of the wholly owned subsidiary's plant in Matumba, East Africa. Reports of problems with the chemical-producing plant had been coming in for the last six months, and they had become more serious in the last two months. Concerned with the future of the plant, Briggs put together a small task force of head office and subsidiary technicians to investigate the problems and recommend solutions.

The report was extremely direct. Quality at the plant was dropping and productivity had fallen. The defective rate of chemical batches had risen from 12 per thousand to 98 per thousand over the past six months. Productivity had decreased by 16 percent in the past quarter.

The statistics troubled Briggs. The plant in Matumba had gone online only a year ago and was equipped with the latest equipment and machinery and the most advanced processing technology. The entire technical side of the operation was run by Milford's engineers, who had several years of experience. The first six months, in fact, had been a great success, and Matumba's productivity had matched Milford's worldwide standards in nearly every way.

After the first two quarters, however, things began to go wrong. One of the most difficult problems was electricity. When the plant was set up, the Matumba government had guaranteed an uninterrupted electricity supply to the plant as a part of the package of incentives it had offered

to attract Milford into setting up an advanced-technology facility in the country. However, much of Matumba's electricity-generating capacity was based on hydroelectric projects, and these were dependent on the degree of rainfall that the country's catchment areas received during the rainy season, during the first four months of the year. This year the rains had failed to come, and water levels in the hydroelectric project reservoirs fell below operating levels. There was nothing the government or anyone else could do to generate power in adequate amounts to meet the country's needs. Bound by its promise and eager to maintain a hospitable environment for overseas investment, Matumba authorities had given high priority to the Milford plant's power needs. Despite their best efforts, however, the plant had no power for one day a week in the past four months, and in the past six weeks, production had to be shut down for two days a week. To keep up production volume and minimize production losses because of the plant shutdown, the production managers had reduced the number of quality-control checks both at the point of raw-material feeding and at final-production testing. The electricity shortage also resulted in the malfunctioning of the plant's temperature control systems at two stages of the production process, which was also affecting quality.

The task force had come up with two options, both of which assumed that the electricity situation in Matumba was not likely to improve soon, and that over the long term, it could fluctuate considerably, depending on the pattern of

continued

Case 16.1 (*continued*)

annual rainfall. Moreover, if Matumba's drive to attract other overseas companies to the country met with even moderate success, the demand for industrial consumption would go up sharply, and Milford would lose its most-favored status in this regard. The government was already under criticism from some quarters of the political opposition for bending over backward to please Milford. The opposition was actively calling for retracting Milford's privileged access to the country's generating capacity in times of scarcity.

The first option recommended that the company set up a captive power station, which, in effect, meant the building of a complete power-generating facility to supply electricity exclusively to Milford's plant. The plant would cost an estimated $16 million to build and could be completed in about a year and a half. The facility would ensure that the chemicals factory would receive an uninterrupted supply of electricity, which would lead to consistent production performance and progressively higher productivity standards.

The other option was to modify the subsidiary's technological processes to be less dependent on electricity and to meet its energy needs from other sources, especially natural gas, which was readily available in Matumba at relatively inexpensive rates. Although using natural gas was relatively cheaper, even after taking into account the costs involved in modifying some of the plant's technological processes and equipment, the option did pose some difficulties. The processes using natural gas were not as advanced as those using electricity, and there could be a marginal decline in product quality, even though the production volume could be maintained at the

same level. Another issue was safety. Although Milford's safety standards were quite strict and well developed, it was possible that they could be compromised at the subsidiary level. The main problem was the safety orientation of local employees. Most had little experience in working in such a plant. A comprehensive safety training program and continued emphasis on safety consciousness could reduce the risks significantly but not eliminate them.

Briggs looked at the report, which concisely put together the main pros and cons of each option and closed with a clear and strong emphasis on the need for early action. "We'll have to decide within the next few weeks," thought Briggs. "Before the Germans and Italians come in and set up their operations, we have to dig in and dominate; it will be impossible to do it later." The next morning the members of the technical operations committee received a notice of a policy meeting to be held Thursday in the main conference room to discuss the problems at the Matumba plant. Attached to the notice was a copy of the report with a request for each member to read it before the meeting.

DISCUSSION QUESTION

1. Assume that you were a member of the Milford technical operations committee. What questions would you raise at the meeting? Which of the options would you suggest? In your opinion, could Milford take other approaches to resolve these issues?

CASE STUDY 16.2
INTERNATIONAL CREDIT BANK

The annual performance review meeting at the headquarters of International Credit Bank had not gone very well for Gregory Fuller, regional vice president for Asia. He had expected trouble at the meeting, but he had not expected the kind of intensely negative feedback he received from Timothy Martin Jr., the bank's president and chief executive officer. Fuller's area of responsibility included the bank's overall operation in southern and Southeast Asia, and the bank had not done very well in the region during the past two years. Martin was extremely upset about this, because the entry of International Credit Bank into this region was his idea, and he had visualized spectacular growth for the bank in this region, which he felt was going to be the main growth area for the next two decades. In fact, Martin had felt that the only real chance for the bank to grow internationally was in this area and other options were almost nil. Africa had been doing so badly that even such international lending agencies as the World Bank were losing heart. On the other hand, Latin America has also been plagued by economic troubles over the years. He, for one, was not going to commit the bank to that part of the world, at least for now, which meant that for the foreseeable future Latin America was forbidden territory for any international expansion plans for International Credit Bank.

International Credit Bank was a major commercial bank based in the United States. Founded in 1920, it had survived the Depression years and become an important player in the international banking markets by the 1960s. The bank's international approach, exemplified by its strong presence in Europe and Australia, had enabled it to grow rapidly in the 1970s and the early 1980s. Commercial banks in general, however, were hit by the growing securitization of international financial markets, and International Credit Bank was no exception. Although it was a large bank, it was quite conservative in its approach and did not wish to set up overseas investment banking subsidiaries to take advantage of new opportunities that were becoming available in the financial markets. As a matter of policy, the bank had decided to expand its commercial banking operations into other countries, both to keep growing and to offset the decline in its European commercial banking business.

The bank, and especially Martin, had great expectations from its move into the Asian countries. The growth prospects were good, the infrastructure was in decent shape, and the Asian economies had, for the most part, recovered from their financial crisis of the late 1990s. Most countries had proven to be good hosts for foreign direct investment and had done very well on the international front, especially in exports. The region had seen improvement in its banking sector, primarily as a result of the Asian financial crisis. Both the increasing domestic prosperity, led by industrialization, and rapid international trade growth signaled important opportunities for a commercial bank such as International Credit Bank, which had excellent facilities for financing both domestic and cross-border transactions.

The bank faced few problems in establishing a presence in most of these countries. Correspond-

continued

Case 16.2 (*continued*)

ing banking relationships were already there, and the bank's Southeast Asia representatives had maintained excellent contacts with the senior government officials in these countries. Approvals for establishment of branches were therefore fairly easy to come by, and within two years the bank had a network of seven branches in four countries of the region. Early business development was greatly facilitated by the presence in all four countries of a number of international companies that were the bank's clients in Europe and North America. After the initial progress, however, the bank's business did not increase as rapidly as Martin had anticipated. His frustration grew as after three years of relatively rapid expansion the bank witnessed only very slow growth for two years. What was worrying Martin was that despite a 100 percent ownership of all the branches, productivity per employee in the branches in Asia was consistently lower than in the branches in Europe and North America. In the performance review meeting he had let his concerns be known quite clearly to Fuller, who had come up with one major reason to explain this problem.

According to Fuller, the bank was growing slowly not because there was not enough business or because the local management was not expending enough effort to obtain new business, but because the local management did not want to take on new business until it was certain that it could handle it effectively and efficiently. At this point, all branches had portfolios that were up to their maximum capacity, and any abnormal expansion of business would have an adverse effect on the quality of work, which could severely damage the excellent reputation that International Credit Bank had built up over

the years in the region. When Martin pointed out that they could expand business with the existing and available resources because the productivity was low, Fuller became quite upset. He said that it was unfair to measure productivity of branches in southern and Southeast Asia using the same criteria used for branches in Europe and North America. Fuller pointed out that there were a number of special constraints on the branches in the region, one of which was a very low level of computerization. Only the lending officers and the branch managers had personal computers and even they had problems in working with these. Martin knew that these branches had at least some form of computerization and asked why they could not increase their level of computerization now. He asked Fuller to go back to the central MIS division of the bank and put together a plan for fully computerizing the seven branches in the region.

Fuller wasted no time following up. Three days later he was flipping over a short but well-documented report from the MIS department on the issue of fully computerizing the seven branches in Southeast Asia. The report suggested that over the next six months, nearly all operations of the branches could be fully computerized. Retail checking and savings, discounting of commercial bills of exchange, letters of credit, accounting and maintenance of ledgers, payroll and benefits, maintenance of credit records and profiles, and information and backup all could be put on a single integrated system. Moreover, if the system worked, these branches could be hooked up with the bank's dedicated communication system using a satellite network channel. The initial costs would be comparatively high,

continued

Case 16.1 (*continued*)

because external consultants would be required to install, debug, and test the system and train the staff. System maintenance would also be an important cost factor, because the hardware supplier did not have a full-service office in two of the four countries to be covered by this project.

As Fuller read the report, one doubt after another rose in his mind, and Fuller began to feel uneasy about the whole project. Just then, the phone rang. It was Julia Peterson, Martin's executive assistant. It appeared that Martin had seen a copy of the report and was excited about it and wanted Fuller to stop by and discuss it right away. Oh no, thought Fuller, as he collected his ideas en route to Martin's plush office. This is going to be quite a difficult job if Martin has made up his mind on this. In any case, I have no choice but to say my bit, since there is no way I am going to take the blame for this whole thing if it goes awry, when I had opposed it in the first place.

Martin welcomed Fuller quite warmly, apparently very pleased with the prospect of his branches in Asia being fully computerized and ready to make the productivity gains he had been seeking for so long. "This is going to really get us a jump start on the competition," he told Fuller. "It seems none of the foreign banks in that part of the world are fully computerized yet. So with one stroke not only will we improve our productivity and increase our business, but we'll also get ahead of the competition. And I am sure the local governments are going to love this, since we will be bringing in high technology. The costs do appear quite high, but then that is to be expected. You can't really get the returns unless you make the investment and I believe this is one investment that is really worth making. Maybe we should have done so earlier, but I guess bunching these

costs along with startup costs would have killed us. Anyway, better late than never, and in this case, it is earlier than the competition. I am sure you agree, don't you, Gregory?"

Fuller spoke with some difficulty. It was obvious that there was a crisis in his mind. Here was the boss, upset with him over the performance of the bank region, now wanting to boost it through a means that Fuller did not think was correct. Nevertheless, he must be honest with himself and Martin and speak his mind. "Well, sir," he began, "the project is technically sound as it is conceived, but there are a number of problems on the ground in these countries that suggest that we should not commit ourselves so rapidly and fully to the type of computerization and automation that has been suggested by the MIS people. These guys are technically sound, but they really do not have an appreciation of the realities as they exist in the field. I know you are concerned about performance there and are of the view that the answer lies in rapid computerization and automation of the operations. Nevertheless, I feel very strongly that we should not ignore the problems that may arise and install a system that may cause more harm than good."

"Well," said Martin, sounding a bit dubious, "it's really your area. Why don't you specify the problems you feel are going to arise and let me have a small executive brief on this by Tuesday morning."

DISCUSSION QUESTION

1. Prepare a short brief on what problems might arise in fully computerizing the operations of branches in Southeast Asia.

PART V

SOCIAL AND
ETHICAL ISSUES AND THE
FUTURE OF INTERNATIONAL
BUSINESS

Ethical Concerns: Multinationals and the Earth's Environment

CHAPTER OBJECTIVES

This chapter will:

- Review the major environmental concerns affecting the global community and the implications they have on multinational corporations at home and abroad.
- Identify new challenges and opportunities that MNCs face as a result of growing environmental concerns.

EMERGING ENVIRONMENTAL CONCERNS

National and international concerns about the environment have increased dramatically over the past decade. Although damage to the earth's environment has been an issue in development and industrial policies in many countries for the past several years, it has not been in the forefront of international attention; other issues, such as economic growth, industrialization, population growth, and poverty, have occupied center stage.

Concern for the environment has grown for several reasons. First, damage to the environment is becoming increasingly visible. A number of environmental and ecological disasters, including several involving large MNCs, have attracted worldwide attention. Second, environmental action groups have become more powerful. The ability of these groups to influence public policy has increased substantially following sustained support, both political and financial, from different sections of society that are more concerned with the environment than ever before. Third, a number of international bodies, such as the United Nations and the World Bank, and national governments have demonstrated their responsiveness to the issue by establishing environmental guidelines and, in the case of governments, by passing laws aimed at protecting the environment.

Concerns for the environment have wide-ranging implications for MNCs in both their home and host countries because not only are MNCs affected by general environmental guidelines but they are viewed as one of the prime sources of danger to the world's environment. This view is valid to a significant extent, given the fact that MNCs influence approximately 25 percent of the world's assets by their actions and affect, in one way or another, approximately 70 percent of internationally traded products and 80 percent of the world's land devoted to the cultivation of export-oriented crops. In many developing countries, MNCs are the prime source of industrial activity. Even where their share in total industrial activity is not large, they are the most visible and therefore the first focus of attention for environmentalist and similar groups.

These developments present both challenges and opportunities for MNCs. The challenges arise in the form of new considerations that MNCs must bear in mind while making investment and operating decisions and the additional costs they must incur to ensure that their operations are environmentally safe and comply with host-country regulations. In some instances, MNCs may be required to close or completely modify the production of certain plants for environmental reasons. Along with these challenges are new opportunities. Concerns with the preservation of the environment call for new types of products and new lines of business and, consequently, create new markets.

SOCIAL RESPONSIBILITY OF BUSINESS

Economists have long debated what constitutes the social responsibility of business. Some, like the economist Milton Friedman, believe that the primary purpose of any business is the maximization of corporate profits. Others believe that a business has an inherent responsibility to, for example, maintain an acceptable work environment for its employees, provide a living wage, provide adequate health benefits to its employees, and reduce the amount of pollutants that stem from the manufacturing of its products. Countries experiencing rapid industrialization, such as India and China, often experience a deterioration in water- and air-quality levels as a by-product of the increase in the burning of fossil fuels such as coal, petroleum, and natural gas.

As is discussed in this chapter, there are countless examples of corporations' ill effects on the environment, but there are almost as many responses to such problems. Some countries, such as those in the European Union, believe in taking unilateral action to reduce their levels of pollution, while other countries, such as the United States and Australia, have expressed the desire to include the rapidly industrializing countries in any agreement regarding pollution control. While economists still debate whether a business has the moral responsibility to protect the environment, it seems that many nations of the world have already assigned this task to manufacturers the world over.

MAJOR ENVIRONMENTAL ISSUES

GREENHOUSE GASES

Greenhouse gases contribute to global warming by trapping heat in the earth's atmosphere. It is predicted that if such gases continue to accumulate at the present rate, they will lead to an increase in the atmospheric temperature by 1.4°C to 5.8°C by the year 2100. This warming could have a disastrous impact on the world's ecological systems and lead to a rise of sea levels by as much as 3 feet (1 meter) and cause the flooding of low-lying coastal areas, many of which are industrial and urban centers with a high population concentration. The gases that contribute most to global warming and the *greenhouse effect* include carbon dioxide, methane, and nitrous oxide, with the first two accounting for approximately 70 percent of the warming effects.

A major source of carbon dioxide accumulation in the atmosphere is industrial combustion of fossil fuels. MNCs are major users of fossil fuels in a number of ways. They extract, refine, and transport much of the world's supply of fossil fuel and are significant consumers of such fuels, both as an intermediate and final source of energy. Table 17.1 illustrates the main economic activities that contribute

Table 17.1

Economic Activities and Global Warming

Activity	Contribution to Global Warming (%)
Energy use and production	57
Industrial	22
Transportation	20
Residential/commercial	15
Use of chlorofluorocarbons	17
Agricultural practices	14
Deforestation and other modifications	9
Other industrial	3
Total	**100**

Source: U.S. Environmental Protection Agency.

to global warming. The production of greenhouse gases as a direct or indirect result of transnational corporations' operations is shown in Table 17.2.

DEPLETION OF THE OZONE LAYER

The earth's environment is protected by a layer of ozone gas in the stratosphere that shields the earth's surface from potentially deadly ultraviolet radiation. In recent years the ozone layer has been seriously damaged by human-made chemicals, especially chlorofluorocarbons (CFCs). CFCs are used to lower temperatures in refrigerators and air conditioners and are utilized in making aerosol and foam propellants. Some CFCs also contribute to global warming, and these and similar chemicals are projected to account for 15 percent to 20 percent of global warming between 1991 and the middle of the twenty-first century. The depletion of stratospheric ozone leads to the accumulation of tropospheric ozone, which is a contributor to global warming through the greenhouse effect.

MNCs have been found responsible for a large proportion of this damage, because they are the main producers of products using and producing CFCs and other chemicals that damage the ozone layer. In fact, all major manufacturers of CFCs are multinational corporations, and the focus of world attention has been quite sharp on this aspect of their activity.

DEFORESTATION

The disappearance of the world's forests has had and is likely to continue to have extremely dangerous ecological consequences. The scale of the problem has already assumed alarming proportions. According to one source, every year 6 million hectares of dry land turns into nonarable desert. More than 11 million hectares of forests are depleted every year, an area approximately the size of Cuba.

Deforestation has a number of adverse global environmental effects. The loss of forest cover on mountains and hillsides decreases the soil retention capacity, which leads to rainwater washing valuable topsoil into rivers, reducing their depth and making them prone to flooding. The lack of forest cover reduces an area's potential rainfall and limits the supply of oxygen, which means that carbon dioxide increases proportionately and adds to global warming.

MNCs have been viewed as responsible for deforestation in many countries for a variety of reasons. Many MNCs are large producers and transporters of timber and timber products. Others have been associated with large industrial and civil construction projects that have been established on former forestlands.

HAZARDOUS WASTE

The production, handling, transport, and disposal of hazardous industrial waste have become of serious concern in many countries, given the risks they

Table 17.2

Greenhouse Gas Production

Gas	Amount of Gas Generated by Transnational Corporations (approximate % of total amount generated)	Significant Sources of Greenhouse Gases
CO_2	50	Emissions from automobiles
		75% of oil and gas and 50% of coal use in OECD countries
		50% of fossil fuel use in developing countries
Methane	10–20	50% from oil and gas production and use
		50% from coal mine emissions
Chlorofluorocarbons	66	Use of aerosol sprays, car air conditioners, solvents, and refrigerators in OECD countries
Other (such as nitrogen oxides and ozone)	50	Emissions from automobiles
		75% of oil and gas use in OECD countries
		50% of coal use in OECD countries
		50% of fossil fuel use in developing countries

Note: A designation of transnational corporation involvement is not meant to exclude involvement by others in the emissions of greenhouse gases, for instance, in their use of cars or other consumer goods. The estimates are designed to indicate an order of magnitude of emissions, which could be affected by measures taken by transnational corporations, whether self-initiated or government mandated.

Source: United Nations Economic and Social Council, Commission of Transnational Corporations.

carry both for the quality of the local environment and for general public health. According to the U.S. Environmental Protection Agency, "Uncontrolled hazardous [waste] sites may present some of the most serious environmental and human health problems the nation has ever faced." Concerns about hazardous industrial waste are now worldwide, the problem being equally serious in many less-developed countries, where regulations relating to the disposal and treatment of hazardous waste are not as well established. Hazardous wastes are generated by a wide variety of industries, in both developed and developing countries. Table 17.3 illustrates some of the key industries in industrializing nations that produce hazardous wastes.

Several ecological accidents and disasters involv-

ing hazardous industrial wastes have shown how serious this threat is becoming. For example, thirteen children died in 1981 from mercury poisoning in Indonesia after eating fish caught in a tributary of Jakarta Bay. Mercury levels in the water, polluted by chemical and heavy-metal wastes from nearby factories, were found to be more than 60 times those deemed safe by international standards. Similarly, a company in Mexico was forced to close after it was discovered to have been pumping highly toxic chromium wastes directly into the aquifer in the Mexico Valley area, threatening the water supply of nearly 20 million people. A critical issue in hazardous waste disposal is the transport of the waste. Companies in countries with heavily regulated hazardous waste disposal methods attempt to circumvent the regula-

Table 17.3

Industries Producing Hazardous Wastes

Key Manufacturing Industries for Industrializing Nations	Hazardous Wastes Produced
Metal finishing, electroplating, etc.	Heavy metals, fluorides, cyanides, acid and alkaline cleaners, abrasives, plating salts, oils, phenols
Leather tanning	Heavy metals, organic solvents
Textiles	Heavy metals, toxic organic dyes, organic chlorine compounds, salts, acids, caustics
Pesticides	Organic chlorine compounds, organic phosphate compounds, heavy metals
Pharmaceuticals	Organic solvents and residues, heavy metals (especially mercury)
Plastics	Organic solvents and residues, organic pigments, heavy metals (especially lead and zinc)

Source: H. Jeffrey Leonard, "Hazardous Waste: The Crisis Spreads."

tions by transporting the wastes to other developing countries with little or no regulations.

MNCs have been accused of not paying enough attention to the problems of hazardous waste in host countries that do not have well-developed environmental control regulatory frameworks. This issue has been brought into the spotlight by several ecological problems and disasters in developing countries that have occurred because of MNC laxity in observing environmentally safe procedures for the disposal and treatment of hazardous wastes generated by their overseas plants. Perhaps the most tragic environmental disaster was the leak of lethal methyl isocyanate gas from Union Carbide's pesticide plant in Bhopal, India, in 1984, which caused more than 2,500 deaths and serious impairment to several thousand more people.

POLLUTION

The problems of industrial pollution became increasingly serious in the late 1980s as industrialization expanded and intensified. Air pollution occurs primarily from emissions from factory chimneys,

while water pollution occurs primarily because of the discharge of industrial effluents into local water bodies. In many countries the air has been so polluted at industrial centers that the local residents have increased incidence of respiratory and other diseases. In other countries, water pollution has ended the use of local rivers, lakes, and bays. Table 17.4 provides an estimate of the countries that emit the highest levels of water pollutants per day.

KYOTO PROTOCOL

In an attempt to curb the collective emissions of greenhouse gases to achieve cleaner air worldwide, a multination agreement called the Kyoto Protocol was signed in 1997. The *Kyoto Protocol* was adopted in the third session of the Conference of Parties to the United Nations Framework Convention on Climate Change, in Kyoto, Japan. The agreement required that 55 countries, which must represent at least 55 percent of the industrial world's greenhouse-gas emissions in 1990, must ratify the agreement for it to take effect. The goal of the Kyoto Protocol is to reduce the collective emissions of

Table 17.4

Water Pollutants (thousands of kilograms of organic emissions daily)

1	China	6,204.2
2	United States	1,968.2
3	India	1,582.3
4	Russia	1,485.8
5	Japan	1,332.3
6	Germany	792.2
7	Indonesia	752.8
8	Brazil	629.4
9	United Kingdom	569.7
10	Ukraine	499.9

Source: Economist, Economist Pocket World in Figures, 2005.

greenhouse gases by 5.2 percent from 1990 levels, while the European Union has agreed to reduce its emissions by 8 percent by 2010.

The European Union has been a strong proponent of the Kyoto Protocol, and the agreement has also been ratified by Japan and Canada. The United States and Australia have not ratified the agreement, so in order to meet the original minimum signatory requirements, Russia needed to ratify the agreement, which it did in November 2004.

MNC RESPONSES

Multinational corporations, for valid reasons, have been held responsible for their contribution to the increased environmental problems the world faces today and are called on to adjust virtually every aspect of their activities.

ESTABLISHING IN-HOUSE ENVIRONMENTAL ETHICS

MNCs' approach to battling environmental pollution and ecological degradation is dependent

to a large degree on the corporation's ethics. The corporation's response to these problems depends on what it perceives to be its responsibility. MNCs have tremendous political leverage, particularly in the smaller LDCs, which are in need of their technology, industrialization, and economic growth. Environmental laws are less developed in LDCs, while public awareness of environmental issues there is limited, and there are few channels for the effective and voluble expression of public opinion. The ruling powers in LDCs generally tend to have almost universal authority, and their decisions are difficult to challenge, which allows MNCs to establish environmentally unsound projects, should they decide to do so, as long as they have the confidence of the local authorities. Many studies have shown that MNCs have tended to locate their more polluting plants in developing countries to escape the strict environmental standards and regulations imposed by developed countries.

It is extremely important for MNCs to take a responsible approach to the environmental issue. Many corporations have adopted such an approach and have voluntarily restricted their environmentally unsound operations and even stopped production of environmentally unsafe products. Many others have not.

RELOCATION OF PRODUCTION

In the past, MNCs' location decisions were principally dependent on techno-economic criteria: raw material supply, infrastructural facilities, availability of a trained workforce, proximity to markets, availability of transportation, and so on. Now decisions to establish plants must evaluate potential effects on the environment. Not only must the economic consequences (such as feasibility and rate of return) be forecast, but plans must be made to protect the local environment. Thus, while permission from a government was sufficient in the past to establish a factory in a host country, MNCs are now likely to be required to discuss their site plans with local representatives to take into consideration their concerns about a plant's actual and potential impact on the local environment and ecological balance.

MODIFICATION OF TECHNOLOGY

Traditionally, the main motivator of technological change was a search for more advanced and economically efficient technologies that would generate new and better products at lower costs. More recently, however, technology development has also focused on environmental safety. Technologies in development must be monitored in regard to their environmental consequences.

RAW MATERIAL USE

Raw material use is an important focus of technological modification. The raw materials currently in use may not be available in the future, principally for two reasons: They may be nonrenewable, as are fossil fuels, and their use may result in consequences that are harmful to the earth's environment. As con-

cerns with the environment grow, MNCs are called on to look at raw materials in terms of not only their monetary price but their ecological consequences as well. Limitations imposed by these considerations exert pressure on MNCs to use technologies that reduce industrial waste, maximize consumption efficiency of raw materials, promote recycling of waste and used products, and concentrate on more durable and lasting products.

ENERGY USE

Energy use is another important area of concern in the general technological modifications that MNCs will have to undertake as part of their response to environmental imperatives. Typical approaches in this area include gradual phasing out of energy-inefficient technologies and introduction of technologies based on clean, renewable, and environmentally safe sources of energy (for example, solar power and hydrogen), as opposed to those based on polluting, nonrenewable sources, generally limited to fossil fuels. The problem has been complicated by nuclear accidents at Three Mile Island in the United States and Chernobyl in the Ukraine, which have placed a major question mark over the future of nuclear energy as an alternative to conventional fossil fuels. The small nation of Iceland has been successful in the use of hydrogen power. Approximately 70 percent of Iceland's energy needs are met by geothermal and hydroelectric power. Iceland has a vast pool of geothermal energy beneath its surface, which allowed for the successful experimentation over the years with alternative sources of energy. All of Iceland's homes are heated via these clean energy sources, and only its transportation industry still requires oil and gas. Recently, Shell opened a hydrogen station in the country, and buses that run on hydrogen power were also introduced (see Figure 17.1).

Energy sources are likely to grow more expensive and scarce, while patterns of energy use are likely to

Figure 17.1

Source: Courtesy Shell Hydrogen—www.shell.com/hydrogen.

be under increasing scrutiny from a number of different quarters, including environmental groups and the media. MNCs must ensure that they use energy sources in an environmentally sound manner, which will require substantial investments in new or modified equipment, such as energy-efficient industrial furnaces, boilers, and exhausts, and new equipment to control atmospheric emissions, such as air filters and gas treatment chambers. Energy use will have to be modified not only in production, but also in all other facets of activity, including transportation.

ENVIRONMENTAL RESTORATION

The response to the environmental challenge cannot be limited to in-company modifications in production, technologies, energy, product mix, or location decisions. It must extend beyond the corporation, because the environmental impact of the operations of industrial concerns affects the local community and, in an aggregate sense, its home or host country. Company responses must be designed to compensate for aspects of environmental regeneration that are most directly and visibly linked to the areas of the corporation activities. For example, companies that use substantial quantities of wood would be called on to support local and national reforestation and social forestry programs. Companies that have had a role in adding to atmospheric pollution would have

to support programs that attempt to remedy the consequences of such pollution, such as the cleanup of lakes and other freshwater bodies damaged by acid rain, or international agreements such as the Kyoto Protocol. More generally, it is becoming a growing responsibility of corporations to foster environmentally responsible behavior both among their employees and in the communities in which they are located.

POLLUTION DISCLOSURE

Environmental disclosure will be an important responsibility of MNCs in the future. MNCs will have to remain aware of and appropriately informed about the environmental impact of their activities through an efficient internal information system. This data would have to be shared with the outside world, both voluntarily and through mandatory reporting requirements and environmental audits. A touchy issue will be environmental compliance by an MNC's joint-venture partners or partly owned subsidiaries in host countries. While an MNC may prescribe a certain environmental standard for itself and wish to have it replicated by its joint-venture partners or overseas subsidiaries, that wish may not be reciprocal. Similarly, overseas partners may impose more stringent environmental constraints that an MNC may not wish to be bound by. The issue of environmental safety has become an important one in many negotiations for international joint ventures, and environmental responsibilities are often incorporated as fundamental provisions in the terms of agreement. MNCs have become particularly sensitive to this issue because of the dangers of environmentally unsound acts that their joint-venture partners might commit, for which they might have to take the blame in both their home and host countries, and which could damage their reputation for environmental responsibility in other countries.

It is extremely important that MNCs disseminate information on their own about the consequences, both favorable and unfavorable, of their operations on the environment. Proper disclosure of such information will be extremely important in maintaining the environmental image of a corporation and facilitating a feeling of confidence among different groups—local governments, creditors, consumers, suppliers, investors—in the firm's environmental soundness. Proper disclosure of the environmental status of a firm's activities also has an important damage-control role, inasmuch as it informs the public about possible dangers. Any harmful consequences for the environment emanating from MNC activity would be much more damaging to a firm if it became known that the MNC had chosen to suppress prior information it had about such a possibility.

IN-HOUSE
ENVIRONMENTAL TRAINING

As a part of overall corporate planning, the environmental consequences of all future company activities should be assessed well in advance. A serious commitment to this type of oversight will enhance the corporate image.

One way of demonstrating this commitment is to include the corporation's environmental approach in its mission statement and corporate objectives. Any business plan intended for external audiences should include company-defined environmental goals, as well as specific plans for implementation. Planning for environmental safety must be comprehensive, covering future investments in plants and other physical facilities, use of natural resources, treatment of industrial wastes, prevention of environmental damage, protection of water resources, and prevention of accidents.

No plan can be successfully implemented if the operating-level staff is not actively educated. This is all the more true of plans for environmental soundness and safety because operating-level staff are likely to view the plans as peripheral to their central functions, not because of their antipathy to the environment, but simply because of their perception of its relative importance in the context of their work. MNCs must therefore engender a sense of commitment to environmental safety and responsibility among management and staff to elicit optimal cooperation in the achievement of the company's environmental objectives.

Personnel must also be informed about the nature of the environmental problems that confront the world, in general, and the environmental consequences of their activities as company workers, in particular. One way to give meaning to this exercise is to spell out ways in which employees could contribute to overall environmental safety in their own tasks. To ensure that these guidelines are taken seriously, firms must establish an incentive structure that encourages employees to monitor environmental standards and provide practical suggestions on how the company's environmental performance could be improved. A reward structure could also be established on a group or unit basis, through which the group could be rewarded on the basis of the environmental safety or standards it is able to maintain over a given period of time. It is essential to involve employees, at both management and staff levels, if any environmental safety program is to be successful.

MNC Opportunities

While the environmental challenges facing MNCs are daunting, a number of opportunities have also arisen. Many MNCs have been quick to anticipate the trends in the world's regulatory, economic, political, and social environments and have been positioned to derive the maximum advantage from them.

New Consumer Products

As the world grows more environmentally conscious, there is an increasing need for environmentally safe products. This demand points to the opening of new markets, first in developed and later in developing countries. Environmentally safe products have already made their appearance in many countries and embrace a wide range, from personal goods to consumer durables. Whole Foods Market is an upper-end grocery store that specializes in selling natural and organically grown food products. The company, which started in Austin, Texas, in 1980, now has approximately 200 store locations throughout the United States, Canada, and the United Kingdom, and proudly displays on its Web site that it has been ranked in the Fortune 100 Best Companies to Work For since 1998. While Whole Foods Market sells products free of preservatives, additives, and colorings, the company has also gone to great lengths to reduce the amount of energy consumption in its store locations, to promote recycling of paper, glass, and plastic, and to collect reusable items for recycle such as batteries, light bulbs, and computer equipment. As mentioned on the company's Web site, numerous store locations have utilized solar power for almost one-quarter of the store's energy needs.

New Technologies

Firms specializing in technology development are already receiving large orders for new, environmentally safe technologies in a wide range of industries. Environmental-control technologies are in particular demand. Furnaces that burn cleaner, more efficient production processes, and technologies to treat toxic emissions and effluents are all in great demand. Automobile manufacturers have been selling hybrid automobiles, which run on a combination of gasoline and a rechargeable battery, for the last few years, a trend likely to continue given these vehicles' fuel efficiency.

New Industrial Products

Today's plants require a large number of mechanical modifications to meet environmental standards. Water-treatment plants, emission-control filters, waste-management systems, and the like represent new markets and opportunities that are going to expand across the world.

Substitute Products

A number of products that are in wide use but are considered dangerous to the environment are likely to be phased out and replaced. Certain types of plastic products that were found to be resistant to biodegradation, for example, have been replaced with other polyurethane foam products, which either are biodegradable or can be recycled.

New Energy Sources

A number of companies are intensively researching the development of new sources of energy for the future. Along with developing energy sources, firms are attempting to develop new devices and products that run on such sources of energy. One of the most important examples of such an energy source is solar power, which is clean, environmentally safe, and virtually unlimited. Working models of solar-powered automobiles have been developed and other solar-powered products have been in use for several years. As mentioned above, environmentally conscious companies such as Whole Foods Market have implemented solar power in their stores in an attempt to save money while utilizing a clean source of energy. Additionally, oil giant Shell has embraced the concept of the hydrogen fuel cell enough to open a hydrogen station in Iceland.

ENVIRONMENTAL CONSULTING

Corporations specializing in environmental technology, design, and management and similar areas are already flooded with contracts and offers to develop environmental safety programs in several different countries. This area is likely to grow rapidly as industrial concerns, local and national governments, and communities attempt to upgrade the environmental quality of industries, neighborhoods, and other aspects of everyday activities. The growing support from the developed countries for such concerns has enabled the collection of substantial funds from various charitable and other foundations to be used to finance such services across a broad spectrum of countries.

THE ENVIRONMENT IS CENTER STAGE

The environmental issue has clearly moved from the periphery of MNC concerns to center stage. The environment now has to be factored into almost every decision, and top management can no longer simply delegate the responsibilities in this area. It is an issue for the headquarters of every MNC to consider when planning global and local strategies, whatever the internal organization structure of the business. MNCs that take an enlightened approach to this issue are quick to capitalize on opportunities while managing risks effectively and are likely to end up the winners. Unlike other forms of corporate activity, however, it is not enough if one corporation wins and another loses. Everyone must win if the earth's fragile and currently endangered environment is to be nurtured and sustained.

SUMMARY

Environmental concerns over greenhouse gases, depletion of the ozone layer, deforestation, hazardous wastes, and industrial air pollution have moved to the forefront of international concern and attention. Because of the significant control and influence that MNCs have over world resources, they are being challenged to operate in more environmentally responsible ways. These challenges include conducting business ethically, conducting environmental impact studies before making plant location decisions, implementing technological modifications to reduce waste and increase environmental safety, developing environmentally safe energy sources, accepting social responsibilities for environmental regeneration, diversifying manufacturing, planning, educating, sharing information, and increasing investment in R & D.

New opportunities, however, are being created as new products and markets designed to meet environmental concerns become available.

DISCUSSION QUESTIONS

1. Why should MNCs be concerned with global environmental issues?
2. What are greenhouse gases?
3. What has been causing the depletion of the ozone layer? What role have MNCs played in this process?
4. What are hazardous wastes? Find some recent examples (from the *Wall Street Journal* or other periodicals) in which MNCs have been involved in either producing or cleaning up hazardous wastes.
5. How can MNCs be more responsible for the global environment? Explain your answer.
6. What new opportunities will MNCs enjoy as a result of increased attention to environmental problems?

BIBLIOGRAPHY

Bruce, Leigh. "How Green Is Your Company?" *International Management*, January 1989, 24–27.

Economist. *The Economist Pocket World in Figures*, Profile Books, Ltd., London, 2005 edition.

Jay, Leslie. "Green About the Tills: Markets Discover the Eco-Consumer." *Management Review*, June 1990, 24–28.

Johnstone, Bob. "A Throw-Away Answer." *Far Eastern Economic Review*, February 1990, 62–65.

"Kyoto Protocol," *The United Nations Framework Convention on Climate Change*, http://unfccc.int/resource/docs/convkp/kpeng.html, accessed April 26, 2005.

Leonard, H. Jeffrey. "Hazardous Waste: The Crisis Spreads." *National Development*, April 1986, 44.

Leonard, Richard. "After Bhopal: Multinationals and the Management of Hazardous Waste." *Multinational Business*, no. 2 (1986): 1–9.

Mahon, John F., and Patricia C. Kelley. "Managing Toxic Wastes: After Bhopal and Sandoz." *Long Range Planning*, August 1987, 50–59.

Roberts, Gerald. "World Energy Outlook: What Managers Should Expect." *Multinational Business*, Spring 1989, 33–36.

Shell Hydrogen. "A Hydrogen Future for Iceland." Brochure. http://www-static.shell.com/static/hydrogen-en/downloads/brochures/brochure, accessed April 26, 2006.

Smith, Douglas N. "EC Toughen Pollution Regulations." *Business Insurance*, March 5, 1990, 21.

Terpstra, V., and K. David. *The Cultural Environment of International Business*. 3rd ed. Cincinnati, OH: South-Western, 1991.

U.S. Environmental Protection Agency. "Policy Options for Stabilizing Global Climates." Draft Report to the U.S. Congress. 1989.

Whole Foods Market. "Environmental Policy." http://www.wholefoodsmarket.com//issues/list_environment.html.

CASE STUDY 17.1

ALAPCO CHEMICALS LTD.

Wilbur Stevens looked in dismay at the mound of toxic waste piled high in a closed-off area near his factory as he was driven past the dumping ground on his way to another busy day at his office in the Los Helios factor of Alapco Chemicals, where he was general manager. Los Helios was a major industrial location in the southern part of Valdina, a small country in Central America that had close ties with the United States and was heavily dependent on U.S. aid for its continued survival. Alapco Chemicals had established its factory in Los Helios in 1934 and expanded operations considerably. The main products of the Los Helios factory were pesticides and insecticides that were in great demand by Valdina farmers, whose crops were in danger from grave damage by weeds and pests that flourished in the hot and humid climate. Alapco was the only important producer of these products in the country and enjoyed a monopoly over the market.

Although the company had shown consistent growth in both sales and profitability over the past decade, recently its environmental record had begun to be called into question by environmental groups, especially those based in the United States. Attention to the environmental problems of Valdina had been attractive for a number of reasons. The air pollution in the country, especially in the area near Los Helios, was among the worst in the world. The country's forests had been almost completely decimated by indiscriminate logging both for revenue and for clearing land for new communities and industry in the small country. The nine main beaches of the country were so polluted by

industrial and municipal waste that they had been declared unfit for swimming. One beach had been totally closed to the general public for the past five years.

A group of environmental activists had focused the blame on the government of Valdina and on local and foreign industry. Until two years ago there was no systematic legislation or even regulation of the environmental aspects of industrial and other forms of economic and development activities. The only regulation was in the form of some weak and often outdated factory codes, which were rarely enforced. Further, the government did not have a separate agency for environmental control, and the issues, if any were raised, were handled by the ministry concerned with a particular industry.

Growing international attention and increasingly visible effects of the environmental deterioration in Valdina had ultimately goaded the government into action. In 2004 environmental legislation was passed that contained guidelines to be observed both by industry and agriculture. Globe-Watch, an active environmental action group in Washington, DC, helped the government draft the legislation, which in its final form turned out to be fairly streamlined and quite stringent.

Enforcement of the legislation, however, was another matter. The government of Valdina, strapped for cash and deep in debt, did not have the resources to establish a system of periodic inspections and follow-ups to ensure that the guidelines were actually being followed. More-

continued

Case 17.1 (*continued*)

over, being dependent on industry, especially the multinationals, to raise revenues, the government hardly had the political will to take stern measures to enforce its decree. As a result, much of the legislation remained merely on paper and any implementation was done voluntarily. Voluntary action was also limited because following the safeguards meant substantial capital outlay toward the purchase and installation of pollution-control equipment in factories or toward modifying a plant or processes to ensure that they caused less environmental damage.

Alapco was one of the main polluters, partly because of the sheer size of its operation (it had the largest single plant in Valdina), partly because of the nature of the chemical-manufacturing process, and partly because some of its processes were quite old and had not been modified to control their effect on the environment. Again, because Alapco was the only producer of some of the chemicals needed by Valdina's farmers and because the company's top executives had extremely close connections with the government, no action was taken to enforce the new regulations, and things remained pretty much as they were for the next year, until Stevens arrived in Los Helios as the new general manager of the plant.

Stevens was a brilliant engineer who held a master's degree in chemical engineering from Carnegie-Mellon University and an MBA from the Massachusetts Institute of Technology. He had worked with a tire company in Great Britain and with a chemical firm in Germany before returning to the United States as operations manager for Alapco's plant in Peoria, Illinois. In Peoria, Stevens had made an excellent impression with the senior management and workers. His

management style and unique abilities had been major factors in turning around the plant's performance within three years from subpar productivity to one of the best among Alapco's fifteen plants. As a result, Stevens had been identified by top management as a potential candidate for the highest levels of the company hierarchy. As a part of the plan to groom him for senior management positions by giving him greater responsibilities and exposing him to an international situation, Stevens was appointed general manager and chief executive officer of the company's plant at Los Helios in Valdina.

On reaching Los Helios, Stevens was struck by the dominance Alapco enjoyed in the country. He was regularly invited to receptions given by senior government officials, and nearly every request he made on behalf of the company was quickly processed with a positive response. The plant was also operating with a reasonable degree of efficiency, considering its rather outmoded technology. Alapco's senior management had, as a matter of policy, continued to use this technology, taking the view that it was adequate to meet the current needs of the market in Valdina and that the introduction of new technology would result in high costs that the company would not be able to recover under the present conditions and market structure in Valdina.

Stevens soon began to feel quite comfortable in his new position. Valdina had an excellent school for children of American expatriates, which were many, and his family had managed to adjust to the new conditions quite well. After a few months, however, he received a group of visitors from Washington who left him feeling quite uneasy. They were members of a delegation from Global-

continued

Case 17.1 (*continued*)

Watch, and they informed Stevens that their group had helped the government of Valdina formulate the environmental policy and that they were, on their own, following up on that legislation. At first Stevens was quite annoyed and stated that this was a matter between his company and the government of Valdina and that if his plant was violating any of the regulations, it was for the government of Valdina to say so and not any third party. Further, he added, not a single letter or any other communication had been received from the government of Valdina on this issue, and he therefore believed that his plant was complying with all government requirements. The environmentalists were very direct. They brought out a list of environmental violations that the operations of Alapco's plant were actually committing every day and compared them to the operations of Alapco's plants in other areas, especially in the developed world. Their presentation made clear that Alapco was following two different environmental standards: one in developed countries and one in the developing countries. As far as Valdina was concerned, the reason for the double standard was the absence of the government's ability or willingness to enforce the legislation.

Stevens saw the point. He had been aware of this problem but he had not seen it in the same light as the environmental group, that is, as an ethical and moral responsibility of his company to their host country. Yes, there were toxic waste dumps just outside the plant and barely three miles from a densely populated residential area. A tropical storm could blow off the waste and cause serious damage. The emissions from the factory's chimneys were far higher in pollutants than those at any of the other plants. The Valdina plant had no effluent-treatment facility and all the chemical waste was routinely dumped into the sea. The problem was that in Valdina, all this seemed natural. Everyone was doing it and no one said anything. Nevertheless, Stevens realized that this was fundamentally wrong and that the company should do something about it.

He called the company's headquarters in Lansing, Michigan, and suggested that unilateral action be taken to improve the environmental standards of the Alapco plant and bring them in line with the other plants of the company. He also submitted a cost estimate and pointed out that while there would be a slight erosion in the profits of the company, the benefits to the host country would be great. The head office, however, did not appear very enthusiastic. Although the members of the senior management team did not say so directly, the message seemed to be, "If we don't have to do it, why should we?"

Stevens was quite disappointed by this reaction. Maybe there is another way out of this mess, he thought as he drove past the waste dump outside the factory.

DISCUSSION QUESTION

1. What would you do in this situation if you were:
   A. Wilbur Stevens?
   B. Director of Globe-Watch?
   C. Minister for industries of the government of Valdina?

CHAPTER 18

Future Issues in International Business

CHAPTER OBJECTIVES

This chapter will:

- Summarize the latest trends in international relations and trade.
- Identify the role that technological innovation will have in creating greater efficiency and productivity.
- Present a forecast of how multinational corporations will evolve in the areas of staffing, management style, and location of manufacturing facilities.
- Offer other issues that will influence the MNC of the future.

WHY STUDY THE FUTURE?

Not only must international business managers manage their operations in the present, they must also anticipate future changes. The need to assess future trends that are likely to impact business operations is obvious. If a business is able to accurately anticipate future trends, it has that much more time to adjust its own business practices and strategies, and when the expected changes actually occur, it will be in an excellent position to respond.

It is difficult to predict how and where changes will occur, but it is useful to assess future trends. Many firms develop sophisticated internal forecasting methods to generate possible scenarios in their areas of interest. Other firms use the services of specialized agencies or consulting firms that concentrate on future analysis.

There are, however, a few identifiable broad trends and resulting scenarios that are likely to have a major impact on the functioning and responses of international businesses.

FUTURE TRENDS AFFECTING INTERNATIONAL BUSINESS

EUROPEAN UNION INTEGRATION

As discussed in chapters 4 and 6, membership in the European Union increased to 25 countries in May 2004. For this union to be successful in the years to come, this expanding group of countries, which come with a variety of economic histories and cultural backgrounds, must figure out a way to succeed without infringing on the national sovereignty of the member states. Small nations such as Denmark have already expressed concern about being engulfed in a large bureaucratic organizational structure headquartered in Brussels, and there are other problems on the horizon. With the inclusion of Cyprus in the European Union in 2004, the problem of Turkey must be resolved. The northern portion of the island of Cyprus has been under Turkish control since the early 1970s, but this portion of the island was not admitted to the European Union when the southern portion of the island was admitted. The Northern Turkish Republic of Cyprus is recognized as a sovereign nation only by Turkey itself; and Turkey has ambitions of joining the European Union in the near term. Originally, Turkey's application for admission to the European Union was stalled, as the country was located primarily in Asia, but with the admission of Cyprus to the European Union, this geographic rationale is not as likely to thwart Turkey's desires. Turkey has also made numerous improvements domestically in terms of human rights, and in the performance of its economy, all with EU membership in mind. If Turkey is eventually admitted into the European Union, it would be the only country with a Muslim majority in the EU. How the integration of Turkey into the European Union is handled could affect the union's relationship with other Islamic countries in the world, as well as the overall relationship between the European Union and the United States.

From an economic perspective, many of the current EU member states have had trouble meeting the "convergence criteria" as outlined in the Maastricht Treaty, with both Germany and France missing the deficit-to-GDP hurdle over the last few years. As with any policy, the failure to invoke punishment for exceeding the agreed fiscal constraints of the European Union will lead to the criteria themselves losing significance. There is already talk of changing the requirements in terms of the convergence criteria, thus making the hurdles less strict in coming years. This seems to make sense as the European Union expands, since the next group of possible EU members includes the likes

of Romania and Bulgaria, whose economic performance over the last few years has been less similar to that of the recently admitted countries. In the aftermath of the Danish veto concerning adopting the euro, all future member states (including the 10 admitted in 2004) must adopt the euro eventually. Some countries, on admission, will require more time to meet the necessary requirements of euro adoption, but none have the ability to opt out of the currency union.

Another area of concern for the future of the European Union is the movement of Britain from its present common law system to the EU-mandated civil law system. As was discussed in an earlier chapter, civil law is more codified, while common law relies on the precedence of decisions in the past to judge contemporary concerns. Should Britain move to the EU civil law system, it will find that its reliance on legal precedence is no longer acceptable and that some of the codified laws practiced in the European Union could in fact differ from what Britain has been used to for centuries.

The final area of concern for the European Union going forward is the successful ratification of the recently completed European Union Constitution. Should any of the member states not ratify the constitution in its current form, yet another revision of this document will be required. Given the recent enlargement of the European Union and the possible new members coming in after 2007, putting together a constitutional document that is agreeable to all member states may become difficult.

THE RISE OF INDIA AND CHINA

As has been discussed numerous times in this text, China and India have come a long way economically in the years since the first edition of this book was written. India, which has undergone much economic reform to reduce the level of protection from foreign direct investment, has become the recipient of many service-sector (especially technological) jobs from the United States and others in the Western world. Likewise, China has also seen an incredible growth in its annual GDP, which some forecast will be higher than that of the United States by the year 2050. Much of China's expansion has come in the manufacturing sector, with China becoming ever more important in industries such as apparel, textiles, and furniture. Given the amount of joint ventures currently being undertaken between China and the Western world, China has been looking for a level of technology transfer from the West that would enable it to begin to manufacture products in some of the upper-end segments of industries where it is only currently the low-cost provider (such as apparel and furniture).

How long GDP expansion in both India and China will continue is not known, but these economies should continue to successfully supplant much of the lower-cost jobs in both the service sector and the manufacturing sector in the Western world, which may increase calls for protectionism in the West in the years to come.

PROTECTIONISM AND TRADE AGREEMENTS

The United States has signed numerous bilateral free-trade agreements over the last decade, and this trend should continue in the near term. Bilateral agreements such as the U.S.-Singapore Free Trade Agreement (FTA), the U.S.-Vietnam FTA, and the U.S.-Chile FTA all promote the protection of certain industries that the United States still deems as strategic, such as agriculture and telecommunications. Over the last few years, there has been an increasing desire for the protection of various industries due to competition from Asia. Some industries, such as the furniture industry, are on opposite sides of the protectionism argument depending on which sector is being considered. Furniture manufacturers in the United States have lobbied Congress for the creation

of protective barriers given the "unfair competition" coming from China, while furniture retailers, who profit from the lower-cost furniture coming from China, have lobbied against such protection.

With the agreed end to the textile quotas at the end of 2004, nations with a high reliance on textile exports, such as Pakistan, have begun to orchestrate their own bilateral trade agreements with the developed world in an attempt to maintain high export levels. Thus, there will be a push from developing countries for the creation of more bilateral trade agreements, something that some economists have referred to as a "spaghetti bowl" of world trade agreements, all having different preferential arrangements depending on what each signatory country has to offer.[1] As the proliferation of bilateral trade agreements increases, the relevance of the World Trade Organization may be materially affected, as this organization does not have the ability to resolve disputes between countries that are not engaged in multilateral trade agreements. While we have discussed numerous multilateral trade associations in this text, such as NAFTA, ASEAN, and the European Union, bilateral trade agreements seem to be the order of the day, and their success could impede the progress of multilateral agreements. However, if the success of bilateral agreements, such as the ones recently signed by the United States, is less important in terms of the percentage of world trade, the influence of the WTO in trade policy will continue to be significant.

DEPRECIATION OF THE U.S. DOLLAR

As was discussed in earlier chapters, the U.S. dollar has been of historical significance in international business. Over the last few years, the U.S. dollar has experienced a significant deterioration when compared to the British pound, the euro, and the Canadian dollar. In fact, former Federal Reserve chairman Paul

Volcker has said that there is a 75 percent chance of a significant currency crisis in the United States within the next five years. While this depreciation is good for U.S. exporters in the short term, as their goods are relatively less expensive when compared to the foreign goods priced in the foreign markets, the long-term effect of the depreciation of the dollar could begin to impact foreign portfolio and direct investment into the United States.

The U.S. economy has certainly been the engine of the world economy over the last decade, and the U.S. consumer's penchant for buying foreign imports has contributed to both the high level of consumer indebtedness and the negative current account balance in the United States since the 1980s. What is not clear, however, is how sustainable the current consumer spending spree is in the United States, and the impact that continued current account deficits will have on the demand for U.S. dollars going forward.

Some economists have predicted that the continued depreciation of the dollar will lead to many countries relying on an "index" approach to their foreign reserves. Rather than holding U.S. dollars as the primary foreign reserve currency, some countries may opt to hold a portfolio of foreign currencies such as the yen, euro, and British pound, along with the U.S. dollar. To correct the downward movement of the U.S. dollar, other economies such as India, China, Japan, and the European Union not only must become sources of imports to the United States but also must become consumers of U.S. products and services in their own right. This will necessitate both effective world trade agreements and structural reforms in many of the aforementioned economies to increase the level of consumption and GDP growth over the next decade.

ENERGY POLICY

The rise of China has brought with it an increased demand for oil over the last few years. As was discussed in Chapter 17, countries such as Iceland have successfully incorporated the use of alternative sources of energy, such as hydrogen, in their economies. But, for the foreseeable future, the continued use of fossil fuels such as oil, coal, and natural gas will dominate energy policy throughout the world. Table 18.1 provides a summary of the largest players in the oil consumption and production markets.[2]

As you can see, the United States is the world's largest consumer of oil, followed by China. Given the high level of industrialization in both China and India recently, and given that this process is expected to increase in the future, both of these countries should exhibit an increase in demand for oil in the coming years. It remains to be seen how the oil-producing countries will handle the increase in world oil demand. Saudi Arabia certainly has spare capacity from what it is currently producing, but many of the world's other primary sources of oil are producing at levels that are either at or approaching their national daily capacities.

GLOBAL RESOURCE DEPLETION

The next few decades are likely to be marked by rapid and far-reaching changes in the world economy that will influence international business in a variety of ways. The world's natural resources are likely to be depleted rapidly, and substitutes will have to be found. The depletion of such natural resources as oil, metallic ores, and minerals will weaken the economic position of those countries that rely almost solely on the export of such commodities for their foreign exchange earnings. On the other hand, exclusive monopoly over the technology used to manufacture substitutes could be acquired by large MNCs, which would increase their international economic dominance.

ENVIRONMENTAL DEGRADATION

At the dawn of the twenty-first century, international concerns about the rapid and extensive deterioration

Table 18.1

Oil Production and Consumption (thousands of barrels per day)

Oil Production				Oil Consumption	
Saudi Arabia	9,817	1	United States	20,071
Russia	8,540	2	China	5,982
USA	7,454	3	Japan	5,451
Iran	3,852	4	Germany	2,664
Mexico	3,789	5	Russia	2,503
China	3,396	6	India	2,426
Norway	3,260	7	South Korea	2,303
Venezuela	2,987	8	Canada	2,149
Canada	2,986	9	France	1,991
UAE	2,520	10	Italy	1,927

Source: Economist Pocket World in Figures, Profile Books, Ltd., London, 2006 ed., p. 53.

of the world's environment had gained significant public attention, and environmental action groups had acquired considerable political influence in many countries, especially in the United States and western Europe. Environmental groups were also active in many LDCs in Latin America, Asia, and Africa.

Much of the blame for the damage to the environment has been, and continues to be, placed on the MNCs. Concerns for the environment are particularly strong in certain areas of ecological damage: harm to the earth's ozone layer, atmospheric pollution, deforestation, pollution of inland freshwater resources and coastal waters, and damage to the marine environment.

There is no doubt that pressures are likely to grow, and they may have several important consequences for MNCs. There is likely to be more stringent official regulation of the pollution and environmental effects of MNCs' manufacturing activities both at home and in host countries. A host country's greater awareness of the harmful effects of manufacturing activity on its local environment is likely to result in tougher environmental standards for MNCs setting up overseas operations. Further, MNCs may be required to reduce the environmentally adverse effects of their existing operations by installing more sophisticated pollution-control equipment or spending more on remedying existing environmental damage.

MNCs must also consider the possibility that environmental activists, who are increasingly influential in many developing countries, will take political action against them. It is indeed possible that while an MNC may meet the environmental standards laid down by the host government and have approval for its manufacturing operation, it may still face strong opposition from environmental activists who could attempt to stall actual implementation in a variety of ways. Such instances have occurred in a number of places around the world and it is possible that this tactic may mark a growing global trend.

For MNCs this scenario implies a need for greater investment in R & D for new environmentally safe production technologies and effective and economical pollution-control methods. Further, since public concern is so widespread, it is important for MNCs to increase their public relations efforts to convince governments and the general public that their operations are not harmful to the environment. Thus, in addition to product image, brand image, corporate image, and social image, the MNC of the future will have to be increasingly concerned with its environmental image.

The concerns with the environment will also open new business opportunities for MNCs of the future. The development of pollution-control technologies and equipment by MNCs would put them in a position to market those to other MNCs and companies in host countries. Further concerns with the environment will open up demands for new types of technologies aimed at solving some of the world's environmental problems and preventing further damage. Recycling, waste management, and reforestation are some of the things that are immediately important. In addition, there is likely to be considerable demand for environmentally sound products, such as biodegradable or recyclable materials. Many major corporations are now developing new products that address these concerns, and most of them are selling well.

INTERNATIONAL TERRORISM

In the aftermath of the events of September 11, 2001, the world must now deal with the threat of international terrorism, which has the potential to disrupt international business in the years to come. Aside from individual terrorist acts, which cause a temporary disruption in business, the Straits of Malacca, which is utilized by commercial shipping vessels on entry and exit from the port of Singapore, has seen a rapid increase in piracy and remains an area of the world that could have a tremendous impact on international shipping if problems such as these are allowed to escalate. The existing international agreements concerning the security and utilization of international waters must be improved to allow for the prosecution of those that disrupt commercial shipping vessels in the area, and modernization must be brought to countries that currently harbor or support international terrorist groups.

THE DOHA AGENDA

One method for reducing the amount of terrorism in the world is increasing the level of modernity and the benefits of such modernity throughout the world. Many of the countries that support international terrorism are in fact failed states. Nations that are not poor but still support terrorism have yet to see the benefits of globalization reach their poorest citizens. The Doha Round of trade negotiations has the goal of improving the lives of those in the developing world ("the South") via increase in trade with the nations of the developed world ("the North"). Some economists, such as Jeffrey Sachs of Columbia University, believe that economic and social improvements in African nations will reduce the likelihood of failed states that may then become havens for terrorists. One primary area of improvement in the Doha agenda can be the reduction of protection of the agriculture industries of the developed world. This is an industry where many developing countries are able to produce products for export, but too often the wealthier countries have protectionist policies in place that do not allow them to sell their products in international markets. Another area of improvement is in the area of trade barriers within the developing nations themselves, as these barriers often prevent the distribution of goods and services that could improve the quality of life for the citizens of LDCs. The French have a saying that it is better to remove the swamps than to swat at mosquitoes,[3] the equivalent of which would be the improvement of the quality of life via increased trade, which in turn will reduce the likelihood of terrorist havens spreading throughout the developing world.

MIGRATION

Given the increased openness of many economies in the developed world, another issue that will require attention in the years to come is migration. With the addition of 10 new members to the European Union, the citizens of all of these new entrants will eventually have the ability to migrate anywhere within the European Union in search of work. Germany, which is the closest geographically to many of the new entrants, has gained a temporary restriction on the number of new immigrants from the east. In the United States, there have been calls for stricter border controls in both Mexico and Canada in the wake of the terrorist attacks of September 11, 2001. Parallel to the concern of too many immigrants in the near term is the potential problem of not having enough immigrants into the Western world in the long run. Many of the developing economies of the European Union, the United States, Canada, and Japan will need new workers in the future given current population trends. The aging of the citizens in the developed world will continue for the foreseeable future and will require either an increased level of job outsourcing to countries with very young populations (such as India or China) or an ease in immigration requirements to ensure that the necessary occupations are filled in the developed world. Some countries, such as Denmark, have begun to raise the restrictions of entry into their countries, while other countries, such as Canada, have increased the granting of citizenship to immigrants in an effort to increase the country's working population.

ACCOUNTING STANDARDS

Over the last few years, there have been corporate fraud scandals in countries such as the United States, Canada, and Russia and throughout the European Union. New legislation, such as the Sarbanes-Oxley Act in the United States, has attempted to correct ethical problems that have proliferated along with the increased openness of financial markets worldwide.

Given the amount of publicity surrounding the violating companies such as Enron, Nortel, Parmalat, and Yukos, the international businessperson should expect more regulation in the future as opposed to less. The successful multinational will keep abreast of these new regulations to determine how best to function under the new regulatory environment.

TECHNOLOGY EXPLOSION: THE INFORMATION ERA

Technology has been one of the most important driving forces behind internationalization of business in the twentieth century. In the twenty-first century, this is likely to be even more so. Many major industrial corporations that have made large investments in technologies—lasers, fiber optics, superconductivity, digital electronics—are likely to find themselves at a significant competitive advantage vis-à-vis their competitors in their own and other countries. The depletion of natural resources and the growing consciousness about the threats to the environment are likely to spur new technological advances in safe and regenerative products.

Technology is also likely to make the working of international business more efficient and more competitive. The revolution in information and communications technology has already made it possible for a large MNC to monitor simultaneously from a single location the operation of hundreds of its locations and offices spread across different countries and time zones. The expected increases in communications and computing power are likely to make this control even more efficient and economical and add significantly to MNCs' business capabilities. In fact, the types of communication and internal and external information services and systems available to a globally oriented company are likely to be an increasingly important factor in the firm's overall competitiveness. The edge provided by the access to advanced information technology will also expand the scope of international business because it will enable corporations to search, locate, analyze, evaluate, and choose new business opportunities and possibilities in different parts of the world with a facility that was not possible in the past.

THE INTERNET

Another area of increased future regulation will more than likely be the Internet. Communist countries, such as China, as well as theocratic governments, such as Iran, have already begun to censor Internet Web sites. Governments around the world will also increase the level of taxation of consumption on the Internet. It is apparent that the Internet will continue to bridge the gap of geographical distance between a given consumer and a given company, and should increase the level of international trade. There are numerous small businesses in the world that are based on the Internet and that connect buyers and sellers throughout the world in a way before unimaginable.

IMPACT OF TRENDS ON MNCS

The multinational corporation is likely to remain the dominant form of corporate organization in international business for several years to come. Its form and manner of operation, however, are likely to change substantially in response to changes and trends in the business environment.

THE MEGACORPORATION

Developments in information, communications technologies, computers, and transportation are likely to shrink the world further and enable easier geographical expansion for major corporations. It is likely that today's corporations, seeking expansion, will utilize these opportunities to increase the size of their operations.

Although developments in technology are going to be rapid and far-reaching, they are also likely to be extremely expensive. Only very large corporations are going to be able to afford the expense of specialized and dedicated computer and communication networks, state-of-the-art manufacturing technologies, and the massive investments needed to build entirely new plants based on the new technologies. These firms will thus have a massive technological and competitive edge over their competitors.

Smaller companies may fall by the wayside, either going out of business or readjusting their operational focus. Mergers and acquisitions are going to continue to be common because major international corporations will attempt to either eliminate or join the competition. Strategic alliances may become more common because major corporations eye the same markets and work out relationships that share resources, strengths, and competitive advantages. Some of these trends are already beginning to surface. There has already been much consolidation of the banking industry in both the United States and in Europe.

GEOCENTRIC STAFFING

The personnel of MNCs are likely to become more geocentric than they are today. As the number of locations of operations increases, the parent office is likely to find it increasingly difficult to secure executives from the home country to fill positions in all locations. Moreover, as overseas personnel join MNCs in increasing numbers, a large pool of well-qualified local and third-country nationals is likely to emerge and be available for deployment in different operational locations of the globally oriented enterprise. In many developing countries, standards of technical and managerial education are rising rapidly. MNCs are finding it useful to recruit personnel locally for manning overseas operations, even at relatively senior levels. The geocentric corporation of the future is likely to have an internationally varied managerial executive cadre that is extremely mobile, regardless of individual nationality.

MULTICULTURAL MANAGEMENT

Management styles are likely to change considerably over the years, as global corporations respond to rapid changes. Corporations of the future are likely to incorporate management styles that will adapt to a host-country sociocultural environment instead of imposing home-country standards and practices. The experience gained managing in overseas locations, cultures, and environments is likely to generate a well-defined international management policy that will be based on a much better understanding of the different sociocultural environments of global corporation operations, which would definitely improve the interface with local governments, clients, and business associates and improve the efficiency and success rate of local operations.

MANAGERIAL TECHNOCRATS

Managers of the future must become technocrats, intimately familiar with the latest in communication and computer technologies, to be able to operate in their hi-tech office environments. There may be a lesser degree of physical effort required because improved communication facilities would cut down the need for the frequent traveling endured by today's international managers. Some indications of this scenario are already available in the form of videoconferencing facilities that are prevalent in many MNCs today. Increasing traffic congestion and rising problems of inner-city living will increase the development of the home office, which would enable a manager to work from home and be in constant touch with the office via advanced telecommunication facilities.

OVERSEAS MANUFACTURING FACILITIES

The growth of overseas manufacturing facilities is likely to continue due to the availability of lower labor costs in potential host countries, and MNCs are likely to be better served by this arrangement. As host governments mature, politically as well as economically, they are likely to prefer direct investment in their countries by MNCs, instead of receiving finished products in the form of imports. Foreign direct investment generally stimulates the local economy, and its benefits can be considerable if the local economy itself is well managed and balanced.

As the trend toward greater openness and market orientation takes root, many host countries are likely to seek direct investment by foreign firms, either by participation in privatization programs of existing state-owned enterprises or by takeovers of loss-making units in the private sector. The benefits of the infusion of new technology and managerial skills and capital gained by the host countries will be recompensed by new business opportunities and a spread of the manufacturing base nearer the market for the MNCs.

Locating production overseas provides access to cheap labor and inexpensive inputs and reduces transit costs. Moreover, a more open and market-oriented government would be less prone to expropriate or nationalize an MNC's assets and, therefore, would not constitute a great political risk. This would provide a much better climate for foreign direct investment.

The one constraint that might inhibit rapid growth of foreign direct investment in many LDCs is the inability of the host countries to generate the foreign exchange resources necessary to enable a repatriation of profits by the foreign enterprises. One way out of this constraint is the linking of new investments by MNCs in foreign-exchange-strapped host countries to commensurate earnings by exports, either of its own products or those of other host country commodities or manufactures. Similarly, debt-equity swaps may result in additional investment, even in countries that are heavily burdened with external debt obligations.

FINANCIAL INTEGRATION

The 1990s saw several major changes in the fundamental relationships between the different international financial markets, which were reflected in new levels of integration, modernization, and globalization. Financial markets of the future are likely to be even more integrated, as existing barriers crumble and the free flow of funds becomes still easier across national borders. While integration and deregulation are characteristic of today's markets only in the industrialized world, the future may see the addition of new markets to the global financial network.

The markets of the newly industrialized countries, the more advanced developing countries, are likely to be increasingly integrated into the global economy. In this scenario MNCs would have an opportunity for a truly global sourcing of funds. The foreign exchange markets would, of course, become much more liquid and complex, because there would be a large number of freely convertible currencies trading on international exchanges.

Concerns with exchange risks and destabilizing capital movements are likely to bring greater emphasis on international cooperation in the supervision of activities, both domestic and international, of financial institutions. The major industrial countries have already agreed on standards of capital adequacy to be observed by banks in their countries via the Basel Accord. Other developing countries, such as Pakistan, are also preparing their banking industries for inclusion in this agreement. Some evidence of a greater opening up of the financial sector to external participation in the developing countries was provided by the Uruguay Round of GATT talks, in which many developing countries agreed to lower barriers to trade in financial services. The increasing openness of the financial sector has continued during the Doha Round under the WTO, and many bilateral trade agreements, such as the U.S.-Singapore FTA, also made advances to this end.

RISING LABOR UNREST

MNCs are likely to meet with increasing demands for higher salaries and wages in most host-country operations as expectations rise along with costs of living. The trends in trade unionism, however, are likely to vary. With the collapse of the Soviet bloc, one of the main sources of ideological and political support for trade union movements in many countries is gone. Trade unions have become stronger in many third world countries, however, especially as worsening living conditions have led to increasing demands for higher compensation levels, while difficult operating conditions have reduced MNC profitability.

MNCs may nevertheless have increasing leverage in dealing with trade unions through their capacity to shift production to different overseas locations. Further, greater use of automated manufacturing processes, especially through the use of industrial robots, may lead to less dependence on human labor on the production floor, which would reduce the bargaining power of trade unions. On the other hand, the developed world could see a rise in trade union membership should the level of job losses increase due to such outsourcing and automation.

THE PERMANENCE OF CHANGE

Given all of the future possibilities discussed in this chapter, the only thing that we can say will definitely happen is change. An increasing level of global competition will require many changes in the competitive landscape in which today's corporations compete. As countries such as India and China become more integrated with the developing world economies, these economies will have an impact on the future course of international business. Thus, more countries will be able to contribute to the progress of globalization, and the multinational corporation will be able to benefit from competing in a truly global market place now and in the years to come.

SUMMARY

International business has changed dramatically in the past decade and will continue to change in the future. Responding to improving surging global democracy, diminishing natural resources, diverging economic conditions, and regional economic integration will require development of new roles and business practices. Global competition and international debt problems will also force change. Increased protectionism may result as the dialogue between the industrialized and less-developed countries becomes more acute. Technology improvements, offering the opportunity to create more efficient enterprises, will continue to be the driving force of internationalization.

Megacorporations will continue to emerge. Multinational corporations will be staffed geocentrically, and management practices will be adapted to incorporate host-country sociocultural attitudes and beliefs. Managerial tasks will focus on high-technology communication and computer technologies and may promote the development of the home office. Overseas manufacturing facilities will become more common, and environmental issues will grow as ecological effects become visible. Greater international cooperation will develop as financial markets integrate and modernize their global networks. Automation may lead to less dependence on human labor in manufacturing facilities.

DISCUSSION QUESTIONS

1. Why is anticipating future trends important to conducting business?
2. What are the major current international political trends, and how might they affect business relationships? How might they affect decision making?
3. How will depletion of raw materials affect international business structures?
4. How does technology affect a corporation's ability to survive and compete in the world of the future?
5. What is a megacorporation?
6. Discuss geocentric staffing as it relates to future recruiting and hiring practices within a multinational corporation.
7. How might you better prepare yourself for the challenges of doing international business in the future?

NOTES

1. Bhagwati, *Free Trade Today*.
2. Economist, *Economist Pocket World in Figures*.
3. Newsworld International, "Interview with Dominique Moisi."

BIBLIOGRAPHY

Behrman, J.N. "The Future of International Business and the Distribution of Benefits." *Columbia Journal of World Business* 20 (1986): 15–22.

Bernum, Cynthia F. "The Making of a Global Business Diplomat." *Management Review*, November 1989, 59–60.

Bhagwati, Jagdish. *Free Trade Today*. Princeton University Press, Princeton, 2003.

Blocklyn, Paul L. "Developing the International Executive." *Personnel*, March 1989, 2–5.

Economist. The Economist Pocket World in Figures, Profile Books, Ltd., London, 2006 edition.

Hayden, Spencer. "Execs Discuss Problems of International Business." *Management Review*, September 1989, 35–38.

Knorr, Robert O. "Managing Resources for World-Class Performance." *Journal of Business Strategy*, January–February 1990, 48–50.

Laczniak, G.R., and J. Naor. "Global Ethics: Wrestling with the Corporate Conscience." *Business*, July–September 1985, 3–9.

Newsworld International. "Interview with Dominique Moisi, Deputy Director of the French Institute for International Relations." *Special Assignment with Bill Cunningham*, January 2005.

"Send Back Your Huddled Masses." *Economist*, December 16, 2004.

Sethi, S. Prakash. "The Multinational Challenge." *New Management*, Spring 1987, 53–55.

PART VI

CASE STUDIES

CASE STUDY 1

The Global Tire Industry and Michelin in 2004

On February 25, 2004, Michelin, the world's leading maker of automotive tires, unveiled lower than expected financial results for 2003. While its European competitors had been able to maintain or increase margins, Michelin's overall operating margin had decreased from 7.8 percent in 2002 to 7.4 percent. Management pointed to increasing raw materials costs and a high exposure to the U.S. market, which had witnessed a decline in SUV tire sales of 3.3 percent. In spite of this, Michelin maintained its forecast of achieving a 10 percent operating margin from 2005 onward.

Michelin had recently announced a string of acquisitions, among them the German tire retailer Viborg, and a 10 percent stake in Hankook, the largest Korean tire maker. There were also successes in Asia, long considered the company's Achilles' heel. It now owned the two leading brands in China and it had recently set up a joint venture with the Indian tire maker Appolo Ltd. Michelin had also mounted an alliance with Bosch, the automotive parts supplier, for the joint development of tire, braking, and chassis systems.

Yet, Michelin faced a number of challenges. Its financial results had failed to exhibit revenue growth, with 2003 sales of €15.4 billion at the same level as 2000 and down 1.8 percent from 2002. It had encountered difficulty in passing on raw materials

price increases to consumers. The company had cited unacceptable pricing demands when it refused to supply GM Europe with certain high-volume tires. Its rationalization plans, announced in 1999, had suffered a setback in 2002 when an industrial tribunal in France ordered Michelin to pay compensatory damages to workers.[1] And it seemed to be lagging behind Continental AG in developing an integrated suite of products around tire and braking systems.

Though Michelin had made great strides since the early 1990s, when it was in financial distress, the tire industry and Michelin were never without significant challenges. Wrote an industry expert, "If an entrepreneur developed a business plan which promised the returns that the tire industry has actually been making over the last decade, no venture capitalist would agree to finance it."[2]

THE TIRE INDUSTRY: A HISTORY

While the concept of an air-filled tire dates from 1846, the tire industry was born at the end of the nineteenth century when several firms started manufacturing bicycle tires in both Europe and the United States. The most innovative companies would later become the industry leaders: Britain's Dunlop invented the original rubber tire, a carcass made of fabric layers; Goodyear, from the United States, patented the first tubeless pneumatic tire in

1903; France's Michelin developed the removable tire; and Germany's Continental was the first to develop tread patterns in 1904.

Quality improved dramatically during the first half of the twentieth century with the invention of the rubber tire. In the 1920s carbon black was introduced, increasing a tire's average life span from nine months in 1910 to three years by 1937. The development of synthetic rubber (butadiene) in the 1930s and 1940s further improved the quality of raw materials while reducing their cost.

MICHELIN'S RADIAL INNOVATION

Most innovations in tires had been incremental, but there was one major exception: Michelin's 1946 radial tire. The radial had up to three times the life span of a traditional "bias" (or "cross-ply") design, and it was reducing fuel consumption dramatically while increasing safety compared to bias tires, which were prone to blowouts. However, production required massive investment in new facilities, and rivals, especially U.S. giants Goodyear and Firestone, which had made huge investments in bias tire production, did all they could to delay acceptance.

The radial did eventually succeed. In the early 1970s, the French company built two dedicated plants (in Canada in 1971 and in the United States in 1975) to make radials. The 1973 oil shock made the radial's fuel savings even more attractive. Eventually, U.S. manufacturers were forced to develop their own radials and invest in new plants. Goodyear, for instance, devoted close to US$3 billion to convert to radial production in the 1970s.

It was now a race for survival, and major tire makers rushed to bring their own radials to market. The results in terms of product quality were often disastrous: Abnormally high rates of tread separations and blowouts forced Firestone to recall its first radial line in 1978 at a cost of US$147 million. In Europe, both Kléber (France) and Metzeler (Austria) had to recall their products.

A PAINFUL ROUND OF CONSOLIDATION

The tire industry now entered a painful round of consolidation. Goodrich and Uniroyal merged in 1986. The two had product complementarities but few manufacturing synergies, leaving little scope for rationalization. After the merger, earnings continued to disappoint. In Europe, Dunlop was left bankrupt after a failed merger with Pirelli and had to find a new partner. In 1984 it sold its European and North American interests to Sumitomo. Pirelli bid US$1.8 billion for Firestone but Bridgestone entered a counterbid and won the day, forking out a hefty US$2.6 billion. Pirelli consoled itself with the acquisition of the much smaller Armstrong Tire.

By 1989, while a price war fed by overcapacity was raging, Michelin overcame its long-standing reluctance to make acquisitions and purchased Uniroyal-Goodrich for US$1.5 billion, thereby becoming the world's largest tire maker. By then, Uniroyal-Goodrich had already sold its European operations and licensed out the Uniroyal brand in Europe to Continental. Also, Continental rebuffed a bid by Pirelli in 1991.

The restructuring of the industry then largely came to a halt. Goodyear, burdened by heavy debt, was the only major player that had not been able to afford a significant acquisition. The price war in the 1980s left the industry reeling, and a period of restructuring and cost cutting followed. By 1993 Michelin, Bridgestone, and Goodyear together had 52 percent of the global market, and the top ten firms had about 80 percent of world production. This would not change significantly throughout the decade (see Exhibit 1.1).

After experiencing a lean period in 1990–93, the tire industry returned to profitability in 1994 as the tire market tightened. Between 1994 and 1998 the retail price of tires rose every year.

Case Studies Exhibit 1.1

Global Tire Company Rankings (in millions of dollars, translated at average annual currency exchange rates)

No.	Company, Headquarters	2002			2001		2000	
		Global Market Share %	Tire Sales	% of Total Corporate Sales	Tire Sales	% of Total Corporate Sales	Tire Sales	% of Total Corporate Sales
1	Groupe Michelin, Clermont-Ferrand, France	19.6	$13,751.70*	95.00	$13,425.00*	95.00	$13,200.00*	93*
2	Bridgestone Corp., Tokyo, Japan	18.9	13,465.00*	*75.00	12,950.00*	74.00*	13,750.00*	74*
3	Goodyear Tire & Rubber Co., Akron, Ohio	18.2	12,300.00*	88.80	12,470.00*	86.70	12,725.00*	85*
4	Continental A.G., Hanover, Germany	7.2	4,795.90	44.60	4,900.00	49.00	4,955.00	53
5	Pirelli S.p.A., Milan, Italy	3.8	2,692.70	39.00	2,530.00	39.00	2,600.00	38*
6	Sumitomo Rubber Industries Ltd., Kobe, Japan	3.7	2,638.40	73.80	2,598.20	72.70	2,783.00	71
7	Yokohama Rubber Co. Ltd., Tokyo, Japan	3.3	2,354.20	71.00	2,272.20	71.00	2,514.00	70
8	Cooper Tire & Rubber Co., Findlay, Ohio	2.5	1,714.00	54.00	1,705.30	54.00	1,802.60	52
9	Kumho Industrial Co. Ltd., Seoul, South Korea	1.8	1,443.80	60.30	1,247.60	61.50	1,235.00	54
10	Toyo Tire & Rubber Co. Ltd., Osaka, Japan	1.8	1,306.50	61.50	1,246.50	60.30	1,322.60	59
11	Hankook Tire Co. Ltd. 5, Seoul, South Korea	1.6	1,301.40	87.50	1,118.90	88.90	1,208.30	92
17	Apollo Tyres Ltd, Kerala, India	N.R.	405	100.00	362.30	100.00	318.30	100

Source: Global Tire Company Rankings, *Tire Business*, September 1, 2003.

* = estimated; N.R. = not ranked

Goodyear led the way in North America with 4 percent increases in November 1994, soon followed by Michelin (3 percent). By 1998 retail prices had increased by an aggregate 13.6 percent in Europe and 21.5 percent in North America. The big change, however, was in the original equipment market, where the indexing of prices resulted in upward corrections of 20 percent or more, enabling Goodyear and Michelin to improve margins.

During the 1990s, many tire companies also moved into the former communist states to create a low-cost manufacturing base and seek growth. Sumitomo and Continental were the first to make acquisitions, followed by Pirelli, Goodyear, and Michelin.

TIRE MARKET SEGMENTS

Eighty-five percent of all tires sold worldwide related to cars and trucks (1.1 billion in 2002).[3] The remaining 15 percent was made up of "specialty tires," comprising bike, motorcycle, aviation, agricultural, and civil works tires. Of the 1.1 billion tires sold in 2002, 838 million were for passenger cars, 284 million were for trucks, and a much smaller quantity was for agricultural or other technical purposes. (Exhibit 1.2 gives historical growth rates per region.)

The tire market was usually segmented along two main dimensions: original equipment versus replacement equipment and cars versus trucks. The first dimension distinguished between tires mounted by a car manufacturer (original equipment manufacturer, OE) and tires purchased when replacing a used tire (replacement tire, RT). The second dimension referred to the type of vehicle to be equipped: cars (and light trucks) versus trucks (heavy trucks and other commercial vehicles). The OE market had always been smaller (29 percent of the tires sold in the car segment and 21 percent in the truck segment) and far less profitable than

Case Studies Exhibit 1.2

World Growth Rates for Passenger Car and Truck Tire Sales, 1995–2002 (average annual % growth)

	Passenger car tires	Truck tires
North America	1.72	3.64
South America	2.22	2.64
Europe	3.12	3.09
Eastern and Central Europe	7.86	1.47
Asia	3.5	1.71
Middle East and Africa	4.02	4.18
Oceania	3.15	7.03
World	2.92	2.71

Source: LMC International, World Tire Forecast 2004.

the RT segment. Also, in the replacement market customer needs were more varied than in the OE segment.

Geographically, about 70 percent of worldwide sales were made in Europe, North America, and Japan.[4] Yet, the fastest-growing market was Asia, with an estimated growth rate of almost 8 percent in 2003. The fastest-growing segment in Asia was the RT market in Thailand, recording in 2003 a 34 percent increase in volume. Growth in China stood at 28 percent. Yet, Japan (still the largest Asian market in volume) remained sluggish and brought the average growth of the Asian market down to 8 percent. In all, the market for tires in 2003 had more than doubled over the last 20 years to reach US$70.6 billion.[5]

HEAVY TRUCKS MARKET

Demand for truck tires was driven by economic conditions. In a recession, trucks drove fewer miles, reducing tire wear (especially since fleets tended to swap tires when trucks lay idle), and demand picked up quickly at the end of a downturn. During 2002, the global truck tire market grew by 5 percent (RT by 4.6 percent and OE by 8 percent). This growth came mainly from Asia. The market for heavy trucks

Case Studies Exhibit 1.3

Market Share Evolution of the Major Car Manufacturers

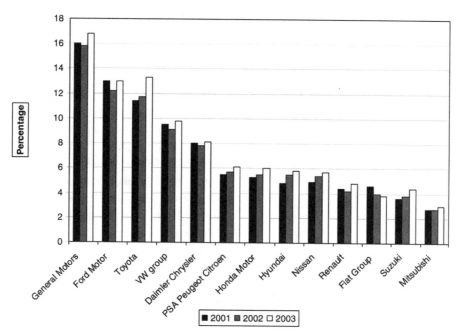

■ 2001 ■ 2002 □ 2003

was geographically split among Europe (21 percent of the volume sold), North America (18 percent), Asia (44 percent), Africa and the Middle East (8 percent), and South America (9 percent).[6]

Truck tires represented less than 3 percent of the operating expenses of a fleet but were related to more than 50 percent of truck breakdowns. Customers were nevertheless price sensitive even if the upfront purchase price mattered less than the actual cost per mile. The major tire manufacturers had recently invested significantly in services for truck companies. For example, they were increasingly proposing tire management outsourcing (inventory management, reporting) and retreading to extend tire life.

The top four truck makers in Europe represented 64 percent of sales.[7] In the RT market, big-fleet operators had gained importance as the industry concentrated. In the United States, for example, 3

percent of the fleet operators commanded 50 percent of the trucks on the roads. In France, 15 percent of the trucking fleet of 150,000 was owned by the large fleet operators (more than 500 trucks).

CARS AND LIGHT TRUCKS

Consolidation in the car industry had led to increasing power in the hands of fewer car companies (see Exhibit 1.3 for sales data), which often regarded tires as commodities. Lately, tire makers had tried to improve their margins by increasing OE prices. Commented J.P. Morgan's David Bradley, "Goodyear and Michelin have been very aggressive about seeking price hikes, but that only works if nobody steps in to fill the breach." When Michelin announced in early 2003 that it would stop supplying tires to General Motors Europe after two clashes over prices, Continental stood ready to take the business.[8]

The RT market, on the other hand, had been characterized by better operating margins and higher volumes (71 percent of tires sold). Also, selling to end customers had made tire manufacturers more sensitive to distribution and marketing issues, leading the main players to vertically integrate. This segment of the car market had enjoyed an average growth rate of 2 to 3 percent per year for the past 10 years. RE volumes across continents were split among Europe (30 percent), North America (39 percent), Asia (21 percent), and Africa, the Middle East, and Latin America (10 percent).

MAKING TIRES

RAW MATERIALS

A tire is made up of about 100 components. Carbon black, which gives the tire its rigidity, makes up about one-quarter of raw material costs. Natural and synthetic rubber accounts for about 50 percent of raw material costs. Increasingly, synthetic rubber is being used for passenger car tires and natural rubber for utility tires. Many tire manufacturers have a degree of vertical integration, owning hevea plantations and synthetic rubber plants, but none is entirely self-sufficient. Steel cord, used for making radial belts and the carcass of larger tires, is also a major component and represents roughly 20 percent of raw material costs.

Natural rubber prices can be highly volatile (e.g., there was a 123 percent increase during 2003).[9] Also, the price of oil affects the synthetic components of the tire. Tire manufacturers therefore had to put in place hedging mechanisms to limit volatility in inputs prices. Yet, the recent fluctuations in oil and hevea supply had put pressure on margins. Also, about two-thirds of purchases were either dollar-denominated or directly affected by dollar fluctuations. Tire makers had set up the purchasing platform Rubbernetwork.com to organize the market for natural rubber.

MANUFACTURING

Tire plants were labor-intensive and only profitable when running at very-high-capacity utilization levels. In 1999 industrywide overcapacity was estimated at nearly 30 percent (see Exhibit 1.4 for plant locations of the major players). However, capacity utilization was very different by region. All the major manufacturers developed their own machinery. Round-the-clock work with three shifts, seven days a week, was a major change introduced in the 1990s. The industry as a whole had probably doubled productivity since 1994, having already done so in the five previous years, and further gains were expected.

Over the last 15 years, the five biggest tire makers had been developing new manufacturing processes that would, they hoped, dramatically reduce capital and labor costs and allow production in smaller batches. These processes were closely guarded secrets. Michelin had led the way with its C3M process. Goodyear's Impact process and Bridgestone's BIRD, the latter believed to be completely automated, also claimed huge savings. "A paradigm shift is taking place," wrote industry expert Neil Mullineux in 1999,[10] adding that the new processes would further widen the gap between the three leaders and the followers.

Implementation had not happened quickly, however. In 2002 Pirelli stated that it would use its new MIRS process only for the manufacture of high-end products. Similarly, Michelin announced the use of its C3M technology in the entry phase of its move into Brazil. It had also announced the use of C3M for manufacture of some top-end tires.[11]

In addition, car manufacturers' move to low-labor-cost countries put additional pressure on tire manufacturers, forcing them to reduce their own costs. This phenomenon, coupled with the

Case Studies Exhibit 1.4

Market Leaders' Plants in Europe, North America, and Asia (includes plants making tires for passenger cars, lights trucks and buses, agricultural, motorcycles, earthmovers, industrial, aircraft, and racing)

	1990		1996		1998		2001		2002	
	Plants	Employees	Plants	Employees	Plants	Employees	Plants	Employees	Plants	Employees
Western Europe										
Michelin	31	70,813	32	50,057	31	62,980	37	64,317	31	64,705
Bridgestone	6	7,160	5	6,715	6	5,930	6	5,788	6	6,087
Goodyear	6	8,975	7	15,300	6	12,357	9	17,195	8	11,600
Continental	9	8,803	12	18,000	10	11,941	12	16,431	11	13,790
Sumitomo	6	70	8	6,665	8	6,401	8		8	4,500
Pirelli	10	11,700	8	7,215	8	7,210	8	6,630	7	5,705
Yokohama	0	0	0	0	0	0				0
Toyo	0	0	0	0	0	0				0
Cooper	0	0	0	0	1	750	1	640	1	700
Kumho	0	0	0	0	0	0				0
North America										
Michelin	15	21,382	13	17,450	15	16,950	15	17,400	15	16,091
Bridgestone	7	10,855	9	11,355	10	13,971	10	12,777	11	11,458
Goodyear	13	19,908	12	20,680	11	16,670	12	20,680	13	18,146
Continental	5	6,335	4	5,609	5	4,334	4	4,509	5	4,858
Sumitomo	3	3,103	2	2,700			2	2,640	2	2,500
Pirelli	3	2,450	2	1,255	1	490	1	630	1	250
Yokohama	1	500	1	831	1	1,138	1	831	1	1,417
Toyo	0	0	0	0	0	0	0	0	1	417
Asia										
Michelin	3	NA	2	450	6	4,351	2	1,300	6	7,464
Bridgestone	12	12,719	13	12,455	17	13,965	15	12,674	17	15,352
Goodyear	5	3,885	9	4,273	9	5,228	8	4,973	9	4,668
Continental	1	1,000	1	1,000	1	500	0	0	3	3,011
Sumitomo	3	3,250	4	2,430	8	9,373	5	4,330	5	4,909
Yokohama	6	5,676	7	6,758	7	5,034	6	6,130	7	5,219
Toyo	2	1,900	3	2,170	2	1,750	2	1,750	2	1,766
Cooper	0	0	0	0	0	0	0	0	0	0
Kumho	1	1,300	2	2,860	2	2,860	2	2,860	3	5,711
Hankook	NA		3	4,590	4	4,357	3	4,310	5	5,757

Source: Tire Business, Global Report 2003, INSEAD Research. The main countries included under Asia are China, India, Indonesia, Japan, Malaysia, Nepal, Pakistan, the Philippines, South Korea, Sri Lanka, Taiwan, Thailand, and Vietnam. Michelin is present in Japan and Thailand; Goodyear in India, Indonesia, Malaysia, Philippines, Taiwan and Thailand; Bridgestone in Japan, Indonesia, Taiwan, Thailand; Continental in Pakistan (until 1996); Sumitomo and Toyo in Japan; Yokohama in Japan (and in South Korea through a joint venture); Kumho in South Korea.

* North America includes Canada and the United States.

expansion of emerging markets such as China and Brazil, led tire companies to relocate manufacturing facilities.

MARKETING

Customers for replacement car tires were commonly divided into three groups (top end, middle range, and low end). The strategy of supplying each segment, also known as "good, better, best," had been implemented in the United States by both Michelin (Uniroyal, BF Goodrich, Michelin brands) and Bridgestone (Firestone, Dayton, Bridgestone brands). Goodyear lacked a middle-market brand but would soon have Sumitomo's Dunlop brand.

The Big Three, which consisted of Michelin, Bridgestone, and Goodyear, were trying to enhance their reputation worldwide. Bridgestone, whose reputation in its home market was excellent, suffered from low recognition in Europe and North America, where Firestone was better known. Michelin was highly reputed worldwide, but its subsidiary brands were not; Goodrich was little known outside the United States, Kléber was strong only in France, and Michelin had relinquished its midmarket Uniroyal brand in Europe to Continental. Consumer surveys reported confusion with regard to the perceived quality of Goodyear's various brands.

Private-brand tires had captured a significant market share but were no longer seen as the major threat. They had grown vigorously in the 1970s and 1980s, especially in the United States, but in the 1990s the majors fought back more aggressively with their own associate brands. In the United States, private-label brands accounted for about 30 percent of the market. Price was an important variable to customers, but it was estimated that only 20–25 percent of buyers sought the lowest prices. Most fell into either the "brand conscious" or "store reliant" categories.

DISTRIBUTION

In the 1990s distribution began to be perceived by tire manufacturers as a success factor in the RT market. Tire manufacturers saw in distribution an efficient way to initiate a pull through to the RT volume and focus on customer retention with better pricing control (particularly in trucks and their fleet management). Tire makers had used franchising extensively to increase their footprint, as their own stores were often loss making or turning only a small profit.

In Europe, the top 25 independent dealers accounted for 25–30 percent of sales, and concentration seemed set to increase as British, German, and other retail chains expanded beyond their home markets, often pooling their purchasing and marketing functions to negotiate better terms. Kwik-Fit was Europe's largest independent retailer, with more than 2,500 shops and several brands: the flagship Kwik-Fit (in the United Kingdom, Ireland, Belgium, and Holland), Speedy (in France, Belgium, and Spain), Pitstop (in Germany), and a group of small chains that kept their local identities.[12] Multinational marketing cooperatives were also growing, with networks such as Point S, Tecar, and Vulcopneu attracting a growing number of dealers in France, Germany, Italy, and Spain with advantageous purchasing conditions and the prospect of regional marketing clout. They were a growing force behind the proliferation of private brands and leading outlets for cheaper tire imports, especially from Asia.[13]

In Japan, distribution was consolidating as the share of mass merchandisers such as Autobacs and Yellow Hat increased. There, too, the growth of chains that negotiated large discounts or bulk orders threatened to erode the pricing power of manufacturers.

PRICING

"Tire prices . . . are below what they were five and ten years ago. And the consumer is getting an unbe-

Case Studies Exhibit 1.5

Tire Manufacturers' Market Share (%) in Europe, 1997, 2000, and 2002 for Cars and Light Trucks/ Commercial Vehicles

	1997	2000	2002
Michelin	27 / 40	27 / 41	24 / 41
Continental	21 / 16	20 / 15	20 / 15
Goodyear-Sumitomo	20 / 17	20 / 18	19 / 18
Pirelli	10 / 6	9 / 6	9 / 6
Bridgestone	9 / 12	10 / 13	10 / 14
Others	13 / 9	14 / 7	18 / 6
Total	100 / 100	100 / 100	100 / 100

Source: UBS Limited, Global Tire Sales and Production, 2003.

Tire Manufacturers Market Share (%) in North America, 1997, 2000, and 2002 for Cars and Light Trucks/Commercial Vehicles

	1997	2000	2002
Goodyear	31.9 / 30	28.5 / 30	25.5 / 29.5
Michelin	22.4 / 20.5	21 / 22.5	20.3 / 23.5
Bridgestone-Firestone	16 / 21.2	17.5 / 20.4	14.5 / 20
ContinentalGeneral	4.3 / 7	5 / 8	4.4 / 8.5
Cooper	18.8 / NA	18.6 / NA	19.5 / NA
Yokohama	NA / 2.3	NA / 1.8	NA / 4
Toyo	NA / 1.3	NA / 1.0	NA / 3.5
Others	6.6 / 13.3	9.2 / 12	15.7 / 11
Total	100 / 100	100 / 100	100 / 100

Source: UBS Limited, Global Tire Sales and Production, 2003.

Tire Manufacturers' Market Share (%) in China, 2001

Michelin	26
Warrior (Michelin)	17
Goodyear	10
Bridgestone	5
Hankook	5
Kumho	1
Others	36
Total	100

Source: Michelin Fact Book. 2002; case writers' estimates.

lievably high-quality, highly technical product for a very, very low price," said *Modern Tire Dealer*.[14] Yet, during the latter half of 2002, the North American market saw a round of price increases as raw material costs escalated in line with oil and natural rubber prices. Michelin's announcement of a price increase in November 2002 was quickly followed by announcements by several of its competitors.[15]

Recently, prices and costs of raw materials had been highly correlated. Tire makers claimed that they had been able to fully compensate for the rise in raw material prices by an increase in tire prices. Many investment banks had been warning that this compensation might be possible only in the short term, particularly in the United States. This was confirmed in the first half of 2003. Tire makers also were commenting that the U.S. market and the truck segment in particular were becoming problematic. Michelin's decision to raise U.S. prices through the second half of 2003 only on its lower brands (with a Michelin brand price increase announced for early 2004) perhaps reflected new caution. See Exhibit 1.5 for the market share positions of the key competitors by region.

MICHELIN AND CIE

"If Michelin became a multinational company it is mainly due to François Michelin's personality. He profoundly marked the company. His personal priorities became the group's priorities. . . ."

Carlos Ghosn[16]

COMPANY HISTORY

Michelin revolutionized tire design with the invention of the radial tire and still enjoyed a formidable technical reputation. It was the least diversified of the Big Three, with 95 percent of its revenues from tires. It also had a small sideline in maps and travel guides.

The company began in 1863 as an agricultural machinery business in Clermont-Ferrand in the Auvergne region of central France, using rubber for seals and joints. The Michelin brothers (André and Edouard) took over the company and in 1889 renamed it Compagnie Générale des Etablissements Michelin. In 1891 Edouard made a removable bicycle tire that could be changed in only 15 minutes. The Michelins promoted their tires by persuading cyclists to use them in long-distance races. In 1898 André realized that a stack of tires with arms would look like a man and designed the now-famous Michelin Man (or Bibendum).[17]

The company started its international expansion in 1905, when it opened an office in London, and soon built factories in Turin (1906) and New Jersey (1908). More plants were opened in the 1920s and 1930s in Germany, Argentina, Spain, Czechoslovakia, and Belgium. Michelin's technological innovations included detachable rims and spare tires (1906), tubeless tires (1930), treads (1934), and modern low-profile tires (1937).

Research conducted during the Second World War by Michelin produced substitutes for natural rubber and new tire designs. The radial, launched in 1946 as the "X tire," was fitted on Citroëns in 1951. In the 1960s, Michelin continued its U.S. expansion and convinced Sears to sell its radials in 1966. Said François Michelin, "If I am not in the States, I will never be one of the leaders." The company decided to manufacture radials in North America and opened plants in Canada (1971) and South Carolina (1975). Michelin was the world's tenth largest tire supplier in 1960, progressing to sixth by 1970 and third in 1974. In 1978 it overtook Firestone to move into second place with 17 percent of the world market.

By the late 1970s, despite its investment in new radial plants, Michelin lagged in productivity as U.S. rivals built increasingly efficient factories. Some competitors were also claiming they made better tires. Pirelli's P6 and P7 ranges and the all-season tires developed by Goodyear were cutting into Michelin's U.S. market share. The second oil crisis in 1980 plunged the company into the red. Between 1981 and 1984 Michelin lost nearly FF9 billion and in 1985 was forced to seek a FF4 billion distress credit; this was arranged at favorable interest rates, rumored to be with help from the French government. In 1985 favorable market conditions also returned the company to profit, which hit a peak of FF2.6 billion in 1988 with the new MX tire generation.

Michelin was late in developing a strategy for Asia. In 1986 it set up a joint venture in South Korea with Woo-Pong that eventually failed. In 1987 the company built a plant in Thailand. Joint ventures in Japan (with Okamoto) and Malaysia followed in 1988 and 1989.

By 1988 Michelin was not producing enough tires in North America, and exports from France posed insoluble logistical problems, not to mention high costs. Its premium ranges had won market share in both OE and RT in the United States, but it lacked access to independent retail outlets. Meanwhile, Uniroyal-Goodrich, which had an excellent distribution network, was looking for a buyer. In 1989 Michelin acquired the company for US$1.5 billion (including US$810 million in assumed debt). The acquisition turned Michelin into the world's largest tire manufacturer and the chief tire supplier to General Motors (supplying more than 50 percent of its requirements).

Uniroyal-Goodrich's entire production facilities had to be restructured at a cost of US$4 billion. In one year, Michelin's debt doubled to FF44.7 billion. Posting a FF5.2 billion loss in 1990, Michelin launched a drastic rationalization program in the United States, closing down bias tire plants inherited from Goodrich, reducing the workforce, and negotiating a new contract with the United Rubber Workers.

In 1991–92 Michelin implemented a new FF3

billion cost-cutting program, laying off 16,000 employees (4,900 of them in France). Another FF3.5 billion cost-reduction plan was unveiled in 1993, with 10,000 more staff laid off in Europe and North America (8 percent of the total workforce); European plants were "specialized," and the Michelin and Uniroyal-Goodrich sales operations in North America merged. By 1995 Uniroyal-Goodrich was at last in working order.

THE "MONSIEUR FRANÇOIS" ERA

Since its foundation in 1898, Michelin had been run by a family member. "Monsieur François," Michelin's charismatic president, reigned over the company for more than 45 years, till 1996, when he handed over the company to his son.

Secret, enigmatic, and unpredictable, François Michelin had been a boss unlike any other. A fellow industrialist described him as "a disconcerting yet engaging man, who provokes admiration and fear."[18] A devout Roman Catholic dedicated to his family, he was as likely to seek help from God as from his managers in times of trouble, and religion tainted the sense of fairness with which he ran his business.

Michelin was known to its employees as "La Maison" and carried an array of values that set it apart from other corporations. François Michelin liked to say "what he knew from the House, he learnt it from the House," underlining the strong, secret, and self-made identity of the company. The company was one of the few worldwide identified by the philosopher R. Horacio Etchegoyen as having its own organic life, its own "soul," and this soul was the result of the men working at Michelin.

CORPORATE CULTURE AND MANAGEMENT

Because of the family ownership structure, Michelin had long been highly centralized and secretive. Until the 1990s there had been no formal organizational chart and the company did not use formal titles (except for the financial director and plant managers). Managers simply introduced themselves as Mr. So-and-So from Michelin (insiders could guess someone's role from his or her place in the internal directory). Departments were known by a one- or two-letter code: SG for Accounting, K for legal, and so on. François Michelin liked to quote the Chinese saying, "You are a prisoner of your next word," and shunned the media and public pronouncements. Speeches were factual, reflecting the company's belief in hard facts. He also believed that "the smallest leak would be suicide."

Instead of *grandes écoles* graduates and MBAs, Michelin recruiters preferred to hire local young engineers who would develop with the company, which offered them a lifelong career. Commented Carlos Ghosn on his years at Michelin, "François Michelin was only interested in . . . the individuals. As well as the facts, the concrete realization of people."[19]

François Michelin, as any other employee, had spent nearly five years learning basic manufacturing and sales skills before taking on the leadership. His credo, often preached to his troops, was "All those who work for Michelin have a common goal: to make the best possible product for the customer."[20] His son Edouard would follow the same path before taking the reins of the company.

As a family-dominated company, Michelin had always been able to take a long-term view and had used this to full effect with its strategic planning. "In Michelin," Carlos Ghosn commented, "there are no short term plans; when things go bad we hold tight till it goes."[21]

Michelin had also felt a particular responsibility for the welfare of employees even though it started laying off staff in the 1980s. (In the city of Clermont-Ferrand itself, the workforce had fallen to 15,000 from a 30,000 peak.) In its early years the company had invested in housing, schools, hospitals, nurseries, and shops, creating a veritable "Michelinville" that it gradually sold or handed over to local authorities. François Michelin took a dim view of trade unions, which he tolerated only as a necessary evil.

While operations reflected his own thriftiness, with modestly equipped premises and ceaseless efforts to save on "unnecessary" expenses, there was one area where nothing seemed too expensive: research and development, often described as "the boss's mistress." François Michelin valued engineering excellence above all else. Inventories were allowed to swell far beyond expected orders to accommodate powerful plant managers. The company's best marketing tool, François Michelin believed, were its products.

OWNERSHIP AND LEGAL STRUCTURE

Surprising to many observers was Michelin's legal structure. Even after Michelin became a global manufacturer, the family remained strongly in control. More than 500 Michelin family members owned a substantial but undisclosed share—variously estimated at between 10 percent and 40 percent—of the holding company, Compagnie Générale des Etablissements Michelin.[22] Control was exerted through the unusual legal status of *société en commandite par actions (corporate partnership limited by shares)* retained by Michelin since it was first founded. Patents and other intellectual property were held by the holding company, which received royalties from the operating company.

The group was headed by three managing partners (*gérants*), who enjoyed extensive powers in exchange for unlimited liability for the company's losses. They received no salary but were paid a substantial share of the profits. It was almost impossible for nonfamily shareholders to dismiss a *gérant*. A nine-member executive committee was created to assist and advise the *gérants*.

The *commandite*, a legal form dating back to the eighteenth century (when seafaring captains used it to raise finances for voyages of bounty), had been ferociously criticized by outside investors. Other French companies (most family-owned businesses) had long since adopted the limited liability (*société anonyme*) structure. The benefits of the *commandite* were described by François Michelin in 1992 as follows: "It allows us to move much faster, to be protected from outside pressure when taking decisions. . . . Do you know that Japan is nothing more than a huge *commandite*, through its banking system? It lets us take a long-term view."

"YOUNG EDOUARD: THE AMERICAN"

> "He will have less to build than to manage, less to conquer than to maintain. He will receive in heritage a powerful but archaic empire, dominating but endebted, worldwide leader but contested."
>
> *Pascal Galinier*[23]

Edouard joined Michelin in 1989, spending three months in training with other cadres taken on that year, followed by four months as a worker at two company plants. He moved up to supervisor, then became production manager at the Puy-en-Velay plant making giant earthmover tires.

In 1991 he was sent to the United States as a *gérant* and worked with Carlos Ghosn (then general manager), the Brazilian executive later known as "le Cost Cutter" at Renault and Nissan. Edouard later earned his spurs as president and chief operating officer for Michelin North America. He described the experience as seminal: "The North American market is hyper competitive. All the tire makers are there, as well as all the OE manufacturers. And distribution plays a huge role: half the market is dominated by private distributor brands."[24] He also said, "In North America we are a younger organization, our teams are smaller and more reactive to the market."[25]

In 1993 "the American," as he was named by Michelin's old-guard employees, returned to Clermont-Ferrand and took on greater responsibilities, soon sharing decision making with his father. A convert to methods such as removing managers to empower employees, he started encouraging new ideas. Asked about his role, he once described it as "speeding up project management and innovation . . . fine-tuning rather than revolutionizing."[26] Before the major reorganization in 1996, he was credited with engineering a €600 million cost-cutting effort launched in April 1993, as well as the 1994 decision to hike OE prices, although he was characteristically modest about his own contribution to the latter: "Let's say that my father paved the way through two years of consistent efforts, and that I acted as catalyst in a decision that was vital for our House."

In 1995 Edouard, described by his father as an "iconoclast" ("I took it as an invitation to be myself"), broke with tradition by putting 4,000 managers through training sessions that stressed the importance of marketing, service, and profitability. He also set up an incentive pay scheme linked to corporate and personal performance for managers, a revolution within Michelin. He wanted to clarify the structure, to allow "Growth, Speed, Responsibility and Profitability" to spread through the firm.

Edouard's new policy was deeply influenced by his American experience. He brought from the United States a willingness to improve relations with investors and outsiders. He instilled in the firm new approaches to the clients and to the markets. "For the first time in Michelin's history, we recognized that Marketing had a role to play within our company. Until that day [when Edouard took the power] it was almost rude to talk about

marketing . . . ," remembered Thierry Martin, one of the managers that worked on the new company structure.[27] Edouard also moved toward improving relationships with the French unions. "Edouard is more willing to negotiate," said a union representative. "Before, with his father, there were no discussions."

REENGINEERING THE HOUSE

It was in 1995 that the company turned its efforts to a wide-ranging reorganization effort under the aegis of Edouard. Managers were asked to carry out cross-departmental audits over a six-month period. By February 1996, Edouard was ready to present the new organization. The company's highly centralized regional structure was replaced with nine so-called tactical operational units (TOUs), each covering a major product line. As profit centers, TOUs were accountable for their results. Each had its own product development, marketing, manufacturing, and sales departments. International coordination was ensured by four regional executives, and 12 "group services" provided support to the TOUs.

The company commented at the time, "The internationalization of the car and tire markets calls for a consistent approach on all continents, while remaining close to the needs of each individual market." Even more surprising to outsiders, Michelin unveiled a new organization chart in which key positions were filled by young executives. Only one area remained under central control: R & D, Monsieur François's main concern and still perceived as the "heart of the House."

In 1999, three months after taking the top job at Michelin, Edouard unveiled excellent first-half results yet, in the same breath, announced 7,500 job cuts across Europe, 10 percent of its European workforce. The announcement sparked off demonstrations and a rebuke from Lionel Jospin, the Socialist prime minister of France. A French tribunal later ruled against some of the redundancies, ordering Michelin to pay damages to the affected employees.[28] Michelin also had to negotiate the implementation of the 35-hour workweek with the French unions. The final agreement provided for the recruitment of 1,000 more workers.

In spite of this, Michelin continued with its rationalization program, announcing closure of three factories in the United Kingdom and Germany that resulted in 1,300 job cuts.[29] In 2002 it announced 2,000 job cuts in North America, representing some 7 percent of its North American workforce.[30] In early 2003 it unveiled plans to cut 1,200 of its 9,550 Spanish workforce while investing €188 million in operations in the country. Michelin's 2003 number of factories stood at 80 in 19 countries.

CONSOLIDATING THE GLOBAL REACH OF MICHELIN

After successfully penetrating the North American markets in the late 1980s, Michelin turned to central Europe and its perennial weak point, Asia. In 1995, it bought a majority interest in Polish tire manufacturer Stomil and the following year acquired 90 percent of Taurus in Hungary. In 1996 it joined forces with Continental to make private-label tires for independent distributors, and in 1997 it acquired 51 percent of German wheel maker Mannesmann Kronprinz. In early 2003, Michelin purchased Viborg, the German tire retailer. In 1999 the purchase of Tire Centers Inc, a distributor and retreader of truck tires, underlined Michelin's determination to become a major player in U.S. retreading.[31]

In China, where Michelin had opened a commercial office in Beijing in 1989, it created a joint venture in Shenyang in 1996 that made radials for the Chinese market.[32] In 1997, Michelin invested in three additional Shenyang joint ventures, which doubled the capacity of car tires to 1.2 million units

per year. In March 2001 Michelin announced the successful conclusion of protracted negotiations for a 70-30 joint venture with Shanghai Tire and Rubber, the largest producer in China. It then merged the four joint ventures in Shenyang into a single entity, Michelin Shenyang Tire Company, in which it held 85 percent of the capital.

Michelin also set up a research center and its regional head office in Shanghai.[33] Its stated goal was to exceed sector growth, lead tire technology, and take a dominant share of both the premium and standard segments of the car and truck tire markets. These moves in China were followed by acquisitions in South Korea. In January 2003, Michelin bought a 10 percent stake in Hankook, the second largest tire manufacturer in Korea and the eleventh largest in the world.

Michelin, however, still lacked a presence in the large Indian market. On December 8, 2003, Edouard Michelin announced, "With this agreement, Michelin fully intends to establish its presence and to grow in India with Michelin technology products, together with a partner with whom we share mutual ambitions, respect and trust." Apollo Tires had been chosen to set up a joint venture (51 percent Michelin, 49 percent Apollo) for radial truck tires in India. Michelin's existing facility in India would be absorbed in the new entity, due to commercialize its first Michelin tires in early 2006.

MICHELIN IN 2004

By 2004, Michelin was unique among the Big Three in making nearly 90 percent of its sales outside its home market (about 47 percent in Europe, 40 percent in North America, and 13 percent in Asia). It marketed a range of 28,000 products, with tires ranging from less than seven ounces (200 g) to more than five tons for all types of vehicles, "from bicycles to the space shuttle." Every day Michelin made more than 830,000 tires as well as more than

Case Studies Exhibit 1.6

Michelin's Cost Structure

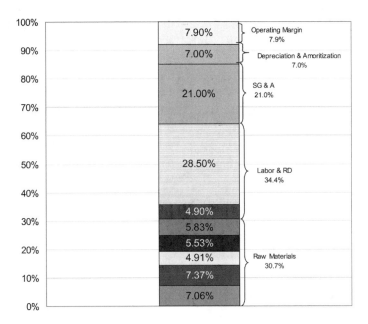

Source: INSEAD research, Company reports, CSFB Company research.

76,000 inner tubes, 2.5 million miles (4 million km) of wires, 88,000 wheels, and 70,000 tourist maps and guides. See Exhibit 1.6 for an overview of Michelin's cost structure.

PRODUCTION

Michelin had stated that it was to selectively introduce C3M in production. C3M was estimated to require about half the capital costs of an equivalent conventional plant with the same capacity, only two-thirds of the labor, and a quarter of the energy required in a conventional process.[34] Manufacturing was completely different: A flow-line process made components in their final form (all rubber parts were built directly onto the drum),

eliminating the conventional batch production of subcomponents.[35] Michelin's stated policy was "to maintain independence in the technological and procurement aspects." It designed and manufactured most of its tire-making machinery itself and was characteristically secretive about development and deployment.

RETAILING

Like other tire makers, Michelin relied on independent retailers for most of its sales but since the 1980s had increased ownership of retail outlets. The outlets also sold other manufacturers' tires and offered a variety of car services: exhaust, shock absorbers, batteries and brakes, cooling systems, air conditioners, and so on.

Retailing also was a means to service truck and car fleets. Tire fleet management services were growing in importance, and Michelin's response was a three-pronged servicing approach: through independent dealers, Michelin-owned Euromaster, and Michelin Direct. The latter involved direct sales to large fleets and on-premise services through Michelin fitters. Michelin and Euromaster were increasingly utilizing fully equipped vans that serviced at the customer site.

The Michelin-owned European retailing operations were consolidated under the Euromaster brand with about 1,350 outlets in nine countries (including 550 in the United Kingdom and more than 300 in France). In early 2003 Michelin added Viborg, a retailing and service chain with 577 branches, including 350 in Germany. This purchase provided Michelin with major retailing positions in all European countries except Italy, Portugal, and Greece.

Michelin also had strong connections with independent retailers. In France, for example, Michelin had a strong relationship with the retailer G6. When Euromaster won service contracts for fleet service, Michelin allocated part of the work to G6 or other preferred independent chains. In contrast, fleet contracts won by Michelin itself were kept entirely in-house (i.e., executed by Euromaster).[36]

On September 30, 2003, the European Court of First Instance upheld a €19.8 million fine against Michelin in a 2001 unfair-pricing case.[37] The commission found that Michelin had breached EU competition law with a complex system of remunerations to its dealers over the sale of truck tires, discouraging them from obtaining supplies from other suppliers. The court declared that "a company in a dominant position, which operates loyalty discounts and bonuses, impedes normal price based competition and infringes community law."[38]

In the United States, Michelin used a multitude of distribution channels, including thousands of independent dealers and mass-merchandiser points of sale (such as Sears, Wal-Mart, and Western Auto Group), as well as major membership clubs. It also serviced more than 50,000 U.S. truck fleets, including UPS. *Modern Tire Dealer* surveyed dealers each year on their criteria for choosing suppliers. The 2002 survey showed that the following criteria stood out (in decreasing order of importance): good service, prompt and speedy delivery, reasonable prices, stock availability, accessible location, brand names, warranties, product knowledge (of their sales staff), and reputation.

RESEARCH AND DEVELOPMENT

Michelin spent 4.5 percent of sales on R & D, far more than any of its rivals. The company strongly believed that its success was due to its commitment to R & D and innovation. Michelin had spent several decades developing C3M and had unveiled it in 1992. New tire concepts were developed at the company's technology centers in Europe, the United States, and Japan, which were equipped with large-scale computing facilities to carry out sophisticated simulations. Prototypes were checked at four testing sites (in France, Spain, the United States, and Japan), re-creating the various conditions in which tires were used.

Despite its leadership position, Michelin had sometimes been slow in implementing its innovations. Improvements in radial design had remained in testing in Clermont-Ferrand while rivals introduced better products in the late 1970s and 1980s. More recently, competitors had managed to catch up in process technology. In 1999 Michelin had been caught off guard by suddenly strong demand for high-performance tires,[39] and in late 2002 Continental had cut into Michelin's market share by capitalizing on the surge in demand for winter tires.

Michelin was always looking for breakthrough

innovations. A major recent innovation was the Energy "green" tire,[40] which reduced rolling resistance by 35 percent[41] and fuel consumption by 5 percent by adding silica to the rubber mix. Michelin also had a highly successful 80,000-mile tire, the XH4 Long Life, for the U.S. replacement market. Its Classic range was aimed at the budget European market, and it had a new high-performance range, the Pilot.[42]

In 1997 the company had introduced its PAX run-flat tire, which could travel 125 miles (201 km) after a puncture. By early 2003 Michelin had formed an alliance with Goodyear, Pirelli, and Hankook to foster the adoption of its PAX run-flat tire. The PAX was available on a growing number of models, starting with the Renault Twingo in 1999 and including the new Audi 8 and BMW's Mini Cooper (supplied by Pirelli).[43] In January 2004, Michelin announced that the major manufacturers Honda and Nissan would propose PAX-equipped vehicles as an option to their customers. Unlike Bridgestone's run-flat tire, Michelin's PAX concept required a nonstandard wheel.

Recently, Michelin had unveiled a 50-50 joint venture in Integrated Safety Systems with Bosch to develop "vehicle dynamics and stability assessment systems." The venture was aimed at combining the respective tire and electronic expertise of the two players. Among its stated objectives was to increase the mobility of Michelin's PAX run-flat tire and wheel system by 2004.

In March 2003 Michelin also unveiled a range of car accessories through a new subsidiary, Michelin Lifestyle Limited, which included foot pumps, air compressors, car mats, wheel trims, and first aid kits. In addition, Michelin identified a range of other products it intended to market—home and travel accessories, cycle accessories, and Michelin-branded clothing.

THE CHALLENGE FOR THE MICHELIN MAN

In recent years, Michelin had become more responsive to the outside world, for instance, allowing journalists to visit some of its factories, "once almost as tough to enter as the no man's land between the two Koreas."[44] Yet the continued secrecy and family control, not to mention the *commandite* structure, still baffled investors and analysts. Commented Edouard Michelin, "I don't feel ashamed of being a *commandite*. I am convinced there is an innovative and modern way to be a *commandite*."[45]

In his first speech as head of the group to the June 1999 shareholders meeting, Edouard Michelin had laid out his strategy: to focus on product performance, globalization, productivity gains, management efficiency, and, lastly, "reliable, reactive control of the group so as to increase its robustness." In a later interview he had emphasized delegation, empowerment, and accountability so as to make time for more important activities, new countries, and strategic opportunities and promised to focus more on customer demand. The task facing Edouard Michelin in 1999 was huge: to usher into the twenty-first century a firm that was coming, from many points of view, straight out of the nineteenth. Said Edouard Michelin about his father, "I think in terms of vision of the industry . . . we are very close. In terms of method, we are very different. That's normal: I represent a new generation."[46]

Four years later, Edouard Michelin had accomplished a lot. Michelin's position in Asia had become much more significant, joint ventures had increased its product development and global reach, retailing had become a major growth vector; substantial investments in marketing had been made, and the corporation had been largely decentralized. Edouard Michelin appeared firmly at the helm of the company. In spite of these accomplishments, Michelin had not taken a large share from either

Case Studies Exhibit 1.7

Tire Sales Forecast for 2006 (millions of units)

	Passenger Cars			Light and Heavy Trucks			
	OE	Replacement	Total	OE	Replacement	Total	Total
North America	75.1	240.4	315.5	20.2	65.6	85.9	401.37
South America	11.7	31.8	43.5	3.7	18.3	22.0	65.57
Europe	85.7	187.0	272.7	12	29.6	41.6	314.30
Central and Eastern Europe	16.0	45.7	61.7	3.7	17.4	21.1	82.85
Asia	72.0	109.4	181.4	30.4	92.3	122.7	304.12
Middle East and Africa	3.3	34.9	38.3	1.9	20.5	22.4	60.67
Oceania	1.7	12.9	14.6	0.4	5.0	5.4	20.04
	265.5	662.2	927.7	72.4	248.8	321.2	1,248.93

Source: LMC International.

Goodyear or Bridgestone at a time when both had been facing significant problems. And the market for tires was not expected to change dramatically (see Exhibit 1.7 for forecast growth rates). Michelin's move into distribution and its venture into wheel-related parts were potentially increasing its stagnant sales base but also had to deliver profitability to improve share price. What else did Eduard Michelin need to do to turn Michelin into the leader of the tire industry?

NOTES

1. *Les echos,* February 11, 2002, http://www.postcom.org/archive/news2002/news02-02.htm (accessed June 10, 2005).

2. Neil Mullineux, *World Tire Industry,* Economist Intelligence Unit, 1999.

3. Michelin, *Fact Book Michelin,* 2002, estdoc.web-michelin.com/repository/DocumentRepositoryServlet.html (accessed June 10, 2005).

4. Michelin, *Fact Book Michelin,* 2002.

5. Crain Communications Ltd., Rubber and Plastics, August 25, 2003.

6. Michelin, *Fact Book Michelin,* 2002.

7. Credit Suisse First Boston Equity Research, Michelin, November 19, 2003.

8. *Wall Street Journal,* September 16, 2002.

9. Credit Suisse First Boston Equity Research, Michelin.

10. Mullineux, *World Tire Industry.*

11. *European Rubber Journal,* 2002.

12. Scotsman Publications Ltd. The Ford Motor Company had bought Kwik-Fit in 1999 for £1 billion but sold it in August 2002 to CVC Capital Partners for £330 million.

13. *Global Tire Report,* 1996–97.

14. Saul Ludwig, *Modern Tire Dealer,* January 1997.

15. Credit Suisse First Boston, November 21, 2002.

16. Carlos Ghosn and Philippe Riès, *Citoyen du monde* (Grasset, 2003).

17. It was shown holding a glass full of nails, with the Latin caption *Nunc est bibendum* (Let's drink now), to underline Michelin tires' greater resistance to punctures.

18. *L'Usine Nouvelle,* September 21, 1989.

19. Ghosn and Riès, *Citoyen du monde.*

20. Freydet and Pingaud, *Les patrons face à la gauche* (Paris: Ramsay, 1982).

21. Ghosn and Riès, *Citoyen du monde.*

22. *Financial Times,* December 20, 1999.

23. Pascal Galinier, "Les héritiers: Edouard Michelin," *Le nouvel economiste,* no. 1005, July 13, 1995.

24. Ibid.

25. Ibid.

26. Ibid.

27. *L'express,* December 4, 2003.

28. *Les echos,* February 11, 2002.

29. Crain Communications, *Rubber and Plastic News,* October 29, 2001.

30. *Business Week,* September 2002.

31. *Modern Tyre Dealer,* January 1998.

32. The joint venture was imposed by the Chinese authorities to promote the exchange of know-how.

33. *Financial Times Information,* March 18, 2003.

34. Crain Communications, *Tyre Business.*

35. One C3M module could manufacture 100 tires per day

with a single mold. Its acquisition cost would be less than €1 million, the processing time was cut by 85 percent compared to traditional methods, and the space required was reduced by 90 percent, the energy by 75 percent, and labor costs by 30 percent. Thirty modules (the size of a plant) could be operated by only 150 people (Alain Jemain, *L'usine nouvelle,* September 24, 2001). Under development are C3M units equipped with several molds.

36. For example, whereas the Euromaster operation serviced only 10,000 of the 90,000 trucks Michelin was contracted to service in the United Kingdom, Euromaster serviced all the trucks contracted by Michelin.

37. *Europe Information Service,* European Report, October 1, 2003.

38. Crain Communications, *Rubber and Plastics News,* October 20, 2003. Michelin was brought to court by the European Commission for having shut other tire makers out of the market between 1990 and 1998. Michelin holds more than 50 percent of the French replacement tire market.

39. *Tire Business,* October 25, 1999.

40. XFE (Xtra Fuel Economy) in the United States.

41. The original X radial reduced rolling resistance over bias designs by 34 percent. Between its launch in 1946 and 1990, manufacturers had managed to reduce rolling resistance by only a further 10 percent.

42. In the United States, high-performance tires as a percentage of replacement units shipped was 15.2 in 2002, up from 9 in 1996 (*Modern Tire Dealer,* annual survey 2003).

43. Reuters, March 9, 1999; and *Modern Tire Dealer,* 2003.

44. *Financial Times,* December 20, 1999.

45. "Edouard Michelin: The New Head of Michelin," *Financial Times,* December 20, 1999.

46. "Edouard Michelin."

CASE STUDY 2

The European Non-Life Insurance Industry and AXA in 2001

"Is big beautiful?" asked John Engestroem, CEO of London reinsurer Liberty Re at an insurance conference in Baden-Baden in October 1997. AXA certainly seemed to believe so. Under the leadership of the legendary Claude Bébéar, AXA grew to become one of the major insurers in Europe. AXA was not alone in having pursued size and acquisitions; many other financial services firms had concluded megadeals: The German universal bank Deutsche Bank had acquired the U.S. investment bank Bankers Trust in 1999; there had been a Swiss-Swiss marriage between the two leading universal banks UBS and SBC in 1998; and a spectacular US$82.5 billion merger of insurance giant Travelers Group and banking powerhouse Citigroup had been concluded in 1998. Echoing the merits of size, Christopher Condron, AXA's recently appointed head of U.S. operations said, "To be a real winner in financial services, you have to be a global company. AXA is one of the rare ones."

Yet, the view that "size is king" was not universally shared. Juergen Zech, then CEO of Gerling, maintained in 1997 that in insurance, size is not as important as in manufacturing because "you have a chance to offset smaller size through better management."[1] Also, the management consultancy firm A.T. Kearney found in a study on the European insurance industry in 1999 that no correlation existed between

the size of insurance companies and superior levels of operating profitability or shareholders returns.

When Henri de Castries, 47, took over from Claude Bébéar as chairman and CEO of the AXA Group in May 2000, many analysts agreed that AXA was geographically better balanced than any of its competitors. Some analysts, however, spoke of AXA as being in a "post binge hangover." Henri de Castries said he wanted to continue growth, though, and explained, "I am not interested in becoming big just for the sake of it. But our competitors are big and size allows us to become a price setter rather than a price taker. A market capitalization of $100 billion will give us more room to manoeuvre."[2]

There appeared to be a need to maneuver, indeed. With the abrupt end of the stock market boom in 2000, insurance companies could not as easily compensate weak operating results by returns from investments of customers' premiums. While the life insurance sector appeared to remain promising, the non-life sector had been profoundly affected by several factors: deregulation, overcapacity, entrenched competitors, structural differences among European countries in the insurance sector, new entrants, deconstruction of traditional insurance activities, impatient shareholders, and so forth. It was in this challenging environment that Henri de Castries had to figure out how to position AXA's amalgam of activities in non-life insurance for profitable growth and shareholder value creation. The case describes the non-life insurance industry in Europe with a focus on automobile insurance and reviews some of the key strategic issues of AXA and its competitors in 2001.

INDUSTRY OVERVIEW

SEGMENTATION: LIFE AND NON-LIFE INSURANCE

The insurance industry was divided into two major businesses: Life insurance and non-life insurance. Life insurance was basically a long-term savings tool. The policyholder paid a regular premium to the insurance company over a period of time (or in a lump sum), thus accumulating capital and earning a rate of return. If the policyholder reached a specified age, he or she began to withdraw regular payments (annuitization) for a given period of time or until his or her death. If the policyholder died prematurely, a beneficiary would receive either the current value of the annuity or the amount paid into it so far, whichever was greater.

Historically, a life insurance policy had been combined with risk protection. In case of the policyholder's early death, a beneficiary would get not only the current value of the actual savings but also a specified amount of money protecting the surviving dependents against financial hardship. These mixed insurance-savings products were not always transparent with regard to the return they offered on the savings. In France, consumer pressure and competition from banks led insurers to split the product into a pure savings instrument and a life insurance. By contrast, in Germany and the United Kingdom, these mixed products were still popular.

Non-life insurance was classified into property and casualty (P&C) and accident and health (A&H). They provided coverage for a specified risk, usually for a limited period. Major non-life insurance classes were automobile, A&H, property, liability, and legal expense. In general, a policyholder paid a certain sum (premium) to get insurance for a specified risk. If the policyholder never faced the event he was insured against, his premium was by and large lost. Some P&C products were compulsory in many countries (e.g., automobile and home insurance). The split between personal and commercial insurance for P&C was approximately 80-20.

MARKET SIZE AND TRENDS

Global insurance premiums totaled US$2443.7 billion in 2000, with 38 percent of global insurance premiums generated by non-life insurance and 62 percent by the life business. The European Union, with 30 percent, was the second biggest insurance market in the world behind the United States (34 percent) and was followed by Japan (21 percent). The biggest insurance market in Europe was the United Kingdom, with a premium income of €220.3 billion (27.9 percent), followed by Germany (€134 billion, or 17.0 percent) and France (€130.4 billion, or 16.5 percent). The seven leading European markets (the top three plus Italy, the Netherlands, Switzerland, and Spain) represented more than 85 percent of the market.

Within Europe, the share of life insurance had been continuously expanding from 50 percent in 1990 to 64 percent in 2000, totaling €470 billion in premiums. The boom in life insurance in the 1990s was a result of both low interest rates and a growing concern in the developed countries about state pension provisions. Unit-linked products,[3] pensions, and other long-term savings products had contributed significantly to the growth of the life business. The nature of products varied among countries, reflecting and exploiting national tax benefits, and so forth.

The EU non-life insurance market stood at €264 billion in 2000. The European Union's six largest markets, Germany, the United Kingdom, France,

Case Studies Exhibit 2.1

Share of Non-Life Insurance Across Major Countries 1992 and 1999

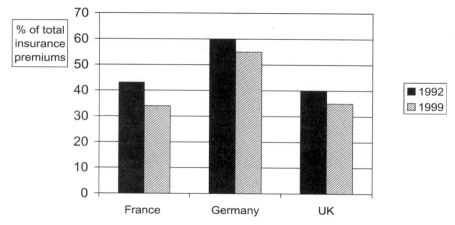

Source: CEA, European Insurance in Figures, 2000.

Italy, Spain, and the Netherlands, represented 87 percent of the EU market. Growth rates in the European Union had been very modest in the 1990s. The average annual growth rate for non-life in the European Union between 1992 and 1999 had been only 1.6 percent, compared to 9.5 percent for the life business. However, there were national differences. While non-life premiums in Germany and France grew at 2.5 percent and 1.8 percent per annum, respectively, during 1992–99, the non-life market in the United Kingdom shrank by 1.3 percent in the same period.[4] Total non-life premiums per inhabitant had been €871 in Germany, €821 in the United Kingdom, and €653 in France in 1999. Also, the relative importance of non-life versus life differed within Europe. For example, the share of non-life in Germany was almost 55 percent in 1999 but represented only 35 percent of the insurance business in the United Kingdom (see Exhibit 2.1).

Non-life premiums tended to evolve with GDP. However, since 1995, premium growth in non-life had lagged behind GDP growth, largely due to price declines. The final phase of European deregulation in 1994 had led to the abolition of price and product control and to the introduction of a single European insurance license. Since 1994, an insurer that had obtained a license in its home country could conduct business in all other EU member states without any additional license.[5] This and the increase in insurance capacity in the late 1990s had put a downward pressure on prices.

VALUE CHAIN IN NON-LIFE INSURANCE

The value chain for non-life insurance was composed of claims payments (procurement), servicing, product manufacturing, and distribution (see Exhibit 2.2). Procurement related to payments to hospitals (health), car repair shops, physically injured people and their lawyers (automobile insurance), and the like. This represented the biggest cost block, ranging from 60 percent to 90 percent of premiums, depending on company and country.

Servicing included ascertaining, inspecting and

Case Studies Exhibit 2.2

Value Chain for Property and Casualty Insurance

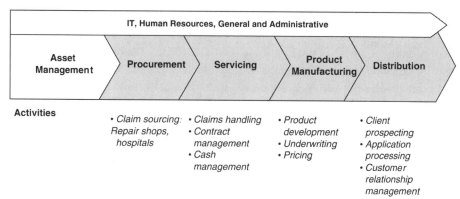

Source: Provided courtesy of Christophe Angoulvant, Vice President & Anne-Ev Enzmann, Associate, A.T. Kearney.

processing claims, reviewing policies after each claim, and invoicing and collecting money. Assessing the veracity of claims was very important, since some customers inflated claims or caused damages themselves. A survey conducted by the Association of British Insurers (ABI) found that fraud added on average 4 percent to the cost of automobile insurance. As many insurance agents were paid on a commission basis, some helped customers formulate their claims so that it would be accepted. Different servicing administration also translated into significant differences in cost. In France, for example, servicing was to a large extent handled by local agents, whereas in Germany, regional offices dealt with the bulk of the servicing.

Product manufacturing was composed of product development, underwriting (risk scoring and selection), and pricing. In the aftermath of deregulation, premiums were increasingly set according to individual risk quality. In automobile insurance, for example, premiums could differ by neighborhood locality, gender, profession, age, car, and so forth to reflect different risks of accidents and thefts. The level of sophistication varied widely among compa-

nies. In France, for example, MACIF segmented its customers living in urban areas into 14 price zones to score various risks, whereas UAP used only 2.

Distribution of insurance products related to attracting clients, processing applications (collecting client information, providing quotes, completing the insurance application), and customer-relationship management. Traditional distribution channels in non-life insurance were tied agents, independent brokers, and a salaried sales force. Tied agents and brokers were independent intermediaries and were remunerated on a commission basis. New distribution channels had developed, including direct sales via telephone and the Internet as well as corporate partnerships with banks and nonfinancial retailers.

Distribution varied widely among countries. In Germany, Spain, and Italy, personal insurance was predominantly distributed via an exclusive network of tied agents. In the United Kingdom, the Netherlands, and Belgium, insurance companies sold mainly through independent channels, particularly brokers. France exhibited a more varied pattern. Since the beginning of the 1980s, mutuals had opened retail outlets with a salaried sales force (direct selling, i.e., without an intermediary) and were competing head-to-head with the tied agents of private insurance companies. In 1999, tied agents and direct selling by mutuals each represented 34–35 percent of premiums. In 1990, the figure for the mutuals was 29 percent, and for tied agents 47 percent. Also in France, sales of insurance in banks and the post office, which had not existed in 1990, had been established as a new distribution channel and generated 8 percent of premiums in 1999.

PROFIT MEASUREMENT IN NON-LIFE INSURANCE

The profitability of a non-life insurance company was determined by the result of its primary activities (underwriting result) and the result of its investment activities (investment result). The underwriting result (or technical result) was calculated as the difference between "paid in" and "paid out": premium income minus claims (payments resulting from insurance contracts) and expenses (distribution, servicing, manufacturing, overhead). By industry convention, the significance of claims was expressed as a percentage of net premiums earned (claims or loss ratio), and so were expenses (expense ratio).

The sum of the expense ratio and the claims ratio was called the combined ratio. It was not unusual to find a combined ratio higher than 100 percent. This meant that for every dollar of premium income the company took in, it had to pay out more than a dollar in claims and expenses. In the United Kingdom, for example, the automobile insurance sector as a whole had achieved underwriting profits in only 2 of the 10 years between 1988 and 1998.

Since there was a time lag between premiums being paid in and claims being paid out, so-called technical reserves were accumulated. They were carried as a liability on the balance sheet to provide for future commitments under existing policies. Till the

day of payout, reserves were invested and generated an investment return. Since the amount of technical reserves was only an estimate of future payments, there was significant room for adjusting earnings. In good years, insurers could increase claims estimates, thus raising reserves and lowering taxable net income, while in bad years, they could report lower technical reserves and thus increase profits.

The investment result was composed of investment income (interest, dividends) and realized capital gains (sale of stocks or bonds that had increased in price). The product of asset leverage (average invested assets as a percentage of net premiums) and investment yield (net investment returns, including realized capital gains, as a percentage of average invested assets) determined the investment result. Asset management was of central importance to insurance companies, and several were among the biggest institutional investors. In the United Kingdom, for example, insurance companies were the largest domestic owner of UK shares, owning 21 percent of all UK ordinary shares. This compared with 18 percent of UK shares held by company pension funds and only 1 percent owned by banks. See Exhibit 2.3 for a profitability breakdown of non-life insurance in the United States, Germany, France, and the United Kingdom.

The balance sheet of an insurance company showed investments as financial assets, balanced by insurance liabilities (technical reserves) and the risk capital provided by shareholders. The EU statutory solvency margin required that an insurer have a level of capital funds of at least 17 percent of net premiums. Since insurers invested mainly in bonds and held them to maturity, the interest rate was a key factor in determining an insurer's investment return. Investment yields of insurance companies were higher in times of falling interest rates, as happened in the 1990s. Insurers in some countries had also used the booming stock markets after 1995 to realize capital gains by selling shares.

Case Studies Exhibit 2.3

Profitability of Major Non-Life Markets

	United States 1996–2000	United Kingdom 1996–99	Germany 1995–99	France 1995–99
Loss ratio	77.5	75.4	70.5	84.5
Expense ratio	27.4	32.5	25.3	22.5
Underwriting result	–6.5	–7.9	1.5	–8.3
Investment yield	7	9	7.2	5.8
Asset leverage	268	273.3	217.3	25.3
Net investment result	18.8	24.6	15.7	15.4
Other expenses/earnings	–0.01	–2.7	–6.6	–1.5
Profit margin (Pre-tax)	12.2	14	10.5	5.7
Tax rate	21.2	24	60.3	41.6
Profit margin (After-tax)	9.6	10.7	4.1	3.4
Solvency	106.1	102.7	145.4	111.5
ROE	9.1	10.1	2.9	3.2

Source: For United Kingdom: *Insurance Pocket Book* 2000. TTP. Sigma 5/2001

Underwriting results in non-life had shown a variable pattern. Periods of high premium rates were followed by periods of low premium rates. It had been estimated that there tended to be a six-year cycle between successive peaks of investment results. Since mid-2000, premium rates had again tended to go up. Underwriting and investment results tended to be negatively correlated. Strong investment results increased the capital funds of insurers, allowing them to lower premium prices. There also tended to be a negative correlation between realized capital gains and the underwriting results, as insurers tended to realize capital gains in times of underwriting losses to smooth earnings.

AUTOMOBILE INSURANCE: A KEY NON-LIFE INSURANCE MARKET

Within non-life, the automobile insurance segment was the biggest segment, exceeding €100 billion in premiums in 2000 and accounting for 28 percent of non-life premium income in Germany, 36 percent in France, and 31 percent in the United Kingdom.

Three countries totaled more than 50 percent of the European automobile insurance market: Germany (20 percent), the United Kingdom (17.5 percent), and France (14.3 percent).[6] However, the share of automobile insurance in total premiums had been declining in the past eight years due to the low average growth rate of 1.4 percent in the period 1992–1999.

Motor insurance, like home or travel insurance, was a relatively simple, standardized product, which did not require lengthy explanation and advice during the selling process. Services on the Internet allowed consumers to obtain price quotes from different providers and to easily compare the policies on offer. One broker report put it bluntly: "We believe the Internet will ultimately lead to commoditization and make it difficult for non-life insurers to generate returns much above the cost of capital."[7]

Automobile insurance consisted of two subsegments: compulsory and noncompulsory insurance. Compulsory third-party liability (TPL) automobile insurance to protect against bodily injury and property damage of third parties was required by law.

Thus, 80.6 percent of all households in Germany held passenger-car TPL insurance in 2000; in the United Kingdom, the figure was 68 percent. Noncompulsory insurance related to comprehensive or semicomprehensive insurance for the insured's own damages and passenger casualty. The split of premiums between compulsory TPL and noncompulsory insurance was approximately 60-40 across Europe in 1999.

Automobile insurance premiums had come down in the second half of the 1990s. Commoditization and deregulation had made competition intense. In addition, insurance companies tended to regard automobile insurance as an entry-level product to capture clients at a young age. While the expense ratios of the traditional insurers in automobile insurance had remained more or less constant over the last 20 years, the claims ratio had increased over time. The frequency of TPL claims had been falling in the last 30 years across most EU markets. However, average cost per claim had gone up quite substantially. In the United Kingdom, for example, average cost per claim had increased by 104 percent over 10 years, from £703 in 1988 to £1434 in 1998. While the retail price index (RPI) had risen by 33 percent between 1990 and 1998, the average cost of spare parts and repair charges had increased by 58 percent and 38 percent, respectively.[8]

Several factors appeared to drive the increasing cost of claims. The value of vehicles insured as well as the cost of labor for car repairs had been rising as cars became more complex. Also, car repair shops were becoming more capital intensive, and car manufacturers had extended into car repair service, gaining market share at the expense of independent shops. "A lot of repairers have been squeezed out of business and the investment required to cope with different systems is enormous," said George Lowe, director of insurance at the United Kingdom's Automobile Association.[9] Also, car manufacturers were increasingly controlling the market for spare

Case Studies Exhibit 2.4

Example of Automobile Claim Expense Categories

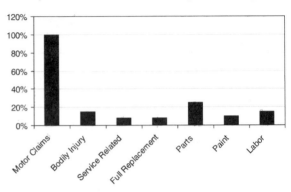

Source: A.T. Kearney analysis.

parts of their brands, obtaining high margins to the detriment of insurers. Finally, personal injury settlements had become more generous as more people went to court to fight for damages. For an overview of automobile claim expenses, see Exhibit 2.4.

COMPETITION

MARKET STRUCTURE

With almost 3,000 non-life companies operating in the European Union, the European insurance industry was still quite fragmented. Yet, compared to the beginning of the 1990s, concentration had increased. The combined market share of the seven biggest players in Europe had increased from 16 percent to 31 percent in the period 1990–1999, and from 18 percent to 39 percent in the six biggest EU markets in the same period. Still, significant differences in concentration trends were observed among the major countries. The United Kingdom had deregulated the insurance industry as early as 1982, and consolidation was well advanced. By 1999, the top five non-life insurance companies represented 55 percent of the market, compared to 32 percent five years before. Similarly in France, the top five non-life companies had a market share of 57 percent in 1999, up from 41 percent in 1990. In contrast, concentration in Germany, where the industry had been deregulated only in 1994 under EU pressure, had progressed at a much slower pace. The market share of the top five had modestly increased from 33 percent in 1992 to 41 percent in 1999.

It was estimated that more than 92 percent of the concentration gain had been generated by mergers and acquistions deals. In 1999, more than 50 percent of all M&A transactions had crossed national borders, whereas at the beginning of the 1990s, the figure had been only around 30 percent. Cross-sector deals into banking remained an exception among non-life insurers. In contrast, some banks had charged forward and had bought insurance companies. For example, Credit Suisse acquired Winterthur in 1997. Only very recently had insurers reacted by investing in banking: German insurance market leader Allianz bought the number three in German banking, Dresdner Bank, in 2001.

COMPETITORS

The competition landscape changed quite significantly in the 1990s. On one hand, a few insurance giants had developed, competing across Europe (e.g., Allianz). On the other hand, within each country, there remained many national players, of which the mutuals (e.g., HUK Coburg in Germany) had carved out a very strong position. In addition, a raft of new players had emerged: companies selling direct to consumers (e.g., DirectLine), retailers offering insurance to their shoppers (e.g., Tesco), Internet portals comparing and selling insurance services, car companies proposing insurance as part of their sales process, and banks selling insurance policies over their counters. The various types of players and a representative firm of each are briefly reviewed next.

The European Insurance Giants

The industry was increasingly populated by a small number of large, broad insurance groups, which had become major market players in all major EU markets: Allianz (Germany), AXA (France), Generali (Italy), Zurich (Switzerland), Royal & Sun Alliance (United Kingdom), CGNU (United Kingdom), and Winterthur (Switzerland), see Exhibit 2.5. Allianz was perhaps the most prominent of this group. In 2000, it was the largest insurance company worldwide based on premiums and was by far the market leader in both non-life and life in Germany, with an estimated market share of 18 percent and 14 percent, respectively. One of the strengths of Allianz in its home market was its superior underwriting capabilities leading to a low claims ratio (see Exhibit 2.6). It believed that its vast historical database derived from a broad product range was key in assessing and pricing the risk per customer. With 55 percent of premiums, the P&C business was at the heart of Allianz's business (the comparable figure for Generali was 35 percent and for CGNU 42 percent).

Mutuals were non-profit-based insurance companies and were owned by their policyholders. They played a strong role in personal insurance products in France and Germany and challenged the private companies as low-cost providers. For example, the top automobile insurers in France, AXA, mutuals Groupama, and MACIF, were competing head-to-head. Mutuals operated mostly on a national basis, although there were two large pan-European mutual alliances in 2001: Euresa and Eureko. Many regarded these alliances to be of a defensive nature, not having a large impact on business performance.

German insurance company HUK Coburg was a good example of how mutuals had developed. In Germany in 1999, mutuals generated 21 percent of premium income, compared to 70 percent for public insurance companies. In automobile

Case Studies Exhibit 2.5

European Market Share of the Biggest European Non-Life Insurers

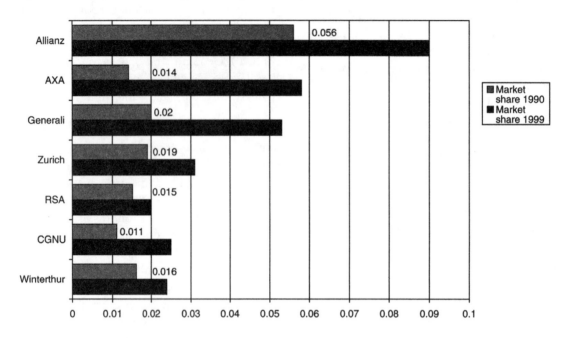

Source: Swiss Re, sigma 3/2000, annual reports.

Case Studies Exhibit 2.6

German Non-Life Market 1999 (excluding health): Top Six Players

	Gross premium (in € millions)	Claims ratio	Expense ratio	Combined ratio
1 Allianz	6,731	70.3	26	96.3
2 Gerling	2,182	85.3	27.1	112.4
3 AXA Colonia	2,161	75.6	28.7	104.3
4 R+V Allgemeine Versicherung	1,905	65.1	32.9	98
5 HDI	1,396	106.4	16.6	123
6 HUK Coburg	1,366	91.2	9.9	101.1
Industry	*53,845*	*75.3*	*26.5*	*101.8*

Source: Federal Supervisory Office for the Insurance System, Germany (BAV), 1999.

insurance, they had increased their market share from 19 percent in 1975 to 28 percent in 1998. Coburg was the number two player in automobile insurance after Allianz and was the sixth largest insurer in non-life. It was founded in 1933 as a mutual automobile insurance society for teachers and priests in Erfurt. By 2001, Coburg was open to everybody, covered all insurance classes, and administered 21.7 million policies. At the heart of Coburg's growth strategy were the so-called trusted persons, part-time agents building on a good personal network to sell insurance. In 2001, Coburg's distribution had 5,500 trusted persons, of which 5,000 were part-time workers and 500 were full-time agents with their own offices. Coburg also had a salaried sales force located in 39 branch offices, four customer service centers, and a mail-order service. In the media, the trusted persons model had sometimes been viewed as controversial: "Again and again there are cases in which an agent sells useless contracts to a customer just to get the sales commission," wrote the *Süddeutsche Zeitung*.[10] Proponents, however, referred to the high customer satisfaction and low rates of cancellations and complaints. This sales approach also turned out to be a very cost-effective distribution channel if the insurer could effectively manage the large number of part-time sales people.

Direct sellers were companies operating over the phone or Internet, avoiding the large investment in field salespeople. Direct sellers had made major inroads in the United Kingdom, representing 34 percent of all personal automobile insurance premiums in 1998. In France and Germany, they had only a 3–4 percent market share in 2000.

Perhaps the most innovative direct seller in Europe was Direct Line of the Royal Bank of Scotland. It had started in 1984 in the United Kingdom when four businessmen used their experience in the insurance and information technology industry to

take a fresh look at private automobile insurance: "Recognizing that the customer wanted simplicity, service and value for money, we dispensed with the middleman, offered direct access by telephone and introduced highly sophisticated computer systems to make transactions swift and simple." The Royal Bank of Scotland backed the new venture, and Direct Line was founded as a wholly owned subsidiary of the bank.[11]

At the core of the value proposition was customer service. In 1985, Direct Line removed the need for cover notes and thus was able to deliver an insurance policy within 24 hours. Directline.com customers could register automobile accident and home insurance claims online beginning in 2001 and could keep track of their claims on a 24-hour basis. The claims registration facility also enabled the settlement of certain claims over the Web. At the same time, innovative technology helped to keep costs down. In 1995, the first Direct Line Accident Management Center started repairing cars. Subsequent centers developed into factory-style operations to provide better, quicker repair service for customers and reduce costs for Direct Line. As a result, the combined ratio of Direct Line was the lowest among the top five UK players: 91 compared to 111 for market leader RSA and 124 for AXA in the United Kingdom. Direct Line relied heavily on marketing and brand management.

In 1993, less than a decade after its inception, Direct Line had become the United Kingdom's largest insurer of privately owned automobiles. In 2001, the Direct Line Group held a market share of 5.6 percent, following CGNU (19 percent), Royal Sun & Alliance (15.4 percent), AXA (8.4 percent), and Zurich (6.7 percent). It had a total of 8.2 million customers. Exhibit 2.7 gives the top five players in life and non-life for Germany, France, and the United Kingdom.

Case Studies Exhibit 2.7

Top Five Players per Country and Segment in 1999

LIFE 1999		NON–LIFE 1999	
Germany	Premium (€ million)		Premiums (€ million)
1 Allianz	8,252	1 Allianz	6,069
2 Hamburg-Mannheimer	2,816	2 Gerling	3,410
3 R+V	2,649	3 AXA-Colonia	2,157
4 Deutscher Herold	2,382	4 R+V (cooperative)	1,917
5 Aachener und Muenchener	2,270	5 HDI (mutual)	1,395
France			
1 CNP	15,803	1 Groupama/GAN (mutual)	7,193
2 AXA	10,824	2 AXA	6,069
3 Predica (Credit Agricole)	7,350	3 AGF (Allianz)	5,024
4 BNP Paribas	6,284	4 MAAF/Mut. Du Mans (mutual)	3,297
5 Assurance du Credit Mutuel	4,632	5 MACIF (mutual)	2,138
United Kingdom			
1 Barclays Life	20,757	1 CGNU	7,994
2 Prudential	15,596	2 Royal + Sun Alliance	4,950
3 CGNU	11,842	3 AXA	3,410
4 Lloyds TSB	7,119	4 Zurich Financial Services	2,339
5 Standard Life	7,046	5 Cornhill (Allianz)	1,476

Source: The European Federation of National Insurance Associations (CEA), European Insurance in Figures, 1999 Data (July 2000).

NEW PLAYERS

In the aftermath of deregulation and helped by advances in technology, a number of new players entered the insurance market: banks, powerful nonfinancial retailers, e-businesses, and the like.

E-Customer Gateways

The advent of the Internet opened up a whole range of new customer services such as online price comparisons. Proprietary financial services portals such as French ZeBank offered automobile insurance in cooperation with AXA. Customer portals such as http://www.virgin.net assembled under the theme "motoring" the sale of new and used cars, car rental, as well as automobile insurance, by referring customers to a selected list of providers (Direct Line, Tesco Car Insurance, Elephant). Financial services aggregators provided a one-stop shopping open architecture where customers could get information, conduct research, and obtain price quotes from multiple providers and be offered application or referral to an agent or provider.

Automotive and Related Industries

Car manufacturers such as Volvo, Peugeot, BMW, and Toyota as well as gasoline retailers had started to offer all kinds of services around the car, including automobile insurance. Volvo, for example, had entered into an exclusive cooperation agreement with If P&C Insurance, whereby If offered branded automobile insurance products to Volvo and Renault customers in Scandinavia. German gasoline retailer Aral announced in November 2001 that in cooperation with the mutual HDI, it would offer a comprehensive insurance package covering everything from breakdown service to car passenger insurance.

Nonfinancial Retailers

Big consumer supermarkets such as Tesco in the United Kingdom or Carrefour in France had also moved into insurance. For example, Tesco offered Tesco Car Insurance and Tesco Car Breakdown Assistance. The insurance policy was branded and distributed by Tesco but manufactured and serviced by UK Insurance Limited. On Tesco's side, automobile insurance was part of the product offering of Tesco Personal Finance (TPF), a joint venture with the Royal Bank of Scotland that was launched in July 1997. By 2001, it had more than 1 million customers and offered non-life and life insurance as well as mortgages, and was already profitable.

Banks

Not to be left behind, banks entered the insurance market with great determination, coining the term "bancassurance." Some industry analysts believed that banks had a competitive edge in selling insurance given their frequent contact opportunities with customers and intimate knowledge of their financial status and circumstances. Also, distribution at bank branches could be up to 50 percent cheaper than agency distribution given the small incremental cost of widening the banking product range.

Banks had been more successful at selling life products than non-life insurance. In Germany in 1999, 5 percent of non-life insurance premiums had

been obtained by banks, compared to 20 percent for life insurance. In France, comparable figures for 1999 stood at 9 percent for non-life and 61 percent for life insurance. So far, few banks had gone for ownership of a non-life insurer. One of the first banks to do so worldwide had been Crédit Mutuel in France, which had set up its own insurance company, ACM, in the early 1970s. Its success in cross-selling insurance was impressive: In the east of France, where it had its home base, 25 percent of its bank customers also held at least one non-life insurance product. By contrast, some other banks that had ventured into insurance had reconsidered ownership. Abbey National, the UK building society, had divested its non-life insurance joint venture with CGNU in January 2001, limiting itself only to offering access to insurance as part of its overall financial retail package.

AXA

AXA traced its origins to the mutual Mutuelle de l'Assurance Contre l'Incendie, which was founded in Paris in 1816. Operations began in 1817 under the name Ancienne Mutuelle, offering fire protection for its members. In 1985, AXA became the corporate name of the group of French regional insurance companies acquired by Ancienne Mutuelle. The choice of the name—short and easy to pronounce in every language—reflected the international ambitions of the group. In 1988, AXA was listed on the Paris Stock Exchange and in 1996 on the New York Stock Exchange. In 2001, AXA called itself "a world leader in financial protection and wealth management." It counted 50 million customers, generated €80 billion in revenues, had €892 billion in assets under management, and achieved a return on equity of 13.7 percent in 2000. With a market capitalization of €55 billion as of July 27, 2001, AXA was the second biggest European insurer behind archrival Allianz. In March 2001, the AXA mutuals owned, directly and indirectly, about 21 percent of the issued ordinary shares, which represented 33.6 percent of the voting rights, with the remainder being publicly traded.

THE BUILDING OF AN EMPIRE—THE BÉBÉAR YEARS

Claude Bébéar (b. 1935), a product of France's elite Ecole Polytechnique, had shied away from the cushy jobs in the French civil service that were favored by many graduates of the *grandes écoles* and had chosen instead to join in 1958 a small and unremarkable insurer. Recruited by a classmate's father who was then the chairman of Ancienne Mutuelle, Bébéar was told he would eventually run the firm—and so he did. In 1975, on the death of the chairman, he was appointed CEO. Driven by the ambition to become the global number one in insurance, Bébéar went on the acquisition trail.

In the 1980s, Bébéar worked to transform the regional insurer into a major player in France. In 1982, he took control of Groupe Drouot, a significantly larger French stock company with a market presence in France and other countries in western Europe. In 1986 and 1988, he acquired two other insurance companies: Groupe Présence and AGP. By 1988, AXA was the second largest French insurer, just behind UAP. The same year, Bébéar was elected "Manager of the Year," the first representative of the financial world to receive this distinction.

In the 1990s, AXA took off to become one of the world's largest insurance groups. A key milestone was the acquisition of Group UAP in 1997, then number one in the French insurance market with positions in Germany, the United Kingdom, Benelux, and Italy. The acquisition of the P&C insurer Guardian Royal Exchange in 1999 provided AXA with critical size in the United Kingdom and Ireland and strengthened AXA's position in Germany. In Belgium, AXA Royale Belge acquired the banking network of Anhyp, the second largest Belgian savings bank.

AXA had first tried to cross the Atlantic in 1989. While the attempt to take over the U.S. P&C insurer Farmers failed, the experience had helped AXA in taking over the mutual Equitable, the fifth largest life insurer in the United States. It was demutualized in 1992 and renamed AXA Financial. By 2000, AXA had bought out all minority interests. Through Equitable, AXA had acquired skills in asset management, which were further reinforced by the acquisition of U.S.-based asset manager Sanford C. Bernstein in 2000. Looking east, AXA acquired the Australian life insurer National Mutual in 1995 (renamed AXA Asia Pacific Holdings), gaining a key foothold in Australia, New Zealand, and Hong Kong. In 2000, Bébéar saw the opportunity to enter the world's largest life insurance market by taking control of Nippon Dantai, ranked as Japan's thirteenth largest life insurer.

Analysts agreed unanimously that AXA had developed an impressive track record of deal making. With a keen eye for value, persistence and patience in the approach, and very fast and efficient execution capabilities, Bébéar excelled at acquisitions. When he stepped down as CEO in early 2000, his company had become the world's largest insurance company by premiums written, had 50 million customers—including individuals, small and medium-sized businesses, institutional investors, and major corporations—and counted 140,000 employees. The AXA share price had risen by more than 200 percent from the beginning of 1987 (€8.80) to the beginning of 2000 (€30.20).

By 2000, AXA showed the strong personal imprint of Bébéar. He had achieved his dream of turning AXA into a global force. Insiders characterized him as a charismatic and effective communicator who was concerned with shaping an AXA culture of local entrepreneurship. Bébéar was also a strong supporter of philanthropy. In recognition of AXA's leadership in this field, former U.S. president George H.W. Bush had presented Bébéar with the Point of Light Award in 1997, the first time that such a distinction had been awarded to a non-U.S. company.

The AXA Group structure under Bébéar was based on the principle "Think global, act local." Everything was decentralized except for a few central functions at group level: planning, reporting, decisions concerning the allocation of shareholders' equity and acquisitions, IT policy, human resources philosophy, executive career management, and the use of the AXA trademark and the corporate image.

AXA IN THE NEW MILLENNIUM—NEW CHALLENGES AND A NEW CEO

In May 2000, Henri de Castries, 47, succeeded Bébéar as chairman and CEO of the AXA Group. A descendant of a military family—his ancestor Charles Eugené de la Croix de Castries had been minister of the navy under Louis XVI—Henri de Castries had first followed the typical career path of the French elite. A graduate of the prestigious universities HEC and ENA, he first served as a paratrooper in the army and then joined the Ministry of Finance. In the prestigious treasury division, he was in charge of sorting out troubled French companies and later, privatizations. Yet, unlike the majority of his peers, de Castries was not parachuted by the authorities to a top job at a private-sector company with strong connections to the state. Instead, he left the finance ministry in midcareer and, after meeting Bébéar, joined AXA in 1989.[12] He was first put in charge of the finance department, then of legal restructurings and mergers. In 1993, he became a senior executive vice president with responsibilities for the group's financial and real estate activities. In 1994, his responsibilities were extended to the

group's North American and British operations, before he became CEO in 2000.

Henri de Castries took leadership after AXA had embarked for years on an aggressive international program of acquisitions—characterized by one analyst as "bulimia": In 2000 alone, AXA had spent €23 billion on acquisitions, or a third of its market capitalization. De Castries, who had worked closely with Bébéar for 11 years, insisted that there would be no changes in strategic direction. However, after de Castries had spent 18 months in his new job, analysts noted that the deal-driven approach of Bébéar had given way to a more team-oriented effort of extracting greater value from existing assets. Acknowledging that managing a very geographically and culturally diversified company was no easy task, de Castries considered his main job "to make all the pieces fit together" and said that "one of the major challenges now is to take advantage of our size." Observed de Castries, "That doesn't mean we won't make new acquisitions. But acquisitions can only be easy and natural if we improve the efficiency of existing operations."[13]

After assuming CEO leadership, de Castries first strengthened his power base and built his new team. The three main priorities as announced in October 2000 were integration, e-commerce, and customer relationship management (CRM). A new department, Group Operations, was created, in charge of exploiting synergies across the group. De Castries hired for the job the former chairman and CEO of Ford France, Claude Brunet. The goal of the so-called Transversal Strategic projects was to leverage scale and increase productivity of AXA.[14] Also, a training scheme was kicked off that would eventually involve 6,000 of the insurer's staff. In a first attempt to make his top managers work more closely together and learn from one another, de Castries invited 250 of the group's executives to a training course in the Amazon jungle in spring 2000—to develop what he called a "multicultural team spirit."

On the operational front, de Castries set his sights on improving service efficiency. Mr. de Castries felt that they had to increase productivity in their factories. He felt that the companies that understood that financial services are industrial business would be at a competitive advantage. In 2000, a global reorganization program was launched with the goal of separating the "servicing utilities" from the distribution network, centralizing procurement and IT, and getting closer to the clients. De Castries also knew that AXA was far from being a leader in adopting new technology and that this was a major driver of productivity. E-commerce would be used to help reorganize processes and develop support systems for the sales force. While e-commerce could be used to acquire new clients, it was not de Castries's first priority.

De Castries also thought that AXA's traditional distribution channels were neither aggressive enough nor sufficiently advice oriented. Henri de Castries believed that the big fight in the insurance business was in distribution. Competitive advantage could be achieved by attracting more customers, selling more products, and keeping our customers for longer periods of time. Henri also believed that AXA should make its networks more advice oriented. While AXA sold on average 1.8 products per customer, retail banks counted 4 to 5 products per customer. Henri calculated that by increasing the number of products sold per client to 3 meant 50 percent more revenues. Thus, it was more effective to increase sales within the existing client base than it was to grow the company via expansion.

To win the fight in distribution, CRM was considered key. Customer knowledge was to be centrally managed, and sales efforts had to be linked to customer profitability. In an attempt to make agents focus on value-adding activities—selling and getting to know the client—pilot studies had been launched in 2001 to test CRM tools. All non-value-adding activities, for example, claims management and contract management, were planned to be transferred to central platforms. De Castries believed in the traditional channels but wanted them to focus on advice and sales of complex products as well as on cross-selling of high-margin products. Routine transactions and less-complex products would be transferred to alternative channels such as call centers or the Internet. In France, the union of tied agents, *Réussir*, had received the proposed changes in a hostile manner. Only after weeks of tough negotiations and slammed doors was an agreement signed in March 2001 approving pilot tests. By the end of 2001, AXA had started to build call centers and transfer claims management to these new servicing utilities.

De Castries wanted AXA to be a world leader in both manufacturing and servicing, and distribution. He told the financial community in May 2001 that he considered AXA a company with factories and a network and that AXA wanted to distribute the products of its factories also via channels it did not own "if this made sense." AXA also wanted its distribution networks to cross-sell to clients what they needed but what AXA did not produce.

The issue of scope also was back on de Castries's agenda in 2001. Did AXA want to become a full-fledged financial service provider and follow the example of archrival Allianz, or should AXA stick to its core business of insurance and asset management? De Castries had sold its investment arm, Donaldson, Lufkin & Jenrette, to Credit Suisse in late 2000. However, the Allianz-Dresdner deal had given fresh blood to the debate about "bancassurance."

In response to the acquisition of Dresdner by Allianz, de Castries told shareholders in September 2001 that "if others think to include all financial services, we do not change our strategy: We continue to think that being a specialist and leader in financial protection rather than a conglomerate is a good choice." De Castries favored distribution

Case Studies Exhibit 2.8

AXA: Consolidated Gross Premiums and Financial Services by Activity (€ millions)

	2000	1999	1998	2000/1999 % Change	% Change on a Comparable Basis*
Life and Savings					
France	12,528	10,555	9,547	18.7	18.7
United States	12,483	10,777	9,181	15.8	4.1
United Kingdom	7,939	7,205	5,140	10.2	−3.7
Asia/Pacific	6,796	2,859	2,975	137.7	14.6
Germany	2,912	2,757	2,408	5.6	2.7
Belgium	1,099	912	921	20.6	20.6
Other countries	2,239	2,025	2,275	10.6	8.8
Total	45,996	37,090	32,447	24.0	8.4
Property and Casualty					
France	4,001	3,926	4,179	1.9	0.0
Germany	3,085	2,766	2,473	11.5	−0.3
United Kingdom	2,683	2,008	905	33.6	1.6
Belgium	1,297	1,285	1,310	0.9	1.5
Other countries	4,513	3,607	3,023	25.1	12.9
Total	15,579	13,592	11,890	14.6	3.7
International Insurance	3,651	3,109	2,833	17.4	10.5
Asset Management	2,984	1,928	1,292	54.8	21.3
Other Financial Services	11,760	10,806	8,236	8.8	33.5
Total Revenues	79,970	66,525	56,698	20.2	10.8

*Restatement of revenues using constant exchange-rate basis, eliminating the results of acquisitions, disposals, business transfers (constant structural basis), and changes in accounting principles (constant methodological basis).

(Continued)

partnerships like the ones with BNP Paribas or Crédit Foncier (AXA distributed their mortgages) in France. Yet, AXA had been disappointed "by BNP's lack of effort in promoting" AXA's products. Following the merger of BNP with Paribas, the bank had placed priority on promoting the services offered by Paribas subsidiaries. According to de Castries, "Who owns the client is a key issue. We do not want to give up client ownership for the sake of cross selling complementary products." Banks also were asking for an increasing distribution margin.[15] Under the pressure of crumbling margins, AXA had withdrawn from its cooperation with BBVA in Spain. For the same reasons, Generali had ended its

relationship with BSCH. See Exhibit 2.8 for general income and balance sheet data on AXA.

THE PROPERTY AND CASUALTY SEGMENT

Regarding the P&C segment, de Castries had always stressed that P&C was a core business. When de Castries took over, 60 percent of non-life premiums were generated abroad, up from 30 percent in 1990.[16] The P&C segment accounted for 19 percent of gross revenues in 2000, contributing 14 percent of net income; growth in 2000 had been 3.7 percent. Profitability in P&C was very different across

Case Studies Exhibit 2.8 *(Continued)*

AXA: Consolidated Net Income by Activity (€ millions)

	2000		1999		1998	
	As Reported	Cash Earnings*	As Reported	Cash Earnings*	As Reported	Cash Earnings*
Life and Savings						
France	385	388	331	335	257	260
United States	1,098	405	266	268	249	250
United Kingdom	158	179	182	189	207	209
Asia/Pacific	73	116	32	40	−75	−54
Germany	39	41	10	14	7	7
Belgium	167	172	186	192	234	236
Other countries	131	136	81	84	57	59
Total	2,051	1,437	1,088	1,122	1,011	1,021
Property and Casualty						
France	274	281	244	253	158	165
Germany	135	159	42	59	69	70
United Kingdom	−162	−150	−5	10	19	19
Belgium	169	191	239	258	136	143
Other countries	−110	−73	33	49	−3	14
Total	578	631	558	629	382	411
International Insurance	137	153	−51	44	44	50
Asset Management	166	211	84	95	95	97
Other Financial Services	121	273	219	156	156	167
Holding Companies	1,123	58	129	−79	−79	−74
TOTAL	4,176	2,763	2,027	1,967	1,609	1,672
Per Ordinary Share (basic)	10.28	6.69	5.73	4.52	4.52	4.78
Per Ordinary Share (diluted)	9.74	6.38	5.40	4.24	4.24	4.48
Impact of Exceptional Operations	1,643		156		—	
Net Income Excluding Impact of Exceptional Operations	2,261		1,865		1,531	
Per Ordinary Share (basic)	5.95		5.28		4.52	
Per Ordinary Share (diluted)	5.69		4.98		4.24	

Note: *Cash earnings represents net income before the impact of exceptional operations and amortization of goodwill.

Source: AXA Form 20F.

The holding company activities consist of AXA's nonoperating companies, including mainly AXA (the Company), AXA France Assurance, AXA Asia Pacific Holdings, and AXA UK Holdings.

(Continued)

Case Studies Exhibit 2.8 *(Continued)*

AXA: Consolidated Statement of Income (€ millions)

	2000	1999	1998
Revenues			
Gross premiums written	79,971	66,528	56,697
Change in unearned premiums reserves	−439	9	32
Net investment results	20,863	15,630	14,069
Total revenues	100,395	82,167	70,798
Insurance claims	−67,564	−56,681	−49,819
Reinsurance ceded, net	1,000	808	381
Acquisition expense	−6,274	−5,616	−4,921
Bank operating expense	−6,509	−5,286	−4,488
Administrative expense	−11,871	−10,577	−8,141
Total benefits, claims and other deductions	−91,218	−77,352	−66,988
Income before tax expense	9,177	4,815	3,810
Income tax expense	−2,773	−1,292	−1,222
Amortization of goodwill, net	−353	−634	−93
Minority interests	−2,124	−858	−974
Equity in income (loss) of unconsolidated entities	−23	−10	11
NET INCOME	3,904	2,021	1,532

AXA: Consolidated Balance Sheet as of December 31, 2000 (€ millions)

Assets		Liabilities	
Total investments	263,448	Future policy benefits and other policy liabilities	182,896
Cash and equivalents	26,065	UK with-profit liabilities	25,111
Broker-dealer related receivables	73	Insurance claims and expenses	39,242
Deferred acquistion costs	8,154	Unearned premium reserve	6,783
Value of purchased business in force	3,724	Securities sold under repurchase agreements	1
Goodwill	15,865	Broker-dealer related payables	279
Accrued investment income	3,986	Short-term and long-term debts:	
Other assets	36,040	Financing debt	9,201
Separate account assets	117,261	Operating debt	4,445
		Accrued expenses and other liabilities	52,803
		Separate account liabilities	117,377
		TOTAL LIABILITIES	438,138
		Minority interests	3,702
		Subordinated debt	8,261
		Mandatory convertible bonds and notes	192
		SHAREHOLDERS' EQUITY	
		Ordinary shares	3,809
		Capital in excess of nominal value	12,379
		Retained earnings and reserves	8,134
		TOTAL SHAREHOLDERS' EQUITY	24,322
		TOTAL LIABILITIES, MINORITY INTERESTS,	
TOTAL ASSETS	474,616	SHAREHOLDERS' EQUITY	474,616

Case Studies Exhibit 2.9

AXA Property and Casualty Operations in 2000: Major Markets

	France € millions	%	United Kingdom € millions	%	Germany € millions	%
Gross premiums written	4,001		2,683		3,085	
Change in unearned premiums reserves	−1		−2		4	
Net investment results	717		376		411	
Total Revenues	4,718		3,057		3,500	
Insurance claims	−3395	81.6	−2369	90.5	−2357	77.3
Reinsurance ceded, net	105		−60		−33	
Acquisition expense	−514	13.5	−694	26.9	−396	11.2
Administrative expense	−500	13.0	−269	10.4	−541	20.6
Operating income	413		−334		172	
Income tax expense	−132		111		5	
Amortization of goodwill, net	−8		−15		−26	
Minority interests	0		77		−17	
Equity in income (loss) of unconsolidated entities	0		0		1	
NET INCOME	274		−162		135	
Combined Ratio*		108.1		128.0		109.1

Note: *Expenses and cost of claims as a % of premiums earned, net of reinsurance ceded.

countries, however. The French AXA subsidiaries had a combined ratio of 108.1 percent, compared to 109.1 percent in Germany and 128 percent (116 percent excluding reserve strengthening) in the United Kingdom in 2000. De Castries's goal was to bring the AXA P&C ratio down from 113.9 percent in 2000 to 104 percent in 2003. See Exhibit 2.9 for more specific data on the property and casualty segment of AXA.

In France, AXA's size did not seem to help much. In claims management of automobile insurance, for example, AXA had agreements with 3,000 repair shops in France but did not get significantly better prices than the mutuals. While the salaried sales force of the French mutuals were able to direct 60 percent of their clients to preferred repair shops, only 30 percent of AXA clients went to AXA partner suppliers, mainly because tied agents would refer their customers to the suppliers they knew.

Against a market growth rate of 3.7 percent in P&C in France in 2000,[17] AXA grew only 2 percent —or 0 percent on a comparable basis. In 1999 management had launched an overhaul of the organizational structure with the goal of creating an integrated, multichannel, "client-centered enterprise," displacing the current structure created in the years 1988–1991. By 2002, AXA still operated in France with four companies built around the different marketing channels: AXA Assurance (general agents), AXA Courtage (brokers), AXA Conseil (salaried representatives), and Direct Assurance (sale by telephone and Internet). For the P&C business, AXA Assurance generated 68 percent of premiums, followed by 22 percent of premiums generated by brokers, 7 percent by specialized networks, and 3 percent direct. General agents also sold 17 percent of life insurance, though the bulk was sold via others channels: brokers (37 percent), direct sales force (36 percent), and other networks, especially corporate partnerships with retailers and banks (10 percent).

AXA planned to improve its French distribution network by means of two complementary measures: reducing the number of general agents and setting up new insurance "boutiques." These boutiques, called Espaces AXA, would be created close to high-traffic sites (high streets and shopping malls) that were not necessarily covered by traditional agencies.

In the United Kingdom, the major concern was that years of underpricing meant that AXA, along with other players in the market, did not have enough reserves to pay the claims. Recognizing "that for some time the property and casualty marketplace has been a tough one" in the United Kingdom and that AXA lost €1 million in the first six months of 2001 in its P&C business, AXA had announced the cutting of 100 jobs among management in November 2001.[18]

OUTLOOK

In the spring of 2002, de Castries did not see many things to be cheerful about. Disappointed with the low levels of profitability, investors had withdrawn from the insurance sector and had sent stock prices down. Given the state of the world economy and capital markets, experts deemed it difficult for insurers to raise new money in the near future. Weak capital markets had reduced the value of insurers' assets, constraining insurance capacity and adding pressure because of shrinking technical reserves. A reduction in insurance capacity had traditionally led to increasing premiums. However, some industry analysts had become skeptical about insurers' ability to raise prices sufficiently given the competitive environment.

Some analysts considered AXA bruised by a slump in equity values, worsening business conditions, and a hefty $550 million bill from the U.S. attacks of September 11. Analysts and investors were getting concerned about the ability of AXA and its new CEO to implement the promised target cost cuts of 10 percent of administrative expenses in

2002 and to achieve the target of a group combined ratio for P&C of 104 percent in 2003. JP Morgan, for example, downgraded AXA from Buy to Market Performer because they saw risks that the restructuring plan may take longer to implement than had been planned

The non-life segment had been underperforming for a long time and some analysts speculated about a sale. However, in the third quarter of 2001, non-life had helped AXA generate earnings in times when consumer confidence in the stock market and unit-linked products had dramatically fallen.

These were challenging times for AXA and its CEO. How would the insurance industry and its profitability develop? Would overcapacity and price competition become a constant concern or would problems ebb away when the economic cycle turned up again? Would the insurance industry favor the giants, or were smaller, more focused firms better positioned to create shareholder value? Did de Castries have the right strategy for AXA? Shareholders certainly were looking for reassuring news as the results of the chosen strategy had not yet translated into remarkable financial results. Would de Castries perhaps be better off spinning off businesses such as P&C, as they were too competitive? Was a more radical approach needed to convince investors that AXA was the leader it said it was, or was AXA on the right track?

NOTES

1. Reuters, October 27, 1997.

2. *Financial Times*, September 2, 2000.

3. Any savings product in which the saver's money bought units in an investment fund and thus the value of the saver's fund was linked to the value of the units. There was no guaranteed return for the saver; income for the insurer was generated by a fee.

4. European Federation of National Insurance Associations (CEA), European Insurance in Figures, 2000, http://www.cea.assur.org/cea/v2.0/uk/accueil.php (accessed March 15, 2004).

5. An EU insurance company was supervised only by the authorities of the country where it had its headquarters.

6. CEA, European Insurance in Figures.

7. Deutsche Bank Equity Research, European Insurers, August 2001.

8. ABI, Market Factsheet: The UK Motor Insurance Market.

9. "UK: Motor—Up to Speed," *Post*, September 28, 2000.

10. *Süddeutsche Zeitung*, March 13, 2001.

11. Direct Line, http://www.directline.com.

12. Two-thirds of the directors of French listed companies have attended one of the handful of *grandes écoles*, which include ENA.

13. *Financial Times*, September 2, 2000.

14. Dow Jones Newswires, March 30, 2001.

15. AXA, press release, January 10, 2001.

16. An example in life insurance was the distribution of life products of Eureko, the alliance of European mutual insurers, in which the Portuguese bank BCP asked for 210 out of the 250 basis points charged as distribution margin.

17. Swiss re, sigma 3/2000.

18. *Les Echos*, January 8, 2001.

The Battle of the Smart Cards in the Netherlands in 2002

Many Dutch banks hoped that 2002 would be a watershed year for the use of smart cards in the Netherlands. Launched with a lot of hoopla in 1996, the cards had thus far failed to take off despite high hopes: The cards' capabilities were impressive. In addition to serving as a payment card, a microprocessor chip embedded on the card enabled it to store large amounts of data and perform calculations. For this reason, it had been predicted that smart cards would eliminate the need for cash, thereby helping cardholders reduce the amount of items that bloated their wallets and allowing banks to streamline operations and build a new revenue stream.

After a five-year bruising battle between the two rival bank consortia, Chipknip and Chipper, the banks decided to converge on the Chipknip standard in an attempt to limit their losses and boost customer and business confidence. There were signs that smart cards were taking off. Indeed, they were increasingly being used for parking, with some cities accepting them as the sole method of payment in parking meters. The use of smart cards in vending machines was also on the rise, and major corporations such as Albert Heijn and McDonald's also began accepting the Chipknip.

However, banks had not yet reached the breakeven point with smart cards, and other payment systems such as "mobile payment" by short message service (SMS) were already being launched. Now that the Chipknip standard had won out, how could banks relaunch the card and multiply its use? How could they generate a profitable revenue stream from the millions of cards that customers had but, so far, had failed to use in large numbers?

THE LAUNCH OF THE SMART CARDS

BACKGROUND: PAYMENT CARDS IN THE NETHERLANDS

One of the basic services banks offered their customers was cash deposits and withdrawals. Banks had invested extensively in branches and personnel to reach out to as large a customer base as possible. This in turn had led to growing cash holding and handling costs. Since banks did not charge customers for these services, cash handling had traditionally been cross-subsidized by revenues from other services.

The automatic teller machines (ATMs) had been introduced to address the cost of cash withdrawals. An ATM took up little physical space, required few operational resources, and provided the customer with 24-hour service. Yet, as long as customers and businesses used cash and checks as their primary modes of payment, banks still faced the high costs of cash handling and inventory. The introduction of bank cards would change this.

In the second half of the 1980s, at least five different pilot studies on electronic payment with bank cards were carried out in the Netherlands. These tests were all conducted independently, with the post office bank (Postbank) and other banks running separate pilot programs, various oil companies participating in the tests, and Albert Heijn, the largest supermarket in the country, conducting a pilot of its own. The payment procedure used in each was the same, however. The customer's card was inserted into a dedicated terminal, which read the information on the magnetic stripe of the card and verified online whether there was enough money in the bank account of the cardholder for the purchase. If the bank authorized the transaction, the money was immediately and electronically "debited" from the cardholder's bank account and transferred to the account of the card accepter (hence the names "debit card" and "electronic fund transfer," or EFT).

All tests were accompanied by difficult discussions among banks, merchants, oil companies, and consumers about who would pay for the infrastructure and operating costs. In the process, participants gained practical experience and quickly realized that standardization on one system would be essential to avoid multiple infrastructures. By the end of 1987, the banks and Postbank had agreed on a standard, and at the end of 1988 they established a common company, Beanet (which later became Interpay), to host a central computer system to which all would call to authorize an EFT.

In 1989, only two years after these bank cards were introduced, approximately 20 million electronic transactions were carried out and more than 1,000 terminals had been installed. In the same year, banks introduced a cash-handling fee for commercial customers, artificially creating an incentive for businesses to keep cash to a minimum. Initially, this led to substantial dissatisfaction among merchants, but in 1991 an agreement was signed in a collective effort to reduce cash-handling costs and stimulate payment by bank cards. Banks provided inexpensive financing to commercial customers to acquire terminals and, following lengthy negotiations, the Post Telegraph and Telephone (PTT) lowered its tariffs for data communication. Also, in 1991 all bank cards were fitted with a personal identification number (PIN) to enhance security. When paying or withdrawing cash with the card, called the Pinpas, the cardholder would now have to enter a code to demonstrate ownership.

To encourage customer use of the cards, banks invested substantially in advertising and public relations. They also rapidly increased the network of ATMs: Between 1991 and 1993, the number of terminals grew by 500 percent. Not only did this make cash withdrawal convenient; it also helped consumers get used to cards with a PIN code. A big breakthrough came at the beginning of 1992 when Albert Heijn began to accept bank cards. By 1995, the annual transaction volume for bank cards was 256 million—well in excess of the predicted 150 million transactions made just three years previously. Albert Heijn accounted for about 45 million of these.

By 1996, there were 23.4 million bank cards in circulation in the Netherlands. Ninety-five percent of individuals age 16 and older had a bank card. More than 50 percent of bankcard holders had a Postbank card, while 36 percent had a card from Rabobank. Thirty-nine percent of individuals age 16 and older held cards from more than one bank, with typically one card from the Postbank. Bank cards were used frequently: 61 percent used their card at least once a week (up from 55 percent in 1994), and the average frequency of use was 64.5 times per annum in 1996. More than 75 percent of bank card owners always carried their bank card with them. A Booz Allen & Hamilton study linked increasing

Case Studies Exhibit 3.1

Terminals and Debit Card Transactions in the Netherlands

	Number of Terminals	Number of Transactions (millions)
1982	90	test
1986	500	N/A
1988	992	N/A
1989	1,000	20
1990	2,000	N/A
1991	4,038	32
1992	10,365	47
1993	25,549	67
1994	47,588	143
1995	73,376	256
1996	96,044	371
1997	108,044*	425*

Source: Interpay Annual Report (March 1994).

*Number projected by Interpay.

Note: The Netherlands population was 14.5 million in 1986, and 15.5 million in 1996.

debit card use to the growth in the terminal network. Exhibit 3.1 shows the uptake of debit cards in the Netherlands.

In 1996, there were more than 76 million other types of plastic cards also in circulation.[1] This translated into the fact that everyone age 16 or older had an average of 6.2 cards, up from 3.7 in 1993. Common card types were credit cards, prepaid service cards, loyalty cards, and membership cards, with higher-income individuals tending to have more cards.

The percentage penetration of households (22 percent) and number (3.3 million) of credit cards in the Netherlands was relatively low and had been relatively stable since 1993. Eurocard/MasterCard was by far the leading credit card, being supported by the banks and with 72 percent of its customers claiming that it was their most important credit card. Visa ranked second, but it had lower usage,

while American Express and Diners Club served small niches of heavy users. Credit card use had been decreasing over time, and by 1996 was 14 times per annum (15.8 in 1994). These transactions mostly took place during travel, in restaurants, and in gas stations. For common purchases debit cards were preferred.

The percentage household penetration of prepaid cards was 40 percent, with most of these being telephone cards. PTT Telecom, the national phone company, had two cards: prepaid phone cards and Scopecards (calling cards). Scopecard penetration was around 6 percent, and its usage frequency was relatively low at 5.1 times per annum on average. Behind phone cards, the second most significant prepaid cards were company cards used in company restaurants.

Loyalty cards had become very popular in the Netherlands: Household penetration had risen from 35 percent in 1995 to 49 percent in 1996, with the total number of cards at 7.7 million. Customers used these cards to collect bonus points by making purchases in the card issuers' stores. These points then could be redeemed for gifts (e.g., frequent flyer programs). The most successful programs in the country were Airmiles (Albert Heijn supermarket, Royal Dutch Shell, ABN AMRO, Vroom & Dreesman (V&D) department store) and Mobil Card. They had a household penetration of 82 percent and 33 percent, respectively. Frequency of usage was almost on par with bank cards: close to 60 times per annum.

Another popular plastic card was the membership card (38.3 million cards). Well over 50 percent of the population owned a medical insurance card (56 percent) and a hospital card (57 percent). When surveyed, about 50 percent of people claimed that they always carried these cards with them despite using them infrequently (60 percent of respondents used them less than four to six times a year).

THE INTRODUCTION OF THE SMART CARD

As the Dutch were getting used to making payments with plastic cards, the banks were preparing the next generation of payment card: the smart card. Early in 1995, they announced the collective launch of a card with an electronic purse called the Chipknip. Cardholders would initially be able to load money onto the card from their bank accounts through small devices situated next to ATMs. Eventually, they would be able to do this at home through devices connected to the telephone or personal computer (via modem). The purse would be on a microprocessor in the card. The magnetic stripe would eventually disappear since all the information required to identify an individual would be encoded on the chip. When a customer used the Chipknip in a shop, a terminal would first prompt the customer for confirmation of the transaction; after the Yes button was pushed, the smart card would transfer the money from the electronic purse to the terminal of the shop. The shop would later connect to the Chipknip back office, which would then credit the shop's bank account. Since there was no need for online verification of the customer's bank account, checkout would be much faster. If the customer were to use this card for small payments (e.g., bus tickets or parking), the shops, the banks, and the individual would need less cash than they had before smart card use. Cash holding and handling costs would thus decrease further.

The system had been orchestrated by Interpay, which had avoided making a substantial investment in the platform technology by licensing the Proton smart card system developed by Banksys, the consortium of Belgian banks. Before the Chipknip was rolled out nationally, a pilot was conducted in October 1995 in Arnhem, a Dutch city with a population of 127,000. In total, 45,000 cards were distributed, including 20,000 from the Postbank.

The pilot was not without problems. Retailers all complained about the high transaction fee of €0.07 per transaction. Though the large retail chains had wanted to negotiate better rates, Interpay refused to do so. Worse, the banks refused to put their logos on the card and also strictly limited the Chipknip card's function to the electronic purse, reasoning that it was necessary to build customer confidence and ease customers into using the cards. In the end, many large and small retailers refused to participate in the pilot. Despite this, Interpay, speaking on behalf of the banks, declared the pilot a success.

During the same period, PTT Telecom had set up two major pilots for upgrading its prepaid disposable telephone card. Its rationale was that since there was money on the card, it possibly had uses other than just paying for phone calls. The impending deregulation of the telecommunications industry added an extra incentive for PTT to explore alternate sources of revenue. In summer 1995, it issued 100,000 Zeelandcards in the province of Zeeland. These cards could be used in payphones, parking meters, and vending machines and on public transportation. PTT also issued 20,000 Studentcards, suitable for several functions at the university. Neither of the cards used the Proton platform.

When, in December 1995, the director of the ING Group announced that Postbank would no longer participate in the Chipknip venture and would collaborate instead with PTT Telecom in building an alternative smart card platform (the Chipper), the banking community was shocked. Given that ING Group had introduced the Chipknip in Arnhem on behalf of all the banks, and that it was the largest shareholder of Interpay (holding 30 percent of its shares), this announcement was particularly surprising. Mr. Minderhoud, a member of the executive committee of Postbank and ING Group, said that the company wanted to give their customers more convenience by developing new services and that the Chipper provided the appropriate platform to accomplish this task. The multifunctionality of the Chipper as well as its home applications are the real benefits of a smart card. Thus, Mr. Minderhoud felt that these two issues gave the customers the convenience that they desire.

Postbank had been one of the pioneers in telebanking in the Netherlands and had developed a base of 850,000 telebanking subscribers (700,000 by phone and 150,000 by PC/modem). Serving its customers from counters in each post office, Postbank saw the smart card as an opportunity to leverage its experience in telebanking.

In response to Postbank's move, the other banks decided within three months that the Chipknip would also be multifunctional and suitable for home applications. Postbank still decided to push ahead with its own smart card, as the company's management believed that the smart card is a tool that could distinguish their bank in comparison with others. Linking with Postbank was also quite convenient for PTT Telecom, since running an electronic purse operation required a banking license, which it did not have. The effect of Postbank's announcement was so strong that the date it took place, December 18, 1995, became known "Black Monday" in the banking community. Why was the financial community attaching so much importance to the smart card? What was at stake?

SMART CARD TECHNOLOGY AND ITS USE IN THE NETHERLANDS

The smart card had several advantages over magnetic stripe cards. First, because the chip was programmable and could perform calculations, it could store and change information. Transactions could therefore be made off-line, cutting time and cost. Second, smart card technology operated on less expensive terminals that therefore could be distributed broadly, including to consumers' homes. Magnetic stripe cards still required very intelligent

and expensive terminals that could scramble data as it was transmitted. The cost of secure data transmissions prohibited wider adoption of terminals from customers' homes. In contrast, information on the smart card was scrambled by a secret key before it left the chip and could be read only by a chip in the terminal of the card accepter. This chip, called the Secure Application Module (SAM), decoded the scrambled information by a master key and subsequently reencoded it before returning it to the cardholder. Moreover, the chip would never use the same key twice. As the intelligence was in the chip rather than in the terminals, the terminals would be less expensive. Data transmission would thus be less expensive and more secure.

The technology also made it possible to replace single-function cards (e.g., membership cards) with a much smaller number of multifunction cards. Customers would be able to use the same card to pay at shop checkout counters and parking meters, register frequent-flyer points, access secure buildings, store medical information, and so forth. These functions could even overlap, as, for example, the card could register a discount in a parking meter if it had been used in a specific shop nearby.

This multifunctionality, however, came at the expense of increased complexity. With traditional plastic cards, the card accepter was typically the card issuer (e.g., the clothing chain C&A). This relationship would change with the smart card technology, especially in the Netherlands, where two smart card initiatives had developed. These technology platform providers supplied alternative technologies to track all transactions carried out with either smart card. For the cards to be successful, the providers also had to develop the cards' capabilities to ensure reliable and fast settlement of accounts. If smart cards lived up to expectations and were widely adopted, the technology platform providers also had to be prepared to transform into huge transaction-processing factories. In the more immediate term, they needed to market their platform to potential card issuers (e.g., banks, insurance companies, retail chains) and to card accepters (e.g., local merchants) to gain acceptance.

It was estimated that the up-front investment for a platform provider was about €180 million,[2] followed by annual operating costs of €25 million per year. A study of smart cards in the health sector provided a second cost reference.[3] It distinguished the cost of "cardware" (the smart card and its personalization) from the cost of running the system (e.g., security management). Total cardware costs for the country's population of 15 million were estimated at €15 million for simple memory chip cards and €120 million for multifunctional smart cards. This assumed a depreciation of cards over four years. Total system costs were estimated to come to €30 million and €180 million, respectively.

Both the Chipknip and the Chipper platforms offered several benefits to card accepters (e.g., C&A), such as faster checkout at the points of sale (no online verification, no counting of change, no separate loyalty cards, no receipt generation, immediate settlement of deposit). It also permitted faster and easier cash deposits, less loss of interest, fewer calculation errors, and less risk of fraud and robbery. In the early stages of plastic card payments, e-purse smart cards were expected to be cheaper than debit cards for small payments. Debit card transactions cost the merchants about €0.10 per transaction, in addition to communication costs (online connection).[4] Credit cards were even more expensive, as about 3 percent of the purchase amount went to the credit card company. With the smart card, transaction costs were reduced to 0.7 percent or 0.8 percent per transaction with a minimum fee for very small payments (€0.05 for the Chipper). Alternatively, accepters could opt for a fixed charge per transaction. For the Chipper and Chipknip, this charge was €0.04 and €0.05, respectively. There also was a monthly charge per terminal of about €7. Yet,

since all transactions were off-line, there would be no communication cost per transaction.

A card accepter could, in return for a license fee, obtain an account or "slot" on every smart card produced on the platform. For example, C&A could license a slot on the Chipper platform. Thus, two customers with Chipper cards issued by different groups (Postbank or PTT Telecom) could use the electronic purse on their card to pay at C&A and participate in its loyalty program. Although participation in a loyalty program was fully voluntary, customers could easily sign up by simply keying in a PIN code at a C&A counter. Subscriptions (e.g., memberships), storage of entrance tickets, and personal information would all be available on given smart card platforms and could be activated by the cardholder.

The card issuers in turn had to decide whether they would sign up with the platform of the Chipper, the Chipknip, or possibly with both. While the decision had already been made by the major banks, several companies (e.g., Albert Heijn, Shell) had to decide whether to issue a smart card, to simply take out a license with either platform and remain a card accepter, to cobrand a card with another issuer, or to stay with simple memory or magnetic stripe cards. It was estimated that a card issuer would need to invest €5 million up front for the infrastructure. The annual operating costs for card issuing, management, help desk, and so on were thought to be about €1.5 million. This did not include the estimated €5–7 cost per card, which was expected to have a lifetime of about three years.

The advantages to issuing the cards included access to the permanent "slots" on them. Whereas a card accepter's customer (licensed on either the Chipper or Chipknip system) could turn off or remove particular loyalty programs altogether, the card issuer's customer did not have this freedom. Further, the issuer could pack other functions onto the card. For example, banks could add debit and credit card functions. Card issuers (e.g., the Airmiles partners) would also own the data generated by the card and could use it for communication and marketing activities, or sell it to third parties. While the issuer could not disclose data on an individual customer, it could provide aggregate data.[5] The data generated as a card accepter would be more restricted as it would be limited to loyalty schemes.

CHIPKNIP VERSUS CHIPPER

Following ING Bank and Postbank's decisions to pursue the Chipper technology, the Interpay banks' initial disbelief transformed into a frantic quest to line up issuers and accepters. By January 1996, however, the Chipper venture announced that the Dutch automobile association ANWB would equip its membership cards in 1997 with a Chipper. The Dutch government agency responsible for scholarships also announced that it would introduce Chipper student cards starting in summer 1996. In February 1996, the food retail chain Superunie, which held a 21 percent market share, declared it would equip its Primeurcard with a Chipper. Then came the announcement the following day by Albert Heijn that it would issue a Chipknip card in autumn 1997. It had even convinced the other Airmiles partners (Shell and department store group V&D) to also introduce a Chipknip. Indeed, Albert Heijn, with its 28 percent share of food retailing in the Netherlands, and Shell, with its 30 percent share of gasoline retailing, were major partners. However, both stressed that they still had many questions about the Chipknip technology, not least about the cost.

Meanwhile, allegations went back and forth over who was to blame for the apparent confusion. The chairman of Interpay, J.J. Verhaegen of Rabobank, was quoted as saying, "The introduction of the Chipper and the Chipknip is similar to having a country with left and right driving at the same time."

His counterpart at Postbank, Kees van Rossum, disagreed: "We will simply have a road network with different makes of cars."[6] To this, Verhaegen countered, referring to the faster introduction of the Chipknip, "The facts of the Chipknip weigh heavier than the vision of Chipper. We will adapt at no cost the debit terminals to accept the Chipknip cards."[7] The head of PTT Telecom, Ben Verwaayen, added, regarding the verbal skirmishing, "I have given up trying to understand the problem. . . . It is obvious to everybody that the Chipper technology is the leading technology. In addition, it is an open standard [the banks can join]. In spite of this, they [the banks] cling to their own system." In light of all this, Albert Heijn retreated from its original commitment to Chipknip, stating that it had assumed that Postbank would also be a partner.[8]

In summer 1996, several other loyalty programs were announced. Rabobank stated that it would launch a Chipknip LOKO (local buying) card that would be a joint savings program bringing together small businesses in given areas. To compete with the Airmiles program, four companies (Esso, Edah, C&A, and Hema) announced that they would introduce a Chipper card in 1997. Also the MKB, the national organization of small and medium enterprises (SMEs), pledged to introduce a loyalty scheme in cooperation with Chipper to respond to the 10 percent loss of SME turnover they estimated the Airmiles program had caused.

As the two platforms were busy getting customers on board, Dr. P. Ribourdouille, a member of the executive committee of ABN AMRO Bank, forecast, "We will be forced to work together and develop a common infrastructure. The consumer will not accept that s/he cannot use the card somewhere. Also costs will be lower. Competition should take place at the level of the functions."

But Mr. Minderhoud, said "I agree that competition needs to take place at that level, but I disagree that cost considerations will force cooperation at the level of the infrastructure. This was the case for the introduction of the Pinpas [debit card] in the 1980s. But chip technology is much more advanced and much cheaper, and therefore such cooperation is not necessary."[9]

While Postbank had officially announced in April 1996 that it would cease cooperating with Chipknip, its sister company, ING Bank, continued to participate in the discussions on the Chipknip as a member of Interpay. In October 1996, ABN AMRO and Rabobank decided it was time to create a new company without the ING Group. Under the aegis of Interpay, Easychip was set up to develop the multifunctional Chipknip. The leading financial daily, *Financieel Dagblad*, observed, "This means the suspicion of the banks has grown so much that they do not appreciate the presence [of ING] anymore."[10] Also, talks between the banks and Postbank on the compatibility of their ATMs were suspended.[11] Meanwhile, PTT Telecom and Postbank committed several hundred people to developing and marketing the Chipper concept.

Efforts to pull the Dutch National Bank (DNB) and the government into the debate failed. Hans van der Wielen of the DNB observed, "We do not want to be the piano player in the Wild West Saloon that is killed by accident. . . . Competition is not bad within the limits of functionality and efficiency . . . competition should take place at the level of the payment services and other functionalities. Cooperation should take place at the level of the infrastructure."[12]

This was no reassurance for Shell. While it maintained its membership in the very successful Airmiles program, it decided it would not launch a Chipknip smart card; it was too expensive. This meant that the Airmiles card would not be a smart card. Other issuers, namely the Superunie initiative of Edah, Esso, Hema, and C&A also decided, due to cost and expected use, not to launch a smart card with a payment function. Edah considered the smart

card cost of €5 too expensive compared to the €2 for a personal client card. It also had doubts about the smart card's forecasted usage.

THE SITUATION IN AUTUMN 1997

By the autumn of 1997, the banks of the Chipknip alliance had installed devices to enable cardholders to reload their card in 4,000 of the nation's 6,000 ATMs. They had also installed 85,000 terminals (accepting Chipknip only) and were targeting 100,000 by the end of the year. The Chipper alliance had equipped the 22,000 PTT Telecom public phone booths with devices that accepted only Chippers to reload the card. The Chipper consortium had no terminals yet but had contracts for 40,000 hybrid (accepting both Chipper and Chipknip) terminals, which would be ready by the end of 1997. There were potentially 450,000 points of sale that could accept electronic payment. These included: 240,000 points in retail, 140,000 in public and in-company vending machines, 10,000 in public transportation, and 9,000 at parking lots. Both platforms were also developing a number of devices that would allow individuals to reload their card at home and use it for home shopping, for example, via the Internet.

The Chipknip platform had stated several times that it would equip its terminals with SAMs for both types of smart card. In August 1996, ING bank mounted a large public advertising campaign announcing that its terminals would have both a Chipper and a Chipknip SAM. ABN AMRO was rumored to have offered Postbank €7 million to put the Chipper SAMs on its smart card terminals, though Postbank apparently had not been tempted by the offer. In response, the Chipper consortium had been very slow in releasing the specifications of the Chipper SAM, prompting the Chipknip group to goad that the Chipper can easily say that they offer hybrid terminals, but we have not seen anything yet. The race to install terminals thus continued. Banks replaced the debit card terminals with smart card terminals at no charge. They also heavily subsidized the terminals of new clients: The price per terminal was reduced from €700 to €150 with the added promise that large-volume customers would receive discounts.

Due to the way the Dutch banking sector had developed, both the Chipper and the Chipknip alliance represented a significant force. In the consumer market, Postbank had a 50 percent market share, while the other two major banking groups, ABN AMRO and Rabobank, shared the rest of the market. In the business market, the ING group, ABN AMRO, and Rabobank each had roughly one-third of the market.

Meanwhile, PTT Telecom stated that it would replace about 100,000 leased telephones with phones equipped with a smart card reader (Chipperphone). They also started selling and promoting the Chipperphones as substitutes for regular phones. The consumer could use this phone to reload the Chipper and make payments from home. The smart card of PTT Telecom, the Scopecard, would have all the functions of the existing Scopecard: domestic and international calling from abroad without cash via a free access number; special phone services such as message service, return calling, interpreting and teleconferencing; and teleorder services such as telegram service, telegift, and flower service. It would also have the standard Chipper services and additional services specific to the Scopecard Chipper: a loyalty function for PTT Telecom savings programs and a memory for up to 16 phone numbers.

In spite of the enormous publicity surrounding the introduction of the smart card, research carried out at the end of 1996 showed that consumers were only partially aware of the advantages of the smart card. Only 30 percent of polled consumers thought a smart card offered more value than the conventional plastic cards. When confronted with a list of propositions regarding smart cards, many respondents seemed to agree that a smart card was something "new" (65 percent) and "smart" (40 percent), but only 35 percent thought he or she could use a smart card. When asked to cite disadvantages of the smart card, many respondents mentioned the risk of loss and theft.

Nor were many consumers clear on the battle between Chipper and Chipknip. The great majority (60–70 percent) of respondents answered incorrectly when asked which company was advertising the Chipper. The Chipper and Chipknip cards were not perceived as being different, yet 10 percent of respondents had said they would consider changing banks because of differences in the functionality of the chip on their bank's card.

A 1996 study by the Economic Institute for Small and Medium Enterprises in the Netherlands (EIMK) shed light on other important smart card customers: local businesses that would need to accept the card. The study found that cash transactions in 1995 still represented about 59 percent of total turnover and 88 percent of all transactions. It was also found that 60 percent of all transactions were for less than €12. The EIMK had also calculated the "external" payment costs (telephone, credit card charges, PIN costs, cash handling, and transport) for the Dutch SME. These had increased from €150 million in 1991 to €250 million in 1995. For all payment methods, the average external cost per transaction in 1995 was computed at €0.06, up from €0.05 in 1991. The cost per cash transaction was estimated at €0.02; for debit cards it was €0.36, and for credit cards it was €2.27. The country's organization of SMEs embraced this study to protest the high cost of smart card payments.

In June 1997, *Financieel Dagblad* reported that of the 4 million Chipknips introduced, very few were actually being used. This was followed by a Postbank announcement that the Chipper would be introduced at a slower pace than anticipated. "We want it to satisfy the very strong requirements of the Dutch National Bank on transactions by phone," said Laman Trip, chairman of Postbank. He also added, "It turns out to be very difficult to develop multifunctionality and use from home." The launch of Albert Heijn's smart card, which had been announced for the autumn, was awaited impatiently. The company had been very secretive about the exact services that would be put on the card.

At the October 1997 conference in The Hague on the "Holland Chipcard Experience," there was widespread interest from abroad on the Dutch experience with smart cards. Foreign visitors were quick to praise the Dutch lead. But the debate at the conference about the "killer" application that would get the Dutch to embrace the smart card, and the fact that many applications might be operational only in five years left some foreigners wondering whether the Dutch were not putting the cart before the horse.[13] Koenraad de Geest of Austrian Payment System Services remarked, "The Netherlands is ahead in developing multifunctional applications for smart cards, but that has more to do with the competition between Postbank and the banking consortium than with the public demand for cards." Gerard Ketelaar of PTT Telecom was more optimistic, however: "1997 will be a breakthrough year for chipcards. By the end of 1998, everyone in the Netherlands will have smart cards. There is nowhere in the world where this is so advanced. . . . By being able to provide a highly reliable means of payment on electronic networks and of identifying the party in the transaction, we have the key to the Internet in our hands."

In the Eye of the Storm: 1998

During 1998, Chipper and Chipknip accelerated the pace of the competition to become the standard. In January 1998, the number of Chipper payment terminals increased to 10,000 and most Postbank cash machines were equipped with a Chipper reloader. The Chipknip consortium was particularly determined. By 1998, some 130,000 card accepters were in place. Both consortia also invested in complementary products to the e-purse, such as telephone cards, parking cards, and loyalty programs. They also tried to leverage their relationships to foster adoption of their system. For example, Postbank leveraged its long-standing relationship with the telecom incumbent KPN (formerly PTT) to quickly expand into telephony chip cards. Banks did the same. For example, ABN AMRO leveraged its relationship with one of the largest suppliers of payment terminals to ensure that the Chipknip system would get priority during the rollout of the terminals. This strategy caused a six-month delay in the introduction of the Chipper system. The most costly method of increasing penetration was to subsidize sales of the payment terminals and card-acceptance technologies. A manager of the largest supplier for payment terminals commented that in those years, company sales were largely paid for by the banks, not by the retailers.

By the end of 1998, virtually all bank cards had either Chipper or Chipknip functionality. However, neither the difference between the systems nor which system was accepted by card accepters was clear to most people. Also, no "killer application" had been introduced that took full advantage of the benefits of the chipcard. The most popular applications thus far were vending machines and company restaurants. Banks also continued to focus more on the potential benefits for chip card accepters rather than the advantages for consumers.

Further, problems in the development of chip card functionality beyond electronic payments (e.g., health records, student cards, public transportation cards) caused a decline in consumer interest. Both Chipper and Chipknip had promised a rapid expansion of the functionalities of their cards. However, integrating these functionalities on one card and ensuring the security of personal information stored on the chips proved to be much more difficult than expected.

At the end of 1998, it became clear that the consortia were in a deadlock. The expected breakthrough in usage of the cards seemed farther away than ever. On average, there were less than 400,000 transactions per week on a total of some 20 million cards.[14] More than 75 percent of the population never loaded money on their cards. The people who did load money used it less than four times a year on average. Some major potential accepters (e.g., McDonald's and Albert Heijn) simply refused to participate.

Although exact numbers were not revealed, between €300 million and €500 million had been invested in the Chipper and Chipknip technologies. Operating costs of both systems combined were estimated to amount to €25–50 million each year, and further investments appeared necessary to expand into new smart card applications.

1999–2001: END OF THE BATTLE

On October 21, 1998, the consortia announced that they were planning to migrate to a common infrastructure, although neither would give up its technology. Over time, all payment terminals in the country were to be equipped with two SAM-chips and additional RAM, enabling them to accept both Chipper and Chipknip cards.

Meanwhile, a 1999 study of merchant payment transaction costs conducted by the National Retailers Association (HBD) raised further questions. It showed that the chipcard remained significantly more expensive than the PIN card and cash. Given transaction volumes and both internal (back office, money transport, cash registers, terminals) and external costs (deposits, contracts with Interpay, data communication, and so on), the cost of chipcard

transactions was estimated at €0.27 per transaction, PIN transactions at €0.22, and cash transactions at €0.10. Worse, if Interpay's waived contract fees were included in the calculation, a chip transaction would cost merchants €0.58.[15]

The first sign of migration to a common platform was in March 1999, when KPN of Chipper began accepting Chipknip in its public telephone booths. In September 1999, KPN exited from the Chipper consortium. Eric Robles, executive vice president of Postbank, commented on the background of the negotiations that followed at the end of 1999:

> After KPN had withdrawn from the Chipper consortium, we [Postbank] were faced with a number of options. We carefully analysed a number of scenarios. First, we could continue to believe and invest in chip card technology and multi-functional services. This was an uncertain, unpopular and expensive option. Our second option was to curtail all new investments and scale down chip-card activity to e-purse functionality only, but leaving the Chipper alive. Third, we could fully exit chip cards to escape the money-losing venture with few negative consequences in terms of customer satisfaction. This appeared to be the most attractive option at the time, if it were not for our commitment to the "Pay-per-Mile" program of the Ministry of Public Transport. We had contractually agreed to have the Chipper enable a new road tax based on mileage from which we could not withdraw without serious repercussions. These scenarios were all unfavourable for the Chipknip consortium since they would either imply prolonged competition between two standards or a likely end of the e-purse in the Netherlands altogether, since the e-purse would no longer be a universal application once 6 million Postbank customers dropped out. Considering the amount of money that the banks continued to pour into multi-functionality for the Chipknip, an end to the e-purse would have been particularly harmful to them. The fourth and final scenario was to migrate to one platform. Thus, realizing that our migration to Chipknip would prevent large write-offs for the other banks, we were able to negotiate a substantial contribution for the conversion.

In March 2001, the Dutch Banking Association NVB announced that the Chipper technology would be dismantled and that Chipknip would become the e-purse standard. The need to convert to the euro and adjust all payment terminals in the country was to be combined with a transition to Chipknip only. On April 15, 2002, the last Chipper payment was made in the Netherlands.

"Just call me God," quipped Dolph Heyning, director of the Name Works, the company that invented the Chipknip name. "It's a pity so few people use the system. Neither do we."[16] The Post-bank appeared to find it difficult to fly under the Chipknip banner. Their card would be called "Chip-pas." Also, they would not equip their debit card with the electronic purse but install it on a separate card. Asked why, the Postbank stated, "It would be easier to give such a card to another person than your debit card."[17]

LOOKING FORWARD: 2002 AND BEYOND

By 2001, smart card usage for payments had increased in the Netherlands. Growing acceptance of the Chipper and Chipknip cards by retailers, parking meters, and catering outlets had pushed transaction volumes up, but only to 22 million, or 0.5 percent of all retail transactions.[18] In January 2002, however, the number of Chipknip transactions increased sharply: Daily transactions doubled in the course of the first six months of 2002. Exhibit 3.2 gives an overview of transactions and terminals in the Netherlands since the launch.

The number of people using chipcards also had sharply increased. While only 12 percent claimed to be using their Chipknip in December 2001, this number had increased to 28 percent by June 2002.[19] Of the people already using Chipknip, 59 percent were using it to pay at parking meters. This was largely due to a number of major cities (including Rotterdam and Nijmegen) converting their parking meters from coins to cards. In these cities, parking

Case Studies Exhibit 3.2

Number of Chipknip Cards in the Netherlands (millions)

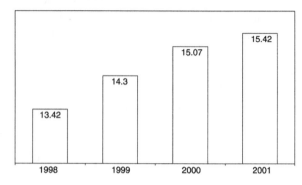

Number of Chipknip Terminals in the Netherlands (millions)

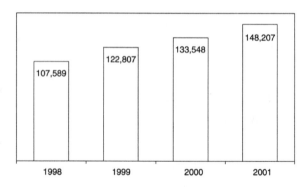

Number of Chipknip Transactions per year in the Netherlands (millions)

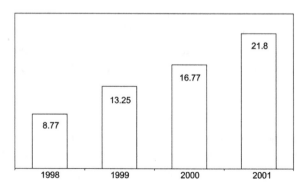

payment by Chipknip doubled from 2000 to 2001.[20] Approximately 50 percent of all users also paid with Chipknip for small groceries.

As things finally began to look up for Chipknip in 2002, Harold Van Eupen of Rabobank commented, "It has taken a long time for people to realize the advantages of chip card payments, but finally it appears to be successful." Albert Heijn's decision to begin accepting smart cards as of November 1, 2001, also spurred hopes that the Chipper would be more widely used. In announcing the decision, the company commented, "As we had to change our equipment to get ready for the euro, it made sense to change now." At the end of 2001, McDonald's and Chipknip also ran a joint campaign to promote the use of Chipknip. However, the experience of Laurus, Albert Heijn's competitor, in accepting the chipcard had not been too encouraging. A company official remarked that "fewer than 1% of our clients use it."[21] For the time being, Albert Heijn continued to use its own paper-based loyalty program of customer cards.

In spite of the impressive growth in the number of transactions, there were several warnings against overoptimism. Robles from Postbank issued one of these, commenting, "I do not believe the e-purse will become profitable in the foreseeable future, but we are staying in the game with Chipknip to keep our options open." Van Eupen of Rabobank added, "Even with this huge increase in transactions, we are still at the very beginning of the adoption curve."[22] Break-even levels were also affected by the reduction of the fee per transaction from 0.8 percent to 0.6 percent, effective from February 2002. These reductions had been forced on the banks by the government sanction of the merger between the two card systems. Even so, the organizations representing small and medium-sized corporations (MKB) and retailers (RND) had been calling for a public watchdog committee to oversee the "monopolist" Interpay.[23]

That parking was really the "killer application" had also been questioned in at least one city. In June 2002 people in Nijmegen were given the option to pay once again for parking with coins. This backtrack followed a stream of complaints from local businesses about the declining number of visits to the city by local people and foreigners. Also, users were unimpressed by meters' tendency to malfunction. Succumbing to the complaints, the city reconverted its parking meters to accept smart cards, credit cards, payment cards, and coins.

The question whether the European standard for electronic payment (EMV) would be compatible with Chipknip was also looming on the horizon. Europay, the organization that managed the international settlement of MasterCard and Eurocard payments, had been trying to create interoperability for electronic purses. Since March 1999, the Europay CLIP electronic purse was compliant with the specifications of the Common European Purse Standards (CEPS). This standard had been developed by Europay in cooperation with Visa and Geldkarte in Germany. CEPS specifications, in turn, were compatible with the EMV standard for terminals, chip design, and applications. By 2005, many retailers and card issuers would be obliged to adopt new EMV standards. They, and not the credit card companies, would then become liable for fraud in cases where there was no compliance with EMV specifications. In 2002, Dutch banks had not yet agreed to use the CEPS/EMV specifications. Migrating from the Chipknip to the CEPS would also imply adjusting all 150,000 terminals and approximately 15 million chip cards.

Trust in electronic payments proved to be another issue. At the beginning of 2002, a large number of PIN-fraud cases emerged in the country. Although experts believed that smart cards were much safer than debit cards—because a chip cannot be copied as easily as a magnetic stripe—the cases provoked widespread mistrust of electronic payment. A move toward EMV raised other security questions. While the EMV standard solved many security problems linked to the current smart cards, hacking experiments had shown that EMV cards were also at risk of being cloned. This could be done, for example, by measuring the chip's power consumption. Though online verification could modify this risk, it would also take away one of the key benefits of smart cards: that they could function off-line. A higher level of authentication was possible (dynamic data authentication, DDA) but would double the cost of the EMV cards, which were estimated to cost €2 each in high volumes. A researcher at the University of Cambridge computer sciences department cautioned that even these increased security measures were no guarantee: "You have to be significantly more determined [to hack], but if you throw enough money at it, every chip will be broken."[24]

Smart cards were also being examined for a variety of new uses, including payment for public transport. In 2002, the Translink Company, which represented about 90 percent of public transport providers in the Netherlands, was planning to invest €1.5 billion in a "proximity electronic card payment system" for most public transport (train, tram, bus).[25] Through Interpay, Chipknip was part of one of the three consortia bidding to participate in this highly complex smart card application. A similar public transport card system had been implemented successfully in Hong Kong. Translink was contemplating introducing a more comprehensive and more complex card system, which potentially could include an e-purse function. In summer 2002, it was unclear whether that card would be complementary with Chipknip.

There was also talk in 2002 that Interpay and Banksys were considering a merger.[26] This appeared to be partly motivated by the expansion of the U.S. card-processing companies First Data Corp. and Total Systems Services (TSS) into Europe and the cross-border expansion of processors from larger European countries. Several of the largest European banks were outgrowing their national borders, where they owned the national bank cooperatives with smaller domestic banks. To save costs, some had started to use third-party processors for issuing and processing cards. Processors had seized the opportunity of the migration of the magnetic stripe card to the EMV card to sharpen their attack on the European market. So far, however, First Data and TSS had been successful, primarily in the United Kingdom and predominantly with credit cards.

Further, some experts were predicting that "mobile payment" was on the horizon and that this could challenge chip payment cards. Customers would be able to pay by sending an SMS, for example, to a vending machine, a parking meter, or a person. This transaction would be settled by the telecom company via the phone bill or against the balance on a customer account that resided in a network. In summer 2001, Postbank and the telecom company Telfort participated in a market test and handed out wireless application protocol (wap) phones. Of the 450,000 phones handed out to clients, 80,000 people used them, to Postbank's and Telfort's surprise, to check the balance of their account (400,000 in one day) or make mobile payments (330,000 in one day). By comparison, Postbank's 7.5 million customers had checked their balance by phone in 2001 about 110 million times.[27]

In 2002, the Chipknip train was finally rolling out of the station. Now that the name and system confusion had been eliminated, Interpay and the banks were hoping that the growth of the first half of 2002 would continue. Would Chipknip be able to silence the critics of smart cards? Would they finally see growth and profits reminiscent of the debit card success?

NOTES

1. Plastic Cards 1996, NIPO Amsterdam.

2. Exchange rates current in summer 2002 valued US$1 at approximately €1.

3. Jaap Akkermans and Marcel Boogaard, "Cost effective solution for Health Cards using in interoperable mixture of memory and processor chips," memo, September 1997.

4. For a small shop owner, this would be the cost of a regular call at €0.10 per minute. For large retailers with an ISDN line, this cost could drop to a couple of cents.

5. The card user remained very well protected with smart card technology, as only the card number (not the customer number or other personal data) together with the time, date, and amount of the payment were stored in the payment terminal when the cardholder used the card. The personal data of the cardholder was stored in the chip and protected by the PIN code. The only way the card accepter or issuer could get this data was by the physical agreement of the cardholder (i.e., keying in the PIN code).

6. *Financieel Dagblad*, March 20, 1996.

7. *Financieel Dagblad*, April 12, 1996.

8. *Financieel Dagblad*, April 16, 1996.

9. *Financieel Dagblad*, June 7, 1996.

10. *Financieel Dagblad*, October 10, 1996.

11. A lack of agreement among the financial institutions meant that the Dutch could use either the ATMs of the banks or the Postbank terminals, but not both, to withdraw cash.

12. *Financieel Dagblad*, October 11, 1996.

13. *The Netherlander*, October 18, 1997.

14. *Interpay Corporate Communications*, July 3, 2002.

15. "De Kassa Rinkelt Niet Voor Niets," *HBD*, 1999.

16. *NRC Handelsblad*, March 6, 2001, 13.

17. *De Volkskrant*, October 17, 2001, 18.

18. *Interpay*, Rabobank.

19. Heliview, customer survey, March 2002.

20. *Algemeen Dagblad*, July 19, 2001. In 2000, 2.5 million parking transactions were recorded by Interpay.

21. *NRC Handelsblad*, October 24, 2001, 18.

22. Case writers' interviews in 2002.

23. *Het Financieel Dagblad*, March 10, 2001, 1.

24. "How Secure Are Smart Cards?" *Card Technology News*, March 1, 2002.

25. "Proximity cards" do not require physical contact with a terminal; an electronic "gate" reads the chip.

26. "Processor on the Prowl," *Card Technology News*, August 7, 2002.

27. *Het Financieel Dagblad*, August 13, 2001, 3.

Bang & Olufsen and the Electronics Entertainment Industry in 2003

"Our concept is so strong in every sense, that we don't have to adjust to the market—it is the markets that have to adjust to us. Nothing communicates as strongly as the products themselves. Above all, every one of them communicates Bang & Olufsen—and every one of them has a strong identity. Any form of communication starts by listening to the signals of the products. Only by creating a communication which matches the company's and the products' values do we avoid confusing the identity. Surprising communication which makes the difference—and whose sender everybody would recognise at any time—that's our vision."

Former Bang & Olufsen CEO Anders Knutsen[1]

On January 15, 2003, the CEO of Bang & Olufsen (B&O), the Danish manufacturer of high-end electronic entertainment products, presented the interim report covering the period June 1 to November 30, 2002. Despite an overall increase in sales of 3.1 percent and an increase in margins from 5.0 percent to 6.6 percent (see Exhibit 4.1), analysts responded by lowering the target price of Bang & Olufsen shares. In recent years, B&O had consistently outperformed other manufacturers of luxury goods while its stock price had underperformed the same group (see Exhibits 4.2, 4.3, and 4.4). Analysts voiced concern about the 19 percent decline in sales in Germany. They also seemed to question whether B&O's recent drive into the U.S. market would ever generate profits.

B&O had an impressive track record of stylish audio and video product innovations. At the same time, it continued to be very focused on a small number of products and was running significant losses in the United States. Would B&O have to retrench to Europe or could it make its magic work around the world? Was its business model sustainable or would it be crowded out by the large electronics companies, which operated globally and leveraged their R and D and marketing capabilities across many product segments? Could it survive as an independent company? These were some of the questions CEO Torben Ballegaard Sørensen was considering in the spring of 2003.

THE MARKET FOR ELECTRONIC ENTERTAINMENT IN EUROPE AND NORTH AMERICA

MARKET SIZE

In 2002, the market for audio and video products in Europe and North America was about €52.5 billion,

Case Studies Exhibit 4.1

Consolidated Financial Statement for Bang & Olufsen, A/S (in € millions; €1=DKr7.42)

	1997–1998	1998–1999	1999–2000	2000–2001	2001–2002	1st half 2003
Assets						
Cash and short-term investments	74.0	17.6	17.5	7.1	22.2	
Receivables (net)	48.4	51.7	67.0	75.2	81.2	
Total inventories	3.1	78.5	78.7	92.4	87.9	
Current assets–total	185.4	147.8	163.2	174.8	191.3	
Long-term receivables	4.0	7.7	5.6	3.8	3.7	
Other investments	2.5	0.0	0.7	0.8	1.1	
Property, plant, and equipment (net)	85.4	97.9	114.2	129.0	122.3	
Other assets	2.2	2.0	5.2	1.9	1.8	
Fixed assets	94.0	107.6	125.7	135.4	128.9	
Total assets	279.5	255.4	288.9	310.2	320.2	364.6
Liabilities and Shareholders' Equity						
Accounts payable	22.7	38.8	38.5	25.1	24.8	
Short-term debt and current portion of long-term debt	45.6	38.7	35.3	58.6	61.9	
Other current liabilities	13.5	9.0	10.8	6.3	6.3	
Current liabilities—total	81.8	86.5	84.7	90.1	92.9	
Long-term debt	26.6	24.8	49.9	52.1	51.7	
Provisions for risks and charges	7.6	5.1	5.0	6.0	7.0	
Deferred taxes	6.7	6.8	6.8	7.3	0.9	
Total liabilities	122.8	123.2	146.4	155.4	152.5	
Minority interest	0.0	0.0	0.0	0.2	0.0	
Common equity	156.7	132.2	142.6	154.6	167.7	
Total liability and shareholders' equity	279.5	255.4	288.9	310.2	320.2	
Number of employees	na	2668.0	2783.0	2776.0	2908.0	
Income Statement						
Net sales or revenues	420.1	455.6	501.7	513.5	567.7	277.4
Cost of goods sold (Excluding depreciation)	241.0	261.5	281.4	290.9	323.6	
Depreciation, depletion, and amortization	19.6	17.7	21.9	23.1	24.9	
Gross income	159.5	176.3	198.4	199.5	219.2	
Administration costs	13.5	14.1	15.8	17.5	16.3	
R&D	32.0	34.2	41.5	40.2	44.9	
Distribution and market cost	77.5	84.1	96.0	105.3	123.2	
Operating expenses—total	383.7	411.7	456.7	476.9	532.9	
Operating income	36.4	43.9	45.0	36.5	34.8	18.6
Non-operating income	10.7	6.8	12.1	2.3	2.4	
Other income/expenses (net)	16.5	(6.6)	3.5	0.5	0.4	
Earnings before interest and taxes (EBIT)	3.6	44.1	60.6	39.3	37.5	
Interest expense on debt	7.6	5.7	15.2	9.1	7.1	
Pretax income	56.0	38.4	45.4	30.2	30.4	18.3
Income taxes	14.5	12.7	12.7	10.3	12.0	
Of which minority share	0.0	0.0	0.0	0.8	1.4	0.3
Net income before preferred dividends	41.5	25.7	32.8	20.7	19.8	11.3
Dividend	13.5	9.0	10.8	6.3	6.3	
Earnings Per Share (nominal DKr10)	17.0	20.0	18.0	12.0	11.0	
Quoted share price on May 31 (DKr)	441.0	462.0	283.0	268.0	235.0	
P/E	26.0	23.0	16.0	22.0	21.0	

Source: Bang & Olufsen annual reports, 2001 and 2002.

Case Studies Exhibit 4.2

Sector Analysis Household Audio and Video Equipment / Consumer Electronics
(1997 to 2001 5-year averages)

Ratios	Company				
	B&O	Loewe	Philips	Sony	Thomson
Profitability Ratios					
Year on year average sales growth (percent)	7.28	3.10	−5.88	−1.70	−0.95
Return on total equity	21.1	16.2	35.1	6.8	15.6
Return on assets	11.7	4.6	14.1	2.4	5.6
Cost of goods sold to sales	58.2	68.6	64.8	60.5	73.2
Gross profit margin	37.5	26.1	29.3	33.5	23
Operating profit margin	8.9	3.6	3.9	3.1	4
Asset Utilization Ratios					
Asset turnover	1.6	1.8	1.1	1	1.4
Inventory turnover	3.7	7.6	4.5	4.8	4.8
Net sales to gross fixed assets	1.9	2.6	1.8	2.1	2.8
Liquidity Ratios					
Receivables percent of current assets	32.8	59.7	43.7	35.1	50.1
Accounts receivable days	41.2	78.9	65.8	57	87.3
Inventory days	98	49.6	79.8	75.7	60.8

Source: Thomson Analytics.

split between video product sales of €32 billion and audio product sales of €20.5 billion (see Exhibit 4.3). The market in these areas for entertainment electronics had peaked in 2000 when total sales had reached €52.9 billion, representing a 0.2 percent growth over 1999. From 2000 till 2002, the industry was stung by the global recession, and sales weakened in both Europe and the United States.

By 2003, the overall economic outlook remained clouded. Growth of video and audio products till 2005 was expected to be around 0.5 percent per year in Europe and around 2 percent in the United States. These growth projections, however, masked a substantial variation across product categories. Sales of analog products were expected to decline, whereas hopes were high for rapid growth of digital and plasma televisions, DVD players, and MP3 players.[2]

MASS-MARKET SEGMENT VERSUS HIGH-END SEGMENT

The electronic entertainment industry was divided into a high-end segment and a mass-market seg-

Case Studies Exhibit 4.3

Market Sizes and Growth Rates (€ millions)

	1997	1998	1999	2000	2001	2002	2003[3]	2004[3]	2005[3]
TV, VCR, DVD, Camcorders [1]									
France	2,650	3,000	3,100	3,320	3,380	3,405	3,435	3,470	3,495
Germany	4,175	4,270	4,155	4,040	4,020	4,220	4,185	4,170	4,150
United Kingdom	1,197	1,260	1,307	1,323	1,528	1,581	1,594	1,619	1,647
Rest of Europe [2]	4,244	4,513	4,530	4,594	4,723	4,870	4,875	4,898	4,916
United States	16,000	16,500	19,300	19,000	17,500	17,950	18,450	19,000	19,700
Total video	28,266	29,543	32,392	32,277	31,151	32,026	32,539	33,157	33,908
Year on year (YOY) growth		4.50%	9.60%	−0.4%	−3.5%	2.80%	1.60%	1.90%	2.30%
Audio [2]									
France	3,545	3,605	3,660	3,695	3,700	3,700	3,720	3,735	3,760
Germany	3,090	2,995	2,950	3,025	3,025	3,030	3,038	3,052	3,070
United Kingdom	844	876	904	929	942	970	1,008	1,017	1,046
Rest of Europe [3]	3,957	3,955	3,975	4,047	4,056	4,074	4,109	4,129	4,167
United States	8,360	8,360	8,900	8,905	8,710	8,700	8,715	8,800	9,050
Total audio	19,796	19,791	20,389	20,601	20,433	20,474	20,590	20,733	21,093
YOY growth		0.00%	3.00%	1.00%	−0.8%	0.20%	0.60%	0.70%	1.70%
Total Europe	23,702	24,474	24,581	24,972	25,375	25,850	25,963	26,090	26,251
YOY growth		3.30%	0.40%	1.60%	1.60%	1.90%	0.40%	0.50%	0.60%
Audio and Visual Performance									
Total United States	24,360	24,860	28,200	27,905	26,210	26,650	27,165	27,800	28,750
YOY growth		2.10%	13.40%	−1%	−6.1%	1.70%	1.90%	2.30%	3.40%
Total Europe and United States	48,062	49,334	52,781	52,877	51,585	52,500	53,128	53,890	55,001
YOY growth		2.60%	7.00%	0.20%	−2.4%	1.80%	1.20%	1.40%	2.10%
Total Japan [4]					13,000	13260	13,525	13,796	14,072
YOY growth						2.00%	2.00%	2.00%	2.00%
Total Asia-Pacific, Middle East [4]					19,800	21,200	22,700	24,300	26,000
YOY growth						7.10%	7.10%	7.00%	7.00%
Total Latin America [4]					6,200	6,620	7,070	7,550	8,060
YOY growth						6.80%	6.80%	6.80%	6.80%
Grand total					90,585	93,580	96,423	99,536	103,133
YOY growth						3.30%	3.00%	3.20%	3.60%

1. *Source:* Euromonitor, Profound Market Briefing June 2002, France, Germany, United Kingdom, and United States TVs, VCRs, and camcorders.

2. *Source:* Euromonitor, Profound Market Briefing June 2002, France, Germany, United Kingdom, and United States audio.

3. Case writers' estimate.

4. *Source:* Customer Market Intelligence, April 2001. Includes both audio and video.

ment. In 2002, the high-end segment represented about 8 percent of the total market[3] (€4.2 billion across Europe and the United States). This segment was projected to reach €4.4 billion by 2005. This trend reflected recent wealth increases among consumers in the 1990s. One example of products in this segment was the jumbo television (30 inches or more), whose share of all color TV sets in Germany had increased from 11 percent in 1998 to 18 percent in 2000.[4] Products tended to have strong lifestyle brands, high quality, high prices, and exclusivity in design and distribution. The German company Loewe and Denmark's Bang & Olufsen had been the only major high-end players. Sony, Philips, and Thomson had been offering some products in the high-end segment but had remained anchored in the mass market.

The mass market in 2002 had a value of €48.3 billion, projected to increase to €50.6 billion by 2005. This segment tended to stress value for money, features, and low prices. The broad scope of this segment forced manufacturers to carry a wide range of products to meet the demands of the many different consumer types. The product life cycle of mass-market products had traditionally ranged between 12 and 18 months.[5] Companies such as Sony, Philips, Thomson, and Panasonic had traditionally been among the key players in the mass-market segment.

REGIONAL DIFFERENCES

In 2002, the North American market for audio and video products was €26 billion, of which the high-end segment represented about €2.1 billion. Total sales had fallen by 6.1 percent in 2001. However, it was expected that growth would return and range between 1.9 percent and 3.4 percent until 2005. The North American market tended to be characterized by intense price competition and a strong focus on marketing. Consumers were often deal oriented and expected to be able to thoroughly test the product in the store before making a purchase. North American customers also tended to have a level of technological literacy higher than that of European customers and often were actively comparing and seeking out product features.

The European market for audio and video products in 2002 stood at €25 billion, of which the high-end segment represented €2 billion. The largest markets were Germany, the United Kingdom, France, Italy, and Spain, totaling more than 85 percent of the entire European market. The European market had not experienced the same drop in 2001 as the North American market but was not expected to realize significant growth till 2005. High-end companies B&O and Loewe had their origin in Europe, reflecting the interest of a segment of European customers in style in contrast to product features.

DIGITAL VERSUS ANALOG PRODUCTS

Digital products were forecast to play an increasingly important role. In 2002, the digital market was projected to grow at rates of up to 20 percent per year and reach a total size in North America of €22 billion by 2005. Digital products had historically offered a 25 to 40 percent higher margin than analog products.[6] Digital TV was forecast to take almost 25 percent of total digital sales. Other promising products included DVD players, home satellite systems, digital camcorders, digital cameras, home theater systems, MP3 players, mobile video, satellite radio, computer software and peripherals, and electronic gaming.

NEW TECHNOLOGIES

The transition from the analog to the digital world continued to change the entertainment electronics market and posed a major challenge to the electronics manufacturers. Five concepts were expected to shape the new electronics entertainment world: affordability, portability, interoperability, accessibility, and compatibility.[7]

Broadband and wireless (Bluetooth, HomeRF) devices already had significantly changed the way people used the Web. Many predicted that these technologies would become the backbone of tomorrow's home automation. Connectivity with smart sensors and cable and satellite operators would have to be designed. For example, video recorders would have to be able to exchange videos over broadband connections.

Other new products included a Moxi digital entertainment system, which aspired to become the central gateway to all other electronic equipment. This system combined a CD and DVD player, a satellite receiver, a cable box, a personal video recorder, and a radio and could connect to other devices via Bluetooth.[8] Also, portable handheld and hard-drive–based products with additional storage capacity were contributing to the convergence of functions. The Panasonic AV-10 contained a camcorder, a camera, an MP3 player, a voice recorder, and a viewer. Satellite radio, especially for cars and trucks, was becoming increasingly popular due to its superior quality, service, and convenience. Other new trends included new display devices such as Mira, a tablet like screen, or T-Mobile, which combined a PDA, a mobile phone, and a digital camera.

THE ELECTRONICS ENTERTAINMENT VALUE CHAIN

RESEARCH AND DEVELOPMENT

R & D had been one of the key drivers of growth in the entertainment electronics market. It had also led to several megabattles among corporations to define the standard. Perhaps the most notable battle was the fight in the video cassette recorder business in the late 1970s and early

1980s among Sony (Beta), Matsushita and JVC (VHS), and Philips (Video 2000). As only one technology (VHS) became the accepted standard in this market, Sony and Philips had to write off their large investments. For Matsushita and JVC, this victory turned out to be a watershed event in their development. Though standards battles still occurred, the major players had tended to more frequently seek codevelopment of technologies. Said Ad Huijser, Philips's chief technology officer, "We have learned our lessons from the past."[9] For example, Sony and Philips had codeveloped and launched the CD and the DVD. The large consumer electronics companies tended to spend between 4 percent and 10 percent of sales on R & D. For Philips, its R & D spending amounted to 9.6 percent of sales in 2002, 10.2 percent of sales in 2001, and 7.3 percent of sales in 2000. For Thomson, R & D spending was 3.7 percent of sales in 2002, 3.5 percent in 2001, & 3.9 percent in 2000 (see Exhibit 4.4 for activity-based expenditures).

MANUFACTURING

Companies such as Sony and Philips had historically manufactured virtually all their components in-house. During the 1990s, this changed dramatically. Outsourcing of basic components became the norm, and even the large manufacturers specialized in a smaller range of key components (e.g., plasma screens), which often were sold to competitors. For example, Bang & Olufsen bought a large range of components from Philips. Because of the increased specialization, both Sony and Philips had significantly reduced the number of production plants worldwide and shifted production to low-labor-cost countries. Since the 1980s, Philips had reduced its number of production facilities from more than 100 to only 14 production sites in 2000.

Case Studies Exhibit 4.4

Supply Chain Expenditures

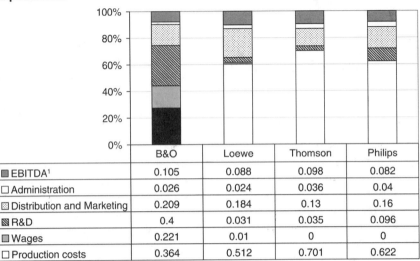

	B&O	Loewe	Thomson	Philips
■ EBITDA[1]	0.105	0.088	0.098	0.082
☐ Administration	0.026	0.024	0.036	0.04
⊠ Distribution and Marketing	0.209	0.184	0.13	0.16
▧ R&D	0.4	0.031	0.035	0.096
▨ Wages	0.221	0.01	0	0
☐ Production costs	0.364	0.512	0.701	0.622

Source: 2002 company annual reports (2001 for Thomson) and case writer's estimate figures for Thomson and Philips are consolidated for all of their activities.
1. Earnings before Interest, Taxes, Depreciation, and Amortization.

MARKETING AND DISTRIBUTION

Manufacturers used a wide range of marketing approaches to sell their products. The major players heavily used TV. On the other hand, companies such as Bang & Olufsen mainly advertised in high-end lifestyle journals and relied on word-of-mouth publicity.

Wholesale distribution of electronics entertainment was typically done in-house through distribution centers dealing directly with large electronics stores and mass merchants. Mass-market manufacturers also sold their products through wholesalers that distributed to the fragmented retail market. This retailer market had been consolidating, however. High-end manufacturers tended to pay particular attention to distribution, as this influenced the buying experience. Bang & Olufsen, for example, had developed a number of stores that exclusively sold their products. Sony also had invested in retail stores but considered these more a marketing and branding investment than a focus for expansion. Some manufacturers had also implemented the store-within-a-store concept. In particular the high-end electronics companies Loewe and B&O had used this concept extensively to differentiate their products.

PRICING

Though pricing in the mass market tended to be very competitive, there remained very significant differences in the prices charged by different manufacturers. For example, Bang & Olufsen charged €20,000 for its 42-inch plasma TV BeoVision 5, whereas Samsung asked €14,500 for its 61-inch top-of-the-line plasma TV. The differences reflected product features, positioning, and branding (see Exhibit 4.5 for price comparisons of TVs from Bang & Olufsen and other industry competitors). Prices tended to decline gradually as new technologies spread.

Case Studies Exhibit 4.5

Comparison of Retail Prices of Different Manufacturers' Color TV Sets

Manufacturer/model	Tube size (cm)	List price (€)	Video rating
WideScreen 16:9—Europe[1]			
B&O Beovision 3	30	3,700	Very good
Philips 36 PW 9525	34	3,056	Very good
Loewe Aconda 9381 ZW	30	2,555	Very good
Grundig MW 82-510/8 DPL	30	1,890	Very good
Plasma TVs—United States[2]			
Pioneer PDP-5030HD	50	14,091	
Sony PFM50C1	50	10,417	
Philips 50FD9955	50	8,181	
Panasonic TH-50 PHD5U	50	8,699	
BeoVision 5	42	20,485	
Loewe Spheros 42-S	42	14,600	
Pioneer PDP-4330HD	42	10,455	
Sony PFM-42B1	42	5,909	
Philips 42FD9952	42	5,727	
Panasonic TH-42 PHD5U	42	5,636	
Medion MD 6018	42	5,400	

[1] *Source:* Deutsche Bank, Bang & Olufsen, and Loewe, April 23, 2002.

[2] *Source:* http://www.Geodatasys.com/tv.htm, March 4, 2003.

KEY COMPETITORS OF ELECTRONIC ENTERTAINMENT PRODUCTS

LOEWE

B&O's most direct competitor was Loewe. The German company was founded in 1923 by Dr. Siegfried Loewe. From its early days, the company focused on technology innovation. It developed the famous Loewe "triple tube," which many considered to be the first integrated circuit in the world. The Loewe radio, equipped with the triple tube, was the first to reach sales of 1 million units in Germany and substantially contributed to the strong growth in broadcast listeners from 1926 to 1930.

Scientists at Loewe focused their R & D on TV technology also. This resulted in numerous innovations, among others the first television in the world to be equipped with a square picture tube (1939), the first recorder in the world featuring a cassette tape (1950), and Europe's first stereo color television (1981). Loewe historically manufactured products with an expected product life cycle of five to six years.[10]

Loewe's products were known for their high quality and elegant design. The company's mission was to offer the best-quality product at all price levels. Loewe brand campaigns often relied on testimonials with double-page ads featuring personalities from the worlds of design, the arts, and entertainment. Though Loewe did not have the luxury lifestyle image of B&O, it had a strong presence in the high-end segment. Its products had received many prizes for quality and design. Since 1981 alone, 78 Loewe products had been awarded 132 national and international prizes. Its product mix was also broader than that of B&O, which had led to a better penetration in the mass

Case Studies Exhibit 4.6

Loewe Versus B&O Product Comparison

	B&O	Loewe
Pricing	Top end	Toward high end
Product line	Focused product mix	Rich product mix
Innovation/new product development cycle	12–36 months	6–24 months
Product life cycle	8 years	5–6 years
Display technologies	Picture tubes, flat screen, plasma	Picture tubes, rear projection, LCD, plasma
Design	Emotional extravagance	Classical elegance
Key competitive strength	Acoustic know-how	Wide range of display technologies
Media	Not a key focus	Strong focus
New products 2002	BeoVision 5 (plasma), MP3 players	Loewe systems (including Bose) rear projection, LCD 50 cm
Long-term focus	Car audio and acoustic research	Product pipeline underlies innovation and technological advances

Source: Bang & Olufsen Annual Report 2002, Loewe Annual Report 2002, Deutsche Bank, "Bang & Olufsen and Loewe," April 23, 2002.

markets.[11] See Exhibit 4.6 for a comparison of Loewe and B&O. Loewe sales in 2001 were €372 million.

In 2002, Loewe established its distribution in the United States. The distribution was set up in cooperation with another high-end manufacturer, Bose, a U.S. sound specialist. Stores were dedicated, offering exclusively the products of Loewe and Bose. Loewe had expected a loss of €0.5 million in the start-up year but had to revise the number to €2.6 million. It explained that the bigger-than-expected losses were mainly due to gaps in its product line. Its key product, the 40-inch flat-screen TV Acordia, had fallen behind the latest standards. It expected that the poor performance would improve once its next-generation flat-screen TV was released in the second half of 2003. To stem the losses, Loewe and Bose decided to sell in their stores the products of other manufacturers also.

Sony

Sony was founded in 1945 by Masaru Ibuka. He established a facility in Tokyo for the repair of radios and also made shortwave converters or adapters that could easily make medium-wave radios into all-wave receivers. The name Sony was initially just a trademark, but in 1957 it was adopted as the corporate name. Demand for the radios was spectacular. Ibuka's team also found the time to develop an electric rice cooker. This was the beginning of a long and impressive history of innovation in consumer electronics.

Sony was the leader of the electronics entertainment industry and offered both a wide range of mass-market products as well as products aimed at high-end consumers (see Exhibit 4.7 for market share data). Sony was known for high quality across its entire product line. It was also known as a leader in the development of new technologies.

Case Studies Exhibit 4.7

Regional Market Share, 2000
(percent, based on revenue)

	Sony	Philips	Matsushita
Europe	21	14	17
North America	27	13	10
Latin America	24	10	19
Asia Pacific (excluding Japan)	15	8	5
Global (excluding Japan)	22	11.8	12.2
Global (including Japan)	22	13	10

By 2002 Sony operated 12 Sony outlet stores in the United States.

In 2003, Sony was locked in a fierce battle with Microsoft in the game console industry. It had successfully overtaken Sega and Nintendo and in 2002 depended for 57 percent of its total profits on this product line. Microsoft, however, had challenged Sony in 2001 for the leadership in this market with the launch of the Xbox. Sony did not want to lose this battle, as its other audio-video businesses had come under profit pressure due to intense competition from other consumer electronics manufacturers.

PHILIPS

The foundation for what was to become one of the world's biggest electronics companies was laid in 1891 when Gerard Philips established a company in Eindhoven, the Netherlands, to "manufacture incandescent lamps and other electrical products." Philips grew to become Europe's largest electronics group. The company had pioneered many technologies and products but had at times faced difficulties turning these into commercial successes. The CD-i technology was one example of this. Philips had gone through rounds of restructuring in the 1990s but had maintained its mass-market focus in consumer electronics. However, similar to Sony, Philips had recently introduced upscale products and in particular their plasma TV's were selling well. On November 25, 2002, Philips announced that its restructuring in the United States was progressing well and that the overall sales through upmarket retailers had risen 145 percent over 2001. Sales of branded TVs were up by 55 percent compared to the previous year. The entry into high-end retailing had been done through strategic partnerships with premium specialty retailers such as Tweeter. In the United States, Philips had attempted to sell to the low end of the mass market under the brand Magnavox while positioning the brand Philips as a premium brand.

OTHER MASS-MARKET PLAYERS

The French company Thomson had been a significant European player though not of the same strength as Philips. It sold a very wide range of mass-market products. In recent years, Thomson had been focusing on the design of its products with the help of several well-known designers (e.g., Philip Starck). The product philosophy was one of creating designs of sufficient quality for the mass market. In 1990, Thomson launched Proscan, a high-end brand, but it did not really catch on with consumers. In 1995, Thomson changed its company name to Thomson Multimedia to reflect its increasing focus on multimedia. In addition to the above electronics companies, many other competitors were offering products: Toshiba, Samsung, Panasonic, Sharp, Pioneer, Bose, Yamaha, Sanyo, Siemens, JVC, and Grundig. Their focus was exclusively the mass market.

BANG & OLUFSEN A/S
HISTORY

B&O was founded on November 17, 1925, by Peter Bang and Svend Olufsen. The first product the two young engineers produced was the world's first radio with a power plug, the Eliminator (1926), a technological leap from the traditional battery-driven radio. Since this first invention, Bang & Olufsen consistently sought to be an innovator.

In 1938 Bang & Olufsen introduced the first mains radio with push-button operation, the Master 38CH. The subsequent launch of the Master Deluxe 39 came with 16 permanent stations. This invention along with the strict use of high-quality materials was instrumental to the development of B&O's reputation for quality. The year 1939 also saw the launch of the BeoLit, the first radio with a Bakelite cabinet. The Beolit was the first product to carry the famous Beo name, which has since labeled all major new products from Bang & Olufsen. In 1940, Bang & Olufsen launched a campaign to sign up authorized Bang & Olufsen dealers to expand its sales in international markets.

Over the years, style and quality became hallmarks of B&O, resulting in numerous international prizes for innovative designs and product quality (especially for acoustics and user-friendliness). Very well known was its 1963 slogan, "B&O, for those who discuss design and quality before price," which was still used four decades later.

Throughout the 1970s and 1980s, Bang & Olufsen continued to develop and produce new and innovative products. The highlight of this era was the development of the groundbreaking BeoLink system, allowing the user to receive audio and video signals in different rooms through a single operating unit by the use of discrete cabling and infrared remote control units. This was the first remote that was able to simultaneously operate all the different products from the same manufacturer. In 1978, 11 Bang & Olufsen products were accepted into New York's Museum of Modern Art. This number had by 2002 grown to 18.

During the late 1980s and early 1990s, Bang & Olufsen experienced a significant financial crisis. While the company had several products on permanent display at New York's Museum of Modern Art[12] and New York's Metropolitan Museum of Art, they had lost financial control.[13] Commented Finance Executive Vice President Peter Thostrup on the situation in 1992, "I can't say that we were a profit-driven company. The products were what the company cared about."[14] Many wondered whether B&O would survive. The crises also forced Bang & Olufsen to sell a 25 percent equity stake to Philips in the early 1990s.

The very poor 1990–91 results led to the replacement of CEO Vagn Andersen with Anders Knutsen. Knutsen had joined the company in 1973 as head of the Personal and Working Environment Department. He had worked his way through the company in various positions. In November 1992, the new CEO presented his turnaround plan, "Breakpoint 1993." The plan focused on tight financial control while maintaining the strengths of B&O in design and R & D. More particularly, Knutsen set out to outsource all noncore activities, considering everything from the cafeteria to the production of transistors. A second focus was the reduction of working capital through just-in-time production and improved efficiency in R & D. The third leg of the strategy was a repositioning of the brand from a top-line electronics brand to a true luxury good. The fourth focus was the streamlining of distribution to increase profitability and ensure that the targeted repositioning could be supported.

The turnaround was a success. When Bang & Olufsen released its 1997–98 results, it also announced that it had bought back the 25 percent equity stake from Philips. In 2000, B&O split the company into five separate units to support Knutsen's strategy (see Exhibit 4.8 for details). By the end of the decade, B&O was again on firm financial footing and had sharpened its business model. It had also sought out new businesses where it could

Case Studies Exhibit 4.8

Result for B&O Business Units (100% owned)

	Revenue			Pre tax Profit		
	2000–2001	2001–2002	2002–2003*	2000–2001	2001–2002	2002–2003*
Audio-visual	481.8	530.5	256.6	27.1	30.9	20.1
Telecom	32.9	35.4	20.8	na	−1.3	na
Mediocom	31.4	40	16.2	4.6	2.2	−0.1
New business	0.3	2.3	1.8	−1.5	−2.6	−1.1

Source: Bang & Olufsen, Annual Report, 2002.
*First half of 2003.

use its competencies in design (e.g., medical devices) and had entered the U.S. market.

BANG & OLUFSEN'S BUSINESS MODEL

Research and Development

Bang & Olufsen carried out fundamental research in the acoustics area, where 250 engineers were actively pursuing new technologies. However, its primary focus remained design (product design, functionality, and systems integration). A remarkable example of this focus was the Be01 remote control, which had only 11 buttons yet could be used to operate all B&O appliances in the house.

Product design had been driven by a small number of very influential designers. This had resulted in very strong design consistency. Standing out were designers Jakob Jensen and David Lewis, who had, more than anybody else, defined the B&O design. The successors to David Lewis were already being groomed by Lewis himself. Bang & Olufsen strongly believed that its designers should not be employees but freelancers. They feared that if designers got too close to Bang & Olufsen, they would start paying too much attention to the problems and limitations in the rest of the organization and could make them lose their creative edge. While most freelance designers that

B&O used had a dominant part of their activities with B&O, they remained independent.

R & D originated from the "Idealand" which was a central hub around which product design was organized. The R & D was very much team based. User interfaces were, for example, developed by an interface designer, a psychologist, a software developer, and a narrator.[15] This team design was a conscious decision to ensure that several perspectives were given due consideration. This team structure had also been a cornerstone of B&O's efforts to develop the coherent and integrated home entertainment system BeoLink (all rooms, one system, one remote).

Considering the high price of the products, B&O customers expected the products to last well into the future. To respond to this, Bang & Olufsen worked with the rule of thumb that each product had to have an expected product life of eight years. B&O had decided that it was more important that their products were flawless than to be the first to launch a new technology. For example, whereas other electronics manufacturers had been competing to get first to market with plasma TV screens, B&O had waited for the arrival of the second-generation plasma screen, which offered better picture quality (BeoVision 5). In the meantime, B&O had devoted its efforts to perfecting the design of the TV.

To secure access to new technologies and components at low cost, B&O engaged in strategic partnerships with Ericson (Bluetooth) and Philips (general components). Philips, in fact, had been a B&O supplier of components for more than 60 years, selling picture tubes, optical discs, and DVD and CD players. Other suppliers were Panasonic (plasma screen), Sony, Hitachi, and Sanyo.

PRODUCTION

Bang & Olufsen had outsourced most of its production to suppliers, buying picture tubes from Philips, plasma screens from Panasonic, and peripheral devices from a range of suppliers. In their facilities in Struer, Denmark, B&O produced PCBs (key electronic components) and surface components, and conducted final assembly and quality control. Emphasized former CEO Anders Knutsen, "No matter which end of the price range you buy, the Bang & Olufsen special standards of quality are part and parcel of the purchase."[16]

One product that analysts and B&O had placed a lot of confidence in was the BeoVision 5 plasma television. BeoVision had been designed by David Lewis, who found his inspiration in the movie *Fahrenheit 451*, which featured a flat wide-screen TV on the wall.[17] The BeoVision had been designed in such a way that it could be attached to the wall, lean against a wall, or stand freely in the room. The television was equipped with a brushed aluminium frame. This was intended to serve the same purpose as a passe-partout for a painting: to direct the eye and render calmness. To provide interior decoration flexibility to the consumer, B&O decided to offer the frame in several colors: natural, black, red, blue, and green.

The frame encapsulated the latest technology ensuring that the picture quality was optimal. Included in these technologies were sensors that would measure the light intensity of the room and adjust the TV settings accordingly. Powerful built-in speakers were located beneath the screen with a possibility of Dolby Digital Surround. The BeoVision 5 was only built to order to meet the customer's individual requirements. Because of the precision required to construct the TV, 1,000 components were assembled by hand before the TV underwent exhaustive testing and quality control.

MARKETING

B&O's marketing efforts were closely aligned with the image it tried to project. First, it did not advertise in mass media or widely distributed publications but only in high-end lifestyle magazines. Second, it communicated two messages. One type of advertising featured no product. The objective was to communicate the values B&O wanted to associate with its products, for instance, "freedom," with reference to the Beolink system. The other type of advertising featured one B&O product (and, exceptionally, several B&O products) in a very sophisticated setting. The overriding theme was picturesque simplicity. The arrival of the Internet had brought another marketing medium, which B&O tapped to project its core values. Since 1995, B&O had also realized numerous product placements in major Hollywood motion pictures (e.g., *The Sum of All Fears, Men in Black II, Minority Report, Vanilla Sky, Unfaithful, Charlie's Angels, Tomorrow Never Dies, Mission Impossible*) and some TV series (e.g., *Sex in the City*).

DISTRIBUTION

Facing increasing competition from Japanese manufacturers in the 1970s, B&O started to develop closer ties with selected retailers. These retailers were offered a partnership referred to as the BeoCenter. To further develop this strategy, B&O created a company called Expo-Competence. This unit specialized in the design of BeoCenters.

Case Studies Exhibit 4.9

B&O Performance in the United States and Canada

	1996–1997	1997–1998	1998–1999	1999–2000[a]	2000–2001	2001–2002[b]	2002–03[c] 1st half
Turnover	20.6	20	22.4	27.6	41.9	51.2	22.1
Loss	na	na	na	−2	−5.5	−10.8	−6.9
B1 Stores	na	na	na	36	55	58	58

Source: Bang & Olufsen, Annual Report, 2001–2002.
[a] 1999–2000 loss is case writers' estimate.
[b] Loss includes a provision of €0.4 million to bad debt.
[c] Loss includes a provision of €3.8 million to discontinuation of stores.

The ultimate product was a complete turnkey shop aimed at the exclusive sales of B&O products.

The distribution approach was further developed when B&O experienced the financial crisis in the early 1990s. It had observed that retailers that carried B&O products alongside products of competitors very often focused on price instead of quality. To overcome this, B&O accelerated the implementation of exclusive distribution channels. It also banned nonexclusive retailers that did not agree to play by B&O's rules. Commented Lars Topholm, B&O CFO, "We got rid of retailers who were discounting. After all we don't sell just technology—we sell magic."[18] As a direct consequence of this policy, B&O reduced its retailer network from 3,000 to 2,000 outlets between 1994 and 1997.

By 2003, B&O had a retail presence in more than 40 countries. The following retail formats could be distinguished:[19]

B1 shops, selling only B&O products

B2 shops, with at least 50 percent of revenues related to B&O products

B3 shops, with 25–50 percent of revenues related to B&O products

C shops, buying at least DKr500,000 worth of products from B&O per year

D shop-in-shops, selling B&O in shopping centers

E shops, chains buying at least DKr500,000 from B&O per year

Except for 30 B1 shops in Europe and 20 B1 shops in the United States, B&O had no ownership in the distribution channel. The remaining B1 stores were run as franchises. B&O placed very specific demands on training.

THE ENTRY OF B&O INTO THE U.S. MARKET

In 1998, B&O opened its first B1 stores in the United States. This signaled its full-fledged entry into this market, targeting the 1.5 percent of American consumers (or 4,125,000 people)[20] for whom B&O thought price was of lesser importance. When B&O entered the United States, it was faced with the challenge of finding a sufficient number of franchisees because of the limited awareness of the brand. This forced B&O to own the majority of its B1 stores, contrary to its normal strategy. The expansion proved to be very costly, leading to a loss in the United States of €3 million in the second half of 2002 compared to a loss of €4 million in the corresponding period of 2001. In addition, provisions of €3.1 million were made to cover the cost of closing stores. This cost had been €0.4 million in 2001 (see Exhibit 4.9 for details on the United States and Canada). Factors in addition to costs that were also raised to explain the negative result were bad management, poorly trained sales personnel, choice of the wrong locations that were either too expensive or had suffered from a rapid change in demographics, and lack of a full product portfolio.

In response, Bang & Olufsen abandoned its exclusive policy and introduced non-B&O-branded products to fill the gaps, such as a 42-inch Panasonic LCD TV. It also changed its objectives for the United States from 100 stores by 2004 to profitability. Said Ole Bek, president of Bang & Olufsen America, "We were looking at a three- to five-year plan, but now we are looking at a six-to seven-, or maybe an eight-year plan."[21] In December 2002 B&O launched its BeoVision 5 (plasma) in the United States, and the reviews were very positive.

Because of its relatively limited public relations budget, Bang & Olufsen did not run large campaigns but relied on cosponsored events in areas local to its stores. CEO Torben Ballegaard remained optimistic: "The market is there. There are plenty of rich people that like our products. We just need to get hold of them. That is our challenge."[22] With this statement he referred to the increasing demand for complete home cinema solutions priced in the range of US$50,000 to US$75,000.

BANG & OLUFSEN NEW BUSINESS DEVELOPMENT

By 2003, B&O had five fully owned business units.[23] The corporate unit was responsible for brand building and group staff functions. In addition to B&O Audio Visual, B&O had created B&O Telecom to develop and market new telephony concepts for dynamic electronic communication in the home; B&O New Business intended to leverage core competencies. It owned 76.4 percent of B&O ICEpower, which developed, produced,

and marketed products based on powerful amplifier technology. Another business unit was B&O Medicom, which targeted the market for medical equipment in collaboration with existing and new partners. The first success had been the development of an insulin injection pen for Novo Nordisk. The pen, which combined design with superior ease of use, had been a great success. A fifth unit was B&O Operations, which handled purchasing, production, and logistics for the B&O Group.

THE CHALLENGE FOR BANG & OLUFSEN

In spite of the confidence expressed by Torben Ballegaard, the stock price of B&O remained depressed. Analysts were impressed with the new products they had seen but remained focused on the sales evolution in B&O's key markets and the problems in establishing a beachhead in the North American market. Was another financial crisis looming or was B&O well positioned to continue its development as an independent manufacturer?

NOTES

1. Anders Knutsen, former (1991–2001) Bang & Olufsen CEO, interview by Danish TV-2, September 1997.

2. Bear Stearns, *Equity Research Investment Report,* Hard Line Retailing: Consumer Electronics, March 2002.

3. Estimate based on Loewe and B&O sales compared with overall European market, and also accounting for Sony's, Philips's, and Thomson's sales in this segment.

4. Deutche Bank, *Equity Research Investment Report,* Bang & Olufsen and Loewe, April 23, 2002.

5. Philips briefing—Consumer Electronic Mainstream.

6. Bear Stearns investment report, "Hard Line Retailing," March 2002, 20.

7. Ibid., 5.

8. Ibid., 8.

9. Jennifer L. Schenker, "Fine-Tuning a Fuzzy Image," *Time,* http://www.time.com/time/europe/digital/2002/03/stories/philips.html. (September 15, 2005)

10. Credit Suisse First Boston Equity Research Investment Report, Consumer Electronics Industry, October 28, 2002.

11. Deutche Bank, Equity Research Investment Report, Bang & Olufsen and Loewe, April 23, 2002.

12. BeoWorld, "David Lewis," http://www.beoworld.co.uk/davidlewis.htm. (September 15, 2005)

13. CFO Europe, "Bang on Target," http://www.cfoeurope.com/199904b.html. (September 15, 2005)

14. Ibid.

15. http://www.arts.warterloo.co/acct/couses/acc646/projects2002/bovssony.htm

16. Knutsen interview.

17. Bang & Olufsen, *Annual Report 2001/02.*

18. CFO Europe, "Bang on Target."

19. Handelsbanken Research Company report on Bang & Olufsen, April 8, 2002.

20. BNY.dk nr.4 "B&O bliver I cowboy land til den bitre ende"

21. http://twice.com/index.asp?layout=print_page&doc_id=&articleID=CA219245

22. BNY.dk nr.4 "B&O bliver I cowboy land til den bitre ende."

23. Bang & Olufsen, *Annual Report 2001/02.*

ABX

Frédéric Le Roy
Professor
Director of ERFI
Associate Professor to Montpellier Business
School–France/CEROM
University of Montpellier I, ISEM

M'hamed Merdji
Professor
Head of Marketing Deparment Groupe Sup de Co
Montpellier
International Business School

Saïd Yami
Associate Professor
ERFI/University of Montpellier I, ISEM

Franck Seguy
Managing Director of Horiba ABX
Parc-Euromédecine

HORIBA ABX, S.A.

In 2003, ABX was the European leader and the fifth largest world provider in the hematology market, which is a particular segment of the in vitro diagnosis (IVD) market. Hematology consists of analyzing the cells of the blood (red blood cells, white blood cells, platelets) to provide a count and differentiation of the types of blood cells. The IVD market developed in France within the framework of a public policy of limitation of health expenditure (indeed, many diseases are detectable by anomalies in the composition of blood).

THE LAUNCHING OF THE COMPANY, 1983–1996

At its creation, in 1983 in Paris, ABX entered the hematology market by making a revolutionary innovation. It gathers the machines (automats), the reagents (consumables that allow the chemical reaction to take place), and the associated services (service after sale, scientific supports, etc.) all in one firm.

ABX entered this market by introducing hematology automats of a size much smaller than that of existing automats and at a much lower price. Automatic cell analyzers introduced by ABX, named Minos, consist of a range of compact and ergonomic instruments, which bring a reliable response to routine control.

Minos was developed by Henri Champseix. He was an engineer in a diagnostic company, and his idea for this technology was refused by the management of the firm. He then met Jean-Edouard Robert, the future chairman of ABX, on a Paris–Dakar rally. Robert was a car copilot and Champseix was a motorbike driver.

Sales of Minos began outside of France, where there was little competition. In three years, ABX saw its sales multiply by 15 and obtained control of 15 percent of the French market, with distribution in more than 25 countries.

ABX received many awards for its innovation. In 1986, ABX received the Marwick Barber-Peat trophy for its advanced technology. In 1988, ABX received the Oscar of export trophy for its sales abroad performance. In 1989, ABX also received the Design Oscar.

These awards resulted in a very significant development. In 1987, ABX opened a new assembly line in Montpellier, France, that enabled the company to multiply its sales by 5. In 1990, ABX achieved sales of FF100 million, with 50 percent of its production intended for export. ABX controlled 20 percent of the French market and distributed its products in more than 75 countries.

In 1990, ABX was acquired by the Swiss group Hoffmann-La Roche and was included in the Roche Diagnosis division. This acquisition made it possible to finance development while maintaining control, since the Swiss group left the existing management team in place.

ABX launched Helios, Argos, and Pentra, three hematological analyzers of average size intended for laboratories and hospitals. ABX also reinforced its position in the "small apparatus" market with the launch of Micros.

In 1993, all ABX activities were moved to Montpellier. In 1995, ABX decided to manufacture its own reagents for the hematology market. Following these developments, in 1995, ABX controlled more than 25 percent of the French market and was represented in more than 135 countries.

THE DEVELOPMENT OF THE COMPANY, 1996–2001

In 1996, the Hoffmann-La Roche group sold its share of ABX to the Horiba Group, which had been the distributor of ABX in Japan for the past 10 years. La Roche wished to disengage itself primarily because of ABX's weak financial results and because the head of ABX would not accept La Roche's proposed restructuring plan.

In 1996, the Horiba Group was based in Kyoto and had annual sales of US$652 million. It employed 3,700 workers. It is an international group, with subsidiary companies in Europe, Asia, and the United States. It specializes in the design, manufacture, and marketing of instruments primarily for industrial or scientific applications.

Horiba started by doubling the capital of ABX, which made it possible to pay its debts and to finance a sales development program. The first effort in that direction related to the distribution network. Until 1996, the network was that of the La Roche group with two exceptions, France (ABX) and Japan (Horiba).

ABX decided to distribute directly in Europe by creating agencies on the continent (in Germany, Austria, Benelux, Great Britain, Italy, Spain, and Portugal). These agencies were started one by one. La Roche maintained product distribution for three years. ABX also built a worldwide network of agencies (more than 85 distributors) and created three subsidiary companies, in the United States, Brazil, and Poland. After 1998, ABX handled its own distribution again.

The second effort related to the production side of the business. In 1997, a reagents production factory was built in Brazil. In 1999, ABX acquired Biochem in the United States. Biochem specialized in hematology and had a factory on the East Coast.

The last sales development effort related to innovation. In 1997, ABX was the first company to introduce a hematological analyzer that allows a completely automated counting of the reticulocytes. It was named the Pentra 120 Reric. The success of the Pentra enabled the company to increase its sales by 78 percent over 1999 levels.

Case Studies Exhibit 5.2

Competitive Positioning

	ABX	BCI	Sysmex	Abbott	Bayer
Very top-of-range		++	++++++		
Top-of-range	+++	+++	++++++	++	++++++
Medium-of-range	++++	++++++	+++++	++++	+
Bottom-of-range	++++++	++	++++	++++	++
Very bottom-of-range	+		++++		

THE POSITION OF ABX IN THE HEMATOLOGY MARKET

The world in vitro diagnosis market was estimated to be US$20 billion in 2003. Exhibit 5.1 shows how the submarkets were segmented.

immunology	41%
biochemistry	39%
hematology	7%
blood grouping	5%
hemostats	3%
other disciplines	5%

Large multinationals are present in the IVD market. The five largest groups are La Roche (US$3.9 billion in sales), Abbott (US$3.6 billion in sales), J&J (US$2.7 billion in sales), Bayer (US$2.1 billion in sales), and Dade-Bering (US$1.6 billion in sales). In comparison, ABX had sales of US$100 million.

Hematology accounted for 7 percent of the IVD market, or approximately US$2.7 billion. This market is very concentrated, since five companies carry out 88 percent of the sales. The first four competitors were, in 2003, Beckman Coulter (40 percent of the market), TOA Sysmex (20 percent), Abbott (10 percent), and Bayer (9 percent). ABX was just behind Bayer and occupied the fifth place in the world (9 percent of the market).

ABX entered the market by proposing to customers an automat of much smaller size at a cost lower than those proposed by the competitors. ABX was thus located primarily at the middle to low end of the price range. It was less present at the top of the range and completely absent from the very top of the range.

Among its competitors, only Abbott had a similar position. Beckman Coulter was located primarily at the middle and top of the range and was present at the very top of the range. Bayer developed especially for the top-of-the-range market, and Sysmex was present in all price ranges, with a strong position at the top of the range and the very top of the range (see Exhibit 5.2 for a breakdown).

POSITIONING OF THE COMPETITORS IN THE HEMATOLOGY MARKET

The segments experiencing strong growth, however, were at the top of the range and the very top of the range, and to a lesser degree, the middle of the range and the very bottom of the range. The bottom-of-the-range segment was declining, and it represented the essential positioning of ABX. It is thus symptomatic that, in 2003, the products most sold by ABX were Micros and Pentra 60, whereas the more recent and more sophisticated products, such as Pentra 80 and Pentra 120, were sold in lesser quantities.

THE ENTRY INTO THE BIOCHEMISTRY MARKET

The sales development in hematology seemed insufficient to the top management team of ABX. To develop the company beyond this simple market, the decision was made, in 1999, to enter another IVD market: biochemistry. Biochemistry is the scientific discipline that explores the chemical reactions that, by their juxtaposition and their interactions, allow the maintenance of life.

The entry of ABX into this market was achieved by the acquisition of the biochemistry arm of La Roche (the Mira line). La Roche needed to divest its holdings in this area, per the rules of the European Community, due to its merger with Boehringer. It gave up its biochemistry segment only in the European Community. ABX must remain within this geographical area for two years before being allowed to expand.

ABX gave back to La Roche the machine stock La Roche had previously installed (referred to as machines for hire) and the postsale service contracts. Despite its divestiture from biochemistry, La Roche was committed to providing the line of reagents to ABX for 18 months. The challenge for ABX was thus twofold: It had to develop its own line of machines and reagents at the same time.

To develop its reagents, ABX entered into a partnership with Bio-Meyrieux. Bio-Meyrieux had been developing a line of reagents for many years. ABX acquired these products and now sells them under its own brand. However, this solution exposed ABX to a strong dependence vis-à-vis its competitors. ABX then decided to manufacture its own line of reagents. In May 2000, ABX launched its own line of clinical chemistry reagents both in France and for the international markets.

In the same way, ABX made the decision to manufacture its own biochemistry automats, by hiring technicians, engineers, data-processing specialists,

and so forth. In 2000, ABX invested €6 million in Montpellier for the construction of six buildings, which increased the size of its site by 50 percent.

FROM DIFFICULTIES TO REVIVAL, 2001–PRESENT

In 2001, ABX manufactured 6,200 automats (25 percent of worldwide production) and 40 tons of reagents. However, ABX's situation was difficult. The company was heavily in debt and had to finance the construction of the new buildings as well as the recruiting to develop its biochemistry division. Moreover, Bio-Meyrieux decided to reconsider its partnership by not allowing ABX to sell Bio-Meyrieux's biochemistry reagents under its own brand.

The threat of bankruptcy led Horiba to acquire, in 2001, 100 percent of the capital stock of ABX. Immediately, the authorized capital was increased by €35 million to €44 million. Following this integration, in dissension with Horiba, Jean-Edouard Robert, the chairman and founder, left the company in 2002.

In August 2003, ABX acquired Biopep, a company specializing in coagulation, and built a new R & D center in Montpellier. At the end of 2003, ABX launched its first biochemistry automat, the Pentra 400.

To develop its sales, ABX created a policy of original equipment manufacturing (OEM), which consists of selling its automats, as well as the reagents, to its competitors, which market them under their own brands. Thus, ABX Micros 60 was marketed under the name Advia 60, with the graphics and colors of Bayer. ABX thus hopes to profit from Bayer's sales network. To Bayer's advantage, it can also sell products that are not manufactured by ABX.

ABX placed large hopes in the OEM policy. The general idea was that the IVD industry could be divided into two types of actors in the long term: manufacturers of materials and distributors. ABX would specialize in production, and large multinationals, such as Bayer, would base their strategies more on the distribution side.

THE ORGANIZATION OF ABX

In 2004, ABX's customer base consisted of approximately 25,000 laboratory clients throughout the world. ABX also had four factories or centers of production (France, the United States, Japan, Brazil), and 700 employees, including 468 in Montpellier.

Over the last 20 years, ABX has been structured into three companies: ABX SA, located in Montpellier, with six branches in Europe; ABX Inc., in the United States; and ABX Limitada, in Brazil. The organizational chart includes, on the level of the board of directors, a post of chairman and a post of delegated general manager; these positions are supplemented by a team of operational directors. Six main functions are distinguished for the operational directors:

- *Marketing and lawful business direction*, which includes business law, documentation, communication, and the development of marketing
- *Quality, organization, and information systems direction*, which includes quality systems, organization and methods of management, business data processing, information technologies, and data-processing integration
- *Industrial direction*, which includes the quality of the products, research, development, reagents, purchases and provisioning, production, and logistics
- *Financial direction*, which includes treasury and customer accounts, group subsidiary management control and reporting, and an associated financial director
- *Sales direction*, which includes exporting, training of customers and technicians, and international technical support

- *General administration direction*, which includes employment and formation, legal businesses, general services, hygiene and safety, infirmary, and systems of remunerations

In the Montpellier factory, which is dedicated to the manufacture of automats, the first stage of production is the control of entry, which is divided into two subsets: the control of the electronic subsets and the control of the machine elements. The raw material deliveries are controlled numerically. When this control is not delegated to the supplier, the batches are checked, then labeled with a reference number, the date, and the identification of the person who performed the inspection. They are then placed in stock with clear references to allow the provisioning of the assembly line.

The second stage is factory production. Subset preparation zones are located at the periphery of the production lines: electric, tire and mechanics, optics, laser, synthetic matter, and Plexiglas. In the center, there are four final lines of assembly, each of which corresponds to a given automat. The frame and all the subsets are assembled manually. For each automat there are, on average, four workstations. The operators are cross-trained and can alternate positions to avoid boredom.

The last stage is final quality control. The apparatuses are tested under real-life conditions with human blood to identify any possible dysfunctions. The automats are initially run using water, to check that all the elements function for a sufficiently long period of time (approximately 800 cycles). The automat then passes to hematological or biochemical development, depending on the model.

DISCUSSION QUESTIONS

1. What are the main reasons for the difficulties encountered by ABX at the time of its development?
2. Is the strategy of ABX clear? Does ABX

have a competitive advantage compared to the other firms in its industry?

3. How can we explain ABX's decision to enter the biochemistry market? Was this decision appropriate?

4. Should the company have instead remained specialized in the sector of hematology and have invested financial resources to effect an increase in price range?

5. Will membership in the Horiba Group allow the development of ABX? Would it not be preferable for ABX to be integrated into a leading group of the IVD market, such as Bayer or Abbott?

6. Does ABX have the means of developing by itself? Does it have to cooperate in a more active way with its competitors? Does it have to accentuate its strategy of OEM? On the contrary, does it have to seek to reinforce its own brands?

CASE STUDY 6

Arcelor and the Global Steel Industry

Frédéric Herlin
Key Account Manager, France, Center for Creative Leadership

AN OUTSTANDING YEAR

In February 2005, Guy Dollé, CEO of the steel giant Arcelor, was working from his office, located at the former Arbed headquarters in Luxembourg City. The large palatial building had been erected in the 1920s to symbolize the importance of the Arbed steel company to the tiny nation of Luxembourg, which was stuck between Germany, France, and Belgium. Eighty years later, Arbed—after significant changes not just to the company but also to a bleeding European steel industry—would become one of three top players, together with Usinor (France) and Aceralia (Spain) to engage in a voluntary merger by forming the Arcelor Group in 2001, at the dawn of the third millennium. See Exhibit 6.1 for a recent ranking of the world's largest steel manufacturers.

Consolidation of the fragmented steel industry, with chronic overcapacity, had been the name of the game for the last five decades in Europe. Now concentration continued on a worldwide scale. Arcelor, squeezed by three powerful iron-ore producers and a similarly concentrated automotive industry—its main client—had to gain scale and scope quickly, in order not to see its margins squeezed from both ends of the value chain.

Dollé, 62, had grown up across the border, in Metz, France. For centuries, ore mining and steel-making had forged the economy of this region called Lorraine—hence his pride about being "born in steel." Before announcing the past year's results to the press, he could look back with similar pride at three years of exacting work at the helm of the group, from its very inception. Undoubtedly, the market turnaround since late 2002, with voracious demand from China that propelled world steel prices to all-time heights, had largely contributed to the success (see Exhibit 6.2). The group's net profit had skyrocketed to €2.3 billion. The balance sheet had also been repaired with a net debt/equity ratio of 20 percent. But Dollé found a deeper reason to rejoice: Almost everything had worked according to his strategic plan. The bold combination of three national steel companies into one appeared fully justified by the management gains, which were achieved and exceeded. More important, these good results gave Arcelor enough financial muscle to roll out the

Case Studies Exhibit 6.1

World Steel Rankings: Crude Steel— Output, 2004 (millions of tons)

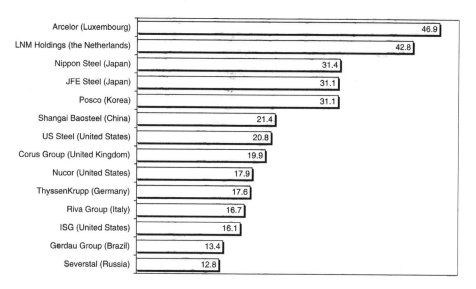

Source: Metal Bulletin, http://www.metalbulletin.com/, accessed September 15, 2005.

rest of the plan. After the group's consolidation and integration—phase one, which took roughly two years to achieve—and the transformation—phase two, which meant putting horizontal structures and practices in place that would allow the myriad of companies (approximately a fully consolidated 450) that formed Arcelor to functionally act as one—he wanted to accelerate the pace toward the third decisive step: global growth.

The group was overexposed in Europe—a declining market for steel—with a dominant market share (35 percent), from which it derived 77 percent of its revenues (see Exhibit 6.3). By contrast most experts predicted that by 2010–15, 80 percent of steel consumption growth would take place in emerging countries. To maintain long-term profitability, Arcelor had no choice but to turn toward high-growth economies. Amid the ongoing concentration in the steel industry, this gave Dollé a clear goal 5 to 10 years from now: making his group one of the four to six global behemoths that would represent 40 percent of total world steel production, each with 80 to 100 million metric tons of annual capacity. It would be a very different company going forward, with doubled output and a much larger international exposure.

Some details in the picture, though, were enough to dampen any feeling of euphoria. Arcelor was about to be dislodged from its world number one ranking by an improbable challenger: Mittal Steel, after Mittal completed its recent acquisition of ISG in the United States (see Appendixes 6.1 and 6.2 for more information on these two competitors). And there were signs from China that the steel pendulum could start to swing back the other way in the year's second half. Dollé knew this to be the moment of truth, when analysts and investors would scrutinize his group's ability to ride out the downward part of the cycle.

Dollé had none of the flamboyant profile of his

Case Studies Exhibit 6.2

World Steel Overview

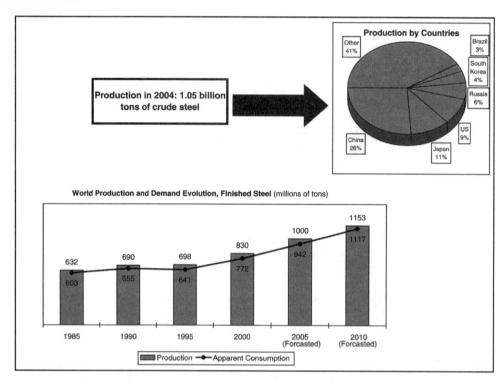

Source: International Iron & Steel Institute, World Steel Institute, World Steel Dynamics, 2005 edition.

industry rival, Lakshmi Mittal. The "steel rajah," whose patiently built empire was a fascinating story of entrepreneurial boldness, made headlines not just in the financial press but also in tabloids that reported the lavishness of his daughter's wedding at a French castle, or the record price tag—US$130 million—paid for the family's neoclassical mansion in London's fashionable Kensington.

By contrast, Arcelor's Dollé, in his shy, sometimes rugged style, initially appeared as an improbable choice to head the merged Arcelor group. After graduating from the elite Ecole Polytechnique in France, he had spent most of his career in field assignments, first as a research engineer, lastly as

the technical director of the coastal plant at Usinor Dunkirk. He quietly made his way to deputy CEO of Usinor—the final merger of the largest French steel producers—in 1999. Only when his impetuous boss, Francis Mer, was called by French president Chirac to take the job of French minister of finance, did the veteran Dollé, hitherto first mate of the Usinor ship, step forward—neither by ambition nor by an appetite for money.

Yet his straightforwardness made him a suitable man for the mission ahead. There was no light at the end of the tunnel when Arcelor was founded. Crisis had hovered about the European steel sector ever since the first oil shock in 1974. Dollé could

Case Studies Exhibit 6.3

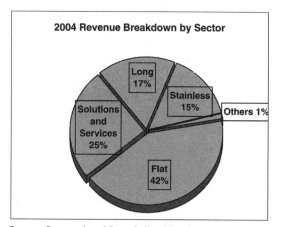

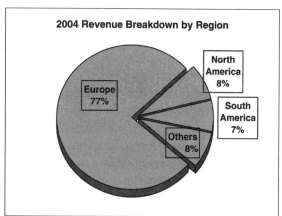

Source: International Iron & Steel Institute, World Steel Institute, World Steel Dynamics, 2005 edition.

carry bad news, as well as significantly downsize the workforce if needed, as he did by the late 1980s as the head of the Sollac steel unit in Lorraine. He was dubbed a "serial decision maker," with a simple, intangible method: first coldly analyze and cross-check data, then, once a conclusion could be inferred from the facts, unflinchingly execute the plan, from an inner sense of duty.

THE HISTORY OF THE EUROPEAN STEEL INDUSTRY: RISE, FALL, AND RESTRUCTURING

Today's European Union of 25 member states had actually been "forged in steel": on April 18, 1951, a proposal made by French foreign minister Robert Schuman was enacted in the Treaty of Paris. It established the European Coal and Steel Community (ECSC), a single market space for steel, coal, iron ore, and scrap for initially six member states: France, Germany, the Benelux countries, and Italy. The common market was officially opened in 1953, under the impulse of Jean Monnet, the other founding father of today's European Union, who

presided over the High Authority of the ECSC. Coupled with postwar reconstruction dynamics, it boosted a dynamic, European-wide competition and proved essential in strengthening the European steelmaking sector.

Two decades of spectacular and continuous expansion ensued. They were stopped short by the oil shock of 1973. A severe decline followed for European steelmakers, faced not only with a drop in demand—just when many had completed massive capacity enhancements with brand-new coastal or greenfield steel plants (France, Spain)—but also concurrent with process innovations such as the electric arc furnace (EAF), which eliminated the need for the hot, costly phase of oxygen-based steel production. Overcapacity caused a quasi-suicidal price war among European steel majors in an effort to fight the low-cost "Bresciani." The Bresciani were small, independent steelmakers from the region of Brescia, Italy, who pioneered the use of minimills and the EAF for basic long carbon steel products and wire rod. To make matters worse, the rise in steel production from emerging countries made European steelmakers less competitive in a glutted world market.

In the late 1970s, various restructuring programs were developed with European Community (EC), state, and regional intervention funds, as capacity and workforce reduction had to be compromised with the traditional strong job-security level in many EC countries. In Luxembourg, for instance, the state voted subsidies for Arbed and other local steel producers to finance "extraordinary" work of general interest to keep staff at work (in the anti-crisis division for example). In France and Belgium, early retirement schemes were granted with state aid, forcefully pensioning workers as young as 50. In regions such as Lorraine, whose lifeblood had always been ore mining and steel-making, this caused social unrest and a long-lasting trauma. The obsolete state of many plants, notably for blast furnaces and rolling mills, became all too obvious. Experts called by governments, such as top executive Jean Gandois, or McKinsey & Co., were severely critical of some production facilities in Belgium, Luxembourg, and France. Isolated efforts were initiated by large European steelmakers to find synergies, under both the search for remedies and the pressure exerted by the EU commission. Launched in 1977, the Davignon plan, named by the EU commissioner who sponsored it, amplified such measures, mostly by encouraging self-limitation or reduction of production capacities, and enacting steel import quotas, as well as price protection mechanisms within the European Union. But the self-discipline imposed on European steel mills became lax with time. Moreover, some countries, such as France, Belgium, and Italy, pumped public funds of all kinds into their steel industries, or even took over the shareholders' role (e.g., the Usinor nationalization in 1981). This severely hampered rival private companies and distorted the rules of the free market as established by the EU Treaty of Rome. External factors worsened the situation: Inflation raised the cost of money needed to modernize plants, and the increase in the cost of raw materials (iron ore, coke) and of energy and transport in the wake of the second oil crisis pushed input prices up. An abysmal period followed (1980–85), which led the EU commission to declare "a state of obvious crisis" in the iron and steel industry, authorizing it to enforce compulsory production quotas.

Painful restructuring efforts continued in the coal and steel sector in the European Union for the rest of the decade. In the 1990s, new technologies and modern production processes became widespread. Old blast furnaces were modernized, closed, or gradually replaced by electric steel plants (which convert scrap by use of the EAF). The sector took off slowly again. The EU commission considered once and for all—except for stringent transition periods granted to new EU member countries—state aid for investment and restructuring in the steel industry to be incompatible with rules of the common market. This led to the privatization of Usinor in France in 1995. Spain, like its European counterparts, had a long history of restructuring and consolidating its own steelmakers. Membership in the European Union committed Spain to further reducing its steel output and overall capacity. Aceralia Corporación Siderúrgica (ACS) was assembled from the reorganization of the CSI group, a 1994 merger between AHV (Bilbao) and Ensidesa. In 1997, the Arbed Group (Luxembourg) established a strategic alliance with Aceralia. In 1999, concentration in the European Union reached a climax with three major moves: British Steel and the Dutch firm Hoogovens joined destinies into the newly created Corus group, the first full, cross-border merger in steel. Usinor (France) took a controlling stake in Cockerill-Sambre, the main Belgian producer. In Germany, ThyssenKrupp AG was formed by the merger of Thyssen with Friedrich Krupp.

As a result, between 1975 and 2000, approximately 700,000 jobs had vanished in the EU steel industry, a 70 percent decline in employment (see Exhibit 6.4). This painful medicine made the patient thinner but kept him alive.

Case Studies Exhibit 6.4

Employment in the Steel Industry, Selected Countries, 1975–2000 (thousands of employees)

	1975	1980	1985	1990	1995	2000
Country						
European Union	958	92	561	434	321	277
Japan	447	380	349	305	252	197
United States	457	399	238	204	171	151

Source: International Iron and Steel Institute, http://www.worldsteel.org, accessed on September 15, 2005.

This was the background against which Arbed, Aceralia, and Usinor decided to merge.

THE EARLY YEARS: A STEEL DISCIPLINE

When the group was formed, an obvious objective was to achieve synergies among the group's units, and thereby significant costs savings. The implementation of synergies started immediately after the merger was approved by the EU commission. Annual cost savings—€200 million at the end of 2002—were to reach €700 million in 2006. Major synergy programs included:

- A strong focus on the purchasing function, which favoured total cost of ownership (TCO) reduction in a bid to bring costs down, and a base of best-in-class suppliers whose performance would be regularly reviewed. In the beginning of 2003, the group had formed Arcelor Purchasing, a distinct legal entity with the mandate of negotiating purchases for all its companies.
- A progressive optimization and reconfiguration of upstream production facilities. The new management team had conducted several studies, from which its inland (landlocked) blast furnace sites in Europe appeared to be no

longer viable. As a consequence, their costly relining would not be financed, and they would all close during the 2004–10 period. The decision was announced years ahead in order to efficiently manage the necessary, socially painful transitions. Future investments would focus on the more competitive large-scale coastal mills. Downstream production (cold rolling, high-value-added coated products) would be organized on a strategy of specialization.

Compared to the three founding companies on a stand-alone basis, the merger enabled capital expenditure savings close to €350 million over four years (2002–5). Synergies would also extend beyond the group in the form of alliances, whether local or global, in geographic areas—or expertise domains, or both—where Arcelor was not in a dominant position. Through one of its founders (Usinor) the group had signed a global strategic alliance with Nippon Steel, which was reaffirmed following the formation of Arcelor. Its main focus was the automotive industry, from where it moved on to cooperation in stainless steel and construction steel. Arcelor and Nippon Steel would exchange licenses to expand their respective product portfolios. They also carried out studies along with automakers to design innovative steel solutions for new vehicles. In the stainless steel sector, the cooperation led to the development of special products for exhaust systems. Nippon Steel and Arcelor also forged an agreement with Tata Steel (Tisco) of India to better reach the Indian automotive industry. The same approach was used later in China with Baosteel.

Another decisive departure from past practices was "management by margins." Consistent with the promotion of new, high-value products, and instructed by the woes of previous price wars in Europe, the Arcelor management team had made a clear choice of prioritizing margin over volume. What Guy Dollé called the "Arcelor effect" (but which was also enforced by its European competitors) was that as soon as a drop in apparent consumption (real consumption + inventory buildup) was detected, the group would cut back production to maintain high prices for its products, and wait for inventory levels to come back to normal. In February 2005, a slowdown initiative was launched, to reduce the output of the European units in line with a faltering EU demand (–14 percent in flat products which include sheets, plates, and slabs of steel), due to high inventory levels, and the softening of real steel consumption. A reduction in output of roughly 1.5 million tons was decided. A set of drastic measures included the stoppage of a blast furnace in Stahlwerke Bremen, a much lower output at the hot (liquid) phase in Cockerill Sambre, Belgium, and a prolonged standstill of a blast furnace of EKO Stahl.

GOING FOR GLOBAL GROWTH

In 2004, the group posted €30 billion in revenues and employed 95,000 people in 60 countries. It was the number one steel producer in Europe and South America, with a total output of 47 million tons of crude steel. But it was largely absent from North America, Russia, and Asia, except for a number of joint ventures with local producers, essentially in its core market: flat carbon steels to the automotive industry, for which it was the world leading supplier with a 15 percent market share. Its steel was used in one out of every two cars in Europe. Arcelor's other principal markets were general industry, the construction sector, household appliances, and packaging.

Compared with its counterpart in the supplier and customer industries, concentration had always been weak in the steel industry. The top 10 companies supplied less than 30 percent of world production, while the top 10 automobile producers had 95 percent of the world market (see Exhibit 6.5) and the top 10 manufacturers of electric household appliances 80 percent. This resulted in a structural trend toward lower prices for most steel products, as customers were able to play one steelmaker against another. Despite mergers (in the creation of ThyssenKrupp, Corus, and Arcelor), and vigorous restructuring and cost-reduction exercises, a significant proportion of achieved savings had been absorbed by the steady fall of sales prices on world markets.

Against this backdrop, Guy Dollé and his chairman, Joseph Kinsch, wanted to see in the brighter skies of 2004 a tipping point, not just in terms of the cyclical nature of the activity, but also in terms of structural industry trends. The merger of Mittal and ISG pointed, in a way, in the same direction as the recent strengthening of Arcelor in Brazil and Latin America. For steelmaking to achieve sustainable profitability, only big players were likely to survive.

Biggest of all was China. Its GDP had grown by more than 8 percent annually over the last two decades. In 2003 and 2004, China had increased its steel production by 40 and 50 million tons, respectively—the equivalent in each year of two years of production for the Arcelor group, and almost half the European production. This increase of more than 20 percent annually in two consecutive years made China the foremost steel-producing nation, with more than one-quarter of world production. From the end of 2003, this situation had

Case Studies Exhibit 6.5

Industry Concentration: Comparing Steel with Other Sectors (10 top producers worldwide)

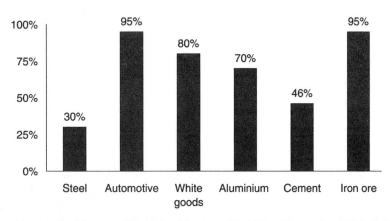

Source: International Iron & Steel Institute, World Steel Institute, World Steel Dynamics, 2005 edition.

generated a very strong demand for raw materials, ore, coke, and maritime freight on the world markets, and hence spectacular price increases for both raw materials and steel products. Nevertheless, the highest price for steel after indexing for inflation reached the level of only 1991—which was still below historical peaks.

The year 2004 had been one of expansion for Arcelor. It now had a majority stake (73 percent) in CST of Brazil, and a brand-new plant had been inaugurated in Vega do Sul. A 73 percent stake was also held in Acindar, Argentina. In the United Kingdom it had acquired the hot-rolled steel sheet-piling business the of Anglo-Dutch Corus Group. In Belgium, foundations were laid for a new electric steel shop in Charleroi, with an investment of €240 million. In China, a joint venture with Nippon Steel and Shanghai-based Baosteel had been launched to seize the tremendous growth opportunities offered by the Chinese market. The new operation, located in Shanghai next to Baosteel's upstream production facilities, was to operate at an annual capacity of 1.7 million tons of flat carbon steel, of which 900,000

tons consisted of cold-rolled steel and 800,000 tons consisted of dip zinc-galvanized sheet.

Arcelor was irreversibly engaged in pursuing global growth. It focused on fast-developing economies: the so-called BRIC group of emerging countries (Brazil, Russia, India, China). Guy Dollé liked to relabel the acronym—first coined by Goldman Sachs—BRICET, adding eastern Europe and Turkey to the list. The declared objective was to increase the group's exposure in these countries to 50 percent of revenues versus the 23 percent of today. Another reason to invest there, although Arcelor had no declared intention to integrate vertically, was that the growth potential of BRIC was often coupled to an easy access to large sources of raw materials (iron ore, coal, natural gas), thereby minimizing transport and energy costs in a time of skyrocketing prices (see Exhibit 6.6). The group's financial objective was to achieve an average pretax return on capital employed of 15 percent over the cycle (three years).

Arcelor also aimed to significantly reduce its gearing ratio (net financial debt/equity). This was

Case Studies Exhibit 6.6

BRIC Growth Potential

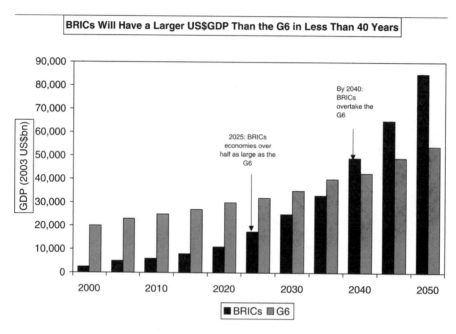

Source: Goldman Sachs Global Economics Paper Number 99: Dreaming with BRICs: The Path to 2050, http://www. gs.com/insight/research/reports/99.pdf,

effectively achieved at the end of 2004, with a ratio of 0.20, despite a major acquisition financed through an increase in capital. The debt had come down from €6 billion in 2001 to only approximately €1 billion, thanks mainly to strong cash flow and profits linked to higher steel prices. The debt level objective was a 30 percent to 50 percent gearing ratio—the group could therefore afford plenty of external growth. It was prepared to spend at least US$3.5 billion in the next two years on acquisitions. It was keen to purchase Erdemir in Turkey and Kryvorizhstal in Ukraine, two state-controlled steel companies due to be privatized in October 2005. But these companies were also eyed by other industry leaders, in particular Mittal Steel. Each auction was valued at up to $2 billion.

The main strategic guidelines for the group could be articulated as follows:

• Further optimize its European production tool through synergies. For flat carbon steel, this implied the phased transfer of the (hot) liquid production phase to the more cost-efficient coastal sites (Sidmar, near Antwerp, and Dunkirk), with the closure of a first continental blast furnace in Liège, Belgium, scheduled in May 2005. For the Stainless Steel Division, construction of a new steelmaking plant (Carinox) in Charleroi, Belgium, was to be completed soon, upstream of the existing hot rolling mill of Carlam. This new investment concentrated the production of stainless steel, allowing economies of scale, and the closure of two less-competitive plants.

- Manage the business portfolio by pulling out of nonstrategic activities, as was already done for small welded tubes and stainless steel activities in the United States and Thailand. What had started as a compulsory divestment from certain production units for the EU commission to authorize the creation of the group was now a continuous exercise of cleaning and optimizing the portfolio of activities throughout the world.

- Propose the same product and service offering worldwide in response to the request of global customers. A good example was the construction of a cold rolling and galvanization plant for automotive products in Shanghai, China, as a joint venture (12 percent stake) with Baosteel and Nippon Steel.

- Enrich the portfolio of products, thanks to synergies between products and markets in different sectors, and through well-focused R & D efforts. For instance, the group had created a special team—BCS: Building and Construction Support—to better serve the construction industry, trying to combine the offerings of the flat carbon and long carbon sectors. This resulted in new solutions for the construction industry, such as multistory structures employing beams and composite formwork from cold-profiled sheet.

- Accompany customers through their development, best illustrated by Arcelor working closely with carmakers, starting at the vehicle design stage.

- Ensure growth through targeted acquisitions that reinforced Arcelor's geographic presence and market shift, away from Europe. The best illustration of this strategic move was its brilliant execution in South America, where

within three years, Arcelor's South American activities grew from 4 percent to 13 percent of the group's overall turnover and delivered more than 25 percent of the group's profits. Due to this success, Guy Dollé liked to label Arcelor a "European-Brazilian" steelmaking group.

ARCELOR'S EUROPEAN COMPETITION

The merger that created Corus brought together Hoogovens' highly efficient plant near Amsterdam and a clutch of British Steel plants of less than optimal size. It provided a welcome rationalization of the sector, but the company's subsequent attempt to merge with CSN, a Brazilian steelmaker, fell apart. A few months later a split developed within Corus over plans to sell its Dutch aluminium operations to Pechiney, in France. Corus's Dutch supervisory board objected to the sale on the grounds that the proceeds would be used to prop up the ailing British business. The arrival of Philippe Varin, a long-serving Pechiney executive, as chief executive in May 2003 ushered in greater harmony and faster progress in solving the company's problems. Jobs were cut, UK operations were concentrated on three main plants, and productivity was increased. Some warned, however, that if Corus did not establish a global growth strategy it could lose its independence. It ranked as the number eight steel producer in 2004, with an output of 19.9 million tons.

ThyssenKrupp Stahl (TKS) was another, though somewhat atypical, example of the "second league" players. As the tenth-largest steelmaker in the world, it produced far less than Mittal or Arcelor (17.6 million metric tons of crude steel in 2004), but it was a world leader for stainless steel and held fourth place in the world's quality flat steel market. Although accounting for about two-thirds of profits in 2004, steel was only one of five company branches, sitting alongside everything from shipyards to elevators and car parts to bearings. Executives trumpeted the group's diversified nature, saying its conglomerate status protected it better from the vagaries of the steel cycles. But analysts said it rubbed the other way as well—it benefited less from the peaks of the cycle with businesses such as car parts, where it was an end user. The Duisburg plant also illustrated both the company's strengths and its weaknesses. Having restructured all its European operations into one site following the merger between Thyssen and Krupp in 1999, the group was ahead of its rivals in cost reductions. But, having done the hard work, it had little flab left to cut, and by having one main central plant, it lacked the flexibility of other groups. For instance, TKS had decided to build a 4.5 million ton steel-sheet-producing plant with CVRD in Brazil, due to start production in 2008. But because it came several years after Arcelor opened a similar site (Vega do Sul), many analysts felt it came too late.

TKS illustrated another point about European steelmakers: With their high production costs and wages, they could not compete internationally in mass-produced steel. Innovation and added value were necessary because high-quality basic steel was available from emerging countries at lower prices. The only hope for European companies that could not go for global growth was to concentrate on special, higher-grade steel.

Two fundamental tendencies could therefore be observed on the international steel market: consolidation into larger corporate units aimed at creating greater efficiency, particularly with regard to overhead costs, sales structure, and purchasing, and achieving global leadership with market niches.

Other companies of respectable size followed in the European rankings: Riva of Italy, Germany's Salzgitter (the largest single supplier of flat steel to Mercedes), and Austria's Voestalpine. By taking over Mannesmann AG tube works, Salzgitter had

been able to expand its own pipe business by many times in one blow, while benefiting from the strength of the Mannesmann brand.

A new round of consolidation was expected, and most of these midsized producers looked at each other as potential partners. All of them denied the existence of concrete talks and officially rejected the idea in the short term. But the perspective of not being part of the future "big players" club of four to six steel giants by 2010 put pressure on them to join the merger carousel—or lose out.

Arcelor, because it had already achieved critical world size at its inception, and focused as it was on its BRICET strategy, was not interested in another large European deal. "One must be out of his mind to invest in Europe," Dollé said bluntly. Acquiring a large target in its main perimeter, the EU countries, was neither attractive (mature market) nor realistic, given the fact that the EU commission would prohibit any merger resulting in an industry concentration level exceeding a specific threshold, by the firm's market share or by the so-called Herfindahl-Hirschmann Index (HHI), an internationally recognized measure of market concentration.

THE ARCELOR ORGANIZATION

From its inception, the company was organized into four main divisions, or core activities:

- Flat carbon steel
- Long carbon steel
- Stainless steel
- Distribution, transformation, trading (DTT)

FLAT CARBON STEEL

An empire within the empire, the flat carbon steel (FCS) sector provided the group with more than half its turnover. It had approximately 10 percent of the world market share for the production and sale of flat carbon. It generated more than €16 billion of revenue in 2004. FCS covered the full range of flat carbon steel, including slabs, heavy plates, hot-rolled coils, cold-rolled coils and metallic and organic coated steel, as well as formed and welded blanks. These products were used in the automotive sector and in industrial applications such as construction, civil and mechanical engineering, processing industries, household appliances, and packaging. See Appendix 6.3 for a primer on the steel industry.

Organized by geographical production clusters in five business units (north business unit for Germany and Flanders; center business unit for Belgian Wallonia and northern and eastern France; south business unit for southern France, Spain, and Italy; Brazil business unit; and packaging business unit), FCS was structured into only two divisions in marketing terms: Arcelor Auto, which specialized in supplying the automotive industry, and Arcelor FCS Commercial, which served all other industrial customers.

The packaging business unit, Arcelor Packaging International (API), was the world leader in packaging steel, in terms of both volume and technological sophistication. In an increasingly mature market threatened by competing materials such as aluminum and plastics, API was developing new products and working with customers to build and defend the role of steel as an ideal packaging solution. It had plans to address all participants in the chain, such as designers, bottlers and canners, and distributors, emphasizing the reusability and food safety of steel packaging. A new rapid-cooling process for continuous annealing reduced the weight of steel packaging, which made it more attractive.

LONG CARBON STEEL

The long carbon steel division comprised three main specialties (heavy long products, light long products, and wire-drawing activities). The main outlet for long products was the construction sector, as well as the railway industry.

STAINLESS STEEL

The stainless steel division incorporated the production, processing, and distribution of stainless steel flat and long products, nickel alloys, and special plates. It produced virtually the entire range of stainless steel products and alloys in Europe, Asia, and the Americas. Key markets were domestic appliances, automotive exhausts, and construction.

DISTRIBUTION, TRANSFORMATION, TRADING (DTT)

With 11,000 employees and a presence in more than 50 countries, the Arcelor group's distribution, transformation, trading sector (DTT) distributed and finished a full range of flat and long products and "steel solutions" for custom projects. Although the majority of products sold were supplied by the group's plants, DTT would source between 30 percent and 35 percent of its needs from third parties. It was to be renamed A3S—Arcelor Steel Solutions and Services—to emphasize its customer-driven and value-added orientation. The activity was built around an impressive network of depots, service centers, and manufacturing sites, located for the most part in western Europe—its historical market. It intended to grow in central and eastern Europe, where it had begun to invest. It had a business unit specializing in supplying custom steel solutions for the construction of major civil engineering, public works, and offshore projects, such as port facilities, underground parking lots, and tunnels.

A STRATEGIC MARKET: THE AUTOMOTIVE INDUSTRY

As its top global supplier by far, Arcelor had to defend a stronghold: the automotive market for high-grade flat carbon steel products. Maintaining its supremacy implied joint developments with customers and led to long-term partnerships. This had a short-term downside: a larger share of annual or multiannual sales contracts in a year of sharp increases in spot prices (for products with delivery lead times less than three months), with limited immediate gains. The trade-off, though, was a growth path more stable and sustainable through cycle downturns.

A global offering benefited global automotive customers in economies of scale and reduced costs and financial risks. When it did not have a significant presence, in Brazil, for example, Arcelor would provide its Extragal Z technology (galvanized steel for external auto components) to automakers throughout the world via local joint ventures: with Dofasco in Canada and the United States, Borcelik in Turkey, Severstal in Russia, Tata Steel in India, Nippon Steel and Baosteel in China, and so on.

Arcelor would also set up cross-disciplinary "customer teams" to provide technical assistance to automakers from the preliminary project phase right through car production engineering, with resident engineers based at its main customers' auto manufacturing facilities.

Arcelor also liked to emphasize its indirect contribution to the Kyoto Protocol carbon dioxide reduction targets by helping reduce the weight of automobiles. In particular, its research programs were aimed at the development of ultrahigh tensile steel, which would combine very high tensile strength and increased ease of processing. This steel enabled module weight reduction in the order of 15 percent compared with the high tensile steel it was replacing.

SOUTH AMERICA: THE BEST OF BRIC

The group had been present in Brazil for more than 80 years through Belgo-Mineira, a subsidiary of Arbed, one of the founding companies of Arcelor. Prior to the Second World War, Belgo accounted for 49 percent of the steel produced in Brazil. It was the largest producer of long carbon steel in South America, specializing in drawn wires, rods, and rolled steel products for the civil engineering and construction sectors. In 2001, it had entered the capital of Acindar, an Argentinian steel producer, increasing its participation to 73 percent four years later. In 2002, Arcelor also took a 25 percent stake in Companhia Siderúrgica de Tubarão (CST), in Brazil, the world leader for slabs (semifinished products for flat carbon steel production), with a 20 percent market share. Arcelor would later gain control of CST, increasing its share to 73 percent, and diversify its production into hot-rolled coils. Earlier that year, it inaugurated a greenfield facility in Vega do Sul, in south Brazil, specializing in cold rolling, pickling, and galvanization. One of the largest investments carried out by Arcelor since its creation, Vega do Sul had an annual capacity of 880,000 tons, which was intended mainly for the automotive industry and household appliance manufacturers. The facility received its hot-rolled coils from a CST mill. In 2005 Arcelor finally considered combining all its Brazilian businesses and shareholdings (CST, Vega do Sul, and Belgo) into a single company. After successive share conversions and exchange operations, the new entity, to be named Arcelor do Brasil, would be listed on the São Paulo stock exchange in the fourth quarter of 2005. It would employ 14,500 people, generate revenues of 12.5 billion reais (US$5.5 billion), and produce 11 million metric tons of steel, half of which were intended for the export business.

The result of the consolidation was that it established Arcelor not only as the leading player in the Mercosur market—way above rivals CSN and Gerdau—but also as a highly competitive exporter to the North American downstream market. The group planned to invest a further $4 billion over the next five years in Brazil. It hoped to quickly reach 18 million tons of steel-producing capacity in South America. Guy Dollé was openly enthusiastic about the South American steel "Eldorado," as a blend of increasing consumption, lowering costs, and capitalizing on the availability of raw materials, skilled management, and state-of-the-art production facilities.

NORTH AMERICA: ARCELOR ON THE LOOKOUT

Back in 1950, the U.S. steel industry produced almost 60 percent of the Western world's raw steel. On Wall Street, investors even consulted an index of blast-furnace activity to get a hint on how the stock market might respond. But 50 years later, fortunes had changed dramatically, and more than 30 large U.S. steelmakers had declared bankruptcy in recent years. Out of a total of 1,054 million tons of crude steel produced worldwide in 2004, the United States contributed less than 10 percent (98 million tons). Only 1 out of every 1,000 U.S. workers still worked in steel. Three key reasons could be attributed to the decline: legacy costs (i.e., pension obligations), competition from minimills, and massive imports and recurrent trade protection.

LEGACY COSTS

An ever-shrinking number of active workers were charged with making profits sufficient to support the present and future of an ever-growing number of retirees and dependents. This gradually became a demographic nightmare for steel companies. The foremost example was Bethlehem Steel.

Every time it had to close an outmoded capacity, it accelerated the retirement of long-standing employees and put a new burden on a pension plan that by the 1970s the company had already acknowledged was underfunded. As a result, Bethlehem Steel went bankrupt in 2002 and its six plants were absorbed by ISG, to be acquired two years later by Mittal Steel. U.S. Steel, which remained number seven in the world in 2004, with 20.8 million tons of crude steel produced, survived thanks to a better handling of its legacy costs. For decades it would make aggressive contributions to its pension fund, book these as the deductible expenses they were, and exit with a reduced tax bill.

COMPETITION FROM MINIMILLS

For years, the large U.S. integrated steelmakers looked down on the minimill phenomenon, on the grounds that minimills produced low-quality steel. Yet Nucor, the most successful minimill firm, had been relentlessly advancing to become America's second largest steelmaker—the world's number nine in 2004—with a production of 17.9 million tons. Although minimill output was still mostly low-grade and low margin, the technology for making higher-grade steels in minimills was advancing rapidly.

MASSIVE IMPORTS AND RECURRENT TRADE PROTECTION

Thanks to powerful lobbying, the U.S. steel industry had been able to put off a much-needed consolidation, while Europe and Latin America were forging ahead. Domestic demand helped, growing by nearly 7 percent a year in the 1990s, after almost no growth during the 1980s. U.S. steelmakers did not stay idle, spending billions in plant and equipment modernization over two decades and shedding more than 300,000 workers, nearly three-quarters of their labor force. Productivity grew at twice the average rate for all American manufacturing, and aligned itself with that of Germany and Japan, the world's best, with less than 4 man-hours per ton of steel—down from about 10 man-hours in 1980. Yet U.S. steel prices remained higher than world market prices, attracting a rush in imports. In March 2002, tariffs on imported steel as high as 30 percent were imposed by President George W. Bush. Canada and Mexico were exempt from the tariffs because of penalties the United States would face under NAFTA agreements. Immediately after tariffs were filed, the European Union announced that it would impose retaliatory tariffs on the United States, thus risking the start of a major trade war. The tariffs were originally scheduled to remain in effect until 2005. They were lifted in December 2003, after the WTO ruled against them, saying there was no evidence of dumping and that the tariffs represented an illegal barrier to free trade. Both the issuing and the lifting of the tariffs stirred controversy in the United States. Some of the president's political opponents, such as Representative Dick Gephardt, criticized the plan for not going far enough. For some of the president's conservative allies, imposing the tariffs was a step away from Bush's commitment to free trade. Critics also contended—with some truth—that the tariffs would harm consumers and U.S. businesses that relied on steel imports, in particular automobile manufacturers (in a key swing state, Michigan), and that it would eventually cut more jobs than it would save in the U.S. steel industry—a heavy importer of foreign steel itself. There was a widespread belief on all sides of the debate, confirmed by top Bush administration officials, that politics played a role in the decision to impose tariffs, namely, that the large and important rust belt swing states of Pennsylvania and West Virginia would benefit from the tariffs.

After the Bush administration rescinded the tariffs, steel prices did not come down, as demand was picking up quickly. The price differential on the U.S. market subsisted. For example, a ton of hot-rolled coil steel would sell for a spot price of $693 in the United States in January 2005, whereas the same quantity could be purchased for $575 elsewhere. This seriously harmed some U.S. steel-consuming industries, such as auto-parts suppliers. By September 2005, Delphi Corp. was near bankruptcy.

This was the context in which global players Mittal and Arcelor had to devise their strategy for the U.S. market, the world's second largest after China.

In 1998, Mittal made its first big inroad when it bought an integrated producer called Inland Steel. It reorganized Inland plants to use slab from its ISPAT facilities in Mexico, which lifted production and reduced costs. The acquisition of ISG six years later would allow Mittal to deliver further economies of scale: The new consolidated U.S. operation would own three mills clustered on Lake Michigan, making it easier to centralize management, consolidate material delivery, and optimize production. Thanks to size, the combined company would also have access to larger, lower-cost supplies of ore, coke, and coal.

Arcelor, like Mittal, was looking for assets in the United States, but because of the flat demand for steel, it was patiently waiting for easy pickups at the next cycle downturn. Meanwhile, it was firmly engaged in a niche, high-value strategy, with the objective to become the preferred steel supplier to the North American automotive industry. It had a well-established partnership with the Canadian steel producer Dofasco. In 2005 they were in the final stages to jointly build and operate a greenfield galvanizing line that would supply the growing automotive industry in the United States. With a planned annual capacity of 500,000 metric tons of steel, the facility would produce galvanized products for the visible parts of car bodies, including Arcelor's proprietary product, Extragal. The project grew from the success of an identical galvanizing line at Dofasco's Hamilton operations, which supplied Detroit car manufacturers across the Canadian border.

THE DERAILMENT OF RAW MATERIALS AND ENERGY PRICES

From 2003 onward, input costs for the steel industry literally exploded, affecting iron ore, coke, coking coal, alloying elements (nickel), scrap, as well as energy. In 2005, freight rates were up fourfold compared to 2002. The unabated rise in the price of oil and gas also pushed up the cost of running coking plants, an essential component of the hot-metal route.

The "cold"-metal route, involving steel scrap as a raw material, was also affected. About 42 percent of the steel produced worldwide in 2004 was generated from recycled steel scrap. Because steel is fully recyclable, it can be used over and over again with no downgrading of its qualities. Its magnetic properties make it simple to extract from other materials for recycling. But scrap prices had also rocketed for the last two years.

The most serious threat was to ore: A three-way oligopoly ruled the world's iron ore market with a combined share of 70 percent, whereas the five largest steelmakers, in contrast, controlled only 20 percent of the crude steel market. Around February every year, the three big Brazilian and Australian iron-ore-mining companies would sit down with large European or Japanese steelmakers to thrash out a price for the year. Once settled, the new price was usually accepted across the global steel industry. It had been a comfortable, stable system, and for most of the 1990s, the price of iron ore barely moved. In February 2004, negotiations led to 19 percent increases. The system went out of balance in 2005. "For 20 years, the iron miners have been in a bear market, suffering from under-investment and being pushed around by the steel mills," said an industry expert. "But because of the demand from China, they are now calling the shots." Although China was the biggest consumer and importer of ore, and

the fact that its biggest steel company, Shanghai-based Baosteel, had been negotiating on behalf of the China Iron and Steel Association representing the 13 main Chinese steelmakers, it had little or no influence over the price negotiations with CVRD and Rio Tinto. The China Iron and Steel Association had long tried to organize a cartel among local players similar to the Japanese, to allow the mainland to use its buying power to negotiate lower prices, but thus far had failed. Getting the Chinese steel mills to act in concert, according to a China-based analyst, was like "herding grasshoppers." Baosteel, the biggest producer in China, accounted for less than 10 percent of output.

CVRD (Companhia Vale do Rio Doce) from Brazil, the biggest iron-ore-mining group, and Rio Tinto were both able to seal a 71.5 percent increase in the price of iron ore from Nippon Steel. BHP Billiton was believed to have been pushing for a 90 percent increase on the basis that, due to soaring shipping costs, it was now significantly cheaper for Asian companies to buy ore from Australia.

Baosteel, as well as South Korea's giant steelmaker POSCO, swiftly fell in line with Nippon Steel.

Arcelor first protested loudly at the price increases negotiated between CVRD and Nippon Steel. Together with its European colleagues, it would describe the increase as "totally unreasonable and disproportionate to market conditions, which are not significantly different from 2004." But for all his alacrity, Guy Dollé could only bite the bullet and eventually accept the price hike of 71.5 percent.

CHINA: OPPORTUNITY OR THREAT?

In recent years, China had emerged as both the largest producer and the largest market for steel. Its 1.3 billion people demanded more goods such as cars and kitchen appliances. The country frantically built more bridges, housing blocks, and railway networks. New steel mills cropped up all over the country. Chinese steel production was forecast to total 346 million tons in 2005, up from 273 million tons the previous year, an increase of 27 percent. Such a rate of production was unsustainable. Although Chinese demand for steel had been growing at 30 percent year-over-year during some months of 2004, it was expected to slow to under half that in 2005. Chinese steel prices had already started falling sharply by late 2004, increasing pressure for a shakeout in an industry whose rapid, fragmented growth had been a bellwether for government concerns about an overheating economy. Rising Chinese steel production had an impact on the global economy, driving up prices for imported commodities and shipping freight rates. This left the Chinese government with a dilemma. Officials did not want China to become a large exporter of steel because of the demands on natural resources. However, large closures might affect social stability. The National Development and Reform Commission (NDRC), a key economic ministry, called for closures of smaller, marginal steel mills. Chinese state banks were on notice from Beijing to extend loans solely on a commercial basis, and not to keep unprofitable local steel producers afloat. "A steel factory may be the main employer in a town, and local bank managers would be under intense pressure to offer support whenever needed," explained a Shanghai-based market specialist. The NDRC plan called for a global reduction in annual production to 300 million tons and a cut in the number of manufacturers. The biggest beneficiaries of the NDRC move would be the country's 10 largest manufacturers, led by Baosteel in Shanghai, whose aggregate share of production would rise from 30 percent to 50 percent by 2010 and 70 percent by 2020 under the plan. But some experts greeted the plan with skepticism as a relic of the planned economy that would be impossible to enforce. Ji Yuheng, a steel

industry executive, said that "neither consolidation nor massive closures" were likely for small mills in the short term.

It was in this context that Arcelor contemplated taking a stake worth up to $247 million in Laiwu Steel—a Chinese midsized producer based in the eastern Chinese province of Shandong. Laiwu Steel was expected to double its capacity of beams used in construction with the opening of a new plant at the end of 2005. But the Chinese government's new blueprint for steel, although forcing substantial consolidation of domestic producers and limiting investment in new production capacity to those foreign companies with annual production of more than 10 million tons—some 15 companies—appeared to rule out a controlling stake by foreign groups. It stated, "When foreign companies invest in China's steel industry, in principle, foreign control is not permitted."[1] Li Xinchuang, vice president of China Metallurgical Industrial Planning and Research Institute, which had been closely involved in writing the policy, specified, "There is no specific upper limit on foreign investment. However, the principle is not to let them in as majority holders, especially for the top five primary steel manufacturers." This had to be put in perspective with the declared policy of the Chinese government to generate three world champions in every strategic industry.

Guy Dollé and his team, learning about the new limitation policy, could not immediately decide whether to settle for a minority stake in Laiwu Steel, walk away from the deal, or try to work around the guidelines. Some analysts indeed believed there could be room to maneuver. The policy document statement that foreign takeovers were banned "in principle" could allow Chinese officials to approve some takeovers if the deals brought added benefits. In particular, the authorities might be interested if the foreign company agreed to bring advanced steelmaking technologies to China.

However, Dollé's main concern about China was

its impact on the global steel market: By demanding more and more iron ore to make more steel, and at the same time putting downward pressure on steel prices, China, which had been the engine for high steel prices in the last three years, could make 2006 a rather unhelpful combination of lower steel prices and higher raw material costs. This would be a sure recipe for a cyclical downturn, when some industry analysts were predicting a slump in steel prices already by the second half of 2005.

THE CHALLENGE OF SUSTAINABLE DEVELOPMENT

Arcelor's sustainable development policy was built on the classic definition of the Brundtland report (1987):[2] "development that meets the needs of the present without compromising the ability of future generations to meet their own needs." It was based on the four Ps—profit, people, planet, and partners —which rested on eight principles: profitable growth from steel as a core business, risk management and safety, protection and preservation of the environment, open dialogue with stakeholders, skills development, innovation, strict compliance with existing rules of corporate governance, and responsible citizenship.

The main developmental issue that Arcelor faced—together with other steelmakers—was that out of all heavy industry sectors, steelmaking was one of the biggest sources of carbon dioxide emission, a major contributor to the greenhouse gas effect. With some 50 terawatt hours annual needs (half electricity, half natural gas), Arcelor was also among the top 10 consumers for both commodities in Europe, and the first or second largest in Spain, Luxembourg, and Belgium. However, it generated some 28 percent of its own power needs from the gases produced by the plants.

Carbon dioxide emissions in the steel industry derived mainly from the coal used to make the coke used as a reducing agent and energy source for the blast furnace. In the case of Arcelor, direct emissions of carbon dioxide from iron making amounted to 42.5 metric tons, or about 1 ton per ton of liquid steel. But if one took into account indirect sources such as power generation, total emissions reached 61.3 metric tons or about 1.5 tons per ton of liquid steel. Arcelor had reduced its emissions by 21 percent since 1990, surpassing by far the average 8 percent reduction agreed in the Kyoto Protocol by the European Union. The group, however, felt it was reaching the limits of what could be achieved within the current state of technology and market constraints. One of the major drivers had been the migration of steel production from the blast furnace to the electric arc furnace using recycled scrap. Given the current recycling rates (which determined the quantity of available scrap) and hot-metal quality considerations, further improvements seemed out of reach without any breakthrough innovation in the production process.

Arcelor faced another hurdle in complying with the EU rules to implement the Kyoto Protocol. Allocated country by country, the imposed quotas for gas emission potentially jeopardized the capacity synergies planned across the group, or at least complicated the exercise. And quota overruns, which could in principle be compensated by trading additional carbon dioxide emission rights, could prove very expensive.

Arcelor's official stance stressed the risk that "overzealous" environmental regulation could damage the capability of the European steel industry to compete on a viable basis against steelmakers in the rest of the world, particularly American competitors. It considered the European directive governing carbon dioxide emissions too harsh and discriminatory for European steel firms and had therefore appealed it with the European Court of Justice. The judgment was only to be known by late 2005.

Arcelor, like several of Europe's largest steel manufacturers, had nonetheless responded to the EU commission's call for cleaner steel production methodologies. It would lead a cohort of 47 European companies and organizations into an agreement to launch a cooperative R & D initiative aimed at searching for new steel production processes that would drastically reduce carbon dioxide and other greenhouse gas emissions generated by the process. The consortium, called Ultra Low CO_2 Steelmaking, or ULCOS, would examine a set of concepts for reducing these emissions by 30 percent to 70 percent—an ambitious requirement given the starting situation (up to two tons of carbon dioxide per ton of steel for the integrated route). The first concept solutions were expected by 2010.

EPILOGUE

On June 30, 2006, the Arcelor Board of Directors voted to accept a takeover offer by Mittal Steel Company for $33 billion. The takeover offer, assuming that it receives regulatory approval, would create the biggest steelmaker in the world with about ten percent of the global market. The combined company would produce 100 million tons of crude steel a year and employ more than 320,000 people.

Steel analysts are generally in favor of the Mittal bid, as it is thought that the two companies are complimentary, with few geographic overlaps. The new company is scheduled to be called Arcelor-Mittal. While this potential merger produces a very large company, the strategic issues raised in this case are all afoot: to expand into the China market, to stay ahead of the curve in an ever-changing industry, and to find the best strategic alternatives in the never-ending quest for growth and prosperity that their shareholders desire.

NOTES

1. ME Steel, http://www.mesteel.com/cgi-bin/w3-msql/goto_smotw.htm?u=http://steelmillsoftheworld.com/news/newsdisplay_cntry.asp&v=slno&s=2998 (accessed July 25, 2005).

2. The Brundtland Report, also known as Our Common Future, alerted the world to the need for sustainable economic development that would not deplete natural resources or harm the environment. Federal Office for Sustainable Development, http://www.are.admin.ch/are/en/nachhaltig/international_uno/unterseite02330/ *\(access date May 12, 2005).

DISCUSSION QUESTIONS

1. If you were Guy Dollé, would you decide to pursue the minority share in Laiwu Steel, or would you instead opt to walk away from the deal entirely, or to perhaps try to work around the existing guidelines?
2. What strategy seems most appropriate to handle the demand in the United States?
3. What challenges will the Kyoto Protocol and other environmental initiatives bring to Arcelor in the near future?
4. Given the low gearing ratio, are there any other possible acquisitions on the horizon?
5. What other changes would you recommend so that Arcelor can be successful in a troubled industry in the future?

Arcelor's Challenger: Mittal

Mittal Steel NV was forged in 2004 when publicly traded Ispat International (of which the Mittal family owned 70 percent) purchased Antilles-based LNM Holdings (wholly owned by the Mittals) for roughly US$13.3 billion. In 2005, Mittal would finalize the US$4.5 billion acquisition, announced in October 2004, of International Steel Group in the United States. The new combined entity stood as the largest steel company in the world, with a production of 64 million tons (58 million metric tons) and revenues of US$31.8 billion.

Lakshmi Mittal had learned about the business from his father, Mohan, who started a small steel mill in the 1950s in India. The Mittals looked for opportunities abroad, which led the father to back the son in the purchase of his first steel mill, in Indonesia, in 1976.

From there, Lakshmi Mittal embarked on a growth strategy that saw the company buy up run-down state assets—mostly the remnants of aging, bankrupt post-communist dinosaurs—across the world, from Algeria to Mexico, in the former Soviet Union, and in Poland and Romania. He then would turn these steel mills around. This was achieved by closing inefficient units, reducing costs and payroll, revitalizing management and expertise with teams of Indian advisers, and finding new export markets for the mills' production.

The acquisition of ISG made Lakshmi Mittal the head of, and the lead shareholder (88 percent)

in, the world's largest steelmaker. He was ranked as one of the richest men on earth, worth roughly US$20 billion.

Lakshmi's son, Aditya—a young business graduate from Wharton—was part of his management board, as was his daughter Vanisha.

Mittal Steel manufactured a wide range of products: semifinished steel, flat and long carbon steel products, as well as wire rod, coated steels, tubes, and pipes. It was generally considered a low-end, mass-commodity producer—except in the United States, where it was the biggest maker of high-grade steel sheets for car bodies.

Mittal organized its management predominantly around countries or regions, rather than product groups. Managers in the 14 countries on four continents where the company had plants would swap ideas and pool knowledge and resources through regular meetings and conference calls. If one area was short of iron ore or coal, for example, supplies could be diverted from elsewhere. The group also located export markets for surplus production in its home region.

Mittal's group controlled 40 percent of its iron ore supplies and was self-sufficient in coke, a big edge when these materials were not available at reasonable prices.

In Europe, Mittal Steel mills consisted mostly of former Soviet bloc outdated facilities. As a result of insufficient quality, Sidex, for instance, a mill acquired by Mittal in 2002 in Romania, had been refused a supplier's role to the local Dacia-Renault car plant for its worldwide low-cost best-seller, the Logan. Mittal Steel was therefore considering investing up to US$350 million in Europe to catch up with rivals in one of the world's most coveted steel markets. Production of automotive-grade steel sheets—which are used for car bodies and have to be highly resistant to wear as well as suitable for coating with special high-gloss paint—is among the most technically difficult operations in steelmaking. The decision to produce such high-value-added products was seen as a critical test of Mittal's ability to maximize the potential of his sprawling network of plants on four continents. Worldwide, Arcelor stood as the biggest producer of high-grade sheets for car bodies, making some 10 million tons (9.1 million metric tons) a year, ahead of Mittal, with about 6 million tons (5.4 million metric tons). Companies more advanced than Mittal in auto-grade steel also included Germany's Thyssen-Krupp and Austria's Voestalpine.

Mittal was also looking to expand its presence in China. It had recently bought a 37 percent stake in Hunan Valin Steel Tube and Wire, which it wanted to convert into a majority share.

Even though Mittal Steel ranked as the biggest steel company, only 12 percent of shares traded publicly—a float too small to attract large funds. Lakshmi Mittal had been under pressure to sell some of his stake, and many thought he would do so in the next 18 months. Meanwhile, few stock market analysts monitored the company. Another reason was that it appeared complex, with its disparate network of operations on four continents.

ISG: An American Turnaround Story

Wilbur Ross liked to say that, if the 1990s were the decade of high technology, the 2000s would be the decade of basic industries. In 2000 he left Rothschild, where he had spent twenty years as a bankruptcy specialist, to start his own fund, W.L. Ross & Co. He soon started shopping around U.S. bankruptcy courts.

With 500,000 retirees and a far smaller number of workers, the downsized U.S. steel industry was struggling under the load of legacy costs (i.e., pension obligations). As an example, when Bethlehem Steel filed for bankruptcy in 2001, its declining operations employed only 12,000 workers. But in addition to paying them high union wages, it also had to support the benefits—above U.S. worker average—promised to its 67,000 retirees.

Ross entered the steel business in February 2002 by buying the assets of collapsed giant LTV for US$327 million, including US$127 million in cash and the rest in "assumed environmental liabilities." He got a bargain, paying US$11 per ton of steel-making capacity when most steel companies were valued at US$200 per ton of capacity.

Because LTV had liquidated instead of reorganizing a year after filing for Chapter 11 bankruptcy, Ross did not have to assume any of the legacy obligations. Pensions and retiree health premiums were estimated to add US$30 to US$50 in costs to a ton of steel. Ross avoided billions of dollars in pensions owed to LTV retirees, who instead got reduced checks from a federal agency, the Pension Benefit Guaranty Corp. (PBGC). He also passed off more than US$5.9 billion in retiree health-care costs onto either the former workers themselves or Medicare.

The LTV deal looked even better a few weeks later, when in March 2002, the Bush administration, eager to provide relief to the battered steel industry—concentrated in must-win states such as Pennsylvania and West Virginia—enacted tariffs of 8 to 30 percent for three years on steel imports.

Suddenly LTV, now renamed ISG, looked like it could be a going concern. It rehired 60 percent of LTV's employees and restarted the blast furnaces and mills with a lower cost structure. Ross proclaimed his intention to reduce the number of man-hours required to produce a ton of steel by nearly 70 percent. Negotiating with unions, ISG replaced lifetime pension and health-care benefits with 401(k)s and a tentative deal to tie other benefits to company performance. At ISG, workers received extra pay for beating production goals—a rarity under prior union contracts.

In August 2002, ISG bought Acme's minimill in Riverdale, Illinois, which had closed in 2001. At that time, Wilbur Ross, in a shareholder's meeting, stated that minimills can cost up to $350 million to build, and that they were buying them for about $65 million.

In December 2002, Bethlehem Steel seemed on the verge of liquidation, too. Already bankrupt, the company had stopped making payments to its severely underfunded pension plan. Again, the PBGC agreed to take over the obligations. With one large legacy cost set aside, Bethlehem suddenly looked more attractive to potential buyers. In a similar deal to the one he had offered LTV's former employees, Ross offered Bethlehem's unionized workforce changes in work rules, benefits, and compensation in exchange for preserving up to 60 percent of existing jobs. United Steelworkers of America endorsed the proposal.

In less than two years, Ross and his coinvestors had picked up the assets of five steel producers for a total US$2.1 billion and melded them into International Steel Group Inc. The consolidated company became the largest U.S. steelmaker virtually overnight and looked like it could be profitable again.

In October 2004, Ross agreed to sell ISG to Lakshmi Mittal for US$4.5 billion, half in stock and half in cash; Ross personally pocketed US$300 million. He had been more than a little lucky, buying when steel was less than US$300 a ton and selling when prices topped US$550 a ton. He and his partners retained a US$2.5 billion stake in Mittal's steel empire, but soon Ross turned his attention to replicating his success in coal and textiles.

CASE STUDY
APPENDIX 6.3

Steel: A Short Primer

Steel is an alloy of iron and carbon containing less than 2 percent carbon and 1 percent manganese and small amounts of silicon, phosphorus, sulphur, and oxygen. Steel remains one of the most widely used materials, found in every aspect of our lives, from automotive manufacturing to construction products, from cutlery to refrigerators and washing machines, and from cargo ships to the finest surgical scalpel.

Major steel consumers are the construction sector and the automotive industry. Other key markets include electrical equipment, packaging, electronic components, household appliances, and shipyards. Steel's single biggest customer is the automotive industry, which buys 29 percent of all steel produced, followed by electrical equipment, which takes 10 percent.

Steel is produced in more than 50 countries and on every continent. In 2004, more than 1.1 billion tons (1 billion metric tons) of steel was produced worldwide. The list below provides production statistics for a selection of other materials:

Aluminium	24 million tons (21.9 million metric tons) (2002)
Copper	16.4 million tons (14.9 million metric tons) (2002)
Gold	661 tons (600 metric tons) (2003)
Portland cement	96.7 million tons (87.8 million metric tons) (2000)
Timber	400 million cubic yards (300 million cubic meters) (2001)

Steel currently comes in more than 3,500 different grades with many different properties—physical, chemical, environmental—75 percent of which have been developed in the last 20 years. If the Eiffel Tower were to be rebuilt today, the engineers would need only one-third the amount of steel.

Steel is made via two basic routes:

1. From raw materials—iron ore, limestone, and coke—fed into the blast furnace to produce liquid iron (often called "hot metal" or "pig iron"). The iron that emerges from the blast furnace contains 4-4.5 percent carbon and other impurities, which make the metal too brittle for most engineering applications. The basic oxygen furnace (BOF) process takes this liquid iron plus recycled scrap steel and reduces the carbon content to between 0 and 1.5 percent by blowing oxygen through the metal in a converter to produce molten steel (commonly called "crude steel"). About 60 percent of steel produced today is made by this method, known as the integrated route.

2. From scrap via the electric arc furnace (EAF) method. Used in minimills, this technique is much easier and faster since it requires only scrap steel, which is introduced into an electric furnace and remelted. About 34 percent of steel pro-

507

duced in 2003 was produced via the EAF, or electric, route.

Secondary steelmaking processes are then applied to make fine adjustments to the steel composition, temperature, and cleanness, such as:

Casting: Steel is continuously cast into solid slabs, blooms, or billets.

Primary forming: Operations such as hot rolling are applied to continuous cast slabs, blooms, and billets. Their main purpose is usually to achieve large shape changes, although the steel properties, too, can be significantly altered.

Manufacturing, fabrication, and finishing: A wide variety of secondary operations are applied to give the steel component its final shape and properties. These can be subdivided into processes such as shaping (e.g., cold rolling), joining (e.g., welding), coating (e.g., galvanizing), heat treatment (e.g., tempering), surface treatment (e.g., carburizing), and so forth.

Slabs, billets, and blooms are known as semifinished products. Finished products include (hot- or cold-rolled) flat products, such as plates, coils, and sheet, and (hot-rolled) long products, such as wire, bars, rails, and beams.

A flat steel product can be a plate or a (hot or cold) rolled strip product. Strip width is less than 24 inches (600 mm) for hot-rolled products and less than 20 inches (500 mm) for cold-rolled products. Typically steel is rolled between sets of rollers to produce the final thickness. Plate products vary in thickness from 0.4 inch (10 mm) to 8 inches (200 mm), and thin flat rolled products from 0.04 inch (1 mm) to 0.4 inch (10 mm). Plate products are used for shipbuilding, construction, large-diameter welded pipes, and boiler applications. Thin flat products find various applications in automotive body panels, household appliances, cans, and a whole host of other products from office furniture to heart pacemakers.

A long product is a rod, a bar, or a section—typical rod products are the reinforcing rods for concrete. Engineering products, gears, tools, and the like are typical of bar products. Sections are the large rolled steel joists used in building construction projects. Wire-drawn products and seamless pipes are also part of the long products group.

Glossary

absolute advantage as stated by Adam Smith and David Ricardo, the specialization of each country in the goods that it can produce most efficiently

absolute uniformity theory that proposes that accounting methods be standardized regardless of the different circumstances of different users

accounting exposure degree to which the consolidated financial statements and balance sheets of a company can be affected by exchange rate fluctuations

acculturation not only understanding cultural differences, but modifying or adapting behavior to become more compatible with local culture

acquired group memberships affiliations not determined by birth, such as religious or political customs and practices

act of state doctrine legal principle that holds that sovereign nations can act within their authority considering assets or belongings taken by the state in public actions

ad valorem duty determination of customs duties as a percentage of the value of the goods

advising bank a bank in the country of the exporter that informs the exporter that letters of credit have been made available by foreign banks; an advising bank has no responsibility of payment associated with the letters of credit

African Development Bank (AFDB) headquartered in Ivory Coast, with the objective of accelerating the development process in Africa

Agreement on Trade-Related Aspects of Intellectual Property Rights (TRIPS) an agreement that allowed the creation of domestic laws concerning the protection of intellectual property rights

air waybill a bill of lading accepted by the shipper, indicating that he or she has received the goods and agrees to deliver the goods to the specified airport

alongside upon delivery, placement of goods on a dock or a barge very close to the ship, so that the goods can be placed aboard the ship

American terms prices of currencies quoted in terms of variable units of U.S. dollars per unit of their currency

Andean Community a customs union among Latin American countries

antidumping laws domestic laws that stipulate that a foreign country cannot sell a product at a cost below that of the cost of production (or less than fair value)

arbitrage the process of buying goods in one market and selling them in another market; the profit is determined by the differential between the purchase price of the good and price at which the good is ultimately sold

arm's-length pricing   the same price for affiliates as is charged for unrelated third party buyers

ascribed group memberships   affiliations determined by birth (such as sex, family, age, ethnicity, etc.)

ASEAN Free Trade Area (AFTA)   free trade area formed by the Association of South East Asian Nations in 1992

Asian Development Bank (ADB)   development bank that centers on promoting economic growth and cooperation in Asia and the Far East

Asian financial crisis   1997–98 economic collapse of many Southeast Asian nations due primarily to speculative bank lending in the region

autarky   an economy that does not trade with other nations; a closed economy

average cost pricing   using both fixed and variable costs in figuring the costs of production

back-to-back loans   arrangement for dealing with blocked funds where blocked funds are lent out to a local company, who then arranges for an equivalent loan to the parent company (also known as parallel loans)

backward-bending labor supply curve   phenomenon of a reduction in total labor hours due to higher salaries so that the amount of income remains the same, but the number of hours worked actually decreases

balance of payments (BOP)   an accounting system that reflects one country's financial transactions with the rest of the world

balance of trade (BOT)   the difference between a country's total exports and its total imports

banker's acceptance   a draft drawn on a bank indicating that the bank agrees to pay according to the terms of the agreement

barter   the exchange of goods or services for other goods or services without using money

Basel Accord   system for quantifying loan portfolio risk for major international banks

beneficiary   the person in whose favor a letter of credit is issued or a draft is drawn

Berne Convention of 1886   international agreement protecting the copyrights of literary and artistic works

bid-offer spread   difference between the buying and selling price

bilateral agreements   trade agreements between two countries that are not under the influence of multilateral organizations such as the WTO

bill of exchange   a written order requiring the party to which it is addressed to pay the bearer or another named party a particular sum of money at a future date

bill of lading   a document that acts as both a receipt and a contract between a shipper and a carrier; it acts as a receipt that goods have been received by the shipper and as a contract indicating the terms of the delivery

bimetallism   the period in monetary history during which two metals (gold and silver) were used to determine the values of different currencies

boycott   the blanket prohibition on importation of all or some goods and services from a designated country

brain drain   a term describing the departure of a country's best-educated and most intelligent people

branch offices   offices of a company at locations other than the headquarters

Bretton Woods   the location (in New Hampshire in the United States) where 44 countries, including the United States, established the international monetary system that was introduced to stabilize the international flow of currencies

bribery   payments to government officials, politicians, and political parties to gain favors that are otherwise not allowed by law

brownfield strategy   the entering of a foreign market via the purchase of an existing company

bulldog bonds   foreign bonds sold in the United Kingdom

bundled technology   technology that the owner is willing to transfer only as a part of a package or system

bureaucratic law   system of laws that is set by the current leadership in a country and is subject to change when governments change

call option   option that allows the purchaser to buy the underlying investment

Calvo doctrine   belief that when foreign interests choose to enter a nation and conduct business within that country, they are implicitly agreeing to be treated as if they were nationals and are subject to the laws and decisions of the sovereign nation and have no legal recourse outside of that nation

capital account   in a nation's balance of payments, account that measures the net changes in financial assets and liabilities abroad

cartel   a group of suppliers of a commodity who come together and agree to limit the supply of the commodity and charge an agreed-on price

cash against documents (CAD)   a payment method in which an intermediary processes the title documentation upon receipt of a cash payment

cash conversion cycle   the length of time between the purchasing of raw materials and the receipt of cash after the finished goods have been sold; usually expressed in days and determined by adding inventory days on hand and accounts receivable days on hand, and subtracting accounts payable days on hand

cash in advance (CIA)   a payment method in which the full payment is made prior to the shipment of the goods

cash with order (CWO)   a payment method in which the payment is made when the order is placed

central banks   government institutions that control the growth of the money supply and regulate commercial banks

centrally planned economy   government-directed economic activity of a country through government ownership of the means of production

certificate of origin   a document that certifies the origin of a good

choice of forum   requirement of an international business contract that stipulates the relevant jurisdiction where potential disputes will be settled

circumstantial uniformity   the use of different methods of accounting standards depending on the variations in the economic conditions in a given country

civil law   codified system of laws in the form of statutes

Clayton Act   U.S. law that prohibits the acquisition of stock or assets of another firm if the purchase will reduce the competitiveness in the industry (an antitrust law)

clean letter of credit   letter of credit that only requires presentation of the bill of exchange to obtain payment

cost-plus pricing   an amount is added to the cost of production to determine appropriate pricing at the next level of distribution.

codetermination   a management method that includes representatives of labor in the decision-making process and on the boards of the companies

collective bargaining   the process by which management and labor discuss wages and working conditions

commanding heights   key industries required to effectively control an economy

common agricultural policy (CAP)   a policy of the European Union directed at price supports for existing agricultural programs

common law   a law established through precedents resulting from the cultural traditions of a country

common market   a customs union that also eliminates the barriers that inhibit the movement of the factors of production

comparative advantage   the theory, first introduced by David Ricardo, that even when one country has an absolute advantage in the production of two goods it can still benefit from trade if it trades with a country that has a relative advantage in the production of one good

compound tariff   combination of a specific and ad valorem tariff

confirmed letter of credit   a letter of credit confirmed by another bank that adds its guarantee

consignment   selling of goods by an agent representing the exporter; the agent delivers a payment, net of a commission, to the exporter

constant-dollar accounting   reporting assets, liabilities, expenses, and revenues in terms of the same purchasing power

contract manufacturing   the subcontracting by a multinational firm of the manufacturing operations with a local company via a specified contract

convergence criteria   specific targets of fiscal and monetary performance as specified in the Maastricht Treaty

convertible currency   currency that can be exchanged for another country's currency without the consent of the government

copyrights   exclusive rights of authors, composers, singers, musicians, and artists to publish, dispose of, or release their work as they see fit for a specified period of time

correspondent bank   a bank that conducts business with foreign banks located in its country

cost and freight (C&F)   a term indicating that the cost and freight expense are included in the quoted price of the good; implies that the purchaser must secure insurance for the shipment of the goods

cost, insurance (CI)   a term indicating that the cost and insurance are included in the quoted price of the good; implies that the purchaser must secure shipment of the good

cost, insurance, freight (CIF)   a term that indicates that the cost, freight, and insurance are included in the quoted price of a good

cost method of accounting   the parent only reports income from a subsidiary when the subsidiary declares a dividend to the parent (values subsidiary as an investment)

counterfeiting   illegally using a well-known name on copies of a firm's goods

countertrade   a means of exchange by which one government attempts to limit the outflow of hard currency from the country by providing payment in the form of other goods

countervailing duty (CVD)   an added tariff applied to goods that have benefited from an export subsidy

covered interest arbitrage   earning profits on interest-bearing instruments through differences in the spot and forward exchange rates

crawling peg   a foreign exchange relationship in which a country makes small periodic changes in the value of its currency with the intent to move it to a particular value relative to another currency over a period of time

credit risk insurance   a type of insurance that protects against nonpayment after the delivery of goods

cross border supply   services supplied from one country to another

cross rate   the exchange rate between two countries based on the exchange rate of each currency against a third currency, usually the U.S. dollar

cultural cluster approach   attempt to group cultures based on geographical similarities

cultural universals similar elements that can be found in all cultures

culture the learned beliefs and attitudes that characterize human populations, passed on from earlier generations

culture shock the anxiety an individual experiences when introduced into an unfamiliar situation

currency exchange controls a government's means of determining how much foreign currency citizens or visitors can have and the exchange rate they must pay for it

currency swap an agreement by which currency is exchanged at a specified rate only to be reversed at a future date

current account part of the balance of payment account; measures the aggregate import and export of goods and services

current-cost accounting accounting system with the objective of accounting for the effects of inflation in the costs of assets

customs (1) the process of collecting the duties on exports and imports; (2) the officials who collect the duties

customs union an agreement between two countries that eliminates import restrictions between the member countries and establishes a common tariff for all other countries

date draft a draft that matures a specified number of days after the date it is issued

deemed paid credit an indirect foreign tax credit that can be taken in addition to the direct foreign tax credit to avoid double taxation

deferred payment credit a letter of credit that specifies payment at some time following review of the exporter's shipping documentation

demurrage fees costs for the storage of an exporter's goods at the foreign loading dock

depreciation of a currency a reduction in the worth of a currency when compared to another currency or gold

devaluation a government's decision to reduce the value of its country's currency by increasing the amount of local currency needed to buy foreign currencies

developed countries countries that are more advanced in GNP and living standards

developing countries countries that are technologically less advanced

development banks institutions established in developing countries to foster economic development through investment or loans

direct investments operations that have sufficient foreign ownership such that the firms' management decisions are influenced by the foreign interests

direct lobbying influencing by establishing a liaison or representative office in the capital city and establishing direct contact with local officials and politicians.

direct quote the number of units of the home currency that are required to buy a foreign currency

disposable income the portion of an individual's income available for consumption after taxes

distributor an agent who maintains an inventory of the supplier's merchandise and sells directly to the consumer

documentary letter of credit bank requires presentation of documentation in order to obtain payment

Doha Agenda current round of WTO trade discussions with the focus on improving the performance of developing nations and concerning reducing the remaining barriers to international trade (especially in agriculture)

domestic international sales corporation (DISC) a subsidiary of a U.S. firm established solely for exporting goods; receives special tax incentives to operate

double taxation avoidance treaty agreement between nations where revenues of an MNC

would not be taxed in the foreign country in return for the same treatment in the other country

draft (bill of exchange) the order given by the drawer for the drawee to pay the payee a specified amount at a future date

drawback the refund of duty on imported components used in the manufacture of goods that are exported on completion

drawee the individual or firm responsible for payment of the indicated amount of a draft to the payee

drawer the individual or firm that issues a draft

dual-equity issue listing stock for sale on domestic and international stock exchanges simultaneously

dumping selling goods in a country at a price below the cost of production and freight or, in some circumstances, selling goods in a foreign country at prices lower than those charged for the same good in the home country

duty a tax one country must pay to sell its products in another country

economic exposure the degree to which fluctuations in exchange rates will affect the net present value of the future cash flows of a company

embargo a quota that prohibits all trade between countries

entry mode the manner in which a firm chooses to enter a foreign market

equity method of accounting reporting the value of equity shares (from 20 to 50 percent ownership interest) in a subsidiary on the parent company's consolidated financial statements

ethnocentric strategy focused on the home market only

ethnocentric pricing strategy a pricing policy in which a firm maintains the same prices in all the markets in which it operates that it charges in its home market

ethnodomination when certain ethnic groups control the majority of business interest in a given market

euro the official currency of the European Union

Eurobonds bonds traded primarily in Europe and in a currency different from the currency of the country in which they are sold

Eurocurrency a currency in use in countries other than the nation of origin

Eurodollars U.S. dollars on deposit in banks outside the United States

Euroequity issue stocks sold on stock exchanges solely outside the home country of the issuing firm

Euronext integrated stock market that consists of the stock exchanges in Paris, Amsterdam, Brussels, and others in Europe

European Bank for Reconstruction and Development (EBRD) promotes the economic development of Eastern and Central Europe

European Central Bank (ECB) central bank of the European Union

European Community a common market formed in 1958 for its member nations; in 1991 there were 12 member countries: the United Kingdom, Germany, France, Italy, Belgium, the Netherlands, Luxembourg, Denmark, Spain, Portugal, Greece, and Ireland; later expanded into the European Union

European Court of Justice court through which member states of the European Union can seek redress of disputes

European Economic Area (EEA) common market that includes the members of the EU plus Norway, Iceland, and Liechtenstein

European Economic Community (EEC) a common market for some nations not in the European Union, such as Norway, Iceland, and Switzerland

European Investment Bank (EIB)   pursues goals of regional development and economic and social cohesion within the European Union for current and upcoming members of the EU

European Monetary System (EMS)   system established in March 1979 in an effort to stabilize the currencies of European Community nations

European Monetary Union Union (EMU)   economic integration for majority of European Union member nations which involves movement to the Euro as currency for all members.

European terms   foreign currency prices are quoted in terms of one U.S. dollar

European Union (EU)   group of 25 economically integrated member states

exchange rate   a determination of value using only two currencies

exchange risk   the risk that one currency will be lower in value than it was previously

excise taxes   taxes levied on specific products or industries to achieve desired policy objectives by a host country's government (also known as sin taxes)

export broker   a firm or individual who locates and introduces buyers and sellers for a fee

Export-Import Bank of the United States (Ex-Im Bank)   bank that assists U.S. exporting firms by issuing loans, guarantees, and insurance

export management company   a firm that acts as the export department for other firms

export processing zones   locations where import duties are not levied because the goods are reexported

export trading companies (ETCs)   firms that act as the export departments for other firms

exposure netting   the process of holding two currencies that are believed to be a hedge against each other

expropriation   seizure of property by a foreign government

extraction tax   tax that serves to reimburse a host country for the depletion of a natural resource

extraterritoriality   process by which a government attempts to apply its laws outside its geographic boundaries

factors of production   land, labor, capital, and technology

first to file   patent system in which the first to file a patent in a given country is awarded the patent without the need to prove that it is the inventor

first to invent   patent system in which patent protection is granted to the person or entity that first invented the technology or product

first world   the countries of the developed world, such as the United States, Canada, Japan, and the countries of western Europe

Fisher effect   the observation that in the long run, the real rates of return in countries that have no restrictions on the mobility of capital are the same, but the nominal rates vary in proportion to the expected rate of inflation in a particular currency

floating exchange rates   a process that allows for the valuation of currencies based on the supply and demand of the currencies

force majeure clause   a clause that excuses a party from fulfilling a contract because of conditions beyond its control

Foreign Corrupt Practices Act   legislation directed toward the elimination of bribery between U.S. and foreign firms

foreign direct investment   foreign investment in a firm that constitutes effective control of the firm

foreign earned income   all monies employees receive as payment for services rendered; includes wages, salaries, and commissions

foreign exchange   transactions involving the exchange of one currency for another

foreign sales corporation (FSC) a firm provided for in the tax code that permits U.S. corporations to shelter income derived from exports

foreign tax credit an income tax credit available to citizens or corporations that paid tax abroad on the same income

foreign trade organization (FTO) an organization established in many ex-communist economies that is authorized to import and export goods of a particular industry

foreign trade zones locations determined by the government that do not need to pay tariffs or duties on imports, particularly goods that are assembled and reexported

foreign unearned income income that is derived from overseas investments

forward contract a contract that establishes an exchange for a particular currency to be delivered at a future date

fourth world the least economically developed nations of the world

four tigers Hong Kong, Singapore, Taiwan, and South Korea

franchising a licensing system in which a party is authorized to use the name and create the product of another firm for a fee

free alongside (FAS) a term indicating that the quoted price includes the cost associated with delivering the goods to the desired vessel for shipment

free in (FI) a term indicating that the cost of loading and unloading the vessel is the responsibility of the firm or individual who has hired the vessel

free on board (FOB) a term indicating that the quoted price includes loading the goods onto a vehicle at some particular location

free out (FO) a term indicating that the cost of loading the vessel is the responsibility of the firm or individual who has hired the vessel

free port a port that does not require the payment of duties for use

free trade areas trade agreements that eliminate trade barriers among its members, while members are able to set their own trade policies with nonmember states

free trade zone government-established zones that permit free entry and storage of goods; duties do not need to be paid until the goods leave the zone

freight forwarder a firm that transports goods for export

functional currencies the currency in which the cash flow of the company is generated

General Agreement on Tariffs and Trade (GATT) a treaty intended to limit trade barriers and promote trade through the reduction of tariffs among the signatory nations

General Agreement on Trade in Services (GATS) set of multilateral rules governing international trade in services

general export license a license required to export goods not needing special authorization

geocentric integrated world strategy that is best suited for the majority of markets where a company operates

globalization of markets trend toward one huge global market through increasing volume and the variety of cross-border transactions in goods, services, capital, information, and labor force

GNI per capita gross national income per capita; the amount of the nation's gross national product representing each individual of the total population (also known as GDP per capita)

gold exchange standard a system established at Bretton Woods in which the United States agreed to exchange gold for U.S. dollars at an agreed-on rate

gray-market exports goods that are legally imported from the producing country into another country, and then are reexported to a third country, where higher prices are then charged for the same goods

greenfield strategy   entering a foreign market via starting up a new company

greenhouse effect   rise in global temperatures due to increase in greenhouse gases such as carbon dioxide, methane, and nitrous oxide

greenhouse gases   term used to denoted gases that contribute to global warming by trapping heat in the earth's atmosphere

gross domestic product (GDP)   the aggregate value of a nation's output based on factors of production located within the country but excluding exports and imports

gross national income (GNI)   the aggregate value of all goods and services produced by a country

gross national product (GNP)   the aggregate value of all goods and services produced by a country; also known as GNI

guest workers   authorized foreign labor

hard currency   currency that can be exchanged for other currencies quickly and without government permission

hard technology   physical hardware, capital goods, blueprints, and specifications

harmonization   the process of increasing the compatibility of accounting practices by setting limits on how much they can vary

hedging   using various instruments to protect against exchange-rate risk

high-context culture   culture in which a conversation's context is just as important as the words that are actually spoken

Hofstede's five dimensions of culture   theory that culture can best be described in terms of five primary areas: (1) social orientation (individual vs. collective), (2) power orientation (power tolerant vs. power respect), (3) uncertainty orientation (acceptance vs. avoidance), (4) goal orientation (aggressive vs. passive), and (5) time orientation (long-term vs. short-term)

home-country nationals   citizens of the country in which the headquarters of a firm is located

horizontal integration   business expansion into related product lines

host-country nationals   citizens of the country where a subsidiary is located

hyperinflation   inflation that increases in hundreds or thousands of percent

import substitution   a policy of developing countries to promote the development of industries that are intended to replace the need for imports

indirect lobbying   influencing by buying local officials in the host country who are important in shaping the official attitudes and governmental views of multinational firms

indirect quote   rate quote in which the home currency is expressed as a unit and the price is shown by the number of units of a foreign currency that are required to purchase one unit of the home currency

infant-industry argument   the argument that an industry new to a country, especially a developing country, needs to be protected by tariff walls or risks being destroyed by larger foreign competition before it can grow and develop

inflation   increase in prices over time measured against a certain benchmark, typically known as the base year

Inter-American Development Bank (IADB)   a development bank located in Washington, DC, that is specifically geared toward the development of Latin America

interest-rate swap   exchanging fixed-interest-rate instruments for those with floating interest rates

internalization   retaining information within the company

International Accounting Standards Board (IASB)   group whose aim is to harmonize the rules of accounting used in various countries

International Centre for Settlement of Investment Disputes (ICSID)   group affiliated with the World Bank that provides a forum for resolving disputes between states and foreign investors

International Court of Justice   located in the Netherlands, the primary court of law for countries that have legal questions involving other countries

International Development Association (IDA)   affiliated with the World Bank Group, an association that was established in 1960 to provide long-term funds to the poorest member countries of the World Bank

International Federation of Accountants (IFAC)   group whose aim is to harmonize international auditing principles and procedures

International Finance Corporation (IFC)   a part of the World Bank that loans money for private development in developing countries

International Labor Organization (ILO)   group affiliated with the United Nations that attempts to define and promote international standards regarding safety, health, and other working conditions

international law   rules that govern the activities and policies of nations with other countries; established between individual countries and apply only to countries that have entered into the agreements

International Monetary Fund (IMF)   Bretton Woods–created institution that promotes the expansion of balanced growth of international trade

international monetary system (IMS)   the structures and policies needed for the international transfer and exchange of funds

international trading companies   firms that supply most of the foreign goods to the markets in which they operate

intervention currency   a currency purchased by a government to affect the value of the government's currency

invisibles   services

irrevocable letter of credit   a letter of credit that is payable if all the conditions of the letter of credit are met

Japan Bank for International Cooperation (JBIC)   established and funded by the government of Japan; aim is to provide financial assistance to developing (primarily Asian) countries

J-curve effect   an effect associated with the devaluation of a currency in which the balance of payments actually worsens before it improves, thus the *J* shape of the curve

joint venture   see *strategic alliance*

jurisdiction   capacity of a nation to prescribe a course of conduct for its citizens and to enforce a rule of law on its citizens

just-in-time (JIT) inventory system   an inventory system in which deliveries are made as component parts are needed; a system created in an effort to reduce the costs associated with carrying inventory; also known as *kanban*

kanban   see *just-in-time inventory system*

Kyoto Protocol   international agreement to reduce the collective emissions of greenhouse gases to achieve cleaner air in all parts of the world

lagging   creating deliberate delays with respect to the outflows or inflows (increasing the accounts payable days on hand, for example)

laissez-faire   the concept of freedom of enterprise and freedom of commerce with minimal government intervention in a society's economic activity

leading   the early receipt of goods (or reducing the accounts receivable days on hand for a firm, for example)

Leontief paradox   a discovery by Wassily Leontief that U.S. exports required less capital and more labor than U.S. imports

letter of credit   a credit instrument that guarantees that the importer's bank will pay the exporter on receipt of certain documents

letters rogatory   the means by which courts from other countries request evidence from one country while in another country

licensing   a business arrangement that permits a firm or individual to use the patents, copyrights, and technology of another firm

lingua franca   a foreign language used as a common language in countries that have many languages

lockouts   the closing or locking of the plant by an employer, and the barring of workers from entering the premises

London Court of International Arbitration   legal center that deals with disputes regarding private international commercial transactions

London Inter-Bank Offered Rate (LIBOR)   the interest rate used among large banks on large, overnight Eurocurrency loans

long position   a situation in which a firm makes a purchase of a currency or commodity in the expectation of a future appreciation in its value

Louvre Accord   international agreement made in Paris in 1987 by the G6 countries (United States, Canada, United Kingdom, France, West Germany, and Italy) to hold down the value of the dollar on world markets

low-context culture   culture in which the words used by the speaker explicitly convey the speaker's message to the listener

Maastricht Treaty   agreement that provided the framework for the economic and political integration of the European Union; came into effect in November 1993 and set certain convergence criteria of monetary and fiscal performance that each member country would try to achieve for successful economic and political integration of the EU member states

Madrid Agreement of 1991   international agreement on the protection of trademarks

managed float   a term indicating government involvement in maintaining the exchange rate of a particular currency

management contract   an agreement in which one firm supplies managerial assistance to another for a fee

maquiladoras   in-bond export industry in which components produced in the United States are exported duty-free to Mexico for assembly and then exported duty-free back to the United States for completion

marine insurance   insurance that covers losses at sea that are not covered by the insurance of the carrier

market capitalization   the value of total stocks outstanding at a particular time (stock price multiplied by the number of shares outstanding)

marketing mix   a firm's process of addressing the marketing issues of price, promotion, distribution, and the product

marketing segmentation   the process of recognizing differences among consumers such that the firm can address those particular needs

marking identification   symbols used on cargo

Marshall Plan   program established by the U.S. government following World War II to aid European countries

matrix organization   an organizational concept that superimposes one structure over another to gain both functional and creative expertise

mediation a less formal third party dispute resolution method than arbitration

mercantilism an economic philosophy of the late seventeenth and early eighteenth centuries that encouraged the accumulation of gold and other precious metals

Mercosur Accord customs union among South American nations

money laundering the act of concealing the source of ill-gotten funds by changing them into legitimate business activities and bank deposits

moral hazard a hidden reckless action of external partners who know they will be saved if things go wrong

most favored nation (MFN) a clause in most treaties that requires a trade concession that is given to one country be given to all other countries

multilateral agreements trade agreements among three or more countries that are under the influence of multilateral organizations such as the WTO

Multilateral Investment Guarantee Agency (MIGA) an agency affiliated with the World Bank Group that was established in 1988 to promote overseas direct investment flows into developing countries by providing guarantees against political risks

national competitive advantage theory a theory by Michael Porter that states that successful international trade comes from the interaction of four country- and firm-specific elements: (a) factor conditions, (b) demand conditions, (c) related and supporting industries, and (d) the strategy, structure, and rivalry of a firm

nationalization process in which a host government takes over an operation

net statistical discrepancy errors and omissions in the balance of payments calculation for a given nation

newly industrialized countries (NICs) see *four tigers*

nondiscrimination treatment of foreign enterprises on the same basis as domestic enterprises

nontariff barriers government policies that create restrictions on imports without the use of tariffs, for example, quotas, customs procedures, and safety and quality requirements

NOREX Alliance integrated stock markets of Denmark, Sweden, Norway, Iceland, and a few others

North American Free Trade Agreement (NAFTA) free trade agreement among the United States, Canada, and Mexico initiated in 1994

official reserves account a nation's holdings of monetary gold and internationally accepted currencies

offshoring outsourcing to overseas (or simply non-domestic) markets

oligopoly a market with very few sellers

oligopsony a market with very few buyers

one-step method recording currency transaction using spot rate for the currency in effect on the day of the transaction

open account a method of trade in which the exporter ships without guarantee of payment from the buyer

open insurance policy an insurance policy that covers all shipments over a period of time

options the right to purchase or sell before or on a given date

ordinary shares shares that confer voting rights (on the London and Australian stock markets) and are similar to common stock in the United States

Organisation for Economic Cooperation and Development (OECD) group that publishes economic data, conducts research, and provides policy guidance for its member nations (primarily of the developed world)

Organization of the Petroleum Exporting Countries (OPEC)   a cartel of 11 oil-producing nations

outsourcing   business decision to seek external firms for assistance in one or more non-essential operations

Overseas Private Investment Corporation (OPIC)   a corporation of the U.S. government that insures U.S. business interests overseas against such things as expropriation and the inconvertibility of currency

packing list   a list including quantities and identification of items being shipped

paper gold   see *special drawing rights (SDRs)*

parallel loans   see *back-to-back loans*

Paris Convention   international agreement that protects patents and trademarks

patents   rights granted by governments to the inventors of products or processes for exclusive manufacturing, production, sale, or use of those products or processes; the equivalent to a legal monopoly over the subject matter of the patent for a period of time

pegged exchange rate   a fixed exchange relationship

perils of the sea   an insurance term used to denote marine occurrences such as stranding, lightning, collision, and seawater damage

petrodollars   name for the vast supply of loanable funds coming from oil-exporting countries, which led in part to the Latin American debt crisis of the 1980s

piracy   the use of illegal and unauthorized means to obtain goods, such as copying software

Plaza Accord   international agreement made in New York City (at the Plaza Hotel) in September 1985 that brought down the value of the U.S. dollar

political risk   the risk associated with the political environment of a foreign country; could include social unrest within the country or government actions that alter a firm's ability to operate in the foreign country

polycentric   having strategies in multiple countries without integrating them

portfolio investments   investments for purposes other than control of a company; do not require the physical presence of a firm's personnel or products on foreign shores

predatory pricing   attempt to capture market share by cutting prices below that which is charged in the home market

premium (in forward exchange)   a term indicating that the forward rate exceeds the spot rate

price fixing   collusion in the administration of prices

principle of comity   the principle by which each nation defers to another's sovereignty in the protection of rights of foreign citizens by showing reciprocal respect for other countries' laws and powers with respect to the acts of citizens abroad

primary sector   traditional economic activities such as agriculture and mining

Private Export Funding Corporation (PEFCO)   an organization that lends to foreign buyers in need of financing to purchase U.S. exports

private law   law pertaining to individuals within nation-states typically negotiated via a contract

process technology   knowledge used in the process of making a product or service

product adaptation   modification of the existing product line to take into account the cultural, legal, or economic differences between the domestic and foreign markets

product extension   marketing the same products abroad as are marketed at home, hoping that the foreign markets have tastes and preferences similar to those of the home market

product technology   knowledge used to make a product or service

production factor endowments   assets such as land, labor, capital, management and technological skills, specialized production facilities, and established distribution networks

productivity   the value of the output produced by a unit of labor or capital

progressive taxation   the system of taxation that holds that the more an individual or corporation earns, the higher the tax it pays

protectionism   government intervention in trade markets to protect specific industries in its economy

Protestant ethic   view that work is salvation that has its roots in the Protestant Reformation

public law   the manner in which nations interact according to a legal framework

purchasing power parity (PPP)   a method of determining exchange rates between two currencies based on the purchasing power of similar goods

purposive uniformity   varying the determination of accounting standards according to the diversity of users and the circumstances of the users in a given country

put option   option that allows the buyer to sell the underlying investment

quota   a specified amount of a product that a government will permit to be imported

rationalization   a strategy to achieve economies of scale under which a subsidiary changes its purpose for production from manufacturing for its own market to manufacturing a limited number of component parts for use by several or all subsidiaries

reciprocity   see *principle of comity*

red-chip stocks   equities that are issued on the Hong Kong stock market but are controlled by mainland China

religious law   see *theocracy*

remitting bank   the bank that initiates payment of money

revaluation   an improvement of one currency in value in relation to another

revocable letter of credit   a letter of credit that the opening bank has the right to modify or cancel without notifying the beneficiary

rules of origin   specifications clarifying what actually constitutes member goods and services within a free trade area

samurai bonds   foreign bonds sold in Japan

Sarbanes-Oxley Act   legal requirements for increased financial reporting standards in the aftermath of numerous corporate fraud scandals in the United States

secondary sector   manufacturing and industrial activity

severance tax   see *extraction tax*

Sherman Act   U.S. antitrust law that prohibits monopolistic activities. The goal of this law is to preserve competition in both U.S. and foreign markets

short position   a situation in which a firm makes a purchase of currency or commodity in the expectation of a future depreciation in its value

shunto   spring wage offensive in Japan, when union wage negotiations take place

sight draft   a draft that is payable upon presentation to the payee

sin taxes   see *excise taxes*

Smithsonian Agreement   an agreement reached in December 1971 by the leading 10 industrialized nations that established a new international monetary system

smuggling   the illegal trade and transportation of goods that is devised to circumvent customs duties, quotas, and other constraints on the movement of goods

society   a political and social entity that is geographically defined and is composed of people and their culture

sociocultural   factors that influence both society and culture

soft currency   a currency that cannot be easily converted

soft loans   loans that can be repaid with a soft currency and that charge a low interest rate

soft technology   management, marketing, financial organization, and administrative techniques that can be combined with hard technology to serve the needs of the user

sogo shosha   a Japanese general trading company

sovereign debt   the debt of a national government

sovereign immunity   the immunity of a government from the courts of its own country

sovereignty   principle that individual nations have absolute power over the governing of their populace and the activities that occur within their borders

special drawing rights (SDRs)   also known as *paper gold*; rights created by the IMF that are essentially book entries that represent the right of the country holding them to access resources of equivalent value

specific duties   duties that are assessed based on a physical unit of measurement (per ton, per bushel, etc.) and are stipulated at a specific monetary value

spot exchange   the deliveries are completed within the same day that the deal is struck

spot rate   the exchange rate between two currencies used for immediate delivery

spread (in the forward market)   the difference between the spot rate and the forward rate

spread (in the spot market)   the difference between the quoted buy and sell rates of the foreign exchange trader

standard industrial code (SIC)   a coding system used by the U.S. government to classify goods and services

standard international trade classification   a UN coding system used to classify commodities involved in international trade

steamship conference   steamship operators who agree to charge the same freight rate

straight bonds   debt issued with a fixed interest rate

strategic alliance   business arrangement in which two or more companies join together to form some sort of an operation (see also *joint venture*)

strikes   actions that occur when workers refuse to work and walk out of the place of employment

subsidiaries   companies that are owned by a parent company

subsidies   governmental (often monetary) support of specific industries to make them more competitive in international trade

switch trading   a type of countertrade in which a country unable to pay in a hard currency locates goods for exchange from a third country to pay its debt

target return levels   a method of price setting in which a fixed percentage or level of monetary return is added to the total costs of production.

tare weight   the weight of the container and packaging containing a good

tariff   a tax assessed on goods that are imported or exported from a country

tariff quota   a tariff that requires a higher tax payment after a specified amount of the good has been imported or exported from the country

tax haven   a country with low or no required tax payments on income earned in other countries or on capital gains

tax incentive   a tax holiday or reduction of taxes due granted to a company making an investment

tax treaty   an agreement between two countries concerning the taxation of citizens and corporations of each country operating in the other

technology transfer   process by which knowledge is diffused through learning from its place of origin and introduction to other world markets

temporal method   method of accounting in which monetary items are translated at the current rate, while nonmonetary items are translated at the rates that preserve their original measurement bases

tenor   the time period allowed in a draft

terms of trade   ratio of export prices for a country in relation to its import prices

tertiary sector   services and related industries

theocracy   system of law based on religious beliefs that govern the behavior of a country's citizens

third-country national   citizens of neither the country of a subsidiary or of the parent company

third world   less-developed countries (LDCs)

tied agent   independent intermediary who can only advise a customer on products offered by their firm, society, or insurer

time draft   draft that allows a certain period of time to elapse before payment is made

trade creation   the resulting trading relationships once countries shift from a high-cost producer to a low-cost producer in the same customs union

trade deflection   process by which nonmember nations of a free trade area reroute their exports to member nations with the lowest external trade barriers to access the free trade area at the lowest possible cost

trade diversion   process by which member nations of a free trade area stop importing from lower-cost nonmember states in favor of member states

trademark   design or logo used by manufacturers to differentiate their goods with customers

trade name   name used by manufacturers to differentiate their goods with customers

transaction exposure   the calculation of the loss or gain associated with transferring currencies over national borders; also known as the impact of foreign exchange rates on a company's accounts receivable and accounts payable

transaction statement   a document that specifies the terms between an importer and an exporter

transaction taxes   taxes levied at the time a transaction or exchange occurs

transfer pricing   the price associated with the transfer or sale of goods between related companies or between a parent company and its subsidiaries

translation   the process in which financial statements are restated using a different currency

translation exposure   see *accounting exposure*

transparency   governments should publish all laws and regulations

triangular arbitrage   taking profits from an imperfection in the exchange rates relating to three currencies; buying and selling the same currencies in different markets to make a profit from fractional differences in each market

Triffin paradox   during the gold standard, the more heavy the reliance by the rest of the world on U.S. dollars for the expansion of world trade, the less confidence there would be in the United States', being able to honor its commitment of redeeming dollars for gold

TRIPS   Trade-Related Aspects Regarding Intellectual Property Rights, an agreement created under the GATT

turnkey operation   a contract in which one firm constructs a facility and prepares it for operation and then relinquishes it to its new owners

turnover   an example of a term that has different meanings in different locations ("turnover" means sales in England, but means the replenishment of inventory stock in the United States)

two-step method   accounting for gains and losses for both the business activity and the currency exchange

unbundled technology   technology available separate from the total system of technology

UNESCO   United Nations Educational, Scientific, and Cultural Organization

unilateral transfers   flow of funds or goods for which nothing is expected in return

unitary taxes   taxes imposed by a specific state on the basis of a multinational's multistate or worldwide profits, rather than based on the profits generated from the host state

United Nations Conference on Trade and Development (UNCTAD)   conference established in 1964 to address concerns of developing nations on issues of international trade that affected their economic development

Universal Copyright Convention (UCC) of 1952   an international copyright protection agreement administered by UNESCO

utilitarianism   philosophy that states that moral values are reflected in policies that provide the greatest happiness to the greatest number of people

value-added tax (VAT)   a tax assessed based on an improvement made to the product that increases the value of the product

variable costs   those that vary with the levels of production such as labor or raw materials.

vertical integration   business expansion into areas within the same production chain

visibles   manufactured goods

voluntarism   principle that states that the workers alone will define and pursue their self-interest for the welfare of the enterprise

water's edge taxation   taxation that limits states in taxing the profits of a multinational firm that are generated in the United States, as opposed to worldwide profits

Webb-Pomerene Act   U.S. law that allows for exemption from Sherman and Clayton antitrust laws if domestic firms join together for the purposes of gaining access to foreign markets

wharfage   the fee to use a pier or dock

wholly owned subsidiary   an entry mode in which the investing firm owns 100 percent of the new entity in a host country (see also *brownfield strategy*)

wildcat strikes   strike by workers during an existing contract and with little or no notice to the employer

without reserve   a term indicating that an agent or representative is authorized to make decisions without consulting the group that he or she represents

World Bank   bank established initially to assist the countries of Europe following World War II; now assists in the development of developing countries

World Intellectual Property Organization (WIPO)   international signatory organization formed to protect intellectual property worldwide

World Trade Organization (WTO)   international forum formed in 1995 for resolving trade disputes

xenophobia   fear of the strange or foreign

yankee bonds   foreign bonds sold in the United States

zaibatsu   large Japanese conglomerates that also have trading companies as integral components

Index

Page numbers in *italics* indicate figures and tables

About the Authors

Dr. Riad A. Ajami is the Charles A. Hayes Distinguished Professor of Business at the University of North Carolina at Greensboro (UNCG) and is the director of the Center for Global Business Education and Research in UNCG's Bryan School of Business and Economics. Dr. Ajami is also the editor-in-chief of the *Journal of Asia-Pacific Business*.

Prior to joining the UNCG faculty in 1996, Dr. Ajami served as the Forman Distinguished Professor of International Business at Rochester Institute of Technology, and Ohio State University. Dr. Ajami has had visiting professorships with University of California at Berkeley, University of Pennsylvania, and the Harvard Center for International Affairs at Harvard University. He also has professional affiliations with Hautes Etudes Commercials–HEC (Grande Ecole of Management), France; American University, Beirut; and University of Istanbul, Turkey.

Dr. Ajami sits on the editorial boards of several journals, including the *Transnational Management Journal*, among others. He is a frequent contributor to books on international business and has coauthored *The Global Enterprise: Entrepreneurship and Value Creation*.

His expertise has been sought by national media, including *Nightline*, the *Lehrer News Hour*, *NBC News*, CNN, and National Public Radio.

Dr. Karel Cool is the BP Professor of European Competitiveness, Professor of Strategic Management at INSEAD. His specialized areas of research include industry and competitive analysis, and competitive strategy. Dr. Cool is also a visiting professor of management and strategy at the Kellogg School of Management at Northwestern University. Dr. Cool is the associate editor of the *Strategic Management Journal* and is on the editorial board of the *British Journal of Managemen*, among others. He is also an ad hoc reviewer of many leading journals including *Organization Science*, *Management Science*, and the *Academy of Management Review*.

Dr. Cool's publications include *European Industrial Restructuring in the 1990s*, numerous INSEAD business case studies, and articles in numerous journals, including the *Strategic Management Journal*, *Management Science*, *Organization Science*, *and the Financial Times*. He has also contributed chapters to many other collaborative works in many leading business publications.

G. Jason Goddard obtained his MBA from the Bryan School at the University of North Carolina at Greensboro. Mr. Goddard is an instructor at the Bryan School, and is an editorial board member of the *Journal of Asia-Pacific Business*. He currently teaches an introductory undergraduate course in international business at UNCG, and has also taught the discipline in the MBA program at UNCG. Mr. Goddard also teaches an investment real estate course at UNCG in the Finance and Accounting department. Mr. Goddard is currently employed full-time at Wachovia Corporation, where he has been a commercial lender for over 10 years. He is currently Vice President, and works in the risk management division in Winston-Salem. His dealings in the international arena include providing financing for letters of credit for international transactions, loaning to foreign-owned subsidiaries with offices in the United States, and analyzing and translating financial statements provided by international parent companies, among other experience.

Dr. Dara Khambata holds the Crown Prince of Bahrain Chair in International Finance at the Kogod School of Business at American University in Washington, DC. In addition, he manages a portfolio in 27 emerging markets using data from the International Finance Corporation and the World Bank Group. Professor Khambata has served as a consultant for both public and private institutions.

Dr. Khambata's publications include *The Practice of Multinational Banking*, *The Multinational Enterprise in Transition*, and *International Business: Theory & Practice*. Professor Khambata has also published articles in numerous journals, including *Columbia Journal of World Business*, *Journal of Global Marketing*, *International Journal of Management*, *Asia-Pacific Journal of Management*, *Foreign Trade Review*, *Journal of Economic Development* and *Journal of Developing Areas*, among others.